DATE DUE

6/5/14			

FOLLETT

Encyclopedia of Beat Literature

Edited by KURT HEMMER
Foreword by ANN CHARTERS
Afterword by TIM HUNT
Photographs by LARRY KEENAN

Facts On File
An imprint of Infobase Publishing

Encyclopedia of Beat Literature

Copyright © 2007 by Kurt Hemmer

Facts On File, Inc.
An imprint of Infobase Publishing
132 West 31st Street
New York, NY 10001

Library of Congress Cataloging-in-Publication Data

Encyclopedia of beat literature / edited by Kurt Hemmer; foreword by Ann
Charters; afterword by Tim Hunt.
p. cm.
Includes bibliographical references and index.
ISBN 0-8160-4297-7 (alk. paper)
1. American literature—20th century—Encyclopedias. 2. Authors,
American—20th century—Biography—Encyclopedias. 3. Beat Generation—
Encyclopedias. I. Hemmer, Kurt.
PS228.B6E53 2006
810.9'11—dc22 2005032926

Text design by Joan M. Toro
Cover design by Semadar Megged/Salvatore Luongo

Printed in the United States of America

VB Hermitage 10 9 8 7 6 5 4 3 2 1

This book is printed on acid-free paper.

Dedicated to Linda, Dick, Erik, and Jason.

page iv blank

CONTENTS

FOREWORD

For more than a half-century, writers and critics have been exploring the controversial nature of the concept of a Beat Generation and of Beat literature. The first article on the Beats, "This Is the Beat Generation," written by novelist John Clellon Holmes for the *New York Times* in 1952, provoked so many letters to the newspaper's editor that Holmes spent nearly six months trying to answer them. Since his time, scores of journalists and scholars have offered their different interpretations of Beat literature, and this encyclopedia is a worthy continuation of their spirited conversations on the subject.

Which dozen or so volumes do I consider to be essential among the previous books about Beat literature? Still noteworthy in my estimation are the three earliest critical anthologies, including Beat authors that followed soon after the publication of Allen Ginsberg's *Howl and Other Poems* (1956) and Jack Kerouac's *On the Road* (1957). These three anthologies expanded the reading audience for the Beat writers, providing them a contemporary context and some literary respectability.

The first, Gene Feldmen and Max Gartenberg's edition of *The Beat Generation and the Angry Young Men*, appeared in 1958 and compared the new radical American writers with the group of young contemporary English novelists and playwrights considered their British counterparts.

Two years later Donald M. Allen edited *The New American Poetry*, placing the Beat poets amid their avant-garde contemporaries in the United States. To conclude his anthology, Allen included "Statements on Poetics," a discussion about their experimental aesthetics from Lawrence Ferlinghetti, Philip Whalen, Gary Snyder, Michael McClure, LeRoi Jones, John Wieners, as well as Kerouac and Ginsberg.

The third anthology appeared in 1961 when Thomas Parkinson, a professor of English at the University of California at Berkeley who had encouraged Ginsberg to enroll as a graduate student, compiled *A Casebook on the Beat*. This collection highlighted "the pros and cons of the beat movement—with 39 pieces of beat writing—Kerouac, Ginsberg, and others," along with attacks on and defenses of the Beats by writers such as Norman Podhoretz, Kenneth Rexroth, and Henry Miller.

In the 1970s four books stand out in my estimation. The California poet David Meltzer did extensive interviews with Rexroth, William Everson, Ferlinghetti, Lew Welch, McClure, and Richard Brautigan that were published as a mass-market paperback, *The San Francisco Poets* (1971). After working with Kerouac to compile his bibliography in 1966, Charters published the first full-length biography, *Kerouac*, in 1973, four years after his death.

The first insightful academic study of the writing of Kerouac, Ginsberg, and William Burroughs was John Tytell's *Naked Angels* in 1976. Two years later, Barry Gifford and Lawrence Lee published *Jack's Book*, a fascinating series of interviews with "the men and women who populate the Kerouac novels."

In the 1980s and 1990s commentary on the Beat writers increased from a trickle to a flood, as their work was scrutinized by a growing number of academic scholars who understood that their poems and novels were authentic works of literature. Number eight on my Top Titles' Chart is Tim Hunt's critical study *Kerouac's Crooked Road: The Development of a Fiction* (1981). Hunt's laudable aim was "to reconstruct Kerouac's development from a promising imitator (the Wolfean *The Town and the City* of 1948) into intuitive experimentalist (*Visions of Cody,* 1952) by way of the relatively conventional novel that still mostly shapes our sense of his work (*On the Road* as eventually published by Viking)."

In 1983 appeared *The Beats: Literary Bohemians in Postwar America,* issued as volume 16 in the *Dictionary of Literary Biography,* 700 pages of biographical essays analyzing the work of the major and minor Beat authors.

In 1991 John Arthur Maynard wrote *Venice West: The Beat Generation in Southern California,* an in-depth investigation of the geography that supported a community of dissident writers at midcentury.

That same year appeared *The Portable Beat Reader,* a wide-ranging anthology that celebrated the development and extent of Beat writing. Last on my list of a dozen essential titles, in 1996 Brenda Knight's compilation *Women on the Beat Generation* focused on the work of 40 women writers who are too frequently overlooked in discussions of Beat literature.

In the last half of the 20th century these 12 books about the Beats established the canon of important authors and works; in the first years of the 21st century, new books began to investigate the subject of the Beat literary movement's place in the wider context of American culture.

In 2001 *Beat Down To Your Soul* collected essays, reviews, memoirs, and other material that explored the different aspects of "Beat." In 2002 John Suiter wrote *Poets on the Peaks,* a brilliant book examining how Snyder, Whalen, and Kerouac's work as fire lookouts in the North Cascades contributed to their development as nature writers.

That same year Ronna C. Johnson and Nancy M. Grace edited *Girls Who Wore Black,* interviews with members of three generations of Beat women along with literary analysis from the perspective of gender criticism. Finally in 2004, Jennie Skerl collected essays that challenged the media stereotypes and legends about the Beats, emphasizing the contribution of African-American and female Beat writers.

If the pattern of this unceasing production of books on the subject of Beat literature holds—the attempt to understand their literary achievement in an expanding cultural context by viewing their work from multiple points of view—then this *Encyclopedia of Beat Literature* for Facts On File promises to be the most useful of all. Enjoy!

Ann Charters

INTRODUCTION

Rob Johnson, the William S. Burroughs scholar from the University of Texas Pan-American, began to work on this encyclopedia in 1999. When I took over as the editor, the decision was made to create a work that focused on the literature rather than the lives and culture of the Beat Generation. Too often the legends of the Beat Generation have usurped the primary focus in Beat studies from the texts themselves. What ultimately makes the writers of the Beat Generation important is their art. The *Encyclopedia of Beat Literature* is designed to introduce and guide fans, students, and instructors to some of the most ambitious and stimulating works produced by the Beat writers and their allied contemporaries. This volume should complement the excellent dictionaries, encyclopedias, historical surveys, and biographies already in existence about the Beat movement as well as those to come. Here is a sampling of novels, memoirs, books of poetry, individual poems, essays, and short story collections of some of the best literature that the Beat movement produced. I wanted to call attention to these works as they appeared in their own historical moments, not as dead things collecting dust on shelves but as motivating and living stimulators of the imagination. Both aficionados and novices of Beat literature should find material in these pages that will enhance their appreciation of Beat literature.

The aura surrounding the fantastic and often cinematic lives of the Beat writers at times overshadows the brilliance of their writing. I myself was first lured to the exceptional artistry of Beat writing by the wonderful incandescence of the mytho-logical stories of the Beats' lives. The two—art and life—cannot be separated. But neither should the study of the art be dominated by the study of the lives. After years of studying these countercultural heroes, I thought the time had come to create a work that rigorously examined the work of these artists as a collective movement that continues to thrive. My hope is that this text will help perpetuate and invigorate the ongoing intellectual conversation over what writers and texts are "Beat" and which of them are worthy of continued analysis.

The creation of this encyclopedia truly started for me in the summer of 1992 when I walked into the Brown University Bookstore on Thayer Street in Providence, Rhode Island, and discovered Ann Charters's *The Portable Beat Reader*. I was already determined to pursue a career as a literature instructor, and I wanted to find a genre of writing that would sustain my enthusiasm for the half-dozen or so years required of graduate study. After working intensely on an undergraduate senior thesis on the novels of Milan Kundera and their relation to the philosophy of Friedrich Nietzsche, I had developed a new appreciation for the artistic use of language. I wanted to find something, as William Carlos Williams would say, written in "American." What I found was a genre that I anticipate will not satiate my enthusiasm during my lifetime. Reading Charters's introduction, "Variations on a Generation," and the selection from Jack Kerouac's *On the Road*, which included the mind-blowing line "But then they danced down the streets like dingledodies, and I shambled after as I've been doing all my life after people who interest me, because the only people for me are the mad ones, the ones who are mad to live, mad to talk, mad to be saved, desirous of everything at the same time, the ones who never yawn or say a commonplace thing, but burn, burn, burn like fabulous yellow roman candles exploding like spiders across the stars and in the middle you see the blue centerlight pop and everybody goes 'Awww!,'" I decided on the spot that there was only one place for me to start my graduate studies: the University of Connecticut, Storrs, where Ann Charters taught a course on the Beat Generation. The Beat lives had fascinated me, but it was Kerouac's language, a way of writing that seemed unlike anything I had heard before, that enraptured me.

I have been shambling after the Beats ever since. While at the University of Connecticut, I was able to bring the Beat legend and story-teller Herbert Huncke, with the help of Professor Charters, to campus for a reading. When I picked up Huncke on December 7, 1997, at the Chelsea Hotel in New York and drove him to campus while he entertained me, one of my students, and his friend Jack Walls with stories of the past and words of wisdom, I felt that I had walked into the magical world that I had dedicated myself to studying. Since then I have had the pleasure of organizing readings for Gregory Corso, Michael McClure, Janine Pommy Vega, Ted Joans, and Ed Sanders. I eventually went to Washington State University in Pullman, Washington (where Timothy Leary received his M.S. in psychology in 1946), to work with Tim Hunt, the author of *Kerouac's Crooked Road: The Development of a Fiction,* which I still believe is the finest work of Beat scholarship. Ann Charters's foreword and Tim Hunt's afterword book end this volume and help explain where Beat Studies has been and where it might go. I owe a great deal to these two tremendous scholars.

From them I learned that a starting point for the birth of the Beat Generation could be 1944 when Burroughs, Kerouac, and Ginsberg were all intro-duced to each other through mutual friends David Kammerer and Lucien Carr in New York. Kerouac, Ginsberg, and Carr were studying at Columbia University. Burroughs had followed his friends from St. Louis; Kammerer and Carr, from Chicago to New York. When Carr stabbed Kammerer to death

on August 13, 1944, for unwanted sexual advances in Riverside Park (an event that can be said to be the first of the many infamous [and sometimes hor-rifying] events surrounding the Beats), a bond was formed among their friends, Ginsberg, Kerouac, and Burroughs, that would last the rest of their lives. What could be called the first truly Beat text, an unpublished collaboration between Kerouac and Burroughs called "And the Hippos Were Boiled in Their Tanks," was inspired by this disturbing incident. When this group of friends became close with the Times Square hustler Herbert Huncke in 1946, they were introduced to the term *beat,* which Huncke used to express exhaustion and dejection. Kerouac later combined this mean-ing with "beatitude," making the term *beat* mean exalted spirituality experienced from the travails of existence. In a discussion with John Clellon Holmes in November 1948 about what made their generation distinct, Kerouac said that they were part of a "Beat Generation." The Six Gallery read-ing, connecting the East Coast Beats and the West Coast Beats, in San Francisco on October 7, 1955, by Allen Ginsberg, Gary Snyder, Michael McClure, Philip Whalen, and Philip Lamantia, with Kenneth Rexroth as master of ceremonies and Kerouac and Neal Cassady in the audience marked the begin-ning of a nationwide literary movement of loosely affiliated artists that we today call Beats.

One could do worse than choose January 14, 1967, as the end of the Beat Generation. On this day more than 20,000 people, including Jim Morrison and the other Doors, assembled at the Polo Field in Golden Gate Park, with only two mounted police officers in sight, where the Diggers distributed turkey sandwiches laced with acid pro-vided by Owsley, the Hell's Angels guarded the stage where Ginsberg, Snyder, Lawrence Ferlinghetti, Lenore Kandel, Jerry Rubin, Timothy Leary, the Jefferson Airplane, Big Brother and the Holding Company (featuring Janis Joplin), and the Grateful Dead performed. It was called the Human Be-In, also known as the "Pow Wow" and the "Gathering of Tribes," and it morphed the Beat Generation into the burgeoning Hippie Generation. Leary called out, "Turn On, Tune In, Drop Out!" After Snyder blasted his conch shell to signal the conclusion to the event, Ginsberg helped convince participants to clean the area, and people went to watch the sunset over the Pacific Ocean. But there was no clear break between the Beats and the Hippies. It was the case of an underground movement spreading to the colleges and the suburbs. As Jennie Skerl astutely asserts, it was the first time an avant-garde movement became a popular movement.

In selecting these entries, the contributors and I attempted to choose the best, most famous, and most innovative works associated with the various Beat aesthetics. Beat historian purists might look askance at the inclusion in this encyclopedia of works by writers whose major body of work either comes before or after what has generally been accepted as the period of Beat writing, like Kathy Acker, Oscar Zeta Acosta, Paul Bowles, Charles Bukowski, Jim Carroll, Robert Creeley, Ed Dorn, William Everson, Richard Fariña, Abbie Hoffman, Ken Kesey, Timothy Leary, Charles Olson, Kenneth Rexroth, Hunter S. Thompson, and ruth weiss. It is part of the ambition of this encyclopedia to broaden our understanding of what can be called "Beat." In that effort I have tried to cast a broad net to include popular works by contemporaneous artists that influenced or were influenced by the various Beat aesthetics. Though the Beat Generation came to an end, the Beat movement can be seen as a living thing continuing to this day. As of the publication of this encyclopedia, Beat poets like Michael McClure and Janine Pommy Vega continue to produce some of their best work.

A few scholars and fans will undoubtedly be upset by those works not included in this encyclopedia. This encyclopedia is a sampling of the best works written by the Beat writers and those profoundly influenced by the Beat movement. Other writers who were influenced by the movement are not covered here. Some of the most notable include Helen Adam, Paul Blackburn, Robin Blaser, Chandler Brossard, William S. Burroughs, Jr., Robert Duncan, Jan Kerouac, Kenneth Koch, Tuli Kupferberg, Sheri Martinelli, Joanna McClure, Frank O'Hara, Peter Orlovsky, Kenneth Patchen, Stuart Z. Perkoff, Hubert Selby, Jr., Carl Solomon, Jack Spicer, and Alexander Trocchi. If this encyclopedia inspires conversations about the writers and works I have neglected, I can only think that it is a constructive endeavor. In a conversation with

Beat scholars at a conference in Albuquerque, New Mexico, several years ago, the inevitable question "What makes a writer 'Beat'?" came up. I gave a tongue-in-cheek response that a Beat writer is any contemporary of Allen Ginsberg's who was either championed by Ginsberg or influenced by his poetics. I think there is some truth in this definition, but ultimately there will never be a final definition of *Beat.* Each scholar and each generation will come up with their own definition of *Beat.* In the present time *Beat* has been used quite often as a marketing tool to sell books. This does not necessarily have to be a bad thing. In an age where fewer and fewer young people read for entertainment, anything that can spark more reading should be embraced. If anyone is influenced to read a so-called Beat work because they found the entry on it in this encyclopedia interesting, then I think of that as a success. If calling a work Beat helps more people pay attention to it, then I am all for it.

That is partially why I did not shy away from including Bob Dylan's *Tarantula,* John Lennon's *In His Own Write,* and Jim Morrison's *The New Creatures* in this encyclopedia. I feel that all of these works can be considered "Beat," though I know that there will be some who will frown on the inclusion of these artists, known primarily for being rock stars, in this volume. I feel that work by Lou Reed and Patti Smith could also be considered Beat. Some of the heirs of the Beat Generation are rock lyricists who, like Dylan and Morrison, took the writing of lyrics to a new level after being inspired by Beat literature. Each generation of rock stars seems to include those inspired by the Beats. In the 1960s it was Dylan hanging out with Ginsberg, and Morrison hanging out with McClure; in the 1970s it was Lou Reed, Patti Smith, and the New York punk scene taking Burroughs as their honorary grandfather; in the 1980s it was The Clash performing with Ginsberg; in the 1990s it was Kurt Cobain collaborating with Burroughs; and today it is Black Rebel Motorcycle Club naming their album *Howl* in honor of Ginsberg's famous poem. In the "Rock and Roll" class that I team–teach with Greg Herriges at Harper College, which analyzes certain rock lyrics as poetry, I have the personal dictum: *Lure them in with rock 'n' roll; send them out with Blake, Rimbaud.*

Though not included in this encyclopedia, some works by non-Beat writers are so powerfully connected to Beat literature that they could almost be called Beat themselves. Such works include Norman Mailer's "The White Negro," his controversial and influential essay about the source of the white hipster coming from African-American culture; Tom Wolfe's brilliant Kerouacian telling of the famous ramblings of Ken Kesey, Neal Cassady, and The Merry Pranksters, *The Electric Kool-Aid Acid Test;* Tom Robbins's *Even Cowgirls Get the Blues,* with the presence of Kerouac hovering over it; and *Tripmaster Monkey: His Fake Book,* Maxine Hong Kingston's portrait of a Chinese-American Beat, Wittman Ah Sing. The point I am trying to make by bringing up these texts is that our understanding of "Beat" will become increasingly complicated as time goes by. And that is a good thing.

Though I included such popular classics as Jim Carroll's *The Basketball Diaries,* Richard Fariña's *Been Down So Long It Looks Like Up to Me,* and Hunter S. Thompson's *Fear and Loathing in Las Vegas* in this encyclopedia, I also included neglected classics like Ed Dorn's *Gunslinger,* Brenda Frazer's *Troia: Mexican Memoirs,* and Jack Micheline's *River of Red Wine and Other Poems,* among others. Just because a work is popular does not denigrate it as a work of art, and just because a book is out of print does not mean that it is not potentially worthy of study. These lessons I learned specifically from being a Beat scholar.

Fans and scholars will note that Jack Kerouac is heavily represented in this encyclopedia. As a scholar of "The King of the Beats," I would argue that Kerouac is the seminal literary figure of the movement. The main reason there are so many entries on works by Kerouac is that I feel the Dulouz Legend, his collection of novels that fictionalize his life, which includes *On the Road, The Subterraneans, The Dharma Bums, Doctor Sax, Maggie Cassidy, Tristessa, Lonesome Traveler, Big Sur, Visions of Gerard, Desolation Angels, Satori in Paris, Vanity of Duluoz,* and *Visions of Cody,* can be considered one masterwork. It is one of the crowning achievements of the Beat movement. There are three major ways of approaching this work: (1) in the order that they were written, (2) in the order

that they were published, and (3) in the order that they chronologically follow Kerouac's life.

One of the major mistakes fans, students, and scholars of Beat literature make is viewing the fiction of the Beat writers as autobiography rather than *autobiographical.* This is an understandable mistake considering that the Beat writers themselves, in postmodern fashion, encouraged the blurring of the lines between fiction and autobiography. Unfortunately the mistake of blindly accepting Beat fiction as autobiography has caused many errors in the biographical accounts of the Beats. This encyclopedia tries not to repeat those errors; thus it stresses the distinction between autobiography and *autobiographical.*

I would also like to add that one of the things I appreciate about the Beat movement the most is its inclusivity. If one looks hard enough one will find "Beats" of nearly every walk of life: men and women; gay, straight, bisexual, and asexual; Democrats, Republicans, anarchists, socialists, and communists; whites, African Americans, Latinos, Asian Americans, and representatives from a dozen countries other than the United States. I do not think any other artistic movement has the degree of inclusivity that the Beat movement has.

The contributors for this encyclopedia worked very hard; I would like to thank each and every one of them for their efforts. In particular I would like to thank Jeff Soloway at Facts On File for his help and insight. I would also like to acknowledge certain people who discussed this project with me in person, on the phone, or via e-mail and pointed me in directions about which I would not have known and encouraged me: James Grauerholz, Oliver Harris, Tim Hunt, Ronna C. Johnson, Eliot Katz, Larry Keenan, William Lawlor, Kevin Ring, Bob Rosenthal, and Robert Yarra. Without their help this encyclopedia would not exist. The wonderful conversations I had and the people with whom I became acquainted while working on this project made it all worthwhile. Though I am sure that errors still remain, the contributors and I spent a great deal of time trying to create an accurate, informative, and entertaining text. Those mistakes that remain are my responsibility alone. This has been a labor of love. I hope you enjoy it.

Kurt Hemmer

A

"Abomunist Manifesto" Bob Kaufman (1959)
When it appeared—first as a sequence in *Beatitude,* the San Francisco mimeo-zine BOB KAUFMAN coedited with Bill Margolis, subsequently as a City Lights broadside in 1959, and finally included in Kaufman's first book, *Solitudes Crowded with Loneliness* (1965)—"Abomunist Manifesto" was as significant to the Beat Generation's self-formation as ALLEN GINSBERG's "HOWL." The (in)famous November 30, 1959, article "The Only Rebellion Around" by Paul O'Neil in *Life* magazine on the Beat phenomenon, which brought stereotyped images of the Beat Generation into the mainstream, featured a now-iconic photograph of a white Beat couple and baby in their "pad"; the young man is lying on the floor reading "Abomunist Manifesto."

Characterized by Kaufman's signature puns, wild wit, and blend of politically trenchant street humor and popular culture with high cultural references, "Abomunist Manifesto" is clearly both a manifesto and a send-up of manifestos, both an homage to and a parody of communism's and surrealism's attempts to encode the "mission statement" of a disaffected movement in the deathless language of the literary or historical classic. Analogous to his years-later statement to Raymond Foye, "I want to be anonymous[;] . . . my ambition is to be completely forgotten," Kaufman captures the Beat investment in disinvestment using pithy, memorable language to describe the ephemeral and elusive. It is not surprising, given these piquant paradoxes, that the piece itself plays with many contradictions

in language, in the scene, and even in the project of writing a manifesto. The title alone references not only, most famously, Karl Marx's *Communist Manifesto* and André Breton's surrealist one but also the popular cultural figure of the abominable snowman (also known as the yeti, the sasquatch, bigfoot, etc.), which, as a mythical humanoid or rarely sighted, undiscovered primate, haunted the mid–20th-century North American imagination much as the "specter of communism" haunted mid–19th-century Europe. This humanoid was such a novel concept that none of the terms listed above appears in Webster's 1966 *New World Dictionary.* In a sense "Abomunist Manifesto" resonates with Kaufman's own multiraciality and elusiveness; he plays skillfully on the image of the black person in the eyes of 1950's white bohemia as a mystery, a seductive but scary, sort-of human, sort-of not. To be sure, this element of abomunism was lost on most of its white readership, who saw the abomunist as a lovably nonconformist Beat like themselves— Camus's stranger crossed with Holden Caulfield, an existentialist Huck Finn. "Abomunist" also, importantly, references the atom ("A-")bomb; one of Kaufman's heteronyms in the piece is "bomkauf" (bomb-kopf, or bomb-head; also bomb-cough), another clear reference to the tragedy that, along with the death camps, initiated the era we now call postmodern—that is, the end of the modernist illusion of progress and perfectability, combined with an intensification of modernism's disaffection and hopelessness. An "abomunist" is not only abominable (from the Latin *abominare,* "to regard as an ill omen"), a "frinky" (Kaufman's Afro-American inflected neologism that combines funky, freaky, and kinky) outsider, but also a denizen of that generation living under the shadow of potential global annihilation. Beats were, in a sense, symptoms of U.S. political and social dysfunction: they were regarded as ill omens by the mainstream, and indeed they were symptoms of that mainstream's illness.

"Abomunist Manifesto" itself is divided into 10 sections, each tellingly titled for maximum comedic effect and political edge: "Abomunist Manifesto," "Notes Dis- and Re- Garding Abomunism," "Further Notes (taken from 'Abomunismus und Religion,' by Tom Man)," "$$ Abomunus Craxioms $$," "Excerpts from the Lexicon Abomunon," "Abomunist Election Manifesto," "Still Further Notes Dis- and Re- Garding Abomunism," "Boms," "Abomunist Rational Anthem (*to be sung before and after frinking . . . music composed by Schroeder*)," "Abomunist Documents (*discovered during ceremonies at the Tomb of the Unknown Draftdodger*)," and "Abomnewscast . . . On the Hour. . . ." Each section varies in format, from a list of dictionary definitions or axiomatic definitions of abomunism to newscasts to a hipster Christ's diary to sound poetry, providing an antic romp through the Beat/jazz ethos and more subtly, one might argue, through that of a black nonconformist. One can see influences such as Lenny Bruce, Lord Buckley, and Mort Sahl in the sardonic commentary on current events and retellings of the Gospels in hipster lingo; revolutionary patriots and/or traitors Thomas Paine and Benedict Arnold put in appearances; events like the then-recent discovery of the Dead Sea Scrolls as well as the long-past kidnapping and murder of the Lindbergh baby become matter for absurdist wisecracks.

Barbara Christian, in an early (1972) appraisal of Kaufman's career, has suggested that the "Manifesto" is a deconstruction of all known "isms," that is, contrived attempts to regiment thought into systems, "last words" that claim authority as the only words and that thus become implicated in such final solutions as the atomic bomb. "Manifesto" issues behavioral imperatives in descriptive form:

ABOMUNISTS DO NOT FEEL PAIN, NO MATTER HOW MUCH IT HURTS. . . .

ABOMUNISTS DO NOT WRITE FOR MONEY; THEY WRITE THE MONEY ITSELF. . . .

ABOMUNIST POETS [ARE] CONFIDENT THAT THE NEW LITERARY FORM "FOOTPRINTISM" HAS FREED THE ARTIST OF OUTMODED RESTRICTIONS, SUCH AS: THE ABILITY TO READ AND WRITE, OR THE DESIRE TO COMMUNICATE. . . .

In the compellingly and defiantly nonsensical "Abomunist Rational Anthem," republished in Kaufman's second book, *Golden Sardine*, as "Crootey Songo," language itself disintegrates into presymbolic scraps of sound expressed through outbursts of protest and play:

> Derrat slegelations, flo goof babereo
> Sorash sho dubies, wago, wailo, wailo.

Though it is possible to decode this poem to some degree (*derrat* is *tarred* backward; *slegelations* elides *sludge, flagellation,* and *legislations,* indicating Kaufman's assessment of United States justice; *flow, goof, dubies,* and *wailo* evoke jazz/Beat/drug culture, etc.), the point is not to do so, but to experience the disorientation of babble which at the same time, like jazz argot, encodes protest. Many years later, Ishmael Reed chose "Crootey Songo" as the epigraph for the first volume of the *Yardbird Reader,* indicating the ongoing importance of "unmeaning jargon" (Frederick Douglass's description of the vocables and proto-scat of slave songs) for African American poets.

The whole of "Abomunist Manifesto," in fact, performs an aggressive if playful "unmeaning," as a verb rather than an adjective. "Abomunist Manifesto" unmeans cold war language and ideology, recasting it in a countercultural, minoritarian collage of American cultural detritus.

Bibliography

Christian, Barbara. "Whatever Happened to Bob Kaufman?" *Black World* 21, no. 12: 20–29.
Damon, Maria. "Unmeaning Jargon/Uncanonized Beatitude: Bob Kaufman, Poet." In *The Dark End of the*

Street: Margins in American Vanguard Poetry. Minneapolis: Minn. University Press, 1993, 32–76.

Edwards, Brent, et al., eds. *Callaloo* 25, no. 1 (Special Section on Bob Kaufman): 103–231.

Kaufman, Bob. *Solitudes Crowded with Loneliness.* New York: New Directions, 1965.

Maria Damon

Acker, Kathy (1947–1997)

Postmodern writer Kathy Acker once referred to the Beats as "the first breath of fresh air in [her] life," and she stated repeatedly that WILLIAM S. BURROUGHS was her strongest influence. One of her most famous novels is *BLOOD AND GUTS IN HIGH SCHOOL.* She was a product of the poetry and art worlds but wanted to write fiction. Burroughs became her model of a conceptualist fiction writer. A self-described literary terrorist, Acker used plagiarism (or *piracy,* as she liked to say) as a formal strategy and attempted to use literary forms, especially the novel, as stages for textual performance art.

She was born Kathy Alexander and grew up surrounded by privilege in New York City. Her father deserted her mother before she was born, so the "father" to whom she refers in her work was her stepfather. She attended exclusive schools in uptown Manhattan and as a young teenager began to sneak away downtown to the bohemian East Village. At age 13 she met GREGORY CORSO, who was a neighbor of her then-boyfriend, filmmaker P. Adams Sitney. Some 20 years later, she would invite Corso to visit a writing course that she was teaching at The San Francisco Art Institute, a course in which the students had refused to read books that she assigned because they said all books were passé. None of the students knew who Corso was, nor did they know about the Beats. As Acker told it, "Gregory, in typical Gregory fashion, unzipped his pants while reciting his 'poesia' and played with a toy gun. From then on, all the students read poetry. Gregory lived for two months with the most beautiful girl in the class."

In 1964 Acker was a student at Brandeis University and attended a reading by ALLEN GINSBERG and Peter Orlovsky. She recalled that they performed dressed in towels and that during the evening she "learned more about poetry than [she] had in years of top-level academic training." At Brandeis she met her first husband, Robert Acker, who was a student of Herbert Marcuse. (She would later marry and divorce the composer Peter Gordon.) The Ackers followed Marcuse to the University of California, San Diego, where Kathy was a graduate student in literature and also tutored students in Greek and Latin. It was there that she also met two of her most important mentors, David and Eleanor Antin.

Kathy divorced Robert and returned to New York, supporting herself by working in a live (simulated) sex show, as her family had withdrawn financial support. She returned to San Diego briefly and at some point worked as a stripper and had a role in at least one porn film. She also wrote under the pseudonym The Black Tarantula, going so far as to be listed under that name in the Manhattan telephone directory.

She lived in New York City during the 1970s and was part of the downtown art and literary scenes, as well as the burgeoning punk movement. One of her memories from about 1976 was her appropriately punkish tribute-by-heckling of Ginsberg when he made an appearance at CBGB. Years later, she explained:

> [We] had spontaneously attacked and praised Allen Ginsberg. Attacked him for being established, established in a society which we despised, and for bringing something as boring as real poetry into our territory of nihilism, formlessness, and anarchic joy. We revered him because he, and the rest of the Beats, were our grandparents. . . .
>
> The Beats had understood what it is to feel, therefore, to be a deformity in a normal (right-wing) world. . . . Ginsberg's joy, like our joy, had the sharpness, the nausea, of all that comes from pain, from suffering.

During this post-San Diego period, Acker discovered Burroughs; his cut-up technique became crucial to her development as a writer. In 1989 she told Sylvére Lotringer that she had "used *The Third Mind* [by Burroughs] as experiments to teach [herself] how to write." Acker was anachronising Burroughs's and Brion Gysin's book because the time frame in which she claimed to have been using it was the late 1960s and early 1970s. *The Third Mind* was not published until 1978; however, segments of what eventually composed it were published through small presses between 1960 and 1973, so she likely read early pieces. She also possibly had access to the manuscript. Some of Acker's very early works bear the unmistakable mark of *The Third Mind* (for example, see Acker's "Politics" and diary pieces eventually published in 2002 as *The Burning Bombing of America*). Acker sliced texts with abandon, disrupting logic and merging images and ideas at the sentence and word levels.

Most comparisons of Burroughs and Acker tend to focus on their experimentation becoming their technique and vice versa; the usefulness of the cut-up to demonstrate literary deviance; and their critiques of established systems that brainwash people so that they become instruments of the control machine that language represents.

Burroughs's influence is not as obvious in Acker's later writing but is arguably there on politically and socially important levels because she seems to have gendered Burroughs's theories about the relationship among power, language, and politics. The various personae she projected through her writing, her performances, and her very body reveal increasingly sophisticated and subtle applications of the cut-up technique. The concept became instrumental not only in her attempts to find a language of the body but also in her overall automythographical project as she disassembled layers of patriarchal "myth" which are the result of and, in turn, continue to dictate and underlie the controlling Logos that both she and Burroughs wished to disassemble. Burroughs's "reality studio" was her patriarchal language.

Acker lived in England throughout most of the 1980s and returned to New York City and San Francisco in the early 1990s, continuing to write, teach, and publish until November 1997 when she died in an alternative treatment center in Mexico from complications of metastasized cancer. She was buried at sea—a fitting tribute to a pirate.

Bibliography

Acker, Kathy. "Allen Ginsberg: A Personal Portrait." "Magazine Articles" folder. Box 4. Kathy Acker Papers. Rare Book, Manuscript, and Special Collections Library. Duke University.

———. "Politics." In *Hannibal Lecter, My Father*, edited by Sylvère Lotringer. Semiotext(e) Native Agents Series, 25–35. New York: Semiotext(e). 1991.

———. *The Burning Bombing of America*. In *Rip-Off Red, Girl Detective and The Burning Bombing of America*. New York: Grove Press, 2002.

Burroughs, William S., and Brion Gysin. *The Third Mind*. New York: Viking Press, 1978.

Friedman, Ellen G. "A Conversation with Kathy Acker." *The Review of Contemporary Fiction*. 9:3 (Fall 1989). 12–22.

Lotringer, Sylvère. "Devoured by Myths." In *Hannibal Lecter, My Father*, edited by Sylvère Lotringer. Semiotext(e) Native Agents Series, 1–24. New York: Semiotext(e), 1991.

Bebe Barefoot

Acosta, Oscar Zeta (1935–1974[?])

Can a 1960s legendary West Coast Chicano lawyer–activist truly be thought a member of the Beat roster, not least given his various disparaging remarks about the movement? If, indeed, he can, it might be as a kind of Beat anti-Beat figure on his own ironic self-reckoning the "faded beatnik" or on that of HUNTER S. THOMPSON, "the wild boy . . . crazier than NEAL CASSADY." (Thompson based Dr. Gonzo in *FEAR AND LOATHING IN LAS VEGAS* on Acosta.) Certainly in life, as in his writing, Acosta, like the Beats, plays out a key countercultural role, the maverick, roistering voice from California's supposed ethnic margin.

Whether the sheer theater of his sex-and-drugs personal life; his Oakland, San Francisco, and East Los Angeles law work in domestic and tenants rights and defense of Brown Power militants; his community politics; or his two landmark autobiographical fictions—*The AUTOBIOGRAPHY OF A BROWN BUFFALO* (1972) and *The REVOLT OF THE COCKROACH PEOPLE* (1973)—Acosta embodies a heady, often flamboyant, brew. Life and art overlap, the acting-out both in real time and place and on the page of the persona he at various times designated "Buffalo Zeta Brown, Chicano Lawyer," "The Samoan," and "Dr. Gonzo." On the one hand this interface of self and *chicanismo* and the awareness of his own considerable brown flesh within a white America makes him an unlikely Beat candidate. On the other hand, the Beat argot, "on the road" adventures, search for a transcendent spirituality, and gift for a JACK KEROUAC–style speed of narrative, gives him genuine Beat plausibility.

Acosta, thus, can be construed several ways. There is the Acosta raised in California's Riverbank–Modesto who becomes the legal-aid lawyer after studies at the University of Southern California and qualification for the bar in San Francisco in 1966. There is the air-force enlistee who, on being sent to Panama, becomes a Baptist-Pentecostal convert and missionary there (1949–52) before opting for apostasy and a return to altogether more secular ways and times in California. There is the inmate of Ciudad Juárez, Mexico, in 1968 who was forced to argue in local court for his own interests in uncertain street Spanish (or *caló*) after a spat with a hotelkeeper. There is the tequila drinker and druggie who spent 10 years in therapy, the hugely overweight ulcer sufferer who spat blood, and the twice-over divorcee.

Not least there is the Acosta of the barricades, the battling lawyer of the "High School 13" and "St Basil's Cathedral 21" protests in 1968, each trial of the *vato loco* militants, and the police-cell death of the youth Robert Fernandez and the shooting of award-winning correspondent Reuben Salazar of station KMEX. There is the "buffalo" who runs as *La Raza Unida* independent candidate for sheriff of Los Angeles in 1970 and becomes the friend and political co-spirit of César Chávez and Denver's "Corky" Gonzalez. Finally there is the Acosta who leaves for Mexico in despair at the marring internal divisions of Chicano politics, and there is the eventual *desaparecido* in 1974, aged 39, who was last heard from in Mazatlán, Mexico. His end has long been shrouded in mystery. Was he drugs or gun running, a victim of accident or foul play, or a kind of Chicano Ambrose Bierce who had created his own exit from history?

From a literary perspective there remains the Acosta of *The Autobiography of a Brown Buffalo*

and *The Revolt of The Cockroach People*, the voice who can both speak of City Lights Bookstore as "a hang-out for sniveling intellectuals," yet of himself as a "flower vato," or disrespect Ginsberg and Kerouac even as he reminisces about his own "beatnik days." Beat Chicano or Chicano Beat, Acosta supplies the grounds, however paradoxical, for an affiliation of spirit and art to the movement.

Bibliography
Lee, A. Robert. "Chicanismo's Beat Outrider?: The Texts and Contexts of Oscar Zeta Acosta." In *The Beat Generation: Critical Essays,* edited by Kostas Myrsiades, 259–280. New York: Peter Lang, 2002.

A. Robert Lee

***Angel* Ray Bremser** (1967)
Originally published by Tompkins Square Press and later by Water Row Press in *Poems of Madness & Angel* (1986), this epic prose poem is printed all in capitals. Stanzas are in paragraph form with ubiquitous ellipses, ampersands, parentheses, neologisms, and scat-talk. This monumental exposition of love and lack-love was composed in one night while Bremser was in solitary confinement at New Jersey State Prison in Trenton, New Jersey, on a Stromberg–Carlson typewriter.

Angel analyzes and incarnates vast amounts of human experience. It is dedicated to BONNIE BREMSER (BRENDA FRAZER.) It is about how they met, about youth, and how ALLEN GINSBERG's "HOWL" inspired him. The poem reminds us that Bremser was part of the inner circle of the best minds of his generation. References are made about Ginsberg, Peter Orlovsky, GREGORY CORSO, LeRoi Jones (AMIRI BARAKA), PHILIP LAMANTIA, WILLIAM S. BURROUGHS, and JACK KEROUAC. The influence of jazz is also apparent in the poem, and Bremser evokes George Shearing, John Coltrane, and Dizzy Gillespie. It is an overwhelming foray into a nontrivial mind, conscious of the political realities that separate him from his "angel," their music, their Beat artist-and-poet community. It is rampant with folk and street aphorisms and barrels forward with a monster vocabulary juxtaposing rare adjective–noun combinations as poignant and sensible as they are unfamiliar.

Positioning himself in what would now be called a chauvinistic position as Bonnie's creator, Bremser as poet suggests his muse (Bonnie) relies on him as much if not more so than he relies on her: "I SHAPED HER, LIMNED HER, LIMBED HER, TRIMMED HER, BLUED HER, GREW & SYLPHED & HOPED TO GOD & PROPHECIED HER NIGHTLY & BY DARKNESS EVERYWHERE." Yet the reader understands that it is this angel/muse who is actually getting the poet through the night. Bremser explains his agony: "ANGEL THINKS SHE KNOWS HOW HORRIBLE IT ALL IS! I KNOW SHE HAS A FANTASTIC CAPACITY TO GET INTO THE PAIN & TORTURE OF THAT WHICH IS ALL AROUND HER . . . BUT SHE DON'T KNOW THIS TO ITS SHARP CORE, HER DREAMS ARE AS FLYING WONDERS COMPARED TO MY WAKING WALKS THROUGH THE STYGIAN STINKING VOMITED HALLS OF DOLOROUS SPANG & CRONG MUCK." Bremser's positioning himself as a poet, with the help of his muse Bonnie, is what saves his sanity: "NOBODY KNOWS ANYTHING . . . ONLY THE POETS." As Bremser reminds us, "IT WAS POETRY SAW ME THROUGH."

Andy Clausen and Kurt Hemmer

Autobiography of a Brown Buffalo, The Oscar Zeta Acosta (1972)

In this first of his two first-person Chicano memoirs, the persona assumed by OSCAR ZETA ACOSTA bows in with a suitably Beat gesture of self-exposure: "I stand naked before the mirror," a body of "brown belly" and "extra flesh." Evacuation becomes a bathroom opera of heave, color, the moilings of fast-food leftovers. Hallucinatory colloquies open with "Old Bogey," James Cagney, and Edward G. Robinson. His "Jewish shrink," Dr. Serbin, becomes the therapist as accuser, a Freudian gargoyle. Glut rules—"booze and Mexican food." Abandoning his San Francisco legal aid work he plunges into traffic as though his own on-the-road luminary. He mocks City Lights bookshop as "a hangout for sniveling intellectuals," throws in a reference to Herb Caen as the coiner of "beatnik," thinks back on his

marijuana and first LSD use, and offers himself as "another wild Indian gone amok." Acosta so monitors "Acosta." Despite his avowals otherwise, *The Autobiography of a Brown Buffalo* gives grounds, as it were, for thinking it a fusion of either Chicano Beat or Beat Chicano authorship.

As his "brownskin" odyssey, in his own phrasing, unfolds, this same play of styles becomes even more emphatic. The Beatles's "Help" spills its harmonies and plaintiveness on to Polk Street. His friend Ted Casey tempts him with mescaline. Heroin, or powdered mayonnaise, as he calls it, appears at a Mafia restaurant where he stops for food. Women, his exlover June MacAdoo, Alice, and her friend Mary all weave into his sexual fantasies even as he frets, with reason, at his own male prowess. The diorama is motleyed, as comic-cuts weave between illusion and fact.

So it is, too, on July 1, 1967, that "Acosta" announces himself "the Samoan," a brown hulk, the author as harlequin. "I've been mistaken for American Indian, Spanish, Filipino, Hawaiian, Samoan, and Arabian," he witnesses, adding un-politically correct and ruefully, "No one has ever asked me if I'm a spic or greaser." Is this not "Acosta" as human multitext, Latino lawyer yet Latino outrider, Chicano yet also Beat? Certainly, Chicano and Beat influences collude and compete throughout. On the one hand the narrator looks back to his Riverbank boyhood with its gang allegiance and fights against the Okies: "I grew up a fat, dark Mexican—a Brown Buffalo—and my enemies called me a nigger." He heads into a "future" of the Pacific Northwest with the hitchhiker Karin Wilmington, a journey busy in allusion to TIMOTHY LEARY, Jerry Garcia, and The Grateful Dead, which takes him into the Hemingway country of Ketchum, Idaho. Both come together as he circles in memory back into his Panama years, his onetime Baptist–Pentecostal phase seeking to become a "Mexican Billy Graham."

As he then weaves his way back to Los Angeles the itinerary gives off all the eventfulness of a JACK KEROUAC trajectory: characters like Scott ("a full time dope smuggler and a salesman for Scientology") or the waitress Bobbi to whom he describes his family as "the last of the Aztecs"; the odd jobs, car crashes and blackouts in Colorado;

the remembrance of detention in a Juarez Jail and of a border official telling him, "You don't *look* like an American you know"; and, almost inevitably, the pathway back into California along the iconic Route 66. Chicano adventurer–author, it might be said, elides into Beat adventurer–author, Oscar Zeta Acosta as both *chicanismo*'s own *vato loco* and Beat's own Chicano warrior.

Bibliography

Lee, A. Robert. "Chicanismo's Beat Outrider?: The Texts and Contexts of Oscar Zeta Acosta." *The Beat Generation: Critical Essays,* edited by Kostas Myrsiades. 259–280. New York: Peter Lang, 2002.

A. Robert Lee

Autobiography of LeRoi Jones, The
Amiri Baraka (1984)

With rarely other than liveliest eloquence, *The Autobiography of LeRoi Jones* offers a full, busy, life-and-times of LeRoi JONES/AMIRI BARAKA, one of Afro-America's literary and cultural lead players. It has come to rank with other key works of modern black U.S. life-writing, such as Richard Wright's Dixie-to-Chicago *Black Boy* (1945) and posthumous *American Hunger* (1977), Chester Himes's itinerant self-history *The Quality of Hurt* (1972) and *My Life of Absurdity* (1976), James Baldwin's Bible-cadenced *Notes of a Native Son* (1955), the epochal *Autobiography of Malcolm X* (1965), the five-volume portrait begun in Maya Angelou's *Gather Together In My Name* (1974), and Audre Lorde's *Zami: A New Spelling of My Name* (1982). As for Jones/Baraka and a career spanning his Newark, New Jersey, origins, Harlem, Cuba, and Africa, leaving him not only at the forefront of .postwar U.S. writing but the era's race-and-class politics, he can be said to have had abundant grounds for speaking of his life as the negotiation of "a maze of light and darkness."

In his introduction to the 1997 edition, Jones/Baraka confirms that his text met with a tangled compositional and then publishing history. The "last writing" ended in 1974. The manuscript languished and when eventually published in 1984 was made subject to unwanted editorial cuts. The

1997 version not only restores most of the original but, in the light of his transitions from Greenwich Village–Beat literary bohemian to black nationalist to Marxist–Leninist, inserts passing Marxist commentaries on the life history to date. In this respect he regards this version as "the first complete edition of *The Autobiography of LeRoi Jones.*"

"White nationalism is the dominant social ideology" runs an early observation in the introduction, a foretaste of the tone to follow. He speaks of his own early temptation toward becoming a "white-minded Negro," his rancor at the first marriage with the white, Jewish HETTIE JONES, whom he accuses of telling "self-legitimizing martyr stories," and his early move into and then out of "White Village socialization (the Beat thing)." Once launched into *The Autobiography of LeRoi Jones* proper, for the most part he follows the historical trajectory of his life. Newark supplies the originating site: his postal-supervisor father and the family links to the funeral business; his schooling—the fights, gangs, race lines, and black street; radio and comic-book heroes; athletics; and the early and presiding fascination with blues ("our poem of New World consciousness") and jazz ("the music took me to places I'd never been"). In these accounts, as in the rest of *The Autobiography of LeRoi Jones,* he writes as a mix of memorial prose–poem, black vernacular slang, and frequent riffs of image and rap.

In remembering his move to the Newark campus of Rutgers University, then two years at Howard ("We were not taught to think but readied for super domestic service"), with his follow-on stint as a gun–weatherman in the air force ("disconnection and isolation") and from which he was "undesirably discharged" on grounds of suspected communism, he conjures up his passionate jags of reading, Dostoyevsky to Joyce, Dylan Thomas to Henry James. His return to Newark leads directly into the "hip bohemianism" of Greenwich Village. There, his recollections alight on the flurry of new self-awakenings and affairs ("I was like blotting paper for any sensation"). He thinks back with some affection to hanging-out at Pandora's Box and his own writing and art energies amid such names as CHARLES OLSON, FRANK O'HARA, TED JOANS, Merce Cunningham, John Cage, ALLEN

GINSBERG, and DIANE DI PRIMA, with whom he cofounds the magazine *Yugen*. He summons an unrelenting circuit of small magazines, literary gatherings, readings, scrapes, dope, and drinks parties. His jazz interests, of necessity, persist: the sets and recordings by Coltrane, Parker, Gillespie, Mingus, and Davis; venues like The Five Spot; and his own notes for cover sleeves and reviews. He marries Hettie Cohen. In 1961 he sees the publication of *PREFACE TO A TWENTY VOLUME SUICIDE NOTE* as his first-ever collection.

The "Friends of Cuba" trip with other black writers and notables in 1960, however, in which he witnesses the attempt to forge a socialist order and meets Castro, deepens a "growing kernel of social consciousness" and becomes "a turning point in my life." The resulting transition into Black Nationalism, he recalls, coincides with a simply prodigious literary outpouring, notably the play *DUTCHMAN*, the poetry of *The Dead Lecturer* and *Black Magic*, musicology of *Blues People* and *Black Music*, and the critique of *Home: Social Essays*, which includes the essay "CUBA LIBRE." The same brand of nationalism leads to the abrupt departure from Greenwich Village and Hettie Jones for Harlem, his role in Black Arts Theater, the affiliation and splits with Ron Karenga, the FBI harassment and gun charges, the marriage to Sylvia Robinson/Amina Baraka, and a two-years-later return to Newark. In the light of the 1965 assassination, "Malcolm, Malcolm, semper" becomes his mantra. His home city ("my view was that Newark should be a model for the country") has since remained his base. Its politics span Kenneth Gibson's mayoral campaign—an administration he indicts for its failure to make good on its promises, on education ventures such as the Afrika Free School, and on housing, tenancy, welfare, and other black community issues. In shared vein he looks back to his chairmanship of the National Black Political Convention, held in Gary, Indiana, in 1972, as another "high moment in my life," even though it would mark the beginning of the end of his "nationalist" phase.

For, in its turn, the later parts of *The Autobiography of LeRoi Jones* outline his next transition into Marxist–Leninism, repudiating Karenga's "Africanist" Kawaida doctrines and "one-man domination" in favor of proletarian socialism. "Baraka the Marxist," with a self-conscious touch of parody, he calls himself. Throughout he adds citations from the likes of Mao, administers ideological self-reprimands for his Village ("Never-never-land America") and black nationalist phases ("the deep backwardness of cultural nationalism"), and looks to a revolutionary anti-imperialist and Third World socialist pathway for himself and for the Amina Baraka with whom he has had five children and who serves as a kind of colloquium voice throughout in tackling the world as "a prison for black people."

The Marxism–Leninism arrived at in *The Autobiography of LeRoi Jones* will not be persuasive to all readers. But even those who think it an ideological anachronism would be hard put to doubt the force of mind at work, the commitment and yet the self-interrogation. "Partial evidence" may well be the concluding chapter's gloss on his life and its contexts. That, however, is not to underplay Jones/Baraka's encompassing participant–observer's perspective on his own history, nor the intelligent vigor, the flair, with which he gives it expression.

A. Robert Lee

B

Baraka, Amiri (LeRoi Jones) (1934–)

Few writers, African-American or otherwise and spanning the late 1950s through to the present time, can claim quite so diverse or ideologically marked a repertoire as Jones/Baraka. In the *LeRoi Jones/Amiri Baraka Reader* (1991) he gives due recognition to his "Beat–Black Nationalist–Communist" evolution even though, he also insists, "it doesn't show the complexity of real life." His output has embraced every kind of genre: poetry, story, novel, drama, essay, autobiography, journal editorship, anthology, speech, and a plenitude of nonfiction work from jazz and blues histories to his various critiques of U.S. racism and neocolonialism in Africa and the Third World. It would be hard to doubt that he has been other than a fierce controversialist, hugely articulate in his displays of word and image, and resolute in his political activism. His name, deservedly, figures with those of Ralph Ellison or James Baldwin, Toni Morrison, or Alice Walker, at the very forefront of Afro-America's postwar literary achievement.

Born Everett Leroy Jones in 1934 in Newark, New Jersey, he graduated from Barringer High School in 1951, did a year at Rutgers University at the Newark campus before transferring to Howard University (1952–54), and entered the air force ("Error Farce" he calls it) as a weather–gunner from which after being stationed in Puerto Rico, he was "undesirably discharged" for supposed communist beliefs (1957). He started to call himself "LeRoi" in 1952 to distinguish himself and emphasize the French word *roi*, meaning "King." His move from Newark to Greenwich Village in 1958 unlocked a long nascent literary creativity, aided not least by the "hip bohemianism" of the Lower Manhattan Bleeker and MacDougal Street worlds and a literary-art circuit of small magazines, theater, film, readings, and parties whose luminaries numbered CHARLES OLSON of Black Mountain fame, Frank O'Hara as dean of the New York poets, a black coterie that included TED JOANS, avant-garde dance and music figures such as Merce Cunningham and John Cage, and the Beat connections to ALLEN GINSBERG, DIANE DI PRIMA, and GARY SNYDER. In short order he had cofounded *Yugen* magazine with Di Prima, in 1958 had married HETTIE COHEN (with whom he had two children and divorced in 1965), and had his poetry appear in a slew of modernist and countercultural magazines; he saw a first collection, *PREFACE TO A TWENTY VOLUME SUICIDE NOTE,* which most carries his Beat-phase footfalls, published in 1961. His anthology, *The Moderns* (1963), to which he himself was the only black contributor, confirmed his resolve also to "make it new" in the tradition of Pound, Joyce, William Carlos Williams, Mallarmé, or Lorca. Throughout, as subsequently, and like Langston Hughes, whose attention he was early to win, he has held to a passionate commitment to blues and jazz as the very core of African-American cultural identity above all the musical generation of John Coltrane, Charlie Parker, Dizzie Gillespie, Charles Mingus, and Miles Davis.

Jones/Baraka's Beat-bohemian phase, usually dated as 1958–62, began to close in the light of his 1960 visit to Cuba. That brief stay, written up as "CUBA LIBRE," led as he said to his writings becoming ever "blacker," not least in the face of Klan and other southern violence, the ghetto implosions of cities from Watts to Harlem to Bedford–Stuyvesant, and the rise of Black Power in the form of the Black Panthers, SNCC, and a rejuvenated Nation of Islam. This black nationalist alignment caused him to leave Hettie Jones, move to Harlem, Islamize his name to Amiri Baraka in the wake of Malcolm X's assassination in 1965, help establish the Black Arts Theater in Harlem, and move yet further into local community activism. Charged falsely with building a gun arsenal, and with a new marriage to Sylvia Robinson/Amina Baraka with whom he would have five children, he took up the Kawaida doctrines of Ron Karenga, the imprint of whose uncompromising Africanist ideology can be seen in such plays as *The Slave* (1965) and *A Black Mass* (1965). In 1967 he moved back to Newark, at once a site of origins and family but also of the Kenneth Gibson mayoral campaign, tenancy and school challenges, urban renewal and its ambiguities, and overall black community needs and rights.

None of this slowed his immense literary productivity, whether key verse collections such as *The Dead Lecturer* (1964) with its rallying poem–anthem "BLACK DADA NIHILISMUS," and *Black Magic* (1969), his then hitherto most black cultural poetry collection, or his landmark play DUTCHMAN (1964), a stage parable of destructive black–white interface in the circling New York metro, or the fiction of *The System of Dante's Hell* (1965) and *Tales* (1967), given over to the city as hallucinatory pit or inferno, or his major anthology, edited with Larry Neal, *Black Fire* (1968). Alongside ran an equally fecund body of essay and discursive writing, from the formidable musicology of *Blues People* (1963) and *Black Music* (1967) to the razor-keen cultural critique of *Home: Social Essays* (1966).

But his black nationalism phase would also have its day for him. Ahead lay his move into Marxism–Leninism, the belief that U.S. and allied monopoly capitalism operates at the heart of race and class division and requires its own revolutionary socialist counterthrust. That has been his sustaining ideology, the necessary cultural seam, in

the poetry of *In Our Terribleness* (1970) and the Marxist-impelled *Hard Facts* (1975), the drama of *Four Revolutionary Plays* (1969) and *What Was The Relationship of The Lone Ranger to The Means of Production?* (1978), and the anticapitalist political essay–work of *Daggers and Javelins* (1982). The publication of the *Jones/Baraka Reader* and *The Autobiography of LeRoi Jones*, the latter initially in 1984 and then in a restored and marxianized version in 1997, together can be said to give a working overall portrait to date, both man and authorship.

Jones/Baraka has long seemed a near writer–polemicist whirlwind, at one and the same time poet, man of theater, fiction writer, autobiographer, and editor (notably of *The Black Nation*, 1982–86) with, of late, a turn to opera, the accused radical who has faced and has won two important court trials, and for all the grounding in black community Newark, ongoing public intellectual. The controversialism continues, not least the charges of white baiting and anti-Semitism. For even as he has held important university academic and other appointments, his poem "Someone Blew Up America," written in the wake of 9/11/2001, and his forced resignation as New Jersey poet laureate serve as a reminder that the 70-year-old Jones/Baraka has lost nothing in the way of the resolve to make his art one of challenge. The Beat poet and one-time Greenwich Village resident seems a long way behind. The black Nationalist, to anachronistic effect or otherwise, may well have taken on the mantle of Marxist–Leninist in a post-Soviet and George W. Bush-led America of the new century. But whichever the incarnation there can be little doubting his always powerful creative vitality, the committed, undiminishing call to consciousness.

Bibliography

Harris, William J. *The Poetry and Poetics of Amiri Baraka: The Jazz Aesthetic*. Columbia: University of Missouri Press, 1985.

———, ed. *The LeRoiJones/AmiriBaraka Reader*. New York: Thunder Mouth's Press, 1991.

Lee, A. Robert. *Designs of Blackness: Mappings in the Literature and Culture of Afro-America*. London and Sterling, Va.: Pluto Press, 1998.

Reilly, Charlie, ed. *Conversations with Amiri Baraka*. Jackson: University Press of Mississippi, 1994.

Sollors, Werner. *Amiri Baraka/LeRoi Jones: The Quest For a "Populist Modernism."* New York: St. Martin's Press, 1978.

A. Robert Lee

Basketball Diaries, The Jim Carroll (1978)

Begun at age 12 as a journal, *The Basketball Diaries* depicts a young, talented basketball player and his descent into heroin addiction on the streets of 1960s inner-city New York. In 1995 the book was made into an excellent film by director Scott Kalvert starring Leonardo DiCaprio. In the book *The Basketball Diaries,* like his literary predecessor Holden Caulfield, JIM CARROLL is disillusioned with the adult world and its blindness to what is real and pure. For Carroll, this takes place in the mentally exhausting context of the constant threat of communist attack and nuclear war. Who better to tell it like he sees it than a 15-year-old kid seeking honesty and solace in a diary—a writer unfettered as yet by literary contrivance and at the same time easily forgiven for it. He writes about his diaries:

> Soon I'm gonna wake a lot of dudes off their asses and let them know what's really going down in the blind alley out there in the pretty streets with double garages. . . . I'm just really a wise ass kid getting wiser and I'm going to get even somehow for your dumb hatreds and all them war baby dreams you left in my scarred bed with dreams of bombs falling above that cliff I'm hanging steady to.

His tool for getting even becomes his writing: "maybe someday just an eight page book, that's all, and each time a page gets turned a section of the Pentagon goes up in smoke. Solid." Carroll plans a shock so thorough and real that it will register from suburbia to Washington, D.C.

So Carroll trades home and the metaphorical bomb shelter for the open and more real scene on the streets, taking his education from the tumultuous 1960s of drug experimentation, peace marches, and race riots rather than from his parents or his "barb-wire grade school." Within the first few pages the reader is placed in the middle of young kids fighting and taking drugs, sniffing cleaning fluid to get high, and "snatching hand bags off ladies."

Thinking it less addictive than pot, Carroll first experienced heroin at age 13: "So, as simple as a walk to that cellar, I lost my virgin veins." Realizing his mistake, he writes, "Since I got the facts straight I only use H once in a moon." Yet, what he calls a little "Pepsi-Cola habit" develops quickly into a full-blown addiction, and Carroll likewise moves from snatching handbags to "the fag hustling scene," exchanging sexual acts for money, his grades steadily dropping, his basketball career slowly vanishing.

Blending the disturbing image of a very young addict with the humorous antics of a rebellious and exuberant teen, *The Basketball Diaries* poignantly carries on the spontaneous and confessional tradition of Beat greats JACK KEROUAC and WILLIAM S. BURROUGHS. The final entry finds Carroll on a four-day binge, "thin as a wafer of concentrated rye," his addiction totally taking over. He leaves the reader with a mixed message of hope and despair with these troubling last lines: "I got to go in and puke. I just want to be pure. . . ."

Bibliography

Kuennen, Cassie Carter. "Cheetah and Chimp: *The Basketball Diaries* as Minor Literature." *The Jim Carroll Website.* 1989. www.catholicboy.com.

Jennifer Cooper

Beard, The Michael McClure (1965)

Viewed by many as the most controversial play of the 1960s, MICHAEL McCLURE's work *The Beard* represents one of the finest and most visionary works of his career. The play's title refers to an Elizabethan slang phrase, "to beard," meaning to engage in an argument with someone. In the case of *The Beard,* the argument consists of an extended dialogue between two archetypal American figures: 19th-century gunfighter Billy the Kid and 1930's film sex goddess Jean Harlow. The couple's heated discussion takes place as they encounter each other in the afterlife—an afterlife, early critic John Lahr noted, not based on a "Christian heaven, but a meatier one."

The play's stage setting is sparse, bringing the audience's attention to the actor's language and physical gestures. Seated onstage with only two chairs and a table covered with furs, the walls covered in blue velvet. Harlow and Billy the Kid wear small beards of torn tissue paper to signal their role as spirits in eternity. First seated apart but then growing physically closer as the play progresses, the pair engages in a verbal sparring match around themes familiar to readers of McClure's poetry and essays: the spiritual depiction of humanity as divine versus the biological view of humanity as "meat," and the power of sexuality to merge the two. Hollywood sex goddess Jean Harlow is the embodiment of all that is beautiful, sexual, and feminine, while Billy the Kid, the Wild West outlaw, embodies violence, physicality, and masculinity. The repetitive, rapid-fire, dialogue between the two figures makes up a verbal pas de deux in which both characters flirtatiously size up the other's position. The play's dialogue is stark and terse, providing a realistic grounding to the dreamlike setting and a realistic backdrop for the characters' quest for what Harlow describes as "the real me":

HARLOW: Before you can pry any secrets from me, you must first find the real me! Which one will you pursue?

THE KID: What makes you think I want to pry secrets from you?

HARLOW: Because I'm so beautiful.

Their flirtatious dialogue and actions become increasingly violent and more and more erotically charged. The Kid at first rejects Harlow's ethereal notions that the beauty of the human body is illusory, and he refers to her repeatedly as "a bag of meat." As the play progresses, both characters continue the heated dialogue: part threat, part seduction, part philosophical debate. Echoing each other's words, each of the pair grudgingly comes to see the truth in the other's viewpoint, gradually acknowledging that both sides—meat and spirit, physical and cerebral, male and female—must ultimately be joined. The play ends with a shocking moment of sexual coupling in which the play's tensions are resolved. As The Kid drops to his knees, his head beneath the raised dress of Harlow as he performs cunnilingus on her, the two

opposing forces are ecstatically brought together both physically and spiritually. Harlow's final lines in the play "STAR! STAR! STAR! [. . .] OH MY GOD! [. . .] BLUE-BLACK STAR! [. . .] STAR! STAR!" signal a joyous transcendence as spirit and meat are finally reconciled.

First staged on December 8, 1965, by the San Francisco Actors' Workshop, *The Beard* was targeted from its outset by censors who condemned its "obscene" language and the graphic sexuality of its final scene. Despite the fact that the play had won Obie Awards for Rip Taylor as Best Director and for Billie Dixon as Best Actress, a firestorm of controversy followed the production. During a production of the play in San Francisco, lead actors Richard Bright and Billie Dixon were arrested. Other arrests followed—in Berkeley, Los Angeles, and Vancouver. All in all, the play was the focus of 19 court cases, with charges including obscenity, conspiracy to commit a felony, and lewd and dissolute conduct in a public place. A highly publicized trial in San Francisco resulted in exoneration of the playwright and, more broadly, of all American plays that dared to challenge the status quo. Just as the trials concerning the alleged obscenity of ALLEN GINSBERG's "HOWL" and WILLIAM S. BURROUGHS's novel NAKED LUNCH had broadened the boundaries of what constituted "acceptable" poetry and fiction, McClure's legal battle with *The Beard* had done the same for drama, achieving a lasting victory against the censorship of stage productions.

Bibliography
Lahr, John. *Acting Out America: Essays on Modern Theatre.* Middlesex, England: Penguin Books, 1972.

Marranca, Bonnie, and Gautam Dasgupta. "Michael McClure." *American Playwrights: A Critical Survey.* New York: Drama Book Specialists, 1981, 143–157.

Phillips, Rod. *Michael McClure.* Western Writers Series 159. Boise, Idaho: Boise State University Press, 2003.

Rod Phillips

Beat Hotel Harold Norse (1983)
Originally published in German translation by Maro Verlag in 1975, HAROLD NORSE's *Beat Hotel* is a significant work not simply as an accomplished

collection of cut-up routines but also, ultimately, as a record of one of the most dynamic collaborative scenes in Beat history.

Norse, a friend and devotee to W. H. Auden and William Carlos Williams, had been writing and translating in Italy since the mid-1950s. In 1960 Williams, also a mentor to ALLEN GINSBERG, wrote to tell Norse of a collection of notable young writers who had recently converged on Paris, including Ginsberg, WILLIAM S. BURROUGHS, and GREGORY CORSO. The young Beat writers, who had begun their respective rapid and clumsy climbs to stardom just a few years prior, were all living in a nameless "flea-bag" motel at 9 Rue Gît-le-Coeur, run by a Madame Rachou. Dubbed the "Beat Hotel," (a name originally given to it by Corso) in a famous *Life* magazine article on the Beats, it housed some combination of these and other fellow travelers until 1963, when Rachou sold the hotel she had operated for 32 years.

By the time of Norse's arrival at the Beat Hotel in 1960, coaxed by invitations from Burroughs (Norse originally had rented a room nearby once allegedly occupied by Arthur Rimbaud), Norse began to experiment with the cut-up style of writing that had been discovered by Brion Gysin and made famous by Burroughs. Cut-up routines consisted of literally cutting blocks of text and reassembling the paragraphs or pages to create a less predictable and more random narrative. By allowing chance to become a part of the writing process, Burroughs believed one broke the rational word/image lock and freed one's mind from a certain amount of manipulation. While Burroughs and Gysin often mixed newspaper paragraphs, song lyrics, and the work of other writers into their cut-up experiments, Norse stayed mostly to his own work, creating elaborate narratives that he then rearranged into often hilarious and occasionally brilliant chapters. In doing so, Norse saw himself in the same tradition as John Cage in music or Jackson Pollock in painting, "telescop[ing] language in word clusters in a way James Joyce had pioneered, but with this difference: I allowed the element of chance to determine novel and surprising configurations of language."

The most famous cut-up chapter of his *Beat Hotel* is entitled "Sniffing Keyholes," which is, as he describes in a postscript, "a sex/dope scene between a muscular black youth called Melo and a blond Russian princess called Z. Z." The often-som-

ber Burroughs legendarily laughed out loud when he first read this chapter and attempted (in vein) to convince his NAKED LUNCH publisher, Maurice Girodias of Olympia Press, to publish a book of Norse's cut-ups. Girodias felt the work was too similar to Burroughs's, but eventually the chapters that Norse did not lose along the way were published. At times Norse's cut-ups play like a Georges Braque Cubist painting to Burroughs's Picasso: the untrained eye unable to decipher the difference.

Equal in significance to the book itself are the three postscripts added by Norse. One postscript details the methodology of the cut-ups, while another serves as an abridged memoir of the last days in the Beat Hotel. This last section in particular makes *Beat Hotel* an important artifact from a tremendously important time in Beat history when the international literary community first began to recognize the sensation these writers had created. Norse's prophecy, "the fleabag shrine will be documented by art historians," has come true.

Bibliography
Miles, Barry. *The Beat Hotel: Ginsberg, Burroughs, and Corso in Paris, 1957–1963.* New York: Grove Press, 2000.

Chuck Carlise

Beat Thing, The **David Meltzer** (2004)
It was almost inevitable that DAVID MELTZER would address the subject of "the Beats." One of the most moving images in the Beat Culture and the New America museum exhibit that traveled around the country in 1996 was a Harry Redl image of David and Tina Meltzer with son, just married and barely out of their teens—the classic image of the beatnik family. Although Meltzer has gone on record as claiming much of the interest in the Beats as decontextualized media hype, it is a subject he has circled and circled again. His interviews with San Francisco poets, *The San Francisco Poets* (1971), which has appeared in several editions, is perhaps his most popular book and is often a key text for readers trying to get a handle on Beat writers such as LEW WELCH and GARY SNYDER.

The Beat Thing is Meltzer's attempt to "take back" the Beat movement from the ahistoricizing

David Meltzer at his house in Oakland 2004. *(courtesy of Larry Keenan)*

market forces that have so deracinated it. This is the great work of his mature years, where he pulls together his considerable prosodic skills into a 155-page excavation of recent U.S. history. The poetry is a side show of various voices and forms: machine-gun riffs, a mix of long lines reminiscent of Warne Marsh's cliché-free solos, and jabbing lines that recall the algebra of a Sonny Rollins solo. Although there are spaces of quiescence and reflection, this is a "noisy" poem that often overwhelms the reader with its mud flow of names, places, and things—some recognizable, some part of the historical process the author is trying to deconstruct.

Meltzer is aware of how the reader may respond to the work. In the epilog to the work, Meltzer offers an explanation to his process:

> How easily narrative falls into place, realizes itself through a story-telling historian who sets out to frame a tangled constantly permutating chaos into a familiar & repeatable story w/out shadows or dead-ends; how impulsively memory organizes into a choir to tell a story of what it remembers symphonically, i.e., formally; even experimentalists practice w/in or against forms that have formed their relationship to writing & telling stories; history is the story of writing.

The Beat Thing is organized into three sections. The initial section, "The Beat Thing looms

up," is alternately a deconstruction of received Beat culture in the 21st century ("Beat tour jackets T-shirts numbered prints of Beat photos by Redl Stoll McDarrah framed offered round the clock on Beat shopping channel") and a warm memoir of real people and real places that have yet to be part of any beatnik bus tour. A tour-de-force of bop prosody is found in the section that begins with the question "What about Beat food?":

> bowls of bar popcorn and beer in the afternoon look out the windows at tourists furtive up and down Grant Avenue or tostadas and chile rellenos in Mission tacqueria late at night when mariachi trio walk down narrow aisle breaking hearts.

Maybe Meltzer is suggesting that the money machine has yet to find a way to commodify Beat food. He perhaps is also referencing the often impoverished, seat-of-the-pants lifestyle of the Beats where a meal out was an event to be savored.

The second section is "Beat Thing: A Commentary," which is really the historical context that plays out beneath the beatnik hijinks of the first section. The tone is darker—it almost serves as a displacement of the preceding section:

> . . . . color tv minimum
> wage 75 cents an hour Burn All Reds
> kids wear bead chain dogtags
> Henry Wallace in Brooklyn speaks
> Farmer Yiddish to solidarity cheers . . .
> ah everyone's apart
> together
> "Burn All Reds
> No Mercy For Spies
> Rosenberg Traitors Must Die"

In this short section Meltzer alludes to the appearance of color TV, the low wages of marginal workers, popular front politics, the emergence of rhythm and blues, the Strategic Air Command antimissile defense system, and the communist hysteria culminating in the Rosenberg executions. The final section, "Primo Po Mo" seems an extension of the middle section with Meltzer riffing on "the bomb," jazz, and an emerging gay culture as just a few of the particles whirling about the Meltzer Memory Cyclotron.

So much of Beat literature is barely veiled autobiography, but, oddly, so little of that material is self-reflexive. The major exceptions that come to mind are JOHN CLELLON HOLMES's late writing, MICHAEL McCLURE's *Scratching the Beat Surface,* and Meltzer's *The Beat Thing.* It is Meltzer's work alone that is framed neither as a memoir or a critical essay but rather as a creative text that seems to lie in an interzone between critique, autobiography, and poetry. It is one of the most innovative works to emerge from the Beat community in many years.

Joel Lewis

Been Down So Long It Looks Like Up to Me Richard Fariña (1966)

The jacket of the 1983 reprint of RICHARD FARIÑA's *Been Down So Long It Looks Like Up to Me* suggests that Fariña "evokes the Sixties as precisely, wittily, and poignantly as F. Scott Fitzgerald captured the Jazz Age." Although Fariña's novel presages the 1960s in many regards, it is very much a novel embedded in the prescribed year in which Fariña set its narrative, 1958. One of Fariña's chief accomplishments in *Been Down So Long It Looks Like Up to Me* is the degree to which he captures a cultural moment in transition, juxtaposing a depiction of the late Victorian mores of the Eisenhower administration against a burgeoning, if underground, campus culture of sex, drugs, Eastern mysticism, and what his character Juan Carlos Rosenbloom terms "revolution."

Set in Athene, a thinly veiled facsimile of Ithaca, New York, and the environs of Cornell University, *Been Down So Long It Looks Like Up to Me*'s picaresque narrative centers on the semester-long misadventures of Fariña's alter ego, Gnossos Pappadopoulis, recently rematriculated after a year of ON THE ROAD adventuring in Taos, Las Vegas, and the Adirondacks. The novel chronicles Pappadopoulis's attempts to maintain his "Immunity" and "Exemption Status" in the face of an increasingly politicized campus environment and his own capitulation to romantic love. The novel is threaded with intimations of a malevolent global conspiracy (against immunity and exemption), and near conclusion it wanders into the violent domain of pre-

revolutionary Cuba. Throughout, Pappadopoulis's young verve and Fariña's occasionally over-the-top plot and characters carry the narrative forward.

As Fariña's Cornell undergraduate friend and colleague Thomas Pynchon states in the introduction to the novel's 1983 reprint, "1958, to be sure, was another planet." Composed as it was in the early and mid-1960s, *Been Down So Long It Looks Like Up to Me* is clearly a work that was conceived in the shadow of JACK KEROUAC, if not ALLEN GINSBERG and GREGORY CORSO, characterized as it is by Fariña's manic, NEAL CASSADY-like narrator and Ginsberg and Corso's antic energy and framing of an increasingly sexualized society (and literature). Fariña's narrator at times enacts a vision of maleness that is distinctly Hemingwayesque if not outright brutish. But as Pynchon notes, Fariña's novel taps into a time, a sensibility, and a persona that, despite the novel's flaws, offers a vivid depiction of a new decade's generation, a generation that came of age in the fallout of nuclear testing in the Nevada desert and in the lap of a relatively prosperous if staid culture (versus Kerouac's roots in Depression-era Lowell).

Fariña's novel (like Kerouac's *On the Road*) met largely negative criticism in the aftermath of its initial publication, and for some of the same reasons—it was read as undisciplined, raw work, though Thomas Lask in the *New York Times* granted it "a wild, careering sense of the absurd, a flair for invention, and a wide range of mood." *Been Down So Long It Looks Like Up to Me* exhibits many of the shortcomings characteristic of first novels, and a convincing argument can be made that Fariña's chief strength as a writer was his lyricism, evidenced in the songwriting and music in which he engaged as central pursuit throughout his mid-twenties and up until the time of his premature death, as well as in his posthumously published miscellany *Long Time Coming and a Long Time Gone* (1969). Fariña's enduring position as a cultural figure embodying the energy, virility, and wit of the 1960s, most recently evidenced in David Hadju's *Positively 4th Street: The Lives and Times of Joan Baez, Bob Dylan, Mimi Baez Fariña, and Richard Fariña*, rests secure. But as Philip Beidler has noted, "Fariña's text, on the other hand, has proved a good deal less securely enshrineable."

Bibliography

Beidler, Philip. *Scriptures for a Generation: What We Were Reading in the 60s.* Athens, Ga.: University of Georgia, 1994.

Fariña, Richard. *Long Time Coming and a Long Time Gone.* New York: Random House, 1969.

The Richard and Mimi Fariña FanSite. Available online. URL: http://www.richardandmimi.com. Accessed May 31, 2006.

Pynchon, Thomas. Introduction. *Been Down So Long It Looks Like Up to Me.* By Richard Fariña. New York: Penguin, 1996, v–xiv.

Tracy Santa

Berrigan, Ted (1934–1983)

Ted Berrigan represents the vital link between Beat poetry and the New York School of Poets. A highly visible member of the New York School's second generation (which is associated with the Poetry Project at St. Mark's Church in the East Village section of Manhattan), Berrigan was not only a strong advocate of JACK KEROUAC's writing in numerous classroom and lecture settings; he was one of the first poets to have adapted WILLIAM S. BURROUGHS's cut-up techniques as a strategy for writing poetry.

Berrigan is best known to Kerouac fans as the interviewer of the famed *Paris Review* interview of 1968—the novelist's last major interview. The published interview was culled from more than four hours of a taped interview. Although they were played publicly at Andy Warhol's "Factory" in midtown Manhattan at the time that the interview was published, the whereabouts of the tapes are currently unknown.

Berrigan's background was similar to Kerouac's: a Roman Catholic New Englander from a working-class background. He was born in Providence, Rhode Island, and was raised there and in nearby Cranston. He was educated at Catholic parochial schools and began to attend the University of Tulsa (Oklahoma) while still a private in the United States Army. In Tulsa, he met up with a trio of talented high school students, poets Ron Padgett and Dick Gallup, along with the artist–poet Joe Brainard. Padgett as a high school senior was publishing a magazine called *White Dove Review* that managed to publish submissions received

from such established poets as Kerouac and Frank O'Hara.

When Padgett moved to Manhattan to attended Columbia University, Berrigan and Brainard followed. Berrigan, who in an interview referred to himself as "a late beatnik," scuffled to survive. One of the more imaginative ways of earning a buck was by writing elaborate and questioning letters to famous authors—if they responded, Berrigan would sell the letters to a rare book dealer. Although he had a few legit gigs, after 1966 he supported himself entirely on poetry-related jobs—despite the hardships that decision caused him.

His breakthrough work was *The Sonnets.* Inspired, in part by the cut-up experiments of Burroughs and Brion Gysin, Berrigan created a series of sonnets that were either rearrangements of conventional sonnets or sonnets composed of lines appropriated from other poets—often by such friends as Ron Padgett.

The 1967 Grove Press edition of *The Sonnets* (the original edition was a mimeo chapbook) gave Berrigan a level of attention and notoriety that led to a series of academic jobs, including stints at the Iowa Writers Workshop, Yale University, SUNY Buffalo, University of Essex, and the Jack Kerouac School of Disembodied Poetics. Berrigan published prolifically, ranging from mimeo books to limited-edition letter-press books. His major collections include: *Many Happy Returns* (New York: Corinth Books, 1969), *In the Early Morning Rain* (London: Cape Goliard Press, 1970), *Train Ride* (New York: Vehicle Editions, 1971), *A Feeling for Leaving* (New York: Frontward Books, 1975), *RED WAGON* (Chicago: Yellow Press, 1976), *Nothing for You* (Lenox, Mass., and N.Y.: Angel Hair Books, 1977), and *So Going Around Cities: New & Selected Poems 1958–1979* (Berkeley: Blue Wind Press, 1980).

Never tenured and often working temporary or part-time gigs, Berrigan and his family often endured long spells of poverty. No matter what his financial circumstances were, he always took his role as a poet in the community with utmost seriousness. Even plagued by ill health in the last few years of his life, he continued to give readings, teach classes, and talk poetry to any poet who visited his family's apartment on Saint Mark's Place. He died on July 4, 1983.

Berrigan's connections with Beat culture intertwined his literary influences with his choice of lifestyle. Although a strong advocate of both Frank O'Hara and John Ashbery, he was also strongly influenced by the poetry of Paul Blackburn and CHARLES OLSON—although he was less forthcoming about their influence. The later poetry of his short writing career is more focused on a speech-based poetics and is the source of such popular anthology pieces as "Whitman In Black" and "Red Shift." In fact, Berrigan's influences are rather wide ranging. His *Collected Poems* represents a poetic mind willing to be influenced and open to all influences.

He often said that his political stance was best summed up by Kerouac's quip, "Avoid the authorities." His only extended prose work, *Clear the Range* (New York: Adventures In Poetry/Coach House South, 1977) is a novel that is a cut-up and reconstruction of a Zane Grey western. Although the work has garnered little, if any, critical notice, it stands as a crucial link between Burroughs and KATHY ACKER, Burroughs's most imaginative disciple.

Joel Lewis

Big Sur **Jack Kerouac** (1962)

JACK KEROUAC was ill equipped to deal with the strong responses that his work, especially ON THE ROAD, evoked from both fans and critics in the late 1950s. Critical attacks that savaged both his work and his personal life, the sudden assault of celebrity status, heavy drinking, and the likelihood that he felt guilty about using his friends' lives in his work combined to drive Kerouac to a breakdown in the summer of 1960. *Big Sur,* the novel he wrote about this breakdown, is a remarkable accomplishment, for in this work Kerouac traces the decay—and recovery—of his own rational mind.

Kerouac was aware of the tremendous difference between himself and the image the public had of him after his work burst into print in 1957. In one scene in *Big Sur,* he recounts an afternoon when he is alone with an enthusiastic young man who obviously wants to impress the famous writer: "the poor kid actually believes there's something noble and idealistic about all this beat stuff, and I'm supposed to be the King of the Beats according to the newspa-

pers, so but at the same time I'm sick and tired of all the endless enthusiasms of new young kids trying to know me and pour out all their lives into me so that I'll jump up and down and say yes yes that's right, which I can't do anymore—." He goes on to say that notes on a book jacket (unnamed, but clearly a reference to Grove's first paperback edition of *The SUBTERRANEANS*) mistakenly reported his age to be 25 when he is in fact nearing 40. More than nine difficult years had passed since Kerouac had slipped a roll of paper into his typewriter and hammered out *On the Road. Big Sur* works as a companion piece to this earlier novel; it develops a counterpoint to the *Road* story and underscores the message of disappointment with road life that readers often miss. Taken with *The Town and the City* as opposite poles of the Duluoz Legend (Kerouac's fictional account of his life in novelistic form), *Big Sur* depicts the pathetic and perhaps unavoidable fate of the young man who hitchhiked out of the first novel, disillusioned with his past, into the adventures of *On the Road,* setting him on a course that promised joy and led to defeat.

In *Big Sur,* Jack Duluoz (the Kerouac character) leaves his mother's house for the first time since the publication of *Road,* which had lead to "endless telegrams, phonecalls, requests, mail, visitors, reporters, snoopers" and "drunken visitors puking in my study, stealing my books and even pencils—." At the end of the novel he returns to his mother. At the conclusion of *Big Sur,* Duluoz responds to his mother's question in earlier books: "Why can't you stick to the religion you were born with?" Put in perspective, his mental anguish brought on by problematic drinking is another kind of adventure—certainly a dangerous one—from which he returns to the security of his mother's house (and her religion, too) to write about the experience.

As did Sal Paradise (the Kerouac character) in his first *On the Road* adventures, Duluoz heads from the east of his home to the west of adventure. This time, however, he rides a cushy passenger train that makes his hitchhiking days seem part of a distant past of hardship; yet fame, as this book will show, brings its own misfortune. Duluoz keeps his faith in westward travel. As a group of friends later heads to Big Sur, singing traditional American sing-along tunes, Duluoz recalls some of the spirit that enticed him to head west in the first place: We "lean forward to the next adventure something that's been going on in America ever since the covered wagons clocked the deserts in three months flat—." He plans to go to Lorry Monsanto's (based on Lawrence Ferlinghetti) cabin near the coastal resort of Big Sur. In a gesture that symbolizes contrasts, he retrieves his rucksack with its essential survival gear from the bottle-strewn skid-row hotel room where he has crashed. He takes the bus and a cab to Big Sur, and he must walk the last several miles to the cabin through darkness. The troubling notion that "something's wrong" constantly besets him, while the high cliffside road and the night's impenetrable darkness scare him. Even his trusty lantern cannot breach the darkness. In the morning, he sees another scene that symbolizes the past of the Duluoz Legend: "the automobile that crashed thru the bridge rail a decade ago and fell 1000 feet straight down and landed upside down, is still there now, an upsidedown chassis of rust in a strewn skitter of sea-eaten tires. . . ."

More than most of his books, this novel possesses a strong sense of structure and control. The task at hand presents a rhetorical dilemma for the writer, for Kerouac contends with the difficult task of describing a mental and spiritual crisis—a breakdown in his orderly thinking—in a well-structured book. Kerouac unifies the book one way by consistently undercutting the simple joys he finds in his first days at Big Sur with comments that hint at the dark future. For example, while he may enjoy the babbling playful sounds of the stream as it flows to the sea, he tells that reader that he would hear "in the later horror of that madness night . . . the babble and rave of angels in my head."

The romantic nostalgia that he feels for his childhood, his tight relationship with his mother, his production of confessional, romanticized novels—all these seem out of place in a modern America that sends rockets into space and builds superhighways to conduct travelers quickly and innocuously to their destinations. Unable to find comfort either at Big Sur, where the sea's voice commanded him to find human company, or in the city, where people expect him to buy drinks and meals, he escapes by hitting the bottle. At the time of the events chronicled in *Big Sur,* NEAL CAS-

SADY had been recently released from San Quentin for a marijuana-possession conviction. Although Kerouac denied complicity in Cassady's arrest and faulted instead Cassady's high profile in San Francisco's North Beach bars, Kerouac may have felt some guilt for the arrest since his *On the Road* had made Cassady notorious. Now Cody Pomeroy (the Cassady character) in the *Big Sur* has also changed. Although Cody is not bitter about his time in prison—in fact, Duluoz remarks that he seems "more friendly"—the two men do not have the opportunity or perhaps even the energy to launch into the kind of conversation that they enjoyed in the past. Because of their fame, they have been "hemmed in and surrounded and outnumbered—The circle's closed in on the old heroes of the night." Cody also regrets Duluoz's heavy drinking, sensing that the alcohol is another factor that creates distance between them. Duluoz outlines a matter-of-fact description of the onset of delirium tremens, and in the sections that follow, the reader can trace Duluoz's passage through each stage.

After a series of drunken parties in the city, Duluoz returns to the Big Sur cabin, but this time he brings a gang, only to find that the noise and clamor of the group "desecrate" the purity of the wilderness. The late-night gab fests find a sarcastic natural parallel as Duluoz observes that a "sinister wind" blows that seems too big for the small canyon. Images of death abound, from a series of nightmares to a floating dead sea otter and the mouse that died after Duluoz left out a can of rodent poison. Kerouac infuses every description of events or scenes with a powerful undercurrent of turmoil and threatening portent.

Events make increasingly less sense to Duluoz, and he begins to suspect the motives of everyone around him. After a lengthy buildup, Kerouac concludes the section with a chilling line: "And this is the way it begins." Duluoz's state of mind deludes him into all manners of paranoia, from his friends deliberately plotting to make him crazy to the upstream neighbors he suspects of poisoning the creek water. Duluoz cannot hide in anonymity, as he had done during his *On the Road* days; his name is in the newspapers Monsanto left in the cabin, recent gossip columns have already reported his elopement with a local woman, and he imagines the vacation goers at Big Sur see him as a decadent author "who has brought gangs and bottles and today worst of all trollops." He finds no solace in the city; he regrets instantly his decision to return to Big Sur, and the road between has none of its old romantic charm or power to spirit him into the moment.

As Duluoz's faith in books and writing continues to wane, he notes that for Cody, living life has always been more important than writing about it since "writing's just an afterthought or a scratch anyway at the surface—." On the other hand, Duluoz has often said that writing is the purpose for his existence: "if I don't write what actually I see happening in this unhappy globe which is rounded by the contours of my deathskull I think I'll have been sent on earth by poor God for nothing—." In his descending madness Duluoz begins to see his earlier attempts at writing as finger exercises and dabblings at a serious business. He vexes himself for having been a "happy kid with a pencil . . . using words as a happy game"; now he faces mortality and sees the tremendous seriousness of life as if for the first time. He feels that while he had written the proper words when describing the sensations of life, he has never before plumbed the depths of life's emotions. In the worst of his mental breakdown, he realizes that "the words I'd studied all my life have suddenly gotten to me in all their seriousness and definite deathliness, never more I be a 'happy poet' 'Singing' 'about death' and allied romantic matters." The justification for writing *Big Sur* comes on the last page when Duluoz vows to forgive the people he has been with during his madness "and explain everything (as I'm doing now)." The final sentence in the book sounds a note of completion and finality, since "there's no need to say another word."

In the morning, Duluoz finally falls asleep for a short time and finds that "blessed relief" comes to him almost immediately. His torture has passed, becoming only a memory from which he will create another book. The paranoia that possessed him disappears with neither a trace nor an explanation. Duluoz is as puzzled as Doctor Sax was when "the universe disposed of its own evil" in the novel *DOCTOR SAX*. Almost as a teaser to his subsequent work, Duluoz allows Buddhist images to filter like a mirage across his strong image of the cross as he notes that he feels "Simple golden eternity blessing all," a softened blend of Buddhist and Christian phrases. Readers may wonder whether Kerouac heightened the drama of his night in Big Sur, since the awful nightmares pass so quickly. Yet he himself admits that he does not understand the suddenness of its passing. Again, he has been in the backseat of his own experience, the "Observer of the story," much as Sal Paradise had been in *On the Road*. Kerouac takes himself to the edge of experience, whether that experience is sexuality, drugs, fast cars, bop jazz, religious and spiritual epiphanies, or madness and records the sensations that he feels. He cannot always explain what he sees there. In a sense, he is an American foreign correspondent, if one refers to the unknown interior of human consciousness as "foreign" territory. In *Big Sur*, Kerouac probes deeper and more dangerous depths than in previous works, yet his role is essentially the same.

Bibliography

Theado, Matt. *Understanding Jack Kerouac.* Columbia: University of South Carolina Press, 2000.

Matt Theado

Blood and Guts in High School
Kathy Acker (1978)

This extraordinary book represents three transitional points in KATHY ACKER's career as a writer: (1) her first conscious attempt to gain commercial recognition, which was relatively successful; (2) her departure from cut-up experiments and movement toward some semblance of narrative; and (3) her move away from exploring identity (because she had decided it did not exist) and toward experimenting with plagiarism as a formal strategy. More importantly, the novel contains the seeds for her subsequent work and experimentation.

Through *Blood and Guts,* Acker found a much wider audience. The novel might be thought of as a sort of *ON THE ROAD* for punks, riot grrrls, and cyberfeminists, though the narrator, Janey Smith, transgresses far more than geographical borders on her series of "journeys." If JACK KEROUAC can be seen as a 20th-century Blake or Rousseau, romanticizing the common man and celebrating, to the tune of jazz riffs, the "power" and freedom that make the poor and downtrodden superior to mainstream culture, Acker is a modern-day Marquis de Sade—she is romanticism gone awry. Her "tune" is a cacophony: a punk rocker portrait of victimhood, oppression, and subordination. Where Sal Paradise in *On the Road has* nothing and is all the happier for his lack, Janey Smith *is* nothing—a blank page onto which a variety of male, capitalist oppressors "write" what they want her to be.

In a 1986 interview, Acker said that with *Blood and Guts,* she wanted to go beyond the cut-ups and thematically linked stories that she had been writing and move toward making a narrative, so she simply invented Janey but that Janey did not exist (see Acker interview with Ellis et al.). As Acker acknowledged, Janey has no character: "she's nobody: she's an 'I,' a very empty 'I.' And it was a joke, you know, the empty 'I,' and I linked everything together as if this was her life." Janey Smith is a literary Jane Doe; thus, just as other characters in the novel "write" her into existence, so can the reader. Paradoxically, though, Janey is also Kathy Acker, who herself claimed to have no identity even as she obsessively incorporated her autobiography into her work.

The novel is organized into three sections: (1) "Inside high school," (2) "Outside high school," and (3) "A journey to the end of the night." In part one, Janey is 10 years old and the victim of a variety of horrors ranging from incest to rape, though she appears to be a willing participant on all counts. The father as oppressor is literal as Acker throws a literary molotov cocktail into the traditional family structure, and her so-called rapist is a sadist to her willing masochist. Part two explores the same themes of oppression, but this time the "father" is not a sexual predator. Rather, he is a character named Mr. Linker, but metaphorically Mr. Linker is at least two manifestations of "the Man": a pimp who forces Janey into white slavery as well as a doctor who controls her mind. For Acker, Mr. Linker is the embodiment of the larger culture, which includes but is not limited to the father, the political system, the capitalist economy, the public education system, the church, and even the academy. In part three, the "father" is language

itself, and we see Janey (and Acker) attempting to escape this father subversively: She tries to break the bonds of abstract language through a more visceral language. Much of the narrative in the third section is pictorial, visually similar to WILLIAM S. BURROUGHS's *The Book of Breeething* (1980), and Janey's journey is a romp through Egypt with Jean Genet. Like Burroughs, Acker wanted to escape the constrictions (and the constructions) imposed by language, but for her it was a feminist quest. It is a mistake, however, to align her with the French feminists of the 1970s who sought a feminine language of the body to escape the constraints of patriarchal language. Acker eventually concluded that such a goal is impossible to realize.

Before *Blood and Guts,* Acker attempted to gender Burroughs's theories about the relationship among power, language, and politics by employing his cut-up techniques. *Blood and Guts* represents a departure from the cut-up, but it simultaneously foreshadows what became Acker's return to and increasingly sophisticated and subtle applications of the technique. Where Burroughs was concerned with cutting away at the literal word itself to reveal this unspoken collusion between language and politics, Acker eventually produced more abstract cut-ups in which she cut away at the mindsets and worldviews—the myths—that result from and in turn reinforce the concrete words and texts that were Burroughs's focus and for Acker represented patriarchal culture. In her later works, Acker disrupts and reimagines myths that produce words, simultaneously slicing and resplicing the myths those words produce. Rather than trying to create a new language or get beyond existing language, Acker simply expressed what is forbidden in the language. This has often been misconstrued as pornography and vulgarity, but Acker felt that she was simply laying bare the horrifying reality that lies beneath the surface of so-called civilized society. For her, incest, rape, and S&M relationships are merely metaphors for political and economic realities in capitalistic societies. Where Burroughs tried to dismantle these realities by literally mutilating what he saw as "the Man's" most powerful tool—language—Acker saw that this was futile. Her more sophisticated cut-ups are not mutilations but revelations; they cut away at what is taboo by speaking the taboo, as well as speaking through taboo.

Blood and Guts anticipates these revelations. The most obvious example is Janey Smith's "book report" near the middle of the novel. Through Janey, Acker rewrites Nathaniel Hawthorne's *The Scarlet Letter.* The classic novel, which was written by a white, male literary "father" and has arguably reached the realm of myth in American culture, becomes a cut-up dismantling Acker's own childhood, her own myth of western letters, the culture's myth of Hester Prynne, the myth of formal education, Acker's disappointment in the American political system; her reromanticization of America, and her rewriting of yet another literary myth, Nathaniel Hawthorne—these all form a labyrinthine automythography of both Acker and Hawthorne that transcends time and space. In addition, her appropriations of Hawthorne's and other texts are a taste of what is to come with her next novel, *Great Expectations,* in which she blatantly plagiarizes Charles Dickens's classic text.

Kathy Acker is best understood if all of her works are read as one work, and *Blood and Guts in High School* sets the stage for her lifelong fugue-like textual performance. The novel should be read within the context of her larger project. To dismiss it as juvenile or nihilistic, as some critics have, is to misread and misunderstand Kathy Acker. She is not or was not nihilistic; rather, she ran into society's nihilism and began to deconstruct it as she reconstructed by remythologizing, and she did so through her automythography. For Acker, the personal is indeed political.

Bibliography

Acker, Kathy. *Bodies of Work.* New York: Serpent's Tail, 1997.
———. "Me Talking About Me" folder. Typescript of "An Informal Interview with Kathy Acker on the 2nd April 1986" by F. J. Ellis, Carolyn Bird, Dawn Curwen, Ian Mancor, Val Ogden, and Charles Patrick. Box 4. Kathy Acker Papers. Rare Book, Manuscript, and Special Collections Library. Duke University.
Lotringer, Sylvère. "Devoured by Myths." In *Hannibal Lecter, My Father,* edited by Sylvère Lotringer.

Semiotext(e) Native Agents Series. New York: Semiotext(e), 1991.
Scholder, Amy. "Editor's Note." *Essential Acker.* New York: Grove Press, 2002.
Siegle, Robert. "Kathy Acker: The Blood and Guts of Guerilla Warfare." *Suburban Ambush: Downtown Writing and the Fiction of Insurgency.* Baltimore: The Johns Hopkins University Press, 1989.
Winterson, Jeanette. "Introduction." *Essential Acker.* New York: Grove Press, 2002.
Wollen, Peter. "Don't Be Afraid to Copy It Out." *London Review of Books* 20, no. 3 (February 1998): Available online. URL: http://www.lrb.co.uk/v20/n03/woll0_.html. Accessed May 31, 2006.

Bebe Barefoot

"Bomb" Gregory Corso (1958)

"Bomb" was written by GREGORY CORSO in Paris in 1957 and was first published in 1958 as a broadside by City Lights in San Francisco. The poem was subsequently printed as a foldout in Corso's collection *The HAPPY BIRTHDAY OF DEATH* (New Directions, 1960). "Bomb" is a pattern poem, that is, the printed shape is in the outline of the subject the poem describes, in this case the characteristic mushroom-formed cloud created by the explosion of an atomic bomb. The mushroom shape of the text may also be seen as a visual metaphor suggesting the parasitic nature of the bomb and of death itself, which in the poem is embodied in the bomb.

Contrary to what might be expected of a literary treatment of this grim topic, which was written during the height of the cold war in the late 1950s, Corso's "Bomb" is neither solemn nor angry nor anxious but is, instead, imbued with a wild, irreverent humor. Indeed, the poem is not—as might be supposed—a protest or a dire prediction, a denunciation of or a diatribe against the atomic bomb but rather a delirious declaration of love for it!

Corso's paean to the bomb proceeds in part from his assumed role as jester and prankster, gadfly and maverick, clown and contrarian. In this sense, the poem is written in mischievous defiance of the solemnity surrounding the subject and as a provocation to the sanctimony and the self-congratulatory pacifistic posturing of the Left and the left-leaning literary and artistic avant-garde of the era. Another motive for Corso's unusual treatment of the topic of the atomic bomb is the poet's desire to go beyond foregone conclusions and conventional pieties to undertake an imaginative exploration of the subject, to discover unsuspected connections and latent meanings behind the phenomenon of the bomb.

The essential structure of "Bomb" is that of a temporal progression from the past into the future, accompanied by a dramatic escalation toward a climactic vision of an atomic apocalypse and its aftermath. The argument of the poem consists mainly in its endeavor both to place the atomic bomb in the context of human history and to view it in the perspective of the fundamental energies, processes, sequences, and cycles of the cosmos. The basic devices employed by Corso in the poem are those of apostrophe and animation or anthropomorphization, the poet–speaker addressing the bomb as if it were endowed with human intelligence and human emotions.

The poem begins by introducing the contradictory roles of the atomic bomb in human history. On one hand, the bomb is the "budger of history," while on the other it may well prove to be the "brake of time." The atomic bomb, that is, acts to advance events, giving impetus and urgency to contemporary history, while at the same time representing the potential annihilation of all history and humankind. Yet, whichever of these roles is ultimately enacted by the atomic bomb, the bomb is seen by Corso as being no more than an effect of other much greater forces that act upon it or through it, the expression of energies akin to but vastly more powerful than itself. The atomic bomb is ultimately but a "toy of the universe." In these opening images, time and history, power and death, the limits of the human perspective and of human agency, and our incipient awareness of cosmic forces of a magnitude that far surpass our limited imagination are established as central themes of the poem.

Corso proceeds to trace the history of human weaponry from the Stone Age to the invention of the atomic bomb, showing the diverse ends which various weapons have served: survival and self-defense, criminality and conquest, personal anger and tribal warfare, and resistance against oppression and evil. Weapons, the poet implies, are not in themselves pernicious; rather their nature depends on the uses to which they are put. The same holds true of the atomic bomb: "Bomb / you are as cruel as man makes you." Such a nuanced view of the phenomenon of the atomic bomb—as possible human benefactor, as a tool against tyranny, as well as a menace—would not have been at all well received by the bohemian community or political left of the time. (Indeed, in a letter to a friend, Corso records how during a reading of "Bomb" to a group of students at Oxford University, a member of the audience threw a shoe at him.)

The poet suggests that much of the modish opposition to the bomb has its origins in the fear of death, which is an inevitable component of the human situation. He enumerates other forms of death that he sees as far more likely and equally or even more terrible. Also like the figure of Stubb in Herman Melville's *Moby-Dick* who observes "such a waggish leering as lurks in all your horribles," Corso makes remarks about the strange "impish" and "sportive" aspect of atomic apocalypse. In the fiery wind of the thermonuclear blast, all human vanities will be revealed in their ultimate triviality, and surreal, absurd juxtapositions and metamorphoses will occur:

> Turtles exploding over Istanbul,
> The jaguar's flying foot
> Soon to sink in arctic snow
> Penguins plunged against the Sphinx

Simultaneous with this convulsive beauty, the instant that the atomic cataclysm takes place will also represent the ultimate confrontation between time past and time present, an encounter that Corso comically images as a baseball game with Greek gods, theologians, and Christian and Buddhist saviors as players on opposing teams. If time can in this way be abolished by atomic destruction, the present devouring the past even as the present extinguishes itself, then Corso imagines the same destructive power that is latent in the atom as capable of destroying the entire universe; the planets, the stars and galaxies extinguished; and even the Creator being consumed by His own creation.

From this vision of a final void, Corso quickly turns to another fanciful picture—a hell for bombs, an afterlife in which the shattered, detonated bombs of various nations, formerly enemies, sit together in eternity. The pity that this vision of a despised and damned atomic bomb evokes in the heart of the poet causes him to comfort, to court, and even to make love to the bomb. The climax of this love making is an atomic explosion, rendered in full-volume onomatopoeia: "BING, BANG, BONG, BOOM."

Again, defying reader expectations, the destruction of the world as envisioned by the poet in this passage is not depicted as tragedy but as a joyous release, an ecstatic fulfillment:

Flowers will leap in joy their roots aching
Fields will kneel proud beneath the halleluyahs
of the wind

Nor will this cataclysm be the end, for the parasitic mushroom cloud that feeds off and destroys its host—life—also scatters the spores of new life. This is the sense in which earlier in the poem, the bomb was lauded as a "Spring bomb" clad in "gown of dynamite green." Accordingly, the poet foresees future ages in which strange new empires will arise and new bombs will be invented and venerated. The cycle of creation, destruction, creation will continue on and on; worlds will appear and disappear endlessly. Seen in this perspective, the atomic bomb is but a local and minor manifestation of the mysterious fecundating destructive power of the cosmos that itself began with a "Big Bang"; the bomb is thus a vehicle, a tool, a "toy of the universe."

Quite apart from its content, its provocative, polemical or parodic intentions, "Bomb" is a poem of wild invention, verbal exuberance, and delirium of metaphor. Corso spins off allusions at a furious pace, keeping up a swift flow of disjunction and juxtaposition, mixing lyricism and whimsy, horror and humor, achieving a kind of manic sublimity. The poem ranges widely in human history and culture, drawing in figures and images from classical and Norse mythology, the Bible, fairy tale and legend, sports and popular entertainment, literature and contemporary history. Poetic coinages are frequent: *vulturic, rainlight, untrumpet, mythmouth;* and

extravagant, incongruous images abound: *pimps of indefinite weather, marble helmsmen, jubilee feet, lily door, Death's Mozambique,* and *magisterial bombs wrapped in ermine.*

It is uncertain whether in dropping his "Bomb" on the cold war nuclear disarmament debate Corso really hoped to convince anyone of his eccentric perspectives on the issue or whether—more likely—he was aiming to explode some of the passionately held preconceptions and cherished received opinions associated with the controversy and to blast loose certain of the hardened and humorless ideological positions of the era. Happily, the topic inspired Corso to take a comic romp among the sacred cows, scattering them in all directions.

Bibliography

Corso, Gregory. *An Accidental Autobiography: The Selected Letters of Gregory Corso.* Edited by Bill Morgan. New York: New Directions, 2003.

Miles, Barry. *The Beat Hotel: Ginsberg, Burroughs, and Corso in Paris, 1957–1963.* New York: Grove Press, 2000.

Olson, Kirby. *Gregory Corso: Doubting Thomist.* Carbondale: Southern Illinois University Press, 2002.

Skau, Michael. *"A Clown in a Grave": Complexities and Tensions in the Works of Gregory Corso.* Carbondale: Southern Illinois University Press, 1999.

Stephenson, Gregory. *Exiled Angel: A Study of the Work of Gregory Corso.* London: Hearing Eye, 1989.

Gregory Stephenson

Book of Dreams Jack Kerouac (1961)

JACK KEROUAC kept a journal of his dreams for much of his life, dreams written down nonstop on awakening. *Book of Dreams* is a selection of his dreams from 1952 to about the time of the publication of ON THE ROAD in 1957. Dreams are a central source of creativity for many of the Beat writers (WILLIAM S. BURROUGHS includes selections from his dreams in most of his novels). For Kerouac, the recording of dreams is a logical extension of his theory of spontaneous prose. As he says in his preface to the book, "I wrote nonstop so that the subconscious could speak for itself in its own form, that is, uninterruptedly flowing and rippling—Being half awake I hardly knew what I was doing let alone writing." The book is thus far from crafted prose. It is also Kerouac's most unguarded prose, revealing potentially embarrassing aspects of his inmost personality. The dreams here are the raw material for such books as DOCTOR SAX, *The SUBTERRANEANS, MAGGIE CASSIDY,* and *DESOLATION ANGELS,* showing how close Kerouac's subconscious is to the surface in his spontaneous prose. A word of warning: The reader unfamiliar with Kerouac's life and works from this period will find the book less rewarding than those who do. To understand anyone's dreams, the analyst/reader needs to be familiar with the analysand/writer, and *Book of Dreams* is no exception.

The book begins during a period in the early 1950s when Kerouac was becoming increasingly depressed about not being able to publish his books. In one dream, he is forced to wait outside at a party, and when he awakens from the dream, he finds himself in a fury against the publishing establishment and everyone who is stealing his ideas. In another dream, he returns home to his mother's house at Christmas, and his mother's coworkers in the shoe factory believe he has come home for her Christmas bonus check. The subject of money creates an association with JOHN CLELLON HOLMES (James Watson in *Book of Dreams*) whose novel GO had earned Holmes a $20,000 advance. In his dreams, Jack is suspicious of Holmes and accuses him of stealing his idea for a novel about jazz; Holmes did in fact publish a novel about jazz called *The HORN.*

Kerouac's dreams in regard to his writing force him to confront how sincere he is about not caring if he ever publishes his books, that they are written for him alone. At the same time, his dreams reveal his own insecurities about the value of his work. A dream of watching high school girls walk home turns into a guilt-ridden admission that *Doctor Sax* and *On the Road* are "rejectable unpublishable wildprose madhouse enormities." Such dreams reveal the vulnerable side of the man who writes to such editors and publishers as Malcolm Cowley and Carl Solomon that he is the greatest living writer even if they will not publish him. In his dreams, quite pitifully, he sees newspaper reviews of his own works that he has self-published. As the

unpublished manuscripts piled up in his life (a frequent sight in his dreams), he has to conclude, "I am writing myself to death."

Burroughs believed that Kerouac was no more unhappy than anyone else, and in fact that Kerouac's losses, as they find their way into his dreams, are universal—the death of a sibling, death of a parent, first love, and heartbreak. Especially affecting are his dreams of his first serious love affair with Mary Carney (the subject of *Maggie Cassidy*). He regrets her loss as much as anything in his life. Carney represented a point in his life where everything could have turned out differently for him: He could have been happy and married, but he "let it all go for some chimera about yourself, concerning sadness"—specifically his unhealthy fixation over his brother Gerard's death. Kerouac is writing the novel about Carney at the time of these dreams, but it is hard to tell whether Kerouac dreams of her because he is writing about her or he is writing about her because he is dreaming about her: "My angel doll of long ago, whose blackhaired presence in sunny afternoon bedroom I took for granted."

Anxieties of all kinds surface in the dreams. He has recurring dreams of missing a ship by a few minutes at the docks (a real-life instance of this is recorded in *VISIONS OF CODY*). Because he was working on the railroads during this half decade of not publishing, he has dreams of his ineptitude on the rails. The older men on the railroad are menacing authority figures in his dreams; these dreams are similar to dreams that he has of his failure in the military during World War II, caused by his inability to respect authority. His trouble with authority (and guilt over it) creates dreams from his Columbia football days (another self-created failure). In one, the 30-year-old Kerouac has returned to join the team, and he hopes that the college players will not notice he is an old man.

Some critics and biographers focus on what they believe was Kerouac's repressed homosexuality, and the dream record shows that Kerouac was willing to write about his dream life in this respect (even if, in real life—according to ALLEN GINSBERG and Gore Vidal, among others—he was less willing in his novels to come clean about his homosexual affairs). A famous and controversial dream is that of the "double crapper." Kerouac and NEAL CAS-

SADY are sitting next door to each other in connected bathroom stalls and as Cassady tells a story of a homosexual performing oral sex, Kerouac has an erection that keeps him from being able to stand up from the toilet seat. To him, the effect is comic. A dream involving his mother and "flying snakes" that they are watching ("cockroaches" his mother calls them) leads associatively to Kerouac recalling that *cockroach* was his father's pejorative term for Ginsberg. The flying snakes flop on Kerouac "like the importunate advances of affection from my disgusting friends." A giggling man, maybe Burroughs, causes Kerouac anxiety by trying to "tickle" him in two dreams. In a dream toward the end of the book, Kerouac admits, "I must have been a queer in that previous lifetime."

Not all of his dreams deal with anxiety. Many are straightforward wish-fulfillment fantasies, to use Freud's phrase. Such dreams provide insight into Kerouac's guiltless desires. He calls the "happiest dream of my life" one in which he is about six years old, playing his imaginary games by himself in his Lowell bedroom, and his mother brings him cake, milk, and pies. His deepest desire is to have a home where people visit him and a job on a railroad that goes from Boston to New Hampshire to Lowell. A dream entitled "Happy Dreams of Canada" also shows Kerouac's deep desire to live among his own people in their ancestral land—rather than as a Canuck outsider in the United States where he has to submerge his true identity.

This is not a book that should be considered marginal in the Kerouac canon. Some of his most honest, revealing, spontaneous writing can be found here. *Book of Dreams* is an important part of what Kerouac called the Duluoz Legend, his fictional story of his life. In the foreword of the book Kerouac writes, "The characters that I've written about in my novels reappear in these dreams in weird new dream situations . . . and they continue the same story which is the one story that I always write about." An unabridged edition of this book was published in 2001 by City Lights and should help place *Book of Dreams* within its proper context in the Kerouac canon.

Rob Johnson

Bowles, Paul Frederic (1910–1999)

Though Paul Bowles is not generally known as a Beat writer, his influence on the Beats and his personal relationships with them were significant. His writings are partially responsible for inspiring WILLIAM S. BURROUGHS to move to Tangier. Born on the outskirts of New York City, Bowles, writer, composer, translator, and world traveler, grew up as an only child in a well-to-do family of New England stock. During his childhood and early youth, a painful relationship existed between young Paul and his father, causing the boy at a very early age to withdraw into himself. This process of alienation from others was compounded by the fact that Bowles was kept away from the company of other children until the age of five, at which time, as he says, "it was already too late."

His interior life, however, was always a very rich one, even as a child. In early childhood Bowles started to write stories and fairy tales, and he would improvise music on the family piano to escape from dull, prescribed piano practice. At almost every turn of his development, he was limited and held in check by parental intervention and made to do things that he found unpleasant. It is no wonder that, when asked what freedom meant to him, Bowles should answer, "I'd say it was not having to experience what you don't like." At his first possible chance, he turned his back on rules and control and sought ways in which, without restraint, he could channel his inner expressive urges.

By the age of 17 Bowles had become a published poet in the famous literary journal *transition*, edited and published in Paris. But his primary affinity was for music. For the next nine years he studied and wrote music under the guidance of Aaron Copeland and Virgil Thomson in New York and Berlin. His compositions were mostly incidental music for plays and films and scores for musicals on Broadway. As a composer of nearly 150 distinctive compositions, Bowles is highly regarded for the quality of his work.

During his European travels between the two world wars, Bowles came into contact with many artists of the so-called Lost Generation, including Gertrude Stein, Ezra Pound, Jean Cocteau, Stephen Spender, and Christopher Isherwood. It was under the influence and patronage of Stein that Bowles first went to North Africa, an experience that made a profound impression upon him. He was then 21 years old and felt mysteriously attracted to and enormously excited by the place. Although he went on to travel in Mexico, South America, the Far East, and elsewhere, Bowles would eventually spend the greater part of his life in Morocco; it was there that his preoccupation with the unconscious mind and taste for romantic primitivism would find inspiration and confirmation.

When Bowles—together with his wife Jane Auer—settled permanently in Tangier in 1949, he became a full-time writer; after that time, he only rarely wrote music. His first novel, *The Sheltering Sky* (London 1949), owes its creation to Bowles's first encounter with North Africa. From the beginning, the "insanity and confusion" of the place were to his taste. He was content, as he has said, to "see whatever was happening continue exactly as if I were not there." This was part of his "practice of pretending not to exist," of always being an observer and an outsider, a role it took him many years to relinquish. *The Sheltering Sky* was eventually used as the basis for a film directed by Bernardo Bertolucci in 1990, by which time Bowles was at last enjoying a considerable literary reputation.

Bowles continued to live in Tangier until his death in 1999 and had by that time produced another three novels: *Let It Come Down* (New York 1952), *The Spider's House* (New York 1955), and *Up Above the World* (London 1967). He also published several volumes of short stories, including *The Delicate Prey* (1950), *The Time of Friendship* (1967), *The Collected Stories of Paul Bowles* (1979), *Midnight Mass* (1981), and *Points in Time* (1982); books of poems; and translations of North African folk tales. Among Bowles's short stories, the volume titled A HUNDRED CAMELS IN THE COURTYARD (1962) offers a view of the way that kif (marijuana mixed with tobacco) may transform everyday life.

In terms of literary schools or movements, Bowles is not easily pinpointed. He can be said to occupy a kind of position between the writers of the Lost Generation and those of the Beat Generation, many of whom viewed him as a mentor and precursor. Indeed, several of the Beat writers were drawn to North Africa as well, in search of extremes of experience, of sexuality, and of con-

sciousness. After all, this region at the intersection of Europe and Africa was like a new psychic frontier to be explored. Some of the Beats established lasting friendships with Bowles, including Burroughs, ALLEN GINSBERG, GREGORY CORSO, and LAWRENCE FERLINGHETTI. Also JACK KEROUAC visited Tangier but missed Bowles, whom he met in New York on a later occasion.

Bowles was obsessed with exploring the point at which the savage and the civilized intersect and merge, and in his writing he skillfully explored the possibilities offered by this juxtaposition. In common with the Beats he cultivated an interest in drugs, in dreams, and in altered states of consciousness. Also, like many of the Beat writers, Bowles may be seen as a neoromantic who was preoccupied with romantic primitivism and its cultural manifestations including art, literature, music, and dance. On many occasions Bowles ventured into the Sahara to record tribal music and to observe the trance dancers and their religious observances. At the same time, in contrast to the writers of the Beat Generation, Bowles's fiction appears to be extremely pessimistic and quite devoid of any spirituality. His fictional characters have been viewed as "metaphysically condemned"; he saw outrage, terror, and nothingness as having replaced myth in the modern world, leaving humankind in "a landscape stripped of everything human."

During the latter part of his life, Bowles only rarely visited the United States; he was keen to stay as far away as possible, "far both geographically and spiritually," as he put it. So he remained where he was, suspended between two cultures and two continents, never tiring of exploring North Africa and the terra incognita of the human psyche.

Bibliography

Bowles, Paul. *In Touch: The Letters of Paul Bowles.* Edited by Jeffrey Miller. New York: Farrar, Straus and Giroux, 1994.

———. *Without Stopping. An Autobiography.* New York: G. P. Putnam's Sons, 1972.

Green, Michelle. *The Dream at the End of the World: Paul Bowles and the Literary Renegades in Tangier.* New York: HarperCollins, 1991.

———. "Interview with Paul Bowles." By Daniel Halpern. *The Tri-Quarterly* 33 (Spring 1975): 159–177.

Hassan, Ihab. "The Novel of Outrage." *The American Novel Since W.W. II,* edited by Marcus Klein, New York: Fawcett Publications, 1969.

Birgit Stephenson

Brautigan, Richard (1935–1984)

Although he knew the Beats and they him, Brautigan always insisted that he was not a part of their literary movement. Contemporary literary opinion supports this contention, seeing Brautigan, his work, and his place in American literature as a bridge between the Beats and what is being identified as "counterculture literature."

An American novelist, short-story writer, and poet noted for his idiosyncratic prose style, Richard Brautigan is best known for his novel TROUT FISHING IN AMERICA, his collection of stories *Revenge of the Lawn,* and his collection of poetry *The Pill Versus the Springhill Mine Disaster.* Brautigan was born in Tacoma, Washington, on January 30, 1935, grew up in the U.S. Northwest, and by 1956 settled in San Francisco, California. There he sought to establish himself as a writer, was known for handing out his poetry on street corners, and often participated in "Blabbermouth Night" readings at The Place, a popular gathering spot for artists and poets. His first published "book" of poetry was *The Return of the Rivers* (1957), followed by *The Galilee Hitch-Hiker* (1958), *Lay the Marble Tea* (1959), *The Octopus Frontier* (1960), *All Watched Over by Machines of Loving Grace* (1967), *The Pill Versus the Springhill Mine Disaster* (1968), *Please Plant This Book* (1969), *Rommel Drives On Deep into Egypt* (1970), *Loading Mercury with a Pitchfork* (1976), and *June 30th, June 30th* (1978).

Brautigan's novels include *A Confederate General from Big Sur* (1964), *Trout Fishing in America* (1967), *In Watermelon Sugar* (1968), *The Abortion* (1971), *The Hawkline Monster* (1974), *Willard and His Bowling Trophies* (1975), *Sombrero Fallout* (1976), *Dreaming of Babylon* (1977), *So the Wind Won't Blow It All Away* (1982), and *An Unfortunate Woman* (2000). His short-story collections include *Revenge of the Lawn* (1971) and *The Tokyo-Montana Express* (1979).

Overall, Brautigan is remembered for his detached, anonymous, first-person point of view, his

Richard Brautigan at City Lights Books in San Francisco, 1965. *(courtesy of Larry Keenan)*

autobiographical prose style, and his episodic narrative structure that was full of unconventional but vivid images powered by whimsy and metaphor. For example, *Trout Fishing in America* can be said to represent the novel itself being written by Brautigan, a character in the novel, a place, an outdoor sport, a religion, a state of mind, and a symbol of the American pastoral ideal lost to commercialism, environmental degradation, and social decay. In subsequent novels Brautigan vowed not to write sequels to *Trout Fishing in America* and instead experimented with different literary genres: "historical romance," "gothic western," "perverse mystery," "Japanese novel," "detective," and "memoir." General dismissal by literary critics reversed Brautigan's initial literary success, and his popularity waned throughout the 1970s and early 1980s. He remained popular in Japan, however, and Brautigan visited there for extended periods, finding inspiration for later writings. Despite lack of sustained critical acclaim, Brautigan's work is continually translated into other languages, and he maintains strong interest among readers around the world who are attracted to his unique use of language and autobiographical style. Brautigan died in October 1984, in Bolinas, California.

Bibliography

Barber, John. *The Brautigan Bibliography* plus+ http://www.brautigan.net/brautigan/

John F. Barber

Bremser, Ray (1934–1998)

Like GREGORY CORSO and HERBERT HUNCKE, Ray Bremser was educated on the streets and in prisons. CHARLES PLYMELL went so far as to say that Bremser was more "Beat," in the street sense of the word than was ALLEN GINSBERG. Bremser became one of BOB DYLAN's favorite poets (there is a quick glimpse of Bremser in Martin Scorsese's *No Direction Home* [2005]), and mention of him can be found in the liner notes to Dylan's *The Times They Are A-Changin'*.

Born in Jersey City, New Jersey, on February 22, 1934, to a mother who worked inspecting condoms and a father who supposedly played piano on the ship *Orizaba,* from which the poet Hart Crane suicidally jumped in April 1932, Bremser joined the United States Air Force (like AMIRI BARAKA/LeRoi Jones later did) in 1951 to get some discipline. He was honorably discharged but found himself in Bordentown Reformatory for armed robbery from April 1952 to November 1958. While incarcerated, Bremser became an autodidact. When he heard of the Beat poets Corso and Ginsberg in Paris he sent them his poems. This led to his first published poetry in Jones's journal *Yugen.* When he was released, Jones and JACK KEROUAC made the rounds with him in New York City.

The authorities were looking for a way to bust Bremser after he promoted the legalization of marijuana on Ralph Collier's Philadelphia talk show in 1959, and he was arrested for violating parole for marrying Bonnie Bremser/BRENDA FRAZER,

a woman whom he met at a poetry reading in which he participated earlier that year, without the permission of his parole officer. After serving six months at Trenton State, a letter from the poet William Carlos Williams on Bremser's behalf helped Bremser obtain a release. Soon after he was accused of a robbery that he swears he did not commit and fled to Mexico with his wife and their child with the help of money borrowed from Willem de Kooning's wife, Elaine. Frazer's *TROIA: MEXICAN MEMOIRS* chronicles their time in Mexico.

After being bailed out of jail by Elaine de Kooning's friends in Texas, living with PHILIP LAMANTIA in Mexico, appearing in Donald Allen's *The NEW AMERICAN POETRY,* and splitting with Frazer, Bremser was arrested for marijuana possession, jumped bail, was a fugitive from justice, and turned himself in. He was in prison from 1961 to 1965. His first volume of poetry, *POEMS OF MADNESS,* was published with an introduction by Ginsberg while he was in prison. *ANGEL,* his second book, was published after his release with an introduction by LAWRENCE FERLINGHETTI. Bremser reunited with Frazer, lived in Guatamala, and had a second daughter before splitting again with Frazer. He lived on Ginsberg's farm in Cherry Valley, New York, in the early 1970s, had a son with poet Judy Johnson, and moved to Utica, New York. One of the most mysterious, mythical, and notorious Beat outlaw figures, Bremser died from lung cancer on November 3, 1998.

Beat poet ANDY CLAUSEN has this to say about his friend:

> Ray Bremser was a master neologist and syntax pioneer, a language percussionist, an American Khlebnikov, a jazz and blues poet. His language was an outrageous precision, his intentions to push the limits of humor and pain. His books include *Poems of Madness* (1965) (published later as *Poems of Madness & Angel* by Water Row Press [1986]) in which Allen Ginsberg writes in the introduction, "In Bremser poetry we have powerful curious Hoboken language, crank-blat phrasing, rhythmic motion that moves forward in sections to climaxes of feeling," *Angel* (1967), *Drive Suite* (1968), *Black is Black Blues* (1971), *Blowing Mouth*

(1978), and *The Conquerors* (1998), which will appear in a German translation by Pociao (Verlag Peter Engstler).

Bremser could count Bob Dylan, Elvin Jones, and Cecil Taylor as fans. He was my friend. I regarded him as a compassionate and wise man, even though he was a social and spiritual outlaw—a literary renegade to the end.

He was born in Jersey City, New Jersey in 1934. He was fond of pointing out the hospital from the elevated skyway of exit 14 off the Jersey Turnpike as we headed for the Holland Tunnel, where he hated being stuck because he claimed all the tiles made him have to pee.

His mother was a condom inspector and his father was a pianist in clubs and on cruise ships. When he was fifteen he went to New York City and dug Billie Holliday at Birdland.

He joined the Air Force before graduating from high school and served eighty-nine days of a three year enlistment. It did not work out too well. I will not give all the details of Bremser's traumatic extraordinarily adventurous, defiant, hilarious, and tragic life, this is really the subject for a biography of Proustian dimensions.

Ray told me, "Someone gave me a gun. I walked around with it for three weeks. I thought, 'I have a gun I should use it.'"

The authorities waited two months till he turned eighteen and Ray spent 1952–58 in Bordentown Prison, for armed robbery, where he studied literature, wrote poems, got his high school diploma and corresponded with Ezra Pound, Robert Graves, Gregory Corso, and Ginsberg.

On a recommendation from Ginsberg and Corso, Ray sent poems to LeRoi Jones (Amiri Baraka). The "City Madness" section of *Poems of Madness* was published in *Yugen*. The editors, LeRoi and HETTIE JONES, had a party on Ray's release where he met Fielding Dawson, Diane Di Prima, Ginsberg, Seymour Krim, Franz Kline, and Jack Kerouac, who became a drinking buddy. Ray said, "We never discussed literature."

He told me Ginsberg immediately hit on him: "I told him, 'Allen, I've been in prison for six years. I've never even been with a woman, and that's what I want.'"

Bremser was published in Donald Allen's *The New American Poetry, 1945–1960*, that gave him a certain cache he ardently squandered with erratic behavior. Ray was not a great self-promoter. He was not about literary ego or sycophancy. His stance towards the established powers that rule politics and literature, was cantankerous, defiant, and often unpleasant, but none-the-less, heroic.

He married the writer Brenda Frazer (Bonnie Bremser). They had a sad yet terrific time together. They ran to Mexico to escape the law more than once. Frazer writes about those hard times in *Troia: Mexican Memoirs*, also published as *For the Love of Ray*. Their relationship was on again, off again. Even in Ray's last years he would voice the opinion that some day Frazer would come back to him.

In 1961 Bremser moved in with the legendary David Rattray, where he met John Coltrane and McCoy Tyner amongst others.

From late in 1961 to 1965 Bremser was in Trenton State Prison and later Rahway. The main infractions of his parole violation were: advocating legalized marijuana on Philadelphia TV, a robbery which he swore he did not perpetrate, and, the official reason, getting married without permission.

He and Frazer had two daughters, Rachel and Georgia.

Ray was invited by Ginsberg to The Committee on Poetry farm in Cherry Valley, New York in 1969.

He soon had to leave Cherry Valley and moved to the New Paltz area where he became involved with poet Judy Johnson. They had a son, Jesse Dylan Bremser.

Ray had kicked his addictions except tobacco and alcohol. He went to Utica, New York. I would ask him if he was happy in his little Rutgers St. garret and he would say he was content.

In 1982 he and my family, wife, three kids, and five more passengers made it from Cherry Valley to Boulder, Colorado in an old Chevy van in thirty-one hours. I drove non-stop as Ray kept me company. At the Kerouac Conference Bremser won the informal "Best Poet Award" (judged by Ken Babbs and Ken Kesey, I believe).

He would do occasional readings: St. Marks, The Shuttle, Professor Ginsberg's Brooklyn College reading series, and Unison Learning Center.

In 1995 at New York University he participated in a seminar on Kerouac's work and performed Kerouac's verse and his own to strong applause at Town Hall.

In his later years his output was sporadic. Sometime in the 1990s his apartment and all his literary possessions burned. A few great poems from his later days did survive including the classic "Jazz Suiti" also known as "Born Again," which he wrote after Judy Johnson was saved by Jesus.

His last reading was at a Cherry Valley Beat festival. He read with Mikhail Horowitz from his poem "The Conquerors." The last part had been lost and Ray commissioned Horowitz to pen the fourth section.

When we drove Ray home to Utica he got out of the car and immediately took his place on the porch with the other dole receivers. Ray was about 6' 2" and 120 lbs. at most.

I said, "I'll see you, Ray." He would not even turn his head. I yelled it louder. He would not look our way.

On 3 November 1998, Bremser died. His last words were, "I want to die!" and later in a semi-conscious state, with artist Al Duffy his long time friend playing him jazz tapes, Ray whispered, "John Coltrane."

Andy Clausen and Kurt Hemmer

Bukowski, Charles (1920–1994)

At no time did Charles Bukowski consider himself a "Beat." Even though he shared publications, readings, and the occasional social gathering with prominent Beat figures, he set himself apart from his literary contemporaries. As he told the editor of *Paris Metro* in 1978, "I'm not interested in this bohemian, Greenwich Village, Parisian bullshit. Algiers, Tangier, that's all romantic claptrap." Yet we can still find parallels between his work and that of JACK KEROUAC and ALLEN GINSBERG in their use of autobiographical fiction as a tool for exposing and examining reality. They differ in that Bukowski's view of reality can seem bleak and dark next to the optimistic Kerouac's. While the Beats were communal and spiritual (often embracing Eastern religions and philosophies), Bukowski was solitary and, at times, aspiritual. While many Beats embraced illegal drug use, Bukowski denounced it, preferring alcohol. Yet the Beats seemed to be often on Bukowski's mind in his writings. He was aware that they had achieved a literary fame that he felt he rightly deserved. Yet, in the end, Bukowski is arguably even more popular than some of his Beat peers.

Born Heinrich Karl Bukowski on August 16, 1920, in Andernach, Germany, Bukowski's parents later changed his name to Henry Bukowski when they moved to Los Angeles, California. Aside from a few jaunts out East, Los Angeles was where Bukowski lived most of his life and the place that became the setting for much of his work. His childhood was extremely unpleasant, ranging from violent beatings administered by his father to painful and ugly boils that developed on his face and left lifelong scars. These events served as material for his fourth book, *Ham on Rye* (1982), which chronicles his youth. Direct and vivid scenes describe trips to the hospital where young Bukowski endured needles injected into his boils to draw the pus from them. This scarring, along with his prominent nose and paunch belly, assembled to create a rather unattractive man. The awkward, self-conscious Bukowski found a blissful escape in alcohol that remained a constant companion to him for almost the rest of his life.

John Martin began Black Sparrow Press to publish Bukowski in the 1960s, and Black Sparrow can be called the house that Bukowski built (the press also published many Beat authors). In the December 1976 issue of *Hustler*, Bukowski stated that 93 percent of what he wrote was autobiographical. Much of his poetry and short stories deal with the monotony of everyday life, excessive drinking, playing the horses, and sexually charged (although at times clumsy) encounters with women. Throughout the drudgery he imbues his stories with humor and sharp insights into human interactions. His first novel, *Post Office* (1971), tells the story of Henry Chinaski, who (like Bukowski) spent 12 years working for the post office. His prose style is like his poetry in that it is sparse and powerful, the humor cynical and smart. In *Women* (1978), Bukowski lightly fictionalizes his numerous love affairs, from young female fans who would send him pictures and fly out to meet him to his turbulent relationship with the sculptress Linda King ("Lydia"). After having lost his virginity late in life and only having sex sporadically until the age of 50, Bukowski took advantage of his small celebrity status and the opportunities it afforded him to meet women. These real-life romances (filled with heated drama more often than not) provided wonderful material for his work. To pay the bills, Bukowski wrote pornographic stories for adult magazines and provocative pieces for the independent paper *Open City* and later the *LA Times*. These stories were collected and published by Essex House as *Notes of a Dirty Old Man,* which was reissued by LAWRENCE FERLINGHETTI's City Lights Books. It contains Bukowski's account of meeting NEAL CASSADY and the classic hair-raising car ride with Cassady behind the wheel just a few weeks before Cassady died in Mexico.

Notes of a Dirty Old Man was not the only collection of short stories to be published by City Lights. In 1972 they published ERECTIONS, EJACULATIONS AND GENERAL TALES OF ORDINARY MADNESS. Being a large book, it was later reissued in 1983 as two shorter collections, *Tales of Ordinary Madness* and *The Most Beautiful Woman in Town.* In addition to his connection to City Lights, Bukowski's poems appear alongside two Beat authors, HAROLD NORSE and Philip Lamantia in *Penguin Modern Poets—13* (1969). It was at Harold Norse's request that Bukowski be included in the anthology. The two of them developed a friendship. Other Beat encounters include a benefit poetry reading where he appeared with Allen Ginsberg, Lawrence Ferlinghetti, and GARY SNYDER. That evening, as he had done many times in the past, Bukowski drank himself into a belligerent state and insulted Ginsberg, claiming that he had not written anything "worth a shit"

after "HOWL" and "KADDISH." It was typical drunken Bukowski behavior as insecurity and too much booze combined as a catalyst for lashing out at others. He became notorious for insulting the audience at his poetry readings. Of course, his reputation of volatility enticed fans as they waited in long lines to see the "drunk Bukowski show."

The climax of his popularity came when the film *Barfly* was released. Bukowski wrote that the screenplay that was based on his life and work. Directed by Barbet Schroeder, and starring Mickey Rourke and Faye Dunaway, *Barfly* was only a moderate success, but it remains what mainstream America knows best about Bukowski. The making of the film served as material for Bukowski's fifth novel, *Hollywood* (1989). This book takes a funny, critical look at the entertainment industry from the blue collar, outsider- turned-insider perspective.

Charles Bukowski died on March 9, 1994, after a prolonged battle with cancer. Bukowski biographer Howard Sounes wrote of his body of work, "there is an uncompromising personal philosophy running through: a rejection of drudgery and imposed rules, of mendacity and pretentiousness; an acceptance that human lives are often wretched and that people are frequently cruel to one another, but that life can also be beautiful, sexy, and funny."

Factotum, a movie based on Bukowski's novel, directed by Brent Hamer and starring Matt Dillon, was released in 2005.

Bibliography
Brewer, Gay. *Charles Bukowski.* New York: Twayne, 1997.
Cherkovski, Neeli. *Hank.* New York: Random House, 1991.
Duval, Jean-Francois. *Bukowski and the Beats.* Northville, Mich.: Sun Dog Press, 2002.
Harrison, Russell. *Against the American Dream: Essays on Charles Bukowski.* Santa Rosa, Calif.: Black Sparrow Press, 1994.
Sounes, Howard. *Locked in the Arms of a Crazy Life.* New York: Grove Press, 1998.

Julie Lewis

Burroughs, William Seward (1914–1997)
William S. Burroughs has been absolutely central to the history of Beat literature, and yet his

William S. Burroughs reading *Rigor Mortis* by Mary Kittredge, Lawrence, Kansas, 1994. *(courtesy of Jon Blumb)*

position within the Beat Generation was paradoxical from the outset and has been revised significantly over time.

In relation to JACK KEROUAC and ALLEN GINSBERG, Burroughs came quite literally from another generation (he was a decade older than both of them) as well as from a different social class (*haute bourgeois*), religious background (WASP), and region of the country (the Midwest). Burroughs turned his back on this establishment identity and was well on the way to becoming an "enemy within" his culture when the three future writers first met in the mid-1940s. Burroughs therefore entered the original Beat scene as the sardonic sophisticate, playing the part of the master and instructing his two jejune apprentices with knowledge of both high culture and the criminal underworld. And then, before the end of the decade, Burroughs had gone—leaving cold-war America to escape his criminalization as a homosexual and

drug addict, to begin 25 years of expatriation. While the Beat Generation gathered momentum and attracted media attention at home, Burroughs was writing his first novels in Latin America, North Africa, and the capitals of Europe.

By the time he returned in the mid-1970s, Burroughs had established a literary career that bore little obvious relation to Beat history. Unlike Kerouac, whose oeuvres largely had been completed by the end of the 1950s and whose early death sealed his Beat identity, Burroughs had developed his writing in new experimental directions. On the other hand, his body of work and international reputation now played a vital role in legitimizing Beat literature as a category, even if he was typically cast as the sinister third alongside Kerouac and Ginsberg (as in *Naked Angels*, John Tytell's pioneering biographical–critical study of the Beat Holy Trinity). As the academic field of Beat Studies developed during the 1980s and 1990s, and as the dominance of the "Major Authors" approach faded, Burroughs's increasingly anomalous presence gradually made way for neglected writers who were afforded space by new understandings of Beat culture and by revised critical agendas.

It is true that Burroughs's writing of the 1950s does share key outline features with the mainstream of Beat literature. Like the work of Kerouac and Ginsberg, Burroughs used his biography explicitly to give structure and content to his first novels, while his narratives of outlawed desire and drugs dissented radically from social, cultural, and political orthodoxies. More materially, however, Burroughs's literary identity during that first decade was determined by Kerouac and Ginsberg in two ways central to the history of both Beat literature and Burroughs's biography.

Firstly, Burroughs developed as a writer in the 1950s while living outside America, so that he came to depend heavily on his closest friends during the personal crises and writing blocks of that decade. Ginsberg in particular played an essential role, helping to edit Burroughs's writing and acting zealously as his literary agent to ensure that his works were published. Equally important, Burroughs's acutely felt isolation abroad forced him to making a vital, even desperate, investment of creative energy in his long-distance correspondence with Ginsberg. After the break-up of the original Beat scene in the late 1940s, letter writing became the chief means for many of these writers to maintain personal and cultural solidarity. The paradox in Burroughs's case was that, by generating much of his fiction through letter writing, he actually needed the geographic separation to write so that he became most materially involved in Beat literary and personal relations while most physically removed from any Beat context.

Second, Burroughs's fellow writers fabricated him as a legendary figure through their fictional portraits. This was part of the larger Beat project of group mythmaking but with a crucial difference. Kerouac in particular created a series of highly ambivalent fantasy images of Burroughs that, in his absence from America, inaugurated the mystique of an underground reputation. From ON THE ROAD, where "Old Bull Lee" (the character based on Burroughs) appears as "something out of an old evil dream," to VANITY OF DULUOZ, where he is called "a shadow hovering over western literature," Kerouac mythologized Burroughs so seductively that, when his own writing came to be published, it was seen as the product of this already known quasi-fictional persona. Burroughs's role in the Beat Generation was to be its shadowy, rather menacing dark genius, all the more alluring for being so ambiguously presented.

Since the often sensational dramas of Burroughs's personal life appeared to follow the fantasy role scripted for him, it is no surprise that biographical studies have been mired in mystification ever since. Compounding the difficulties, Burroughs accepted such confusions of fact and fiction for both artistic and philosophical reasons, as well as expedience. His insistence to Conrad Knickerbocker in a 1965 interview for *The Paris Review* that "there is no accurate description of the creation of a book, or an event" (collected in *Burroughs Live: The Collected Interviews of William S. Burroughs 1960–1997*), is a radical warning against received wisdom, urging us to doubt not only the official story of his literary history and biography but also the very possibility of a true account.

William Seward Burroughs II was born on February 5, 1914, in St. Louis, Missouri. The younger of two sons, he was a child of privilege, modest wealth,

and social status, brought up by an oversensitive, doting mother and a rather distant, businessman father. He was also the heir to two upper-middle class families that played significant parts in the modernization of corporate America. His paternal grandfather and namesake was a Northern inventor who, in the late 1880s, perfected the modern adding machine and founded the international company that bore the Burroughs name (although the family connection to the firm was broken in 1929). His mother, Laura Lee, was the daughter of a Southern Methodist minister whose brother, Ivy, also achieved national fame: One of the pioneers of modern public relations, Burroughs's uncle earned the nickname *Poison Ivy* for his machinations on behalf of the captains of American industry. The Burroughs–Lee partnership therefore embodied traditions of American capitalism that their son—seemingly a disaffected insider from birth—would spend a literary career working to subvert.

Nevertheless, after attending Los Alamos Ranch School for Boys in New Mexico, Burroughs in 1932 entered Harvard University, the proper training ground for a man of his class. On graduation in 1936, however, instead of following the expected career trajectory, Burroughs joined what he called the international queer set on a European tour. In Vienna, he stayed to study medicine and then, flouting his family's expectations, married Ilse Klapper, a German Jew, so that she could escape the Nazi occupation (they separated on arrival in New York).

In 1938 Burroughs returned to Harvard to study anthropology and while living there with his boyhood friend, Kells Elvins, made his first mature effort at writing ("Twilight's Last Gleamings," a comic sketch that featured the debut of Dr. Benway, later a key character in NAKED LUNCH). The following summer, Burroughs moved to Chicago and then in the fall moved back to New York to take anthropology classes at Columbia. In April 1940 Burroughs was forced by his parents—who still supported him with a generous monthly allowance—to begin psychoanalytic treatment after a traumatic episode fictionalized a dozen years later in "The Finger." This black-humor short story narrates the incident when Burroughs cut off a finger joint in a futile effort to impress a young man. The tale not only reveals the masochistic nature of Burroughs's sexual desire but, as a template for future "routines" (sardonic, usually comical and dark, sketches), suggests the psychoanalytical basis of his need to write.

Moving back and forth between Chicago and New York during the early 1940s, Burroughs failed to enter the army because of his psychiatric record, tried his hand at a series of odd jobs—private detective, bug exterminator, bartender—and, as he put it in the prologue to JUNKY "played around the edges of crime": "It was at this time and under these circumstances that I came in contact with junk." This is the point in Burroughs's life where the autobiographical prologue to *Junky* stops, and it is important to appreciate that, for more than 30 years, this account provided the stencil through which his biography was read. But despite being factually accurate, the gloss it gives is actually very suspect. Equally important, this influential account of Burroughs's life up to the mid-1940s is perforated by holes, including the largest and most revealing one of all: Like the narrative of *Junky* itself, there is not a word here about the encounters Burroughs would have next in New York City—encounters that would in turn initiate the Beat Generation.

It was in spring 1943 that Burroughs joined a Columbia University circle that included Lucien Carr and David Kammerer, two old friends from St. Louis, and it was through Carr that Burroughs met first Ginsberg and then Kerouac. Together they began to form a still larger circle made up of students, street criminals, and would-be artists, including the Times Square hipster, HERBERT HUNCKE, and two Barnard students, Joan Vollmer Adams and Frankie Edie Parker. The young women turned their 115th Street apartment into a bohemian salon, and, despite his homosexuality, Burroughs struck up an immediate rapport with Joan. Although it was not destined to last long, the original Beat scene was now in place.

In his role as mentor, Burroughs offered Ginsberg and Kerouac an alternative to the conventional curriculum they received at Columbia. He introduced them to esoteric works of literature, philosophy, historiography, and economics—Céline, Cocteau, Korzybski, Reich, Spengler, Pareto—as well as to street-level experience of criminal

subcultures. In summer 1945 Burroughs and Kerouac also had a go at collaborative writing—with "And the Hippos Were Boiled in Their Tanks," based on Carr's notorious killing in August 1944 of Kammerer after supposedly being sexually assaulted—but unlike his younger friends, Burroughs had no sense of his destiny as a writer, and the effort led nowhere.

Forced to leave New York in April 1946 for forging a narcotics prescription, Burroughs returned home to St. Louis and then, to be with his old friend Kells Elvins, bought some land near Pharr, Texas. Burroughs might never have returned to New York to resume his relationship with Joan, but when she suffered a breakdown that summer, he did go back to rescue her from Bellevue. Together with Julie, her young daughter from a previous relationship, Burroughs and Joan settled on a 99-acre farm near Houston. When Huncke visited in 1947, he would find a curiously perverse domestic and rural scene, as Burroughs raised crops, built an orgone accumulator (Reich's invention), and supported an on–off heroin habit. Joan, herself addicted to benzedrine, gave birth to their son, Billy, in July 1947.

In 1948 Burroughs moved his family to Algiers, across the river from central New Orleans, and in the following January, Kerouac and NEAL CASSADY paid a visit that would become a famous episode in the cross-country travels fictionalized in *On the Road.* But firearms and drugs offenses forced Burroughs to move on again, and before the end of 1949 he had relocated his family to Mexico City.

Delighted to have escaped cold-war America, Burroughs enrolled under the G.I. Bill at Mexico City College, explored the local drug and homosexual underworlds, and in early 1950 started to write the book he called "Junk" (first published as *Junkie: Confessions of an Unredeemed Drug Addict* in 1953; retitled *Junky* for the "unexpurgated" edition of 1977). Although Ginsberg would later claim that Burroughs wrote *Junky* in the course of their long-distance exchange of personal letters, in fact he began it more as an anthropological diary, a first-person record of his experiences in addict subcultures during the immediate postwar years. When he did start to send material back to America, it was not to Ginsberg but to Kerouac, whose own first novel, *The TOWN AND THE CITY*, had been published that March. No doubt inspired by Kerouac's example, by the end of 1950 Burroughs had a 150-page manuscript, and 18 months later, aided by his enthusiastic agent Ginsberg, his first novel was published by one of the new pulp paperback houses. The text was poorly produced, heavily edited, and did not even appear either under his own name (he used the nom de plume, William Lee) or with his original title, but the fact of publication now confirmed Burroughs's identity as a writer.

Read as fictionalized autobiography, *Junky* has usually been hailed as one of the original works of Beat literature. However, Burroughs's failure to represent his fellow Beats makes for a telling contrast to the typical work of Kerouac and Ginsberg and reveals the novel's general failure to bear the hallmarks of Beat writing. Above all, far from expressing in free-flowing prose an idealistic desire for communal bonds and spiritual values, the world of *Junky* is cold, solitary, and grimly affectless. Only in the final quarter, set in Mexico and written during 1952, did the narrative thaw significantly. Far from coincidentally, this material overlapped the sequel that Burroughs had just begun, published (after a 30-year delay) as *QUEER*.

But in between the writing of his first two manuscripts came the event that has become the most notorious episode in Burroughs's biography: the catastrophic evening of September 6, 1951, when he recklessly shot and killed his wife, Joan, during a drunken game of William Tell. (The climax to director Gary Walkow's film *Beat* [2000], starring Courtney Love, Keifer Sutherland, Ron Livingston, and Norman Reedus, is based on this infamous episode.) After years of silence or mystification, Burroughs would himself make dramatic claims about the importance of this disaster for his motivation as a writer (see his Introduction to *Queer*), although critics have, quite rightly, suspected his conclusion.

Begun in March 1952, *Queer* shifted to the third-person to fictionalize events during the previous year when Burroughs became infatuated with a young American ex-serviceman from the expatriate bar scene in Mexico City, Lewis Marker. Describing their journey through Central America in pursuit of *yagé*, a fabled Amazonian hallucinogen, *Queer*

presents the breakdown of that relationship and the traumatic disintegration of both Burroughs's alter-ego, William Lee, and indeed the narrative itself, for although *Queer* was begun as an autobiographical sequel to *Junky* and at first seems to be its natural pair—another unabashed, first-hand report from a demonized minority—in fact they are radically divided from one another. This is principally because the second novel, in which Lee is driven by desire, initiates the dark fantasy mode that Burroughs called the routine.

Lee's routines display a visceral black humor charged with not only sexual but with political energies—they allow him to perform his identity as the Ugly American abroad—and the form would shortly become the essential unit of Burroughs's seminal work, *Naked Lunch*. Its impact on *Queer*, however, was to fragment the narrative and make it impossible to complete. The other reason why Burroughs abandoned the manuscript was that Marker had abandoned him—leaving Mexico for Florida—and, as he explained in a letter to Ginsberg, he "wrote *Queer* for Marker": "I guess he doesn't think much of it or of me."

Meanwhile, Burroughs had escaped a prison sentence for the manslaughter of his wife, but he knew it was time to move on again. After leaving their son, Billy, with his parents and following a visit by Kerouac—who worked on *DOCTOR SAX* while Burroughs wrote *Queer*—Burroughs departed Mexico at the end of 1952. He set out, this time alone, on another quest in search of *yagé*. From January to July 1953 he traveled from Panama to Peru on this quasi-anthropological mission through the jungles of Latin America, aided by an encounter with the ethnobotanist Dr. Richard Evans Schultes.

"In Search of Yage" (published in 1963 as the main part of *The YAGE LETTERS*) is presented as a series of epistolary field reports from William Lee, and it has been read as a lightly edited sequence of Burroughs's actual letters to Ginsberg. However, appearances are again deceptive, and it turns out that most of these letters were manufactured afterward from notebooks Burroughs kept on his travels. The fact that, like his second novel, his third would be left unpublished for some years also suggests the difficulty that Burroughs had in maintaining anything resembling a literary career.

Burroughs returned to New York in August 1953, staying in Ginsberg's apartment on the Lower East Side while they worked together on his rough manuscripts. The two men had not seen each other for more than six years, and when Burroughs pressured Ginsberg into an affair, the emotional strain forced Ginsberg to reject his former mentor. In December 1953 Burroughs set out yet again on foreign travels, this time crossing the Atlantic for Tangier.

The North African port city, which would be his headquarters for the next four years, was then an international zone administered by colonial powers, and it drew Burroughs because of its image as an exotic haven for outcasts. Exploiting his privileged status as an American citizen, Burroughs was indeed able to live freely there as a drug addict and homosexual. He met the writer PAUL BOWLES, a longtime resident expatriate, and the painter Brion Gysin, but his chronic heroin addiction isolated him, and he did not befriend either of them at this time.

Burroughs launched himself on a last-ditch effort to make a successful writing career. His creativity, however, was mostly tied to the long letters he mailed Ginsberg, and this desire-driven epistolary process resulted only in a series of increasingly wild routines. Texts such as "The Talking Asshole," written in February 1955, while brilliantly inventive and loaded with both sexual and political meaning, could not give Burroughs what he still looked for: a narrative structure. Throughout 1955 he worked on what he now called "Interzone," trying vainly to reconcile the spontaneous, fragmentary, typically obscene fantasies of his routines with plans for a coherent novel. Ironically—considering the popular myth of its drug-crazed production—it was only when the effort to impose conscious novelistic control failed that Burroughs's innovative creativity prospered and the book found its final form.

Meanwhile, his addiction had reached terminal point, and in spring 1956 Burroughs left for London to take the apomorphine treatment. When he returned to Tangier, cured, Burroughs found that he had also freed himself from his dependence on Ginsberg. In early 1957, Kerouac, Ginsberg, his new lover, Peter Orlovsky, and Alan Ansen all visited Tangier to help type and organize Burroughs's chaotic manuscripts that now went under the title *Naked Lunch*. Although Ginsberg pressed for a more autobiographical structure, Burroughs resisted, preferring the less centered form of a collage of materials.

In January 1958 Burroughs moved to Paris where he met up again with Ginsberg, Orlovsky, and GREGORY CORSO at the so-called Beat Hotel, a Left Bank rendezvous for artists and hipsters. Burroughs continued to work on *Naked Lunch*, despite rejections by publishers—frightened off by its formal disarray and shocking obscenity—including LAWRENCE FERLINGHETTI at City Lights (who did later bring out *The Yage Letters*). After selected episodes caused a censorship controversy when they appeared in *The Chicago Review*, the book was finally published in Paris by Olympia Press, although it took a legal battle and another six years for it to go on sale in the United States. Inevitably, *Naked Lunch* became a *succès de scandale* and an iconic text of the emergent international counterculture.

Naked Lunch completed the Beat Holy Trinity's trio of popular masterpieces—alongside Ginsberg's "HOWL" and Kerouac's *On the Road*—but its publication also marked a turning point in Burroughs's relation to the Beat movement. He now allied himself closely with Gysin, and the two men launched a new experimental project based on what they called the cut-up method. Drawing on European avant-garde traditions of chance procedures and collage practices and investing these techniques with scientific, magical, and political ambitions, the new techniques would keep Burroughs and Gysin busy for the next decade. Former comrades like Ginsberg, Kerouac, and Corso were alienated by it, but Burroughs went on to apply the principle across a whole range of media, experimenting with photomontages, tape recorders, scrapbooks, and even films. He produced hundreds of short texts and an extraordinary trilogy of full-length books that were revised several times: *The SOFT MACHINE* (1961; 1966; 1968), *The TICKET THAT EXPLODED* (1962; 1967), and *NOVA EXPRESS* (1964).

During the 1960s until the early 1970s Burroughs made his home in London, his public profile boosted by an appearance at the Edinburgh Writers conference in 1962 and, the following year, a controversy in the *Times Literary Supplement*. He was steadily acquiring an international underground reputation, although, after *Nova Express,* he did not publish another novel until *The Wild Boys* in 1971. The cut-up project had run its course in London: Burroughs found himself increasingly isolated, drinking heavily, and beset by financial crises. The sale of a huge archive of manuscripts financed his return to New York in early 1974, and, as he turned 60, Burroughs's long career as an expatriate writer now came to an end.

Based in New York, Burroughs rapidly acquired a cult reputation for a new generation as he began to move in celebrity avant-garde and punk-rock-music circles. With practical and editorial support from a new aide, James Grauerholz, Burroughs saw his first full-length novel for a decade, CITIES OF THE RED NIGHT, published in early 1981 to general acclaim. Its success was overshadowed, however, by the death of his son, Billy, from liver failure caused by alcoholism.

In winter 1981 Burroughs moved with Grauerholz to Lawrence, Kansas, and the small Midwest university town became his permanent home. He now launched a new—and lucrative—career as a visual artist, starting with his "shotgun paintings," and published the next two novels of his final trilogy, *The* PLACE OF DEAD ROADS in 1984 and *The* WESTERN LANDS three years later. Burroughs also entered into creative collaborations with a host of young innovative artists, filmmakers, and musicians, from Keith Haring to Kurt Cobain, from Gus Van Sant to Tom Waits.

Just three months after the death of Ginsberg, his lifelong friend, Burroughs died in the Lawrence Memorial Hospital on August 2, 1997. Although a highly contentious figure to the end—his work never mellowed by age—Burroughs not only received major critical attention but also exercised an enormously fertile influence on other writers and artists while leaving behind a unique and indelible cultural presence.

Bibliography

Burroughs, William S. *The Letters of William S. Burroughs, 1945–1959.* Edited by Oliver Harris. New York: Viking, 1993.

——— *Burroughs Live: The Collected Interviews of William S. Burroughs 1960–1997.* Edited by Sylvère Lotringer. Los Angeles: Semiotext(e), 2001.

Harris, Oliver. *William Burroughs and the Secret of Fascination.* Carbondale: Southern Illinois University Press, 2003.

Johnson, Rob. *The Last Years of William S. Burroughs: Beats in South Texas.* College Station: Texas A&M University Press, 2006.

Miles, Barry. *William Burroughs, El Hombre Invisible: A Portrait.* London: Virgin Books, 1992.

Morgan, Ted. *Literary Outlaw: The Life and Times of William S. Burroughs.* New York: Holt, 1988.

Skerl, Jennie. *William S. Burroughs.* Boston: Twain, 1985.

Tytell, John. *Naked Angels: The Lives and Literature of the Beat Generation.* New York: Grove, 1976.

Oliver Harris

C

Carroll, Jim (1950–)

By age 13, Jim Carroll was already experimenting with heroin and writing the journal that would become his acclaimed book, *The BASKETBALL DIARIES*. Gifted at both basketball and academics, Carroll won a scholarship to Trinity, an elite Manhattan private school, where he began to write the sports section for the school paper. There he led a double life, ditching classes, continuing his heroin use, hustling gay men, and snatching purses to support his addiction while his basketball star status slowly diminished.

During this time Carroll kept writing, attending poetry readings and workshops at the St. Mark's Poetry Project, "which assembled such poets as ANNE WALDMAN, ALLEN GINSBERG, and John Ashberry." Finally, by 17, he published his first book of poetry, *Organic Trains,* and landed excerpts of *The Basketball Diaries* in the *Paris Review.* Catching the attention of poet Ted Berrigan, an 18-year-old Carroll was taken to meet JACK KEROUAC who praised the poet saying, "At thirteen years of age, Jim Carroll writes better prose than 89 percent of the novelists working today." Even WILLIAM S. BURROUGHS called Carroll "a born writer." No doubt these experiences gave confidence to the already driven young writer.

After high school, Carroll opted out of college and instead worked for Andy Warhol, dated folk-rocker Patti Smith, and ran in the same circles as Ginsberg, BOB DYLAN, and the proto-punk band, The Velvet Underground. Despite continuing success as a writer, Carroll's heroin addiction began to control his life and in 1973, he took off to Bolinas, California, to kick the habit for good. In his self-imposed exile, Carroll focused on his writing, even beginning to pen rock lyrics originally intended for other artists. He soon found himself onstage with Patti Smith, reading his poetry backed by her band. The crowd loved it, giving birth to Carroll's rocker incarnation, about which he later quipped, "any poet, out of respect for his audience, should become a rock star." The Jim Carroll Band garnered popular and critical acclaim with their first album, *Catholic Boy.* The song "People Who Died" was an instant hit, and *BAM* magazine named the album one of the most popular of 1980. In fact, after the death of JOHN LENNON, "People Who Died" became elegiac, requested nearly as much as Lennon's own "Imagine."

Crossing the terrain between serious writer/poet, local sports star, drug addict, and rock idol, Carroll has well established himself as a modern cult hero. He has published four books of poetry, *Organic Trains, 4 Ups and 1 Down, Living at the Movies,* and *The Book of Nods;* two diaries, *The Basketball Diaries* and *Forced Entries: The Downtown Diaries;* three LPs with The Jim Carroll Band; as well as numerous uncollected works such as "8 Fragments for Kurt Cobain," written after the singer's suicide. In addition to these, information about Carroll's spoken-word albums, films, collaborations with artists such as Pearl Jam, Lou Reed, Sonic Youth, and Blue Oyster Cult and just about everything concerning Jim Carroll can be found via his Web site, Catholicboy.com.

Bibliography

Flippo, Chet. "A Star is Borning." *New York*, 26 January 1981, 32–35.

Kuennen, Cassie Carter. "Jim Carroll: An Annotated, Selective, Primary and Secondary Bibliography, 1967–1988. *Bulletin of Bibliography* 47.2 (1990): 81–113.

———— "The Sickness That Takes Years to Perfect: Jim Carroll's Alchemical Vision." *Dionysos: Literature and Addiction* 6, no. 1 (1996): 6–19.

Jennifer Cooper

Cassady, Carolyn (1923–)

Married to the whirlwind, larger-than-life Beat muse NEAL CASSADY, Carolyn Cassady became a central figure in the lives of Cassady, JACK KEROUAC, and ALLEN GINSBERG, as well as an important Beat memoirist with the publication of her own work. An early version of her memoirs, *Heart Beat: My Life With Jack & Neal,* was published in 1976; Carolyn served as consultant on the weak film version, *Heart Beat,* with Sissy Spacek as Carolyn and Nick Nolte as Neal. A much fuller account appeared as OFF THE ROAD: MY YEARS WITH CASSADY, KEROUAC, AND GINSBERG (1990) and deals with her reminiscences of her trio of conflicting identities. She was foremost the loyal wife of the peripatetic Cassady and mother to their three towheaded children. But she was also the lover and confidante of Kerouac, sometimes up all night participating in the marijuana-and-wine-fueled Beat talking and music sessions that the wildman Cassady encouraged at their home. Throughout her turbulent courtship, marriage, and postdivorce life with the erratic Cassady, Carolyn supported herself and her family through her impressive, award-winning skills as an artist, illustrator, and theatrical and costume designer.

Carolyn Robinson was born in 1923 in Nashville, Tennessee, to university faculty parents who encouraged her education and talents. She won a scholarship to Bennington College, in Vermont, where she received a degree in drama and also studied painting, sculpture, and dance. She next pursued a masters degree in theatre and fine arts at the University of Denver. Arriving in Denver in 1947, she was introduced by a would-be suitor

Carolyn Cassady, San Francisco, 1996. Photographer Larry Keenan: "The *Women of the Beat Generation* book-signing party was attended by many of the women in the book. Neal Cassady's former wife Carolyn is shown in this photograph reading from her book *Off the Road* at the Tosco restaurant/bar in North Beach." *(courtesy of Larry Keenan)*

to his dynamic friend, Neal Cassady. Despite the fact that Cassady was broke, sketchily employed, and already married to 16-year-old LuAnne Henderson, Carolyn found him electrifying and records in her memoir a growing sense of attraction that seemed fated. A little over a year after first meeting him, Carolyn and Neal married in a San Francisco civil service, with Carolyn already pregnant with their first child, Cathy.

Neal, attentive and even courtly at times in his affection for Carolyn, was not always forthcoming to her about his complicated relationships with the individuals whom he had met on his lengthy New York honeymoon with LuAnne; these individuals were to become the central coterie of the

Beat Generation. Some details Neal shared, but others were not revealed to her until the publication of various Beat novels a decade or more after they met. Neal continued to see LuAnne despite the annulment he had obtained to marry Carolyn; his road-trip exploits with his teenage ex-wife appear in Kerouac's ON THE ROAD. Neal explored a sexual relationship with an infatuated Ginsberg during his courtship of Carolyn and traveled with Ginsberg to assist WILLIAM S. BURROUGHS to harvest a marijuana crop on the ranch that Burroughs was sharing with his common-law wife Joan and HERBERT HUNCKE in Waverly, Texas. Carolyn overcame her initial trepidation toward drugs to join the persuasive Neal in experimenting mildly with Benzedrine and marijuana. Yet, Neal sometimes obscured his own degree of dependence on drugs, the addictions of some of his Beat friends, and the wildness of his own exploits in pursuit of "kicks." The strongest contrast throughout Carolyn's candid memoir is between her "straight," traditional, duty-bound persona and Neal's freewheeling ways with money, lovers, drugs, and factual truths.

Neal could perform the role of attentive husband and father, and for periods in the late 1940s and 1950s he worked as a railway brakeman and regularly returned home from rail stints with a paycheck. But his bouts of restless energy continued to whirl him off on sprees and affairs, and Carolyn coped with fatigue and poverty when cast back into the struggles of single parenting. When Carolyn gave birth to their second child, daughter Jami, in 1950, Neal had already proposed to Diana Hansen, a New York model with whom he was living and who was pregnant with his child. Caroline agreed to a divorce, and Neal married Hansen when the divorce was granted but before it was final. For a while Neal shunted between his two legal wives, one on each coast, before reconciling with Carolyn and moving back in with her and their daughters. Their son, John Allen, named after Kerouac and Ginsberg, was born in September 1951. The Cassadys enjoyed a period of domestic peace together, welcoming Kerouac into their home while he worked on *On the Road*, and Neal got him a temporary railroad job. Carolyn and Kerouac had shared a mutual attraction since Neal first introduced them; now they began an affair, under the oddly encouraging eye of Neal who seemed to view

their ménage à trois arrangement as just reparation for his own frequent transgressions. Eventually, tensions arose between Kerouac and Neal, and Kerouac, bitter over his second failed marriage and financial straits, decided to depart for Mexico to preserve both his mental state and his valued friendship with Cassady.

The Cassadys moved to San Jose and later to Los Gatos. A work-injury settlement in 1954 brought Neal $16,000 and helped pay for their new home. The couple also began to study the teachings of Edgar Cayce, a mixture of self-help advice and the occult. They eventually attended lectures given by Cayce's son, Hugh Lynn, and associate, Elsie Sechrist, and tried meditation and analysis together. Sechrist remained Carolyn's counselor throughout the rest of her difficult marriage to Neal, who continued to take lovers, including Ginsberg; Carolyn's memoir includes a scene where she describes her shock on walking in on the two during one of Ginsberg's visits to their home. Eventually, Neal's gambling cost them their savings, and in 1958 Neal was sentenced to a two-year jail term for possession of marijuana. The prison time allowed Carolyn to disengage her affections finally and to bolster her independence. Until his death in 1968 in Mexico, Neal was in and out of her life, feted as a counterculture hero by KEN KESEY and his Merry Pranksters. Carolyn knew of Neal's increasing drug use and mental instability but did her best to supervise his visits and excursions with their children and to manage a tolerant attitude toward his erratic episodes.

After Neal's death, Carolyn continued to support herself and her children through her portraiture and her theatrical design work. In 1984 she moved to England where scholars of the Beat Generation continue to seek her out for interviews and queries. She has appeared as a speaker at numerous Beat conferences and events, sometimes with her son, and has consulted on both feature films and documentaries about the Beat Generation.

Bibliography

Cassady, Carolyn. *Heart Beat: My Life With Jack & Neal.* Berkeley, Calif.: Creative Arts Book Co., 1976.
———. *Off The Road: My Years with Cassady, Kerouac, and Ginsberg.* New York: William Morrow & Co., 1990.

Amy L. Friedman

Cassady, Neal (1926–1968)

One might be tempted to say that if Neal Cassady had not existed, JACK KEROUAC would have had to invent him. But for many students of the Beat Generation, Kerouac *did* invent Cassady. It is the rare Beat aficionado who knows much about Cassady beyond what Kerouac conveys in ON THE ROAD. Casual readers often assume that the character of Dean Moriarty, Kerouac's fictional portrayal based on Cassady, is one and the same with Cassady. Never mind that Kerouac's Cody Pomeray in VI-SIONS OF CODY presents a very different portrait of Cassady, and never mind that JOHN CLELLON HOL-MES's GO, CAROLYN CASSADY's OFF THE ROAD, and Neal's own autobiography *The FIRST THIRD* (1971, rev. 1981) also conjure up someone quite distinct from the so-called Holy Goof of *On the Road*. Dean Moriarty, that "Western kinsman of the sun," remains the version of Cassady with which all other versions must compete. This was true for much of Cassady's life and remains true today.

The son of an itinerant barber and former housemaid, Neal Leon Cassady was born on February 8, 1926, in Salt Lake City, Utah. His early childhood was singularly unpromising, as he makes clear in *The First Third*. His alcoholic father, also named Neal, could not hold a job for long, and the family, including two of Neal's seven half-siblings, scraped by for only a couple of years in Hollywood, California, where the elder Neal had his own barber shop. Their subsequent move to Denver introduced young Neal to the city that he would call home for the rest of his childhood. When the Cassadys' marriage failed, father and son decamped for the Metropolitan, a tenement hotel that catered to bums.

Horrified and fascinated by the likes of Shorty, their legless roommate, six-year-old Neal traveled back and forth between the squalor of his new home and the orderliness of his elementary school. Both realms appealed to him. Since his half-brothers liked to beat him up, leaving home was something of a blessing. He could handle his father's consorts, drunkards one and all, and like a little businessman with a challenging commute, he loved his complicated walk across town to school. In another life in another age, he might have been a class star.

But that path in life was not meant to be his. As a young boy, Neal traveled to California by freight train with his father, a journey that both wearied and invigorated him. There was no forgetting either the color or the torpor of life on the road, as Neal experienced the beat circumstances that would give gritty dimension to the later Beat movement. Back in Denver, he lived primarily with his mother and siblings until his mother's death in 1936. For the next several years, he stayed with a much older half-brother before rejoining his father in 1939.

Shuffled from home to home with so little continuity in his life, Neal began to steal cars at age 14. A master of joyriding, he supposedly stole more than 500 cars between 1940 and 1944. His

Neal Cassady watching out for the cops, Oakland, 1966. Photographer Larry Keenan: "While waiting for Ken Kesey to arrive, Cassady kept a lookout for the cops. Kesey was a fugitive at the time. Cassady asked me, 'What's the heat like around here, man?' Thinking he was talking about the weather, I said, 'Pretty nice.'" *(courtesy of Larry Keenan)*

hobby landed him in the Mullen Home for Boys, and later scrapes with the law earned him short stints in a California juvenile forestry camp (1943) and the Colorado State Reformatory (1944–45). In his down time, he pored over Dostoyevsky and other challenging authors whose works he found in the camp or prison library.

Cassady thus styled himself as an autodidact as well as an auto thief. He hungered for knowledge and aimed high when given a choice of reading materials. Like HERBERT HUNCKE and GREGORY CORSO, fellow Beats whose criminal activities did not prevent them from reading widely and deeply, Cassady was not destined to graduate from high school. His radiant, ruthless intelligence was nevertheless central to his character and to his hold on the intellectuals he would soon meet.

Justin Brierly, a Denver teacher and lawyer, was an important early friend and mentor. In his letters to Brierly from the Colorado State Reformatory, he maintains a rather lofty demeanor, evidently aware of the older man's attraction to him. In a wide-ranging letter dated October 23, 1944, he tells Brierly to pay a small debt for him at a Denver restaurant and then switches to literary matters: "They have the Harvard Classics up here, the five foot shelf of books; I've read about 2 feet of it, very nice, I especially enjoy Voltaire & Bacon (Francis)." From there it's on to prison sports and finally an appalling revelation: a farm accident at the reformatory has left Cassady in danger of losing the sight in his left eye. To this, Brierly evidently responded with great concern in letters to both Neal and a prison warden. In a letter posted a week later, Cassady reports that his vision is on the mend and chastises Brierly for not having known that the former warden had been killed in a car accident and a new one is on duty.

The whole exchange is very much of a piece with Neal's later correspondence with friends and lovers. Though often mired in difficulties of his own making, he held the people around him to high standards of accountability. His own flaws and foibles did not mean that he would cut anyone else any slack. This inconsistency, the stroke of a career con artist, beguiled more people than it alienated.

Hailed by one girlfriend late in his life as "the best lay in the U.S.A.," Cassady would prob-

ably be labeled a sex addict nowadays. His appetite for women, occasional men, and masturbation seemed to know no bounds. Compact, muscular, and radiating great physical warmth (according to Huncke), he racked up conquests the same way he stole cars. For him, both acts were akin to an art form that required frequent practice and deserved notice when done with great skill. His other favored activities also combined athletic prowess with a desire for acclaim. He was proud, for instance, of his ability to skip a rock across water an impressive 20 times. As Cassady biographer William Plummer points out in *The Holy Goof* (1981), such a feat "was perhaps the first of his obsessively attained, hyperkinetic and unmarketable skills, the most famous of which—his virtual emblem in later years—was hammer flipping."

His sexual prowess—the hyperkinetic skill that most defined him—*was* marketable, however. Jumpy and compulsively charming, he seemed always on the brink of orgasm. Just so everyone would know what he was up to, he made a habit of strutting around naked, a detail Kerouac admiringly records in *On the Road*. His occasional forays into hustling did not lead to a career, but such activity contributed to his mystique in the eyes of his writer friends in New York City. Without his virile charisma and impressive sexual history, he would not have attracted the attention of Kerouac, who wanted to (and did) make a hero out of him, or of Ginsberg, who wanted to (and did) make love to him.

When Cassady and Kerouac met in New York City in 1946 through Columbia University student Hal Chase, also of Denver, they took to one another eagerly and obsessively. Kerouac needed to see someone like Cassady to make sense of his own life, and Cassady desperately needed to be seen. It is the story of their mutually needy friendship, of course, that animates *On the Road*. By transforming his buddy into Dean Moriarty, a cartoonish version of the real Cassady, Kerouac established the pattern that was to shape his best books. He would tell the story of a companion—a friend, a brother, or a sweetheart—while simultaneously recording a chapter of his own spiritual autobiography, what he called the Duluoz Legend.

Cassady's parallel friendship with Ginsberg was complicated by Ginsberg's passionate yearning for

Neal Cassady shaving at Ginsberg's, San Francisco, 1965. Photographer Larry Keenan: "Allen Ginsberg did not have a bathroom in his apartment, so Neal Cassady is shaving in Ginsberg's kitchen in this photograph. Cassady had a hard time trying to get some lather from the old bar soap. He had cut his face. When Cassady was introduced to people, he was always introduced with, 'meet Neal Cassady, who is Dean Moriarty from Kerouac's *On the Road*.' I had been looking for a way to illustrate this dual role. While he was shaving, I suddenly realized, there they both were." *(courtesy of Larry Keenan)*

the Denver roughneck. The two traveled together to the East Texas farm where WILLIAM S. BURROUGHS, Joan Burroughs, and Huncke were living in 1947. To Ginsberg's mortification, Huncke set about building a bed that Ginsberg and Cassady could share.

The letters in *As Ever: The Collected Correspondence of Allen Ginsberg and Neal Cassady* (1977) show Ginsberg weighing his desires against a nagging suspicion that Cassady was beneath him intellectually. Realizing this, Cassady made a point of working erudite references into his letters. In 1948 he writes to Allen, "Let us stop corresponding—I'm not the N.C. you knew I'm not N.C. anymore. I more closely resemble Baudelaire." Such claims kept Ginsberg interested.

Ginsberg apparently wanted Cassady to develop into a writer—to become, in effect, his equal if not the new Baudelaire. In a letter to Allen written in August 1948, Cassady reports that he is coming out of his depression and making another stab at writing: "I can, once again, walk into a hip joint, smell hip things, touch hip minds—without crying. As for self-improvement: I'm starting music lessons soon; I'm all set, if necessary, to get psychoanalysis, . . . but, perhaps, more interesting to you—I am writing daily; poorly done, poorly executed, woefully weak ice words I string together for what I try to say, maybe, only one paragraph, maybe different subjects each day, maybe, crazy to try (for I seem to get only further embroiled in style) but, I am trying."

While juggling wives, lovers, and an expanding brood of children and trying to write an autobiography at the behest of his author friends, Cassady still managed to earn a living, usually as a California-based railroad brakeman and to maintain regular contact with both Kerouac and Ginsberg through the mid-1950s. If he did not respect his marriage vows—and his two legitimate wives LuAnne Henderson and Carolyn Robinson and his bigamous wife Diana Hansen could attest to that—he was nevertheless so articulate and convincing on the subject of relationships that his intimates routinely forgave him his infidelities and indiscretions even as they suffered dearly from his callous treatment.

When he seemed to hand over Carolyn to Kerouac in 1952, the ensuing affair had much to do with Neal and very little to do with any real bond between Carolyn and Jack. Because Neal liked complications and diversions, the coupling of his wife and best friend was a welcome novelty, especially since Carolyn clearly still preferred him. She writes about the affair with amused affection in *Off the Road,* portraying herself as a sort of R-rated Lucille Ball caroming between rival suitors. For much of her marriage, she was game for nearly anything that would keep Neal interested and in check. His multiple affairs, the apparent suicide of his lover Natalie Jackson, his gambling away of their nest egg, and his two years in San Quentin prison on a trumped-up marijuana charge—none of this ended their marriage. When they finally divorced in 1963, the breakup was anticlimactic and long overdue.

It is a common misperception that fame destroyed Kerouac, when in fact his decline had begun long before he published *On the Road,* but it seems that notoriety, if not true fame, helped Death track down Cassady during his last days on a trip to Mexico. For the first half of his life, he was nothing if not a survivor, a street kid whose fierce hold on life awed everyone he met. But after joining forces with the lawless KEN KESEY and posing as a so-called Merry Prankster—a dancing elephant of the hippie brigade—he became a parody of his old ebullient self. No longer exhilaratingly brash, joyously profane, and hooked on life, he was just dull, drugged, and headed toward disaster. But

even then, he still managed to inspire Jerry Garcia of The Grateful Dead.

His death of exposure alongside railroad tracks in Mexico on February 4, 1968, a few days short of his 42nd birthday, was poetic justice at its cruelest. Overexposed in so many ways, terminally headed down the wrong track, this tragicomic American clown took his final pratfall in a country where only a handful would know who he was or why his story mattered.

The First Third and his *Collected Letters, 1944–1967* (2004) reveal that Cassady was both more and less than the countless literary images propagated in his name. (The movie *The Last Time I Committed Suicide* [1997] directed by Stephen T. Kay and starring Thomas Jane, Keanu Reeves, Adrien Brody, John Doe, and Claire Forlani is based on the famous "Joan Anderson" letter Cassady wrote to Kerouac in December 1950.) Putting her finger on the paradox of Neal's double life as man and muse, Carolyn Cassady candidly admits in the introduction to the letters, "I find I am as guilty as anyone else of promoting myths about him."

Bibliography

Cassady, Carolyn. Introduction. *Collected Letters, 1944–1967,* by Neal Cassady, edited by Dave Moore, xv–xvii. New York: Penguin, 2004.

———. *Off the Road: My Years with Cassady, Kerouac, and Ginsberg.* New York: William Morrow, 1990.

Cassady, Neal. *Neal Cassady: Collected Letters, 1944–1967.* Edited by Dave Moore. New York: Penguin, 2004.

———. *The First Third and Other Writings.* San Francisco: City Lights, 1981.

Kerouac, Jack. *On the Road.* 1957. New York: Penguin, 1991.

Plummer, William. *The Holy Goof: A Biography of Neal Cassady.* New York: Paragon House, 1981.

Hilary Holladay

"Chicago Poem" Lew Welch (1958)

LEW WELCH's "Chicago Poem," perhaps his most famous and most frequently anthologized piece, is an eloquent statement of the poet's midlife change in direction away from urban, corporate America and toward a more inner-directed and nature-centered existence. Originally published in his small collection *Wobbly Rock* (1960) and later in his posthumously published collected works *Ring of Bone* (1973), the poem details Welch's reaction to his residence in Chicago during the years 1953–57, an extremely unhappy period during which the poet worked as an advertising writer in the city. First drafted in June 1957 near the end of the poet's residence in the Midwest, the poem begins with the first-person narrator (presumably Welch) recalling the gray, dismal landscape of mid-twentieth-century Chicago:

> The land's too flat. Ugly sullen and big it
> pounds men down past humbleness. They
> Stoop at 35 possibly cringing from the heavy and
> terrible sky. . . .

The poem is an indictment—not just of the industrial Midwest but of modern urban life. As an early San Francisco reviewer, Grover Sales, wrote in response to hearing Welch read the poem: "This is not the Chicago of Sandburg but the *Rome* of Juvenal and the *London* of William Blake." In place of Sandburg's 1916 vision of Chicago as "Stormy, husky, brawling, / City of the Big Shoulders," four decades later Welch portrays a hopeless urban atmosphere where men "Stoop at 35" under the horrible weight of their surroundings, and in place of Sandburg's romantic vision of a vital and expansive city, Welch depicts a city fallen victim to its own industrial excesses:

> In the mills and refineries of its south side
> Chicago
> passes its natural gas in flames
> Bouncing like bunsens from stacks a hundred
> feet high.
> The stench stabs at your eyeballs.
> The whole sky green and yellow backdrop for the
> skeleton
> steel of a bombed-out town.

The speaker's only solace is not found within the city but in nature. After five years inside the city, an alternative arises that allows him to "recognize the ferocity" inherent in his urban existence: "Finally I found some quiet lakes / and a farm where they let me shoot pheasant." Away from the city while pheasant hunting or fishing, he is able to differentiate between the humanmade chaos of Chicago's south side and beauty of the Midwestern landscape:

> All things considered, it's a gentle and
> undemanding
> planet, even here. Far gentler
> Here than any of a dozen other places. The
> trouble is
> always and only with what we build on top of it.

As the speaker returns to Chicago after a day in the farmlands, he is determined to condemn the modern city for what it is: a human creation which is no longer under human control—a violent and dangerous monster who now threatens those to whom it once offered shelter:

> Driving back I saw Chicago rising in its gases
> and I
> knew again that never will the
> Man be made to stand against this pitiless,
> unparalleled
> monstrocity. . . .
>
> You can't fix it. You can't make it go away.
> I don't know what you're going to do about it,
> But I know what I'm going to do about it. I'm just
> going to walk away from it. Maybe
> A small part of it will die if I'm not around
>
> feeding it anymore.

The solution, according to Welch, is total resignation from the "monstrocity" [sic] of urban, industrial America, an act that seems to foreshadow much of the 1960s counterculture's rejection of the structures of American society and its embrace of a more nature-centered existence.

Bibliography

Charters, Samuel. "Lew Welch." In *Dictionary of Literary Biography*. Vol 16, *The Beats: Literary Bohemians in Postwar America*, edited by Ann Charters, 539–553. Detroit: Gale, 1983.

Phillips, Rod. *"Forest Beatniks" and "Urban Thoreaus": Jack Kerouac, Gary Snyder, Lew Welch, and Michael McClure.* New York: Peter Lang, 2000.

————. "'The Journal of a Strategic Withdrawal': Nature and the Poetry of Lew Welch." *Western American Literature* 29 (1994): 217–237.

Rod Phillips

Cities of the Red Night William S. Burroughs
(1981)

This first book in a trilogy of novels was published in the 1980s that also includes *The PLACE OF DEAD ROADS* and *The WESTERN LANDS*. Although written late in WILLIAM S. BURROUGHS's life, these three novels are gaining a reputation as being among his best. Ann Douglas in her introduction to *Word Virus: The William S. Burroughs Reader* states flatly that they *are* his best work.

The books are a trilogy in that there are overlapping characters and a consistent set of key ideas, including the continuous revelation of Burroughs's philosophical views on control systems, Christianity's monopoly on spirituality in the West, the move from a One God Universe to a magical universe, time versus space, and the need for humans to evolve to leave the dying planet—Earth being a "dead whistle stop," a death colony run by aliens (Venusians). Unlike most trilogies, there is no real character development in the conventional sense nor are the books linear in the conventional way that most "trilogies" develop. This should not be surprising to readers of Burroughs. Like JACK KEROUAC, he preferred to see his works as one long book. Burroughs also appears to have been able to imagine these works as a whole before writing any of them, meaning that in this trilogy (and in other works), he can freely cut back and forth through time and space, sometimes giving multiple names to the same character and playing similar tricks with geography. This singularity of vision may also suggest to some readers the limits of Burroughs's range: At some point in the reading of all of his works, the reader feels that he has read this book before.

Cities of the Red Night is, like all of Burroughs's books, a blueprint for cracking the codes of reality that restrict us from ultimate freedom. The Urstory he adopts is the history of the 18th-century pirate Captain Mission, "one of the forebears of the French Revolution," as Burroughs says in a foreword, who established the colony of Libertatia and enforced the following Articles: all decisions submitted to a vote, no slavery, no death penalty, freedom of religion. Under these principles, Burroughs says, all of the enslaved people of the world could unite and overthrow despotic governments, slave religions, and other control systems. However, Mission's revolution did not spread, a key failure in the history of humankind, believes Burroughs: "Your right to live where you want, with companions of your choosing, under laws to which you agree, died in the eighteenth century with Captain Mission. Only a miracle or a disaster could restore it." *Cities of the Red Night* is a fantasy involving a "what might have been" plot had Mission succeeded.

Book One introduces the two main parallel storylines in the novel. The first involves a young man named Noah who lives at the beginning of the 18th century in one of the American colonies where he and his father manufacture guns. The book follows the fate of the Blake family and Noah Blake's companions. They are ostracized, evidently for their homosexuality, and Noah and four friends ship out with Opium Jones, a captain whose primary cargo is eponymous. They end up being captured by a "pirate" named Captain Strobe of the *Siren*, whose sailors dress as women to lure in unsuspecting vessels. Noah and his companions are taken to Port Royal where they become conscripted in a plan to free the Americas according to Captain Mission's Articles—thus their name, the Articulated. Noah has been presciently chosen by Strobe and Jones because they seem to know that he will invent the prototype of the modern bullet as well as other sophisticated weapons. This storyline reads like a boy's adventure story.

The other storyline is a mock hardboiled detective story involving several missing persons cases and the recovery of a rare manuscript. The detective's name is Clem Snide, Private Ass-hole. Snide is hired to find a boy named Jerry Green by his father. The boy's decapitated corpse turns up. Snide and his assistant Jim use psychic forces and "sex magic" as well as tape cut-ups and language cut-ups that help them to learn the truth. Jerry has apparently died from "orgasm death," or the red death, a disease attributed to a virus turned malignant by

Cities of the Red Night 47

radiation that was released 20,000 years ago when a meteor crashed in Siberia. The virus has once again become malignant because of radiation released in worldwide nuclear tests. He follows Jerry's trail to London, Tangier, and Marrakech. Jerry, it turns out, was sacrificed in a hanging as part of the Egyptian sunset rite dedicated to Set. Dimitri, a rich employer of Snide, tells him this. Snide, as is the case with Phillip Marlowe and the Continental Op, becomes employed by several parties who seek the same information. While searching for another missing boy, John Everson, Snide travels to Mexico City, where he attends Lola La Chata's annual party. The party brings friends together from Burroughs's own past, including a character based on his lover Kiki and Bernabé Abogado, based on his lawyer Bernabé Jurado. Everson is a patient in an operation to transfer identities, performed by the Iguana Twins, who are also sorceresses in the Noah Blake storyline (several characters overlap in the two stories). The Iguana sister tells Snide that she can give him information which will help him "survive" a suicide mission on which Dimitri has sent him. She hands him a parchment-bound pamphlet entitled *Cities of the Red Night*.

Book Two begins with Clem reading the *Cities* manuscript. Indeed, the novel takes on a postmodern feel as books are read within books and characters begin to write books that we are reading. The manuscript creates an anthropological fantasy from 100,000 years ago, and this lost civilization is at the root of our present-day woes. There were six cities of the red night located in the Gobi Desert (their names are six magical words taught to Burroughs by Brion Gysin, who told him if you repeated them before you fell asleep you would have prophetic dreams). Their populations were stable, based on a one birth/one death formula that was kept constant through the practice of transmigration of souls. Two factors destabilized the civilization. The first was the discovery of artificial insemination techniques, making it possible for a whole region to be populated by the sperm of one male. The second was more serious: A giant meteor fell to Earth, lighting up the sky with a deadly red radiation. Whereas the inhabitants were previously all black skinned, now mutant white people appeared. One of them, known as the White Tigress, took over

Yass Waddah and enslaved all of the males. The males in Waghdas waged war, and the cities were all eventually destroyed and deserted. The books detailing their knowledge of the transmigration of souls fell into the hands of the Mayans, who misread them and "reduced the Receptacle class to a condition of virtual idiocy." The story thus explains the origins of the "Mayan Caper" and mind-control techniques practiced by the indigenous people of the Americas.

The six cities come to represent a path to the afterlife, each with a magical meaning related to the assassin Hassan i Sabbah's motto: "Nothing is true, everything is permitted." These cities also become the points on a pilgrimage that ends in the afterlife: "The traveler must start in Tamaghis and make his way through the other cities in the order named." This pilgrimage corresponds fairly closely to the description of the seven souls in the final book of the trilogy, *The Western Lands*. Thus, throughout these books, Burroughs shows a remarkable ability to create metaphors, codes, and systems that depict the secrets of the universe.

Although Clem has exact copies of these books, the Iguana sisters want him to find the originals because "Changes, Mr. Snide, can only be effected by alterations in the *original*." However, Clem and his assistant (who, like many of the "assistants" in the trilogy, is probably based on Burroughs's collaborator, James Grauerholz) opt instead to "start making books. I write the continuity. Jim does the drawings." One of the books they make details the city of Tamaghis, and in the book, characters from the parallel storyline appear as well. The novel takes on a disorienting, intertextual style. Once again, Clem is hired by another client, this time Blum and Krup, two vaudevillians who appeared in previous Burroughs books. Clem plays dumb: "Books? Me? I'm just a private eye, not a writer." They blindfold him and take him on an adventure that has the feel of an espionage film, such as *The Third Man*, or *North by Northwest*. He meets a CIA operative named Pierson who has a plan to kill off the white race with a biological agent and blame it on brown, black, and yellow races to justify exterminating them. Then he will genetically reengineer the white race as a super race. They hire Clem to write the "scenario."

Here the book becomes a parody of the serious writer-goes-to-Hollywood story (Fitzgerald, Faulkner, Agee in Hollywood): "Blum says he wants something he calls art. He knows it when he sees it and he isn't seeing it." In the script, Snide writes a hanging scene in which Audrey appears; and Audrey later substitutes for Snide in the narrative (they are the same character, in different times). The book's technique is explained in a key observation by Jerry. Clem asks, "Who else is here?" "All the boys from your scripts . . . One foot in a navy mess and the other on some kooky spaceship. You see, there is a pretense this is just a naval station and you never know which is the pretense: spaceship or navy." In Burroughs, names and places can be interchanged, and reality is an illusion, often compared to a film.

Noah Blake and his companions participate in the Articulated's plan to retake the Americas. Captain Strobe is captured in Panama City, but the city is taken by the rebels, thanks in large part to the sophisticated guns designed by Noah. The captured Spanish soldiers are read the Articles and quickly are converted to the cause. Only a small percentage refuse: "Any body of men," says the narrator, "will be found to contain ten to fifteen percent of incorrigible troublemakers. In fact, most of the misery on this planet derives from this ten percent." This statistic will be repeated in *The Place of Dead Roads* when a group similar to the Articulated, the Johnson Family, takes over the Americas. The real enemy in this book turns out to be the Spanish colonizers, and the Articulated steal their ledger books and are thus are able to predict the future behavior of the Spanish. With the Americas freed, Noah and the boys can survey the freed country at will, embodying a pioneer spirit: "We carry with us seeds and plants, plans, books, pictures, and artifacts from the communes we visit."

In Book Three Noah arrives in a frontier town, rents a house by a river, and trains himself as a shootist—a scene that looks forward to a nearly identical episode featuring Kim Carsons in *The Place of Dead Roads.* Noah's encounter with a Venusian reminds him of Captain Strobe, and in the following sections, we return to the character of Audrey, who must travel through the six cities to attain immortality in the City of Waghdas (a scheme very similar to the pilgrimage that must be performed in the trilogy's final volume, *The Western Lands*). As is true of many of Burroughs's books, the characters are now revealed as having multiple identities: Noah, Audrey, and Clem Snide are apparently interchangeable characters. Noah realizes that he must "make preparations for a war I thought had ended," but it is Audrey who is featured in the climactic battle staged at the novel's end.

To get to Wagdhas, Audrey must defeat the matriarchal villains, the Countesses de Vile and de Gulpa, in Yass–Waddah. All of the bad characters in history, including Burroughs's own personal demon—that of the "Ugly Spirit" that he thought killed his wife Joan—are gathered in Yass–Waddah. The battle resembles the climactic scenes in *Nova Express.* "Towers open fire," and the war room at Yass–Waddah is revealed as the "Studio," where the film that keeps human beings enslaved by illusion is created: "It was all intended to keep human slaves imprisoned in a physical bodies while a monstrous matador waved his cloth in the sky, sword ready to kill." Audrey wakes from this battle in mental ward—an intentionally cheap device—repeating the names of the six cities on his pilgrimage. Life is a pilgrimage, but one that may take many lifetimes (thus the multiple identities for characters in the book). Audrey, as Burroughs did after accidentally shooting Joan, tries to write his way out of his human predicament, sitting at a typewriter in an attic room. He meditates on a future that could have been had the Spanish never come over to the Americas in their galleons, a future in which Captain Strobe's social experiment at Port Roger had succeeded. However, Audrey, like Burroughs, is "bound to the past."

Rob Johnson

Clausen, Andy (1943–   )

The author of 10 books of poetry, Andy Clausen was consistently cited by the late ALLEN GINSBERG as one of the most important poets of the next generation. With a lively, oratorical voice that is unforgettable both on the page and in public readings, Clausen's work extends the democratic and imagination-filled traditions of such writers as Walt Whitman, Ginsberg, GREGORY CORSO, the French surrealists, and the Russian Futurists, especially Vladimir Mayakovsky.

Born in a Belgium bomb shelter on October 14, 1943, Clausen moved to Oakland, California, at age two, right after the end of the second world war. After graduating from high school, he became a Golden Gloves amateur boxer and joined the Marine Corps for a short time as a paratrooper. Clausen left the marines in 1966 after seeing Ginsberg on television read "Wichita Vortex Sutra." The line from Ginsberg's anti-Vietnam War poem that particularly caught Clausen's attention and turned him away from militarism was: "Has anyone looked in the eyes of the dead?"

Having read Ginsberg, Corso, and JACK KEROUAC, Clausen became a writer after deciding that Beat poetry (rather than, say, computers) was going to be the wave of the future. He met NEAL CASSADY in 1967, in San Jose, California, when Cassady visited the house where Clausen was staying. The dynamic energy in Clausen's poems would later remind Ginsberg of Cassady. Clausen met Ginsberg for the first time in 1968 after a poetry reading in San Francisco's Glide Memorial Church where Clausen had taken off his clothes. The following day, Ginsberg surprised Clausen by going to his apartment to ask where he had gotten the line in one of his poems, "The five senses are the five wounds of Christ." When Clausen confirmed that he had made that line up, a lifelong friendship was forged. In later years, Clausen also became good friends with many of the others writers associated with the Beat Generation, including Corso, RAY BREMSER, JACK MICHELINE, and JANINE POMMY VEGA.

Clausen married Linda Harper in 1968, and they went almost immediately on the road—to Denver and to Chicago, where they took part in the protests outside the Democratic Party convention. During their time together—until the mid-1980s—they lived in many cities and states throughout the United States and in several Canadian provinces. They had three children—Cassady, Mona, and Jesse—who currently live in the Northwest. In later years, Clausen also lived in Kathmandu and Prague, where he read for Vaclav Hável while Hável was president of the Czech Republic. Clausen has also traveled to India, Thailand, Nepal, eastern Europe, Greece, and Italy, and poems from those travels are included in his book, *40th Century Man: Selected Verse 1996–1966.*

Clausen has worked most of his adult life as a construction worker, a union-member hodcarrier. Numerous other jobs have included cab driver, tire warehouse worker, gandy dancer, and sawmill worker. Now in his early 60s, he is teaching poetry in New York schools and prisons and is currently living in upstate New York with the poet Janine Pommy Vega.

When Clausen published his second book in 1975, called *Shoe-Be-Do-Be-Ee-Op,* Ginsberg wrote him a letter reviewing every poem in the book and telling him how much he enjoyed it. In 1991, Clausen published WITHOUT DOUBT, and Ginsberg wrote in the book's introduction: "His comments on the enthusiastic Sixties, defensive Seventies, unjust Eighties and bullying Nineties present a genuine authority in America not voiced much in little magazine print, less in newspapers of record, never in political theatrics through Oval Office airwaves. . . . Would he were, I'd take my chance on a President Clausen!"

Other volumes of poetry through the years have included *The Iron Curtain of Love* and *Festival of Squares.* He has also released several recordings of his poetry, including *Let It Rip.* Among other literary credits: Clausen is the main subject of a short film by Vivian Demuth called *Dinners with Andy;* he is a coeditor of *Poems for the Nation,* a collection of contemporary political poems compiled by Ginsberg; he has been a coeditor of *Long Shot* literary journal; and he is currently completing a book of memoirs about his experiences with Ginsberg, Corso, Cassady, Bremser, and many other writers associated with the Beat Generation.

When the current mayor of Oakland, Jerry Brown, was running in the Democratic Party primaries for president of the United States in 1988, Ginsberg introduced Clausen to Brown as Ginsberg's political adviser. With an interest in Buddhism and in Left traditions such as anarchism and democratic socialism, Clausen's dynamic, inventive poetry is deeply concerned with examining the varied ills and absurdities of our contemporary culture and exploring visions for a more humane future.

Bibliography

Clausen, Andy. *Festival of Squares.* Woodstock, N.Y.: Shivastan Publishing, 2002.

——. *40th Century Man: Selected Verse, 1996–1966.* New York: Autonomedia, 1997.

——. *The Iron Curtain of Love.* New Brunswick, N.J.: Long Shot Productions, 1984.

——. *Shoe-Be-Do-Be-Ee-Op.* Oakland, Calif.: Madness, Inc., 1975.

——. *Songs of Bo Baba.* Woodstock, N.Y.: Shivistan Publishing, 2004.

——. *Without Doubt.* Oakland, Calif.: Zeitgeist Press, 1991.

Eliot Katz

Coney Island of the Mind, A
Lawrence Ferlinghetti (1958)

A Coney Island of the Mind is a three-part poetry collection by LAWRENCE FERLINGHETTI, publisher of City Lights Books and owner of City Lights Bookstore in San Francisco. The book's enduring popularity has led to dozens of reprintings, with Ferlinghetti's international appeal revealed by numerous translations. Approximately one million copies of *A Coney Island of the Mind* are in print around the world, and the book stands as a signal work of the San Francisco Renaissance and the Beat Generation.

The book opens with a series of 29 poems gathered under a subheading that repeats the title of the volume as a whole. These poems are untitled and are simply numbered 1–29. However, like Shakespeare's numbered sonnets, Ferlinghetti's poems are now often titled in correspondence to their opening lines. The second section is "Oral Messages," which includes seven poems conceived for presentation with jazz accompaniment. The poems are meant to be spontaneous, and the written versions presented in the text are subject to improvisation in performance. The third and final section of *A Coney Island of the Mind* revisits Ferlinghetti's first collection of poems published as Number One in the Pocket Poets Series from City Lights Books: *PICTURES OF THE GONE WORLD* (1955): This third section includes 13 poems, with numbers 1–13 as titles. The three sections give *A*

Lawrence Ferlinghetti, businessman, San Francisco, 1965. Photographer Larry Keenan: "I followed Lawrence around his bookstore, City Lights, one day, noting his attention to detail. He did everything in the bookshop, no job too big or too small. I asked him how he handled being a Beat poet and bookstore owner. He told me that when he comes to work at the store he is all business." *(courtesy of Larry Keenan)*

Coney Island of the Mind the feel of something more than a small book of poems. Ferlinghetti's most popular book is a volume of selected poems from the early years of Ferlinghetti's career as a writer.

Inspired by a positive review of *Pictures of the Gone World* by KENNETH REXROTH in the *San Francisco Chronicle*, Ferlinghetti in 1956 wrote quickly and without revision, compiling a series of 29 poems in open form. He sent the group of poems to James Laughlin, the director of publications at New Directions, and Laughlin replied with enthusiasm, indicating his desire to publish several of the poems in volume 16 of *New Directions,* the magazine he published. Ferlinghetti agreed to the publication of the selections in *ND,* and when Ferlinghetti's controversial publication of ALLEN GINSBERG's *HOWL AND OTHER POEMS* led to a censorship trial and subsequent publicity, including an article in *Life,* Laughlin pursued the idea of publishing a book by Ferlinghetti. Laughlin, however, wanted to produce more than a short book of poems. He urged Ferlinghetti to develop additional material, including selections from *Pictures of the Gone World.* Ferlinghetti at this time was also engaged in performing poetry with jazz accompaniment with Rexroth at The Cellar in San Francisco, and the performances were released as a Fantasy LP. Laughlin liked the recording, and Ferlinghetti submitted the texts of the poems as possible inclusions for the book that Laughlin intended to produce. Thus, *A Coney Island of the Mind* went to press at New Directions not as a brief sequence of poems but as a three-part collection that reflected the various dimensions of Ferlinghetti's developing career.

The title of the collection, as Ferlinghetti indicates on the page opposite the first poem, comes from *Into the Night Life* (1947), a book produced through the collaboration of Henry Miller with Palestinian artist Bezalel Schatz. The book features silkscreen art by Schatz and text by Miller originally published in *Black Spring* (1936). Ferlinghetti borrows the phrase "a Coney Island of the mind" without intention to allude to Miller's text and to derive supplemental meaning from Miller; instead, Ferlinghetti says that the phrase independently suggests the spirit of Ferlinghetti's work—"a kind of circus of the soul."

The subsection "A Coney Island of the Mind" opens with "In Goya's Greatest Scenes," a poem which reveals Ferlinghetti's characteristic linking of visual art with his writing. The poem calls attention to numerous details from Francisco Goya's sequence *The Disasters of War* (1863). The scenes of Goya, Ferlinghetti says, capture the suffering of humankind, with images of "bayonets," "blasted trees," "bats wings," "cadavers," and "hollering monsters." The images are at once "abstract" and "bloody real" and therefore stimulate the imagination to achieve a reckoning with disaster. This rec-

ognition of disaster, says Ferlinghetti, corresponds to contemporary society, which goes forward with "freeways fifty lanes wide" and "bland billboards" that portray "imbecile illusions of happiness." Perhaps the contemporary scene does not include as many "tumbrils" as Goya's scenes, but contemporary citizens drive "painted cars" with "strange license plates" and motors "that devour America." Ferlinghetti's poem ultimately is a warning about society's miserable self-destruction in the same way that Goya's great scenes are warnings about the atrocities of war.

The fifth poem in the opening section—often referred to as "Sometime During Eternity" in consideration of the opening line—builds energy by discussing profound subject matter with low, hip language. The topic is Christ, the crucifixion, and the foolish need of people to feel sure that their religion is the real religion that has the full endorsement of Christ himself. The treatment of the topic has wit because Galilee is referred to as "some square-type place" where a man who is "some kind of carpenter" claims "that the cat / who really laid it on us / is his Dad." This carpenter is too "hot," and people gather to stretch him on a tree "to cool." In time, people design their own replicas of this tree, and they implore "*the* king cat" to come down from the tree so that he can join in the performance of "their combo." The irony, however, is that the cat does not come down, and the "usual unreliable sources" that provide the news proclaim that the cat is "real dead." Ferlinghetti's poem mocks the hypocrisy of humans who forsake Christ and then want Christ to save their souls.

The 14th poem in the opening sequence—often referred to as "Don't Let That Horse"—returns to Ferlinghetti's appreciation of great works of art, but this poem is much more playful than "In Goya's Greatest Scenes." Ferlinghetti seems to call attention to *The Equestrienne* (1931) by Marc Chagall, specifically Chagall's work in completing the painting. Ferlinghetti imagines Chagall's mother imploring Chagall not to let the horse in the painting eat the violin, but anyone who observes the painting, which Ferlinghetti comically mistitles "The Horse with Violin in Mouth," can see that the violin is under the horse's jaw, not in his mouth, and the horse's consumption of the violin is not a possibility because the horse has flowers in its mouth. Ferlinghetti further imagines that upon completion of the painting, Chagall jumps up and into the painting, mounting the horse, riding away, and "waving the violin." Chagall gives the violin to "the first naked nude" he meets and there are "no strings / attached." This joke concludes the poem, but Ferlinghetti's comical reference to a devil-may-care Chagall is perhaps funnier if one understands that the original painting depicts a surreal yet elegant and serious vision of love.

Perhaps the most memorable work in the opening section of *A Coney Island of the Mind* is the 15th poem, also known as "Constantly Risking Absurdity." The poem discusses the risks of the creative performance of a poet by making an extended comparison between the poet and acrobats in a circus. The poet is a tightrope walker on a "high wire of his own making." The poet, if he fails to discover "taut truth," may in the eyes of his audience be deemed absurd. At a "still higher perch" is Beauty, who must make a "death-defying leap." If the poet fails to catch "her fair eternal form," then the poet is a failure, and like acrobats who crash to the floor below, the poet may "die" in the midst of performance. In Ferlinghetti's view, the poet (or acrobat) is "a little charleychaplin man" who can rise to exquisite levels of artistry, but if anything goes wrong, he can sink to humiliating levels of foolishness. The business of being a poet is a risky business; yet the successful taking of risks makes artistic achievement possible.

The second section of *A Coney Island of the Mind* is "Oral Messages," and in this sequence the first poem is "I Am Waiting." The title becomes a refrain in the poem as Ferlinghetti develops a catalog of all the changes for which he is waiting: an end to oppressive governments, an end to repressive religions and religious leaders, an end to apocalyptic atomic weapons, a renewal of concern for protecting the environment, and an end to racial segregation. Ferlinghetti would like to have all of these adjustments to society capped off by "a rebirth of wonder." He wants the imagination to take a central place in human existence so that life can truly be satisfying and rewarding. Because the poem is meant to be heard with jazz accompaniment, not read from the page, Ferlinghetti sets

his short lines with a consistent left-hand margin, not spacing the lines and varying indentations as he does in the first group of poems. Presented with music, "I Am Waiting" successfully conveys the witty spirit of dissent that Ferlinghetti takes pride in. He challenges society to see its flaws and finally do something about them.

Also included in the section "Oral Messages" is "Autobiography." Though the poem makes reference to scenes from Ferlinghetti's youth, including his "catching crayfish in the Bronx River," his riding of an "American Flyer bike," his delivery of newspapers, and his military service, the poem explores more completely the shaping of a Beat attitude. Ferlinghetti admits, "I had an unhappy childhood." He adds, "I looked homeward / and saw no angel." Ferlinghetti repeatedly insists that he is leading a "quiet life" and that he spends time in "Mike's Place," yet he reads "the papers every day" and senses "humanity amiss / in the sad plethora of print." To his employer, Ferlinghetti is "an open book," but to his friends, he is "a complete mystery." He says that he has "read somewhere / the Meaning of Existence," but he cannot remember exactly where. The text develops an extensive catalog of references to myths, history, and literature, often with witty twists of wording, creating a dry humor that relentlessly questions daily life.

Of all the poems in the "Oral Messages" section, "Dog" is the most perennially popular. The poem establishes an extended comparison between the Beat artist and a dog that roams the streets of San Francisco without inhibitions. The refrain in the poem is "The dog trots freely in the street" and Ferlinghetti provides an extensive list of things that come into the dog's view, including drunks, trees, ants, puddles, and cigars. However, the dog goes well beyond the normal range of a dog's consideration as he determines that he "has no use for" police officers and that Congressman Doyle of the House Un-American Activities Committee is "discouraging," "depressing," and "absurd." The dog is an intellectual who contemplates reality and ontology and is ready to offer his opinion. The dog is a relentless investigator of the world, and like the dog on the RCA Victor label, he peers "into the / great gramophone / of puzzling existence," expecting complete and meaningful answers.

The final section of *A Coney Island of the Mind* is a selection of poems from *Pictures of the Gone World*, the small poetry book that Ferlinghetti published in 1955. The opening poem, simply titled "1," describes a woman hanging wash. This activity may seem dull and ordinary, but Ferlinghetti discovers sensuality in the woman who struggles with sheets "with arms upraised." Her breasts are visible, and the wind presses the wet and "amorous" sheets against her. She joyously frees herself and pins the sheets to the line. Ferlinghetti then enlarges the scene, capturing the view of the harbor beyond the woman and her sheets. On the water are "bright steamers" and they are bound for "kingdom come." With this enlargement of the scene, Ferlinghetti reminds the reader of the contrast between the vibrant life of the woman and the inevitable slow course of time that will bring her vitality to an end.

A similar contrast is developed in "11"— sometimes known as "The World Is a Beautiful Place." The poem begins with robust irony as Ferlinghetti says that the world is beautiful but quickly short-circuits that beauty by referring to death, starvation, ignorance, violence, vanity, racism, and foolishness. Nevertheless, Ferlinghetti reasserts the beauty of the world, noting that life includes fun, love, music, flowers, dances, picnics, and swimming. The world seems to offer plenty of opportunities for people to engage in "'living it up,'" yet at the end of the poem Ferlinghetti provides a stinging message: Death is always lurking in the background, and just when life seems to be at its peak, one must be ready to meet "the smiling / mortician."

The dark mood of the poems selected from *Pictures of the Gone World* is also shown in "12," which begins "Reading Yeats, I do not think / of Ireland." When reading Yeats, Ferlinghetti thinks of the elevated public transit in New York and the absurdity of the sign that prohibits spitting. Ferlinghetti imagines the bizarre world of the people who live near the elevated tracks: "an old dame" who waters her plant, "a joker in a straw" who is on his way to Coney Island, and "an undershirted guy" who sits in a rocking chair and contemplates the passing trains. Some who read Yeats may think of "Arcady," but Ferlinghetti instead thinks "of all the gone faces / getting off at midtown places."

Life seems to reflect the words that Ferlinghetti once saw in pencil within a book of Yeats's poetry: "HORSEMAN, PASS BY!" These words refer to the startling epitaph on the gravestone of W. B. Yeats, taken from the final lines of "Under Ben Bulben" (1939): "Cast a cold on eye / On life, on death. Horseman, pass by!"

A Coney Island of the Mind remains a remarkable combination of wordplay, allusions, hip language, rich alliteration, freedom in the distribution of lines on the page, and freedom from standardized punctuation. Ferlinghetti is a dissenter, and he questions the wrongs and evils of society and seeks to correct such wrongs and evil through wit and humor. Though his work is plain enough for any reader to enjoy, it is also sufficiently complex to elude the final analysis of the finest scholar.

William Lawlor

Lawrence Ferlinghetti, Hunter's Point Studio, San Francisco, 2004. *(courtesy of Larry Keenan)*

Corso, Gregory Nunzio (1930–2001)

Poet, novelist, and playwright Gregory Corso was born on March 26, 1930, in New York City to Fortunato and Michelina Corso. Abandoned during his first year by his teenaged mother, Corso grew up in a series of orphanages and in a succession of foster homes. Both at school and at home, he was frequently subjected to beatings and to other harsh punishments, often unjust and undeserved. Running away from home repeatedly, living in the streets of New York by day and sleeping on rooftops and in the subway by night, Corso was caught and brought home again and again until he was finally sent to a reform school for two years. He also spent "3 frightening sad months" in the Bellevue mental hospital, a child among adult inmates, and later, at the age of 12, spent five months in the New York city jail, the infamous "Tombs," where he was beaten and abused by the other inmates. Corso's youthful misfortunes culminated when at the age of 17 he was sentenced to three years in Clinton State Prison for robbery.

At the same time, at intervals during this period of intense, direct experience of the "woe and plight of man," Corso was also experiencing events of quite another order. Beginning at the age of five, he was subject on occasion to strange sensations and perceptions, waking visions and vivid dreams. The most remarkable of his visions included an

Gregory Corso, Marin headlands, 1978. Photographer Larry Keenan: "Gregory Corso was one of the many poets reading at the Whole World Jamboree. Ginsberg, Orlovsky, Meltzer, and more were all there. The event lasted for 3 days. We all camped out, played, and ate together." *(courtesy of Larry Keenan)*

apparition of the figure of God among the clouds above the city, an apparition of a dying Indian mounted on a horse amid the city traffic, and another of fiery lions surrounding him as he awoke at night on a rooftop. These revelations of an unknown reality provided him with psychic sustenance.

During his confinement in the Tombs, for example, in the face of the unrelenting cruelty and the terrible isolation to which he was subjected, Corso was able to maintain an inner life of beauty and vision: "when they stole my food and beat me up and threw pee in my cell, I, the next day would come out and tell them my beautiful dream about a floating girl who landed before a deep pit and just stared."

Corso's imaginative, visionary faculty also prepared him to receive and to respond to what he has named the "books of illumination," proffered him by fellow prisoners during his incarceration at Clinton Prison. These books, which were to prove so vitally important to him, included *The Brothers Karamazov* by Fyodor Dostoyevsky, *The Red and the Black* by Stendhal, and *Les Misérables* by Victor Hugo, together with works by Thomas Chatterton, Christopher Marlowe, and Percy Bysshe Shelley, and the "1905 Standard Dictionary . . . with all the archaic and obsolete words." Through the medium of these works, Corso was brought into contact at last with his own verbal imagination, and the experience may be said to represent the true birth of his spirit and the inception of his vocation as a poet.

Released from prison in 1950, Corso returned to New York City where soon afterward—following a chance meeting in a bar in Greenwich Village—he formed a friendship with the young ALLEN GINSBERG, to whom he showed his prison poems. Ginsberg expressed admiration for Corso's work, encouraged him in his poetic vocation, and introduced him to other poets and writers, including JACK KEROUAC and WILLIAM S. BURROUGHS. Under the influence of Ginsberg, Corso began to moderate the archaic–romantic tenor of his poetry and to compose in a more modernist style.

In the years immediately following his release from prison, Corso moved between the West Coast and the East Coast of the United States, supporting himself by working as a laborer, a junior reporter (for

The Los Angeles Examiner), and a merchant seaman. He settled for a time in Cambridge, Massachusetts, where as an unofficial (unenrolled) student he attended classes at Harvard and availed himself of the university library. At length, Corso began to attain some degree of recognition for his literary work, and in 1954 his first published poems appeared in *The Harvard Advocate* and *The Cambridge Review.* At the same time, a play by Corso, *In this Hung-up Age,* was performed. The following year Corso's first volume of poems, *The Vestal Lady on Brattle* was published in Cambridge by Richard Brukenfeld.

The circulation of Corso's debut volume was quite limited (of 500 copies printed, 250 were lost). Accordingly, the book attracted little notice. A copy of *The Vestal Lady on Brattle* did, however, come to the attention of the poet and critic Randall Jarrell, then poetry consultant for the U.S. Library of Congress, who was sufficiently impressed with it to write to Corso to invite the young poet to visit him at his home in Washington, D.C. Corso's poetry also impressed poet and publisher LAWRENCE FERLINGHETTI who solicited poems from him for a volume to be published in the City Lights Pocket Poets Series.

Corso continued to travel, back and forth from East Coast to West Coast, to Mexico, and then to Europe where he made Paris his base for further journeys. In Paris, Corso lived for long periods at the now famous "Beat Hotel"—then a nameless, shabby 13th-class establishment—where he collaborated with Burroughs in literary experiments and wrote a novel, *The American Express,* published by the Olympia Press in 1961. While Corso was living in Paris, his second collection of poems, *Gasoline* (1958) was published by City Lights.

Gasoline was the book that established Corso's reputation as a poet, both in the United States and internationally. Though neither widely nor particularly favorably reviewed in literary journals, the collection soon found an enthusiastic readership, quickly selling out of the first printing and passing through numerous subsequent printings. Indeed, since the date of its first publication to the present time—for nearly 50 years—*Gasoline* has remained constantly in print. During the years that followed this literary breakthrough, Corso confirmed his uncommon and original poetic gifts with the publica-

tion (by New Directions) of two strong collections: *The HAPPY BIRTHDAY OF DEATH* (1960) and *Long Live Man* (1962).

It was, however, during this same fertile period that Corso became addicted to heroin, a factor that contributed significantly to his somewhat chaotic life and limited poetic output thereafter. In the decades that followed, Corso often lived a hand-to-mouth existence, committing acts of petty theft, selling his notebooks and manuscripts to university libraries and private collectors to support his heroin habit, and yet somehow managing to travel and write and even to marry and father children.

Fueled by his prodigious intake of drugs and alcohol, Corso became infamous to some and celebrated by others for his unpredictable and outrageous public behavior. He was often loud, rude, discourteous, and disrespectful, while at other moments he was capable of being sincere and generous. At times, Corso's wisecracks and pranks were aimed at deflating the pretensions of fellow poets, self-serving literary pundits, and self-appointed gurus, while on other occasions his inconsiderate behavior seemed merely spiteful and mean spirited. Probably the traumas of his early years contributed to his psychic instability.

Appearing at increasingly long intervals, further collections of Corso's poems were published during the 1970s and 1980s. *Elegiac Feelings American* (1970) was followed 11 years later by *Herald of the Autochthonic Spirit* (1981). Finally, in 1989, Thunder's Mouth Press brought out *Mindfield: New & Selected Poems,* which contains generous selections from the poet's previous volumes but only seven new poems. The next year Corso appeared as an unruly stockholder in Francis Ford Coppola's *The Godfather: Part III.* Roger and Irvyne Richards took care of Corso for more than a decade at the end of his life. Between 1989 and Corso's death at age 70 on January 17, 2001, no new volume of poems was published, though until the time of his death Corso remained active as a lecturer and as a performer at poetry readings. Near the end of his life, a private detective hired by producers of a documentary film found clues that led to Corso being reunited with his mother for the first time since he was a baby. Corso's daughter, Sheri, took care of him in Minnesota before he died.

Robert Yarra, Corso's friend, suggested that Corso be buried in Rome. Hannelore DeLellis, Yarra's friend in Italy, helped this dream become a reality with additional financial support from two of Corso's ex-wives, others including Yarra, and a fundraiser organized by Patti Smith. According to his wishes, Corso's ashes were buried in Rome in the city's *cimitero acattolico* (non-Catholic cemetery), in a tomb near his beloved Percy Bysshe Shelley. Corso's epitaph is taken from his poem "Spirit," which appeared in *Herald of the Autochthonic Spirit*:

> Spirit
> is life
> It flows thru
> the death of me
> endlessly
> life a river
> unafraid
> of becoming
> the sea

In 2003 New Directions issued *An Accidental Autobiography: The Selected Letters of Gregory Corso,* edited by Bill Morgan. This thick volume with notes and commentary by the editor offers many insights into Corso's life and thought, as well as into the composition of individual poems. It remains to be seen whether a biography of Corso will be undertaken. Corso's contribution to American letters has been assessed and examined in various critical studies, and among the current generation of literary critics there seems to be agreement that Gregory Corso was a distinctive and vital voice in American postwar poetry and that his work has enduring value.

A documentary, *Corso: The Last Beat,* directed by Gustave Reininger, is scheduled for release in 2007.

Bibliography

Corso, Gregory. *An Accidental Autobiography: The Selected Letters of Gregory Corso.* Edited by Bill Morgan. New York: New Directions, 2003.

Miles, Barry. *The Beat Hotel: Ginsberg, Burroughs, and Corso in Paris, 1957–1963.* New York: Grove Press, 2000.

Olson, Kirby. *Gregory Corso: Doubting Thomist.* Carbondale: Southern Illinois University Press, 2002.

Skau, Michael. *"A Clown in a Grave": Complexities and Tensions in the Works of Gregory Corso.* Carbondale: Southern Illinois University Press, 1999.

Stephenson, Gregory. *Exiled Angel: A Study of the Work of Gregory Corso.* London: Hearing Eye, 1989.

Gregory Stephenson

Creeley, Robert (1926–2005)

Called "a Beat before the Beats" by biographer Ekbert Faas, Robert Creeley's poetry mirrored, even suggested that of his Beat contemporaries, though he did not officially intersect with the group until his career was well underway. An eccentric man with one glass eye, Creeley lacked the Zen mindset that characterized many of the Beats and was known for his surly demeanor, ever-readiness for a fight, and overbearing personality. Even JACK KEROUAC admonished him to stay out of fights and "Be a happy drunk like me!"

An academically gifted student, Creeley earned a scholarship to the prestigious Holderness School in New Hampshire. Though he was expected to work toward a career in veterinary medicine, it was at Holderness, where he edited and wrote for the school papers, that his talent in letters became clear. Deciding to pursue a writerly life, he applied and was eventually accepted to Harvard where he quickly became an "unkempt, chainsmoking freshman" dissatisfied with his poetic education. Eventually suspended from Harvard for misconduct and poor grades, he set off for a year as an ambulance driver in the American Field Service in India. It was on the return from this trip in 1945 that Creeley finally composed his first poem, aptly named "Return":

> Quiet as is proper for such places;
> The street, subdued, half-snow, half-rain,
> Endless, but ending in the darkened doors.
> Inside, they who will be there always,
> Quiet as is proper for such people—
> Enough for now to be here, and
> To know my door is one of these.

Soon after, Creeley began to share poetry and literally thousands of letters with poet

CHARLES OLSON, who brought Creeley on as faculty at the experimental Black Mountain School of North Carolina. There he became contributing editor of Black Mountain's *Origin* and then *Black Mountain Review,* which published the likes of WILLIAM S. BURROUGHS, ALLEN GINSBERG, and KENNETH REXROTH. By 1956, Creeley would visit San Francisco during the height of its poetry renaissance, befriending many Beat writers, including Kerouac.

Through his closeness with poets like Olson and Kerouac, Creeley's own theory and practice of poetry solidified, as reflected in his vast catalogue of critical writings. Through Olson's poetry and their many correspondences early in his career, Creeley began to develop the ideas he first gleaned from reading Ezra Pound and William Carlos Williams, writing that "form is never more than an *extension* of content" and that the "things" of poetry "must be allowed to realize themselves in their fullest possible degree." Kerouac's writing then augmented these thoughts. As Faas writes, "Kerouac had the ability to translate present sensation into immediate, actual language," a gift Creeley greatly admired. Creeley's poetry, lectures, and criticism have since been definitive of modern American avant-garde writing.

Creeley's major works of poetry include: *Just in Time: Poems 1984–1994. Life & Death, Echoes, Selected Poems 1945–1990, Memory Gardens, Mirrors, The Collected Poems of Robert Creeley, 1945–1975, Later, The Finger,* FOR LOVE: POEMS 1950–1960, as well as copious editions, works of prose, and critical essays.

Robert Creeley died on March 30, 2005, from complications of respiratory disease.

Bibliography

Creeley, Robert. *The Collected Essays of Robert Creeley.* Berkeley: University of California Press, 1989.

Edleberg, Cynthia. *Robert Creeley's Poetry: A Critical Introduction.* Albuquerque: University of New Mexico Press, 1978.

Faas, Ekbert, and Maria Trombacco. *Robert Creeley: A Biography.* Hanover, N.H.: University Press of New England, 2001.

Jennifer Cooper

"Cuba Libre"   Amiri Baraka (LeRoi Jones) (1960)

If the years 1958–62 can be agreed to represent LeRoi Jones/ AMIRI BARAKA's Beat phase, then "Cuba Libre," which arose out of his 1960 visit to Cuba in the company of such black intellectuals as Harold Cruse, Robert F. Williams, Julian Mayfield, and John Henrik Clarke under the auspices of the Fair Play for Cuba Committee, marks his transition into black nationalism with Marxism to follow in the 1970s. First published in *Evergreen Review,* it would become a mainstay of the collection *Home: Social Essays* (1966), along with such writings as "The Legacy of Malcolm X, and the Coming of the Black Nation" (1965) and "State/meant" (1965). No longer for him Greenwich Village, the bohemian art scene, or HETTIE JONES—his white wife and coeditor of the avant-garde literary journal *Yugen* (1958–62), which published ALLEN GINSBERG and others, or his one-time sense that the Beats were his fellow outsiders. Rather the call now lay in committed, interventionist black politics.

DUTCHMAN (1964), his landmark play set on the circling New York metro in the "underbelly of the city" and a mythic reenactment of the destructive violence which so often has shaped America's black–white interface, gives one expression. Another lies in the poem "BLACK DADA NIHILISMUS," in *The Dead Lecturer* (1964), with its heady, millennial vision of black redress against white-supremacist abuse within a West he designates as "gray hideous space." "Cuba Libre" helps greatly in understanding Jones/Baraka's ideological shift, his impatience with Beat's apoliticality, as he had come to regard it, and the need for a Third World alliance against the United States and western imperialist world order.

Told as though a diary of events, "Cuba Libre" begins from a gathering of the group at New York's formerly named Idlewild Airport, then the day's delay over tickets that he believes were likely finagled by the Federal Bureau of Investigation (FBI), and the next-day flight to Havana and the Presidente Hotel. Determined not to be taken in by "official" Cuba and as he gets to know his fellow members of the group—especially Robert Williams as NAACP militant leader from Monroe, North Carolina, and the painter Edward Clarke—he undergoes a furtherance of his own already rising political consciousness. Each sequence in the visit weighs keenly with him, whether the Casa de las Americas and an encounter with the guide-translator Olga Finley and the subdirector and architect Alberto Robaina, or the Ministry of Education where he learns of progress toward national literacy, or the National Agrarian Reform Institute whose remit is the redistribution of land, or finally the Ministry of Housing with its challenges to meet the needs of a largely rural, poor citizenry. Evidently exhilarated at the solidarity he meets, he prepares with the others for the anniversary of Fidel Castro's conquest of the Moncada Barracks on July 26, 1953. En route to the other side of the island by crowded train and truck, he hears endlessly the cries of "Fidel," "Venceremos" and "Cuba Sí, Yanqui No," debates revolution and imperialism with one Señora Betancourt, and makes his way with the others through intense heat to meet and hear Castro ("He is an amazing speaker, knowing probably instinctively all the laws of dynamics and elocution").

The cross-island journey and back, despite his own dehydration and dysentery, serves as rite of passage, the community socialist belief and fervor, his own exchange of words with Castro, and Castro's unsparing indictments of the Monroe Doctrine, Batista, Eisenhower, and Nixon. He displays a rising scorn for Western consumerism and for the "vapid mores" and "vested interest" of the United States. His conclusion argues that "the Cubans, and other *new* peoples (in Asia, Africa, South America) don't need us, and we had better stay out of their way." The Beat years, important as they may have been in the development of the LeRoi Jones shortly thereafter to become Imamu Amiri Baraka, seem already far behind, a genuinely prior time.

A. Robert Lee

D

Dark Brown Michael McClure (1961)

In JACK KEROUAC's novel *BIG SUR*, Kerouac's narrator Jack Duluoz praises "Dark Brown" by Pat McLear (a character based on MICHAEL McCLURE) as "the most fantastic poem in America." *Dark Brown* is McClure's first book-length poem. The work depicts the poet's quest toward clarity and a sense of rebirth, following a lengthy series of sometimes dark peyote visions that are chronicled most fully in McClure's 1961 collection *The New Book / A Book of Torture.*

Whereas *The New Book / A Book of Torture* represented McClure's struggles with the dark peyote visions of "HELL PAIN BEWILDERED EMPTINESS," *Dark Brown* offers what William King has called "a psychic restructuring" through which the poet discovers and finds renewal in a strong unifying force in nature. This universal force, which McClure refers to as "Odem"—a German word for the spirit of beasts—or the "Undersoul," is the visceral bond which ties together all forms of life. Reminiscent of Ralph Waldo Emerson's transcendentalist concept of the "Over-Soul," McClure's undersoul provides a vision of clarity and unity in a chaotic universe: "Unclouded one. / Undersoul. Odem, Dark brown, Umber, Beast. / The undersoul a star!" By embracing this universal mammalian life force, the poet discovers within himself "the deep and / singing beast" and the "undamning" of his creative powers:

THE BODY AND SPIRIT ARE ONE I AM
energy!.

As in much of McClure's work, this acknowledgment of humanity's connections to the forces of the natural world contains a strong element of what Walt Whitman had called the procreant urge of sexuality. *Dark Brown* is steeped in sexual energy and in the raw physicality of sex. As McClure writes in the introduction to the poem, the notion of love as ethereal—a product of the mind or the soul—is illusory: instead, he writes, "Love is body beating upon body, the *confrontation* of face and face or shoulder and shoulder. I say *Love* is not a dream or mind-invention."

While critics and censors found the raw language of *Dark Brown* to be offensive, it was the two graphically erotic codas included after the title poem, "Fuck Ode" and "Garland," that spurred the most controversy. Perhaps more graphically sexual than any work in the Beat canon, these two works offered a compelling depiction of human sexuality as both sacred and erotic: "Freed / Of all lies the face is pure. The gestures are imm- / ortal." As a result of its graphic sexual content, the 1961 Auerhahn Press version of the book was at times sold under the counter in plain brown wrappers in some bookstores. Despite the censors' early objections, the poem's vitality and energy endure, making McClure's *Dark Brown* one of the finest long poems of the Beat era.

Bibliography

Phillips, Rod. *Michael McClure*. Western Writers Series 159. Boise, Idaho: Boise State University, 2003.

Stephenson, Gregory. "From the Substrate: Notes on Michael McClure." *The Daybreak Boys: Essays on* the Literature of the Beat Generation. Carbondale: Southern Illinois University Press, 1990: 105–130.

Rod Phillips

DESERT JOURNAL ruth weiss (1977)

From 1961 to 1968, RUTH WEISS labored on what was to become her masterwork, DESERT JOURNAL, a collection of 40 poems, a record of a journey of self-discovery in the inscape of the creative mind. The text, illustrated with line drawings by artist Paul Blake, who became weiss's life-partner in 1967, is indebted to both modernism and Beat postmodern aesthetics. weiss limited the composition of each poem to a single page of paper, reminiscent of but not directly inspired by JACK KEROUAC's basic method for the construction of many of his blues poems, allowing her internal processes to determine the content. The result is the creation of the illusion of the unrestrained moving mind, the many facets of consciousness revealed as a sparkly gem. The appropriation of myth, especially the biblical stories of Moses and Jesus wandering in the desert, faintly undergird the structure of the poem in the tradition of high modernism. The collection's mixture of languages (real and imaginary) and its dreamlike setting also link weiss to the heritage of writers such as T. S. Eliot, Ezra Pound, and Gertrude Stein, whose signature use of repetition and word inversion is unmistakably present in lines such as

    pain is the first step
    into the desert

    absence of pain
    is the desert

    not have where
    is the desert

    not to have where to dance
    is the desert

    the desert becomes the dance.

The speaker, whose gender shifts throughout the text, concludes the inner journey as the human fe-

male principle propelled toward the male principle of divine light. Not overtly sectarian, DESERT JOURNAL's triumphant release of the human form fits beautifully with the spiritual pursuits of many Beat writers, particularly their study of Buddhism and the Gnostic traditions of Christianity and the kabbalah. DESERT JOURNAL, now out of print, was published in 1977 by Good Gay Poets in Boston.

weiss's poetry and prose reflects her affinity for a fascinating range of literary, musical, and cinematic texts. The influence of Stein can be seen in her love of word play, often daring to revel in the nonsensical and surreal. Johann Goethe, Johann Schiller, Rainer Maria Rilke, Edgar Allen Poe, Djuna Barnes, Francois Truffaut, Frederico Fellini, Billie Holliday, Django Rhinehart, and Charlie Parker all blend in her voice to create a vibrantly subtle vision of mystical confession.

The characteristic that most distinctly renders her work "Beat" is her use of a spontaneous method of free association akin to Tristian Tzara's Dadaism, William Butler Yeat's automatism, jazz improvisation, and Buddhist intuition. She also believes deeply in the collaborative nature of artistic production, and many of her readings are performances involving collaboration with jazz and other musicians (including classical guitarists) and the audience members themselves. She will spend hours in rehearsal with musicians prior to a performance to establish a simpatico relationship of sound and narrative enabling the final improvisational performance to flow in unfettered synchronization.

Bibliography
Grace, Nancy M. "ruth weiss's DESERT JOURNAL: A Modern-Beat-Pomo Performance." In Reconstructing the Beats, edited by Jennie Skerl, 57–71. New York: Palgrave Macmillan, 2004.

Nancy M. Grace

Desolation Angels Jack Kerouac (1965)

Ellis Amburn, JACK KEROUAC's last editor, called Desolation Angels Kerouac's "lost masterpiece, the final flowering of his great creative period in the fifties: the true voice of Kerouac." Dan Wakefield, writing for The Atlantic in July 1965, stated,

"If the Pulitzer Prize in fiction were given for the book that is most representative of American life, I would nominate *Desolation Angels*."

Part One covers Kerouac's 63 days as a fire lookout on Desolation Peak in 1956 and his subsequent reentry into the world in San Francisco, where the San Francisco Poetry Renaissance is about to begin. Kerouac wrote Part One in Mexico City at the same time that he was writing *TRISTESSA* and *MEXICO CITY BLUES*. In Part Two, Kerouac looks at the Beat innocents abroad, describing their adventures in Tangier, London, and Paris. Part Two was originally a separate book entitled "An American Passes Through." Amburn saw the market for a really big Kerouac book and suggested to Kerouac that both books be published together under one title. Kerouac agreed. Seymour Krim wrote an introduction to the book that attempted to do for Kerouac what Malcolm Cowley had done for Faulkner: provide an overview of Kerouac's life work that showed the interconnectedness of his books.

In Part One, at the urging of GARY SNYDER (Jarry Wagner in the novel), Kerouac signs on for a fire lookout job in the isolated mountains of Western Washington. His post is on Desolation Peak. There he attempts to live the life of a Buddhist monk or a hermit like Han Shan or like one of his boyhood idols, Thoreau, who lived on Walden Pond. What Kerouac learns from this experience is that deep inside of himself is a void of loneliness and, most embarrassing, boredom. He also discovers that to write, he needs characters, not mountains. About half of the brief chapters here are fantasies about what he will do when he returns to San Francisco or travels to Mexico.

Still, Kerouac does gain some key insights that will influence him for years to come. He gains enlightenment and peace from the knowledge that the world is an illusion and that it all passes *through* him. He also writes some of the first environmental protest literature when he argues that the only reason that he is paid to spot fires is so that Scott paper will not lose any of the beautiful trees they cut down to make toilet paper. Here, too, Snyder is an influence. Kerouac admits Snyder's influence and reminisces about their dharma bum days (*The DHARMA BUMS* precedes this book in chronological

order), but he breaks with Snyder sometime during these two months by wanting to embrace society, not withdraw from it: "Yar give me society, give me beauteous faced whores." This is in fact the advice that WILLIAM S. BURROUGHS had given him about Buddhist withdrawal and monkishness: it was an Eastern, not a Western practice.

The events of Kerouac's life seem orchestrated to create scenes with the greatest possible meaning. He goes into the solitude of nature at the moment when the ecological consciousness is being formed on the West Coast by Snyder, KENNETH REXROTH, MICHAEL McCLURE, and others; he returns to San Francisco at the very moment that the San Francisco Poetry Renaissance is underway, a mad social and cultural moment. He is there for both, and the contrast between the former and the latter (desolation versus society) creates great tension but also great energy in the opening sections of Part Two.

Part Two takes Jack Duluoz (Kerouac's persona) down the mountain and back into the city (San Francisco), a descent which has a ring of exile to it, of paradise lost. The sad truth that he has had to admit to himself following his experiences on Desolation Peak is that "the vision of freedom of eternity which I saw . . . is of little use in cities and warring societies such as we have." (In fact, he makes it back to the city just in time to become entangled in a war between old-school and new-school poets). The experience of solitude works on him like a drug that has sharpened his perceptions: down from the mountain, he rediscovers American popular music, *Time* magazine, and alcohol—about which he concludes, "[T]here is no need for alcohol whatever in your soul."

En route to San Francisco, Duluoz hitches a ride to Seattle, where he watches a burlesque show and drinks with a crowd of bum "angels." He needs "humanity," he realizes, and he wants to "wake up" everyone he meets with speeches about what he has learned on the mountain. To him, all of humanity looks the way it does in a Chaplin film—angels without wings. This defamiliarization is similar to the new vision Kerouac has of New York when he returns from having been out West: Travel (in this case isolation) has always sharpened and reawakened his senses.

Duluoz's feet, it turns out, are too battered from his trip down the mountain to hitchhike past Seattle, and he takes a bus to San Francisco. Back in San Francisco, he wanders anonymously for a while before inevitably hooking back up with his "gang" at The Cellar and The Place: Rob Donnelly (Bob Donlin), Mal Damlette (Al Sublette), Chuck Berman (BOB KAUFMAN), Raphael Urso (GREGORY CORSO), David D'Angeli (LAWRENCE FERLING-HETTI), Irwin Garden (ALLEN GINSBERG), Simon and Lazarus Darlovsky (the Orlovsky brothers), and Rene Levesque (Robert LaVigne). The plot of the book centers on several conflicts. For example, Raphael and Cody Pomeray (NEAL CASSADY) need to be brought together as friends, in the spirit of Beat brotherhood and inclusiveness. Garden wants to bring *everyone* in the arts together (even in bed), East and West Coast, to start a social revolution. However, he cannot even bring the warring poets from East and West together for a photo in *Mademoiselle* magazine—"Flaming Cool Poets." Two holdouts are Patrick McLear (Michael McClure) and Geoffrey Donald (ROBERT DUNCAN), who insist on being photographed separately. Garden's ultimate plan, which is realized in Book Two, is to take this artistic and cultural movement—that is, the Beat consciousness—international. Yet, the book is hardly a history of the budding San Francisco Poetry Renaissance; it is, to use Kerouac's key phrase throughout the book, more as if he "passes through" this fascinating time and place as it "passes through" him.

Book Two of *Desolation Angels* was originally a separate book, and a few signs of the books being separate remain. For example, the Randall Jarrell character has different names in the two books, and the NORMAN MAILER character goes by his real name in Book Two, although in Book One he is Harvey Marker. Kerouac also seems to have forgotten his caustic remarks about Jarrell's 1956 poetry reading in Berkeley, for he admires the poet greatly when he visits him in Washington, D.C., a year later. The style of Book Two is also different from that of Book One, which was written in a spontaneous, bop style atop a Mexico City roof during an uninterrupted period of great peace that produced some of his finest writing: *Tristessa* and *Mexico City Blues*. Book Two was written five years later in a

Mexico City hotel, and it reads more as if it were a memoir, albeit a memoir covering the lives and travels of some of the most interesting and talented people in the 20th century. Still, Book Two lacks Kerouac's signature undercurrent of meaning and inevitability (what he calls "the holy contour of life") that runs through his earlier spontaneous prose: in his works from the 1950s, he is able to write spontaneously but with intention and form, even if it is coming through uncensored. In Book Two, he simply appears to have less urgency to say what he has to say. There is, in other words, some key element subtly lacking that makes Book Two less of an achievement than the first.

Part One of Book Two, "Passing Through Mexico," is written from the distance of a very long five years in Kerouac's life. He looks back on the first part of *Desolation Angels* and says that at that time in his life, he was seeking a balance between "doing nothing" (in the Buddhist sense) and being in life at the same time: Going down the mountain and heading to San Francisco allowed him to test his ability to "see the world from the viewpoint of solitude and to meditate upon the world without being imbroglio'd in its actions." He heads to Mexico City to write and finds on his return there that he has forgotten a "certain drear, even sad, darkness" about the country: In his later work, Kerouac no longer romanticizes Mexico and the "fellaheen." As he had done previously, Duluoz lives on the rooftop of Old Bull Gaines's (Bill Garver) apartment. This is Kerouac's longest portrait of his old junky friend from the mad Times Square, mid-1940s days, when Gaines/Garver stole overcoats to keep himself in junk. As is recounted in *Tristessa*, Duluoz makes junk runs for Gaines, empties his toilet for him, and writes in the afternoons and evenings. In the mornings, he watches Gaines shoot up and nod out, and he listens to his endless lectures drawn from H.G. Wells's *Outline of History*. Years later, even Kerouac cannot understand his lifestyle at the time—"I was bound to live my own way"—but it led to three great books being written during that period. In a crucial passage, he describes his real contribution to literature from those days: "I was originating a new way of writing about life, no fiction, no craft, no revising afterthoughts."

The peace of this writing life is broken by the Lakofsky Brothers, Raphael Urso, and Irwin Garden, who arrive in Mexico City after a two-week stay in Guadalajara at the home of Alise Nabokov (Denise Levertov)—"a dull woman poetess," says Duluoz. Urso hates Mexico, seeing it as doom ridden and full of death. This famous group of American poets wanders through Mexico's slums and is whistled at admiringly by students for being so obviously who they are—great young American writers. They sit atop the pyramids and discuss the great Mayan and Aztec peoples and their blood-lust. At the end of the book, Garden plots Duluoz's next move: "Irwin . . . always directed me in some ways." They will all return to New York where it is time for Duluoz and all the other Beats to become famous. Duluoz realizes that the difference between him and Garden is Garden's interest in politics and changing the world, a world which for Duluoz (in his Buddhist phase) is illusion. Garden evidently does not sense the reluctance and fear on Duluoz's part about becoming famous.

Part Two of Book Two, "Passing Through New York," develops Duluoz's fears of becoming famous. In this second part, he recalls his father's prophecy that Garden would betray him. However, this "betrayal" does not take place until the end of the book, when *Road* (ON THE ROAD) is published, but Garden is not there to guide him through the dangers of fame. First, Duluoz details the 3,000-mile trip back to New York in an overloaded car that is being shared by him, the Darlovskys, Garden, and two businessmen also headed to New York. They arrive exhausted and broke and with nowhere to stay. The ever-resourceful Garden looks up the two Ruths (Helen Vendler and Helen Weaver) in Chelsea and gets the gang inside their apartment. Duluoz and the Ruth character who is based on Helen Weaver are instantly attracted to each other. This is the lover whom Garden promised Duluoz would meet in the previous book. Duluoz describes his physical relation with Ruth in mock metaphors and claims to have given her the first "extase of her career." This book contains some of Kerouac's most lamentable misogynistic ramblings, the kind of material that made another girlfriend from this time complain that she loved Jack but despised the "woman-hating stuff." Later, Ruth's psychiatrist

urges her to dump Duluoz, and he ends up living with another woman, Alyce Newman, who realizes that Duluoz is going to be a famous writer and offers to protect him. Foolishly, by the end of the book, he has turned her down.

Of greatest interest to literary historians here is Kerouac's rather shame-faced description of his stay at the Washington, D.C., house of Varnum Random (Randall Jarrell), whose poetry he had dismissed at a Berkeley reading described in Book One. To Kerouac, Jarrell's poetry was the antithesis of his own. Random, Duluoz, and Urso (who is also Random's guest) have a spirited discussion about the merits of Duluoz's "spontaneous" prose, with Random and Urso weighing in against it—this in spite of the fact that Corso's first successful poems are clearly influenced by Kerouac's theory. Random says, "Well, it'll probably become a popular gimmick, but I prefer to look upon poetry as a craft." Duluoz replies by saying that "craft is crafty. How can you confess your crafty soul in craft?" Kerouac demonstrated his theory by writing, in one afternoon, the poem series entitled "Washington, D. C. Blues," in Jarrell's living room. Later, Kerouac felt as if he had taken advantage of his host, whom he ended up admiring in spite of his traditional approach to poetry.

In visiting Jarrell, who was at that time the "National Poet," it is apparent that Kerouac was on the verge of no longer being a fringe literary figure. However, Duluoz says ominously, "I foresaw a new dreariness in all this literary success." Disaster strikes almost immediately. Leaving D.C., Duluoz loses his treasured pack with all of his unpublished manuscripts and openly weeps. The bag is returned, but this incident must have impressed Duluoz with the importance of getting his manuscripts in print. Visiting his mother at his sister's house in Florida further inspires him to be a success, but at the same time, he knows success lies through the men his mother and father have warned him against—Garden and Bull Hubbard (William S. Burroughs). At the end of Part Two of "Passing Through," these are the very men whom he goes to see in Tangier, Morocco, in Part Three of Book Two, "Passing Through Tangier, France, and London."

This trip was intended to be one in which the Beats went international. However, Duluoz is poisoned by cyanide-laden hashish in Tangier, and his "youthful brave sense of adventure" changes to "complete nausea concerning experience — in the world at large." He sees this as a defining turnabout in his life view. Before he is poisoned by the hashish, though, he spends a happy week in the company of Hubbard, who is in the middle of writing his masterpiece, *Nude Supper* (*NAKED LUNCH*). Duluoz describes Hubbard's writing process as one of entertaining himself until he "suddenly double[s] up in laughter at what he done." The pages of the manuscript strewn about the floor and patio of Hubbard's Tangier apartment, but Duluoz collects them and types up fair copies. He is tremendously impressed by the "book": No American writer, he says, was ever more honest than Hubbard is in *Nude Supper*. Scenes from the manuscript he is typing are so horrifying that they give Duluoz nightmares. When he asks the meaning of the hanged boys in the book, Hubbard says even he does not understand what he writes, as if he is "an agent from another planet but I haven't got my orders yet." Burroughs said years later that this is essentially the situation of all writers.

Hubbard eagerly awaits Garden's arrival in Tangier, for he is in love with him. Duluoz describes Hubbard's maudlin pining for Garden. The opium seems to affect Hubbard, too, and when Irwin arrives, it is an anticlimax. By this point, Hubbard seems to have come to the conclusion that his melodrama with Garden is "silly." He refuses to play tourist guide for Garden and his lover Simon Darlovsky (Peter Orlovsky), but the two travelers draw Duluoz down from his rooftop writings with childish calls of "Jack-kee!"

As they tour Tangier, Duluoz and Garden see members of an international "hip" scene among the young Arabs, and they believe that their own work is partly responsible for an international Beat movement. As Burroughs would later say, the real contribution of the Beat movement may well have been its breaking down of the barriers between races and countries. By contrast, says Duluoz, "one look at the officials in the American Consulate . . . was enough to make you realize what was wrong with American 'diplomacy' throughout the Fellaheen world:—stiff officious squares with contempt even for their own Americans." He suggests

that the Americans get out of their limousines and move to the native quarters (from the suburbs) and share a kief pipe with the natives.

In his letters about this trip, Kerouac is much more enthusiastic about the places to which he goes and people whom he meets—much more the "youthful adventurer" than you see here. In fact, his trip to Paris and London is covered in a mere eight pages in *Desolation Angels*. In France, Urso makes Duluoz spend all of his money in a trendy "subterranean" bar. He sees enough of England to decide that the Angry Young Men are far less interesting than London's Teddy Boys. With money from *Road*'s British publication, he leaves as soon as he can: "I wanted to go home."

Part Four of Book Two, "Passing Through America Again," reveals that Duluoz's life at this point seems mistimed in a way that contrasts with the serendipitous events of the first book. He comes back to America and decides to move his mother from Florida to Berkeley—a move that she does not really want to make and is really, he admits, just a way for him to be closer to Pomeray. Several chapters are a defense of his love for and devotion to his mother, a relationship that had been criticized by his friends as far back as 1944 when Burroughs performed an amateur psychoanalysis of Kerouac. He attacks his "fellow writers" who all hate their mothers and accuses them of ignoring their mothers' devotion to them and their simple humanity. One of the critics of Kerouac's relationship with his mother is JOYCE JOHNSON in *MINOR CHARACTERS* (1983), who is identified here as Duluoz's girlfriend Alyce. Still, Johnson points out that Memere is the only woman whom Kerouac ever took on the road, and the ending of *Desolation Angels* includes a marvelous account of their trip from Florida to northern California, in which Duluoz ushers his mother through scenes that he has witnessed many times in Mexico, New Orleans, and Los Angeles. Through her eyes he sees the holiness of the converted Indians in Mexico as well as the evil of Los Angeles's downtown sidewalks. Fortunately, "every evil dog in evildom understands it when he sees a man with his Mother, so bless you all."

The end of the book compresses a lot of Kerouac's experiences. His mother is no sooner in Berkeley than she is writing back to her daughter in Florida. Duluoz is given a jay walking ticket and sees California as a police state (as Kerouac writes to Snyder, too, in letters from this time period). In a remarkable and factually accurate scene, the first copies of *Road* arrive, and he has the unopened book in his hand at that moment when Pomeray, Slim Buckle (Al Hinkle), and Joanna (Luanne Henderson) (some of the "heroes" of the book) all walk in on him. Duluoz sees a golden halo around Pomeray, which he has seen on only a few other occasions, and knows Pomeray is an "angel." However, Pomeray cannot meet Duluoz's eyes, and just a few months later, suddenly famous and conspicuous, Pomeray is busted for marijuana possession. Duluoz denies responsibility for Pomeray's misfortune (Cassady would spend two years in jail), claiming that the bust was a "karmic" punishment for Pomeray's "belting" of his daughter, a scene Duluoz witnessed.

The book ends with Duluoz running back to Mexico just after he has moved his mother to Florida once again. There he discovers that his friend Gaines committed suicide when he could not score any morphine. A huge earthquake rocks his hotel that night: "It's all over," he believes. The coda has him back in New York where he, Simon Darlovsky, Urso, and Garden are all now famous writers. Duluoz, however, hopes for a "new life," a quiet one with his mother, and says good-bye to the Desolation Angels. Duluoz says he is feeling "peaceful," which Joyce Johnson has called Kerouac's "white lie to provide a sense of closure." The ending of the book reflects Malcolm Cowley's complaint that the narrator is a "ghost," and Kerouac says that this was the point: After coming down from the mountain, he saw in a vision that they were all angels, just passing through, and through which, in turn, life passed.

Bibliography

Amburn, Ellis. *Subterranean Kerouac: The Hidden Life of Jack Kerouac.* New York: St. Martin's Press, 1998.
Johnson, Joyce. Introduction. *Desolation Angels,* by Jack Kerouac. New York: Riverhead Books, 1995, vii–xvii.
Wakefield, Dan. "Kerouac, Leary and Whoever." *Gentlemen's Quarterly,* April 1991, 218–225, 263–264.

Rob Johnson

Dharma Bums, The Jack Kerouac (1958)

Ann Charters says that the autumn of 1955, which JACK KEROUAC spent in Berkeley, California, was probably "the three happiest months of his life." This is the time period and the setting for Kerouac's follow-up novel to *ON THE ROAD*—*The Dharma Bums.* Staying with ALLEN GINSBERG in his Berkeley cottage, Kerouac met many of the poets and artists of the emerging San Francisco Renaissance. He climbed mountains with GARY SNYDER and passed around a jug of wine and yelled "Go!" as Ginsberg read the famous opening section of "HOWL" at the seminal Six Gallery Reading on October 7, 1955. Most importantly, Kerouac found a group of like-minded poets who were deeply into Buddhism, including Snyder and PHILIP WHALEN. Snyder gave Kerouac the phrase that became the book's title, *dharma* meaning "the path" or "the law" or "the practice," and the word *bums* referring to the antimaterialism and humility of the followers of Buddha. In a more obvious sense, Henry Miller understood the title exactly when he said of the book, "We've had all kinds of bums in our literature but never a dharma bum like this Kerouac."

In typical fashion, Kerouac wrote the novel in 10 marathon sessions, fueled by Benzedrine. Today it is one of Kerouac's most popular novels, and in the 1960s and 1970s it was a Bible for the "rucksack revolution" of the hippies. However, the book has been maligned as a quick cash-in on the success of *On The Road.* Oddly, the accusation that it was a "potboiler" was first made by Ginsberg, who hoped that Kerouac would not abandon his "spontaneous" style for the more accessible style of *The Dharma Bums.* When the book was viciously attacked in the press (*Time* magazine's critic suggested the title be changed to "On the Trail: How the Campfire Boys Discovered Buddhism"), though, it was Ginsberg who brilliantly defended the book in the *Village Voice,* placing Kerouac's style in the "plain-language" tradition of William Carlos Williams and likening its achievement to that of the novels of Louis-Ferdinand Céline and Jean Genet. Today it seems apparent that Kerouac sacrificed some of his "spontaneous" methods to achieve a more noble goal—that of introducing young America to an alternative spiritual path in life.

The hero of the novel, Japhy Ryder, is based on poet and environmentalist Gary Snyder. It is unclear how willing a role model Snyder was for the book. By the time it appeared, Snyder must have been aware that Kerouac's previous hero, NEAL CASSADY (as Dean Moriarity in *On the Road*) was serving five years to life for possession of two marijuana cigarettes. In letters, Kerouac explained to Snyder the care he had taken to alter the facts about Snyder's life to protect his anonymity. When the book appeared, Snyder was apparently thrilled, as were key popularizers of Buddhism such as Alan Watts, who even revised his lukewarm opinion of "Beat Zen" in his 1958 article "Beat Zen, Square Zen, and Zen." A few months after the book's release, Kerouac sensed a silence from Snyder and wrote to him in Japan. Snyder replied that he "liked" the book but did not think that Kerouac understood Buddhism because of Kerouac's strictures against love and sex: "Nobody ever said anything against love or entanglement but you." The rest of Snyder's response—in which Snyder jokes that all authors will have their "tongues torn out in hell"—is often quoted out of context to suggest a real enmity toward Kerouac. Kerouac replied that the book was not "as bad as you think" and that it was "just so fucking typical of what's wrong with official Buddhism" that Snyder would criticize it.

In the jacket copy Kerouac wrote for Viking, he stressed that the book should not be associated with the "beat" movement and that the Buddhism of the book represented "an exciting new way of life in the midst of modern despair." He was very serious and hoped that the lifestyle that he depicted through these dharma bums would provide a model for young people and would eventually create a revolution in consciousness that would lead to a better world—the one common goal of all the Beat writers, it could be argued. However, by distancing himself from the Beats and by refusing to repeat himself in style or content, Kerouac frustrated a publishing industry that was ready to exploit his art for easy profit. Unlike *On the Road*, *The Dharma Bums* never made it onto the *New York Times* best-seller list.

Ray Smith (based on Kerouac himself) narrates the story, which begins in Los Angeles in September 1955. Smith looks back on the events of the past few years, but the perspective is of someone who has grown more than the short num-

ber of intervening years would suggest. "I was very devout in those days," he says, a practicing Buddhist dedicated to becoming "an oldtime bhikku in modern clothes wandering the world." He calls himself a dharma bum, meaning a religious wanderer, a phrase he later attributes to Japhy Ryder, the greatest dharma bum of all. Ray jumps a train from Los Angeles to San Francisco ("the Midnight Ghost") and meets a little bum who shares a cold night with him and says a prayer by Saint Teresa. He, too, is a dharma bum, says Ray. At Santa Barbara, he leaves the Midnight Ghost and camps on the beaches, spending "one of the most pleasant nights" of his life camping, cooking out, and star watching. The book appears to contain descriptions of many of the happiest and most pleasant experiences in Kerouac's life.

Ray soon introduces the reader to Japhy Ryder, who was raised in a log cabin in Oregon and whose interest in Native American myth later led him to study anthropology. He specialized in Oriental religion and "discovered the greatest Dharma Bums of them all, the Zen lunatics of China and Japan." In a conversation with Ryder, Smith makes an important distinction about his own particular brand of Buddhism: Zen Buddhism, he maintains, is "mean," with children being punished for not answering their master's riddles; "old-fashioned" Buddhism emphasizes compassion, he says. Such sentiments are in part why Watts later revised his opinion on Beat Zen as angry. Smith arrives in San Francisco and Berkeley on the eve of the Six Gallery Reading. To get there, he hitches a ride with a blonde wearing a bathing suit and driving a convertible (see the title story of Kerouac's *Good Blonde*). Smith takes up a collection to buy wine for the reading and sets the tone by yelling "Go" and drinking deeply. The readers include Alvah Goldbook (Allen Ginsberg), Ike O'Shay (MICHAEL McCLURE), Warren Coughlin (PHILIP WHALEN), Francis DaPavia (PHILIP LAMANTIA), and Ryder. Rheinhold Cacoethes (KENNETH REXROTH) is the master of ceremonies. Surprisingly, Smith does not find Goldbook's reading extraordinary (though most accounts of the actual reading emphasize how Ginsberg stole the show). Smith likes the poetry of Ryder the best (Snyder read "A Berry Feast," among other poems) because there was something "earnest and strong and humanly hopeful" about Ryder's work, compared to the cynicism and daintiness of the other poets' works.

Smith moves with Goldbook into a Berkeley cottage. He visits Ryder's "shack" about a mile away, up in the hills, and finds him translating the "cold mountain" poems of Han Shan (*The Dharma Bums* is dedicated to Han Shan, whose works Snyder translated). Han Shan is a 12th-century Chinese poet who, in Ryder's words, "got sick of the city and the world and took off to hide in the mountains." Han Shan becomes the model for the dharma bums. The book becomes a kind of how-to manual on dropping out of society and living a free lifestyle in the dharma-bum way. In fact, much of the book seems more or less calculated to provide a very seductive model of such an alternative lifestyle. Goldbrook and Smith see in Ryder "a great new hero of American culture," much in the same way that Kerouac had already created a hero out of Cassady in *On the Road*. Ryder tells Smith, and by extension a whole generation of eager youth, "You know when I was a little kid in Oregon I didn't feel that I was an American at all, with all that suburban ideal and sex repression and general dreary newspaper gray censorship of all our real human values." Buddhism fills this void of meaning in his life. Ryder is a mountain climber, a poet, a visionary, and a scholar. He is also a legendary lover and introduces Smith to an oriental style orgy, which he calls "yabyum" sex, with a partner they all share named Psyche (identified in letters as a woman named Neuri).

Famously, Kerouac describes a mountain-climbing trip he took with Snyder and a Berkeley librarian named John Montgomery (Henry Morley here). They scale a peak in the Sierras called the Matterhorn (40 years later Snyder returned there, and his picture atop the peak is on the front of the *Gary Snyder Reader*). This episode is among Kerouac's funniest pieces of writing. Morley forgets his sleeping bag (a key error in the high-altitude coldness) and forgets to drain the car radiator to prevent it from freezing; he carries on a non-sequitur monologue that only Ryder and Smith can understand—just barely. Most of the men whom they see in the mountains are deer hunters, and they believe that Morley, Ryder, and Smith are lunatics

for wanting to climb the sheer face of the Matterhorn rather than to hunt and drink. The humor thus makes the point that such simple acts arouse suspicion and derision in a world that values only violence and commerce.

Smith and Ryder learn from each other in this section. Smith learns how to climb without exhausting himself by watching Ryder leaping like a mountain goat. He also learns basic lessons about ecology (Snyder was an early, prescient environmentalist) and how to write a haiku. From Smith, Ryder says he has learned how to write "spontaneously," and years later Snyder would say of Kerouac that his spontaneous prose style was particularly adaptable to the writing of haikus, allowing Kerouac to write great haiku poetry without having to practice it for years. Similarly, ROBERT CREELEY credited Kerouac with freeing him from poetic conventions through the practice of spontaneous writing. Ryder also says that Smith has awakened him to the "true" language of Americans—"which is the language of the working men, railroad men, loggers." Smith's most profound lesson from Ryder takes place during their frantic and exhausting final ascent of the last 1,000 feet of the mountain. Smith says, "I had really learned that you can't fall off a mountain."

This mountain climb is arguably the most famous in American literature and also contains some of the best outdoor and nature writing by an American author. Few writers have captured the experience of hiking and camping with more zest and freshness than Kerouac. The tea that they brew on a high ledge is the "best" that he has ever had; the simple meal and pudding afterward makes the "best" meal that he has ever had. When they finally make it back down the mountain and reenter civilization, the breakfast that they eat is beyond compare as well. The final descent of the mountain captures the alternating moods of joy and peace and fear and exhaustion on their long hard climb and hike. At the bottom, Smith feels "happy," a word seldom typed by Kerouac. Keith Jennison, Kerouac's editor at Viking, said that the book made him "cry," and it may well have been during these powerful, moving, and funny chapters.

Back from their mountain climb, Japhy and Ray meet up with Coughlin and Goldbook, drink a lot of wine, and plot what they call the "rucksack revolution." As Japhy explains, "[S]ee the whole thing is a world full of rucksack wanderers, Dharma Bums refusing to subscribe to the general demand that they consume production and therefore have to work for the privilege of consuming, all that crap they didn't really want anyway. . . . I see a vision of a great rucksack revolution thousands or even millions of young Americans wandering around with rucksacks. . . ." Japhy's vision has been justifiably cited as a forecast of the hippie movement of the 1960s, and although it is difficult to know the degree to which this book was responsible for the countercultural movement of the 1960s, it is undeniable that there is a link. Interestingly, the key member of the group here who would become a 1960s guru—Goldbook (Ginsberg)—says "balls on that old tired Dharma." Ginsberg had not yet become a practicing Buddhist.

As a contrast to the idealism of the "rucksack revolution," Kerouac tells the story of the suicide of Rosie (Natalie Jackson), Cody Pomeray's (Neal Cassady) girlfriend. Her vision of the future, also frighteningly accurate, is of a police state, and in her paranoia to escape from the police, she first tries to slit her wrists with broken glass and then jumps from a ledge to her death. Jackson's suicide provides a good example of how much Kerouac fictionalized reality: In reality, Jackson had killed herself out of despair over having defrauded CAROLYN CASSADY of thousands of dollars to finance Neal's horse-racing and gambling habit.

After Rosie's suicide—which in real-life was a reminder to the West Coast poets of how dangerous the East Coast "Beat" life could be—Smith needs to leave the dharma bums scene and return to his sister's home in North Carolina. He and Ryder listen to an African-American woman preaching Christianity from the street corner, and Ryder challenges Smith's love for Jesus. They part friends, though, and Smith jumps on board the Midnight Ghost back to Los Angeles. This trip is also described in a poem that Kerouac sent in a letter to Snyder. Outside of Los Angeles, Smith camps in the river bottom in Riverside, just beyond the burning smog of the city. A truck driver named Beaudry picks him up and takes him all the way to Springfield, Ohio. Beaudry sees Smith's

dharma-bum way of living and is convinced that his ideas are simple and sound, even if he himself cannot practice them. Later, Smith will write to Coughlin that he believes that their revolution really is spreading because of incidents such as this with Beaudry. Still, Smith is hardly a proselytizer of the revolution, wishing instead to step "around" it. When he arrives at his sister's doorstep in North Carolina, he spies on his family through the window and concludes, "People have good hearts whether or not they live like Dharma Bums."

With his family in North Carolina—his sister, his mother, and his brother-in-law—he enjoys watching midnight Mass on television and reading from Saint Paul. He finds the disciple's words "more beautiful than all the poetry readings of all the San Francisco Renaissances of Time." Still, his daily meditation and dedication to doing nothing concerns his family and the neighbors, who wonder what he is up to. Tension is created between Kerouac's Buddhist belief in life as illusion and the sadness of "trying to deny what *was*." Here Kerouac's genius for writing about levels of consciousness is showcased. The section on North Carolina ends with Smith having a profound vision of Dipankara Buddha (who looks like John L. Lewis, connecting him to Ryder) in which he learns the truth that "Everything's all right. . . . Form is emptiness and emptiness is form." After this revelation, he finds himself able to enter a deep trance state that gives him the power to heal his mother's allergy attacks. Smith backs away from such powers, not willing to shoulder the responsibility that they bring and also mindful of the prideful thoughts that the power instills in him.

Smith decides that it is time to return to the West Coast to prepare for his summer as a fire lookout in the Cascades. He leaves North Carolina and hitches through the South and through Texas. In the mountains outside El Paso, he camps, and after a rowdy but unfulfilling night in Juarez, he returns to his campsite and realizes that "I had indeed learned from Japhy how to cast off the evils of the world . . . just as long as I had a decent pack on my back." A tall-tale-telling Texan gives him a ride all the way to Los Angeles; once again, a ride stolen on the "Midnight Ghost" takes him into Northern California.

Smith says, "If the Dharma Bums ever get lay brothers in America who live normal lives with wives and children and homes, they will be like Sean Monahan." The Monahans (Locke and Linda McCorkle) live in a communal style and have very simple needs. Christine "was an expert on making food out of nothing," and their two daughters are "brought up to take care of themselves." Sean works as a carpenter only when he needs to, and the rest of the time meditates and studies Buddhism. Their communal style of living is the prototype of 1960s communes throughout the country. Ryder lives in a small hermitage on a hillside above the Monahan's house. Smith rejoins him there, and a change seems to have taken place in Ryder: He says that he "ain't happy little sage no mo and I'm tired." When Smith tries to tell him about his meditations in the Carolina woods, Ryder says it is all "just words," an attack that is essentially a questioning of Smith's writing career. The next day, however, Smith's enthusiasm has recharged Ryder, and he is back to normal. Living together again, it is clear that Smith's Buddhism is not Ryder's Buddhism, that they are "dissimilar monks on the same path." Smith practices "do-nothing," whereas Ryder's Buddhism is active. They also disagree on sex, which Ryder is much more open about than Smith. Smith believes that sex is strongly connected to death, a position that Kerouac maintains in his letters to Snyder throughout the 1960s and that is the basis of their fundamental disagreement over Buddhist practice. They also fight over Smith's heavy drinking, but this issue is resolved when Ryder goes to a Buddhist lecture and everyone becomes happily drunk on sake. "You were right!" says Ryder. In reality, it was Kerouac's drinking that ultimately separated him from the West Coast Buddhists, and their attempts to help him stop drinking were unsuccessful.

Ryder is due to leave for a year's study in Japan, and his friends throw him a farewell party that goes on for days. Many of the San Francisco literati attend. Cacoethes holds forth with opinions on America's greatest living poets, who include himself and Ryder but not Smith: "He's too drrronk all the time." Arthur Whane (Alan Watts) tells Smith that Buddhism "is getting to know as many people as possible." Smith is amused to see Goldbook and George (Peter Orlovsky) standing

naked and having a conversation with Whane and Cacoethes, both in suit and tie.

Ryder and Smith abandon the endless party to hike one last time together in the hills above Marin. They share their future dreams, and Ryder tells Smith that his lifework will be a poem entitled "Rivers and Mountains Without End," a book that Snyder finally published in 1996. Ryder/Snyder also followed through on his vision of having a "fine free-wheeling tribe in these California hills." He also accurately predicts that Smith/Kerouac will ultimately abandon Buddhism and will be "kissing the cross" on his deathbed. Both believe in the "rucksack revolution" to come, but it is clear that Smith enjoys the vision more than the reality and is not a joiner. In many ways, these future visions of society are in line with earlier "visions" written about by Kerouac, such as Lucien Carr's Yeats-inspired vision, or Sammy Sampas's ideal of the "Brotherhood of Man." Kerouac finds himself drawn to such visionaries but realizes that he is ultimately an outsider to all movements. Smith and Ryder return to the Monahan's cabin, and Ryder goes to the store to buy the exhausted Smith a Hershey's bar, one final act of kindness. Smith sees off Ryder at the boat, and Ryder's last act in America is, literally, to throw Psyche off the boat into the arms of her friends.

With Ryder departed, Smith hitchhikes north into Oregon and Washington and takes up his post as firewatcher on Desolation Peak in the Cascade Mountains. Readers interested in reading Snyder's parallel experiences at this time can see his journal entries on his Japan Trip in 1956 in *The Gary Snyder Reader*. Although the two are separated by an ocean, Smith finds himself seeing the Cascades through Ryder's eyes. In fact, he almost learns more about him in his absence than he did in his presence. Slowly, Smith makes the experience his own. Kerouac's descriptions of the setting here are among the greatest nature writings in American literature. He understands now the true beauty of Han Shan's "cold mountain" poems. In his diary, he writes "Oh I am happy!" as if it is a great surprise to him that he could be happy. The book ends with two visions. The first occurs during deep meditation when Avolokitesvara, the Hearer and Answerer of Prayers, tells Smith, "You are empowered to remind people that they are utterly free." He sees a shooting star as verification and looks at the "innumerable worlds" in the Milky Way and pronounces these worlds as *"words."* The vision thus reinforces his faith in his personal quest as a writer. The second vision is that of a little old bum whom Smith recognizes as Ryder, and he thanks Ryder aloud for having guided him "to the place where I learned all." "The vision of the freedom of eternity was mine forever," he says. Kerouac's experiences in the Cascades are covered at greater length in DESO-LATION ANGELS and are depicted as much darker than he allows himself to reveal at the end of this upbeat novel. Here, Kerouac concentrates on the influence that Gary Snyder has had on his life and the great debt he owes to this American hero.

Rob Johnson

Di Prima, Diane (1934–)

For Diane di Prima, arguably the one female writer most readily identified with the Beat literary movement, "the best travel has always been in the realm of the imagination." Although not initially part of JACK KEROUAC, ALLEN GINSBERG, and WILLIAM S. BURROUGHS's Beat fraternity, she forged a bohemian life that paralleled theirs in many respects, and by the late 1950s she had become part of the Beat literary circle. Her life story is one of total dedication to literary freedom, personal liberation, and the struggle for those systemically marginalized. During a career of almost a half-century, she has emerged, in the words of poet Marge Piercy, as "one of the giants of American poets."

Di Prima was born in 1934 in Brooklyn, New York, into the Catholic Italian middle-class family of Francis and Emma Mallozzi di Prima. However, it was her maternal grandfather, an anarchist, who seems to have been the major influence on her vocation as a poet. He instilled in her at an early age a love of art, music, and literature, especially that of Dante Alighieri, and by the time di Prima turned 14 years old, she knew that she was destined to be a poet.

She attended Hunter High School in New York and then Swarthmore College from 1951 to 1953 where she studied physics. During these

Diane Di Prima at City Lights Books in San Francisco, 2003. *(courtesy of Larry Keenan)*

years, she avidly read John Keats, Percy Bysshe Shelley, Lord Byron, Shakespeare, and Edna St. Vincent Millay. By 1953, however, her interest in formal education had considerably waned, and she moved to the Greenwich Village, Lower East Side neighborhoods of New York, intent on developing her life as a poet. The 1950s and 1960s were extremely prolific years for di Prima, who earned money to support herself by modeling and other odd jobs, all the while fashioning around herself a community of artists and libertarians that included dancer Freddie Herko, choreographer James Waring, and writer Sheri Martinelli, a confidante of Ezra Pound's. Through Martinelli, di Prima established a correspondence with Pound who was incarcerated in St. Elizabeth's Hospital, where she visited him several times. She also met LeRoi Jones (now AMIRI BARAKA), assisting him and his then wife HETTIE JONES with the publishing of the literary journal *Yugen* and books for their Totem Press.

In 1958 Totem Press published di Prima's first collection of poems, *This Kind of Bird Flies Backwards*. This volume speaks with a distinctly Keatsian voice mixed with Poundian abbreviations and Beat vernacular (for example, *dig, hip, flip, baby-o,* and *cool*). The collection stands as a prelude to her mature DINNERS AND NIGHTMARES (1961), in which she reveals the squalor and luxury of her life as a woman poet. Many of the selections in *Dinners and Nightmares* demonstrate her wry humor as it services astute observations of political and social inequities. In "The Quarrel," for instance, the female narrator silently addresses her lover/artist who refuses to help her with the housework: "I got up and went into the kitchen to do the dishes. And shit I thought I probably won't bother again. But I'll get bugged and not bother to tell you and after a while everything will be awful and I'll never say anything because it's so fucking uncool to talk about it. And that I thought will be that and what a shame." *Dinners and Nightmares* is a highly experimental collage of genres, including plays, conversations, interior monologues, free verse, and lists, a postmodern text long before that term become mainstreamed. It remains a powerful testament to the complications and triumphs of Beat bohemia for women.

With LeRoi Jones, di Prima also published the *Floating Bear* (1961–69) arts newsletter, named for the boat in A. A. Milne's *Winnie the Pooh*. *Floating Bear*, while published with the slimmest of budgets and what is now considered antiquated mimeograph technology, served an essential role in shaping and maintaining the various literary schools that are now associated with the mid–twentieth-century avant-garde. With Alan Marlowe, di Prima's first husband, she also cofounded the New York Poets Theatre and the Poets Press, publishing texts by Jean Genet, Audre Lorde, and Herbert Huncke. Her work with both *Floating Bear* and the Poets Theatre led to confrontations with the FBI concerning obscenity charges. These exciting and turbulent years are covered in MEMOIRS OF A BEATNIK, her quasi-fictive autobiography, published in 1969 by Olympia Press—The Traveler's Companion, Inc. Recently, she has chronicled the period in a more conventional memoir: *Recollections of My Life as a Woman: The New York Years* (2001).

As di Prima developed as a poet, she was also intent on having a family, although she was not concerned about pursuing it in a conventional middle-class manner—she did not consider it necessary to have a husband to have children. She had long practiced free love (both heterosexual and homosexual), and she continued to act independently when she gave birth to her first child, a daughter, Jeanne, in October 1958 without the legal sanction of marriage. She had a second daughter, Dominique, fathered by LeRoi Jones in 1961. Since then she has had three more children: Alexander, Tara, and Rudra. She has also been married and divorced two times and now lives with her life partner, Sheppard Powell, in San Francisco.

All of di Prima's literary works exemplify her deep belief that one cannot separate one's life as an artist from other duties, responsibilities, and desires. In particular, many of her strongest poems are unafraid to claim a female artist's need for a domestic life and her struggles to construct that family compatibly with poetic production. Her most important poem in this regard is "Brass Furnace Going Out: Song, after an Abortion" (1960), which draws on lyrical surrealism to express the mother's love for all life as she speaks to the spirit of the lost fetus:

> the lion pads
> along the difficult path
> in the heart of the jungle
> and comes to the riverbank
> he paws your face
> I wish he would drink it up
> in that strong gut it would come
> to life . . .

The poem is sometimes read as an anti-abortion poem, a reading that di Prima vehemently rejects, and while "Brass Furnace" directly addresses the act of abortion, its allegiance to the symbolic and surreal also speaks to the creation of art—the need for Keatsian beauty and truth in all aspects of one's life.

As the Beat Generation evolved into the Hippie Generation, di Prima moved a great deal, traveling across country with her children, staying at TIMOTHY LEARY's experimental commune at Millbrook, New York, and joining the San Francisco mime troupe called the Diggers, a political activist group that among other activities distributed free food to the indigent. These years, which she has called her warrior years, led to the publication in 1971 of *Revolutionary Letters,* a collection of poems that she often performed on the street. Lines such as this list from letter #19—"1. kill head of Dow Chemical / 2. destroy plant / 3. MAKE IT UN-PROFITABLE FOR THEM / to build again / i.e., destroy the concept of money"—exemplify the angry and extremely idealistic vision of the collection, which reflects the tenor of what some call the second civil war in United States history. The messages conveyed in these poems, with di Prima's signature use of typewriter abbreviations, colloquial language, and uppercase, may strike some as outdated today, but the letters remain valuable cultural critique, illustrating what critic Anthony Libby describes as "extreme left meeting extreme right in the romance of violent revolution or anarchy."

Di Prima had also begun a serious commitment to the study of Zen Buddhism by the time that she settled in San Francisco, studying with Shunryu Suzuki, Katagiri Roshi, and Kobun Chino Roshi. Her interest in the magical arts attracted her to Tibetan Buddhism, and she became the student of Chogyam Trungpa Rinpoche in 1983. These practices have remained central to her process of moving from arts and political activism into a more contemplative, spiritual state of artistic production. They have also contributed significantly to her evolving aesthetics. For instance, she has said that in the creation of texts such as *The New Handbook of Heaven* and *The Calculus of Variation,* both blendings of poetry and prose, she acted as "receiver," rejecting the polishing of the language in favor of the visionary quality of the text, a process that she describes as "accepting dictation" and "the moving mind."

For the last 30 years, di Prima has pursued what may become her master work, *LOBA,* a multilayered vision of woman as the wolf goddess, spanning thousands of years and mixing the sermonic, hermetic, and the vernacular to create a kaleidoscopic vision of female myth and reality. *Loba,* shape-shifting into a myriad of forms such as Kore, Lilith, Eve, the Virgin Mary, Kali-Ma, and Emily Dickinson, began as an essential exploration of female power. Through the vast mythological spectrum that Loba signifies, however, the collection has become a more contemporary portrait of the multifaceted nature of gender identity. Methodologically, the collection exemplifies poet Robert Duncan's idea of composition by field: "[T]he poem," she wrote, "can include everything; and each 'thing' (image, stanza, song, quote, blob of light) has equal weight in the Field . . . implying, like within an ideogram, the unsaid commonalities, which themselves form other dimensions." The first eight parts of Book I were published in 1978; Books I and II were published in 1998 by Viking Penguin. Book III is in progress.

Today, di Prima, teaches two private writing classes each year. She has also taught poetry at Naropa University in Boulder, Colorado, and in the masters program that she helped to found at the New College of California in 1980. Her more than 30 books exemplify a fundamental message from "RANT" (1984), one of her most-often quoted poems, regarding the inevitable fusion of the domestic, political, and artistic spheres of life:

> There is no way out of the spiritual battle
>   There is no way you can avoid taking sides
>   There is no way you can *not* have a poetics
>   no matter what you do: plumber, baker,
>   teacher

Bibliography

Charters, Ann, ed. *The Portable Beat Reader.* New York: Penguin Books, 1992.

di Prima, Diane. *The Calculus of Variation.* San Francisco: City Lights, 1972.

———. *Dinners and Nightmares.* New York: Cornith Books, 1961.

———. *Loba.* New York: Penguin, 1998.

———. *Memoirs of a Beatnik.* New York: Olympia, 1969.

———. *Pieces of a Song: Selected Poems.* San Francisco: City Lights, 1990.

———. *Recollections of My Life as a Woman: The New York Years.* New York: Viking, 2002.

———. *Revolutionary Letters.* San Francisco: City Lights, 1971.

———. "The Tapestry of Possibility." Interview, by Ann Charters. *Whole Earth* (Fall 1999). Available online. URL: http://www.findarticles.com/p/articles/

mi_m0GER/is_1999_Fall/ai_56457596.   Accessed
September 2005.
———. *This Kind of Bird Flies Backwards.* New York:
Aardvark Press, 1957.
Kirschenbaum, Blossom S. "Diane di Prima: Extending
La Famiglia." *MELUS* 14, nos. 3–4 (Fall/Winter
1987): 53–67.
Knight, Brenda. *Women of the Beat Generation.* Berkeley,
Calif.: Conari Press, 1996.
Libby, Anthony. "Diane di Prima: 'Nothing Is Lost;
It Shines in Our Eyes.'" In *Girls Who Wore Black:
Women Writing the Beat Generation,* edited by Ronna
C. Johnson and Nancy M. Grace, 45–68. New
Brunswick, N.J.: Rutgers University Press, 2002.
McNeil, Helen. "The Archaeology of Gender in the Beat
Movement." In *The Beat Generation Writers,* edited
by A. Robert Lee, 178–199. London: Pluto, 1996.
Moffeit, Tony. "Pieces of a Song: Diane di Prima" (In-
terview). In *Breaking the Rule of Cool: Interviewing
and Reading Women Beat Writers,* edited by Grace,
Nancy, and Ronna C. Johnson, 83–106. Jackson:
University of Mississippi Press, 2004.
Waldman, Anne. "An Interview with Diane di Prima."
In *The Beat Road,* edited by Arthur and Kit Knight,
27–33. California, Pa.: Unspeakable Visions of the
Individual, 1984.

Nancy M. Grace

Dinners and Nightmares Diane di Prima
(1961)

DIANE DI PRIMA published her prose-and-short-
story volume *Dinners and Nightmares* when she was
27 years old, three years after her first poetry collection, *This Kind of Bird Flies Backwards,* appeared.
Brooklyn-born di Prima had left Swarthmore College
for the excitement of New York's Greenwich Village,
and the exuberance of starting a life among fellow
struggling poets, artists, and musicians flows from
her eclectic mixture of journal, dreams, dialogues,
and poems. Poet ROBERT CREELEY, in his introduction to the 1974 edition of *Dinners and Nightmares,*
cites both the "clarity" and the sense of an artist still
sifting and searching: "Growing up in the fifties, you
had to figure it out for yourself—which she did, and
stayed open—as a woman, uninterested in any possibility of static investment or solution."

Di Prima can be both starkly descriptive and
surprisingly witty and funny. The book's first section, "What I Ate Where," is an honest prose depiction of the daily and domestic struggles of the
starving artist: All artistic context in di Prima's life
takes a backseat to food. She remembers specific
shared and spartan meals, as well as rare incidences
of indulgence. Typical is an entry from "fall—1956"
in which she recalls "garbage soup which was everything cheap thrown in a pot." At times the meals
take place in a group "pad," but there are also times
when home was a key to someone else's "pad"
where she was allowed to "crash" if she needed.

There are 13 "Nightmares" and five "Memories of Childhood," all written in di Prima's casual, colloquial, (and often unpunctuated) style.
Friends, lovers, and family members make appearances in the former, which a critic applauded as an
exercise in "existential sarcasm." "Memories" is an
allegory of a young boy who is terrified that only he
can see a warrior who stands ready in his neighborhood to drop an atomic bomb. The series of "Conversations" reflects a life of worthy companionship
in the bohemian community, but it also plumbs
the difficulties of poverty and inequality. In "The
Quarrel" she rails silently to a lazy boyfriend about
housework: "I've got work to do too sometimes,"
she thinks to herself, "I am sick . . . of doing dishes.
. . . Just because I happen to be a chick."

The final section, "More or Less Love Poems,"
contains warm lyrics to lovers (perhaps real, perhaps invented) and ends with a welcome song to a
soon-to-be-born baby. It is a mark of the young di
Prima's confidence in her artistic identity that she
tells her child: "Sweetheart / when you break thru
/ you'll find / a poet here." Di Prima would go on to
publish many acclaimed works of poetry.

Amy L. Friedman

Doctor Sax: Faust Part Three Jack Kerouac
(1959)

JACK KEROUAC wrote *Doctor Sax: Faust Part Three*
(published by Grove Press in 1959) primarily in May
and June 1952 while living in Mexico City with WIL-
LIAM S. BURROUGHS. He had, though, been thinking about the material (much of it derived from his

childhood in Lowell, Massachusetts) and the basic concept at least as early as 1948. On October 19, 1948, soon after completing *The TOWN AND THE CITY*, he wrote Hal Chase that he was then "writing three new novels": one was an early attempt at *ON THE ROAD*; a second was to be called "The Imbecile's Christmas"; and the third was to be "'Doctor Sax' (dealing with the American Myth as we used to know it as kids . . .)."

By March 9, 1949, Kerouac had made enough progress to send "the first two chapters of what was now titled *Doctor Sax: the Myth of the Rainy Night*" to Mark Van Doren. In the letter Kerouac explains that the novel,

> is about children and glee; townspeople; a river flooding; and mysterious occurrences, in and about a "castle of life" (with many levels, from dungeon to attic) where "concentrations of evil" foregather (wizards, vampires, spiders, etc.) for a Second Coming in the form of a giant serpent coiled under the castle miles deep. Doctor Sax is the caped fighter against these evils (chiromancer, alchemist of the night, and friend of the children): the Old Wizard (modeled after the original 15th century Faust) his arch-enemy and leader of the gnomes, Zombies, and heretical priests of the castle. There are naturalistic elements interwoven, such as Doctor Sax being, by day, disguised as the football coach of the local high school and referred to in the sports pages as "Coach Doctor Saxon, the Wizard of the Merrimack Valley." There are also fumbling, awkward, apprentice vampires who never quite step into the supernatural sphere; a masquerade play for the children in which real gnomes and monsters appear onstage without their realizing it; one great monster, Blook, who is actually terrified of the children; and giant Mayan spiders that appear with the flood a natural phenomena; and many goings on on various levels, including the scholarly absorptions of a certain Amadeus Baroque who eagerly seeks to understand all this. It turns out "t'was but a husk of doves," serpent, from which, on golden

Easter morning (after climactic midnight events, dins & earth tremors, featuring Doctor Sax's sudden tender change of mind in the rainy night of the river), beautiful doves fly forth—and everybody "good or evil" was mistaken.

While *Doctor Sax* as Kerouac finally wrote it lacks some of these elements (in the actual novel Doctor Sax is not, for instance, a football coach "by day"), this prospectus does anticipate the novel's general outline. In the early chapters Kerouac engages his early childhood (including his sense of a shadow figure who he later crystallizes into Doctor Sax) through a series of memories of events, people, and places; his childhood dreams; and the way these dreams and memories intertwine in his adult efforts to engage this past. The final sentence of the opening chapter—"Memory and dream are intermixed in this mad universe"—underscores the importance of these perspectives and this process. As the novel develops, Kerouac moves between additional childhood scenes and scenes of gothic fantasy (often comic and parodic), involving such figures as Count Condu, the Wizard, and the Castle where they await the emergence of a great snake, which the Wizard, Count, and Doctor Sax anticipate will be an apocalyptic, all-devouring force of evil and which also functions, implicitly, as an image of the child's growing awareness of sexuality, sexual energy, otherness, and death.

Jackie (Kerouac's childhood alter ego in the novel) imagines Doctor Sax both as part of this gothic world and as an adversary to it who tries to protect him, children, and the community from evil and loss, even as he tries to function as a guide to its mysteries. In developing these alternate realms (actual childhood, gothic fantasy, and their various intermixtures) through the middle of the novel, Kerouac works in a series of stylistic experiments and burlesques, at one point presenting the world of Jackie, the child hero, as a kind of movie script and at another presenting a flashback involving the Castle through a found manuscript (ostensibly written and lost by Doctor Sax, then recovered by Amadeus Baroque) in a manner that parodies the narrative and textual frame of such allegorical fantasy–adventures as Edgar Allan Poe's *The Narrative of A. Gordon Pym*.

Two scenes dominate the latter part of the novel. In the first, a relatively naturalistic section, the Merrimac River floods Lowell in the spring of 1936. The still childish Jackie at first welcomes the excitement of the river's power and how the flood disrupts the routine world of Lowell by closing the schools and factories. As the flood persists and its human cost becomes more apparent, Jackie begins to recognize the river's destructive power and its cost to his friends and their families (and indeed to Kerouac himself, since this flood destroyed his father's print shop). This recognition that the flood is not simply a moment of freedom from the ordinary but the destruction of the ordinary drives an awareness of self and community that is less childish and less self-absorbed. The flood is, in turn, followed by the "climactic midnight events" (rendered as gothic fantasy) in which Doctor Sax enlists young Jackie Duluoz as his protégé and as witness for his confrontation with the evil Wizard and his failed attempt to destroy the "great world snake" with the magic potions that he has concocted through his years of Faustlike study (in the novel Doctor Sax and the Wizard are each explicitly figures of Faust, the one finally positive and benign, the other demonic). While Jackie and Lowell must suffer the actual destruction of the flood, they are in the end saved from the apocalyptic evil of the snake by an immense eagle that carries off the snake as it emerges from beneath the Castle, at which point Doctor Sax concludes in "amazement" that "The Universe disposes of its own evil!" Jackie, on what has become a bright Easter morning, goes home "By God" with roses in his hair. As in the scene with the actual flood, young Jackie in confronting the snake moves from childish glee to an awareness of guilt, mystery, sexuality, death, and otherness that leaves him poised between the child's world and the adult's.

Even though Kerouac's March 9, 1949, letter to Van Doren shows that he already had many of the book's scenes and figures visualized, its general shape in mind, and something of the significance of the elements, his work journal from spring 1949 shows that he was soon having doubts about the project and how to develop it. In the entry for March 25, he describes *Doctor Sax* as "a poem, a description of darkness, a midnight lark" and sees it as "capping" *The Town and the City*; he also imagines it as "sandwiched between" *The Town and the City* and his initial attempts at *On the Road*. This positioning underscores the importance of *Doctor Sax* to Kerouac at this point. In *The Town and the City*, World War II disrupts the world of family (associated with the "town") and leads to a more chaotic world (associated with the "city") that is exhilarating in its freedom and independence but also isolating and threatening. In the novel "town" and "city" function as a dialectic, each with positive features and each with negatives (for the child, for instance, the experience of the town provides stability and a matrix of identity through its continuity with past generations and the nurturing of family, but this world is also—especially in contrast to the fluidity and possibility of the city—a world of constraint). In the March 25 journal entry, Kerouac seems to imagine a similar dialectic, only now the two poles of past stability, with its tendency to become sentimental and nostalgic, and present flux, with its potential to become nihilistic and oppressive, are each to be developed separately in its own novel. The potential sentimentality of the *Doctor Sax* material is perhaps one reason why Kerouac, in the March 25 journal entry, characterizes the book he is trying to write as a kind of poem, and the potential sentimentality of a poem derived from childhood memories and fantasies is even clearer in Kerouac's journal entry from the next day, March 26, where he worries that the theme of *Doctor Sax* "is too frivolous for me sometimes" and also "too influenced by mystic, mad ALLEN G[INSBERG]." He laments, "The thing is so beautiful I can't abandon it," then adds that "the idea is so *loony* I can't *get on* with it."

Kerouac's correspondence shows that he continued to mull over the "Great World Snake" and his Lowell material, but his letters also indicate that he was unable to "*get on* with" *Doctor Sax* until May 1952. Several factors explain the delay. Kerouac was, for one thing, "on the road" for much of this period, and when he was not, he was working primarily on various versions of *On the Road*. For another, it was not until he discovered "spontaneous prose" (the approach he later summarized in "The Essentials of Spontaneous Prose") in late October 1951 that he had a way to immerse himself in his childhood material while yet developing it without becoming overly *"loony"* and sentimental. In a May 18, 1952, letter to Ginsberg, Kerouac describes how beginning to write by "sketching," his initial term for "spontaneous prose," led him to abandon his efforts to revise the version of *On the Road* that Viking eventually published and to work instead on a much more experimental version of his "Road book"—the version published posthumously as *VISIONS OF CODY*. In the letter Kerouac encourages Ginsberg to read the just-completed *Cody* and explains that he is finally ready to write *Doctor Sax*: ". . . now I know where I'm headed. I have 'Doctor Sax' ready to go now . . . or 'The Shadow of Doctor Sax,' I'll simply blow on the vision of the Shadow in my 13th and 14th years on Sarah Ave. Lowell, culminated by the myth itself as I dreamt it in Fall 1948 . . . angles of my hoop-rolling boyhood as seen from the shroud." These comments show that Kerouac, by the time he actually drafted *Doctor Sax*, no longer thought of it as a book that would portray "boyhood" or nostalgically celebrate such matters as "hoop-rolling." He was, instead, concerned with his memories of childhood and their emotional and symbolic implications for him as an adult. The "myth" he "dreamt" in 1948 when first trying to write *Doctor Sax* was not a myth of childhood but rather a myth derived *from* childhood, and his 1948 myth (at least as finally developed in *Doctor Sax* in 1952) reflects his adult awareness. It is driven by his adult need to come to terms with death, sexuality, evil, otherness, and doubt. The child may sense and project these issues in his play and fantasies with a naïve immediacy that the adult can no longer manage, but the child is unable to fully define, engage, or resolve them. Kerouac's remarks in his May 18, 1952, letter to Ginsberg suggest, that is, that he had come to realize that his real interest in the material was less in fictionalizing his early adolescent "vision of the Shadow" than in exploring that vision through the subsequent myth of "Doctor Sax"—or even more that his real interest in the material was the way that it could support an exploration of the dialectical interplay of the child's vision and the adult's myth.

The importance of both the child's perspective and the adult's perspective implicit in these comments in turn help explain the significance of spontaneous prose for *Doctor Sax*. Kerouac's remark to Ginsberg that he expected to write *Doctor Sax* by "blow[ing]" on his material shows that he planned to write it using the same approach that he had just used for *Visions of Cody*. In "The Essentials of Spontaneous Prose" he notes that in writing spontaneously the "language" of the text is to be the result of, an "undisturbed flow from the mind of personal secret idea–words, *blowing* (as per jazz musician) on subject of image." In spontaneous prose the writer engages each element of his material from his immediate interest at the moment of writing and explores that element or occasion, what he terms the "image–object," through an associational improvisation—much as a jazz musician improvisationally explores and elaborates a bit of melody, a riff, or the harmonic possibility of a chord. In *Doctor Sax*, then, the scenes, events, and fantasies of Kerouac's Lowell childhood become the image–objects for a series of improvisations in which the adult speaker/writer/narrator engages the past but from the immediacy of the present. The way Kerouac follows the final "sentence" of the text, "By God" with "*Written in Mexico City,/Tenochtitlan, 1952/Ancient Capital/of Azteca*" underscores the adult narrator's presence in the novel, places the narrator (and the novel) in a specific place and time, and emphasizes the narrator's complex relationship to the novel's multiple dimensions of time and reality: These include the adult present of the writing; the mythic and historical worlds of pre-Columbian Mexico (*Azteca*); the people and events of his Lowell childhood; young Jackie's childhood fantasies; and Kerouac's adult-inflected improvisations, celebrations, satires, and burlesques as he reimagines these fantasies and interweaves them with elements from popular culture, literature, religion, Freudian psychology, myth, and politics.

The demands and risks of spontaneous prose as an approach are implicit in Kerouac's comments in his October 27, 1954, letter to Alfred Kazin. Following a brief excerpt from *Doctor Sax*, Kerouac notes that the book was "scribbled swiftly" and explains that "The main thing, I feel, is that the urgency of explaining something has its own words and rhythm, and time is of the essence—Modern Prose." Spontaneous prose, as Kerouac understood and practiced it at its peak of intensity in *Doctor Sax,* required emphasizing immediacy and intensity rather than planning, control, and subordination. To engage, explore, and express his simultaneous, multiple relationships to his childhood through both the child's and the adult's perspective, he had to write "swiftly" and with a sense of "urgency." This approach in part explains the book's at times rapid shifts in tone and style, its kaleidoscopic invocation and recombination of both popular culture elements (pulp westerns, B-movies, and so forth) and literary allusion (in the climactic confrontation with the snake, for instance, Doctor Sax's manner and language at times echo Ahab's confrontation with Moby-Dick). The shifts enable Kerouac to project the mythic depth in the pulp figure of The Shadow and imagine as well the potential for arcane comedy in the tragedy of Ahab (which finally complicates that tragedy rather than diminishing it). The practice of spontaneous prose also suggests why an improvisation can seem to break off without resolving. Writing Ginsberg on November 8, 1952, about the composing of *Doctor Sax,* Kerouac notes not only that it "was written high on tea without pausing to think" but also that Burroughs, with whom he was staying at times, "would come in the room and so the chapter ended there." Once the imaginative engagement and immediacy is disrupted (Burroughs "com[ing] in the room"), the associational arc is lost, and the improvisation has to be abandoned. But whatever the risks, demands, and discontinuities, the process of spontaneous prose provided Kerouac with a way to subvert both the impulse to sentimentalize the child's world and the impulse to trivialize it. It, thus, provided a way to move beyond the dilemma Kerouac expressed in his journal entries of March 25 and 26, 1949, to cast *Doctor Sax* as a kind of poem "capping" *The Town and the City* and yet keeping it from becoming *"loony."*

Bibliography

Kerouac, Jack. "Essentials of Spontaneous Prose." *The Portable Jack Kerouac.* Edited by Ann Charters. New York: Viking, 1995.
———. *Selected Letters: 1940–1956.* Edited by Ann Charters. New York: Viking, 1995.
———. *The Windblown World: The Journals of Jack Kerouac, 1947–1954.* Edited by Douglas Brinkley. New York: Viking, 2004.

Tim Hunt

Dorn, Ed (1929–1999)

Ed Dorn had the great fortune of being mentored by both CHARLES OLSON (his intellectual father who wrote *A Bibliography on America for Ed Dorn,* a tutorial reading list for Dorn to study the West) and KENNETH REXROTH. Many of his poems are politically charged, and like his friend ED SANDERS who helped inspire Dorn to become a cultural revolutionary, he did not shy away from making poetry and political responsibility synonymous. His empathy with the plight of Native Americans is well documented (one of Dorn's grandfathers was half Indian and half French Quebecois), and his translations of Latin American poets are noteworthy. Dorn was one of the few students to actually graduate from Black Mountain College, receiving a B.A. in 1954 (ROBERT CREELEY was the outside reader of his final exam).

Born in Villa Grove, Illinois, on April 2, 1929, to a woman who was abandoned by a NEAL CASSADY–like railroad brakeman, Dorn spent time at the University of Illinois, Urbana and Eastern Illinois University, where art professor Ray Obermayr suggested that he look into Black Mountain College in North Carolina. Initially interested in becoming a painter and wanting to avoid the Korean War, Dorn enrolled at Black Mountain College (where he became interested in Wilhelm Reich, a figure of interest also to WILLIAM S. BURROUGHS) before Olson became the rector. After a hiatus of a few years, Dorn returned to Black Mountain College and became determined to graduate. Olson encouraged Dorn to pursue a career as a poet.

Dorn came under the influence of Rexroth when he moved to San Francisco in 1956. He met JACK KEROUAC and ALLEN GINSBERG (both Dorn and Ginsberg worked as baggage handlers in the same Greyhound Bus Terminal immortalized in Ginsberg's "In the Baggage Room at Greyhound" in HOWL AND OTHER POEMS). Dorn later became close with LeRoi Jones (AMIRI BARAKA), who thought Dorn was one of the most intelligent men he ever met and one of the few white men who understood him. (Baraka broke his close ties with Dorn after he read Dorn's poem "An Address for the First Woman to Face Death in Havana—Olga Herrara Marco," about a woman who was accused of being an enemy of Cuba and whom Castro initially sentenced to death. Baraka called the poem "counter-revolutionary," though the two would continue to correspond.)

Dorn left his wife Helene for his student Jennifer Dunbar, the sister-in-law of Marianne Faithfull. In 1968 they witnessed firsthand the student revolts in Paris. While a prolific writer of poetry and prose, Dorn taught at Idaho State University, Pocatello; University of Essex, Colchester; University of Kansas, Lawrence; University of California, Riverside; University of California, San Diego; and the University of Colorado, Boulder. His masterpiece, *GUNSLINGER*, was published in complete form in 1975. It is one of the great American epic poems of the 20th century.

Dorn died of pancreatic cancer at his home in Denver, Colorado, on December 10, 1999.

Bibliography

Clark, Tom. *Edward Dorn: A World of Difference.* Berkeley, Calif.: North Atlantic, 2002.
McPheron, William. *Edward Dorn.* Western Writers Series. Boise, Idaho: Boise State University, 1988.

Kurt Hemmer

Dutchman Amiri Baraka (LeRoi Jones) (1964)

Incendiary, outrageous—if these adjectives are woven indelibly into the spirit of Beat literature, then AMIRI BARAKA's *Dutchman* might be one of the most perfect literary productions of the Beat era. From Melville to Dickinson to Whitman to Eliot to Steinbeck to Ellison to Miller to Sexton to Plath to Baldwin, it is in the American literary tradition to challenge tradition, and in this way the Beat writers of the post–World War II era were delighted to fall in step with their literary forebears and contemporaries, to write comically and bitterly of America's pressure-packed homogeneity and its paranoid racism, sexism, homophobia, and

anticommunism. But where JACK KEROUAC defies the stasis of a nine-to-five, man-in-the-gray-flannel-suit lifestyle, Baraka, in *Dutchman*, puts on trial the Kerouacs themselves. Where ALLEN GINSBERG pokes fun at the half-truths of such magazines as *Time* and *Life* and tells the military–industrial complex to "Go fuck [itself] with [its] atom bomb," Baraka thumbs his nose not only at conservativism but also at liberalism, not only at racists but also at persons who fancy themselves to be racially enlightened. "You great liberated whore! You fuck some black man, and right away you're an expert on black people. What a lotta shit that is," screams Clay, Baraka's aptly named hero, a usually quiet young man who reshapes himself, as the play draws toward a close, into a perfect manifestation of black American rage on the loose. In *Dutchman*, Baraka simply assumes the benightedness of Eisenhower-like conservatism; thus, he scarcely addresses it, choosing instead to attack what the author appears to perceive as a more subtle, and therefore more lethal, threat: liberalism and the phoniness of its legions. A one-hour film version—directed by Anthony Harvey and starring Al Freeman, Jr., and Shirley Knight—appeared in 1966. This low-key, black-and-white adaptation more than recreates the utter joylessness of Baraka's play. Too, the madness that is, in Baraka's view, native to American race relations comes to monstrous life in the bizarre physical antics of Knight (Lula) and the spit-filled, maniacal tirade of Freeman, Jr. (Clay) in the play's closing moments.

Dutchman—for which Baraka (then known as LeRoi Jones) won an Obie Award in 1964—begins and ends in a speeding New York City subway car, and the suggestion here might be that the race relations manifest in this play are running swiftly and smoothly through the bowels of American life, that the interchange between Clay Williams and Lula, though altogether noxious, is sadly representative of a foundational, irreversible disconnection that always has and always will characterize black–white relations in the United States. It is possible, too, that Baraka's underground setting references the seething distrust and enmity snaking beneath the sometimes placid surface of a country presumably on the rise, racially speaking, under John F. Kennedy and Lyndon Johnson. Things may appear to be nearly tolerable in the United States in the grand era of Martin Luther King, Jr.'s massive march on Washington and the Civil Rights Act of 1964, but if the black man should finally, truly, *comprehensively* speak his mind, white America (employing the assistance of innumerable black traitors) will quickly silence him forever.

It is important to note, too, the play's obvious reference to U.S. slavery, which Baraka feels is alive and well in the latter decades of the 20th century. The dragon of slavery lies squarely at the foundation of black–white relations in the United States and prohibits a pure union between the two main characters in *Dutchman.* They do indeed enjoy at the close of the first act a short-lived fantasy of a one-night stand, one in which racial baggage plays no part. Sadly, however, the best they can do is "pretend" to be "free of . . . history." America's past and present—either faintly or directly—are ever-present, waiting and willing to spoil what might otherwise develop into an unbridled human-to-human exchange. Furthermore, as Lloyd Brown points out, this hopelessness and its link to both U.S. history and mythology is contained even in the play's title: "The underground setting recalls the holds of the slave ships, and this image is reinforced by the title itself: the first African slaves were reportedly brought to the New World by Dutch slave traders. . . . The Dutch reference may also be linked with the legend of the *Flying Dutchman*—the story of a ship doomed to sail the seas forever without hope of gaining land." The fabled *Flying Dutchman* is "doomed" to sail endlessly, remaining landless, exactly because it is the ship that commenced the slave trade between Africa and the New World. Likewise, Clay and Lula—and, by extension, all blacks and all whites—are doomed for eternity in Baraka's pessimistic world view to flounder in any effort to achieve peaceful coexistence.

Speaking of slavery, Clay is a 20th-century reincarnation of Nat Turner—nearly. Turner, an unassuming and much-trusted slave, nurtured a glowing coal of hatred in his heart for the institution of human bondage and for a select crowd of whites whom he viewed as slavery's representatives. He finally and famously enacted his long-suppressed rage; for this, he was caught and killed, but not before leaving a sensational impression of fear in the bellies of whites in and around antebellum Virginia. Like Turner, Baraka's Clay is—throughout the overwhelming majority of his brief lifetime—a quiet, seemingly nonthreatening black man who moves rather freely, albeit separately, among white people. He is well spoken and conservatively dressed in his "three-button suit and striped tie"—clothes, Lula mockingly says, that come from a tradition that "burn[ed] witches" and "start[ed] revolutions over the price of tea." Like Turner, Clay possesses deep-seated rage that rarely sees the light of day and that has much to do with the double life he and other blacks are forced to lead even a whole century after their emancipation. But unlike Turner, Baraka's Clay, after verbally assaulting (and physically slapping) his white adversary, stops short of the act of murder that would, he claims, free him from a kind of lunacy. He does indeed force Lula to heed his fiery monologue, in which he explains (in foul language, at a shrill pitch) that black art—music, poetry, and so on—is a coping mechanism, that Charlie Parker, Bessie Smith, and others are moaning into their horns and singing and "wiggling" in dark rooms only to avoid having to walk out on "Sixty-seventh Street and . . . [kill] the first ten white people . . . [they see]." Black art, in other words, is black rage reconfigured. The simple, rational black person—the nonartist—randomly kills whites, who deserve it; but the black artist, Clay declares, is too decent to commit murder, and so he or she foregoes his or her own lucidity and rechannels his or her murderous passion into song, literature, and/or any other form of creative expression, the subtext of which is typically a coded notice for whites to "kiss . . . [black America's] unruly ass."

Again, though, Clay chooses the non-Turner route, screaming but then sighing, retreating, and remaining (he thinks, at least for a moment) "Safe with . . . [his] words," coiled away in repression and semimadness. The fact that he has exposed his truer feelings and the sanctum sanctorum of black semi- and subconsciousness, however, is more than enough to rally Lula into action, and she stabs and kills Clay, possibly because he has proven to be neither of the two black selves with which she is comfortable: (1) the Uncle Tom figure, and (2) the personification of raw sexual potency, a black phallus with whom she can "rub bellies on the train. The nasty. The nasty. Do the gritty grind. . . ." If Clay cannot fulfill those stereotypes, and if he *can* manifest the sort of resentment that engenders Nat Turner-like rebellions and Watts-like riots, he must be done away with, and mainstream America (in the guise of a beautiful but reptilian white female, a score keeper who zealously maintains a ledger of the names of her victims) must continue its quest to seek out and destroy other signs of black manhood.

In accordance with absurdist drama, Clay Williams and Lula are "types," as Baraka seems to be scarcely interested in investing these characters with individual peculiarities and multiple ambiguities. Rather, throughout the majority of the play he casts Clay as the collective black sellout who wishes to cause no public disturbances, who wears "narrow-shoulder clothes . . . from a tradition . . . [he] ought to feel oppressed by," who fancies himself to be a "Black Baudelaire" (perhaps an allusion to the Beat poet BOB KAUFMAN being called the Black Rimbaud in France) and who falls easily and speedily for Lula, the collective white racist and emasculator, the Evelike figure who eats apple after apple, and whose sexuality is clearly a kind of forbidden fruit for the black man. One wonders if Lula is also representative of Baraka's former Beat associates and white friends/lovers—people who were happy to thumb their noses at racist conventions and (seemingly) embrace black culture, though Baraka felt, in the early and middle 1960s, that he could continue his deeply involved relationships with whites, even counterculturalist whites, only at the risk of failing to understand and to realize his own black self. Each moment spent fraternizing with white intellectuals—indeed, each moment spent cohabitating with his white wife, HETTIE JONES—rendered him more and more a Clay-like "Uncle Tom" and drained ever further the energy that he could have been aiming toward the cultivation of a black-nationalist spirit. Likewise, each moment that Baraka's Clay spends flirting with Lula, sinking more deeply into her python wiles, leaves him increasingly vulnerable to white hatred and, worse, increasingly *less* black. For Clay, to associate with Lula is to forfeit self-awareness. Again, Baraka takes few pains to individualize these characters. Lula—at least at some level—unmistakably

stands for the boundless trouble awaiting any black man who desires agreeable contact with white people, particularly white women. Clay, of course, is essentially a graphic illustration of a handful of "types": the quiet, whitenized "would-be poet," the black fool; the finally honest and therefore livid, homicidal black nationalist.

Like so many literary pieces of the Beat period, then, *Dutchman* offers insight into the life of its author. The play appeared in 1964, the year before Baraka left Greenwich Village for Harlem and his white wife (and their three children) for the nonattachment that he might have felt necessary to develop his ever-growing, ever-fervent politicism. In subsequent years, he would also leave his old name, Everett LeRoi Jones, for a newly adopted one: Amiri Baraka, which means "Blessed Prince." He would, moreover, leave his white friends, the Beats, for his black brothers. In fact, the text of *Dutchman*, in undertones and overtones, documents Baraka's break from the white Beats. The author seems to have in mind Ginsberg—the Beat pontiff—when he bitingly derides, through Lula, "all those Jewish poets . . . who leave their mothers looking for other mothers, or others' mothers, on whose baggy tits they lay their fumbling heads. Their poems are always funny, and all about sex." Of course, Clay's fierce monologue provides an even more cutting, crystal-clear departure from Ginsberg and company: Very near the play's conclusion, Clay morphs into a newly minted mouthpiece for black nationalism and decries the stunning irony of white people's love for black cultural icons—Charlie Parker, especially—who seethe with hatred for Euro-America. There can be no doubt that Clay, in this sudden fury, is voicing Baraka's newfound distaste for the white Beats, almost all of whom openly celebrated the Harlem music scene in general and Parker in particular: "Charlie Parker? Charlie Parker. All the hip white boys scream for Bird. And Bird saying, 'Up your ass, feeble-minded ofay! Up your ass.'"

It is difficult to overlook the coldness of these divorces, but before we condemn Baraka utterly, it is wise to remember that Melville was a less-than-responsible husband and father, particularly during the months he spent laboring over *Moby-Dick* in the Berkshires—in relative solitude, in varying moods of irritability, unhappy to be burdened by the distracting needs of his wife and children whom he uprooted (from a somewhat more convenient life in New York City) and dragged along. In fact, it is not inappropriate to reference Melville here. The latter's interest in residing in the Berkshires during the composition of his masterpiece was largely rooted in the fact that Hawthorne, whom Melville viewed as a kind of demigod and literary soul partner, lived nearby. Baraka's relocation to Harlem, the center of black American life, was also a separation from a circle of persons who (presumably) misunderstood him to a newer, more empathic circle, and this was a milieu in which he could, he felt, create without impediments. This is to explain, not to justify: It is not, as we know, uncommon for artists to forsake their human ties and to immerse themselves bodily into their respective obsessions. In an ironic but very real sense, Baraka's break from his family and his Beat associates crystallized his Beat stature, for nothing is more Beat than this: to live, as Clay does in *Dutchman,* as a changing organism, whatever the cost; to decry the restrictions inherent in the traditional institutions of commitment; to voice—and to stand for and live out—a principle, whatever it might be.

Bibliography

Baraka, Amiri. *The LeRoi Jones/Amiri Baraka Reader.* Edited by William J. Harris. New York: Thunder's Mouth Press, 1991.

Benston, Kimberly W. *Baraka: The Renegade and the Mask.* New Haven: Yale University Press, 1976.

Brown, Lloyd W. *Amiri Barka.* Boston: Twayne, 1980.

Sollors, Werner. *Amiri Baraka/LeRoi Jones: The Quest for a "Populist Modernism."* New York: Columbia University Press, 1978.

Williams, Sherley Anne. *Give Birth to Brightness: A Thematic Study in Neo-Black Literature.* New York: Dial, 1972.

Andrew J. Wilson

Dylan, Bob (1941–)

Born Robert Zimmerman in Duluth, Minnesota, Bob Dylan has recently been described by *Newsweek* critic David Gates as "the most influen-

Bob Dylan in concert, Berkeley, 1965. Photographer Larry Keenan: "This photograph is from the first half of the concert." *(courtesy of Larry Keenan)*

tial cultural figure now alive." The particulars of Dylan's life and self-creation are well documented in dozens of works of criticism, biography, and social history, some prominent examples of which include Robert Shelton's *No Direction Home* (1986), Clinton Heylin's *Bob Dylan: Behind the Shades* (1991), and David Hajdu's *Positively 4th Street: The Lives and Times of Joan Baez, Bob Dylan, Mimi Baez Fariña, and Richard Fariña* (2001). Adopting the name *Bob Dylan* shortly after arriving at the University of Minnesota in 1959, Dylan served an apprenticeship in American folk music and a marginal livelihood in Minneapolis before departing for New York City in December 1960, "hustling uptown," as Shelton puts it, in Times Square for two months before arriving in Greenwich Village and launching a career as a folk performer there in 1961.

Dylan's musical antecedents are well known—among them Woody Guthrie, Jack Elliot, and the countless performers who contributed to Harry Smith's *Anthology of American Folk Music* (1952). Less readily identified are the literary models who influenced Dylan early in his career. Beat writers figure prominently in this group. Dylan's work, in fact, served as a lynchpin which connected the work of Beat writers in the 1950s to literature and culture of the 1960s. As Shelton notes, "The union of poetry and folk music in Greenwich Village during 1961–63 held, thanks in part to Dylan, [who] coupled folk and beat poetry." Dylan's writing in his novel/prose poem TARANTULA, composed in late 1964 and early 1965, is heavily indebted in process, style, and content to the work of WILLIAM S. BURROUGHS, JACK KEROUAC, and GREGORY CORSO. His landmark recordings of this period, including *Bringing It All Back Home, Highway 61 Revisited, Blonde on Blonde,* and the *Basement Tapes* display a spontaneity, consciousness, and surrealistic humor that is kin to the best Beat writing. Dylan's debt to Beat literature became more explicit over time. His 1975 Rolling Thunder tour was to include Ginsberg, and photo documents from the tour famously include a portrait of him showing respect at Kerouac's grave in Lowell.

Dylan's recently released memoir *Chronicles, Vol 1* offers further and candid insight into the formation of Dylan's persona and his connection with the Beats. Recounting a conversation with Archibald MacLeish, Dylan states, "At some point, I was going to ask him what he thought about the hip, cool Ginsberg, Corso, and Kerouac, but it seemed like it would have been an empty question. He asked me if I'd read Sappho or Socrates." The Beats were

Bob Dylan playing the piano, Berkeley concert, Berkeley, 1965. Photographer Larry Keenan: "I was at the concert with my date along with Michael McClure, Allen Ginsberg, some Hells Angels and assorted others. I used my dad's Diner's Club card to buy the whole row for us. Everyone paid me back. Ginsberg introduced me to Dylan after the concert and we made arrangements to do a photo session at City Lights Books." *(courtesy of Larry Keenan)*

the seminal figures Dylan identified as his literary antecedents. Dylan's narrative strategy in *Chronicles*—his self-effacement as well as his self-awareness—is strikingly similar to Kerouac's late period recapitulation of his youth in *VANITY OF DULUOZ*, a narrative whose candor and baldness seems in retrospect to serve as a conscious move on Kerouac's part to dethrone himself as "King of the Beats." Dylan's *Chronicles* serves a similar de-mythologizing function—fracturing a traditional life narrative and audience expectations only to reveal surprising and fresh aspects of a life that many readers might have assumed they already knew and understood.

Bibliography

Dylan, Bob. *Chronicles, Vol 1.* New York: Simon & Schuster, 2004.

Gates, David. "The Book of Bob." *Newsweek,* 4 October 2004, 48.

Hajdu, David. *Positively 4th Street: The Lives and Times of Joan Baez, Bob Dylan, Mimi Baez Fariña, and Richard Fariña.* New York: North Point, 2001.

Heylin, Clinton. *Bob Dylan: Behind the Shades.* New York: Summit, 1991.

Shelton, Robert. *No Direction Home: The Life and Music of Bob Dylan.* New York: Da Capo, 1997.

Tracy Santa

E

Erections, Ejaculations, Exhibitions and General Tales of Ordinary Madness Charles Bukowski (1972)

Though generally known as a poet and novelist, CHARLES BUKOWSKI was an outstanding short story writer. LAWRENCE FERLINGHETTI, who was one of the first to recognize Bukowski's talents, published *Erections, Ejaculations, Exhibitions and General Tales of Ordinary Madness,* dedicated to his young girlfriend Linda King, through City Lights Books. The volume was later broken up into *Tales of Ordinary Madness* (1983) and *The Most Beautiful Woman in Town & Other Stories* (1983). The stories first appeared in the magazines and journals *Open City, Nola Express, Knight, Adam, Adam Reader, Pix, The Berkeley Barb,* and *Evergreen Review.* Bukowski's staccato prose and maverick grammar take us through the underbelly of city life that is full of horror and humor. Though most of the stories are classic examples of Bukowski's stark realism, some of them are highly imaginative and surreal.

"Animal Crackers in My Soup" is one of the great works that is uncharacteristic of Bukowski's hard-boiled and hung-over style. The story is about a man named Gordon who is down and out. He encounters Crazy Carol, who has a house full of zoo animals that she takes care of. Gordon becomes one of the creatures that she nurses back to health. He learns that Carol has sexual relations with all of her animals. Bukowski describes very graphic sex scenes between Carol and a snake, Carol and a tiger, and Carol and Gordon. The short story is partially pornographic and reads like something at which even *Penthouse* forum readers would blush. Yet, this material is ingeniously combined with a political message. Carol is trying to create a Nietzschean Superman or Superbeast with all the best characteristics of the zoo animals with which she mates. Carol's animals all get along because she exudes a love that they all adopt. The world that surrounds Carol and Gordon is described as vile and decadent, and for it to survive, there needs to be a new creature who will not be self-destructive like human beings. After going out for supplies, Gordon and Carol come back to find that the animals have been brutally shot to death by the vicious humans who are wary of Carol. Shortly thereafter, Carol's child is born: an amalgamation of the animals and Gordon. The story ends with a hydrogen bomb being dropped on the city, San Francisco. Carol was too late. Yet, we can appreciate this story as an experimental attempt on Bukowski's part to write a politically pertinent piece of pornography.

One of the more interesting aspects of these short stories is the commentary Bukowski and his characters make on writers. The Beat writers and their associates come up several times, and it was obvious that the Beats were on Bukowski's mind while he wrote these stories. ROBERT CREELEY, who was also published alongside Bukowski by Black Sparrow Press, receives the brunt of Bukowski's ire. "I do suppose," writes Bukowski in "Eyes Like the Sky," "that the biggest snob outfit ever invented was the old Black Mountain group. and Creeley is still feared in and out of the universities—feared and revered—more than any other poet. then we have the academics, who like Creeley, write very carefully. in essence, the generally accepted poetry today has a kind of glass outside to it, slick and sliding, and sunned down inside there is a joining of word to word in a rather metallic inhuman summation or 'semi-secret' angle. this is poetry for millionaires and fat men of leisure so it does get backing and it does survive because the secret is in that those who belong really belong and to hell with the rest. but the poetry is dull, very dull, so dull that the dullness is taken for hidden meaning. . . ." In "My Stay in the Poet's Cottage," Bukowski writes that Creeley is one of the poets who puts him to sleep. "Bukowski is jealous of [ALLEN] GINSBERG," he confesses in "I Shot a Man in Reno." In "Eyes Like the Sky," he writes, "Ginsberg, meanwhile turns gigantic extrovert handsprings across our sight, realizing the gap and trying to fill it. at least, he knows what is wrong—he simply lacks the artistry to fulfill it." Ferlinghetti, Jack Hirschman, Denise Levertov, Robert Duncan, CHARLES OLSON, NEAL CASSADY, JACK KEROUAC, PHILIP LAMANTIA, TIMOTHY LEARY, BOB DYLAN, GREGORY CORSO, WILLIAM S. BURROUGHS, and HAROLD NORSE (whom Bukowski praises) are all mentioned in this collection.

The success of the book occasioned a flight to San Francisco in September 1972 that started with the audience throwing bottles at the hostile Bukowski during his reading and ended with a drunk Bukowski destroying Ferlinghetti's apartment. Norse told Ferlinghetti after, "Didn't I warn you?"

Bibliography
Sounes, Howard. *Charles Bukowski: Locked in the Arms of a Crazy Life.* Edinburgh, Scotland: Rebel, Inc., 1998.

Kurt Hemmer

Evening Sun Turned Crimson, The
Herbert Huncke (1980)

This is HERBERT HUNCKE's major book, written in notebook form in the early to mid-1960s. Compared to *HUNCKE'S JOURNAL*, this book is more thorough and appears to be less cobbled together than its predecessor. Huncke's third book, *GUILTY OF EVERYTHING*, is constructed from a series of interviews rather than from his notebooks. *The Evening Sun Turned Crimson*, then, is the most realized of his works. The book was published by Cherry Valley Books. Huncke had been a friend with the publishers, Pam and Charles Plymell, since the late 1960s. The first edition of 1,000 (in paperback) featured cover art of a junkie jabbing a needle in his arm as he sat atop a New York skyscraper. Huncke hated the cover and asked for a new edition, and for obvious reasons the original needle-and-skyline edition is now very collectible. The second edition uses a photo of Huncke taken by longtime companion Louis Cartwright.

The book covers Huncke's life up to the mid-1960s. Two long autobiographical sections detail his early life and travels in the 1930s as a young man. As in *Huncke's Journal*, many of the chapters are sketches of the fascinating characters whom Huncke knew and with whom he associated in New York from the 1940s through the 1960s, as well as characters whom he met in prison and in mental hospitals. The Beats are also a central part of the book. Huncke discusses his relationship with WILLIAM S. BURROUGHS in two long sections, and he gives an account of the incident that led to his and ALLEN GINSBERG's arrest in 1949. However, as is true of *Huncke's Journal*, this book is valuable for many reasons other than the fact that Huncke was a friend of the Beats. Huncke, like Neal Cassady, made an art of his life.

The title story introduces one of the book's main themes: loneliness. T. S. Eliot called Huckleberry Finn's the loneliest voice in American literature. Huncke's voice is just as lonely. He is in many respects Huck Finn—a picaresque hero with a conscience and an acute sense of loneliness. Here, his parents leave the "extremely precocious" five-year-old Huncke alone overnight in a country cabin: "I felt the intenseness of my being alone," he writes, "and although I've suffered acute awareness of loneliness many many times throughout my life, I've never sensed it quite as thoroughly or traumatically as on that evening when all the world turned into burning flame." Many of the characters described in the book are desperately isolated and alienated, in part because of their fierce independence. In response, they form misfit bands of drug addicts, criminals, homosexuals, and artists. In many ways Huncke's real "family" was the Beats and the members of the various scenes to which he belonged.

Huncke's actual family history is recounted in two autobiographical essays at the beginning of the book. He writes about his parent's divorce, his father's dislike of him, his closeness to his grandmother who taught him to appreciate the fineries in life, and his adventures with dissipated Chicago youth in the 1920s. His home life, he says, illustrates the difference between appearance and reality in the American family of the 1920s. His closest bond was with his maternal grandmother, who had lived on a ranch out West and told him cowboy stories. His father resented the grandmother's affection and accused her of turning him into a "sissy." (His father would later disown Huncke for his homosexual appearance and behavior.) Huncke watches his parents sail through the roaring twenties. However, the depression hit, and he says that the country under FDR "began coming alive with a whole set of new rules."

Living with his mother after her divorce, he is essentially free to do as he wishes—she is no disciplinarian, as the father was. The father remarries and has more children and neglects Huncke. He and his mother become more friends than mother and son. She was only 16 when he was born. He hangs out with other children of divorced parents, a particularly wild crowd of kids in 1920s Chicago. His jazz-age stories of sex, drugs, and alcohol show a side of life in the 1920s that you do not find in the comparatively tame (and upper-class) accounts by Ernest Hemingway and F. Scott Fitzgerald.

In fact, Huncke's distinction as a Beat storyteller first and later as a writer is that he *did* tell these stories, not hide them or obfuscate them. This is all the stuff that the establishment writers left out, considering it unpublishable or subliterary. You certainly get that here in Huncke's anecdote "New Orleans, 1938" in which a man asks him to watch him have sex with a prostitute. He does not pay her, but does pay Huncke a dollar for watching. In his sad story of the "Tattooed Man," he profiles "an ex-junky freakshow worker and poet." One of Huncke's most memorable portraits is "Elsie John," a friend of Huncke's during his youth in Chicago.

Elsie John, a "giant" with long hennaed hair, bright lipstick, and eyelashes that he beaded with mascara, exhibited himself as a hermaphrodite. He was also a heroin addict. The cops bust Elsie John for possession, and Huncke gets off because he is only 17. Forty years later, Huncke remembers the cruelty of the police and Elsie John's suffering.

Huncke's book is also particularly informative and entertaining about the history of drug use. He records, for example, how following the crackdown on "croakers" (doctors who would write false prescriptions) in the early 1950s, junkies began to commit more crimes and more violent ones—the kind of crime unheard of in the 1940s and earlier. Drug use leads Huncke into other absurd situations. One of the best chapters in the book is "Sea Voyage," a comic misadventure describing Huncke and Phil White's (the "Sailor" in Burroughs's books) attempt to "kick" their junk habits by shipping out on a tanker bound for Honolulu. They immediately make friends with a young gay man who fancies Phil White and supplies them with morphine syrettes stolen from the lifeboat medical kits. In the Caribbean, they buy a white-faced monkey named Jocko. Of course, his use of illegal drugs has less humorous consequences—imprisonment, violence, sickness, the death of friends. After he is busted for possession one day after he has been released from a six-month prison stay, he vents his frustration against the system that so severely punishes "victimless" crimes.

Two characters familiar to the student of the Beats receive full portraits here—Vickie Russell and Burroughs. Huncke shows himself to be uniquely sympathetic to the lives of women of the Beat Generation. "Detroit Redhead, 1943–1967" immortalizes Russell, who became famous as the six-foot-tall pot-smoking redhead described in newspaper accounts of the arrest of her, Little Jack Melody, and Ginsberg when they tried to outrun the cops in a stolen car, wrecked the car, and were eventually busted. Huncke first meets her at Bickford's restaurant when she is about 18 years old, and she tells him her life story, which epitomizes in many ways the double standards applied to women and men in the 1940s. Such standards literally force women such as Vickie to live outside of the law. Vickie becomes hooked on junk, loses her apartment, and moves into an apartment building on 102nd Street that is the weirdest building of all in which these people lived—complete with stairways that lead to dead-end walls and a colony of out-of-work midgets. Huncke provides a complete portrait of her, as he did for many of the women of the Beat Generation (in contrast to other Beat writers, who merely sketch Joan Vollmer and Elise Cowen but who are fully and sympathetically treated in Huncke's memoirs). The last time he sees her is at the trial revolving around the Ginsberg affair. Later he learns that she broke down and asked her father for money and help. Years later when Huncke talks to a mutual friend of theirs in 1967, he finds out that Vickie is a housewife and head of the PTA in a Detroit suburb. Huncke, himself never able to make such a transition in the "normal" world, ends the piece wondering "what she has done about all her dreams and how she managed to curb her enthusiasm for excitement and adventure."

Through Vickie, Huncke met Bob Brandenburg, and it was through Brandenburg that Burroughs first met Huncke and White. In "Bill Burroughs" and "Bill Burroughs, Part II," he tells the history of their friendship. Huncke and White had just returned from the sea voyage during which they had unsuccessfully tried to kick their habits and were living in an apartment on Henry Street when Brandenberg brought Burroughs by. When he first saw Burroughs, cold-eyed, conservatively dressed, and ignorant of the underworld lingo, Huncke thought that Burroughs could be from the Federal Bureau of Investigation or an undercover cop. However, when Burroughs told them that he had two cases of morphine syrettes that he wanted to unload, they dropped their reserve. Burroughs, recalled Huncke, asked if either knew how to use the syrettes, and if so would they show him. Burroughs and White became friends immediately. A week later Huncke saw them together and they told him that "they were making the hole [stealing from drunken businessmen in the subway] together as partners, with Bill learning to act as a shill and cover-up man for Phil." Within a couple of months, Burroughs had a drug habit that, according to Huncke, he approached in the style of scientific research rather than as "kicks." Through

Burroughs, Huncke became good friends with the core Beat writers.

Of all the members of this group, Joan Burroughs was Huncke's favorite. She was beautiful and brilliant, but Huncke was never convinced that Burroughs loved her. Therefore, when the close group of friends broke up in 1946, with Ginsberg going to sea, Kerouac home to his mother, and Burroughs and Joan to Texas, Huncke chose to accept their invitation to Texas, less for Burroughs's friendship than for Joan's. In fact, he may well have been trying to protect Joan as he had done with other women in relationships with men he did not trust.

The Evening Sun Turns Crimson is marked by epiphanies in which Huncke replays crucial insights that he has gained at the expense of his own suffering and humiliation. Throughout the book, Huncke applies the "factualist" eye of the junky but combines that with a recall of the emotional memories stirred by the facts, thus making the book quite different from, say, Burroughs's emotionless, hard-boiled account of many of the same incidents in *JUNKY.*

Rob Johnson

Everson, William (Brother Antoninus)
(1912–1994)

William Everson entered the Beat movement through his association with the San Francisco Renaissance. He had come to Berkeley in 1946, a displaced farmer who had lost his grape vineyard along with his first wife, Edwa Poulson, as unintended result of his conscientious objector stand against World War II and subsequent four-year internment in the camp at Waldport, Oregon. Born in Sacramento on September 10, 1912, as middle child of Francelia Heber and Louis Everson, he had lived the first three decades of his life in Selma, south of Fresno. He had begun to write poetry during high school, inspired by a teacher, an inspiration that was later deepened by the powerful works of Robinson Jeffers. His first two books of poetry, *These Are the Ravens* (1935) and *San Joaquin* (1939), consisted largely of nature poems reflecting this inland valley life of seasonal plantings, crop harvests, weather patterns, and life of the soil. At Waldport he had gained experience at printing which, along with some typesetting for his father a printer, would become a lifetime involvement. There he joined other poets and artists in publications mostly questioning inner violence and its outcome in war.

In Berkeley, under the mentoring and editing of poet KENNETH REXROTH, he published his first comprehensive collection, *The Residual Years* (1948) at New Directions. Here also, having already moved from his father's agnosticism to Jeffers's pantheism, he found himself, beginning in a mystic moment at Christmas mass, converted to the Catholic faith of his second wife Mary Fabilli. Ironically, according to church law, they were forced to separate because of the previous divorces of each, and he thence attached himself to the Oakland Catholic Worker, a pacifist, anarchist, lay organization founded by Dorothy Day and Peter Maurin and dedicated to antiwar activism and feeding, clothing, and sheltering the poor.

At this point, by a kind of inevitable spiritual logic, in 1951 he joined the Catholic Dominican Order as the lay Brother Antoninus, dedicating himself to the communal reciting of the Divine Office (consisting largely of the biblical poetry, the psalms) and a daily work schedule. Here, with the help of a Washington hand press he had bought during the war, he established his reputation as a fine press artist printing the highly prized *Psalter Pii XII* and published three volumes of his conversion poetry—in 1959 *The Crooked Lines of God,* poems of religious initiation; in 1962 *The Hazards of Holiness,* poems probing his desolate "dark night of the soul"; and, finally in 1967 the provocative sequence *The Rose of Solitude,* addressing the necessary role of eroticism and integration of *anima* for authentic mystic life.

In 1956 he began his first public readings as a Dominican in which he found great power to spellbind and move. He wrote: "I become for this brief time transcendentally myself. . . . It is this realization of my poems as vehicles for establishing contact between God and other souls that gives me the understanding of their prophetic character."

Also in 1956, he was present in Rexroth's San Francisco apartment when *Life* magazine covered Renaissance/Beat poets' readings, featuring MICHAEL McCLURE, PHILIP LAMANTIA, and others including Antoninus. And in the second issue of *Evergreen Review* (1957), Rexroth introduced the "San Francisco Scene," placing Antoninus significantly within it alongside Robert Duncan and ALLEN GINSBERG, calling him "probably the most profoundly moving and durable of the poets of the San Francisco Renaissance," finding in him a witness against "all the corrupting influences of our predatory civilization." In 1959 *Time* magazine did a story on him as the "Beat Friar."

A victim of recurring nightmares and deep depression, in 1956 Everson had come upon the writings of Freudian theorists and, under the tutelage of English Dominican father Victor White, a psychoanalyst and theologian, had opened himself to Jungian analysis, which was to direct much of his thinking and writing for years to come, involving especially his relationship with women and his search for his authenticating *anima.* With this focus came the third woman pivotal in his life, Rose Tannlund, whom he counseled and who introduced him as Beat poet and monk to the teeming San Francisco social life, being herself not his lover but a revelation to many levels of his psyche and about whom he wrote his astoundingly erotic and mystic sequence-poem *The Rose of Solitude.* As the 1960s passed, he became more and more a counselor to those who came to his Oakland abbey. His readings were multitude and their venues went international.

As these counselees multiplied, he became involved with one of them, Susanna Rickson, a relationship that morphed into an affair in 1966 and led to his dramatically leaving the Dominican Order in 1969. He married her and shortly thereafter moved to Santa Cruz where he began the third era of his life, teaching handpress printing and lecturing on the vocation of poet at the University of California campus. Here his vesture changed from the dramatic black and crème Dominican habit to a frontier buckskin jacket, broad hat, and bear-claw necklace, and his life role changed from monk to shaman. He published 13 books of his own poetry, including the anthology *Blood of the Poet* and the epic of his life, *The Engendering Flood;* eight books of criticism and collected forewords and interviews, one examining regionalism (*Archetype West*); and edited, published, and, in the case of the majestic and prize-winning *Granite and Cypress*, printed six books of poetry by his mentor Robinson Jeffers. In 1981 Parkinson's disease forced him to leave presswork and teaching but not his far-flung readings. He died at Kingfisher Flat, his home, on June 2, 1994.

As can be seen, Everson lived his life in three discreet stages in three landscapes that comprise what is sometimes described as a classic Hegelian thesis, antithesis, and synthesis: farmer in the San Joaquin valley, Beat monk in the San Francisco Bay Area, and senior teacher and shaman at Santa Cruz where the mountains meet the sea. His powerful prophetic poetry, agonized yet serene and sure, is fittingly gathered in three collected volumes: *The Residual Years* (1997), *The Veritable Years* (1998), and the *Integral Years* (2000).

Antoninus/Everson identified with and yet tempered and qualified the Beat movement. After suffering four years of imprisonment for his opposition to war, he briefly belonged to a commune in Marin. He then embraced anarchy and pacifism with the Catholic Worker before he donned monk's clothing in rejection of his contemporary world's values. His asceticism was totally countercultural. Especially in his internment, Catholic worker, and monk stages, he embraced the word *beat* as it is sometimes understood from Jesus's Beatitudes of Matthew 6:3–10—"Blessed are the poor, those that mourn, the meek, justice seekers, the merciful, the pure of heart, peacemakers, those persecuted pursuing the right." He composed and broadcast as much challenging poetry as any Beat including Ginsberg. Even in his monk days, he exalted sexuality (coining "Erotic Mysticism" as sexual imagery inciting encounter with God) when correctly channeled and sacramental in intent. He was to his confreres and to all who knew him friend, counselor, teacher, mystic, shaman, and outstanding bard.

Bibliography

Bartlett, Lee. *William Everson: The Life of Brother Antoninus.* New York: New Directions, 1988.

Brophy, Robert, ed. *William Everson: Remembrances and Tributes.* Long Beach: The Robinson Jeffers Newsletter, 1995.

Gelpi, Albert, ed. *Dark God of Eros: A William Everson Reader.* Berkeley, Calif.: Heyday Books, 2003.

Robert Brophy

F

Fall of America: Poems of These States, 1965–1971, The Allen Ginsberg (1972)

A major volume of "road" poems, *The Fall of America* won the prestigious National Book Award for Poetry in 1973. Conceptually, it is ALLEN GINS-BERG's most ambitious full-length book of poems. The book was composed as a travelogue documenting Ginsberg's travels in the United States from 1965 to 1971. In his afterword, Ginsberg dedicates the book to Walt Whitman, whose warning of American materialistic decline in his major prose work, *Democratic Vistas,* is one of the primary inspirations for *The Fall of America.* Whitman predicted, with some urgency, that the United States needed an imaginative renewal to sustain itself in the increasingly industrialized end-of-the-century modern world; the "soul" of the American imagination was found, for Whitman, in literature. As a poet who saw himself to be a 20th-century heir of Whitman's visionary voice, Ginsberg set out in *The Fall of America* to survey what Whitman called these States and to dramatize the causes of what he saw as their decline and potential for reascension. Despite Whitman's dire cautions in *Democratic Vistas,* his optimism leads him to forecast a 20th century in which American entrepreneurial spirit and technological know-how "lead the world"; of this future, he writes, "There will be daily electric communication with every part of the globe. What an age! What a land!" The text of *The Fall of America* suggests that Ginsberg hears the echoes of this optimism, but in an era dominated by the Vietnam War and what Ginsberg saw as governmental pro-paganda that propped the war, "daily electric communication" had corrupted "these States."

Ginsberg's project in *The Fall of America* is to recuperate language. As much as Ginsberg distrusts American technological advancement in these poems—with technology serving the war effort in what he once termed the electronic war of Vietnam—the composition process of this book itself depended on the use of technology. Most of the poems in this book were composed with the aid of a state-of-the-art reel-to-reel tape recorder. The poet's immediate thoughts were spoken into the tape recorder, while the machine also picked up random background sounds and news from the car radio (see also "WICHITA VORTEX SUTRA"). All language on the tape recorder, not just Ginsberg's words, was incorporated into the poems, and Ginsberg used the on–off clicking sound of the tape recorder to determine the line breaks in the poem. One of the most important technical aspects of this book, then, is Ginsberg's improvisatory composition process. Ginsberg's career is framed by his efforts to loosen poetic voice by combining the need to revise with a determination to honor the productions of spontaneous composition. In his teaching and interviews, he often repeated the words of his first Buddhist teacher, Chögyam Trungpa Rinpoche, who advised artists that one's "first thought" is one's "best thought." *The Fall of America,* with its improvisatory "auto poesy" at the core of its creation, marks perhaps Ginsberg's only sustained book-length spontaneous composition.

The book is divided into five sections. Each section explores a landscape that, in a significant nod to Whitman, is both physical and psychological. Section I, "Through the Vortex West Coast to East 1965–1966," is important for its introduction of the major theme of the book itself—the malleability of language and meaning, and the responsibility of literary artists to take a direct role in the shaping of culture through words. Revising Whitman's declaration that literature is the country's soul, Ginsberg proclaims early in "Beginning of a Poem of These States," the first poem in the book, that radio is "the soul of the nation." Of course, if radio is the soul of the United States, this is so in *The Fall of America* only through the imaginative labor of the poet who recontextualizes the musical and rhetorical snippets of wartime America into coherent, though deliberately fragmented, verse. Music from the radio is incorporated to frame the road optimism and war weariness of the opening poem, in songs ranging through "California Dreaming," "Eve of Destruction," "Universal Soldier," and "Can You Please Crawl Out Your Window?". In this first poem, too, Ginsberg introduces the role that his increased study of Buddhism would play in the book, where the groundlessness of Buddhism is a preferred mode of vision to Judeo-Christian monotheism: "I have nothing to do . . . Heaven is renounced, Dharma no path, no Saddhana to fear." Ginsberg offers a bibliographic note at the beginning of the book, stating that his long poem "Wichita Vortex Sutra," originally published in 1968 in *Planet News,* belongs sequentially in this section of the book. Along with "Iron Horse," another of Ginsberg's separately published Buddhist-inspired poems of this road pilgrimage, "Wichita Vortex Sutra" was added to *The Fall of America* sequence by Ginsberg in his 1984 volume, *Collected Poems 1947–1980.* According to Ginsberg, he included "Wichita Vortex Sutra" and "Iron Horse" in *The Fall of America* section of *Collected Poems* to fill conceptual "gaps" in the original publication history of his work. Because Buddhism plays such an important role in these poems, their 1984 addition to *The Fall of America* sequence represents Ginsberg's later effort to reinforce the activist impulse of *The Fall of America* with the religious authority of Buddhism and the literary authority of the epic form.

"Zigzag Back Thru These States 1966–1967," Section II of the book, extends further a theme introduced in the first section—that late 20th-century capitalism depends on an interconnection of a country's war and leisure economies. In "Autumn Gold: New England Fall," Ginsberg bemoans that "[e]ven sex happiness" is "a long drawn out scheme / To keep the mind moving" until, at the Veterans Hospital, "we can all collapse, / Forget Pleasure and Ambition." The link between war and spectacle in the American economy is significant in *The Fall of America* and in much of Ginsberg's later work. A poem such as "War Profit Litany," which ends this section of the book with an "accounting" that merges the everyday transactions of ordinary citizens with war combat, prefigures later work on this same theme, such as "Who Runs America?" from the 1977 volume *Mind Breaths.*

"Elegies for Neal Cassady 1968," Section III of the book, explores the psychological landscape of the poet as figure for that of the United States. Written a week after NEAL CASSADY's death, the title poem of this section elegizes Cassady as a "Tender Spirit" who now rests "story told, Karma resolved," and concludes of their on and off romantic involvement: "My body breathes easy, / I lie alone, / living." Ginsberg includes in this same section of the book "Please Master," the sexually charged counterpart to "Elegy for Neal Cassady." "Please Master" stages the symbiotic quality of sadomasochistic sexual practice as a symbol for the occasional romantic relationship between Ginsberg and Cassady. Cassady is the self-evidently controlling master having his way with a submissive Ginsberg in this poem. The poem is more than just a private elegy for Cassady. Seen as overly explicit in its time, the poem's assertions of male–male desire in retrospect anticipate gay activist literature of the period that would follow the Stonewall uprising of 1969.

One of the last poems in Section III, "Grant Park: August 28, 1968," closes with a question that resonates into Section IV of the book: "Miserable picnic," Ginsberg writes of the police riot at the Democratic National Convention in Chicago, "Police State or Garden of Eden?" Section IV, "Ecologues of These States 1969–1971," whose title puns on the pastoral form of the *eclogue,* pits the poet's increased feeling of "police state" autocracy against his continued, Whitman-inspired idealism. In "Over Denver Again," written a year after Cassady's death, Ginsberg represents a "Denver without Neal" as a stultifying inorganic tundra where "insects hop back and forth between metallic cities." The need for a human community central to Whitman's vision is under duress in this section. In *Democratic Vistas*, Whitman argued that homosocial comradeship, or "adhesive love," as he called it, offered a democratic "counterbalance" to "offset" American materialism and spiritual decay. Ginsberg is inspired by Whitman's words, but the culture of America in the Vietnam era produces division rather than adhesion. In this section, for instance, Ginsberg writes of the *Apollo* Moon landing, an action in which Whitman, arguably, would have extolled in his poetics of manifest destiny— yet Ginsberg's celebration of the event takes place in solitude, "In a Moonlit Hermit's Cabin," as stated in the title. What Ginsberg earlier described as the "electronic war" continues, and Ginsberg laments that the Moon landing has taken national consciousness, the soul of the nation for Whitman, and transformed it into vulgar nationalism: "Two 'Americans' on the moon! / Beautiful view, bouncing the surface—'one quarter of the world denied these pix by their rulers'! / Setting up the flag!" These words are echoed later, in "Death on All Fronts," when Ginsberg puns on the phases of the Moon, noting that a "new Moon looks down on our sick sweet planet." The Moon, symbol of poetic imagination, has been colonized; the American flag has been planted on a "new" Moon that will never be the same. The poems in this section are notable, too, for their continued return to the poet's private grief over Cassady's death and, in October 1969, the death of JACK KEROUAC. Ginsberg's autobiographical impulse at times overwhelms the poems in this section. In so doing, the poet's trust in naming, seen in his belief earlier in the book in the transformative power of mantra speech, becomes simple name-calling. In "D.C. Mobilization," Ginsberg describes the White House five days after the Kent State shootings as flat, abstracted "Iron Robot"; and in "Ecologue," America is described simply as a "Country / full of pricks."

As if to remind readers that American exceptionalism is a fiction, the final section of the book, Section V, "Bixby Canyon to Jessore Road," closes with "September on Jessore Road," a long poem in quatrains that narrates the movement of millions of suffering refugees on the main road between Bangladesh and Calcutta. Ginsberg details the starving condition of these refugees and asks why U.S. funds that perpetuate the Vietnam war effort cannot be diverted to aid those "[m]illions of children" with "nowhere to go." To be sure, the political sentiment of "September on Jessore Road" is consistent with the literary–activist impulse of *The Fall of America* and its inspiration, *Democratic Vistas*. However, beginning with the private elegies in Section III, it is questionable whether Ginsberg's book can sustain the polyvocal experiments in private and public utterance that open *The Fall of America*. In her review of the book, Helen Vendler notes that the poems are characterized by "the disappearance or exhaustion of long-term human relations." Whether this loss of human connection is a deliberated dramatization of American decay or a symptom of the poet's private loss is the primary legacy of "Ginsberg's ardent atlas," Vendler's description of the encompassing ambition of this book.

Bibliography

Ginsberg, Allen. *Howl: Original Draft Facsimile*. Edited by Barry Miles. New York: HarperCollins, 1986.

———. Interview with Michael Aldrich, et al. "Improvised Poetics." *Composed on the Tongue: Literary Conversations, 1967–1977*. San Francisco: Grey Fox, 1980, 18–62.

Schumacher, Michael. *Dharma Lion: A Critical Biography of Allen Ginsberg*. New York: St. Martin's, 1992.

Trigilio, Tony. "'Will You Please Stop Playing With the Mantra?': The Embodied Poetics of Ginsberg's Later Career." In *Reconstructing the Beats*, edited by Jennie Skerl, 119–140. New York: Palgrave Macmillan, 2004.

Vendler, Helen. "Review of *The Fall of America*." *The New York Times Book Review*, 15 April 1973, 1. Reprinted in Lewis Hyde, ed., *On the Poetry of Allen Ginsberg*. Ann Arbor: University of Michigan Press, 1984, 203–209.

Whitman, Walt. *Leaves of Grass*. Edited by Michael Moon, Sculley Bradley, and Harold W. Blodgett. 2d ed. New York: Norton, 2002.

Tony Trigilio

Family: The Story of Charles Manson's Dune Buggy Attack Battalion, The
Ed Sanders (1971)

This true-crime classic, republished as *The Family* (Thunder's Mouth Press 2002), rivals Vincent Bugliosi's *Helter Skelter: The True Story of the Manson Murders* (1974), the number one true crime best-seller of all time. Thomas Myers writes, "The fact that *The Family* is part information overload, part hard-boiled detective novel, part hip jeremiad, and part schlock monster movie only makes it more intriguing as moral statement." While Bugliosi's excellent account of the Tate–LaBianca murders of August 1969 comes from the perspective of the prosecuting attorney who was able to convince the jury to give the death penalty to all those prosecuted for the murders (later commuted to life sentences after the death penalty was revoked in California), Sanders's book reveals more of the complexities of the case, including detailed connections between the Manson Family and the counterculture, biker gangs, other unsolved murders, and satanic groups.

In August 1969, Sharon Tate (wife of director Roman Polanski), Jay Sebring (hairdresser to many movie stars and JIM MORRISON), Abigail Folger (heiress to the Folger coffee fortune), Woytek Frykowski, Steven Parent, Leno LaBianca, and Rosemary LaBianca were murdered on two consecutive nights by Tex Watson, Susan Atkins, Patricia Krenwinkel, and Leslie Van Houten, members of Charles Manson's cult known as The Family. Some people viewed these murders and the ensuing trial of Manson and his female followers as the death of the 1960s. "And no detached reporter has Sanders within his data," writes Myers, "for in his subject he seemed to have found his own version of Poe's William Wilson, his counterculture doppelganger who was the antithesis of ethical principle and moral conscience—the gestating beast in the belly of peace and love." Disturbingly, Manson has even called himself a beatnik.

Bugliosi argues that the murders were committed to start a race war, "Helter Skelter," that was partially conceived by Manson after hearing The Beatles' "White Album." Sanders does not buy this explanation, nor the popular theory that the murders were committed to resemble the Gary Hinman murder committed by The Family member Bobby Beausoleil to help Beausoleil beat his case. The murders, originally thought to be connected to drug trafficking, baffled detectives. At first, Sanders thought The Family might have been set up by the police because they were a countercultural organization. After spending time reporting on Manson's trial and researching the case for the *Los Angeles Free Press*, Sanders came to see The Family as more diabolical than he could have ever imagined:

> The more I dug into this case the more upset I became over what these people and their connective groups had done and were still doing. I was revolted by some things I learned while researching this book. I realized that during my years in the counterculture I had sometimes behaved imperfectly, and had strayed from portions of the Judeo-Christian tradition in which I was raised. But what I came across seemed to me to be evil, and you don't have to be perfect—in fact you can be quite imperfect—to be revolted by practitioners of deliberate evil.

Though Sanders does not provide a clear explanation for what he thinks are the true motives behind the Manson murders, he does suggest it has much to do with the group's involvement with Satanism.

For a year and a half Sanders studied The Family, even spending time with many of the members and sleeping at their compound. This experience led to an aesthetic insight:

> As I wrote hundreds upon hundreds of pages of notes, I began writing them in verselike, indented clusters. Thus, say, when I described an encounter with a member of the Family, I jotted it down with line breaks! I supposed at the time it was in honor of my mentor, the bard CHARLES OLSON, who had passed away in early 1970. Olson's work combining poetry and history, and his friendship, had thrilled my early years. All of my note pages written in open field verse clusters (which, of course, I transformed into lines of prose) would lead in a few years to my manifesto called *Investigative Poetry*.

This poetic theory led to Sanders's book-length poems *Chekhov, 1968: A History in Verse, The Poetry and Life of Allen Ginsberg*, and the multivolume *America: A History in Verse*. Sanders writes:

> My mentor, the great bard Charles Olson, had written about a "Saturation Job," as a rite of passage for a writer of substance. In a Saturation Job, Olson pointed out, you studied one subject, whether a place or a person or persons, "until you yourself know more about that than is possible to any other man. It doesn't matter whether it's Barbed Wire or Pemmican or Paterson or Iowa. But *exhaust it*. Saturate it. Beat it. And then U KNOW everything very fast: one saturation job (it might take fourteen years). And you're in, forever."
>
> For me, researching the Manson group was my "Saturation Job."

Sanders credits detectives Charles Guenther and Paul Whiteley, who were investigating the Hinman murder for eventually breaking the Tate–LaBianca case.

Ultimately, Sanders's book exposes more questions than it answers. The author continues to work and think about The Family, and it is quite possible that he will have more to say about them in the future.

Bibliography

Myers, Thomas. "Rerunning the Creepy-Crawl: Ed Sanders and Charles Manson." *The Review of Contemporary Fiction* 19, no. 1 (Spring 1999): 81–90.

Kurt Hemmer

Fariña, Richard (1937–1966)

Richard Fariña's death at the age of 29, two days after the publication of his novel BEEN DOWN SO LONG IT LOOKS LIKE UP TO ME (1966), curtailed an ambitious and eclectic body of journalism, short fiction, poetry, and song. David Hadju's *Positively Fourth Street* (2001) argues the significance of Fariña's role in the urban folk music revival of the early to mid-1960s. Less clearly defined is Fariña's literary legacy. The body of his literary work is slender—aside from his novel, his work is represented only by the collection *Long Time Coming and a Long Time Gone* (1969) and a number of uncollected poems, stories, essays, and an unpublished play, *The Shelter*. Despite the brevity of his career, Fariña's work identifies him as a young writer whose depiction of bohemian culture of the late 1950s augured cultural upheaval in the 1960s in much the same manner as better known and earlier work of JACK KEROUAC, ALLEN GINSBERG, and WILLIAM S. BURROUGHS. With KEN KESEY and RICHARD BRAUTIGAN, Fariña's work stands as a link between Beat literature of the 1950s and the counterculture of the 1960s.

Born in Brooklyn to an Irish mother and a Cuban father, Fariña attended Catholic elementary school and the competitive Brooklyn Technical High School, from which he matriculated to Cornell on a scholarship as an engineering major in 1955. He left Cornell in 1959 without receiving his degree, having established a strong friendship with fellow undergraduate Thomas Pynchon, who would dedicate *Gravity's Rainbow* to Fariña. In 1960 Fariña married popular folksinger Carolyn Hester, and through engagement in Hester's career, Fariña took up the dulcimer and began to write songs. His poetry meanwhile reached a national audience in 1961 with publications in the *Atlantic Monthly* and the *Transatlantic Review*. A story, "The Vision of Brother Francis," would be published in 1962 in *Prairie Schooner*. Fariña spent much of 1962 on the road in Europe with and without Hester. According to Hester, he began seriously to draft *Been Down So Long So Long It Looks Like Up to Me* in London that year. Fariña separated from Hester in 1962 and married Mimi Baez, whom he had met in Paris, the following year.

Fariña recorded an album of traditional folk songs with Eric von Schmidt and BOB DYLAN in London in January 1963. On the basis of a demo recorded by sister-in-law Joan Baez in November 1963, Fariña was signed to a publishing contract with Vanguard Records. Richard and Mimi Fariña debuted as a duo at the Big Sur Folk Festival in June 1964, mixing guitar and dulcimer instrumentals with allegorical ballads ("The Falcon") and topical songs of social protest ("Birmingham

Sunday"). Their first album *Celebrations for a Grey Day* was recorded in Manhattan in autumn 1964 and would be followed with the late 1965 release of a second LP, *Reflections in a Crystal Wind*, which would be noted by the *New York Times* as one of 10 best folk albums of the year.

In between recordings and performances with Mimi, Fariña had by early 1965 finished *Been Down So Long It Looks Like Up to Me* in the cabin the couple shared in Carmel, California. Fariña's *bildungsroman* featured his alter ego, Gnossos Pappadopoulis, and was set in a college town very like Cornell's Ithaca, New York, in the late 1950s. His frank treatment of sexual episodes in the novel caused some concern, and according to Hadju, some of the more ribald episodes were struck from the narrative.

On April 30, 1966, Fariña attended a book-signing party in Carmel Valley for his novel, which had been released that week. Later that evening, in the midst of a surprise 21st birthday party that he had arranged for Mimi, he departed on the back of an acquaintance's motorcycle for a brief ride. Returning to the party shortly thereafter, driver Willie Hinds failed to negotiate a turn, and he and Fariña were thrown from the bike. Hinds escaped with minor scrapes. Fariña died instantly of a blow to the head.

Mimi Fariña was to release an LP of prior recorded songs (*Memories*), which included Fariña's send up of Dylan, "Morgan the Pirate." Aside from the posthumous collection *Long Time Coming and a Long Time Gone, Esquire* published Fariña's "Ringing Out the Old Year in Havana" in September 1969. An underdistributed film of Fariña's novel followed, as did a 1970s New York musical production *Richard Fariña: Long Time Coming and a Long Time Gone. Been Down So Long It Looks Like Up to Me*, reprinted in 1983 with an introduction by Thomas Pynchon, remains in print in the Penguin Twentieth Century Classics series.

Bibliography

Cooke, Douglas. "The Richard & Mimi Fariña Website." Available online. URL: http://www.richardandmimi.com. Accessed September 2005.

Fariña, Richard. *Long Time Coming and a Long Time Gone*. New York: Random House, 1969.

Hajdu, David. *Positively 4th Street: The Lives and Times of Joan Baez, Bob Dylan, Mimi Baez Fariña, and Richard Fariña*. New York: North Point, 2001.

Pynchon, Thomas. Introduction. *Been Down So Long It Looks Like Up to Me*, by Richard Fariña. New York: Penguin, 1996, v–xiv.

Tracy Santa

Fast Speaking Woman   Anne Waldman   (1975)

Fast Speaking Woman is not ANNE WALDMAN's first poetry book, but it brought her to the wider notice of readers especially connected to Beat movement writing. It was published by LAWRENCE FERLINGHETTI's City Lights Books in 1975 as Number 33 in the prestigious Pocket Poets Series after Ferlinghetti heard Waldman read the title poem in San Francisco at a Buddhist benefit with ALLEN GINSBERG. Poem and performance were so evocative that Ferlinghetti wanted a photograph of Waldman for the cover of the book to display her as "the manifestation of woman," as she put it. Even by then, Waldman preferred the title poem in performance over its life on the page. When she was backstage during BOB DYLAN's legendary Rolling Thunder Review tour of 1975–76 and was challenged by Mohammed Ali to demonstrate her bona fides as a woman poet, Waldman offered that poem, spontaneously declaiming, "I'm the woman walking down the backstage with Ali." A list–chant poem, "Fast Speaking Woman" was written on the run and subject to extensions and modifications as it was performed, a capacity enhanced by the poem's structure in anaphora and litany. More than 30 pages long, the poem is based on vibrating incantatory repetitions of the declarative enunciation "I am," an anaphoric proliferation of limitless claims for women listed in the following manner, as in "I'm a fast speaking woman / I'm a fast rolling woman / I'm a rolling speech woman / I'm a rolling-water woman." It is arguably Waldman's most accessible—perhaps because most mnemonic—and well-known poem, and it served to site her as a Beat poet, albeit third generation, in spite of her frequent insistence that she is a second generation New York School poet.

"Fast Speaking Woman" is a hybrid of historical moment and poetic influences that typifies

Waldman's work: The urgent exclamatory poem fits with her second-wave feminism as well as with the "hot" school of Beat Generation writing. The poem is indebted, as is evident from its look on the page and from Waldman's performance of it, to Ginsberg and "HOWL"; as do many Waldman "list" poems, it visibly descends from Beat poetic styles of Whitmanic declamation and prophecy as interpreted and epitomized by Ginsberg. Its signifiers describing the woman of its title are ever exchanging among themselves, making it a poem as seemingly "interminable" in the motion of its lines as in its composition, which Waldman described as enduring for some time in an unfinished state.

The ultimate feminist or woman-centered innovation on Beat poetics in "Fast Speaking Woman" is the work's relationship to its sources, especially Maria Sabina, the Mazatec Indian shamaness in Mexico whose chants Waldman has interwoven into her lines. Waldman constructed the poem intertextually, using Sabina's refrain—"water that cleans as I go"—as a "place to pause and shift rhythm and acknowledge the cleansing impulse of the writing," as she notes in an accompanying essay about the poem in the 1996 revised edition. Waldman constructs a litany/list poem that speaks with multiple voices, enacting by the pastiching in of others' voices its claimed relation to women as a caste—the poet-speaker is many Everywomen at once. Waldman's collage of Sabina into her Beat poem accomplishes the transfiguration of Beat aesthetics by the infusion of a woman's material and spiritual discourse, which works to integrate women into the male mythoi of Beat Generation writing.

The other poems of the original edition of *Fast Speaking Woman* have multiple inspirations but most are, as Waldman has noted, "relevant & resonant with the notion of 'chant.'" "Pressure," signed "Lower East Side / 1972," is a list poem that pivots from a catalogue of places and environments to the phrases that give them desperate urgency, "no way out," "no escape," "no way no way," "no return no way off / no way out of midnight." "Notorious" is a list-chant of a woman's repute—"known for her mouth, splendid temper tantrums / squeezed head, nostalgic lips & antelope eyes / known for her nonsense hands & big calves / known for laughing"—that invites identification with the poet herself in a kind of imaginative biography. "Musical Garden," a list of "New Year's Resolutions 1974," continues the practice of listing chanted, repeated commands, here organized around the restrictive clause "can't give" and making reference to literary artists, as in "Can't give you night mail, telephone ringing, / talking about [JACK] KEROUAC . . . Can't give it up, foxy, classy, flashy / . . . can't give it up yet won't give you up yet / can't give it up!" The delirium of refusals comprising New Year's resolutions makes a provocative turn on resolves for improvement as the poet embraces the new year with the determination not to amend or forgo pleasures, habits, desires, artists which form her life. In poems added in the revised edition, such as "I Bow at Bodhgaya" and "Red Hat Lama," a 1973 trip to India is commemorated. Other poems recognize figures identified with the Beat Generation. In "Lines to a Celebrated Friend" the list of advice and commands to the elder poet concludes with "No one's smarter or more enlightened or more famous / For heaven's sake Allen, pull up those baggy pants," a tribute that makes the beloved man Ginsberg visible under the mantle of the esteemed poet, another kind of biography of the female speaker, his acolyte.

The global reach of the poems in *Fast Speaking Woman*, the spiritual openness and far-flung search for understanding, typify the mature poet's body of work, even if the list–chant form is far surpassed by the complex vocalisms, visions, pastiches, and hybridity of the later *IOVIS*. Waldman's gambit in this Pocket Poets Series collection is to foreground women as poets, spiritual channels, and human beings in Beat Generation consciousness and culture. She claims to have always profited from her connection with the famous men of the Beat movement, having "never felt an ounce of condescension" from them, but women artists were not much recognized in the Beat heyday. "Fast Speaking Woman" brought women poets to the attention of Beat Generation writers, publishers, and readers, as Waldman brought a distinctive, self-aware feminine energy and presence to the all-encompassing, uncensored free verse form of the classic Beat poem with her ground-breaking list–chant verses.

Bibliography

Buschendorf, Christa. "Gods and Heroes Revised: Mythological Concepts of Masculinity in Contemporary

Women's Poetry." *Amerikastudien/American Studies* 43, no. 4 (1998): 599–617.

Charters, Ann. "Anne Waldman." In *The Dictionary of Literary Biography.* Vol. 16, *The Beats: Literary Bohemians in Postwar Society,* edited by Ann Charters, 528–533. Detroit: Gale, 1983.

Johnson, Ronna C., and Nancy M. Grace. "Fast Speaking Woman: Anne Waldman." In *Breaking the Rule of Cool: Interviewing and Reading Women Beat Writers,* edited by Nancy M. Grace and Ronna C. Johnson, 255–281. Jackson: University Press of Mississippi, 2004.

McNeil, Helen. "The Archeology of Gender in the Beat Movement." In *The Beat Generation Writers,* edited by A. Robert Lee, 178–199. East Haven, Connecticut: Pluto Press, 1996.

Puchek, Peter. "From Revolution to Creation: Beat Desire and Body Poetics in Anne Waldman's Poetry." In *Girls Who Wore Black: Women Writing the Beat Generation,* edited by Ronna C. Johnson and Nancy M. Grace, 227–250. New Brunswick, N.J.: Rutgers University Press, 2002.

Talisman: Anne Waldman Issue 13 (Fall 1994/Winter 1995).

Ronna C. Johnson

Fear and Loathing in Las Vegas: A Savage Journey to the Heart of the American Dream Hunter S. Thompson (1971)

A significant portion of *Fear and Loathing in Las Vegas* is set on the road, but the particular version of self-discovery that HUNGER S. THOMPSON gives the reader is vastly different than the version JACK KEROUAC offers in his own *ON THE ROAD.* The notion of finding the American Dream is central to both works, and both works also offer radically nontraditional interpretations of what exactly the American Dream consists. But while Kerouac's vision calls for a reconsideration of values and a reinvigoration of spirit, Thompson's vision of the American Dream is one that embraces the absurdity, alienation, and despair of modern culture and revels in it. *Fear and Loathing* argues for a form of salvation and individualism that is found not through ascetic denial and avoidance of the corruption and temptations of modern society but through ecstatic submersion in them. Thompson's book is extremely literal in its interpretation of the

American Dream. It does not pursue the idealistic rhetoric of what the American Dream is supposed to be, but rather it explores the real American obsessions with violence, drugs, sex, and commercialism. In Thompson's version of the American Dream, the id reigns supreme. To be realized most fully, the individual must take self-indulgent egoism to its furthest limits.

Fear and Loathing opens, with a nod to the ancient epic tradition of beginning in medias res (in the middle of things), with Raoul Duke—Thompson's pseudonym throughout the book—and his attorney (based on OSCAR ZETA ACOSTA) on the road to Las Vegas in a red convertible Cadillac in the midst of a massive drug binge. The epic conventions continue with a description of the contents of their luggage—a mind-boggling collection of drugs. Also, as in all epics, *Fear and Loathing* features a quest of discovery to the underworld, albeit a metaphorical one. Through the course of their experiences, Duke and his attorney will delve into the underworld of American culture to seek its very essence. The difference in *Fear and Loathing,* however, is that the underworld and the surface of American culture are one and the same. The truth is readily available for anyone with the intestinal fortitude to discover it. As Duke himself explains, "But our trip was different. It was a classic affirmation of everything right and true and decent in the national character. It was a gross, physical salute to the fantastic *possibilities* of life in this country—but only for those with true grit. And we were chock full of that." This speech is delivered, while under the influence of many powerful drugs, to a hitchhiker who recoils in abject terror and eventually makes his escape from the Cadillac. In an ironic reversal of what the usual interpretation of "right, true, and decent" might be, Duke and his attorney indulge almost exclusively in what would usually be seen as deviant behavior. Thompson's point throughout *Fear and Loathing* is that this so-called deviant behavior is precisely what is at the heart of American character, and anyone who does not recognize it is not living authentically.

The actual plot of *Fear and Loathing* involves very little actually happening, at least not in the traditional sense. Ostensibly, the book is centered around Duke's assignment of reporting on a desert race called the Mint 400. After this event is "covered," a new assignment—reporting on the National District Attorneys' Convention on Narcotics and Dangerous Drugs—occupies the second half of the book. Duke's assignments, however, provide no more than a pretense for being in Las Vegas and recklessly indulging in a random series of drug-fueled adventures and misadventures that more appropriately capture the version of the American Dream that Thompson has in mind. Thus, instead of events that contribute to a typical literary structure of conflict and resolution, Duke and his attorney cruise the boulevards of Las Vegas; wander through casinos; check into, inhabit, and destroy hotel rooms; watch television; rent cars; leave the city; and return, and, above all, consume massive amounts of mind-altering drugs. *Fear and Loathing* is a chronicle of these "adventures," the people whom they encounter along the way, and Duke's commentary on how their experiences reveal our true national character. Invariably, their actions always amount to some sort of legal transgression or challenge to the establishment. Thus, the one motive that actually impels Duke and his attorney from place to place is the evasion of any authorities who might discover and bring to a firm halt their activities.

Drugs of all sorts play a primary role in *Fear and Loathing,* and for Duke and his attorney, act as a kind of perpetual conduit for their quest of knowledge. For Thompson, drug use in the 1970s is markedly different from the 1960s, and this difference becomes one of the principle themes of the book. In the 1960s, such avant-garde figures as TIMOTHY LEARY, ALLEN GINSBERG, and KEN KESEY advocated consciousness expansion, whether through mind-expanding drugs or political activism or paying attention to the kinds of writing that would come to be referred to as Beat literature. But Thompson views 1960s idealism as having no place in the realities of the 1970s. Ginsberg and the other Beats failed in their attempts to seek and foster a better, different reality. A classic example is Ginsberg's and Kesey's involvement with motorcycle gangs, chronicled in Thompson's earlier book titled *HELL'S ANGELS: A STRANGE AND TERRIBLE SAGA.* Rather than the utopian social integration of mutual understanding sought by Ginsberg, the ideological differences of the disparate

groups resulted in the Angels attacking the ranks of an antiwar protest. Rather than utopia building, Thompson argues that "we are all wired into a *survival* trip now." He blames Leary and the like of "crash[ing] around America selling 'consciousness expansion' without ever giving a thought to the grim meat-hook realities that were lying in wait for all the people who took him too seriously. . . . All those pathetically eager acid freaks who thought they could buy Peace and Understanding for three bucks a hit." With the illusions of the 1960s shattered, the 1970s represent a coming to terms with our true identity and as a culture—one that has already achieved its final version of the American Dream. It may be a savage dream, but for Thompson, it is far better to recognize and admit to ourselves the true nature of our dreams than to live according to false ones.

Bibliography

Carroll, E. Jean. *Hunter: The Strange and Savage Life of Hunter S. Thompson.* New York: Dutton, 1993.

McKeen, William. *Hunter S. Thompson.* Boston: Twayne, 1991.

Perry, Paul. *Fear and Loathing: The Strange and Terrible Saga of Hunter S. Thompson.* New York: Thunder's Mouth, 1992.

Thompson, Hunter S. *The Proud Highway: Saga of a Desperate Southern Gentleman, 1955–1967 (The Fear and Loathing Letter, Volume One).* Edited by Douglas Brinkley. New York: Ballantine Books, 1998.

Whitmer, Peter O. *When the Going Gets Weird: The Twisted Life and Times of Hunter S. Thompson.* New York: Hyperion, 1993.

Luther Riedel

Ferlinghetti, Lawrence (1919–)

Writer, publisher, bookseller, painter, activist, newspaper columnist, and navy veteran, Ferlinghetti's most famous works are the poetry collections *PICTURES OF THE GONE WORLD* (1955) and *A CONEY ISLAND OF THE MIND* (1958), but he is also the author of plays, travel books, columns, reviews, and novels. City Lights Bookstore in San Francisco and City Lights Books, the publishing house responsible for the Pocket Poets Series, have been under

Ferlinghetti's direction for more than a half-century, providing opportunities for publication, promotion, and sales to Beat writers in particular and to dissident and experimental writers in general. As an activist, Ferlinghetti has fought against censorship, overpopulation, militarism, racism, and worldwide economic and environmental abuses and in favor of freedom of expression, human rights, and just treatment of developing countries. Although he is clearly tied to the Beat literary movement as a writer, publisher, and bookseller, his career goes well beyond Beat boundaries, making him a noteworthy figure in the arts of the second half of the 20th century.

Ferlinghetti, the youngest of five brothers, was born March 24, 1919, in Yonkers, New York. His father, Charles Ferling, died seven months before Ferlinghetti's birth; his mother, Clemence Mendes–Monsanto, entered a mental hospital soon after Ferlinghetti's birth. Before the child was a year old, his mother's aunt, Emily Mendes–Monsanto, took responsibility for the child, left her husband, and made a new home in France. Thus, Ferlinghetti's first language was French, but in 1924 he and his great-aunt Emily returned to Bronxville, New York, where Emily Mendes–Monsanto tutored the children of the Bisland family. In 1925 Mendes–Monsanto disappeared, leaving Ferlinghetti in the care of the Bislands. During his youth, Ferlinghetti went by his father's name, Ferling, but in writing a review for *Art Digest* in 1954, he reclaimed the full family name of Ferlinghetti and used it thereafter.

Ferlinghetti attended Riverside Country School, Bronxville Public School, and Mount Hermon High School, a private school near Greenfield, Massachusetts (the birthplace of HERBERT HUNCKE). Interested in Thomas Wolfe, Ferlinghetti enrolled at the University of North Carolina at Chapel Hill, completing a degree in journalism in 1941. After returning from military service, he attended Columbia University in New York (as did JACK KEROUAC and ALLEN GINSBERG before him) in 1947, writing a thesis about painter J. M. W. Turner and the influences of John Ruskin on Turner. In 1947 Ferlinghetti took advantage of the G. I. Bill to pursue doctoral studies at the Sorbonne in Paris. In 1949 he completed in French a dissertation entitled "The City as Symbol in Modern Poetry: In Search of a Metropolitan Tradition."

Lawrence Ferlinghetti, San Francisco, 1965. Photographer Larry Keenan: "This photograph was taken in the basement of City Lights. Ferlinghetti told me that City Lights used to be a Holy Roller church and that he had left up the Biblical tracts on the walls. While posing for me in front of 'I Am the Door' Ferlinghetti pulled his coat up to reveal the 'door.'" *(courtesy of Larry Keenan)*

Ferlinghetti's military service (1941–45) earned him distinction and had lasting influence on him. During the invasion of Normandy, he was the commanding officer on a sub chaser, and before leaving the navy, he earned the rank of lieutenant commander. His tour of duty let him see the world, including England, France, both coasts of the United States, the Pacific Islands, and Panama, but the most indelible impression was made in Japan, where he saw the devastation of the atomic bomb in Nagasaki only six weeks after the explosion. This horrible scene made Ferlinghetti an unshakable opponent of war and its horrors.

In 1951 Ferlinghetti married Selden Kirby–Smith, with whom a romance had developed aboard ship en route to France and later in Spain. The couple soon moved to San Francisco, eventually establishing residence in North Beach. The couple had two children: Julie, born in 1962; and Lorenzo, born in 1963. The marriage ended in divorce in 1976.

In San Francisco in the 1950s Ferlinghetti successfully entered the literary community. He taught briefly at the University of San Francisco, wrote reviews of poetry readings for the *San Francisco Chronicle,* and entered the poetry circles of KENNETH REXROTH and Robert Duncan. In 1952 Ferlinghetti met Peter Martin, editor of *City Lights,* a literary magazine, and in June 1953 they became co-owners of City Lights Bookstore. By 1955 Martin sold his interest in the store to Ferlinghetti, who went forward as the lone owner of the bookstore and director of publications for City Lights Books.

Ferlinghetti launched the Pocket Poets Series in 1955 with *Pictures of the Gone World.* The second book in the series was Rexroth's *30 Spanish Poems of Love and Exile* (1955), and the third was Kenneth Patchen's *Poems of Humor and Protest* (1955).

On October 7, 1955, Ferlinghetti attended the legendary reading at the Six Gallery in San Francisco, where Rexroth was moderator and where Ginsberg for the first time read a portion of "HOWL" in public. Ferlinghetti, imitating Ralph Waldo Emerson's response to Walt Whitman, sent a telegram to Ginsberg: "I greet you at the beginning of a great career. When do I get the manuscript?"

HOWL AND OTHER POEMS (1956) became the fourth book in the Pocket Poets Series. The book was printed in England, and the United States Customs seized copies. The prosecutor declined to pursue the case and released the seized copies, but San Francisco authorities entered the case, arresting Ferlinghetti and his associate, Shig Murao, for selling obscene material. The American Civil Liberties Union posted bail and provided legal defense, and after a well-publicized trial, on October 3, 1957, Judge Clayton Horn declared that *Howl and Other Poems* was not obscene. Made notorious through the controversy, the book sold well and became a classic of Beat literature, with Ferlinghetti emerging as a champion of free expression.

With this new fame, Ferlinghetti hoped for a publication of his own, and James Laughlin, the head of New Directions, took an interest, publishing some selections by Ferlinghetti in the magazine *New Directions* and encouraging Ferlinghetti to develop a full-size manuscript. In 1958 Laughlin published Ferlinghetti's *A Coney Island of the Mind,* which included a new sequence of poems, a group of poems intended for performance with jazz accompaniment; a selection of poems from *Pictures of the Gone World. A Coney Island of the Mind* sold well and enjoyed enduring popularity.

By 1960 Ferlinghetti became an important editor in the world of small literary magazines. With BOB KAUFMAN, John Kelley, William J. Margolis, and Ginsberg, Ferlinghetti edited *Beatitude,* a mimeographed publication of great freedom and expression. With DAVID MELTZER and MICHAEL McCLURE, Ferlinghetti edited *Journal for the Protection of All Beings,* a magazine emphasizing political and social views. Under Ferlinghetti's direction, *City Lights,* the magazine originated by Peter Martin, became *City Lights Journal.* Ferlinghetti also continued his work as editor and publisher for City Lights Books, producing new volumes in the Pocket Poets Series and publishing numerous other books as well, including KADDISH AND OTHER POEMS (1960) by Ginsberg and BOOK OF DREAMS (1961) by Kerouac. Although Ferlinghetti enjoyed many successes as a publisher, he also chose not to publish ON THE ROAD by Kerouac and NAKED LUNCH by WILLIAM S. BURROUGHS, thereby missing the opportunity to publish the three signal works of the Beat Generation: *Howl and Other Poems, On the Road,* and *Naked Lunch.*

To provide a retreat for private reflection, in 1960 Ferlinghetti purchased some land in Bixby Canyon near Big Sur in California. A small and simple cabin on this land became the setting for Kerouac's novel BIG SUR (1963) after Ferlinghetti arranged for Kerouac to spend time enjoying privacy. In the novel, the character Lorenz Monsanto is based on Ferlinghetti.

Ferlinghetti also resumed his world travels, venturing to various countries where communism was emerging: in Latin America, he visited Cuba, Chile, and Nicaragua; in Europe he traveled to Germany, France, Spain, and Russia; he even took an agonizingly long train ride across Siberia. In the United States during the 1970s, Ferlinghetti intensified his activism, allying himself with the United Farm Workers, antinuclear protests, and campaigns against whaling.

Although Ferlinghetti never lost sight of his identity as a painter, his successes as an author, publisher, and activist overshadowed his painting for many years. Nevertheless, Ferlinghetti's writings frequently included references to great works of visual art, including works by Goya, Monet, Pissaro, and Klimt. In 1994, at "The Beats: Legacy and Celebration," a conference held at New York University, Ferlinghetti's paintings were included in a special exhibition. Ferlinghetti also had showings at the George Krevsky Gallery in San Francisco and at various other galleries.

At about the time of "The Beats: Legacy and Celebration," Ferlinghetti's *These Are My Rivers: New and Selected Poems* (1994) was published by New Directions. The collection revealed Ferlinghetti's standard practice of blending familiar works from his career with a selection of new material.

How to Paint Sunlight (2001) reveals the painter's perspective in Ferlinghetti's work as he refers various times to patterns of light in the city. In *Life Studies, Life Stories* (2003), one can see Ferlinghetti's drawings. In *Americus, Book I* (2004), Ferlinghetti turns his attention again to the American political and social scene with characteristic humor and satire.

Honors have accumulated for Ferlinghetti, especially in San Francisco, where in 1998 he became the city's first poet laureate. In 1994 an alley in San Francisco was named Via Ferlinghetti. In 2003 Ferlinghetti was given the Robert Frost Memorial Medal, was the recipient the Authors Guild Lifetime Achievement Award, and was made a member of the American Academy of Arts and Letters.

William Lawlor

"First They Slaughtered the Angels"
Lenore Kandel (1967)
This epic poem is a graphic protest against martial violence, social and spiritual desecration, and political oppression. Collected in Kandel's 1967 book *Word Alchemy*, the poem derives from an earlier period of composition centered in Beat aesthetics and cultural expression, the register in which the poet first raised voice and vision. The poem is spoken by a collective narrator—"we"—who represents survivors of an unspecified holocaust, the "angels" left after the first slaughter. These survivors have been witness to surreal barbarity ("the bellies of women split open and children rip their / way out with bayonets") and slaughterhouse cannibalism ("the cherubim are gone / they have eaten them and cracked their bones for marrow"), the work of the murderous invaders of the title line. The poem seeks revenge and swears defiant resistance to the dark forces seeking to impose conformity and surrender at any cost.

The five-section epic depicts war zone destruction, watchful hidden resistance, and then a regrouping, as if telling of a descent into hell that is followed by a rise from the underground ("we are rolling away the stones from underground, from the / caves") to "do battle" in revenge. This journey is voiced in terms of Beat Generation themes and aesthetics and gives way to the emergence of a new-age suggestive of the sixties counterculture, so the poem seems to span the two countercultural bohemian eras of its time. Beat Generation nihilism and dour cold-war predictions depict the celestial slaughter, as divine allusions mix with earthly locations ("who flushed St. Peter's keys down the mouth of a / North Beach toilet?") and contemporary slogans ("in an effort to make friends and influence people"). The cold-war fifties of bomb shelters and nuclear paranoia ("radioactive eyes") mingles with domestic retreats to Levittowns of "dishwashers and milltowns." Junkies, catatonics, and androgynes make appeals for deliverance, but only a weary and wary hope is permitted.

The poem's performance of signature images and verse forms from WILLIAM S. BURROUGHS and ALLEN GINSBERG, which typify Kandel's Beat-inflected works, align it with the early postwar hipster manifestations. Kandel's evocations of Burroughs's visions of totalitarian torment ("the penises of men are become blue steel machine guns / they ejaculate bullets, they spread death as an orgasm") are modified by surrealist images evocative of "HOWL": "standing spreadlegged with open sphincters weeping soap suds / from our radioactive eyes / and screaming / for the ultimate rifle / the messianic cannon / the paschal bomb." Uses of anaphora and long-lined catalogues also make reference to Ginsberg and his Whitmanic borrowings. The "Moloch" section of "Howl" comes through in a skillful passage that likewise blends its enunciation and form: "Lobotomy for every man! / and they have nominated a eunuch for president / Lobotomy for the housewife! / Lobotomy for the business man! / Lobotomy for the nursery schools! / and they have murdered the angels." The poem writhes in contempt for oppression.

This 1950s-inflected epic envisions the 1960s in the febrile aftermath of the angels' holocaust. Rising like Lazarus from the grave, the hipster–warrior survivors, emboldened by vision ("peyote-visioned eyes"), vow confrontation and revenge: "we shall stare face to face with naked eyes." From the cold war to the dawn of the antiwar counterculture of the love generation, the poem's jaded witnesses testify against the slaughter of "angels," the affliction or "armageddon" of the narration.

Bibliography

Cook, Bruce. *The Beat Generation: The Tumultuous '50s Movement and Its Impact on Today.* New York: Scribner, 1971.

Gifford, Barry, and Lawrence Lee. *Jack's Book: An Oral Biography of Jack Kerouac.* New York: St. Martin's Press, 1978.

Johnson, Ronna C. "Lenore Kandel's *The Love Book:* Psychedelic Poetics, Cosmic Erotica, and Sexual Politics in the Mid-sixties Counterculture." In *Reconstructing the Beats,* edited by Jennie Skerl, 89–104. New York: Palgrave Macmillan, 2004.

Wolf, Leonard. *Voices From the Love Generation.* Boston: Little, Brown, 1968.

Ronna Johnson

First Third, The Neal Cassady (1971)

This autobiography is one of the least discussed books to come out of the Beat movement. This is not without irony since its author, NEAL CASSADY, was the human bonfire before which Beat leaders JACK KEROUAC and ALLEN GINSBERG warmed their eager hands. In the early, heady years of their association, Kerouac and Ginsberg could not get enough of this all-American oddball. They thrilled to their new friend's antic behavior and virile charisma.

In a 1952 letter to Ginsberg, Kerouac went so far as to include the reform school alumnus–car thief–inveterate womanizer–railroad brakeman in the "genuine literary movement" at hand. Although he would go on to make Cassady famous as the basis for the fast-talking Dean Moriarty in ON THE ROAD, Kerouac believed that Cassady was much more than a muse; he thought that his beloved friend was a real writer who just needed to sit down and get to work. But the mere act of sitting down did not come easily to the frenetic Cassady, and writing was not his calling, as it was for Kerouac.

Still, Cassady set to work on an autobiography in 1948. According to CAROLYN CASSADY, the most enduring of his several wives, he wrote *The First Third* sporadically in a period of six years. In the second edition of *The First Third* (City Lights, 1981), she explains that her husband's "last concentrated efforts to rewrite" occurred in 1954 when he was laid up with work-related injuries. Ginsberg and City Lights publisher LAWRENCE FERLINGHETTI were urging him to finish the book and get it into print, and Carolyn was glad to help out: "We worked together on it from the beginning, but I made as few suggestions as possible to guarantee the book would reflect his thinking and his style exclusively, for better or for worse." City Lights finally published *The First Third* in 1971, three years after Cassady had died a few days shy of his 42nd birthday.

It seems that he had originally intended to write a more complete autobiography, but his preoccupation with detail created a major hindrance. The revised text in the second edition, which incorporates Cassady's annotations and additions discovered after his death, stands at 138 pages. The prologue recounting his ancestry and his parents' failed marriage takes up roughly a third of the narrative. The remaining three chapters cover Cassady's childhood travails in the company of his father, an alcoholic bum. At the end of the book, Cassady has reached the ripe age of seven. Cassady had barely made a dent in his life story when he set it aside for good.

The First Third is an undeniably flawed book. For starters, the title is a misnomer since the book covers only the first *sixth* of the author's sadly truncated life. More important, the story lacks the spontaneous ebullience that Kerouac admired in Cassady's letters, and it is short on introspection, opting instead for a relentless cataloguing of occurrences. Yet it is also undeniably interesting, even apart from the author's fame and famous connections, and deserves consideration as a true Beat text.

Reading it, one senses what made Cassady a legendary monologuist. His recollections of Denver's streets in the 1930s are photographic in detail, and his depictions of Depression-era bums are unsentimental without being cruel. Like HERBERT HUNCKE, another Beat-movement raconteur and icon, Cassady had a vast fund of unusual experience on which to draw. When he was six, his father took him away from the household where they had both been beaten up regularly by Cassady's bullying half-brothers. Fleeing to a flophouse called the Metropolitan felt like a step up at the time. "Yes, without a doubt, I had a matchless edification in observing the scum right from the start," Cassady writes with cheerful cynicism. "Of course, being with brow-beaten men, surly as they sometimes were, I gained certain unorthodox freedoms not ordinarily to be had by American boys of six. Also, my usually-drunk father (or on his way to that condition) was of necessity a bit lax in his discipline. Still, I didn't often take advantage of him, since I really loved the old boy."

Young Cassady and his father shared a top-floor room at the Metropolitan with "Shorty," a double amputee who slept on a three-foot shelf and supported his alcoholism by begging. Although Shorty "stank of body smell and was very ugly, with a no-forehead face full of a grinning rubber mouth that showed black stubbed teeth," he did not prey on Cassady. But Cassady did encounter child molesters, and sex with little girls was part of his early experience as well. Cassady does not gloss over these encounters, though they do not seem to have been of great importance to him. Instead, it is the relationship with his father to which he returns repeatedly.

On one occasion, father and son had become separated on a freight train hurdling east from California. Imagining that he had lost his fa-

ther forever, Cassady was beside himself with fear and misery, only to discover belatedly that his father had hopped aboard another car on the same train. None of the other bums in Cassady's car had thought to suggest this possibility, nor had the elder Cassady attempted to yell out reassurances. The frightening episode left Cassady emotionally bruised but wiser. As a very young boy, he realized that he had more intelligence and foresight than his father and his father's kind.

The question that *The First Third* implicitly asks is, what would young Cassady do with his keen mind and insatiable curiosity about the world? This sliver of an autobiography points accurately toward a life of hardship and adventuresome scrappiness. Though he eventually moved back in with his mother and his siblings, his primary bond was with his father, a bond that Kerouac commemorated in the elegiac allusion to "old Dean Moriarty, the father we never found" at the end of *On the Road*. Given the family history recounted in such detail in the prologue, perhaps *The First Third* is more accurately seen as a memoir about the elder Neal Cassady rather than an autobiography. Indecisive and inadequate in so many ways, "the old boy" was still the great love of his son's difficult life.

Hilary Holladay

For Love: Poems 1950–1960 Robert Creeley (1962)

For Love, ROBERT CREELEY's first volume of collected poems, is widely accepted as one of his finest. Divided into three sections, 1950–1955, 1956–1958, and 1959–1960, the poems trace a tumultuous period of the poet's life—from marital turmoil with his first wife, their separation and divorce, to love's reentrance upon meeting and marrying his second wife. Alternately tender and tragic, the poems represent, as Cynthia Edleberg argues in *Robert Creeley's Poetry: A Critical Introduction*, the poet's determination to understand love while mapping its confusing terrain. In addition, as Arthur L. Ford suggests in his analysis of *For Love*, Creeley also struggles to negotiate the sometimes conflicting goals of marriage and the life of a poet.

The poems in Part 1, the most cynical of the volume, were written during the disintegration of Creeley's first marriage. Opening with "Hart Crane," and "Le Fou" for CHARLES OLSON, Creeley establishes himself in the company of accomplished poets, while also adding ideas of friendship and profession to his thoughts on love. But the third and fourth poems, "A Song," and "The Crisis," establish what is to be the volume's major theme: mapping the love of man and woman, husband and wife, and what feels now like a song, then like a crisis. His growing disillusionment with love and emotion become apparent in such poems as "The Immoral Proposition" where the poet decides that "If you never do anything for anyone else / you are spared the tragedy of human relation- / ships." In "The Operation" he calls love and marriage "just an old / habitual relationship" and even compares the two in "The Business" to a barter, "a remote chance on / which you stake / yourself."

Parts 2 and 3 trace the final disintegration of Creeley's first marriage and his love and remarriage to his second wife. Thus, as Edleberg points out, the poet executes the tricky maneuver of transferring his love from one woman to another, augmenting his theme of love's elusiveness. In "Love Comes Quietly," that transfer appears complete:

> Love comes quietly,
> finally, drops
> about me, on me,
> in the old ways.
>
> What did I know
> thinking myself
> able to go
> alone all the way.

Here, though "finally" implies relief and "drops / about me, on me, / in the old ways" retreats to ambiguity, Creeley understands love's necessity in his life, with all its vagaries and misunderstandings.

The final and title poem in *For Love* seems to sum up Creeley's explorations. He concludes that love changes from day to day, moment to moment, and despite "tedium" and "despair" and the desire "to / turn away, endlessly / to turn away," everything the poet knows "derives / from what it

teaches me." Thus, even without a definitive answer, "into the company of love/ it all returns," for good, for bad, *for love*.

Bibliography

Edleberg, Cynthia. *Robert Creeley's Poetry: A Critical Introduction*. Albuquerque: University of New Mexico Press, 1978.

Faas, Ekbert, and Maria Trombacco. *Robert Creeley: A Biography*. Hanover, N.H.: University Press of New England, 2001.

Ford, Arthur L. *Robert Creeley*. Boston: Twayne, 1978.

Jennifer Cooper

Frazer, Brenda (Bonnie Bremser) (1939–)

One of the most intelligent, resourceful, and talented women of the Beat Generation, Frazer is most well known for writing the underground classic TROIA: MEXICAN MEMOIRS (1969), published as *For the Love of Ray* (1971) in England. Frazer started life far from the Beat world that she would embrace and eventually leave. She was born in Washington, D.C., on July 23, 1939. Her father worked for the Department of Labor, and her mother was a depressed housewife who would be institutionalized and administered shock treatment. Frazer dropped out of Sweet Briar College and briefly attended Georgetown before joining the Beat scene. On March 21, 1969, she married Beat poet RAY BREMSER, whom she had first met after a poetry reading in Washington, D.C., a reading that featured Bremser, GREGORY CORSO, ALLEN GINSBERG, LeRoi Jones, Peter Orlovsky, A. B. Spellman, and Cecil Taylor. Ray's long prose poem "ANGEL" is about Frazer. After violating parole, Ray spent six months in Trenton State Prison. A letter from William Carlos Williams helped him get out. When Ray fled to Mexico in 1961 to escape incarceration for a crime that he claimed he did not commit, Frazer followed him with their baby daughter, Rachel, who was later given up for adoption. Frazer recalls, "The reason the law was after us was because Ray had been accused of an armed robbery he didn't do. . . . My testimony and the fact that a fellow parolee was with us that night were both inconsequential. We were desperadoes because Ray had just served 6 months for violating parole by getting married without permission and talking on the radio about marijuana. . . . We were desperados because we'd just had a baby and couldn't face another separation and what seemed like a set up." Elaine de Kooning, the wife of Willem de Kooning, lent them money. Sent back to Texas after an arrest in Mexico, Ray received bail money from Elaine de Kooning's friends and escaped to Mexico again to stay with Beat poet PHILIP LAMANTIA. Frazer's life on the run with Ray was recorded in *Troia*.

After leaving Ray, she raised their second daughter Georgia. In the 1970s she spent time on Ginsberg's farm in Cherry Valley, New York, and had an unconventional relationship with a married dairy farmer, who had two sons with her. In the 1980s she worked for the Department of Agriculture as a soil scientist. Frazer has been published in the Beat journals *Fuck You: A Magazine of the Arts, Blue Beat, Down Here*, and *Intrepid*. She is presently working on the prequel and a sequel to *Troia*; the trilogy is tentatively entitled "Troia: Beat Chronicles."

Bibliography

Grace, Nancy M. "Artista: Brenda (Bonnie) Frazer." *Breaking the Rule of Cool: Interviewing And Reading Women Beat Writers*, edited by Nancy M. Grace and Ronna C. Johnson, 109–130. Jackson: University Press of Mississippi, 2004.

Hemmer, Kurt. "The Prostitute Speaks: Brenda Frazer's *Troia: Mexican Memoirs*." *Paradoxa* 18 (2003): 99–117.

Kurt Hemmer

G

Get Home Free **John Clellon Holmes** (1964)
This third novel by JOHN CLELLON HOLMES was
his favorite and arguably his best but also his least
known. Written between January 1961 and October 1962, it succeeded in getting Holmes out of a
frustrating writer's block. The story follows May
Delano, Dan Verger, and Paul Hobbes (Holmes's
persona), who were all characters from Holmes's
first novel GO. The major theme of the novel is
sexuality as spirituality. *Get Home Free* is in part a
sequel to *Go*. In *Go*, Delano was partially based on
JACK KEROUAC's first wife Joan Haverty, who was
living with Bill Cannastra (Agatson in *Go* and in
Get Home Free) at the time of Cannastra's death
in a subway accident. Though only a type in *Go*,
Delano is one of Holmes's most fully realized characters in *Get Home Free* and is representative of
Holmes's newfound feminism. Verger was based
on Russell Durgin, a friend of ALLEN GINSBERG's,
whose book collection was pilfered by HERBERT
HUNCKE. Hobbes, the voyeuristic chronicler of
Beat life in *Go*, is also a major character in *Get
Home Free*, although all we hear about *Go*'s visionary poet Stofsky (based on Ginsberg) is that he has
taken a straight job in advertising, and all we hear
about the larger than life novelist Gene Pasternak
(based on Kerouac) is that he has taken a bus to
Mexico.

In part one of the novel, "New York: The
End," Verger moves into Agatson's old loft with
Delano after Agatson's death, and the legendarily
wild parties that typified Agatson's self-destruction
become an "Autumn of bad parties." Holmes presents Verger's existentialist speeches and his belief that excess is a sign of "a spiritual need" with
a backward-looking irony. Delano is also weary of
hearing Verger's speeches. The two break up, with
Verger going back to his hometown in New England, Old Grafton, and Delano returning South.

In Part Two, as he did in *Go*, Holmes creates
characters who are representative of their generation, this time as they move from the drunken
1940s to the hungover 1950s: "the frantic postwar
years when nothing seemed worth one's time but
Third Avenue beers and Times Square bop, Harlem pot and Village sex; when the jangled rhythm
of the war carried over into the fake peace, and
we all wanted wild things, strange things, any extreme of spirit, and (all unknowing) prepared to
put our hopes underground for the fatuous Fifties.
All the night-long talk, and nerves, and drink, and
exhaustion had burned me down until I was clear
and minimal." To come to terms with his stagnant
life, Verger flees New York for his hometown of Old
Grafton (Holmes's hometown of Old Saybrook),
where he tries to decide whether to return to New
York or to take the trip to Europe that he has long
promised himself. He stays with his mother but falls
into his New York habits of dissipation and spends
his time trailing around after the town drunk, Old
Man Molineaux. Old Man Molineaux's great mistake in life is that he failed to leave home and go
to sea, as he always dreamed. Verger takes his cue
and resolves to go to Europe after all but not before
he witnesses Molineaux drinking himself into such
a state that he has to be hospitalized. Verger learns

from Old Man Molineuax (who could be Verger in 30 years, and who also resembles Verger's father) that you have to "come to terms with the hateful past. . . . Otherwise people just take out their disappointments on one another like we did, like my mother and father did."

The third part of the novel is a brief transitional section in which Verger and Delano meet up briefly while Verger prepares to leave for Europe and Delano prepares to head back home to small-town Georgia. There she hooks back up with the old crowd and talks them into going to a bar on the African-American side of town where they used to party as teens. The southerners try to explain to her that race relations in the South are more sensitive because of the emerging civil rights movement than they were five years earlier, but she does not listen. It is a typical setting for a Holmes novel, a moment between being and becoming.

At the bar, the novel's one major coincidence occurs—Hobbes, the Holmes character from *Go*, is playing piano for a young, blind, African-American singer, who could be out of *The HORN*. Hobbes tells Delano over drinks that he had to leave New York before he became a conformist with a straight job. The times, he says, are ones in which you want to be *out* of step, not in. Hobbes takes her back to a ramshackle antebellum mansion where musicians, drug users, and interracial couples hang out. Hobbes, it turns out, has developed a heroin habit. He and Willie, a converted Moslem from Detroit, argue about whether or not whites can ever truly understand the reality of being black. Hobbes urges him to forget the color of his skin, and Willie replies that the moment he does that, he will be lynched. Apparently, Willie makes his point, for later, when Hobbes tries to make generalizations about his "generation" (as he did unselfconsciously throughout *Go*), he realizes that such generalizations cannot include both blacks and whites, whose experiences are so different. In this sense, the novel addresses Holmes's and Kerouac's roles as the labelers of their generation, and Holmes, quite appropriately, points out that *beat*, in spite of its roots in jazz, was primarily associated with white writers. The book thus serves to reflect the assumptions of Hobbes's two previous novels. It also features a self-revealing moment that must be Holmes's own

confession about the New York crowd chronicled in *Go*: "I used to wonder," Hobbes tells Delano, "what was behind all your eyes, all of you, and I know I was never a part of it." Holmes's detractors, quick to say that he presents a "square" picture of the Beats must, therefore, come to terms with Holmes's own acknowledgment of his outside status among these outsiders.

At the end of the fourth part of the book, Delano comes to a kind of Buddhist recognition that heaven is right under her nose, already there. She has this satori on the verge of exhaustion from all-night marijuana smoking and moonshine drinking. She is "beat," she says, but "that need not be bitter simply because it is bleak."

In part five, Delano returns to New York from the South, and Verger returns to New York from Europe. Almost without trying, they find themselves together again. As Holmes says in his 1987 introduction, "I wanted to think they had a chance for provisional happiness, a temporary reprieve, knowing for a certainty they would have made one last try for it." As *Go* described the moment between being and becoming when "hot" jazz turned to "cool," here Holmes describes this existential couple's movement from exhaustion to a tentative new life. In larger terms, he describes a society also in transition: "It is an ambiguous time," Holmes writes in his introduction, "of affluence and lethargy, prosperity and conformity, false gaiety and deep unease."

Holmes considered this book to be his best novel of the three he completed before his death in 1988. Critics often point to *Get Home Free* as being one of the few works by a Beat writer in which race relations are addressed as a central topic (Kerouac's *The Subterraneans* being another). Holmes agreed, believing that the book was ahead of its time in this respect. Kerouac, who kept Holmes as a friend while discarding most of his other friends from the 1940s in the 1960s, praised the book in a December 11, 1963, letter which included a blurb for the book jacket: "Here is my blurb for GET HOME FREE and every word I mean—I like it, and some parts of it are *great*." He particularly likes the reappearance of Hobbes as a piano player in the South and says that it made him "realize you actually dream such drizzly stuff for your vision of America, that, in fact, you're a maniac." He also singles out the "Negro–White party down South" for praise. When the book received poor reviews, Kerouac wrote to Holmes on October 16, 1964: "Had your reviews of FREE sent to me and read them and commented to Sterling [Kerouac's agent, Sterling Lord] you were being treated like me. . . . down to the bone, publishing has been taken over by out-and-out con men who are the Mephistopheleses to your Faustian effort. No mind. Autumnleaf laurel you." It is one of the rare moments when Kerouac expressed his empathy for the plight of a fellow Beat author.

Rob Johnson

Ghost Tantras **Michael McClure** (1964)

MICHAEL McCLURE's collection *Ghost Tantras* may represent the poet's most innovative and bizarre experimentation with language. The book includes 99 poems written using McClure's trademark "beast language," an invented idiom based on the sounds of animals and divorced from normal human discourse, and yet still communicative on some deeper biological level. The lexicon of McClure's beast language is varied and expressive in ways which at times surpass more traditional forms of poetic discourse. Ranging from anguished howls, to roars of sensual delight, to affectionate purring, the invented vocabulary of *Ghost Tantras* is at its most effective when read aloud.

McClure had long been intrigued by the utterances of other animals—and the way that human discourse could often be seen in light of the way that other creatures communicate. Beast language is, at its core, yet another of the poet's devices for weaning readers from their human assumptions and societal conventions, a way to bridge the gap between human and animal, between mind and the physical body. As critic Gregory Stephenson notes, McClure's beast language poems are "shamanistic invocations, incantations, evocations of the beast spirit, of mammal consciousness."

The collection features a striking cover photograph by Wallace Berman of McClure, almost unrecognizable, in half-human, half-beast makeup, a clue to the melding of human and nonhuman

language contained in the poems. In some of the pieces, such as the first poem in the collection, beast language makes up almost the entirety of the stanza, allowing the poet to immerse the reader in a new language in which the tone and textures of the spoken word become more important than vocabulary and meaning of the written text:

> GOOOOOOR! GOOOOOOOOOO!
> GOOOOOOOOOR!
> GRAHHH! GRAHH! GRAHH!
> Grah gooooor! Ghahh! Graaarr! Greeeeer!
>   Grayowhr!
> Greeeeee
> GRAHHRR! RAHHR! GRAGHHRR! RAHR!
> RAHRIRAHHR! GRAHHHR! GAHHR!
> HRAHR!
> BE NOT SUGAR BUT BE LOVE
> looking for sugar!
> GAHHHHHHHH!
> ROWRR!
> GROOOOOOOOOOH!

In most cases in *Ghost Tantras*, beast language is interspersed with traditional human speech. The results are a fascinating, if at times unsuccessful, experiment in broadening the boundaries of poetic discourse, as in this passage from chorus 39, dedicated to Marilyn Monroe on the occasion of her death:

> I hope you have entered a sacred paradise for full
> warm bodies, full lips, full hips, and laughing
>   eyes!
> AHH GHROOOR! ROOOHR. NOH THAT
>   OHH!
> OOOH . . .
> Farewell perfect mammal
> Fare thee well from thy silken couch and dark
>   day!
> AHH GRHHROOOR! AHH ROOOOH
>   GARR

As Lee Bartlett notes, concerning McClure's beast language collection: "The poet uses language to transcend language, probably a losing proposition." Still, *Ghost Tantras* represents one of the boldest experiments in 20th-century literature, ranking with WILLIAM S. BURROUGHS's cut-up

texts, JACK KEROUAC's *VISIONS OF CODY,* and ED
DORN's *GUNSLINGER* as a work of visionary innovation.

Bibliography

Bartlett, Lee. "Meat Science to Wolf Net: Michael
McClure's Poetics of Revolt." *The Sun Is But a
Morning Star: Studies in West Coast Poetry and Poetics.* Albuquerque: University of New Mexico Press,
1989, 107–123.

Phillips, Rod. *Michael McClure.* Western Writers Ser. 159.
Boise, Idaho: Boise State University Press, 2003.

Stephenson, Gregory. "From the Substrate: Notes on
Michael McClure." *The Daybreak Boys: Essays on
the Literature of the Beat Generation.* Carbondale:
Southern Illinois University Press, 1990, 105–130.

Rod Phillips

Ginsberg, Allen (1926–1997)

Along with GARY SNYDER, Allen Ginsberg is the
central poet of the Beat Generation and is one of
the most popular U.S. poets of the 20th century.
He also served as a de facto literary agent for many
Beat writers, as an intermediary between these
writers and potential publishers. Moreover, Ginsberg is a figure who participated in major schools of
contemporary American poetry, including the San
Francisco Renaissance, the Black Mountain poets,
the Confessionals, and the New York School. He
also is a major figure in American gay literature.
Ginsberg's influence on American culture, too,
has been wide. He was a leader in the antiwar and
drug decriminalization movements of the 1960s
and 1970s; he is one of the most widely known
Buddhist converts in the ongoing cultural dialogue
between the Buddhist East and Judeo–Christian
West; and he was among the major voices in the
antinuclear movement, the struggle for gay civil
rights, and the Democratic Left's opposition to the
rise of the Religious Right in the United States. His
political activism, in addition to his explicit borrowing from Whitman as an internationalist symbol of American poetic speech, has given Ginsberg
perhaps the most global reach of all Beat poets,
and his work has been translated into more than
22 languages.

Allen Ginsberg chanting at his apartment. *(courtesy of
Larry Keenan)*

Ginsberg was born on June 3, 1926, in Newark, New Jersey, the son of Louis Ginsberg, a poet
and schoolteacher, and Naomi Ginsberg. Louis's
family was active in Socialist circles, and Naomi's
in the Communist Party. His childhood background offered him early identifications with the
literature and politics of the socially disenfran-
chised: the working class, immigrants, Russians,
and Jews. Ginsberg's early years were marked by
his mother's deteriorating mental condition, the
narrative of which is recounted in his long poem,
"KADDISH." He was just six years old when she
was hospitalized for the first time, and she entered
Greystone Mental Hospital for what would become
a two-year hospital stay when Ginsberg was 11. He
was kicked out of Columbia University because of
his association with the stolen-goods ring involving HERBERT HUNCKE, who had stashed property in

Ginsberg's apartment. As a condition of his readmittance to Columbia, Ginsberg agreed to be sent to the Columbia Presbyterian Psychiatric Institute for psychiatric treatment. There, he met Carl Solomon, to whom "HOWL" was dedicated.

A catalyst in Ginsberg's development as a visionary poet was his alleged William Blake vision of 1948, an experience that he has recounted in numerous interviews and that serves as an allegory for his 1961 poem "The Lion for Real." He was alone in his apartment and had just finished masturbating when he was overwhelmed by the voice of Blake reciting the poem "Ah! Sunflower." As he mentioned in his 1966 interview with the *Paris Review,* Ginsberg felt as if "some hand had placed the sky but . . . the sky was the living blue hand itself. . . . God was in front of my eyes—existence itself was God." Later, in the Columbia bookstore, the feeling persisted. Ginsberg felt that he, the clerk, and the customers "all had the consciousness, it was like a great *uncon*scious that was running between [sic] all of us that everybody *was* completely conscious." For Ginsberg, this event, whether real or hallucinatory, authorized him to write visionary poetry in the tradition of Western prophecy. However, the vision also had a damaging effect on his life. He spent the next 14 years obsessively trying to recapture the feeling of this vision through drug use, and it was not until a meeting with Tibetan lama Dudjom Rinpoche on his travels to India in 1962–63 that he stopped. Up to this point, his efforts to relive the Blake vision through drug use were marked by anxiety, and drugs had not returned him to the vision. However, as he stated in his dedication remarks to *Indian Journals,* Dudjom Rinpoche's remarks during their 1963 meeting helped him shake his attachment to the vision: According to Ginsberg, Rinpoche said, simply, "If you see anything horrible don't cling to it if you see anything beautiful don't cling to it." Rinpoche's advice was significant for Ginsberg as he crafted "The Change," a poem that appropriates language and imagery from the Buddhist Sattipathana Sutra as it dramatizes his effort to work through his attachment to the Blake vision. He repeated Rinpoche's words frequently throughout his career, in interviews and lectures, and applied them often to discussions of drug use, the poetics of visionary experience, and Buddhist doctrinal questions.

On graduation from Columbia, he worked for a time at public relations firm, eventually moving to San Francisco to begin graduate school. In the Bay Area, he began to focus more on poetry, eventually becoming one of the central figures in the San Francisco Renaissance. He also met his lifelong companion, Peter Orlovsky, in San Francisco. His first major poetic success was *HOWL AND OTHER POEMS,* with the title poem garnering enormous attention both for its rupture of prevailing New Critical aesthetic modes and for its ensuing obscenity trial, detailed below, which Ginsberg and his publisher, LAWRENCE FERLINGHETTI, won. Soon after the publication of *KADDISH AND OTHER POEMS,* Ginsberg began a series of international travels that disillusioned him from Soviet-style communism and introduced him to Eastern religious thought, especially Buddhism, to which he would convert in 1972. He spent most of his life based in New York City in a lower East Side apartment and shuttling back and forth between New York and Boulder, Colorado, where he cofounded the Jack Kerouac School of Disembodied Poetics at Naropa University. He died of liver cancer at age 70 in his New York apartment, surrounded by friends, associates, and Gelek Rinpoche, his last Buddhist teacher, who performed Tibetan rituals for the dying for him.

Although Ginsberg's reputation was built on lifelong accomplishments in poetry and political activism, his original goal in life simply was to become a labor lawyer. As recounted in "Kaddish," his ride on the ferry from his home in Paterson, New Jersey, to take his freshman entrance examination at Columbia University was a turning point in the development of a poetry that would emphasize his equally spiritual and political interests. He "[p]rayed on ferry to help mankind if admitted" to Columbia. He uttered this prayer in the name of some of the most important political and literary figures in his young life. It was a "vow" inspired by Nicola Sacco, Bartolomeo Vanzetti, Norman Thomas, Eugene V. Debs, John P. Altgeld, Carl Sandburg, and Edgar Allan Poe. At this period in his life, the young Ginsberg was sure that he would make a mark on the world—but as a lawyer, not a poet. According to one of Ginsberg's biographers, Barry Miles, this vow on the ferry "gave direction to Ginsberg's activities over the years, and that he used it as a benchmark whenever he was confused by a choice of courses of action."

Of course, Ginsberg's time at Columbia University is known not for studying law but instead for how it planted the seeds for the Beat Generation. While at Columbia, he met and became close with Lucien Carr, WILLIAM S. BURROUGHS, NEAL CASSADY, and JACK KEROUAC, and together they would form a "new vision," as they called it, for literature—what would become the Beat Generation. As both vow and prayer, Ginsberg's thoughts on the ferry affirm the activist impulse that would sustain the body of his work. That "benchmark" moment offers a window into the major concerns of his poetics of social change and religious questing.

The social and religious directions of his poetry are functions, too, of the environment in which

"Bad Company," San Francisco, 1965. Photographer Larry Keenan: "Robbie Robertson, Michael McClure, Bob Dylan, and Allen Ginsberg in the alley behind City Lights Books." *(courtesy of Larry Keenan)*

he grew up. His earliest and most famous poems in *Howl and Other Poems* (1956) and *Kaddish and Other Poems* (1961) document his struggles with his mother, who was a great inspiration to him but also was mentally ill and subject to numerous breakdowns; and his disappointment with his father, a locally renowned poet in New Jersey who preferred the quiet middle-class life of a schoolteacher despite the family's socialist-communist background. These early books, too, are windows into the poet's efforts to find a place for his homosexual identity in the repressive pre-Stonewall United States.

The family's political views resembled those of many Jewish immigrant families in the East Coast at the time, and for Ginsberg the influence of his Judaic background always would be a part of his political poetry. Early in his career, during the composition of "Howl," he began to envision himself as a poet-prophet in the literary tradition of Whitman and Blake. This form of self-representation could be seen as the perfect fusion of his earliest political and religious impulses because it is a literary tradition that finds a voice in the earliest social and spiritual concerns of the early Hebrew prophets of the Bible. Although the word *prophecy* has come to mean in common speech simply the ability to predict future events, the definition of the word from which Ginsberg took his identity was much more nuanced. The early biblical prophets were seen as forces of social and spiritual change. They were said to be subject to the direct influence of God, who spoke through them so that they might instruct the culture to turn away from socially and spiritually destructive practices. Prophets were visionary figures who served as intermediaries between everyday people and the word of God. It is from this biblical definition of *prophet* that Ginsberg wrote "Howl" and "Kaddish." In "Howl," he is concerned with reaching back to the visionary speech of prophecy to find language for the "secret heroes" of the Beat Generation—figures such as Kerouac, Cassady, Burroughs who were beaten down by the constraining culture of cold-war America. "Kaddish" is Ginsberg's elegy for his mother; it rewrites the Hebrew Kaddish prayer for the dead in speech described both as "prophesy as in the Hebrew Anthem" and "the Buddhist Book of Answers."

After "Kaddish," Ginsberg continued to write poems framed by the Western prophetic tradition. However, he increasingly emphasized how Western religiosity might be modified—at times, transformed—by traditions such as Hinduism and Buddhism. By the 1970s, Ginsberg's poetry became identified more with his Buddhist practice than with his Jewish background. In 1972, he took Tibetan Buddhist Bodhisattva vows with Chögyam Trungpa Rinpoche, and he began formal Buddhist study and practice with Trungpa, with whom he worked until Trungpa's death in 1987. Ginsberg formed the Jack Kerouac School of Disembodied Poetics within Trungpa's Naropa University (then Institute) in 1974. Naropa would become the first accredited Buddhist college in the United States. Ginsberg ran Naropa's Poetics Department, the academic name for the Kerouac School, and taught there and as Distinguished Professor at Brooklyn College through the end of his life. His classes at Naropa included Blake, the Beat Generation, Spiritual Poetics, Meditation and Poetics, and Spontaneous and Improvised Poetics. Ginsberg's study and practice with formal Tibetan Buddhist teachers continued after Trungpa's death, and he was a close student of Gelek Rinpoche, who was with Ginsberg when he died on April 5, 1997.

Ginsberg's many conflicts with governmental legal institutions began with the censorship trial over the book *Howl and Other Poems*. Seized by customs inspectors because of its frank portrayals of sex (both heterosexual and homosexual) and drug use, the book was at the center of a landmark U.S. obscenity case. State Superior Court Judge Clayton W. Horn eventually ruled that *Howl and Other Poems* could not be obscene—thereby sparing Ginsberg's publisher, Lawrence Ferlinghetti, and City Lights Bookstore clerk Shigeyoshi Murao from a jail term—because any work of art that possessed "some redeeming social importance" was protected by the Constitution.

In 1965 Ginsberg was expelled from Cuba and Czechoslovakia because of his outspoken support for free speech and sexual freedom in those countries. He publicly declared his outrage with Fidel Castro's persecution of homosexuals at Havana University. He was roused in the middle of the night and deported from Cuba. He then flew to Europe's Eastern Bloc, where more than 100,000 people in Prague crowned him "King of May" (*Kral Majales*) and led him through the streets of the city on a chair placed on the back of a flatbed truck. Ginsberg was viewed by the Communist Czech government as an outsider agitating a counterrevolutionary student movement. The police seized his notebook, and he was flown out of the country to London. His disillusionment with both sides of the cold war was dramatized best in "Kral Majales" (1965), his account of the trip to Czechoslovakia: "And *tho*' I am the King of May, the Marxists have beat me upon the street, kept me up all night in Police Station, followed me thru Springtime Prague, detained me in secret and deported me from our kingdom by airplane." When he returned to the United States, he was placed by the Federal Bureau of Investigation on its Dangerous Security List. As early as 1961, the U.S. Drug Enforcement Agency had begun a file on the poet, and afterward he was under periodic surveillance. Ginsberg was strip-searched for drugs on arrival in New York from the Czechoslovakia trip. As he waited for the authorities, Ginsberg managed to see the files that were on the table in the observation room. As biographer Michael Schumacher has reported, one of these documents went so far as to state, with no attribution, that both Ginsberg and his life partner, Peter Orlovsky, "were reported to be engaged in smuggling narcotics."

Still, Ginsberg maintained an active public profile as both an artist and activist. In 1966 he testified before the U.S. Senate on The Narcotic Rehabilitation Act of 1966. The stated purpose of the hearings was to establish sentencing and rehabilitation guidelines for federal drug offenses. Ginsberg testified on his experiences with hallucinogenic drugs such as LSD and *ayahuasca* and urged the Senate, in vain, to keep LSD a legal drug for scientific experimentation and controlled adult use.

Ginsberg's reputation as a poet and social critic was confirmed with the publication of *Howl and Other Poems* and *Kaddish and Other Poems*. He continued an output of poems significant to contemporary American poetry until his death. Ginsberg's major works of the 1960s include his long-poem Buddhist explorations "Angkor Wat" and "The Change," both written during a 1962–63

Allen Ginsberg, Michael McClure, and Bruce Conner chanting at Ginsberg's apartment, San Francisco, 1965. Photographer Larry Keenan: "After meeting Ginsberg for the first time, I was not in Allen's Fell St. apartment long before he rolled up the rug, sat down, and chanted mantras for around an hour. During that time Peter Orlovsky, Michael McClure, Bruce Conner, and I joined in. With this photograph, I wanted the viewer to have the feeling of what it was like to sit down and join in the chanting with the Beats." *(courtesy of Larry Keenan)*

trip through Asia, and "WICHITA VORTEX SUTRA," from *Planet News* (1968). His most notable poems of the 1970s include the work collected in FALL OF AMERICA: POEMS OF THESE STATES (1973), which won the National Book Award for poetry; and *Mind Breaths* (1978), a collection of Buddhist-inspired poems, including the well-known title poem from the collection which reflected his formal study and practice with Trungpa. The poet's literary output of the 1980s and 1990s, including *White Shroud* (1986) and *Cosmopolitan Greetings* (1994), reflects his continued desire to stretch the art form of the poem on the page to include songs, prayers (Eastern and Western), and chants.

White Shroud is especially significant for the poems "White Shroud" and "Black Shroud," both sequels to "Kaddish." In his later years, his efforts to blur the boundaries between poetry and popular music resulted in musical recordings of Blake's *Songs of Innocence and Experience;* collaborations with members of the bands The Clash and Sonic Youth; and recordings of his own poems put to music, such as Paul McCartney and Philip Glass's rendition of "The Ballad of the Skeletons," from Ginsberg's last book of poems, *Death and Fame: Final Poems* (1999).

Death and Fame collects a series of poems written as his body was giving out to liver cancer.

These poems are important for their acknowledgment that Ginsberg's reputation as a contemporary Whitman-inspired poet of the body is, like any other aspect of the politics of literary reputation, a construction. The poems demonstrate, through his body's wasting away, that Ginsberg always celebrated a body both ecstatic and anxious for its mortality. In poems such as "Here We Go 'Round the Mulberry Bush," "Bowel Song," and "Hepatitis, Body Itch," he celebrated the impermanence of the body in the language of abjection. In speaking with candor about the body, Ginsberg also dramatized Buddhist teachings on the body he had received from Trungpa and Gelek Rinpoche, both of whom advised their students to give up their attachments and aversions to corporeal pleasure and pain. In published remarks on Ginsberg's death, Gelek Rinpoche praised Ginsberg because he "put his heart and soul toward the benefit of people." Remarking that Ginsberg was responsible for bringing many Westerners to Buddhism, Rinpoche emphasized the need "to remember his concern, his message and his teaching, honesty, openness."

Bibliography

Ginsberg, Allen. *Collected Poems, 1947–1980.* New York: Harper & Row, 1984.
———. *Cosmopolitan Greetings: Poems 1986–1992.* New York: HarperCollins, 1994.
———. *Death and Fame: Last Poems, 1993–1997.* New York: HarperCollins, 1999.
———. *White Shroud: Poems, 1980–1985.* New York: Harper & Row, 1986.
Miles, Barry. *Ginsberg: A Biography.* New York: HarperCollins, 1989.
Schumacher, Michael. *Dharma Lion: A Critical Biography of Allen Ginsberg.* New York: St. Martin's, 1992.

Tony Trigilio

Go John Clellon Holmes (1952)

This first novel by JOHN CLELLON HOLMES is also the first "Beat" novel ever published, a roman à clef with portraits of some of the most important Beats before they became famous in the mid-1950s. It introduced the label "Beat Generation" to readers. Rather than spontaneous sketches, *Go* delivers well-crafted portraits of JACK KEROUAC (Gene Pasternak), ALLEN GINSBERG (David Stofsky), NEAL CASSADY (Hart Kennedy), and HERBERT HUNCKE (Albert Ancke) as struggling artists and visionaries. Holmes portrays himself as Paul Hobbes, the Beat legend Bill Cannastra as Bill Agatson, and WILLIAM S. BURROUGHS (offstage) as Will Dennison. The portrayal of Ginsberg is particularly interesting when examined alongside the poem "HOWL," which depicts many of the same events found in *Go*. The novel was originally entitled "The Daybreak Boys," the name of a 19th century New York gang, and was composed from 1949 to 1951. Gilbert Millstein, who would later write the famous review of Kerouac's ON THE ROAD that appeared in the *New York Times,* also praised Holmes's novel in the *Times,* but it was neither a critical nor a commercial success and was more or less forgotten until the emergence of the Beats as a significant artistic movement.

However, Millstein's reading of the book prompted him to ask Holmes to define a word that was frequently used in the book—*beat.* Holmes's "This is the Beat Generation," first published in the *New York Times Magazine* on November 16, 1952, marks the first definition of the Beat Generation. In the article, Holmes credits Jack Kerouac for coming up with the label. Still, *Go* saw print long before Kerouac's *On the Road.* Therefore, as Seymour Krim writes in his afterword for the republished edition of *Go,* "We've got to revise our opinions—the print assault of the Beat Generation was a joint charge, and John Clellon Holmes and his *Go* was every bit as important to commandeering the bourgeois printing presses as Kerouac's *On the Road* and Allen G.'s [Ginsberg's] *Howl.*" Holmes even suggested that the completion of *Go* was partially responsible for Kerouac's *On the Road:* "Jack read *Go* over the two years during which I wrote it, two years during which he was unsuccessfully trying to get *On the Road* on the road, and it was *after* he finished reading my first draft in early March of 1951 that he began what would be the final, twenty-day version of his own book, completed in late April of that year. I don't mean to suggest any influential connection between the two books (they rarely overlap in their material), but only to say that perhaps my rather darker view of 'beat experience' was a view he couldn't share—that he found alien to his own perception—and that these objections may have provided him a needed impetus." While *On the Road* is often characterized by naïveté, *Go* is cautious not to romanticize Beat indulgences. As James Atlas writes, "[W]hat distinguishes *Go* from Kerouac's own hectic testimony is its sobriety."

The first part of the novel is called "The Days of Visitation" and begins with Gene Pasternak waking up at five in the afternoon in the Manhattan apartment of Paul and Kathryn Hobbes. The highly excited poet Stofsky bursts in on Hobbes and Pasternak, who are discussing Pasternak's gloom about the fate of his unpublished novel (Kerouac's *The TOWN AND THE CITY*). Stofsky's party in this section is based on Ginsberg's 1948 July 4th party at his apartment in East Harlem. Kerouac first met Holmes at this party, and this party introduced Holmes to other Beats as well. Though he often focuses on his relationship with his first wife Marian (Kathryn in the novel), for much of *Go,* it is the relationships with Beat friends that drive the novel forward.

Hobbes (whose name reflects his strongly rational approach to life) describes the Beat characters he meets through Pasternak and Stofsky as having a "thirsty avidity for raw experience" that distinguishes them from the typical intellectuals who are more interested in judging others than in actually living. Readers of *Go* generally find Stofsky to be the most interesting character in the book, and several scenes are devoted to him. In an early scene, Stofsky, acting like a character in a Dostoyevsky novel (Holmes says Dostoyevsky was a primary influence on *Go*), comes to Hobbes's apartment to announce that he believes in God. He has come to this realization from reading William Blake's poetry. Stofsky's observation that "all systems are just mirrors" reflects the title of a collection of early poems by Ginsberg, *Empty Mirror* (1961). Later that evening, Hobbes finds himself in Agatson's neighborhood and drops in on him at his loft. Holmes's description of Agatson at home in his loft is the best account we have of the self-destructive Bill Cannastra's lifestyle. Cannastra was one of Tennessee Williams's lovers in the mid-1940s, and his wild behavior was notorious. Kathryn and Hobbes's dis-

cussion of sex and infidelity in this section should be looked at in the light of the Kinsey sex survey—which revealed in frank terms the true sexual behavior of Americans behind closed doors—and Wilhelm Reich's belief that orgasms were a healthy way of relieving stress and anxiety. As Hobbes says, justifying his wife's hypothetical infidelity, "It would be better than frustration."

The second part of the book is called "Children in the Markets," and as the title suggests it reveals the Beats as lost children in the overwhelming city. At a marijuana party, both Hobbes and Kathryn end up with other people. Kathryn goes off with Pasternak—although Holmes later said that an affair between Kerouac and his wife never happened. Twenty-five years after the book was published, he realized on rereading it that the Kathryn/Pasternak affair was his way of justifying his own adulterous relations in his first marriage—which, in the novel, are rendered only as a Platonic pen-pal relationship. Homosexuality is discussed somewhat more openly than infidelity. Stofsky's description of his father's repulsion over his confession that he is homosexual is an accurate portrayal of Louis Ginsberg's reaction to his son's similar confession: His father assumed that Ginsberg meant that he was a pederast.

Hart Kennedy's arrival is a highlight in this section. Kennedy gives the book its title as he sways to jazz music urging, "Go!" The Beats cruise Times Square looking for Ancke to buy some marijuana. Kennedy shares his philosophy that "Life is Holy" and, in general, sounds remarkably like Dean Moriarty, Kerouac's depiction of Neal Cassady in *On the Road*. Holmes stresses what Kerouac only suggests by showing Pasternak imitating Kennedy's behavior and adopting Kennedy's philosophy of life. Holmes also provides the most detailed account of Cassady's brief stay in New York at the end of 1948 and beginning of 1949, before he went back out on the road to visit Burroughs in New Orleans. The party described in this section was based on a New Year's Eve party thrown by Ginsberg. Kennedy's ecstatic reaction to jazz at an after-hours club can be compared to Kerouac's similar descriptions in *On the Road*. Both Kerouac and Holmes wished to write novels about jazz, and Holmes ended up actually writing *The HORN*.

In *Go,* Hobbes listens with interest to Kennedy's philosophy, but Kennedy's moral relativism does not appeal to Hobbes's strong sense of morality. Later, Stofsky accuses Hobbes of being a "liberal" in the sense that Columbia professor Lionel Trilling uses the term in *The Liberal Imagination:* someone who values important ideas more than men. Another chapter centering on morality concerns Ancke's theft of some valuable books owned by a friend of Stofsky's from Columbia. Kathryn, observing how Kennedy lives off Dinah's salary says, "That's the *beat* generation for you!" Holmes also provides an interesting description of how Kennedy survived in New York by shoplifting food. There is a particularly unflattering scene when Kennedy gets into a fight with Dinah and hits her in the face—in the process breaking his thumb, just as Neal Cassady broke his thumb in a fight with Luanne Henderson in San Francisco. Such scenes reveal that Holmes was not afraid to be critical of the Beats in this novel and seldom romanticized their actions.

Holmes's novel—once the identities of the real-life characters is decoded—is thus an invaluable account of the complicated relationships among the Beats. It is a fascinating account of the Beats' experiments with alternative lifestyles. After sleeping with Kathryn, Pasternak goes "on the road" with Kennedy to visit Dennison. Kathryn visits her mother, and Hobbes, stung by his wife's recent infidelity (in spite of his professed immunity to such feelings), tries to pay her back by having sex with a woman named Estelle. They party at the Go Hole, and Holmes, a very astute cultural observer, captures the moment when "hot" jazz gave way to a "cool" attitude. Kerouac describes a similar change in the underground atmosphere in *The SUBTERRANEANS.* Hobbes is impotent with Estelle, and after Kathryn discovers some love letters to another woman, she threatens to leave him.

The third and final section of *Go* is called "Hell," which reflects where Hobbes feels the antics of the Beats are leading. A key subplot of this section involves Stofsky allowing a group of criminals to stash stolen goods in his apartment. (In real life, and under similar circumstances, Ginsberg was arrested for possession of stolen goods.) Holmes's account of Ginsberg's arrest was the only such literary account available to his friends in 1952, for Ginsberg was institutionalized and subsequently "reformed" for a time. CAROLYN CASSADY remembers reading *Go* and learning the details of what happened. Huncke's account of the events can be found in *The EVENING SUN TURNED CRIMSON.* Stofsky's dream of talking with God is reflected in poems from this time, which are filled with his yearning to actually see and know God. This desire is still present in later poems where the desire is occasionally somewhat fulfilled.

When Pasternak returns from San Francisco, another key moment in Beat history is depicted. Kerouac's novel *The Town and the City* was accepted for publication on the very same day that Holmes's first novel (still unpublished) was rejected. As Holmes says, "The day when Pasternak's novel is accepted and Hobbes' is rejected happened precisely as it is reported here—one of the odd coincidences that characterized my friendship with Kerouac." Ironically, Kerouac's enthusiasm about actually being able to make a living as a writer would be reversed by the time *Go* appeared in print in 1952. By then, Kerouac had three books rejected for publication (including *On the Road*) and would not be in print again for another five years.

In yet another party description, Hobbes, Pasternak, and Kathryn go to Agatson's loft to celebrate his self-proclaimed last birthday. Agatson's self-destructive antics match eyewitness accounts of Cannastra's behavior. A phone call interrupts the party, and they learn that Stofsky and the others have been arrested. Agatson does not care and takes to the street in search of more beer. Holmes's detailed description of the car wreck that led to the arrest of Ginsberg and Huncke might have come from Ginsberg himself or, perhaps, from a copy of the account of those events that Ginsberg wrote for his lawyer. As Holmes portrays Stofsky here, he is beginning to wonder whether or not Ancke, Winnie, and Little Rock were really the types Blake had in mind when he valorized the "naked and outcast." Holmes shrewdly locates Stofsky's motivation for associating with these criminals in his desperate need for love that his own mother was never able to give him (see "Kaddish," by Ginsberg). In the end, it appears that Stofsky was destined to go through his masochistic punishment.

Ginsberg may well have courted such a disaster: As he told Tom Clark in the *Paris Review* interview, his Blake vision instructed him to pass through "the Gates of Wrath" (in Blake's poem "Morning") to come out the other side into a higher state of consciousness. His arrest and subsequent trial and institutionalization were those "gates." If the novel truly reflects reality, Holmes might have got the story of the arrest from Ginsberg while he was on parole awaiting trial. Stofsky tells Hobbes that the newspaper accounts of his adventure were inaccurate; accounts of the Ginsberg fiasco were printed in the April 23 edition of several New York newspapers, including the *Daily Mirror, Herald Tribune, World-Telegram, New York Times,* and *Daily News.* Lionel Trilling, called Bernard here, is the Columbia professor who agreed to write Ginsberg a character letter. Stofsky says the conditions of writing such a letter were that he swear allegiance to "society"—the liberal society that Trilling described in his famous book, *The Liberal Imagination.* Hobbes's reaction is one of horror: Stofsky is being strongarmed into renouncing his own beliefs by a member of the so-called intellectual establishment. Burroughs's reaction to these events was similar. "Howl," written seven years later, can be seen as a repudiation of the "society" Trilling forced Ginsberg to join.

The novel ends with a depiction of one of the key events in the early history of the Beats—the death of Bill Cannastra. As Pasternak says in the novel, he had been with Agatson the night before until they were thrown out of a bar for fighting. In fact, Kerouac, Lucien Carr, and Cannastra were involved in a bar fight on October 12, 1950. Kerouac lost track of the drunken group later that night, but Carr and Cannastra continued drinking until early the next morning. They ran out of money and decided to take the subway to Carr's apartment. As the subway train began to move, Cannastra thought he saw a friend on the platform and he impulsively stuck his head (and most of his body) out of the train's window. He realized too late that he was stuck and yelled for help, but his head was smashed against a subway pillar and his body was dragged beneath the train. Cannastra's death was a shock and a warning. As Ginsberg wrote to Cassady, "Everybody . . . got all big theories and week-long drunks,

everybody's pride was beaten for a week. As in Greek tragedy, the purging of pity and terror." *Go* is the only Beat work to feature Cannastra as a central character.

In *Go,* Hobbes struggles to make sense of Agatson's death, seeing in Agatson a "hopelessness" that could only lead to an ironic view of the world and thus to violence and self-destruction. His life (and death) reveals a "faithlessness" and spiritual poverty that Hobbes sees in all of the Beats to a greater or lesser degree. Agatson's death thus characterizes the early Beats as existentialists to a greater degree than Holmes would admit in his subsequent article about the Beats, "This is the Beat Generation," in which he claims Beat has a strong spiritual dimension and is not a nihilistic or existential philosophy. This is in fact true to the extent that Hobbes himself is no existentialist at the end of the novel. He renounces "the death of hope," and on the ferry ride back to the city, he comforts Kathryn and looks into the distance for a "home" he cannot quite see.

Rob Johnson and Kurt Hemmer

Guilty of Everything: The Autobiography of Herbert Huncke Herbert Huncke (1990)

Unlike his previous works, *Guilty of Everything* is not taken from HERBERT HUNCKE's notebooks; instead, it is a transcription of a series of interviews that was supplemented by excerpts from his previous writings to create a continuous, chronological flow. Perhaps not surprisingly, considering Huncke's fame as an oral storyteller, Huncke's written style and his style of speaking are almost indistinguishable. The manuscript knocked around in various forms beginning in the late 1960s. The book covers Huncke's life from childhood in 1920s Chicago to the late 1960s. Because this book, unlike his previous ones, is chronologically arranged, it is in many ways the best single source of his life and times.

The book begins when Huncke is 12 and runs away from home, taking the trains out of Chicago to the end of the line. He wants to go to Greenfield, Massachusetts, where he was born, and on to New York City. He makes it as far as Geneva, New York, but is picked up by the police, who think he is a hardened case and put him in jail. His father takes him back home, but Huncke is not the same, having gotten a "taste of the outside world, and I knew they couldn't trap me much longer in any one place." Around this time, he reads *The Little White Hag,* a book about Chinese heroin addicts, and using a kind of Huck Finn logic, he believes that even though everyone at the end of the book went to hell, "It sounded like a pretty interesting way to go to hell to me."

The book proved to be prophetic: As a teenager, Huncke overdoses on heroin, and while his dispassionate friends wait for a doctor to arrive, they take his clothes off and put women's underwear on him. After Huncke has recovered, his father comes to the hospital to pick him up. He stands, his pants drop, and there he is in panties. His father cannot believe it, takes him home to his mother, and tells her, "I'm through, I've had my fill. He's beyond me." His father's hatred of Huncke's homosexuality would create a permanent rift between them. When a friend from grade school is killed by undercover Treasury men during a dope deal, Huncke, still in his early teens, confesses to his mother that he is a "dope fiend." He asks her to help him taper off to quit; she is shocked but agrees. Huncke's relationship with his mother becomes closer to that of brother and sister.

From 1934 to 1939 Huncke "didn't do anything but float around the country." Sometimes he could find heroin; other times he could not. He visits New York, where he feels most at home, and moves there permanently in 1939. His hangout becomes Times Square. He learns to steal from a 42nd street hustler named Roy. They break car windows and steal luggage but are caught. Huncke goes to jail for the first time. "When I came out of my first experience [in prison], I was a whole new dude. You don't have the same enthusiasm. You no longer believe in people quite the same way." Huncke had always had the ambition to be a writer and had in fact excused his underworld excursions as "gathering material" for a book. When he reached the conclusion that he himself could not write, he determined that he "would encourage others that I would meet who could write." This was a key decision that ultimately led to his friendship with the Beat writers.

The book provides an account of his first meeting with the Beats, such as WILLIAM S. BURROUGHS, JACK KEROUAC, and ALLEN GINSBERG. Burroughs, Huncke says, "was so methodical about everything that I felt his approach came from a purely scientific standpoint. . . . He became a drug addict principally as a result of research." "Kerouac," he recalls, "was a typical clean-cut American type. He looked to me like the Arrow-collar man." He meets Ginsberg through Burroughs. Ginsberg was only 20 years old and "wasn't sure what he was to become." Huncke met the rest of the early Beat characters at Joan Adams's (the future Joan Burroughs) apartment. Huncke recalls the "clique" as featuring "Oscar Wilde types who were very effete and very witty," and he was often intimidated into silence by them. He immediately liked Joan; in fact, for many years, he was much closer to her than to Burroughs. As is true of his portrayal of the women of the Beat Generation in his other books, Huncke shows a unique awareness of these women.

In 1946, while sitting in Chase's cafeteria, Huncke is asked by a girl if he would like to meet Dr. Alfred Kinsey, who was conducting his famous sex survey. He meets the doctor and agrees to talk with him if he will pay him for his time, the first of many occasions throughout the rest of his life when Huncke would be paid to tell his stories. Huncke says that Kinsey was "a very intriguing man, a man that I learned respect." He finds himself able to tell Kinsey stories that he has never told anyone else, including one about a 20-year-old man who masturbated in front of him while staring at pictures of a little girl. Huncke adds that the man wanted to sodomize him, but Huncke refused (he was nine years old), and that the experience had the effect on him years later that when he would masturbate in that he would envision this man's huge penis. Such discussions with Kinsey were apparently therapeutic for Huncke. He ended up introducing Burroughs and Ginsberg to Kinsey and says, "I pretty much made his Times Square study." Huncke first came to realize what "an extraordinary person" Burroughs was as he listened to Burroughs and Kinsey talk and debate. Sessions between Kerouac, Ginsberg, Burroughs, and Kinsey—arranged by Huncke—no doubt freed these writers to discuss sex openly and explicitly in their works.

In early 1947 Ginsberg told Huncke that Burroughs and Joan had sent him a letter inviting Huncke to come down to Texas and visit them on their farm near New Waverly. Huncke accepted the invitation and made the trip by bus. Huncke, Burroughs, and Joan lived there from January to October of 1947. Burroughs wanted to grow marijuana and opium, but he had no marijuana seeds, the opium flowers would not grow, and the experiment was mostly a bust. Huncke spent a lot of time talking to Joan. During their stay, William S. Burroughs, Jr., was born. Huncke was never quite sure at the beginning if the child was Burroughs's because he never saw the two "intimate" together. In describing this year in East Texas, Huncke also tells the story of Ginsberg and NEAL CASSADY's visit to the farm. Cassady joined Huncke and Burroughs in their trip back to New York in a jeep that Burroughs had bought. Cassady drove, of course, and talked. He admitted to Huncke that he was "terrified of becoming a queen or a homosexual." Huncke told him it was silly to worry about such things. He calls Cassady a "gentle" man.

Guilty of Everything also contains Huncke's most detailed description of the "bust" involving himself, Ginsberg, Little Jack Melody, and Vickie Russell. According to Huncke, the day before they were all busted, he and Melody had broken into an apartment and stolen some goods, which they then hid in Ginsberg's apartment. That night they celebrated Kerouac's contract for *The TOWN AND THE CITY* at JOHN CLELLON HOLMES's apartment. Huncke got "smashed" and does not remember how he came to wake up in the Clinton Hotel the next morning. Returning to Ginsberg's apartment, he finds no one at home and sensed trouble. Ginsberg and Russell arrived minutes later, frightened and disheveled, and told the story of Melody trying to outrun a "cruiser" that spotted them for making an illegal U-turn. They crashed, and Melody was apprehended. Ginsberg had left his notebooks in the car, though; soon the cops were at his door, and all three were arrested—Huncke for possession of drugs and stolen goods. At the station, they connected Huncke to 52 burglaries, but he boasts that he and his accomplice Johnnie must have committed at least 100. Only Huncke went to prison for the affair.

This was his first "extended bit," and he was in prison until 1953. When he returned to New York, the "bebop" scene was in force and heroin was once again easily procured. When he met Ginsberg again, Ginsberg told him that his psychiatrist had warned him to have "nothing to do" with him. And he didn't. During this period, he meets GREGORY CORSO for the first time, and although he admires Corso's poetry, he never forgives him for leaving him sick and without heroin on one occasion—an act he repaid a few years later when Corso was in the midst of withdrawal symptoms himself, and Huncke held out on him.

From 1954 to 1959 Huncke was in prison for breaking into an apartment. Huncke read about the Beats in a *Life* magazine article, and because photos of Ginsberg in the article were taken at the Gaslight coffee shop, Huncke goes there to find him after he is released. Instead, he meets RAY and Bonnie BREMSER (later BRENDA FRAZER), who have heard Ginsberg tell stories about him. They direct Huncke to the now-famous poet. As opposed to their reunion in 1953, this time Ginsberg opens his arms and is very helpful to Huncke. Reunited with Ginsberg, Huncke became part of the world surrounding Ginsberg and Orlovsky's apartment. He lived near Ginsberg in an apartment with Janine Pommy Vega, Bill Heine, and Elise Cowen, and Ginsberg advised Huncke to use methamphetamine (the New York drug of choice in the early 1960s) as a substitute for heroin. At the time, Scottish writer Alexander Trocchi was at the center of the Avenue C meth and art scene, and he and Bill Heine were close associates. Huncke says that he did his best writing on meth and that much of it has survived and is presumably in his previous books. Several factors broke apart the scene: Ginsberg and Orlovsky went to India; Trocchi left; Heine abused Vega, and Huncke had to hide her out. Most importantly, the pushers caused a shortage and raised the prices, setting off a crime wave.

In late 1964 Burroughs returned to New York, famous and surrounded by adulators. Huncke had read *NAKED LUNCH* but found "his satire a little too biting, a little too cold. . . . [H]e's forgotten the human element somehow." Burroughs sees Huncke at a party and calls him a "damn fool" for continuing to use drugs. Later, in an aside to Huncke, he confesses how boring he finds the commotion over him. Huncke, however, is able to trade on his friendship with Burroughs. He earns a hundred dollars from the hostess of a reception for Burroughs by telling her a story about him—and lying that Burroughs called her a "charming lady."

In the closing section of the book, which takes place in 1968, Huncke finds himself more and more in the public eye. He appears on *The David Susskind Show* as a specimen drug user, and instead of warning people away from drugs, he says that he has shot up methamphetamine and heroin and has smoked a joint before the show. Susskind evidently liked him, for he helped Huncke place his first story in a national magazine ("Alvarez," in *Playboy*.) Subsequently, his old friend and roommate, poet JOHN WIENERS, invited Huncke to read on a program with Ginsberg and himself at Buffalo University. Although he found the faculty stuffy, he said the "younger people, the students, are fantastic." In his later life, Huncke found himself increasingly drawn into public life, as a writer, performer, and as a source of information on his Beat friends.

More than a historical curiosity for Beat enthusiasts, *Guilty of Everything* is an artifact that shows precisely how exceptional Huncke was as a storyteller and allows us a better understanding of the influence he had on friends such as Kerouac, Ginsberg, and Burroughs.

Rob Johnson

Gunslinger Ed Dorn (1975)

ED DORN began to work on his mock-epic masterpiece *Gunslinger* shortly after seeing John Sturges's *The Magnificent Seven* (1960) and noting the success of Sergio Leone's "spaghetti westerns," *A Fistful of Dollars* (1964), *For a Few Dollars More* (1965), and *The Good, the Bad, and the Ugly* (1966), starring Clint Eastwood. James K. Elmborg explains the nexus between Dorn's character, Gunslinger, and the cultural milieu that help generate this apparition:

The Gunslinger, as Western archetypal figure, resides in the collective consciousness of the American people as a cross between a metaphysical hero and an existential outlaw.

He is a man without a past, living outside the law, surviving on his wits and integrity—albeit, an integrity which sometimes appears fairly askew to those whose interests are more of the work-a-day world. Dorn's Gunslinger functions like this archetypal hero of Western films who seems to come from nowhere to solve the problems of a small town, problems its citizens are unequipped to face because they have become too implicated in the structures that created the problems. The *Lone Ranger, Heaven without a Gun, High Noon,* Clint Eastwood's spaghetti Westerns, and a whole genre of class-B movies have imbedded the saloons, gunfights, showdowns, dance-hall girls, loyal horses, and the gunslinger—all the stage props of this genre—in our collective memory.

For Dorn, the Gunslinger represents one facet of the American soul. Dorn realizes that the cowboy–outlaw is part of the American mythology that influences the American psyche.

Dorn started writing *Gunslinger* while working as a visiting professor at Essex University in England. The first book of *Gunslinger* was published in 1968 by Black Sparrow Press and represented a departure from the influence of CHARLES OLSON on Dorn's poetry. The second book appeared in 1969. The Frontier Press published "The Cycle," a subsection of *Gunslinger*, in 1971 and the third book in 1972. *Bean News*, a mock–newspaper related to the poem, was published by Hermes Free Press in 1972. In 1975, Wingbow Press published the completed poem of four books as *Slinger*. Duke University Press brought the complete poem back into publication in 1989 as *Gunslinger*. Elmborg writes, "I think *Gunslinger* is perhaps the most important poem of the last half of the twentieth century." Thomas McGuane declares, "*Gunslinger* is a fundamental American masterpiece." Yet, despite the high praise from most commentators, the poem is relatively obscure.

In Book I the Gunslinger and his horse (who can speak and smokes marijuana) meet "I" (a character rather than a personal pronoun), Lil (a cabaret madam), and a poet who all join the Gunslinger heading to Las Vegas in search of Howard Hughes.

Book II has the group in a stagecoach picking up a hitchhiker named Kool Everything, who has a batch of acid that they pour into "I" when they believe that "I" has died. "The Cycle" is a transition piece that follows Book II and describes Howard Hughes's trip from Boston to Las Vegas. Book III has the company journey to Four Corners, where they have been informed that Hughes will go, rather than Las Vegas. Book IIII [sic] fails to provide the expected confrontation between Hughes and the Gunslinger, as two forces controlled by Hughes, the Mogollones and the Single–Spacers, battle each other while the Gunslinger sleeps. Hughes escapes, and the Gunslinger takes leave of the company.

Dorn uses an eclectic array of sources for the language of the poem. "A kind of cool, sardonic tone pervades the work," writes Michael Davidson, "created mostly out of sixties hip jargon, scientific argot, newspeak, bureaucrateze, computer printout, comicbook dialogue and western slang." The inspiration for the characters comes from pop culture. Davidson observes, "*Slinger* features a cast of characters out of TV westerns, Zap comics, *The Scientific American*, Star Trek, *The Wall Street Journal* and the narratives of frontier exploration."

Though Hughes appears to be the antithesis of the Gunslinger, he is more beneficially read as the dark side of the same cosmic force that spawned the Gunslinger. Together they are the Janus-face of American individualism: corporate brutality and outlaw resistance. The Gunslinger is unable to resolve the problem of the robber baron Hughes at the end of the poem because he is also a representative of the American individualism that has created a character like Hughes in the first place. In *Gunslinger* Dorn is putting a mirror to the face of America and pointing out that the American individualism that we glamorize in our mythic portrayals of American outlaws comes from the same source that contributes to the soullessness of our capitalist society.

Bibliography
Davidson, Michael. "Archeologist of Morning: Charles Olson, Edward Dorn and Historical Method." *ELH* 47 (1980): 158–179.

Elmborg, James K. *"A Pageant of Its Time": Edward Dorn's Slinger and the Sixties*. New York: Peter Lang, 1998.

Kurt Hemmer

H

Happy Birthday of Death, The
Gregory Corso (1960)

In *The Happy Birthday of Death,* GREGORY CORSO deploys passion, humor, and the resources of his fertile, quirky imagination against all the various agencies that debase the human spirit and impair true life. In a series of longer poems, each centered upon a single concept, the poet denounces and ridicules the faults and failings that obstruct the development of humankind, while in the shorter lyrics of the collection he presents epiphanic glints and glimpses, praises the heroes and martyrs of visionary consciousness, and affirms the sovereign power of life.

The longer, reflective poems of the volume, "MARRIAGE," "BOMB," "Hair," "Food," "Death," "Clown," "Power," "Army," and "Police," eschew formal organization, reasoned argument, and explicit formulation in favor of verbal virtuosity, extravagant invention, anarchic humor, and intensity of emotional conviction. The poems are less meditations or discourses on their themes than they are imaginative explorations, proceeding by associative leaps and oblique correspondences, by expansions and fusions and transformations.

The principal and most central in this series of free-wheeling meditative poems is "Power," which may be read as an enunciation of Corso's poetics and of his conception of the role of the poet and of poetry in the world. The poem turns upon the contradictory duality inherent in the word *power,* which means both the possession of control, authority, or influence over others and the ability to act or to produce an effect. By exploring the nature of the concept of power, the poem elucidates the irreconcilable dual nature of the world as material or as spiritual reality.

The poem opens with the declaration that "We are the imitation of Power," which I understand in a Platonic sense, that we may each of us choose to seek or to embody either mundane or transcendent power. This idea is amplified in the first and second stanzas in which the insufficiency of the senses to perceive truth is asserted. In this way, true power exists in the spirit and is exercised through the imagination. With his declaration "I contradict the real with the unreal," Corso expresses in essence the guiding principle of his art: the rejection of the tyranny of the real and an assertion of freedom from limitation, from causality, from "impossibility." The poet (together with his counterparts and allies) is, in Corso's view, a prophet of the ideal, the transcendental, an "ambassador of Power."

It is the poet's task to liberate humanity from all forms of oppression and to redeem the ravaged world, the "Awful blank acreage once made pastoral by myths." Against the violence, indifference, banality, dullness, and despair of the fallen world, the poet possesses two weapons: vision and humor. By means of vision he may remythicize the drear, bleak wasteland of the world, restoring it again to fertile, pastoral Arcadia, and by means of laughter he can defy and deflate the forces of Death-in-Life and oppose the institutionalized repression of the human spirit.

The theme of humor is taken up again in the poem "Clown." Here, the poet contrasts the vital

position occupied by the jester or court fool in medieval society with the current low estate of the
clown. Corso characterizes the present era as a
spiritual winter but prophesies a vernal renewal to
be ushered in by the clown, the "good mad pest of
joy" whose "red nose / is antideath."

Certain of the more malign aspects of our frozen age, our winter of the spirit, are treated by the
poet in "Bomb," "Death," "Army," and "Police." The
titles speak for themselves, and taken as a group
the poems communicate a vision of an infernal era,
dominated by destructiveness, negation, violence,
and oppression. Enthroned in human consciousness
like a baleful and obscene deity sits "Horned Reality its snout ringed with tokens of fear / pummelling
child's jubilee, man's desire" ("Police").

If armies, wars, bombs, prisons, and police are
external, historical manifestations of the fallen
world that we inhabit, then the individual, internal
manifestations of our fallen condition include such
traditional deadly sins as vanity and gluttony, anger
and despair. These impediments to human spiritual
development are given a humorous treatment in
"Hair" and "Food." The former poem takes the form
of a lament by an unnamed narrator who alternately
rages and weeps at the loss of his hair through baldness. The comic effect of the poem derives from the
exaggerated emotion and the hyperbole provoked
by an essentially trivial event. Corso's theme here is
that of human vanity, the blinding conceit that engenders in the mind of the narrator (and by extension all of us) blasphemy, anger, abjectness, despair,
and envy. False values and self-infatuation are here
shown to perpetuate the illusion of the real.

"Food" follows the development of another
persona–narrator from fastidious, abstemious ascetic to voracious, insatiable glutton. The poem
dramatizes and derides the extremes of denial and
indulgence in relation to physical appetite. The two
positions are seen as being equally absurd and un-
tenable. Both serve only to confirm appetite rather
than transcending it, and both represent essentially
life-denying attitudes, dogmatic, deviational obsessions that narrow and distort consciousness and
thus impede expanded vision.

The shorter lyrics of the collection treat a variety of themes, most of which are centered around
the struggle between vision and the real, the ten-

sion between transformation of the self and the
loss of hope and purpose when vision fails. Poems
such as "How Happy I Used To Be" and "On Pont
Neuf," treat the dark aftermath of the visionary
experience, the acute sense of loss, the feeling of
exile and forfeiture, the frustration and despair
attendant on finding oneself trapped again in the
raw, drear, unyielding material world.

Despite such occasional moods of dejection
and disconsolation, the poet continues to resist
and endeavour and contend, striving against the
agencies of negation, cultivating his sources of
strength and inspiration. The spirit of abiding vitality, of renewal and vision, and of the miraculous redemptive principle latent in the world is frequently
imaged by Corso as a young girl or a young woman.

This figure—innocent sorceress, elusive muse,
and mythic apparition—assumes various guises in
Corso's poems. In "The Sacré Coeur Café," she is
envisioned as Cosette, the heroine of Victor Hugo's
Les Misérables. Sitting in a café, the poet awaits her
appearance and dreams of following her, serving
her, sacrificing himself for her, "little Cosette—the
size of eternity." Another incarnation of the same
figure is glimpsed in the form of a lovely "childgirl"
in the poem "Written in Nostalgia for Paris" and is
pursued by him through the streets of the city. In
yet another incarnation she is reverently awaited
in a park in "Spring's Melodious Herald," where
the poet expresses his hope that her "primordial
beauty" will overthrow "winter's vast network."
Embodiment of hope and of regeneration, Corso's
child–woman is a radiant enigma, appearing unexpectedly and fleetingly, anticipated incessantly.

The motifs of confinement and persecution,
familiar from earlier collections of Corso's poetry,
continue to be employed by the poet in *The Happy
Birthday of Death*. In "For K.R. Who Killed Himself in Charles Street Jail," Corso elegizes a friend
and fellow–poet who represents for him the type of
visionary quester destroyed both by the inner tor-
ments inevitably engendered by the spiritual quest
and by the abuse and persecution inflicted upon
such persons by an uncomprehending materialist
society. More hopeful variants of these motifs occur
in the poems "Transformation & Escape" and
"1953," in which escape from confinement may be
read as an allegory of human spiritual liberation.

Corso makes engaging and effective use of sports as a metaphor for metaphysics in two poems, "Dream of a Baseball Star" and "Written While Watching the Yankees Play Detroit." In the first of these, the legendary baseball hero Ted Williams serves as a representative of the spiritual struggle to exceed the limitations of the physical world, while in the second poem baseball provides a trope for the cosmic struggle between spirit and all that impedes and confines it. In both poems, Corso affirms the ultimate deliverance, elevation, glorification and transfiguration of the human spirit, prophesying final victory and liberation.

Corso's metaphysics is of his own eclectic, syncretic, eccentric variety; he is not an expounder of doctrines, dogma, or systems. Indeed, he is disposed to be deeply suspicious of all that presents itself as being absolute, definite, fixed, or final. There are, of course, coherent and consistent ideas implicit in his work, but he chooses not to codify them, knowing that "the letter killeth but the spirit giveth life." The poet expresses this fundamental attitude in the poem "Notes after Blacking Out":

All is answerable I need not know the answer
Poetry is seeking the answer
Joy is in knowing there is an answer
Death is knowing the answer

The Happy Birthday of Death is a search for answers, a poetic inquiry into life, into the human heart, into the world and the cosmos. What is discovered and celebrated by the poet and what lingers afterward in the mind of the reader is a magical sense of the world, a sensation and an awareness that the objects and events of the world are charged with a mystery and a meaning beyond their immediate material qualities. At the same time the collection is an undermining, a discrediting, a rebuke, and a rebuttal to all that is inimical to freedom and growth, to beauty, vision, liberty, desire, and delight.

The poems in this collection may be seen to represent a culmination of Corso's poetic development and mythopoeic vision, effectively extending—through the imaginative scope afforded by the longer poems—the range of tone and technique in his poetry while maintaining its essential integrity of theme. *The Happy Birthday of Death* brings to fullest expression the whimsy, the audacity and the gravity, the boldness of metaphor and the richness of invention that give to Corso's work its unique character.

Bibliography

Corso, Gregory. *An Accidental Autobiography: The Selected Letters of Gregory Corso.* Edited by Bill Morgan. New York: New Directions, 2003.

Miles, Barry. *The Beat Hotel: Ginsberg, Burroughs, and Corso in Paris, 1957–1963.* New York: Grove Press, 2000.

Olson, Kirby. *Gregory Corso: Doubting Thomist.* Carbondale: Southern Illinois University Press, 2002.

Skau, Michael. *"A Clown in a Grave": Complexities and Tensions in the Works of Gregory Corso.* Carbondale: Southern Illinois University Press, 1999.

Stephenson, Gregory. *Exiled Angel: A Study of the Work of Gregory Corso.* London: Hearing Eye, 1989.

Gregory Stephenson

Hell's Angels: A Strange and Terrible Saga
Hunter S. Thompson (1966)

In spring 1965 HUNTER S. THOMPSON began an association with the notorious motorcycle gang known as the Hell's Angels. He maintained close relations with integral members and factions of the group for slightly more than a year, gaining an insider's perspective on the Angels' daily activities as well as their group dynamics, motivations, and collective ethos. Thompson began his association to research the national phenomenon of the Angels for a magazine article in *The Nation.* Once the article was published, however, he was inundated with requests for a more complete, book-length account of his experiences. The resulting *Hell's Angels* became Thompson's first book and one of the best examples of his trademark "gonzo journalism" methodology. For Thompson, gonzo journalism entails not objective, detached reporting but rather becoming intimately involved with the subject being reported. In fact, the reporter's involvement with the subject becomes equally what the story is about as the subject itself. *Hell's Angels* is a remarkable record of the gang's history up to and including the mid-1960s and provides trenchant insights into their cultural significance, but the book is no less a story of Thompson's personal interaction with the Angels and how that relationship impacted him and the Angels themselves. In some ways the book can be seen as the inspiration for MICHAEL McCLURE's work on *Freewheelin' Frank: Secretary of the Angels, as Told to Michael McClure by Frank Reynolds* (Grove 1967), but Thompson's story is a much more in-depth sociological study than the one Freewheelin' Frank provided for McClure.

Although prominent in national headlines for much of the mid-1960s, the Hell's Angels were famously secretive about their inner workings and distrustful of all outsiders. By virtue of being candid in his intentions, being completely nonjudgmental, and willing to meet the Angels on their own terms, Thompson was quickly adopted as a virtual honorary member. Thompson relates many minor discussions and encounters with various important members and spends about a third of the book reporting his account of his participation in the July 4, 1965, gathering at Bass Lake near Yosemite National Park in California. Thompson uses his account of this gathering to portray the Angels as they actually are in contrast to their maligned national image. Throughout the book Thompson never attempts to suggest that the Angels are entirely innocent, benevolent, or beyond reproach; in fact, part of their reputation as dangerous, lawless, and merciless thugs is well deserved. But he also goes to great lengths to show that they in no way live up to the public hysteria that accompanies the Angels wherever they go. He dissects many of the major news stories that were directed toward the Angels during the 1960s and proves the outrageous accusations contained therein to be almost universally without merit. However, Thompson also shows that the Angels media frenzy is a phenomenon that the group—in part, at least—embraces and encourages.

Prior to this period, the Angels were a barely existing, loosely organized group with little sense of self-identity or purpose. Once the national media turned their focus toward the Angels, their membership swelled, and they were galvanized by their new reputation as infamous and dangerous criminals. To conservative Americans, the Angels became a force

tantamount to the barbaric Huns (as they were often described), wreaking destruction on everything in their path. The Angels welcomed publicity of any kind but were especially receptive to the kind of attention lavished on them by radical political factions and the liberal intelligentsia, who portrayed them as antiestablishment heroes. Toward the end of Thompson's association, the Angels were welcomed into the San Francisco Beat circle that included KEN KESEY, ALLEN GINSBERG, and NEAL CASSADY. Gang members were almost always to be found at Kesey's perpetually on-going parties; however, their presence ultimately created an atmosphere of uneasiness. Thompson writes that although radically antiestablishment, the Angels are essentially archconservative in their political leanings and vehemently denounce the viewpoints that are held by most Berkeley liberals. This tenuous alliance ultimately ended when the Angels attacked an antiwar demonstration.

Thompson explains the Angels phenomenon entirely as a media creation and one that he himself played a large role in creating. Once their public image was fixed, the Angels both reveled in their newfound celebrity and fought against the way they were portrayed. In the end, Thompson painted an almost tragic picture of a group that was swept up and transformed by forces beyond its control. When they were revealed to be neither the demonic thugs nor the iconoclastic heroes that others wanted them to be, the cultural spotlight quickly turned away, and the Angels were left once again to search for their own purpose and identity. Ultimately, Thompson suggests, this is their very dilemma: What gives them identity and purpose is exactly their lack of and inability ever to find identity and purpose. Thompson quotes one member on his dislike of being called a loser: "Yeah, I guess I am, but you're looking at one loser who's going to make a hell of a scene on the way out." After a year in their midst, nothing came closer for Thompson to epitomizing the negative essence of who the Angels are and what their purpose is.

Bibliography

Carroll, E. Jean. *Hunter: The Strange and Savage Life of Hunter S. Thompson.* New York: Dutton, 1993.

McKeen, William. *Hunter S. Thompson.* Boston: Twayne, 1991.

Perry, Paul. *Fear and Loathing: The Strange and Terrible Saga of Hunter S. Thompson.* New York: Thunder's Mouth, 1992.

Thompson, Hunter S. *The Proud Highway: Saga of a Desperate Southern Gentleman, 1955–1967 (The Fear and Loathing Letter, Volume One).* Edited by Douglas Brinkley. New York: Ballantine Books, 1998.

Whitmer, Peter O. *When the Going Gets Weird: The Twisted Life and Times of Hunter S. Thompson.* New York: Hyperion, 1993.

Luther Riedel

"High" Philip Lamantia (1967)

This 19-line, two-stanza poem explores solitude, a favorite subject for the Beats. In the first line PHILIP LAMANTIA alters the spelling of the word *solitude*. He substitutes the letter *o* for the letter *e*,

Poet Philip Lamantia, San Francisco, 1999. Photographer Larry Keenan: "Philip Lamantia was one of the first two Beat poets I read. . . . While attending a George Herms exhibit, I got a chance to meet and to photograph him." *(courtesy of Larry Keenan)*

then adds an *o* to the end of the word *beat* to create a rhyming musical phrase *beato solitudo*—that strikes a romantic note from the start.

For Lamantia and the Beats, to be "beat" meant to be beaten down to the very depths of society. "Beat" also meant to be lifted up spiritually—to be "beatific," as ALLEN GINSBERG and JACK KEROUAC said. The "I" in Lamantia's poem is beaten down; in line nine he says, "I am worn like an old sack by the celestial bum." He's also "high," which in the lingo of the Beat subculture meant to be on drugs and in a state of heightened awareness. In the first part of the poem, the "I" who speaks exhibits the traits of someone who is both on drugs and lost. Lamantia often felt lost and sought refuge in solitude. The "I" here might be the author, and yet it is perhaps unwise to assume that "High" is autobiographical. Lamantia urged readers not to take his work as an account of his experiences. What we can say with assurance is that the "I" feels that his familiar world—"the wall of my music" as he aptly depicts it—has been "overturned" by the universe itself. There is a sense of alienation and at the same time a sense of abundance and freedom that is conveyed by the images of "the lark of plenty" and the ovens that "overflow the docks." The word *neant*, which appears in the fifth line in the phrase "ovens of neant," is French and appears in "Le Gout Du Neant" by Charles Baudelaire, one of Lamantia's favorite 19th-century poets. Lamantia enjoyed word play and even coined words of his own—such as *ONGED*, which appears capitalized in "High" in line 13, and makes one think of unhinged or singed. After its spirited beginning, the poem slows down. "This much is time," the poet exclaims. "High" shifts mood and tone. Now, the poem portrays a surreal landscape that is meant to shock readers into recognizing the horrors of the world. Lamantia capitalizes the word *Eagles* and thus reminds us that they serve as the symbol of American military might. Here, however, the mighty, invincible Eagles "crash thru mud." The image might remind readers who lived through the Vietnam War that thousands of American planes were shot down and crashed and that the American military seemed to be stuck in Southeast Asia. In this world of war it is no wonder that the poet seeks the peaceful refuge that is offered by solitude. The "I" has been crazed by the world around him. "I'm mad," he explains. Lamantia uses the word *mad* to mean longing or desire, as well as insane or crazy. So the "I" is insanely eager to embrace solitude, which now seems so real and so tangible that he addresses it as "you." But how will he get to solitude? At first, the speaker does not know. Indeed, he is stuck—"wedged in this collision of planets." It is a difficult situation that leads him to exclaim, in everyday street language, "Tough!" The way out, the poem suggests, is through art and expression. "I'm the trumpet of King David," he says. An Old Testament poet and musician and a mighty warrior who defeated Goliath in combat with his slingshot, King David serves as a symbol of the heroic artist triumphing over adversity. Biblical scholars have said that Jesus of Nazareth was a descendant of King David, and so Lamantia links the Old Testament with the New Testament, Jews and Christians. Amid collision and crash, the "I" in the poem makes himself into an instrument—a trumpet—and expresses his anguish. The Beat poets admired jazz musicians, and Lamantia's King David with his trumpet is an Old Testament version of a hip horn player. Finally, the first stanza ends with a violent image that has all the force of a terrifying nightmare: "The sinister elevator tore itself limb by limb." It is an image worthy of the surrealist masters—André Breton and Salvador Dali—since it takes a machine—an elevator—and gives it the attributes—limbs—of a living organism. One can imagine Lamantia's elevator descending out of control, tearing itself apart, and perhaps killing its passengers.

The last stanza provides a remarkable sense of closure. Relying on repetition and rhyme (head/bread and break/make)—Lamantia pulls the poem together. "You cannot close / You cannot open," he writes, as though summing up the human condition. We can never be complete, cut off, and shut down from others nor totally vulnerable and accessible. Human beings live on the edge, never entirely at rest or safe, Lamantia suggests. That thought is enough to drive anyone crazy—"You break your head," he writes. But from that kind of head splitting emerges something sacramental and redeeming. That is what the last four words—"You make bloody bread!"—indicate. "Bloody bread"

encourages readers to think of Christ, his miracles, and his time on the cross, and so the poet's use, in line five, of the place name—*Veracruz*—which literally means "true cross"—is hardly accidental. It is the true Christian state of solitude that Lamantia seeks. Christ himself was "high" on the cross. Beaten down by the Romans who crucified him, he rose up in a state of beatitude. For Lamantia, solitude is a spiritual place in which one is alone and yet, paradoxically, connected to all creation. Out of solitude comes art, and art makes the poet feel exalted and in a state of grace.

Bibliography

Frattali, Steven. *Hypodermic Light: The Poetry of Philip Lamantia and the Question of Surrealism.* New York: Peter Lang, 2005.
Raskin, Jonah. *American Scream: Allen Ginsberg's "Howl" and the Making of the Beat Generation.* Berkeley: The University of California Press, 2004.

Jonah Raskin

High Priest Timothy Leary (1968)

TIMOTHY LEARY's legendary *High Priest* is an important chronicle as a guide to the psilocybin-and-LSD guru's philosophical and scientific thinking about the psychedelic experience. Reading alternately like a sacred text, a half-finished textbook, and a memoir of the early 1960s, the book is a classic of counterculture and drug literature as well as providing a bridge between the Beats and the later radicals of the psychedelic revolution.

High Priest essentially documents 16 trips that are complete with various "guides," an *I Ching* reading to open each chapter, and numerous marginalia to expand further on the experiences described therein. "Guides" with whom Leary works at various points in the book include ALLEN GINSBERG, WILLIAM S. BURROUGHS, CHARLES OLSON, and Aldous Huxley, and included alongside the narration are quotes from magazines articles, short thoughts by Leary, and excerpts from other related books. Leary's purpose for compiling the book was essentially to capture the mystical, quasi-religious, deeply subjective, experiential, and irrational world of psychedelics, and perhaps more importantly, to expand upon their beneficial use in social, psychological, rehabilitative, and spiritual ways.

Leary, who coined the phrase "tune in, turn on, drop out" and who was a hugely influential voice in the counterculture move to question all authority, essentially saw psilocybin, LSD, and psychedelic culture as directly opposed to the culture of control that he saw in most power structures. In *High Priest* he writes, "Everyone who isn't tripping himself because he's too scared or tired is going to resent our doing it[;] . . . the essence of ecstasy and the essence of religion and the essence of orgasm (and they're all pretty much the same) is that you give up power and swing with it. And the cats who don't do that end up with the power and they use it to punish the innocent and happy. And they'll try to make us look bad and feel bad."

High Priest goes on to document Leary's theories of a natural order to psychedelic discovery, like a rebirth experience "where you come back as a man." The book's first two trips/stories set the tone for this, chronicling first a nonchemical death/rebirth that he felt he had undergone during a physical illness and then the story of his discovery of psychedelic mushrooms in Mexico.

The sixth trip features Ginsberg—first walking around naked with Peter Orlovsky and then telephoning JACK KEROUAC—and introduces the idea of "turning on" the world, the plan for the psychedelic movement. Following several philosophical or scientific trips (particularly the seventh and ninth, which spotlight, respectively, how the irrational, religious experience of psychedelics are at odds with rational thinking and the potential benefits of psychedelic therapy for incarcerated prisoners), Burroughs makes an appearance. Initially Burroughs seems to embody the theory that every person comes from a slightly different evolutionary, "tribal" level of thinking; however, in the end, Burroughs removes himself from the experiments and openly disapproves of how Leary and his followers handle the mushroom therapy in which they are engaged. Burroughs would later call Leary "[a] true visionary of the potential of the human mind and spirit." The following trip features the famous image of Michael Hollingshead's mayonnaise jar of LSD and describes how Leary (taking here his first hits of the drug) was forever changed.

Ultimately *High Priest* serves as an important link to the very earliest days of psychedelic culture and a philosophical guidebook to experimentation within it, as well as providing a fascinating chronicle of a hugely important moment in the history of the American counterculture.

Chuck Carlise

Hoffman, Abbie (1936–1989)

Hoffman was not only a uniquely powerful activist but also a literary link between the Beat Generation and the baby-boom rock and rollers that came after. Abbott Hoffman was born on November 30, 1936, well before the baby boom got going in 1946. He began life in Worcester, Massachusetts. He was the son of a well-to-do Jewish family, but he loved the street-fighting ethos of the Worcester working class and shared much of the worldview of JACK KEROUAC, the seminal Beat writer from nearby Lowell.

Hoffman's Brandeis University degree in psychology, awarded in 1959, seemed a logical career link to a life as a clinical psychologist. (At Brandeis he came under the influence of the philosopher Herbert Marcuse.) He married and had two children and seemed on the road to a reasonably calm middle-class existence.

But his passion for social justice led him to early political activism. He traveled to the South to fight for civil rights, often putting himself in significant physical danger in places like Americus, Georgia. Confrontations between white racists and black activists, with their northern allies such as Hoffman, often erupted into violence.

Hoffman's theatrical genius and gift for passionate, compelling prose and speech embraced the Beat traditions of Kerouac and poet ALLEN GINSBERG, whom he knew well. Abbie acknowledged no artistic boundaries, and the stream-of-consciousness style of the Beat poets were at the center of much of what he wrote and said. His writings in *REVOLUTION FOR THE HELL OF IT* (1968) and *Steal This Book* (1971) reflected the free-form, stream-of-consciousness style that the Beat poets pioneered and perfected, alongside jazz music and the Living Theater performances that were revolutionizing the life of the stage.

As seriously as he took the issues of war and social justice to which he devoted his life, Hoffman never forgot the power or politics of humor and good theater. He vowed first and foremost never to be boring and viewed as his most important right the ability to "Shout 'Theater!' in a crowded fire."

His political masterstrokes were profoundly literary and theatrical and bridged the gap from the downbeat free-form of Beat poetry to the wild, unruly, confrontational energy of rock and roll and the psychedelic drugs whose use he helped pioneer.

When he and Jerry Rubin (with whom Abbie founded the Youth International Party [Yippies] in 1968) showed up at a hearing of the House Un-American Activities Committee (HUAC) carrying toy guns and dressed as American and Third World revolutionaries, the boldness of the theatrical coup collapsed the committee's ability to intimidate.

When he and Rubin tossed cash from the visitor's gallery at the Wall Street stock exchange, they caused pandemonium and created one of the lasting antimaterialist images of the 1960s.

Hoffman carried his Beat/rock activism right to the end. When he was forced to go underground as a result of a drug bust (Hoffman claimed he was framed) in 1973, he assumed the identity of "Barry Freed" and went to work saving the St. Lawrence River from environmental destruction. As a wanted fugitive he had his picture taken with the governor and the U.S. senator from New York. He then helped President Jimmy Carter's daughter Amy demonstrate against the Central Intelligence Agency, probably a first for this country.

When he died of an apparent suicide on April 12, 1989, from a barbiturate overdose in New Hope, Pennsylvania, friends and enemies alike speculated on whether it was actually murder. For Abbie Hoffman, the Beat/rock theater of even his death probably made profound sense. Hoffman is the subject of director Robert Greenwald's *Steal This Movie* (2000) starring Vincent D'Onofrio and Janeane Garofalo.

Harvey Wasserman

Holmes, John Clellon (1926–1988)

John Clellon Holmes (born March 12, 1926, in Holyoke, Massachusetts) was an important figure in the original circle of Beats in New York in the late 1940s and early 1950s when he was a close friend of both JACK KEROUAC and ALLEN GINSBERG, whom he met by chance in 1948 at a Fourth of July party. From 1949 through 1951, while Kerouac was working on different versions of ON THE ROAD, Holmes was writing GO, a novel that, like *On the Road*, features characters based on Kerouac, Ginsberg, and NEAL CASSADY and that dramatizes their nonconformity and search for value, intensity, and transcendence. Unlike *On the Road*, *Go* (published in fall 1952 by Scribners) is set primarily in New York and emphasizes what was happening off the road during this period. Perhaps because *Go* was more conventional in its style and narrative structure, Holmes was able to publish his Beat novel more quickly than Kerouac was; *Go* appeared five years before *On the Road*. While it was seen as promising, *Go* had relatively little impact until *On the Road* helped make the Beat Generation a media phenomenon. Holmes later published two more novels: *The HORN* (1958), and GET HOME FREE (1964).

Like Kerouac, Holmes was acutely aware of the fluidity and rootlessness beneath the surface of conformity in post–World War II America. The son of John McClellan Holmes, Sr., (a salesman) and Elizabeth Franklin Emmons (a descendant of Benjamin Franklin), Holmes grew up primarily in Massachusetts, but his father's economic difficulties during the Depression and his parent's unstable marriage, which ended in divorce in 1941, meant that the family (Holmes had two sisters, one two years older, the other seven years younger) moved frequently and were occasionally separated. While the family's moves were primarily within New England, Holmes also lived as a child in New York, New Jersey, and Southern California. When he was 15, he returned to California, supporting himself for the summer as a movie usher and as a lifeguard; then he returned to New York, dropped out of high school, and took a job in the subscription department of *Reader's Digest*. In June 1944 Holmes was drafted and entered the U.S. Navy Hospital Corps. Following basic training, he married Marian Miliambro, a *Reader's Digest* coworker. Holmes spent the last year of the war working in naval hospitals in San Diego and Long Island, caring for the physically and mentally wounded and working his way alphabetically through a list he had developed of a major writers (he had reached the W's by the time he was discharged in June 1945 for recurrent migraines). Following his discharge, Holmes studied briefly at Columbia University on the G.I. Bill and set about to become a writer. He published several early poems and essays in *Partisan Review, Poetry,* and other mainstream journals before his friendship with Kerouac and Ginsberg led him away from his efforts to become part of the more academic literary establishment.

In *Go,* an account of this period, the central character, Paul Hobbes, is both drawn to the nonconformity of the Beat characters who are his friends and yet never fully gives himself over to it as he tries (and ultimately fails) to become part of the Beat scene while preserving his marriage. Like his persona Hobbes, Holmes, too, participated in the fluidity of the Beat rejection of restrictive moral codes without ever fully giving himself to it, and his marriage to Marian Miliambro, similarly, failed to survive his attempts to negotiate these two worlds. In *Go* Holmes the writer and Hobbes the character are deeply engaged in the Beat Generation but not, finally, fully aligned with it. The book's strength is its meticulous observation, the candor of its analysis, and its generally lucid style. Where WILLIAM S. BURROUGHS, Ginsberg, and Kerouac emphasized vision and experiment, both personally and aesthetically, Holmes emphasized reflection and a certain degree of critical distance and control. If his innate reserve and awareness of the needs of others kept him from giving himself as fully as some other Beats to personal and artistic experimentation, these same traits, which cast him as both an insider and outsider to the group, made him perhaps the most acute observer of the Beat scene and its most astute analyst.

In late 1953 Holmes married Shirley Allen, and the couple used the proceeds from the sale of the paperback rights to *Go* to Bantam Books to purchase a house in Old Saybrook, Connecticut, which they renovated and made their permanent home in 1956. In and around developing *The Horn* and *Get Home Free,* Holmes helped to pay the bills by writing speeches and ad copy and by writing essays and stories for large circulation magazines. His piece "This Is the Beat Generation," published

November 1952 in the *New York Times Magazine,* remains an important document, and from the late 1950s through the 1960s his essays on contemporary culture and society figured prominently in such magazines as *Esquire* and *Playboy.* In 1967 E. P. Dutton published *Nothing More to Declare,* a collection of what would now be termed creative nonfiction and that gathered Holmes's most important essays on the Beat Generation, as well as new essays evoking and analyzing his relationships with Kerouac and Ginsberg, as well as such significant 1950s cultural figures as Jay Landesman, who founded and edited the journal *Neurotica,* and Gershon Legman, whose critiques of the dialectic of sex and violence in contemporary American culture challenged America's chaste image of itself in the 1950s. The pieces on Kerouac and Ginsberg remain among the most insightful and sympathetic introductions to these two key Beat writers.

Holmes's next project underscores his growing involvement with creative nonfiction in this period. Holmes was deeply troubled by the Vietnam War, and in May 1967 he and Shirley left for Europe with thoughts of settling there permanently. During the next eight months they visited cities in Great Britain, France, Germany, and Italy. The trip became the basis of a series of travel essays that, like his earlier pieces on the Beat scene and his Beat friends, imaginatively participate in the immediate moment, while yet standing back and reflecting on such matters as the war, the nature of place, exile, friendship, and belonging. Although he managed to place some of these essays in magazines (ranging from *New Letters* to *Playboy*), there was little market at the end of the Vietnam War for pieces such as these, and Holmes was unable to find anyone who was willing to publish the whole set, "Walking Away from the War," as a book until the University of Arkansas Press included it intact in *Displaced Person: The Travel Essays* (1987), the first in a three volume series, *Selected Essays by John Clellon Holmes.* The work originally gathered in *Nothing More to Declare* is included, along with a number of previously uncollected pieces and introductions written specifically for the series, in the second and third volumes: *Representative Men: The Biographical Essays* (1988) and *Passionate Opinions: The Cultural Essays* (1988).

A few years before the trip to Europe that was chronicled in "Walking Away from the War," Holmes had begun to teach as a writer in residence at various universities. Holmes began this phase of his career in 1963 with a stint at the Iowa Writers Workshop. He also taught at Brown University and Bowling Green State University before accepting a permanent position at the University of Arkansas in 1977, where he taught (spending the school year in Fayetteville and the summers in Old Saybrook) until health problems led him to retire. Holmes died March 2, 1988, in Middleton, Connecticut, following a series of surgeries and treatments for what began as lip cancer. Holmes continued to write until the very end of his life. In addition to the new writing included in *The Selected Essays*, he returned to writing poetry and worked on a final novel. In the years since his death, excerpts from Holmes's reportedly extensive journals have appeared in some journals.

Holmes's reputation as a Beat writer rests primarily on *Go*; his essays such as "This Is the Beat Generation" (1952) and "The Philosophy of the Beat Generation" (1958), which attempt to explain the Beat phenomenon; his interpretive portraits of Ginsberg and Kerouac ("The Consciousness Widener" and "The Great Rememberer") from *Nothing More to Declare*; and several later memoirs in which he traces the later years of his friendship with Kerouac. The importance of these texts is clear. They are firsthand accounts of Beat experience and key Beat figures written by a peer who was never willing to let his desire to celebrate his friends overwhelm his desire to understand them and to probe the cultural, historical, and aesthetic significance of their careers and their work. In these pieces, Holmes sees the Beats as they saw and understood themselves while also seeing the Beats as others saw them, and he treats this divide as itself worthy of mapping, bridging, and interpretation. Holmes, in this work, is our most insightful and empathetic commentator on the early Beats. But in focusing on *Go* and such pieces as "The Great Rememberer," it is all too easy to overlook the cumulative achievement of his three volumes of *Selected Essays*, which deserve to be recognized as major texts in the Beat canon.

In part, the importance of these essays is formal and historical. They help document the im-

portance of the Beat project to the emergence of the New Journalism of the 1960s, typified by Tom Wolfe's early work (their closest approximation in the Beat canon is Kerouac's LONESOME TRAVELER). The essays are also important because they so fully and transparently convey Holmes's voice and sensibility (*Get Home Free* is the only one of his novels that approaches the best of his essays in this regard). In the pieces from "Walking Away from the War," Holmes's sensitivity to the details of place, responsiveness to the implications of mood, and awareness of the complexity of consciousness have a kind of moral weight that at moments might be termed Jamesian. Also, in "Clearing the Field," the memoir that introduces *Passionate Opinions*, Holmes probes his memories of the later 1940s with such candor, yet compassionate lucidity, that it becomes the most compelling glimpse we have into the social and historical moment from which the Beat Generation emerged. Finally, the importance of these essays is that many of them do not focus specifically on the phenomenon of the Beat Generation or on Beat writers. They deal with the sexual revolution and the despair of the Vietnam era. They reflect on such forefathers as W. C. Fields and talk perceptively about such writers as Nelson Algren (in some ways a precursor of the Beats) and Norman Mailer who shared some of their concerns. In these essays Holmes, in part because his eye and critical intelligence ranges well beyond Beat figures and Beat practice, projects a vision of his era in which Beat consciousness and Beat concerns are informed by the broader cultural field and become, as well, representative of it. In Holmes's vision, the achievement and significance of the Beats is that they are simultaneously authentically distinctive and individualistic and yet representative of their place and time. This paradox is, at root, Emersonian, and Holmes signals his awareness of this by titling the second volume of his *Selected Essays* after Ralph Waldo Emerson's 1850 collection of essays: *Representative Men*. By invoking Emerson, Holmes signals what is implicit throughout his essays: that the individualism of the Beats matters not because it is eccentric but because it is spiritually genuine, grounded authentically in primary experience, and *representative*. In his essays, then, Holmes enacts the case for the cultural importance of the Beats and the significance of their aesthetic achievement—both in those essays that have explicitly Beat occasions and in those that do not.

Bibliography

Holmes, John Clellon. *Displaced Person: The Travel Essays (Selected Essays, Volume I)*. Fayetteville: University of Arkansas Press, 1987.

———. *Representative Men: The Biographical Essays (Selected Essays, Volume II)*. Fayetteville: University of Arkansas Press, 1988.

———. *Passionate Opinions: The Cultural Essays (Selected Essays, Volume III)*. Fayetteville: University of Arkansas Press, 1988.

———. *Night Music: Selected Poems*. Fayetteville: University of Arkansas Press, 1989.

Tim Hunt

Horn, The John Clellon Holmes (1958)

The Horn is JOHN CLELLON HOLMES's masterpiece, his most internationally popular novel, and one of the most underappreciated classics of the Beat Generation. The idea for the novel, originally called "The Afternoon of a Tenor Man," started in the early 1950s when both Holmes and JACK KEROUAC desired to write novels about jazz. *The Horn* focuses on a neglected, great saxophonist Edgar Pool and tries to capture the authentic world of black jazz. Pool is based partially on the jazz legends Charlie Parker and Lester Young. KENNETH REXROTH, writing for the *Saturday Review* of August 2, 1958, praised Holmes's novel and compared it favorably to Kerouac's ON THE ROAD, which had appeared a year earlier: "[T]he characters in *On the Road* don't have to live that way. The Negroes of *The Horn* do, and they don't like it a bit." Kerouac considered *The Horn* an excellent novel and Holmes's finest work Though the publication of *The Horn* allowed Holmes to share some of the attention that the Beats were receiving in the late 1950s and received positive critical reviews, there has been very little scholarly attention given to the book.

The chapters of *The Horn* are divided into two forms: the chorus and the riff. The chorus chapters are major installments in the work as a whole,

while the riffs take the form of extended soliloquies or monologues by characters. The book ends with a coda. It opens with quotations from Herman Melville and Charlie Parker. The Melville quotation links jazz greats with the writers of the U.S. Renaissance, a scheme that is developed throughout the book. The Melville quotation celebrates the democratic ideal of the nobility of the outcast. The Parker quotation is a key one for the Beat philosophy. There is no line between life and art, says Parker: "If you don't live it, it won't come out of your horn."

Holmes says that he wrote the first chorus, "Walden," in five nonstop installments in 1952. It was the "easiest" writing he had ever done up to that point. The tenor saxophonist Walden is obviously linked to Henry David Thoreau—although the connection between the two is vague. The chapter begins the "morning" (which for jazz men is the afternoon) in New York following an epic horn battle on stage at an after-hours club called Blanton's (a clear reference to the popular after-hours 1940s jazz spot called Minton's). Walden, a young saxophonist who is still finding his style, "cuts" in on the great Edgar Pool, known simply as "The Horn." In the process of overcoming the older player, Walden finds his true style for the first time. That next afternoon when he awakens, he realizes that he has now chosen a path in life, just as Pool had at one point. This choice will make him one of the outcasts in America "self-damned to difference," as the narrative warns. The soundtrack for all outcast Americans at this time is the emerging musical form known as Bop. The chapter introduces Geordie Dickson, a vocalist who is discovered by The Horn when she is just a 16-year-old girl living in the South. She runs away with Edgar, and he teaches her the techniques of jazz vocalizing. Cleo is a young man playing piano for the band in which The Horn sits at The Go Hole (a club central to Holmes's first novel, GO). In the riff, Cleo follows Pool out of the club and listens to an afternoon-long, Benzedrine-fueled monologue by The Horn. To Cleo, Pool is a jazz legend incarnate, and in his mind he rehearses the 60-odd years of jazz history in which Pool is such an important figure. Pool's thoughts reveal that although men did not "cut" one another in his time—as Walden had done him that morning—he does not resent Walden's act because Walden truly "blew." Still, the act has struck a final chord in him somehow, and he begins his quest, which will last the rest of the novel, to raise enough money to go home to Kansas City, Missouri (where two of the real-life counterparts to Pool had lived, Charlie Parker and Lester Young).

In the "Wing" chorus, Walden is frantic because he knows that his "cutting" of Pool may have finally sent Pool over the brink into self-destruction. He goes looking for Pool's old friends, hoping that they can tell him of Pool's whereabouts and alerting them to the potential danger Pool faces. He first looks up Wing Redburn, whose name links him to Melville, author of *Redburn*. Wing, as Melville did in the mid-1850s, retired from the pure, artistic life and took a day job (Melville in the Customs House, Wing as a studio musician). Walden's presence is thus a reproach to him for having "sold out," but his presence also reminds him of the old days when he, Junius, and Curny were all in a band with Pool. Pool tells the younger musicians that they are competent players, but they do not understand the blues, lacking life experience. When the band breaks up because of Pool's notorious unreliableness, Pool perversely heads South and meets a girl named Fay Lee (whose name recalls Edgar Allan Poe's Annabel Lee just as Edgar Pool recalls Edgar Allan Poe). She represents for him his chance at capturing the "pure line" of music, the spontaneous, natural tone that Pool has captured, but he turns his back on her and returns North. When Walden shows up, all of this floods back to him as he watches a young vocalist have to sing his lines from a carefully scripted score. The moment signals within him a generational change: Pool was a father figure to him during a time of social disruption in which many young men needed such father figures. Now, he is that figure. Pool and Cleo, in the riff, drink in a Times Square bar around the corner from the Go Hole. Pool schemes ways to raise the $50 he desperately needs to buy a bus ticket but refuses to sit in at the Go Hole for a quick $25: Pool has lost his confidence. Instead, he decides to con all of his old friends for money.

The first friend Pool hits on in the "Junius" chorus is Junius Priest. Several attributes of Ju-

nius connect him with Thelonius Monk (including the name). Monk was one of the founders of Bop, and, like Junius, he worked out his revolutionary sound on keyboard and collaborated with a saxophone player (Dizzy Gillespie). As did Monk, Junius lives at home with his mother. Monk, who created the dark-shaded persona of the Bop artist, withdrew from the scene in the 1950s, and so does Junius, but here Holmes shows Junius withdrawing because of a fear that he is overly influenced by Pool and because he fears that he will succumb to the self-destructiveness that seems inevitably to characterize rebels and pioneers such as Pool. Pool and Junius's meeting in Los Angeles (Holmes transplants the East Coast scene to the West, just as Kerouac does in *The SUBTERRANEANS*, no doubt for legal reasons) reveals the appeal of these Bop pioneers as role models for the Beat Generation writers, whose coming together resembles the revolution described as follows: "For, like Junius, all their ideas were running on that way, Edgar's way, and they instantly recognized in each other that same rash and exhilarating discontent that was so like the sudden cool storm-smell that often hung, motionless, in the air those afternoons, and was somehow so prophetic of a new and imminent reality." The idea that there could be a revolution in art created by such outsiders must have been of great inspiration to the Beats. Certainly, Bop was the soundtrack of their early lives. In the following riff, Cleo meditates on the 60-year rise of jazz in America. The riff gives Holmes a chance to showcase his remarkable ear for tracing ideas from song to song.

In his scheme of associating each major character with a writer from the U.S. Renaissance, Holmes connects Geordie Dickson with Emily Dickinson in the "Geordie" chorus. The real-life jazz counterpart to Geordie is Billie Holiday. The chapter recounts Geordie's thoughts immediately after Pool, still searching for money, has left her apartment. She is 35, and Pool makes her feel it, having first met him when she was barely in her teens. She was a young girl in the South, the victim a year earlier of a white gang rape, and he was a sideman in a swing band. She follows him up North, and he encourages her to sing, to "blow" her own song and forget her terrible Southern past. He coaches her as a singer until one day she realizes that "the singing had become important in itself." They hit their stride during World War II, playing the jazz clubs along 52nd street in New York. Pool's success, however, has come too late: He has worked in obscurity for too long to now face his success with anything other than irony—an attitude that links Pool with the fate of Kerouac, Holmes's close friend, who also experienced success too late. Success also breaks up Geordie and Pool. Their lives become an endless series of "hip" parties. They begin to shoot heroin as well. Still, she follows him out to the West Coast where the heroin makes her lose interest in life, including singing. One day she chains herself to a bed and kicks her habit cold turkey in the course of three days. Pool continues to get high, however. One night, she wakes up to find him poised with a needle at her arm, attempting to readdict her. Pool is eventually committed to a hospital for treatment, and Geordie moves back to New York where she builds a solo career and only occasionally sees Pool. As she thinks back on their life and times, she realizes that she has lost the outrage she felt at her Southern upbringing, whereas Pool can never lose his outrage; in fact, it is this rage that inspired his music and kept him going. In the riff, Pool and Cleo continue searching for money for Pool's ticket home. They hit on Billy James Henry, a Julliard-educated musician who plays in a combo with Cleo at the Go Hole. Henry is on to him and coldly refuses any money. Pool realizes that there is one last old friend to whom he can turn.

The epigraph to the chorus "Curny" is from *The Adventures of Huckleberry Finn:* "Goodness sakes! Would a runaway nigger run *south?*" Curny Finnley presents a similar contradiction, as he is a jazz musician who dresses the part of a Southern aristocrat and even adopts their mannerisms, albeit ironically. Curny, a name derived from *Colonel,* is a character whose energy and sense of humor hides his musical genius. He, Wing, and Junius had played with Pool in the early 1940s, and now Pool finds him at a recording session that is being produced by his manager, Mr. Willy Owls. Curny tries to make commercial music but always lets his wit and sense of humor get away from him, leading jazz aesthetes to dub him "a comedian with a trumpet."

Still, he is a favorite with the young and hip listeners. Holmes contrasts him with the gloomy "poet" Pool (think of Edgar Allan Poe). This chapter is an excellent inside look at a recording session, even if the session is spoiled by Pool's inappropriate and disruptive behavior—which Curny brilliantly deflects. Curny keeps telling Pool that he can cash a check for him when he is done recording, but Pool does not want him to think that the money is to "lush" (drink), and he suddenly leaves. The chapter ends on the revelation that Pool has hocked his horn, a sign of just how serious his situation is.

As Wing and Walden continue looking for Pool in the "Metro" chorus, their search leads them to the man who knew Pool before any of them did, the tenor saxophonist Metro Myland. The quotation introducing this chapter is from Walt Whitman, and Myland turns out to be the most visionary and spiritual musician presented here—a true transcendentalist. Metro is several years younger than Pool, and they first meet one bitterly cold night when they are both hoboing across America and hop the same freight car. Pool is 18 and tells the boy his story of how he has run away from home rather than take his father's advice and become a railroad porter. His plan is to return home with the money he has saved, buy a horn, and turn his mother's woodshed into a practice studio (thus the term *woodshedding* to describe a player's practicing). The freight car is freezing, and Pool teaches Metro to stay warm by singing and dancing. Later, in one of the novel's most remarkable scenes, a young white girl jumps the same freight, and to stay warm, she makes love to both men. Metro never forgets the sight of a tear frozen in the corner of her eye, and the clearness with which he sees that next morning remains a revelatory vision to him throughout his life. At Kansas City, Missouri, Pool makes Metro jump off with him, and thereafter, for a year, he tags along behind Pool. Back at home in Kansas City, Pool moves in with his mother, who fails to understand how serious he is about becoming a horn player. Pool buys his first horn at a pawnshop. At the time (early 1930s), for a variety of reasons, Kansas City had become a jazz capitol of America. In this respect, his story resembles that of both Charlie Parker and Lester Young, both of whom grew up in Kansas City and began to play there at about this time. Pool studies the famous jazz players and imitates their fingering on his leg. His woodshedding is progressing when, unfortunately, his father returns once again to live with his mother. His father tells Pool to get a job that is appropriate for a black man, and Pool tells him that horn playing knows no black or white. Metro first realizes how much Pool wants to play when he watches him onstage, desperately repeating the one song he can play ("Comin' Virginia") but playing it to each new rhythm as it changes. Pool's humiliation makes him give his horn away—to Metro. The end of this chapter makes the point that Pool's rage, which has been his source of inspiration, ultimately fails him. The riff takes place in the kitchen of the Go Hole, where Pool negotiates to play two sets for $130 and a bottle. A young trumpeter named Kelcey Crane refuses to play with the clearly drunk Pool.

In the "Edgar" chorus, Pool is insulted by Kelcey Crane's refusal to play alongside him, but Pool realizes that Crane's refusal reminds him of himself as a younger man. The scene turns comic as the drunken Cleo falls off the piano bench while playing; the Julliard-trained Billy James is beside himself at Cleo's and Pool's lack of professionalism. The audience of young listeners flings Pool's own sneering, ironic attitude that they have learned from him back at him. Pool realizes that without the sympathy of the audience, he can no longer play. He tries mightily to blow something that will show the crowd that he still has "it," but he only briefly reaches what was once effortless brilliance on the tenor sax. Billy James walks offstage in disgust, and the set ends. Pool cannot remember having ever "pulled a five" (walked out) on another musician.

Between sets, in the second "Edgar" chorus, Pool sets out to recruit a crowd of sympathetic listeners for his second set at the Go Hole. He goes to the Paradise Club next door and almost gives up on finding anyone among the unfamiliar crowd of young faces when he spots Geordie, having dinner with one of her ubiquitous, young white escorts. He tells her that he is sick and needs help, and she thinks that he is suffering once again from drug addiction. This misunderstanding causes him to be rude to her, and he leaves the club. Almost immediately he thinks that he could have said something nice to her instead, and he realizes that Cleo has also been trying to help him, and he could have thanked him, too. Such thoughts show that as Pool comes ever closer to physical collapse, his fierce pride—that has both created him and destroyed him—begins to break down. Pool stops off at a bar on the way back to the Go Hole for a second set, and once again his request for money is misunderstood, this time by Curny's manager, Mr. Owls, who believes that Pool wants "lush money" (drinking money). Pool leaves the bar after a drink that will be his last. He enters the Go Hole and hears that the trio has started without him. He suddenly realizes that his body can take no more, and he feels himself collapsing. Still, the brilliant solo being played by Kelcey pierces the fog in his brain. He sees two young white listeners (could this be the apparition of Holmes and Kerouac?) hearing the same brilliance, and this ties him to them: "They loved the thing he loved." Then, dismayingly, he hears himself onstage: Walden is playing his own solos, note for note, on a cover of "Junius Sees Her." Wing holds Pool back from going onstage. Pool listens in shock as he is paid tribute to as if he is already dead. It is at this moment that the years of self-abuse catch up to him, and he collapses with a stomach hemorrhage. All of his friends converge on him as he goes down.

In the last section of the book, a coda called "Cleo," Holmes draws conclusions about the significance of jazz and the situation of African Americans in a segregated America. Cleo seems to see in Pool's fading eyes the knowledge that all of the race hatred in the United States will fade only when "the two sundered halves are yoked again: the male, the female; the black, the white, yes." "Yes" becomes the refrain of the chapter and is indeed the refrain of the book. It is the "yes" of NEAL CASSADY in *On the Road,* the primal yes of Walt Whitman. Holmes concludes: Jazz captures American desire and American protest. Jazz celebrates America. At the end of the book, Cleo finds The Horn's pawn ticket for his tenor saxophone, but he does not redeem it. He leaves the horn there as a legacy for some future musician who will purchase it just as Pool had bought his first horn in a Kansas City pawnshop in the 1930s.

Rob Johnson

Hotel Wentley Poems, The   John Wieners
(1958)

This primary document of the San Francisco Beat sensibility was written between June 15 and 21, 1958, and was published in October of that year by Dave Haselwood and Andrew Hoyem's Auerhahn Press. Wieners had moved to San Francisco with Dana Duerke, his lover of six years, after spells at Black Mountain College and in Boston. During a brief stay at the Hotel Wentley on the Polk Gulch, Wieners composed the eight works collected as *The Hotel Wentley Poems;* another three poems from this set were included in a *Selected Poems* of 1986, edited by Raymond Foye.

Wieners's milieu in this period included the poets JOANNE KYGER, ALLEN GINSBERG, Stuart Perkoff, Jack Spicer, and Robert Duncan, and artists Wallace Berman and Robert LaVigne (whose portrait of Wieners appears alongside "A Poem For Painters" in the Auerhahn edition). In this company some of Wieners's dominant concerns formed: drugs, candid sexuality, lyric glamour, and careful registry of immediate environment. Their coalescence in *The Hotel Wentley Poems* gives this first publication of Wieners's a complexity of attentions that are made tight by the focused steadiness of its sentences and line breaks and that are made social by the address of each title: "A poem for vipers," "A poem for painters," and "A poem for museum goers" (in a 1977 interview with Charley Shively, he describes them humorously as "after dinner addresses").

"A poem for record players" opens the sequence in characteristic Wieners shifts between "Details / but which are here" ("The pigeons somewhere / above me, the cough a / man makes down the hall") and gnostic confrontation: "oh clack your / metal wings, god, you are / mine now in the morning." The adherence to these multiple juxtaposed concerns is purposeful and keen, lyrical but never rhapsodic. The most commonly excerpted poem from *The Hotel Wentley Poems,* "A poem for painters" affirms this adherence as a credo:

>My poems contain no
>wilde beestes, no
>lady of the lake, music
>of the spheres, or organ chants.

>Only the score of a man's
>struggle to stay with
>what is his own, what
>lies within him to do.

It is emphatic in this poem that the activity of positing and repositing "what is his own" (akin to CHARLES OLSON's "that we are only / as we find out we are") is the writing's actual propulsion, loading each line with a hesitant insistence to "stay with what we know" as it is earned in the poem's trajectory. Attendant to that is the Duncanian assertion in "A poem for vipers" (WILLIAM S. BURROUGHS explains in his glossary to JUNKY that a "viper" was then hip lingo for a marijuana user): "The poem / does not lie to us. We lie under its / law, alive in the glamour of this hour." (Duncan's "Despair in Being Tedious" [1972] has a palpable *Hotel Wentley* feel in its final stanzas). This receptivity to the "law" of the poem "in" time may contribute to the strongly auditory atmosphere of these poems, to the reader's sense that the writer is "listening" for the next line. Wieners's next book, *Ace of Pentacles* (1964), would bear the dedication "For the Voices."

Under these obligations of emotional and cultural accuracy, Wieners unflinchingly tracks narcotic and sexual proclivity. Methedrine and heroin were especially abundant in late 1950s San Francisco, and Wieners took to them with enthusiasm, noting the circumstances of their use:

>I sit in Lees. At 11:40 PM with
>Jimmy the pusher. He teaches me
>Ju Ju.
>[. . . .]
>Up the street under the wheels
>of a strange car is his stash—The ritual.
>We make it. And have made it.
>For months now together after midnight.

(The following year, Wieners was selling heroin in matchboxes on Scott Street, causing him to be described by Wallace Berman as "Grand Duchess of the five / Dollar matchbox.")

The conditions of these transactions are portrayed not romantically but factually as instances of what Wieners later called "the present gleams." Likewise his presentation of his homosexuality, in his relationship with Dana ("A poem for the old man") and in 1950s gay culture ("A poem for cock suckers," censored by the printer in the first edition as "A poem for suckers"). "A poem for the old man" petitions "God" to "make him [Dana] out a lion / so that all who see him / hero worship his / thick chest as I did," an especially tender paean to his lover's attributes. "A poem for cock suckers" offers a more ambivalent scenario that points to the homosexual's cultural disenfranchisement:

> Well we can go
> in the queer bars w/
> our long hair reaching
> down to the ground and
> we can sing our songs
> of love like the black mama
> on the juke box, after all
> what have we got left.

Bold clarity and longing saturate the language of *The Hotel Wentley Poems* and dimensionalize the poet's documenting eye to bring the work to the pitch of a very present-tense testimony; in this respect, its courageousness is its enduring salience. The book won immediate admiration from poets of such diverse affiliations as Jack Spicer, Allen Ginsberg, and Frank O'Hara and so rapidly became a "classic" that in later years Wieners refused to read from it in public.

Thomas Evans

How I Became Hettie Jones Hettie Jones
(1990)

"I won't say I didn't cry. I cried a lot, and that, of course, is therapeutic," HETTIE JONES has said when asked about the process of writing her memoir, *How I Became Hettie Jones*. The story of her years as a young woman in New York City's avant-garde, the memoir presents the revolutionary interracial world that Jones entered when she became involved with and then married the African-American poet LeRoi Jones (AMIRI BARAKA) in 1958. Unlike the traditional memoir of the spouse of a famous person, however, Jones's memoir takes it cue from second-wave feminism, focusing on her emerging develop-

ment as a writer and her efforts to defy institutional and cultural apartheid. In a finely crafted narrative, Jones constructs a female self that heals the wounds caused by her parents' racism (they virtually disowned her after the marriage) and her husband's decision to divorce her (he could no longer live with a white woman), leaving her a single mother with two children to raise.

Wanting the memoir to be a woman's book, Jones used the trope of "home" to structure the narrative, although she manipulated the term so that it escapes clichéd domesticity. Home in *How I Became Hettie Jones* is her parents' home in Laurelton, New York—the one which she knew from an early age that she had to leave. It is the jazz and literary scenes of the Village and the Lower East Side where she has lived for almost 50 years, and it is all those places where what Jones calls "things in terms of race" came together. It is also the four apartments in which she and her family lived during those years. Morton Street, 20th Street, 14th Street, and Cooper Square materialize in the memoir as personally charged place names titling the four major sections of the book. Home is ultimately the memoir itself, a "sobersided alternative," as Susan Brownmiller called it, to LeRoi Jones's AUTOBIOGRAPHY.

In addition to her struggles to first live independently, first as the wife of a black revolutionary poet and then as a single mother of mixed-race children, *How I Became Hettie Jones* chronicles her experiences with reproductive rights, harsh socioeconomic and social justice systems, jazz at the Five Spot, the production of the literary journal *Yugen,* the loss of her Jewish heritage, and the many friendships, male and female, that sustained her. Shifting past- and present-tense perspectives, Jones presents a congenial, forgiving, yet assertive voice sprinkled with her characteristic black vernacular, weaving together memories, short fantasies, and self-reflexive passages. Interspersed throughout are poems by LeRoi and other writers she knew at the time, such as Ron Loewinsohn, ROBERT CREELEY, and PHILIP WHALEN. She inserts her own writing as well—snippets of letters to her friend Helene Dorn, four poems, and a short narrative about the poet CHARLES OLSON that she had written in secret while married. With these texts, Jones uses the memoir as a generator of self-knowledge, probing questions about whether she truly is a writer and why she did not write more.

Hettie Jones, San Francisco, 1996. Photographer Larry Keenan: "This photograph was taken at the *Women of the Beat Generation* book-signing party. Hettie Jones is shown in this photograph reading some of her work at the Tosco restaurant/bar in North Beach." *(courtesy of Larry Keenan)*

The embedded texts serve as bridges that are essential for both author and reader to move back and forth through time and to understand how tricky memory is and ultimately how difficult it is to ever know one's past. In Jones's hand, these disparate artifacts of material culture function like pieces of this mosaic, creating a unique and long unseen vision of Beat literary and cultural history.

As a women's book, *How I Became Hettie Jones* makes careful note of other women like Jones who have been elided from Beat history. The list is massive and includes the poet Sarah Blackburn; playwright Aishah Rahman; poet Bonnie Bremser (BRENDA FRAZER); DIANE DI PRIMA; poet Rochelle Owens, who was featured in *Four Young Lady Poets* published in 1962 by Totem and Corinth presses; Rena (Oppenheimer) Rosequist; Elaine Jones (later Kimako Baraka, LeRoi's now-deceased sister); and writer JOYCE JOHNSON, one of Jones's closest friends at the time and remaining so today. Interracial couples are also raised from obscurity: Ia and Marzette Watts, Vertamae Smart-Grosvenor and Bob Grosvenor, and Garth and Archie Shepp feature prominently. By writing these individuals back into Beat history, Jones illustrates how important that history has been to the disruption of gender and racial binaries in post–cold war U.S. culture.

Despite the heartbreaks that led to the many tears that Jones shed while writing the memoir, *How I Became Hettie Jones* is not a sad or spiteful book. As reviewer Alix Kates Shulman noted, "[B]arely a hint of rancor or bitterness remains in this judicious, fair-minded book." Instead, Jones's story proclaims the need for pleasure, joy, and even euphoria, all found in her children, her marriage, her work, her apartments, and her friends. With good humor and relentless self-exploration, she claims outright the fact that time left her husband "like any man of any race, exactly as he was, augmented," while she, "like few other women at that time, would first lose my past to share his, and then, with that eventually lost too, would become the person who speaks to you now." In recovering and creating through writing that becoming, Jones validates the strength of human beings to live full lives under difficult circumstances. The memoir makes trenchantly clear that something essential remains in each human being, even while one's name may change, as did hers—from Hettie Cohen, her birth name; to Hettie Jones, her married name; to LeRoi Jones's white wife, her name according to many literary histories; to H. Cohen-Jones, as LeRoi placed it on the *Yugen* masthead. Through language and memory, all those selves can achieve authenticity, and one may even find that a single name, such as *Hettie*, centers them all.

Bibliography

Brownmiller, Susan. "The Bride of LeRoi Jones." *The New York Times Book Review.* 11 March 1990, 12.

Grace, Nancy M., and Ronna C. Johnson. *Breaking the Rule of Cool: Interviewing and Reading Beat Women Writers.* Jackson: University Press of Mississippi, 2004.

Johnson, Ronna C., and Nancy M. Grace. *Girls Who Wore Black: Women Writing the Beat Generation.* New Brunswick, N.J.: Rutgers University Press, 2002.

Shulman, Alix Kates. "Keeping Up With Jones." *The Nation,* 16 March 1990, 425–427.

Watten, Barrett. "What I See in *How I Became Hettie Jones.*" In *Girls Who Wore Black: Women Writing the Beat Generation,* edited by Ronna C. Johnson and Nancy M. Grace, 96–118. New Brunswick, N.J.: Rutgers University Press, 2002.

Nancy M. Grace

"Howl"   Allen Ginsberg   (1956)

First published in the volume HOWL AND OTHER POEMS, "Howl" is the best-known poem of the Beat Generation. Along with JACK KEROUAC's ON THE ROAD and WILLIAM S. BURROUGHS's NAKED LUNCH, it is considered one of the principle works of literature that launched the Beat Generation.

Ginsberg read the first part of the poem at the now-famous Six Gallery reading in San Francisco on October 7, 1955, alongside KENNETH REXROTH, GARY SNYDER, MICHAEL McCLURE, PHILIP WHALEN, and PHILIP LAMANTIA. This reading is considered by critics to be the primary event that inaugurated as a literary force the San Francisco Poetry Renaissance, a reconsideration of new critical aesthetics in favor of open-field avant-garde poetry. The creative locus of U.S. poetry seemed to shift from the East to the West Coast after the Six Gallery reading, prompting reviewers such as Richard Eberhart to write in 1956 that the "West Coast is the liveliest spot in the country in poetry today. It is only here that there is a radical group movement of young poets." The autobiographical material of "Howl" also has been credited with helping to give birth to the Confessional movement in U.S. poetry. After spending time on the West Coast in 1957, Robert Lowell, one of the earliest of the group who would be known as the Confessionals, noted that the personal material of "Howl" exerted a great effect on him, and he felt encouraged to begin "writing lines in a new style"—material that would become *Life Studies,* one of the most important volumes of poetry in the Confessional school.

The protagonists of Ginsberg's poem reject the social, religious, and sexual values of post-World War II U.S. capitalist culture. Ginsberg joins their misery to a vision of spiritual attainment, creating a movement in the poem from suffering to redemption. Section I of the poem is an elegy for those whose lives have been degraded by the social, religious, and sexual containment of cold-war United States. Ginsberg writes that they are "the best minds of my generation" and they have been "destroyed by madness" in their efforts to live within these structures of containment. Ginsberg's use of the repetitive anaphora, inspired by his reading of Walt Whitman and later in his career a model for his incorporation of Buddhist mantra speech, gives this first section the feel of a chant or spell. He said later that this litany, anchored by repetition of *who* at the beginning of each line, was part of his effort to "free speech for emotional expression"—to give voice to those silenced by the cultural practices of cold-war United States. Ginsberg coined the term *one speech-breath-thought* to explain that the beginning and the end of each of these lines or strophes was determined by the exhalation of the poet's breath. In this way, too, Ginsberg's one speech-breath-thought poetics inaugurated in "Howl" a career-long emphasis for expressing the Buddhist triad of body–speech–mind in the form and content of his poems. The first 72 anaphoric lines of Section I culminate in an invocation to Carl Solomon, the inspiration for the poem, with whom Ginsberg spent time in 1949 in the Columbia Presbyterian Psychiatric Institute and who is a central figure in Section III of the poem. "[A]h Carl," the poet writes, as if taking a breath, in line 73, "while you are not safe I am not safe and now you're really in the total animal soup of time." Section II ends with a vision of what would become Beat poetics: Ginsberg's effort, a la Cézanne, to create "incarnate gaps in Time & Space through images juxtaposed," and in the process to "recreate the syntax and measure of poor human prose."

Section II pivots on Moloch, the Canaanite god to whom parents burned their children in sacrifice—re-created in "Howl" as the sacrifice of Ginsberg's generation to the cold-war "military–industrial complex." As a figure in "Howl" for the physical and psychological effects of compulsory postwar capitalism, Moloch emerges from "Ashcans and unobtainable dollars," and "Boys sobbing in armies." He is a creature "whose soul is electricity and banks." For Ginsberg, America's psyche is "pure machinery" that produces Moloch's military-industrial complex and whose armaments can destroy the world.

Section III is structured as a call-and-response litany between the speaker of the poem and Solomon. The two are committed in "Rockland" asylum in Section III, with the name *Rockland* echoing the dry, sparse hardness of Moloch. Solomon is a figure for the postwar counterculture, those who distrust the sense-bound reason of the industrial United States and who are deemed mad for their inability to conform. Their supposed madness is, for Ginsberg, a sign of their spiritual health in the poem—they are represented by "the madman bum and angel beat in Time" in Section I and are devoured by Moloch in Section II. They speak again in Section III, in an apocalyptic conversation that leads to Ginsberg's vision of redemption in the final line of the poem. An addendum to the poem, published as "Footnote to Howl," celebrates the visionary cleansing that follows these final lines of "Howl."

As a result of the poem's explicit homosexual and heterosexual imagery, in 1957 U.S. customs officials seized copies of the book in which it appeared, *Howl and Other Poems,* and tried Ginsberg's publisher LAWRENCE FERLINGHETTI and City Lights Bookstore clerk Shigeyoshi Murao on charges of obscenity. Nine witnesses from the San Francisco literary community testified on behalf of the social importance of the poem; the prosecution countered with two witnesses. Later that year, Judge Clayton Horn ruled the book "not obscene" because of its "redeeming social importance," a ruling often cited as a landmark judgment on the subject of artistic expression in the 20th century.

Bibliography

Breslin, Paul. *The Psycho-Political Muse: American Poetry since the Fifties.* Chicago: University of Chicago Press, 1987.

Ehrlich, J. W., ed. *Howl of the Censor.* San Carlos, Calif.: Nourse Publishing Company, 1961.

Ginsberg, Allen. *Howl: Original Draft Facsimile.* Edited by Barry Miles. New York: HarperCollins, 1986.

Hyde, Lewis, ed. *On the Poetry of Allen Ginsberg.* Ann Arbor: University of Michigan Press, 1984.

Portugés, Paul. "Allen Ginsberg, Paul Cézanne and the Pater Omnipotens Aeterna Deus." *Contemporary Literature* 21 (Summer 1980): 435–449.

Raskin, Jonah. *American Scream: Allen Ginsberg's 'Howl' and the Making of the Beat Generation.* Berkeley: University of California Press, 2004.

Trigilio, Tony. *"Strange Prophecies Anew": Rereading Apocalypse in Blake, H.D., and Ginsberg.* Madison, N.J.: Fairleigh Dickinson University Press, 2000.

Tony Trigilio

Howl and Other Poems Allen Ginsberg (1956)

The scope and range of ALLEN GINSBERG's first book of poems, *Howl and Other Poems,* is often lost in celebrations and attacks on the long poem "HOWL" itself. "Howl" is, after all, so loud that it can drown out in the other poems in the small collection as a whole. William Carlos Williams's preface to the book situates Ginsberg's first volume immediately in the early modernist tradition but with a forward-looking vision of the effect of Beat poetry on contemporary American letters. As Williams puts it, Ginsberg "proves to us, in spite of the most debasing experiences that life can offer a man, the spirit of love survives to ennoble our lives if we have the wit and the courage and the faith—and the art! to persist." The poems in the book also placed Ginsberg as a poet in the prophetic tradition of Walt Whitman and William Blake. As the book achieved increased acclaim, Ginsberg's acknowledgment of these influences revived interest in the visionary tradition of American and British romanticism in the wake of its rejection by high modernism and New Criticism. Its role in shaping Ginsberg's reputation as a political poet of the new American avant-garde and his eventual legacy as a cultural translator of Buddhism in the West also was inaugurated in this book. Indeed, his dedication to the book describes as much. He acknowledges the "spontaneous bop prosody" of JACK KEROUAC; the work of WILLIAM S. BURROUGHS, whose "endless novel" NAKED LUNCH "will drive everybody mad"; and NEAL CASSADY, whose autobiography *The First Third* "enlightened Buddha." Ginsberg's good friend Lucien Carr was also acknowledged on the original dedication page but had Ginsberg remove his name in an effort to keep his privacy. Ginsberg affirms at the close of this dedication that the Beat aesthetic is both a spiritual and cultural enterprise: "All these books," he says of Kerouac's, Burroughs's, and Cassady's volumes, "are published in Heaven."

Williams's final words in the introduction forecast with some accuracy what will follow in the pages to come: "Hold back the edges of your gowns, Ladies, we are going through hell." This commentary significantly prepares the reader for the sufferings of the protagonists of "Howl." Section I of the title poem catalogues the miseries of the poem's protagonists; Section II mythologizes the cause of their debilitating cultural condition in Moloch, "the heavy judger of men"; and Section III dramatizes the potential for redemption in the apocalyptic, conversational call-and-response be-

tween the speaker of the poem and Carl Solomon, with whom Ginsberg spent time in the Columbia Presbyterian Psychiatric Institute in 1949. The following poem in the book, "Footnote to Howl," is constructed as a sequel in which the poet returns from the pilgrimage of "Howl" to affirm the holiness of the world as a lost condition that can be reclaimed from the suffering produced by Moloch: "The bum's as holy as the seraphim! the madman is holy as you my soul are holy! . . . Holy forgiveness! mercy! charity! faith!" The anaphoric repetition of "Holy" in "Footnote to Howl" is a direct response to the same repetition of "Moloch" in Section II of "Howl," suggesting that the unholy condition of the world can be transformed at the level of language—a trust in the power of naming that Ginsberg revisits later in his career, more skeptically in "KADDISH" and with an almost mystical trust in "WICHITA VORTEX SUTRA."

The communal vision expressed in Section III of "Howl" and, subsequently, in "Footnote to Howl" recedes into solitude and loss in the following poem, "A Supermarket in California." This is Ginsberg's most well known of his many homages to Whitman in poetry and prose. Although Ginsberg self-fashioned his reputation as a liberator of American sexual mores, this is one of many poems, such as the earlier "Love Poem on Theme by Whitman" and, later, "Angkor Wat," in which the speaker's sense of himself as a sexual being is fraught with anxiety, longing, and loneliness. A quiet alternative to "Howl" and "Footnote to Howl," this poem opens with the speaker dreaming of Walt Whitman on his walk to the supermarket. His physical hunger brings him to the market, but this destination is a screen for the hunger of desire—for the sexual tension that has caused him to reflect on his gay forefather, Whitman, in the first place. The poet is "self-conscious" and full of "hungry fatigue." He finds a phantasmic Whitman cruising the supermarket stock boys, "poking among the meats in the refrigerator." Whitman's desire is Ginsberg's, too, as often is the case, politically and sexually, in Ginsberg's homages. Thus, when Ginsberg's speaker imagines himself followed by the store detective, the supermarket becomes a figure for cold-war policing of sexual desire in the United States, where McCarthyism questioned homosexuality as anti-American. Eventually, Ginsberg unites with Whitman, and the two walk the supermarket together in the poet's imagined scene, presumably "eyeing the grocery boys" together. Their walk might seem an act of liberation for a poet such as Ginsberg writing in a gay tradition—doing so in Whitman's long-line catalogue form, but with candor that would have been foreign in Whitman's era. Nevertheless, Ginsberg emphasizes of himself and Whitman that they will "both be lonely" in a culture in which digressions—literal and physical—from the sexual status quo produce alienation. In the final strophe of the poem, Ginsberg's speaker reminds himself of the difference between Whitman's America and his own and states with deep loss that the price, for Whitman, of being a precursor poet to subsequent generations was a life on the sexual margins as a "lonely old courage-teacher."

The next two poems recontextualize traditional poetic pastoralism in light of the modern, industrial world. In both "Transcription of Organ Music" and "Sunflower Sutra," the distrust of machinery and technology in "Howl" and the wistful solitude of "A Supermarket in California" are reenvisioned in terms of vision and community. Written from notes taken while listening to Bach's Organ Prelude and Fugue in A Minor, "Transcription of Organ Music" traces the sublime rise and fall of the music as a figure of the cyclic death and rebirth of natural phenomena. Yet in an inversion of traditional pastoral poetry, the ground for the poet's analogy is not nature itself but the artificially reproduced music coming from his record player. The epiphany of the poem—its imagined community between artist and audience mediated by "the presence of the Creator"—is produced by the ordinary artifice of the wiring in the speaker's home. He writes, "The light socket is crudely attached to the ceiling, after the house was built, to receive a plug which sticks in it alright, and serves my phonograph now. . . ."

"Sunflower Sutra" dramatizes this fusion of artifice and nature in the form of a Buddhist sutra, or scriptural narrative. The occasion for the poem was a walk Ginsberg took with Kerouac and PHILIP WHALEN in a San Francisco railyard. The three found an abject sunflower beaten down by the dirt and grime of the trains, "crackly bleak and dusty with the smut and smog and smoke of olden locomotives in its eye." Echoing his own auditory vision of Blake reciting "Ah! Sunflower" in Harlem in 1948, the sunflower in this poem is a catalyst for the poet's transformative vision of himself and his environment. As he does in "Footnote to Howl," Ginsberg constructs a world of machinery and industry in "Sunflower Sutra" that can redeem the natural world rather than, as Moloch, consume it. "Sunflower Sutra" directs its visionary experience inward; but in a revision of the pastoral form from which it borrows, the speaker of the poem sets out to renovate a world in which nature and artifice are coequivalent. The final strophe of the poem famously states this equivalency in one long breathless line reminiscent of Whitman's poetics: "We're not our skin of grime, we're not our dread bleak dusty imageless locomotive, we're all golden sunflowers inside, blessed by our own seed & hairy naked accomplishment-bodies growing into mad black formal sunflowers in the sunset. . . ."

In the next poem, "America," Ginsberg revisits Whitman's idea of America as a poetics of possibility—where, in Whitman's words, "The United States themselves are essentially the greatest poem." One of Ginsberg's major works, "America" is situated in *Howl and Other Poems* as a culmination of the tension between the exterior and interior modes of vision—material reality and the imagination—of the preceding poems. The external and internal combine in "America" to such an extent that it should come as no surprise to readers that halfway through the poem, the speaker declares, "It occurs to me that I am America." The poem's idealistic belief in American potential gives way to a realization of the limits of romantic possibility. In this way, the poem resembles the arc of Whitman's career from the exuberant first edition of *Leaves of Grass* through the dire futurism of *Democratic Vistas*. Romanticism is overwhelmed by nationalism in "America" as the poem moves from short, clipped, comic lines—"America why are your libraries full of tears?"—to adversarial argument, as when the speaker warns, "America stop pushing I know what I'm doing." All the same, the poem never wavers from the absurd, and in this way "America" is a precursor to the goofy political satire of later poems such as "Kral Majales" (1965), "Plutonian Ode" (1982), and "C'mon Pigs of Western Civilization, Eat More Grease" (1999). The cold war is reduced in this poem to theater of the absurd and is rendered in affected language that reminds readers that the presumed birthright of American exceptionalism is based on the colonial conquest of native lands: "The Russia's power mad. She wants to take our cars from out our garages. / Her wants to grab Chicago. Her needs a Red *Reader's Digest*. Her wants our auto plants in Siberia. Him big bureaucracy running our fillingstations." Anticipating the later strategies of writers and theorists who reappropriated the epithet *queer* into the study of gay literature known as queer theory, Ginsberg engages America in an argument to turn its own evaluative terms against it. The speaker of the poem takes his adversary, America, at its word that he is an alienated other because of his sexuality; yet he uses this otherness as a mode of resistance—the same hierarchy of values that alienates him. Proclaiming that he "better get right down to the job," the speaker closes the poem with a vow straight from American utilitarian rhetoric—but for its proud assertion of the speaker's homosexual identity. "America," he promises, "I'm putting my queer shoulder to the wheel."

Howl and Other Poems established Beat poetics as a new generation's avant-garde. As often is the case with experimental work, this book received mixed reviews by the established critics of its era. In this way, perhaps M. L. Rosenthal's 1957 assessment (reprinted in *On the Poetry of Allen Ginsberg*) states the case best for the extremes of both attraction and aversion to the book from critics. In a literary period dominated by the depersonalized mode of new critical poetics, the autobiographical focus of Beat literature was radical in itself, and this focus on autobiographical selfhood, jarring for its time, was more unsettling in the case of *Howl and Other Poems* because of Ginsberg's emphasis on an apocalyptic breakdown and reconstruction of the self in the narrative thread that runs through the book. Rosenthal writes, "Ginsberg may be wrong; his writing may certainly have many false notes and postures. . . . But that is all beside the point. The agony, in any case, is real; so are the threats for the future that it signals."

Bibliography

Breslin, James. "The Origins of 'Howl' and 'Kaddish.'" *Iowa Review* 8, no. 2 (Spring 1977): 82–108.

Ehrlich, J. W., ed. *Howl of the Censor.* San Carlos, Calif.: Nourse Publishing Company, 1961.

Hyde, Lewis. *On the Poetry of Allen Ginsberg.* Ann Arbor: University of Michigan Press, 1984.

Raskin, Jonah. *American Scream: Allen Ginsberg's 'Howl' and the Making of the Beat Generation.* Berkeley: University of California Press, 2004.

Schumacher, Michael. *Dharma Lion: A Critical Biography of Allen Ginsberg.* New York: St. Martin's, 1992.

Trigilio, Tony. *"Strange Prophecies Anew": Rereading Apocalypse in Blake, H.D., and Ginsberg.* Madison, N.J.: Fairleigh Dickinson University Press, 2000.

Tony Trigilio

Huncke, Herbert (1915–1996)

Herbert Huncke introduced the Beats to the term "beat." "Huncke was a crucial figure," writes Ted Morgan in *Literary Outlaw: The Life and Times of William S. Burroughs,* "a sort of Virgilian guide to the lower depths, taking [the Beats] into a world that provided an alternative to the right-thinking banality of Columbia and its so-called teachers. Huncke was the first hipster, who had been on the street since age twelve, and who was basically the victim of police persecution . . . an antihero pointing the way to an embryonic counterculture, which would arise from this Times Square world of hustlers." Huncke was born in Greenfield, Massachusetts, in 1915. The family moved to Chicago where his father, Herbert Spencer Huncke, ran a precision tool shop. His mother, Marguerite Bell Huncke, was the daughter of a prosperous rancher in Laramie, Wyoming. Huncke was less interested in his father's tools than he was with wandering the streets of Chicago. He felt rejected by his father, even though late in life he wrote his father a letter (never sent) in which he told his father that he always loved him and that he understood the reasons behind his harsh discipline. Huncke was sexually molested as a boy, a story he first revealed to Alfred Kinsey as part of his sex survey in 1946 (see GUILTY OF EVERYTHING). When his parents were divorced in 1927, Huncke fell into a wild lifestyle of free sex, of drug and alcohol abuse, and of hoboing around the country. He had a particularly open relation with his mother, with whom he lived after the divorce, admitting his homosexuality as well as his heroin addiction to her. He taught her how to smoke marijuana and gave her tips about sexual techniques. He first learned about heroin from reading a book called *The Little White Hag,* and through his Aunt Olga's connections in Chicago's Chinatown, he learned where he could easily keep supplied in high-quality drugs. Huncke also had a close relationship with his maternal grandmother, who was wealthy, and it was through her influence that he acquired a refined sensibility about the finer things in life, evidenced in his writings. In the 1930s Huncke traveled to the West. He also traveled to New Orleans and Detroit, learning about jazz.

In 1939 Huncke moved to New York City and decide to live in the Times Square area simply because it was the only part of New York about which he had ever heard anything. He would live there for the rest of his life. In the New York of the 1930s and early 1940s, he lived as a male hustler, picking up sexually frustrated businessmen in Bryant Park. He also picked up his heroin and morphine habit again. He was a friend and associate of many of the Times Square grifters, con men, and prostitutes at the time, including Vickie Russell, Little Jack Melody, Phil White, and Bob Brandenberg.

It was through Brandenburg, a want-to-be gangster who worked at a drugstore soda fountain, that Huncke first met WILLIAM S. BURROUGHS. Burroughs had acquired a machine gun and several cases of morphine syrettes, and Brandenburg told him that White and Huncke would know how to dispose of them. Huncke was initially suspicious of Burroughs, who dressed conservatively and did not know the language of the underworld. However, when Burroughs allowed Huncke to shoot him up with morphine, he was convinced of Burroughs's trustworthiness. Burroughs introduced Huncke to ALLEN GINSBERG, JACK KEROUAC, GREGORY CORSO, NEAL CASSADY, and many other members of the Beat group. In Kerouac's case, Huncke with his "beat" lifestyle of living on the street, came to represent a whole generation's attitude toward society. The Huncke of these years is captured as Junky in Kerouac's The TOWN AND THE CITY,

Burroughs's Herman in JUNKY, and in John Clellon Holmes's GO as Albert Ancke. Huncke is also the figure Ginsberg had in mind when he wrote, "dragging themselves through the negro streets at dawn looking for an angry fix," the second line of "HOWL."

Huncke, in turn, introduced these writers to the underworld, and Burroughs's hardboiled style and subject matter of *Junky* and QUEER can be attributed in large part to this association. In this regard, Jack Kerouac is often quoted as saying (in a letter he wrote to Neal Cassady on September 13, 1947), "[Huncke] is the greatest storyteller I know, an actual genius at it, in my mind." Huncke, as Jerome Poynton concludes, was "remarkably apt at contributing to the intellectual growth of his friends." In fact, and in spite of his sense of being intellectually inferior to the Beats, Huncke not only continued to inspire these artists but also, during this period, began to write the sketches and keep the notebooks that would eventually be published as The EVENING SUN TURNED CRIMSON and HUNCKE'S JOURNAL.

On and off during the 1940s Huncke worked as a merchant seaman. At one point, he and Phil White shipped out to kick their junk habits (see *The Evening Sun Turned Crimson*). In 1947 Huncke lived as Burroughs's farmhand near New Waverly, Texas, where they attempted to grow opium poppies and had some success growing marijuana (see *Guilty of Everything*). A few years later, Huncke was also involved in the crime that led to Ginsberg's stay at the Columbia Presbyterian Psychiatric Institute, which is where he met Carl Solomon and the inspiration for "Howl" began (see *Guilty of Everything*).

Huncke spent most of the 1950s in jail for possession and for burglary charges: He probably committed more than 100 burglaries in the New York area in the 1940s and 1950s. Many of his best writings describe his experiences in various prisons. While he was in jail, his Beat friends became famous, and Huncke would read about them in the newspapers. He appears to have been genuinely happy that they had reached the potential he had always seen in them. None of the Beats wrote Huncke in prison, nor did they visit him, a fact he did not hold against them.

When he returned to the "outside" in the early 1960s, his social life revolved around Ginsberg and Peter Orlovsky's apartment on Avenue C in what was being called the East Village. Here he met the poet JANINE POMMY VEGA and the visual artist Bill Heine, inventor of the tie-dye process (see *Huncke's Journal*). When Ginsberg and Orlovsky went to India for an extended stay in 1961, this methamphetamine-fueled scene in the Village fell apart. By 1964, when Burroughs returned to New York a world-famous author, Huncke began to be able to trade on his literary association with the famous Beats. He was paid simply to tell stories about them and throughout the rest of his life was able to more or less live off his storytelling abilities.

Irving Rosenthal, who had published parts of *NAKED LUNCH* in *Big Table* in 1959, worked with Huncke on revising his work for publication, and in 1965 *Huncke's Journal* came out with The Poets Press, started by DIANE DI PRIMA. Perhaps the best portrait of Huncke appears in Rosenthal's novel from a few years later, *Sheeper* (1967). In 1968 Huncke became an overnight media celebrity by appearing on the David Susskind television show and openly discussing his addiction to heroin and use of other illegal drugs. Out of this appearance came his first mainstream publication when "Alvarez" was published in *Playboy*.

By this point in his life, Huncke was no longer a criminal and was on a methadone maintenance program (his 100-milligram daily dose a lethal one for most people). His constant companion beginning in these years was photographer Louis Cartwright, who was murdered in 1994. More of Huncke's work was published in the 1970s, including two of his best-received stories, "Elsie John" (a hermaphrodite he knew as a young man) and "Joseph Martinez," which were published in a limited edition by Huncke's Chicago friend, R'lene Dahlberg. In 1980 his work was collected in the classic *The Evening Sun Turned Crimson*. *Guilty of Everything* (1990) is a transcript of interviews with Huncke, although there is very little difference discernible between his written style and his oral style of storytelling. Unpublished and fugitive pieces are gathered together in the final section of *The Herbert Huncke Reader* (which also includes the texts of his previous books) published to wide acclaim and very positive critical reception in 1998.

Huncke died at the age of 81 in 1997. In the latter years of his life, his rent at the Chelsea Hotel was paid by the Grateful Dead, and he was surrounded by a group of young admirers who more or less traded off the responsibility of his care. By then, he was not only a link to the Beats but also to a bygone era of hobo jungles, prohibition, New York before the war, and the Village before it was "The Village." Huncke's most profound influence on the Beats was similar to Neal Cassady's—as a muse, as a picaresque "character" who gave the mostly middle-class Beats a view of a world that—at the time—they could only observe but to which they could never fully belong. Unlike Cassady, however, Huncke did apply himself more or less seriously as a writer, and his three books are essential reading for fans and scholars of the Beat Generation. In fact, Huncke must be considered one of the dozen or so key personalities and writers in the whole Beat movement.

Bibliography

Huncke, Herbert. *The Herbert Huncke Reader*. Edited by Benjamin G. Schafer. New York: William Morrow and Company, Inc., 1997.

Morgan, Ted. *Literary Outlaw: The Life and Times of William S. Burroughs*. New York: Henry Holt and Company, 1988.

Rob Johnson

Huncke's Journal Herbert Huncke (1965)

This is one of the more important memoirs by a male writer from the Beat Generation. DIANE DI PRIMA first published *Huncke's Journal* in 1965 as the second book to appear on her Poet's Press list. HERBERT HUNCKE, who always liked di Prima, had run into her on the street the year before, and she asked him if had anything she might be able to publish. He went home and gathered up odd essays and fragments of a memoir dating from 1948 to 1964 and gave them to her. They were written—scrawled—in loopy handwriting in a school notebook. The first edition of 1,000 copies sold quickly. A second edition, published in 1968 with a brief introduction by ALLEN GINSBERG, ended up being distributed for free along Haight Street in San Francisco, where di Prima had moved.

Although the book was assembled from Huncke's "journal," it is less a diary of Huncke's life than a series of character sketches and pointed anecdotes drawn from his experience. He is conscious that his strength as a writer lies in the storytelling of the bizarre nature of many of these experiences and that he has lived in a way that few do who are ever able to bring back the stories alive. As WILLIAM S. BURROUGHS says in his foreword to *The Herbert Huncke Reader,* "Huncke had adventures and misadventures that were not available to middle-class, comparatively wealthy college people like Kerouac and me."

Huncke's own selection for his "strangest" experience—and he qualifies this by saying many others would equal it—is the story "In the Park," drawn from his teenage years when he liked to wander through Chicago's Olmsted Park. There he is abducted at knifepoint by a degenerate who forces him to watch him masturbate as he looks at a picture of a naked young girl. This is a terrible story, dangerous and sad. Huncke can sympathize, though, with even the lowest, most maniacal of human beings: "He was unquestionably an excellent example of just what can happen to a human being in a society geared to greed and power where the human element is almost entirely ignored except in lip service to man as an individual." In other words, "the human element" needs to be restored to our relations with each other to better understand—and prevent—the kind of terrible human he encounters. This story is not just a shocking one, though: It is expertly told, dramatically paced, and not nearly as sensational as the events it describes.

Huncke's range is not limited to the bizarre, though. "Ponderosa Pine" is a beautiful description of the mountains and forests of Idaho, one of the many places he passed through in his hoboing years during the late 1920s and early 1930s. In this story he takes a ride in a Model T with the 17-year-old son of a forest ranger. The drive is spectacular, but they are caught in a storm and the car is wrecked. Huncke tries to tell the boy's father of the beauty of what they had seen, but the forest ranger is un-

impressed by Huncke's rhapsodizing over the scenery and the sublimity of the storm that they rode through in the high mountain passes. "I guess he had decided I wasn't a very stable kind of person," says Huncke. Huncke's honesty leads him to discover a meaning in the story that was very similar to the feeling Wordsworth reveals in "The Prelude" when he realizes that he has crossed the Alps without even knowing it, missing a longed-for experience. Here, in retrospect, Huncke is not quite sure if there "really wasn't any Ponderosa there at all." But it doesn't matter: The image of these pines has stirred the beautiful memory years later in a self-described "old drug-soaked city character like myself."

An aspect of *Huncke's Journal* that makes it almost unique among the writing of the Beats—with the possible exception of a few episodes in Kerouac's novels—is his close and sympathetic documentation of the lives of the women he knew. Countless women whose lives would have otherwise gone unrecorded appear in these pages. Huncke *listened* to them and can still see them in his mind's eye—down to very specific details of the kinds of clothes they wore. "Cat and His Girl" is one of Huncke's sensitive and detailed portraits of girls and women in the scene. This is the story of an interracial romance. The girl's father has her institutionalized because she wants to marry a black man: "You see my mother and father think I am insane. They have had me locked up twice." Even when she and her boyfriend are both holding down jobs and trying to succeed in their lives, the father manages to break them up: "I know how to handle niggers," he threatens the young man. Such pressures lead Cat into drugs, and she becomes a prostitute to support her habit. Her ex-boyfriend sees her around occasionally; often she is bruised from the beatings that her clients give her. The young man confides in Huncke that they never really had a chance: "All she really wanted was love." Huncke's moral applies generally to the lives of the free-spirited young women (and men) he knows: "I could only think of how tragic the story was and of the vast amount of stupidity and cruelty inflicted on the two of them and how little chance she ever had of discovering any kind of happiness."

For many of the young people in his stories, Huncke hovers about as a kind of guardian angel, an observer who has seen it all and wishes he could protect the vulnerable young men and women who were going through the kinds of experiences he had in the 1920s and 1930s. In "Frisky," he is part of the Bleecker Street methamphetamine scene that has attracted "unusually beautiful" girls, some as young as 14 years old. When one of them is about to shoot up, he has a premonition, but fails to act on it. The girl dies of an overdose.

Several sections of the book record Huncke's memories of the early 1960s East Village methamphetamine scene, and describe the lives of his roommates on Ave C—JANINE POMMY VEGA, Bill Heine, and Elise Cowen. Vega is one of Huncke's favorites. Allen Ginsberg and Peter Orlovsky hold this scene together with their influence, but when they sail for India, the scene falls apart. Huncke's description of all-night, sometimes three-or-four-day-long meth sessions, in which they "were assembled with minute attention to detail," are probably the best record available of this early 1960s drug subculture. Huncke's own reaction to the drug is that it is as if his "whole self was imbued with all that was happening around—the scene, the people, and many layers of consciousness just awakened." Here and elsewhere Huncke says of the use of speed, heroin, marijuana and other drugs that they are directly responsible for expanding his consciousness.

JACK KEROUAC often credited Huncke with introducing him to the word *beat* as it applied to a particular kind of person on the scene, and *Huncke's Journal* captures that quality of "beatness" throughout. Huncke himself turns to thievery even though he "didn't like the idea of being a thief—but neither did I like the idea of being respectably a slave." Huncke was "beat" when the writers of that generation were still in childhood, and when the Beats themselves were becoming prominent writers in the 1950s, Huncke, their former companion, spent the decade mostly in various prisons. There he read about the furor over Ginsberg's "HOWL" and of Kerouac's success with ON THE ROAD. The Beats did not visit him nor write him in prison, but Huncke did not hold this against them. "Halowe'en" describes his return from prison to New York and being welcomed back by the intellectuals and artistic community of East Village, including Ginsberg, Orlvosky, Vega, and many

other Beats: "They—those of them—creative and basically honest—at least as they understood honesty—had moved forward and had started speaking aloud—and had written great poems and books—and the world had made a place for them—because of their beauty and fineness, and because they are beautiful and good they were kind in their knowledge of me and welcomed me back and—now part of Bohemia—asked me to join them attending several Hallowe'en parties and I accepted." He captures the special quality of his bohemian friends by saying how good it was to be back among spiritual people—"inner value in this instance referring to God and love and openness and a search for peace—both individually and collectively." Beat, argued Kerouac, meant "beatitude," and Huncke's observations here support his claim.

Huncke returned to the East Village at the time of the Cuban missile crisis, and reading his time capsule account of 1961 illustrates how the ideas of the peace and love movement of the 1960s were already very much in the air: "Yesterdays headlines—our great American president states, 'We now have sufficient bomb power to blow Russia off the face of the earth.' . . . Enough of hate—breeding hate—resenting each other—we need more love." Many of the ideas expressed by Huncke in this book will move from the margin to the center very quickly, resulting in widespread protest against the Vietnam War, the establishment of the nuclear-freeze movement, and the emergence of a strong environmental movement around the world.

Bibliography
Burroughs, William S. Foreword. *The Herbert Huncke Reader*, by Herbert Huncke, edited by Benjamin G. Schafer. New York: William Morrow, 1997, ix.

Rob Johnson

Hundred Camels in the Courtyard, A
Paul Bowles (1962)

The four so-called kif stories (kif is a mixture of cannabis leaves and tobacco), "A Friend of the World," "The Story of Lachen and Idir," "He of the Assembly," and "The Wind at Beni Midar," that constitute the collection A *Hundred Camels in the*

Courtyard represent an attempt to describe aspects of "contemporary life in a land where cannabis, rather than alcohol, customarily provides a way out of the phenomenological world." The stories demonstrate the traditional belief among Moroccans that the kif smoker will always outsmart the drinker of alcohol, an intoxicant that is thought to "dull the senses." Kif, on the other hand, is "the means to attaining a state of communication not only with others, but above all with the smokers themselves." The title of the short story collection, incidentally, is taken from an Arab proverb claiming that "a pipe of kif before breakfast gives a man the strength of a hundred camels in the courtyard."

In his autobiography PAUL BOWLES has described how much pleasure the writing of these four stories gave him. He would start out by inventing problems of literary narrative and then find ways of resolving them:

> Let us say that I started out with four disparate fragments—anecdotes, quotations, or simple clauses deprived of context—gleaned from separate sources and involving, if anything, entirely different sets of characters. The task was to invent a connecting narrative tissue which would make all four of the original elements equally supportive of the resulting construction. It seemed to me that the subject of kif smoking, wholly apart from the desirable limiting of possibilities it implied, would provide as effective cement with which to put together the various fragments. By using kif-inspired motivations, the arbitrary could be made to seem natural, the diverse elements could be fused, and several people would automatically become one. I did four of these tales, and then there seemed to be no more material.

While kif smoking plays a part in all four of the stories, it is only in "He of the Assembly" that Bowles attempts to approximate in prose the state of *M'Hashish,* that is, of being intoxicated by kif, a condition with which he was himself well acquainted. Bowles does so by means of a nonlinear and hallucinatory narrative technique. The reader enters into the world of kif, as it were, a

world where such distinctions as internal/external, dream/reality, subjective/objective, and past/present/future dissolve. Simultaneously, the overall structure and composition of the story is carefully orchestrated into seven paragraphs that, as Bowles has explained, are "built into four levels—level 1 is the same as level 7; 2 is the same as 6; 3 the same as 5, and 4 is a kind of interior monologue, told in the first person, which is the crucial part, which is the center—or top, if you like—of the pyramid." It appears that Bowles's background as a composer of music becomes especially pronounced in this carefully executed story.

In "He of the Assembly" (a literal translation of the Arab name Bouyemi) the dominant motif is that of the eye. At the beginning of the story He of the Assembly, in a state of *M'Hashish,* is trying to place somewhere in his past the phrase "the eye wants to sleep but the head is no mattress." Throughout the story the other protagonist, Ben Tajeh, is haunted by having, or perhaps not having, received a letter containing the phrase "the sky trembles and the earth is afraid, and the two eyes are not brothers." Eyes are mentioned throughout the text, suggesting the theme of vision, and at the end of the narrative He of the Assembly looks "across his sleep to the morning," emphasizing the final intersection of the levels of vision: physical and psychic.

Bowles's main aim in this story is to communicate to the reader the experience of being *M'Hashish.* Among the main characteristics of that experience are an altered sense of the physical body, a severance of the bonds between mind and matter, and a feeling of well-being, gaiety and calm. To Charles Baudelaire the hashish experience was a disturbing one, a "confusing fury" as opposed to opium, the "gentle seducer." Baudelaire also found hashish to have the effect of enfeebling the will power, of riveting the attention on trivial and minute detail, and of magnifying the sensation of time and space. The reader of "He of the Assembly" will find all of these states of consciousness embedded in the story.

In the other three kif stories the recurrent motif is that of the clever kif smoker who gets the better of a friend or an enemy who is invariably a drinker of alcohol. Sometimes this is done by using poison or magic, as in "A Friend of the World" and in "The Wind at Beni Midar"; or it is done by sheer cunning, as between the two friends in "The Story of Lachen and Idir." A subordinate theme of these stories is the changing social and political conditions of Morocco, which contribute to a sense of confusion of identity in the minds of the protagonists, a confusion aggravated by living concurrently in the old and the new Morocco.

In all four of the stories a recent change in attitude toward kif smoking on the part of the Moroccan authorities is stressed. The Koran does warn against "befuddlement of the mind," but "it does not mention herbs." The stories repeatedly accentuate the fact that the opposition to kif comes not from religious injunctions but from a government focused on modernization. Bowles looked with regret at the passing of a more tolerant attitude toward kif. However, with his usual caution, he also warned against overindulgence, pointing out that "apparently you can't keep it up and not be mindless."

Bowles's work in undertaking translations from the Moghrebi (one of the languages spoken in Morocco) into English may have suggested to him the use of nonlinear narrative structures and techniques, as explored in A Hundred Camels in the Courtyard. Given that he regarded the writing process as an excursion into the unconscious, he felt that the use of kif had been an unfailing aid to him. He explained that "the kif is simply the key which opens a door to some particular chamber of the brain that lets whatever was in there out. It doesn't supply the matter. It liberates whatever's in, that's all."

Bowles's kif stories represent perhaps the clearest link between his writing and that of the Beats, in whose work cannabis figures prominently as a source of insight. From WILLIAM S. BURROUGHS's JUNKY and NAKED LUNCH, to ALLEN GINSBERG's HOWL and JACK KEROUAC's ON THE ROAD, the benign and revelatory effects of marijuana are celebrated. Indeed, not only did these authors write about marijuana, but they frequently used the drug as an aid in their writing.

Similarly, the interest of many Beat writers in interior states, including dreams and visions, and in the intuitive mind and spontaneous, instinctual life of "primitive" people, has a counterpart in Bowles's fiction. Such interest is anticipated in Bowles's

novel Let It Come Down (1952) and is confirmed in the kif stories collected in A Hundred Camels in the Courtyard.

Bibliography

Bowles, Paul. Without Stopping. An Autobiography. New York: G. P. Putnam's Sons, 1972.

Ebin, David, ed. The Drug Experience. New York: Grove Press, 1965.

Hayter, Alethea. Opium and the Romantic Imagination. Berkeley, Calif.: Faber & Faber, 1968.

Stewart, Lawrence D. Paul Bowles—The Illumination of North Africa. Carbondale: Southern Illinois University Press, 1974.

Birgit Stephenson

"Hymn to the Rebel Café" Ed Sanders
(1993)

From the ancient poet who "came in a skiff / across the Nile / with satires in his pocket" to such 20th-century rebels as Jean-Paul Sartre and Janis Joplin, "Hymn to the Rebel Café" praises the unruly tradition of chaos seekers, musicians, artists, and thinkers who have reshaped history's paradigms—and the venues that have supported them. In this poem, ED SANDERS celebrates the relentless spirit of rebellion throughout human history.

> He opens,
> They were planning a revolution
> To end want & hunger
>
> They were plotting a new form of thinking
> They were arguing in blue smoke
> A direction for art
> They were ready to change the world, "to topple the towers// in the rebel café."

For Sanders, more than just the individual rebellious spirit but also any gathering of the like-minded serves to incubate insurgent thinking. Thus he uses the café both literally as a locus for such groups and symbolically as a churchlike venue to frame his poem. Just as a church is any space where two or more gather in religious concert, the café functions here in rebellious concert where hymns of holy maintenance are replaced with ideas for widespread change. In calling his poem a hymn, Sanders ironically praises the rebel from the pews of the oppressor.

In addition, most of Sanders's poems were written in the bardic tradition, to be performed, often with the aid of special lyres designed by Sanders himself. Thus, in concept, the poem is literally hymnlike. As Dan Barth writes, reviewing the work after hearing Sanders perform the poem, "Of course it is impossible to capture [the performed poem] on the printed page, but it's the next best thing and a good approximation. The line breaks correspond well with breaths and stops." "Hymn to the Rebel Café" is intentionally infused with music.

Sanders sings the praises of the modern cafés that have acted as venues and safe havens for artists, bohemians, and radicals. He hails "The Philadelphia Taverns / of 1776," the "Café Royale / on 2nd Avenue" and "Austin's Fox Bar, Paris 1904." He goes on: "Hail to the Stray Dog, to the Café Trieste! / Hail to the, o Total Assault Cantina! / Salutes, o Greater Detroit Zen Zone! / Hail, o Sempiternal Scrounge Lounge of Topeka!" The list continues.

Unlike churches, however, cafés are far more volatile and prone to the whims of the market and to the scrutiny of the state to which its denizens stand in constant opposition. Sanders writes, "We'll have to keep on / opening & closing our / store fronts, our collectives, / our social action centers / till tulips are in the sky."

Yet the rebel café will never be totally gone; it will only shift from one location to another because, again like the church, it is not a location so much as the intention of its members. Sanders closes, "The cafes come / The cafes wane / but the best and the final rebel café / is inside the human brain."

Bibliography

Barth, Dan. Review of *Hymn to the Rebel Café*. Literary Kicks: Available online. URL: www.litkicks.com. Accessed May 31, 2006.

Jennifer Cooper

I

In His Own Write John Lennon (1964)

At the very breaking point of worldwide Beatle-mania, JOHN LENNON, who was directly afterward dubbed the "clever" Beatle, added to his notorious pop-chart success with a literary best seller, bearing a name donated by Paul McCartney, *In His Own Write*. (Apocryphal or not, the story goes that it was originally to be called "In His Own Write and Draw"—except at the last minute the multiple puns seemed unnecessarily awkward.) Published by Jonathan Cape in the United Kingdom and by Simon and Schuster in the United States, it was an instant international success and won the Foyles Literary Prize. Said the *Times Literary Supplement*, "Worth the attention of anyone who fears for the impoverishment of the English language and the British imagination." Lennon was hailed as a new literary voice, while similar accolades were bestowed upon BOB DYLAN as a serious balladeer and spokesman for his generation. Amid the bombast, a quiet rivalry between the two was established.

Lennon's poems, word play, and comical drawings were the accumulated satirical jabs and musings of a young man on the road, a young man capable of much more than just constructing pop songs or sending shivers up teenage girls' spines with his dynamic vocals. A slim volume, *In His Own Write* is the essence of what it is to be all things Liverpudlian—inordinately irreverent, riotously yet subtly funny, fiercely individualistic, and naturally theatrical. With his gift of cutting dialogue, Lennon mocks hypocrites, mediocrity, the banal, and the sanctimonious, and he does it with savagely wicked glee. Critics and fans alike were quick to point out his obvious influences—James Joyce (Lennon said that he had never heard of him), Edward Lear (him either), Chaucer (said that he had never read him). He did admit to being partial to Lewis Carroll and even later wrote his "I Am the Walrus" as a response to Carroll's "The Walrus and the Carpenter."

Foyles Bookstore held a literary luncheon in Lennon's honor at the Dorchester Hotel in April 1964. Not since George Bernard Shaw had been similarly honored had so many requests for invitations been received. When the young author, hung-over from his own previous night of revelry, was called to make a speech, he stood, mumbled something incoherent, and sat back down. Explanations of what he actually said conflict with one another. It could have been, "God bless you," "It's been a pleasure," or "You've got a lucky face"—this last an expression of gratitude made by Liverpool panhandlers after having received a handout.

So popular was Lennon's maiden literary voyage that he was asked for more, and in 1965 *A Spaniard in the Works* was published. This undertaking required more immediate attention, as there were no verses or drawings left, and Lennon was required to start his writing anew. Once again the results were well received and publicized (in the movie *Help!* Lennon appears in one vignette shamelessly kissing a copy of the book), and by the end of the decade American writer Adrienne Kennedy had adapted both Lennon works as a play, *In*

151

His Own Write, directed by Lennon's close friend, actor Victor Spinetti, at the Old Vic Theatre.

Lennon takes aim at mainstream life and values in his two collections and often the attacks are not only uproariously funny but vitriolic as well, perhaps even mean spirited. He ranks with the best of his American precursors of the Beat Generation, those who had had enough of being marginalized or ignored or ridiculed simply because they were different or because they held different views and a hope for a more inclusive society.

Bibliography

Brown, Peter, and Steven Gaines. *The Love You Make: An Insider's Story of The Beatles.* New York: Signet, 1983.
Coleman, Ray. *Lennon.* New York: McGraw Hill, 1984.
———. *A Spaniard in the Works.* New York: Simon & Schuster, 1964.
———. *Skywriting by Word of Mouth.* New York: Harper & Row, 1986.

Greg Herriges

"In Memory of Radio"   Amiri Baraka   (1959)

First appearing in *White Dove Review* in 1959, "In Memory of Radio" is perhaps AMIRI BARAKA's (LeRoi Jones) most famous poem. Later collected in *PREFACE TO A TWENTY VOLUME SUICIDE NOTE*, this work connects Baraka's understanding of the duality of the black experience in America with the slipperiness of popular culture. With "maudlin nostalgia" that is apparent in other poems such as "Look For You Yesterday, Here You Come Today," Baraka looks beneath the surface of American popular culture in what David L. Smith describes as "the most fundamental of Christian dilemmas: the knowledge of good and evil." Wondering at the divinity of Lamont Cranston, the alter-ego of The Shadow in the mystery 1930s radio program by that name, Baraka both looks back at the innocence of childhood and raises the specter of the black experience in an American society with a distinctively white consciousness. "Shadow" is not only black vernacular English for an African American, the very word suggests a kind of invisibility.

Baraka conjures the images of violence, both physical and epistemological, against blacks when he mentions Goody Knight. As John Hakac has pointed out, California governor Goodwin "Goody" Knight was in part responsible for keeping Caryl Whittier Chessman on Death Row for more than a decade. When the poem was first published in 1959, international outrage flamed over the inhumanity of this process. Knight neither issued any stay of execution nor pardoned Chessman. He simply provided a rhetoric of social stability behind which a mechanism of injustice could grind. The image of Goody Knight acts as a metaphor for the popular culture that the poet ponders, the surface of harmony hides no real altruism. Demonstrating through his hallmark typographic slight of hand, Baraka shows the double nature of love: "Love is an evil word. / Turn it backwards / see, see what I mean? An evol word."

Remembering his childhood love for such programs as *Red Lantern* and *Let's Pretend* leaves the poet feeling uneasy. He mourns the loss of his innocence, being able to believe in the surface of things. As for pretending, the poet still does "Thank God!" Like the programs themselves, his love for popular culture had an underside. He had to give it up or be subsumed by the dominant hegemony. "It is better to have loved and lost / Than to put linoleum in your living room?" However, the poet frets at his own impotence in the face of the myths of American culture, a recurring theme in *Preface to a Twenty Volume Suicide Note,* and admits complicity with it.

Bibliography

Hakac, John. "Baraka's 'In Memory of Radio'." *Concerning Poetry* 10, no. 1 (1977): 85.
Hudson, Theodore. *From LeRoi Jones to Amiri Baraka: The Literary Works.* Durham, N.C.: Duke University Press, 1973.
Smith, David L. "Amiri Baraka and the Black Arts of Black Art." *boundary 2* 15, nos. 1/2 (Autumn, 1986–Winter 1987): 235–254.
Sollors, Werner. "Does Axel's Castle Have a Street Address, or, What's New? Tendencies in the Poetry of Amiri Baraka (LeRoi Jones)." *boundary 2* 6, no. 2 (Winter 1978): 387–414.

Stephanie S. Morgan

Interzone **William S. Burroughs** (1989)

This collection gathers material WILLIAM S. BUR-ROUGHS wrote after completing *JUNKY* and *QUEER*. The title is derived from Tangier's status as an "international zone" during the time that Burroughs lived there. Originally, this material was part of what would become the *NAKED LUNCH* manuscript, but very little of the actual text of *Interzone* appears in *Naked Lunch;* nor does Burroughs avail himself of this material in the cut-ups trilogy that followed *Naked Lunch.* The work collected here thus provides a key transition between the linear, hard-boiled style of *Junky* and the surreal, poetic, fragmented style of *Naked Lunch.* Along with *Queer* and *The YAGE LETTERS, Interzone* is crucial reading for those who wish to come to *Naked Lunch* by following the author's early development. Certainly, a familiarity with the earlier works enables a much more informed reading of the difficult *Naked Lunch.*

In his introduction to *Interzone,* James Grauerholz, Burroughs's longtime companion and editor, says that *Interzone* is based on an early manuscript version of *Naked Lunch* rediscovered by Bill Morgan in 1984 among ALLEN GINSBERG's papers at Columbia University. "Interzone" was in fact the working title of *Naked Lunch.* Grauerholz included the material from this lost manuscript that had not been previously published and supplemented it with work from the same period that he found in Burroughs's collections at the University of Arizona, Columbia, and the University of Texas at Austin. Many of these pieces were first written in letter form to Ginsberg. The most significant find in the manuscript at Columbia is entitled "Word," a literary bloodletting that reads as if Burroughs is purging himself to transform himself.

From the collection at the University of Arizona, Grauerholz includes "Twilight's Last Gleamings," first written with Kells Elvins in 1938. Based upon the sinking of the *Morro Castle* in 1935, this story of a captain and his crew sneaking aboard the lifeboats of a sinking ship exists in various shorter versions in other works by Burroughs. This is one of Burroughs's favorite stories, and he uses it often as a metaphor for what happens when the "ship of state" goes down: Those responsible for sinking it jump ship and leave the passengers to die.

In the next story, "The Finger," a man cuts off the end of his finger to impress a woman. Although written in the third person about a character named Lee (Burroughs's mother's maiden name), the story is clearly an autobiographical retelling of Burroughs's own attempt to impress his boyhood love Jack Anderson. However, Burroughs worried that the homosexual angle would render the story unpublishable and changed the object of desire from male to female. In later years, Burroughs would further obfuscate the facts, claiming, for example, that the finger end was blown off in a chemistry accident. The straightforward, factual presentation of the act of cutting off one's finger reflects the emotionless, junk-influenced style of *Junky.*

"Driving Lesson" has a similar style and is also about his relationship with Anderson. The Burroughs character is called "Bill," and he and Jack carouse in the bars of East St. Louis. Bill comes to realize that Jack is stupid and asks Jack if he would like to drive his car, even though Jack has little experience behind the wheel. As if to prove his point about Jack's stupidity, Bill encourages him to drive so fast and recklessly that Jack ends up totaling Bill's father's car. The clear self-destructive urge of Bill is not commented upon. His father takes him home and makes little of the incident, since neither Jack nor Bill was seriously hurt.

"The Junky's Christmas" has actually been anthologized in collections of holiday stories. As is true of the previous two stories, this one was written in a letter to Ginsberg (circa mid-1950s) with the hopes that he could have it published. It is the story of "Danny the Car Wiper" who, on Christmas Day, comes out of a three-day jail sentence junk-sick and broke. When Danny finally scores, he gives up his junk to a young man in the flophouse apartment next to his who is suffering horribly from kidney stones. A Christmas miracle occurs for Danny when he suddenly feels "a warm flood" pulsing through his veins, and he thinks that, because it is Christmas, he must have *"scored the immaculate fix."*

The remaining stories in this section are all set in Tangier and are only loosely related. Grauerholz selected them from among the letters Burroughs sent to Ginsberg. "Lee and the Boys" is

Burroughs's most extensive picture of his life with Kiki, the Spanish boy who appears in many of his works: "Like many Spanish boys, Kiki did not feel love for women. To him a woman was only for sex. He had known Lee for some months, and felt a genuine fondness for him, in an offhand way." A second brief Tangier story, "In the Café Central," sketches a crowd of sybarites and scavengers who live in hotel lobbies, prey on the rich, and delight in each other's humiliations. One anecdote here has to do with Tennessee Williams, an unapproachably famous guest in Tangier, who is nonetheless approached by one of these sybarites and rebuffs him. Burroughs eventually met Williams, and they became friendly. The related "Dream of the Penal Colony" casts Tangier metaphorically as a place inhabited by colonists who are actually prisoners. The colonists can be recognized by "the penal colony look: control, without inner calm or balance; bitter knowledge, without maturity; intensity, without warmth or love." This useful list of characteristics reveals Burroughs's growing ambivalence about Tangier, which had originally appealed to him (as had Mexico) as a place of total freedom. The intrigue and secret-agent plot here will surface in the passages of *Naked Lunch* that are set in Tangier.

Burroughs wrote "International Zone" in response to Ginsberg's suggestion that he might be able to sell a magazine article about his Moroccan experiences and observations. Burroughs would later reject the essay as far too conventional, but it is hardly so and can hold its place with the very best travel writing of the period. It is also a revealing self-portrait of Burroughs as fatally defeated character. For Burroughs and the other desperate characters living there, the "special attraction of Tangier can be put in one word: exemption. Exemption from interference, legal or otherwise. Your private life is your own, to act exactly as you please." Such freedom was crucial for Burroughs at this period, having been successively run out of America and Mexico. Burroughs would eventually leave Tangier because he felt the walls closing in after Morocco gained independence and Tangier was no longer an international zone.

The "Lee's Journals" section of the book is mostly drawn from letters that Burroughs sent to Ginsberg. During this period, Burroughs drew no

line between the writing of letters and the writing of his books, and he depended on Ginsberg to collect and edit his work. The "journals" detail Burroughs's development of the novel that would become *Naked Lunch*. They testify to Burroughs's heavy self-criticism of his work, show how thoroughly he revised his work, and how willing he was to cut out any material that was not up to his high standards. For example, many of the "routines" included here were cut from *Naked Lunch*.

These journal entries also reveal Burroughs's dedication to creating a new kind of self-referential novel. As he says of himself in "International Zone," he is in a "larval" stage, ready to change into something but not knowing what: "What am I trying to do in writing?" he asks in "Lee's Journals." "This novel is about transitions, larval forms, emergent telepathic faculty, attempts to control and stifle new forms. . . . I feel there is some hideous new force loose in the world like a creeping sickness, spreading, blighting." While in *Junky*, *Queer*, and *The Yage Letters* he reconstructed his past; he writes that the new novel "is an attempt to create my future. In a sense, it is a guidebook, a map." Such notes suggest that *Naked Lunch* is a more personal book than has been understood before: It is literally Burroughs's guidebook for his life.

Burroughs saw the writing of *Interzone*/*Naked Lunch* as decidedly antiliterary. He says in "Lee's Journals" that until he was 35 and wrote *Junky*, he "had a special abhorrence for writing, for my thoughts and feelings put down on a piece of paper." To overcome this hatred of literary novels and of their self-revealing "feelings," Burroughs wrote in a hard-boiled style in *Junky*, displaced his "feelings" in the "routines" of *Queer*, and put together an epistolary novel in *The Yage Letters*. Throughout these journal entries, he struggles to articulate a form of novel writing that will not disgust him. Essential to his concept of the novel is its fragmentary nature and its self-referentiality: "The fragmentary quality of the work is inherent in the method and will resolve itself as necessary. That is, I include the author Lee, in the novel, and by so doing separate myself from him so that he becomes another character." Such notes show that the radical form of *Naked Lunch* was thoroughly thought-out beforehand. "The Tangier novel," he writes, "will consist of Lee's impressions of Tangier, instead of the outworn novelistic pretense that he is dealing directly with his characters and situations. That is, *I include the author in the novel.*" He will not, as some other novelists do, pretend that the author is hidden. Another key to the technique of *Interzone/Naked Lunch* is the "routine" that he first developed in *Queer.* The routine allows for the "uncontrollable, the unpredictable," and the dangerous to enter into the novel. Such explicit technical discussions of the writing of *Naked Lunch* are invaluable, and scholars of *Naked Lunch* will find the "Ginsberg Notes" section here to be central.

"Word" is the longest piece in *Interzone* and quite possibly are the words that JACK KEROUAC typed that gave him nightmares when he visited Tangier in 1957. In many ways, this manuscript can be seen as a rehearsal for the kind of "antinovel" that Burroughs has sketched out in the "Ginsberg Notes" and other journal entries. It does take on the kind of mosaic form that Burroughs sought. But the work is decidedly undisciplined, too: "This book spill off the page in all directions." "Word" is more than anything else the record of Burroughs's first sustained attempt to unleash his "word hoard." The method is purgative; the metaphors, not accidentally, scatological. Like *Naked Lunch,* there is great poetry in these pages, too. Yet, the overall feel of this key, transitional work is that Burroughs wrote it for himself, with no hope of ever getting it published.

Bibliography

Grauerholz, James. Introduction. *Interzone,* by William S. Burroughs. New York: Viking Penguin, 1989. ix–xxiii.

Rob Johnson

Iovis Anne Waldman (1997)

The publication of *Iovis I* in 1993 and *Iovis II* in 1997 signaled ANNE WALDMAN's emergence as a major voice in 20th-century poetics. Often called her master work, *Iovis,* subtitled *All Is Full of Jove,* began in 1985–86 as Waldman's exploration of male energy, both an attack on and a celebration of the power of the word as material form to shape and reshape human culture at universal and personal levels. The 600-page poem takes its name from a passage in Virgil's Eclogues: *Iovis omnia plena,* which Waldman translates as "All is full of Jove." Jove is a generative for Jupiter, the name of the god who ruled over all other gods in the Roman pantheon. Drawing most explicitly in titular form on ancient Roman and Greek epic as reservoirs of western history and values, *Iovis* also belongs to the contemporary long poem responding to these classical structures, specifically William Carlos Williams's *Paterson,* Ezra Pound's *Cantos,* CHARLES OLSEN's *The MAXIMUS POEMS,* T. S. Eliot's *The Wasteland,* and H. D.'s *Helen in Egypt.* Working within, against, and beyond these tradition and antitraditions, Waldman, a long-time feminist, drew extensively on Buddhist philosophy, collected personal and family stories, and drew on many cultural myths to capture, as she has described, "the vibration, or patterned energy, of one woman on this planet as she collides with all apparent and non-apparent phenomena."

Iovis is a distinctly nonlinear text, both visually and narratively. Drawings, double word columns, diversified spacing between lines, varied indentations and typescripts, typewriter signs, circled passages, boxes, letters, essays, short lyrics, brainstormed thoughts, and crossed-out words characterize *Iovis* as a hybrid of modernist collage art, modernist and Beat multimedia productions, the folk and middle-class hobby of scrapbook making, the game-board jigsaw puzzle, and the academic commercial encyclopedia. No single voice, setting, scene, or plot dominates. Instead, *Iovis* manifests an aesthetic of juxtaposition, multidimensionality, and inclusiveness, all of which in combination like the scrapbook or collage or encyclopedia presents the illusion of infinite, uncensored openedness. Within *Iovis,* one encounters the voice of many different languages as well as the narrative perspectives and discursive conventions of the epic, meditation, manifesto, autobiography, creation myth, spells, charms, incantations, personal letters, ethnography, lyric, dream narrative, Burroughsian cut-ups, political treatises, Jungian archetypes, and many other forms to create a harmonizing cacophony (or both/other) that speaks to Waldman's Buddhist understanding of the nondualistic source of the universe. In this mélange of the male–female that was configured through the material of paper and ink, critic Rachel Blau de Plessis identifies as the overarching plan of *Iovis I* and *II*—as well as book *III* that is now in progress—the "hermetic bisexual hermaphrodite or androgynous twins" in meditation.

Iovis as an exploration of the struggle of women writers to acquire self and cultural affirmation makes Waldman's second-wave feminist efforts significant to more recent generations through the inclusion in *Iovis II* of a letter written in 1994 by the young poet Kristen Prevallet. In the letter, Prevallet recounts an incident in a poetry class taught by ROBERT CREELEY in which he rejected her assertion that *Iovis* was an epic. Prevallet's dilemma—like that of Waldman 30 years earlier, Plath and Sexton a decade or so earlier, and H. D. and Gertrude Stein during the first half of the century—remains how to deal with the male ego that fails to recognize the personal as the universal and the political, the male ego that still manages to set the agenda for artistic standards of excellence—and thus recognition.

These issues are addressed throughout the poem, coalescing at one point in an essay in *Iovis II* on women artists of the Beat Generation. Waldman, not unlike many of the women writers associated with seminal Beat figures, expresses some ambivalence toward this heritage. She legitimizes the Beat world's long-held focus on individual independence as important to her own development as a writer, but she is not afraid to recognize their sexism, racism, and the extremely limited roles that women played in this milieu. Consequently, *Iovis* wholeheartedly affirms the women's movement for helping Waldman achieve her own subjectivity, while simultaneously it gratefully practices Beat aesthetics while harshly judging their gender values.

Iovis, Waldman admits, is written to "save" the self, as were many Beat texts as well as texts by countless women authors for centuries. By revising not only the male-authored epic but also other genres to tell her personal story, Waldman has crafted a *body poetic* in which she is "the context of those before me who worshipped a goddess whose eyes were mirrors. One eye reflected the 'inside,' the other the gorgeous & dark phenomenal world. Take your pick. Both, both." As the poetic body in and through which the ritual of self and cultural history is endlessly repeated and rewritten, *Iovis* is a poem as process that in Waldman's own words is meant to "soar and be told."

Bibliography

Christopher, Lee. "An Interview with Anne Waldman." *AWP Chronicle* 28, no. 1 (December 1995).

DuPlessis, Rachel Blau. "Anne Waldman: Standing Corporeally in One's Time." *Jacket* 27 (April 2005). Available online. URL: http://jacketmagazine.com/27/w-dupl.html. Accessed September 2005.

Puchek, Peter. "From Revolution to Creation: Beat Desire and Body Poetics in Anne Waldman's Poetry." *Girls Who Wore Black: Women Writing the Beat Generation*, edited by Ronna C. Johnson and Nancy M. Grace. New Brunswick, N.J.: Rutgers University Press, 2002: 227–250.

Waldman, Anne. "Anne Waldman." In *Contemporary Authors Autobiography Series*. Vol. 17. Detroit: Gale, 1993.

———. Interview. "Fast Speaking Woman: Anne Waldman," by Ronna C. Johnson. *Breaking the Rule of Cool: Interviewing and Reading Beat Women Writers*, edited by Nancy M. Grace and Ronna C. Johnson, 255–277. Jackson: University Press of Mississippi, 2004.

———. "Feminafesto." In *Kill or Cure*. New York: Penguin Books, 1994, 142–146.

———. *Vow to Poetry: Essays, Interviews, and Manifestos.* Minneapolis, Minn.: Coffee House Press, 2001.

Nancy M. Grace

J

Joans, Ted (1928–2003)

Author of more than 30 verse collections culminating in *Teducation: Selected Poems 1949–1999*,
performance poet, surrealist, troubadour, vintage
jazz aficionado: Afro-America has known few
more engaging Beat presences than Ted Joans.
Not all of his career can be designated Beat.
Other key aspects of his creativity connect into
lifelong surrealist and music interests ("Surrealism is my point of view" and "Jazz is my religion"
were to become his mantras) and the frequent
itinerant venturings into Europe and Africa. But
throughout the late 1950s and 1960s and their
aftermath, Beat serves as an unmistakable energy
within his poetry.

Alongside LeRoi Jones/AMIRI BARAKA, BOB
KAUFMAN, A. B. Spellman and Archie Shepp, he
also gave meaning to the notion of black Beat,
the firsthand-lived seams of black art and history
in a movement customarily thought of as forming
around the axis of ALLEN GINSBERG, JACK KER-
OUAC, WILLIAM S. BURROUGHS, GREGORY CORSO,
and LAWRENCE FERLINGHETTI and in which *black*
often enough became more metaphor than actual
life. Echoing Ginsberg's "HOWL," Joans would write
in an autobiographical essay of 1996, "I too have
known some of the best Beat minds of that generation." Indeed he had. He was also himself one of
those minds.

His July 4, 1928, birth to parents who were
Mississippi riverboat entertainers was auspicious in
a number of ways. He found his own independence
in Greenwich Village; began his writing career in

Ted Joans, San Francisco, 1996. Photographer Lisa
Keenan: "I am a fan of Ted Joan's work. I was telling
him how much I liked his small, powerful, painting of
Charlie Parker that was in the Whitney Museum's Beat
Culture exhibit at the de Young Museum." *(courtesy of
Lisa Keenan)*

157

Beat Poems (1957), *Jazz Poems* (1959) and two early signature collections, *Black Pow-Wow: Jazz Poems* (1969) and *Afrodisia: Old and New Poems* (1969); became a Village presence for his birthday spectaculars and studio and other gatherings; and took part in Fred McDarrah's Rent-a-Beatnik circuit, where "beatniks" were rented to suburban parties. He has long acknowledged Ginsberg as having got him into café- and public-reading mode. Manhattan, besides Harlem, also meant art galleries such as the Guggenheim and MOMA as well as friendships with Frank O'Hara and Jackson Pollock. Paris gave him access to André Breton and French surrealism. Africa meant, above all, Mali's Timbuku, along with the Tangier of PAUL BOWLES and Jane Bowles and Burroughs, the sub-Sahara of Dahomey and Cameroon, and a host of cities to include Marrakesh to Accra. Mexico drew him on account of the mural and canvas work of Diego Rivera and Frida Kahlo, and Cuba, too, drew him in the person of the surrealist painter Wilfredo Lam. Through to his last years in Seattle and Vancouver where he died in 2003, his poetry continued to reflect this inspired blend of jazz, Europe, Africa, and Beat. A Joans reading, whether blueslike, his own kind of rap, or one of his incantations, was always "spoken," easeful, and yet at the same time full of sharpest irony and wit.

The hallmarks of the verse were observable from the beginning. It could be the sexual wordplay of a surrealist love poem such as "Sanctified Rhino" (the rhino became his favored icon). It could be the weave of inside allusion and temper in his jazz tribute to Charlie Parker, with whom he once roomed, in "Him the Bird." It could be the vivid, panoramic Africa lore of "Afrique Accidentale." It could be the smack at racist ill-temper or bias in such satiric shorter pieces as "Uh Huh" or "Two Words." As to Joans's Beat focus, "The Wild Spirit of Kicks" gives witness to his friendship with Kerouac ("Old Angel Midnight singing Mexico City Blues") and "The SERMON" to the working desiderata of Beat life ("you must have a copy of Jack (on the road) Kerouac"). If one can now speak of Afro-Beat as indispensable to any true reckoning of the Beat movement overall, it could not be more engagingly embodied than in the life and poetry of Ted Joans.

Bibliography

Fox, Robert Elliot. "Ted Joans and the (B)reach of the African American Canon." *MELUS* 29, nos. 3–4 (Fall–Winter 2004): 41–58.

Lee, A. Robert. "Black Beat: Performing Ted Joans" In *Reconstructing The Beats,* edited by Jennie Skerl, 117–132. New York: Palgrave, 2004.

A. Robert Lee

Johnson, Joyce (1935–   )

It is fair to say that writer Joyce Johnson deserves considerable credit for bringing to center stage women artists from the Beat Generation. With the publication of MINOR CHARACTERS, her memoir of coming of age in the New York Beat scene of the 1950s, Johnson gave voice and a cultural history to women who had long been invisible. She herself was one of those women who had found a home in the Beat arts community, making important literary contributions to it, but whose presence had been elided from Beat histories until she reinserted her own story of self discovery.

Johnson was born in New York City on September 27, 1935. Her mother, Rosiland Ross, came from a Jewish family that had immigrated to the United States from Warsaw, Poland, in the late 1800s. Her father, Daniel Glassman, who had immigrated from London, England, was also Jewish. He worked as a bookkeeper and auditor for the Metropolitan Tobacco Company in New York City. Johnson's mother, who had studied voice prior to becoming a housewife and mother, made sure that the young Joyce Glassman also got an early start in the arts, enrolling her in dramatic movement classes as well as the Professional Children's School where Joyce became a child actor. At the age of 10, Joyce also began to take private weekly piano and composition lessons, her mother intent on transforming her into "a kind of Rodgers and Hammerstein combined," Johnson has written. While in high school, she managed to compose three full-length musical comedies, but it was only during her senior year at Barnard College, which she entered in 1951, that she quit the piano, finally confronting her mother with the truth that she did not want to pursue someone else's dream.

As Johnson recorded in *Minor Characters*, a world more adventuresome than the Broadway musical attracted her. As a 13-year-old, she and a friend would ride the bus downtown to spend Sunday afternoons in Greenwich Village where the bohemian art world flourished. A secret desire to write also occupied her thoughts. Even as a preschooler, she had composed poems and dialogues, dutifully recorded by her Aunt Leona Ross in *The Book of Joyce Alice Glassman*. In college, she took literature and creative-writing classes. She also became friends with Elise Cowen, an intelligent and troubled young poet, who introduced her to ALLEN GINSBERG and the burgeoning Beat Generation movement. Johnson left Barnard in 1954, only one course short of her degree requirements, using her secretarial skills to find jobs in publishing so that she could concentrate on becoming a novelist, including taking a novel-writing workshop taught by Hiram Hayden at the New School.

In January 1957, while working on her novel and paying her rent as an employee of the MCA Literary Agency, Johnson had a blind date set up for her by Ginsberg that would redirect her life once again. She received a telephone call from JACK KEROUAC, asking her to meet him at the Howard Johnson's on Eighth Street. She said yes, bought him a hotdog, and began a two-year relationship with Kerouac, during which she witnessed the publication of ON THE ROAD and his transformation into an unprepared media icon. Johnson first wrote about those experiences in *Minor Characters*, also using the memoir to discuss her own coming of age as a woman artist and to document the lives of other women in the Beat circle, such as Edie Parker, Joan Vollmer Adams Burroughs, Elise Cowen, HETTIE JONES, and Mary Frank. Her correspondence with Kerouac was published as *Door Wide Open: A Beat Love Affair in Letters, 1957–1958* by Viking Penguin in 2000.

Johnson's relationship with Kerouac ended in late 1958. She continued to work on her novel, which he had encouraged her to do, and in 1962, her efforts came to fruition: *Come and Join the Dance*, the first Beat novel written by a woman, Joyce Glassman, was published by Antheneum Press. *Come and Join the Dance*, which has been out of print for many years, is based to a large extent

on Johnson's Beat bohemian experiences during her late teens and early 20s. The novel illustrates Johnson's early apprenticeship to the fiction of Henry James and through psychological realism presents from the perspective of a female protagonist key elements of Beat culture, including hipsterism, gratuitous sex, and cold-war existentialism. The novel helps to fill in gaps in the master Beat narrative by placing women artists in the scene and illustrating how they helped to integrate Beat ethics and aesthetics into their personal lives. *Come and Join the Dance* does not claim female emancipation as did many first- and second-wave feminist texts; rather through its characterization of the Beat woman as subject, the book anticipates the emergence of the women's movement in the late 1960s and early 1970s.

That same year, she met James Johnson, a young, married, abstract expressionist painter named from Painesville, Ohio. They soon moved into a New York City loft together where he could paint while she worked as a copyeditor at William Morrow and he completed a turbulent divorce. Joyce and Jim were married in December 1962, but he was killed on December 9, 1963, when the motorcycle that he was riding crashed into a truck just a short distance from their home. After Jim's death, Johnson went to Europe to escape familiar haunts, but by October 1964 she had returned to her editing job with William Morrow, and that month she met another young painter, Peter Pinchbeck, a native Londoner. A year later, Johnson became pregnant, and she and Peter married. Their son Daniel was born on June 15, 1965.

Johnson has said that her writing stagnated during these years, and it was not until the early 1970s when she separated from Pinchbeck that she began to write again. As a single mother, she also continued to work in publishing, adding Dial, Atlantic Monthly Press, and McGraw-Hill to her résumé and editing important civil-rights books including ABBIE HOFFMAN's REVOLUTION FOR THE HELL OF IT, Ron Kovic's *Born on the Fourth of July*, and Ann Moody's *Coming of Age in Mississippi*. She also edited for posthumous publication Kerouac's VISIONS OF CODY.

Johnson returned to fiction writing with the publication of *Bad Connections* in 1978. The novel portrays the confusion and ambivalence of the white, middle-class housewife named Molly in the 1960s as she fights to raise her child and seek sexual and political liberation. Eleven years later, Johnson published *In the Night Café* (1989), which she considers her best work: As lyrical fictive–autobiography, *Café* returns to Beat-era themes to explore the life of Joanna Gold, a young mother married to a talented and destructive abstract painter, Tom Murphy. A chapter of the novel about the son Nicky was published earlier as "In the Children's Wing," winning the O. Henry Prize Award for Best Short Fiction in 1987.

The genre of documentary nonfiction has also drawn Johnson's interest, and her report of the controversial murder of six-year-old Lisa Steinberg, *What Lisa Knew: The Truth and Lies of the Steinberg Case*, was published in 1990. The sad, brief life of the little girl, the trial of her nonlegal adoptive father Joel Steinberg, and the complicity of his partner Hedda Nusbaum are chronicled in the book, which received both positive and negative responses from feminists.

Most recently, Johnson has revisited the genre of memoir, bringing out *Missing Men* (2004), which narrates memories of her father, James Johnson, and Peter Pinchbeck. All her books reflect her introspective nature, her relentless determination to establish self and community with equanimity and to speak for the best of Beat values: honesty, and integrity and artistic liberation.

Bibliography

Glassman, Joyce. *Come and Join the Dance.* New York: Antheneum, 1962.

Grace, Nancy M., and Ronna C. Johnson. *Breaking the Rule of Cool: Interviewing and Reading Beat Women Writers.* Jackson: University Press of Mississippi, 2004.

Johnson, Joyce. *Bad Connections.* New York: Putnam, 1978.

———. *In the Night Café.* New York: Dutton, 1989.

———. *Minor Characters: A Young Woman's Coming of Age in the Beat Orbit of Jack Kerouac.* New York: Penguin, 1999.

———. *What Lisa Knew: The Truths and Lies of the Steinberg Case.* New York: Kensington, 1990.

———. *Missing Men.* New York: Viking, 2004.

Johnson, Joyce, and Jack Kerouac. *Door Wide Open: A Beat Love Affair in Letters, 1957–1958.* New York: Viking, 2000.

Johnson, Ronna C., and Nancy M. Grace. *Girls Who Wore Black: Women Writing the Beat Generation.* New Brunswick, N.J.: Rutgers University Press, 2002.

Nancy M. Grace

Jones, Hettie (1934–   )

Hettie Jones, née Cohen, remains convinced that she was not destined to spend her life in the Laurelton, New York, of her birth. Even as a small child living with her Jewish, middle-class parents and an older sister, Hettie sensed that a different world awaited her. When little, she dreamed of becoming a cantor, but that vocation was closed to women at the time. So she listened to the counsel of her mother. Born Lottie Lewis, she volunteered for the Red Cross, Girl Scouts, and Zionist causes, showed her daughter how to sew and iron, and cautioned her to "marry someone who loves you more." Her father, Oscar Cohen, taught both his daughters how to fly-fish, catch, and throw, taking Hettie to Yankee Stadium, Ebbets Field, and the racetracks, all the while reminding her that life is not found in books. The roles she was to play in the Beat movement and the Civil Rights movements of the 1960s were still unimagined, but she knew that something greater awaited her—Hettie "had to *become*."

To break the circle of home, she eschewed attending Vassar and elected instead to matriculate in 1951 at Virginia's Mary Washington College. At the small, all-girls school, she was introduced to the theater, participating in set and costume design as well as acting. The Spanish poet and dramatist Frederico García Lorca became one of her favorite writers. She also published prose nonfiction in the college's literary journal. More importantly, segregation and discrimination based on color made itself known to her for the first time. She was the only Jewish student, often mistaken as Puerto Rican, and her years in the South brought her face to face with the deep inequities of invidious social divisions between blacks and whites.

In 1955, after graduating with a degree in drama, she briefly attended Columbia University before moving in 1957 to Greenwich Village, where she found a job as subscription manager for the *Record Changer*, a magazine for record collectors. It was at the *Changer* that she met a young African-American man, a graduate of Howard University as well as a writer and jazz enthusiast: LeRoi Jones (AMIRI BARAKA). He had been raised in a middle-class home in New Jersey and shared Hettie's interest in Franz Kafka; the two soon moved in together; they married on October 13, 1958. Their lives as a mixed-race couple in mid–20th-century United States, even in the liberal enclave of the Village, were not easy, often requiring painful personal sacrifices. They sometimes encountered hostility from strangers on the street, and even from close relatives, such as Oscar and Lottie Cohen, could not accept the fact that their daughter had married a black man; this created a long-standing rift between Jones and her parents. LeRoi's family, however, welcomed her unconditionally. This mixture of public and private responses to their union left Jones in virtually unchartered territory—there were no self-help books for those, like Jones, who had crossed the color line.

Despite the difficulties, Jones proudly recalls the era as one of personal liberation, a time in which she learned to be self-supporting, to acknowledge herself as a sexual being, and to wear the kind of clothes she liked despite the fashion trends. Living in the center of the New York art world at the height of the Beat movement affirmed her desire to self-express, bringing her into contact with a pantheon of art personalities. Her husband was making a name for himself as a poet, jazz historian, and radical playwright, and their apartment quickly became a gathering place for painters, musicians and writers, including Franz Kline, Fielding Dawson, JACK KEROUAC, ALLEN GINSBERG, and DIANE DI PRIMA.

Jones herself was writing poetry in secret, and although her husband encouraged her to write critical texts, she balked at that idea, electing instead to support the endeavors of others. A job as a copy editor at the *Partisan Review* allowed her to bring home a regular paycheck so that LeRoi could devote his time to writing and other political activities. When he founded Totem Press and *Yugen*, one of the most influential small-press literary journals to emerge after World War II, it was Hettie who provided the

physical labor, typing and laying out other people's poetry. She was also the primary caregiver for their two daughters, Kellie and Lisa, born in 1959 and 1961, respectively. Jones, however, blames no one for holding her back as an artist; nothing, she says, "but my own voice held me hostage."

The early 1960s saw the rise of the black-nationalist and black arts movements, and as LeRoi become more involved in both, he distanced himself from the Beat movement—and from his wife, as well. By middecade, Jones found herself abandoned by a husband who believed that her skin color compromised his political status. LeRoi's numerous infidelities, including an affair with di Prima, who had been Hettie's friend, also took its toll on the marriage. They divorced in 1965. Jones retained custody of the two children and stayed on in the Lower East Side, making a life for herself and her family through freelance editing and teaching.

In 1990, Jones published HOW I BECAME HETTIE JONES, a memoir of her early years in the avant-garde, but like other second-wave feminist memoirists, Jones chose not to subordinate her story to that of her more famous husband. Instead, she recovered her history and that of many other young women, including JOYCE JOHNSON, Helene Dorn, and Aishah Rahman, who fought against racial prejudice and stereotypes that constrained sexuality, intellect, and economic independence. The memoir features some of her own poetry, written in secret, evidence that early on she had mapped out a literary life for herself.

It was only after the divorce, however, that she dared assert her own voice as a writer, encouraged by the young male poets who had studied with Joel Oppenheimer as part of the St. Mark's Poetry Project. Jones began to read publicly, and by the mid-1970s she was writing short fiction and a great deal of poetry. The wages that she earned writing adolescent literature also enabled her to spend more time at home with the children. She published her first poetry chapbook, *Having Been Her*, in 1981. *Drive*, her first full-length book of poems, came out in 1998 and won the Norma Farber Award for a first collection of poetry. A second collection, *All Told*, followed in 2003.

Influenced by LeRoi's poetry and the avant-garde literature she read as an editor for Grove Press,

Jones describes her poetry as musical expressions of her state of mind, constructs that adhere to CHARLES OLSON's theory of projective verse and open field composition. Her short stories and adolescent fiction, tending toward morality tales, focus more explicitly on the intersection of gender and race, especially motherhood and mixed-race individuals.

A strong belief in art as a vehicle to promote social justice compels Jones to use her talents in the service of others. In 1988 poet JANINE POMMY VEGA invited her to teach a prose workshop at Sing-Sing, which she agreed to do. Since then Jones has taught at the Bedford Hills Correctional Facility for women, editing collections of prison writing, such as *Aliens at the Border* in 1997.

In 2004 she helped Rita Marley write her own memoir, *No Woman No Cry: My Life with Bob Marley* (Hyperion).

Jones continues to write, teach, and advocate for those less fortunate. Her dedication to a life that seamlessly blends the aesthetic with the political and domestic testifies to the importance of Beat and other mid–20th-century avant-garde philosophies in American culture.

Bibliography

Grace, Nancy M., and Ronna C. Johnson. *Breaking the Rule of Cool: Interviewing and Reading Beat Women Writers.* Jackson: University Press of Mississippi, 2004.

Johnson, Ronna C., and Nancy M. Grace. *Girls Who Wore Black: Women Writing the Beat Generation.* New Brunswick, N.J.: Rutgers University Press, 2002.

Jones, Hettie, ed. *Aliens at the Border: The Writing Workshop, Bedford Hills Correctional Facility.* New York: Segue Books, 1997.

———. *All Told.* New York: Hanging Loose Press, 2003.

———. *Big Star Fallin' Mamma: Five Women in Black Music.* New York: Viking, 1995.

———. *Drive: Poems.* New York: Hanging Loose Press, 1998.

———. *How I Became Hettie Jones.* New York: Dutton, 1990.

———. "This Time It Was Different at the Airport." *Art Against Apartheid; Works for Freedom.* Ikon Second Series 5/6 (Winter/Summer 1986): 150–153.

Nancy M. Grace

Josephine: The Mouse Singer Michael McClure (1978)

Based on the short story by Franz Kafka, "Josephine the Singer, or the Mouse Folk," MICHAEL McCLURE's play *Josephine: The Mouse Singer* ranks as one of the playwright's most successful works. Michael Feingold writes in his preface for the published play: "For German readers, Kafka's is the language that gives the lie to language, the syntax that denies the utility of syntax. And what else is McClure doing when he throws away grammar, and even words, and writes in growls and snarls and pipes instead? Giving the lie to language, in an American rather than a German way. Every writer knows that the point of what you express is the inexpressible; the words are only the vehicle that gets you to that point." Like other McClure plays from the period, such as *Gorf* (1974), *Spider Rabbit* (1969), and *Apple Glove* (1969), *Josephine: The Mouse Singer* features fantastic costumes, surreal imagery, and a pronounced blurring of the lines that separate humans from other species. Heavily influenced by his reading of French dramatist Antonin Artaud's book *The Theatre and its Double,* McClure's plays often move beyond traditional staging and costumes in an effort to break through the audience's intellectual filtering and social conditioning to engage them at the very roots of human experience, thus giving the experience of theater the surreal quality and insight of a dream.

Despite the fact that all the play's characters represent mice dressed in Edwardian and Victorian costumes, *Josephine: The Mouse Singer* is perhaps McClure's most conventional play—if the term can be used to describe any of his work—in terms of plot and dialogue. The play's central figure is a gifted singer in a community of tone-deaf mice, but this artist's talents endanger her fellow creatures and lead several to suicide.

The play, like Kafka's story before it, raises the central questions of the artist's proper role in the community, the role of free expression, and whether art, no matter how brilliant or beautifully crafted, should take precedence over society. But, as critic Michael Feingold points out in the play's preface, whereas Kafka tended to view the nonhuman world as "a source of horrified fascination," McClure's lifelong affinity for the nonhuman world allows for a rewriting of the play in which "Kafka's nightmare view of life turns out to contain an ecstatic joy." *Josephine: The Mouse Singer* won the *Village Voice* Obie Award for the best play of the year, though its run in November 1978 was very short at the WPA Theatre. Numerous successful productions since its debut season have established it as one of the classics of U.S. avant-garde theater.

Bibliography

Artaud, Antonin. *Theatre and Its Double.* New York: Grove Press, 1958.

Marranca, Bonnie, and Gautam Dasgupta. "Michael McClure." *American Playwrights: A Critical Survey.* New York: Drama Book Specialists, 1981: 143–157.

Phillips, Rod. *Michael McClure.* Western Writers Series 159. Boise, Idaho: Boise State University, 2003.

Rod Phillips

Junky William S. Burroughs (1953)

This first novel by WILLIAM S. BURROUGHS is his most accessible work. While many readers have difficulty with Burroughs's later novels, this one resembles the straightforward, hard-boiled prose of Dashiell Hammett. The book was started in Mexico City and was originally called "Junk" under the pseudonym "William Dennison," the name of the character based on Burroughs in JACK KEROUAC's *The TOWN AND THE CITY.* The novel was published under "William Lee" (Lee being Burroughs's mother's maiden name) as *Junkie: Confessions of an Unredeemed Drug Addict* bound back-to-back with *Narcotic Agent* by Maurice Helbrant. The 35-cent pulp books sold more than 100,000 copies. An unexpurgated and expanded edition was printed in 1977 as *Junky.* The book is often read as Burroughs's anthropological examination of the drug underworld.

One of the important historical references that Burroughs makes in this novel is to the Harrison Narcotics Act of 1914, which prohibited the supply of opiates in the United States. Harris informs us that Burroughs's uncle Horace Burroughs had become addicted to morphine through medical treatment and committed suicide shortly after the Harrison Act came into effect, presumably because he was unable to handle the criminalization of morphine use. Though Burroughs does not single out the Harrison Act in *Junky* as the determining factor that pushed addicts into a life of crime, he does argue that the police state created by drug laws is at least as dangerous as the addictive drugs themselves.

In the later part of *Junky,* Lee, Burroughs's persona, jumps bail after being convinced that he has no chance for escaping a drug conviction. He writes, "I saw my chance of escaping conviction dwindle daily as the anti-junk feeling mounted to a paranoid obsession, like anti-Semitism under the Nazis. So I decided to jump bail and live permanently outside the United States." Burroughs had seen the anti-Semitism brought by Nazism in Austria and Yugoslavia in the mid-1930s after he graduated from Harvard. His first wife, Ilse Klapper, was a German Jew whom he had married to bring her to the United States to save her life from the Nazis. For the rest of his life Burroughs would be wary of political groups who used paranoia under the guise of social cleansing truly to exert more control over the populace. Though our modern sensibilities make it difficult for many readers to view drug addicts as victims, Burroughs tries hard in his novel to place some of the responsibility for the problems that are associated with drug use on the United States government. Many of the junkies whom Burroughs depicts in *Junky* and his other novels have a code of ethics that is portrayed as superior to the code found in the straight world.

Although the book is an early Beat classic, Burroughs's writing in *Junky* was not as much inspired by his Beat friends as by the memoir *You Can't Win* (1926) by Jack Black. There are no references to ALLEN GINSBERG and Kerouac in the novel, though there is a striking portrait of HERBERT HUNCKE as the character Herman, and none of the characters in *Junky* is an aspiring artist or bohemian. They are the street denizens about whom Burroughs had fantasized after reading *You Can't Win.* Burroughs had hoped to find a life for himself among the criminal underground that had fascinated him as a youth. In his foreword to the 1988 edition of Black's book, Burroughs writes, "I first read *You Can't Win* in 1926, in an edition bound in red cardboard. Stultified and confined by middle-class St. Louis mores, I was fascinated by this glimpse of an underworld of seedy rooming-houses, pool parlors, cat houses, and opium dens, of bull pens and cat burglars and hobo jungles. I learned about the Johnson Family of good bums and thieves, with a code of conduct that made more sense to me than the arbitrary, hypocritical rules that were taken for granted as being 'right' by my peers."

Burroughs does not find the honorable John-sons for whom he was looking in *Junky* (he would later create them fictionally in *The PLACE OF DEAD ROADS*, the second novel of his the Red Night trilogy), but what he does describe is one of the most candid depictions of the narcotics under-world ever told. What is particularly striking about Burroughs's work is that he does not recant his decision to become part of the drug underworld. Ginsberg writes, "[T]he author has done what he has set out to do: to give a fairly representative and accurate picture of the junk world and all it involves; a true picture, given for the first time in America, of that vast underground life which has recently been so publicized. It is a notable accom-plishment; there is no sentimentality here, no at-tempt at self-exculpation but the most candid, no romanticization of the circumstances, the dreari-ness, the horror, the mechanical beatness and evil of the junk life as lived."

Ginsberg, the strongest supporter of Bur-roughs's work, put the manuscript in front of his friend from the Columbia Presbyterian Psychiat-ric Institute, Carl Solomon, who had inspired the poem "HOWL" and was the nephew of the owner of Ace Books. Although the publishers saw the book's marketability, they had some reservations about the content of the novel and forced Burroughs to write an introduction which emphasized his patri-cian upbringing. This gave "Lee" a legitimacy that he would otherwise lack, the publishers felt.

The early readers of *Junky*, however, knew that they were reading a book by a man who knew what he was talking about. Burroughs's miniessay on marijuana, for example, is the kind of straight talk that readers loved about the book. Nowhere else was there information on drugs that was accurate and unclouded by government or church moralistic propaganda. Burroughs makes the reader wonder

at the source of all the misinformation. Today the novel rings as true as it did then. Telling the truth about drugs in 1953 was a revolutionary act; it still seems so today, which is perhaps why the book has not lost its relevance and ability to shock with its straightforwardness and common sense based on experience. For example, director Gus Van Sant consulted *Junky* to attain the realism of the drug world in his movie *Drugstore Cowboy,* which is based on James Fogle's novel about pharmaceutical drug addiction. Burroughs, appropriately, has a cameo in the film as an old junky priest, "Father Bob."

The language of Burroughs's novel is that of drugs and crime. To "beat" someone is to steal from them, not related to Kerouac's definition of *beat* as related to "beatitude." Burroughs's catalog of junky jargon is reminiscent of Jack London's fascination with the argot of the hobo. In fact, the cultures are similar. They both have a linguistic base. The junky culture is fascinating because of its language, and the language is its culture. Clearly, this was material for writers, the same way that whaling and confidence men and their system of symbols and signs and secret codes were material for Melville 100 years before. In a sense, *Junky* is what Kerouac wanted to do with his writing: make his life into a story using subterranean language.

In addition to Burroughs's use of language, the sexuality of Burroughs's character Lee is also of extreme importance. Sexuality seems to have been sublimated by the pursuit of narcotics. Attitudes toward homosexuality in the novel are ambivalent. Burroughs shows simultaneous attraction and re-pulsion. He is generally very drunk before he will submit to his desire to sleep with a man. A startling omission is the lack of descriptive detail regarding Burroughs's wife Joan, whom Burroughs had ac-cidentally killed when he tried to shoot a glass off the top of her head in 1951. When Lee's wife ap-pears, it is suddenly, and she exits quickly; in fact, there are almost no women in the book, and there is only a minor reference to his children. Burroughs leaves out his whole married life. Why? This curi-ous omission points to the fact that this "straight-forward" book is also a deceptive one. True of many of the Beats' writing styles, Burroughs's style seems to leave nothing out, but in fact there is great deal of omission, distortion, and invention.

Junky also foreshadows the use of the grotesque and the supernatural that will become major features of Burroughs's later writings. Though they are easy to miss in this work of literary realism, odd instances of prose that prefigure the style found in *NAKED LUNCH* occasionally surface. Looking for junk on the streets of Mexico City, Lee reminisces about the junk neighborhoods that he has known and a particular type of character that he always finds there. He writes, "So this man walks around in the places where he once exercised his obsolete and unthinkable trade. But he is unperturbed. His eyes are black with an insect's unseeing calm. He looks as if he nourished himself on honey and Levantine syrups that he sucks up through a sort of proboscis. What is his lost trade? Definitely of a servant class and something to do with the dead, though he is not an embalmer. Perhaps he stores something in his body—a substance to prolong life—of which he is periodically milked by his masters. He is as specialized as an insect, for the performance of some inconceivably vile function." Passages like this one separate Burroughs distinctly from the hard-boiled writers who inspired him.

The end of the book takes up what will become a fertile subject for the writers of the 1960s—the growing police state in America. Burroughs is the originator of this in postwar American fiction, but he is also in line with his contemporaries such as Aldous Huxley and George Orwell. What happens is that addiction is criminalized and junkies have to flee to Mexico to be "free." His analysis of police-state tactics in the war on junkies is incisive and very revealing about our society. He points out, for example, the ludicrousness of pushing junk on children, who would be terrible "customers," but the feds insist the junk is being peddled in playgrounds. The novel ends with Lee quitting junk and moving on to search for a different kind of drug: *yagé*, which supposedly induces a telepathic state in users. Lee is more attracted to this: "What I look for in any relationship is contact on the nonverbal level of intuition and feeling, that is, telepathic contact." *Yagé* will give him this, he hopes, but this also explains his attraction to the culture of the junky, which is often nonverbal. One junky simply can spot another, "feel" where there is junk, a feeling he compares to water-witching. The glossary Burroughs includes points forward to his later interest in language as a "virus." Of the slang defined in the book Burroughs writes, "It should be understood that the meanings of these words are subject to rapid changes. . . . A final glossary, therefore, cannot be made of words whose intentions are fugitive." In other words, language can never grasp what it is trying to express because the meaning is "fugitive."

Junky succeeds on pure dare because of its subject matter. That it remains of interest is partially because Burroughs developed a style that captured the underlying symbolic meaning of the whole culture of junk. As a Beat book, it is a harsh critique of a police state that seeks to criminalize what Burroughs considers a victimless crime. The book's point of view—that of someone far outside normal society—has great appeal to readers who want to radically reexamine our society. Burroughs thus successfully did what Kerouac wanted to do and what Kerouac would later do, partially inspired by this novel: use his own life as the basis of his writing. Yet, Burroughs's life was far more dangerous and iconoclastic than Kerouac's.

Bibliography

Harris, Oliver. Introduction. *Junky: The Definitive Text of "Junk,"* by William S. Burroughs. New York: Penguin Books, 2003.

Johnson, Rob. "William S. Burroughs: South Texas Farmer, *Junky,* and *Queer.*" *Southwestern American Literature* (Spring 2001): 7–35.

Murphy, Timothy S. *Wising Up the Marks: The Amodern William Burroughs.* Berkeley: University of California Press, 1997.

Rob Johnson and Kurt Hemmer

K

"Kaddish" Allen Ginsberg (1961)

The title poem of ALLEN GINSBERG's 1961 volume, *KADDISH AND OTHER POEMS*, "Kaddish" is the poet's autobiographical elegy for his mother, Naomi Ginsberg, who died in 1956 after a series of mental breakdowns during the last 20 years of her life. The poem rewrites the Kaddish prayer for the dead as it recalls Naomi's tumultuous life and reimagines her death as visionary and redemptive. "Kaddish" reenvisions the spiritual meaning and value of the Kaddish prayer. In so doing, the poem also exposes the brutality of postwar mental-health care—including Naomi's electroshock treatments and lobotomy—and the politics of religious and sexual identity. Naomi's worsening mental illness occurs as the young Ginsberg in the poem realizes that he is gay, and it coincides with his emerging disillusionment with traditional U.S. religious institutions. "Kaddish," along with "HOWL," stands among the vanguard poems of what would become known as the Confessional school of contemporary American poetry. As with all Confessional poems, this one accounts for more than just a gesture of personal purging or grieving. As Ginsberg later wrote, his exploration of the "eccentric detail" of his family in "Kaddish" was part of a larger process of exploring the political meaning of family in cold-war United States. For Ginsberg, the discomfort that readers might feel in reading his abject family narrative might heighten their awareness of the complex conjunction of sanity and madness in the contemporary American family. "I realized it would seem odd to others," he said, "but *family* odd, that is to say, familiar—everybody has crazy cousins and aunts and brothers."

The poem is framed by Ginsberg's conjunction of his Judaism and his nascent Buddhism—as he puts it in the opening section, his effort to combine "prophesy as in the Hebrew Anthem" and "the Buddhist Book of Answers." Ginsberg had what he saw as good reason to fill gaps left behind by Judaism. The Kaddish was not recited at Naomi's grave because the required minimum of 10 Jewish men, a *minyan*, was not present, as mandated by Jewish law. His father, Louis, provided him with an English-language translation of the traditional Hebrew Kaddish prayer with a note that both affirmed and authorized his son's desire to revise the prayer: "Those chants therein," Louis wrote, "have a rhythm and sonorousness of immemorial years marching with reverberations through the corridors of history." Despite this affirmation of his son's literary strategy, Louis also hesitated at the role Buddhism played in reenvisioning the racial and religious identity at the core of the poem. In a 1971 newspaper interview, Louis said, "People ask him why he, as a Jew, follows the Buddhists, and he says he wants to preach idealism of the human race, to take the best of all religions. I say that's a good idea, but before I do that, I want to study more and explore more of my own Jewish heritage."

Section I recalls Naomi's youth as a young Russian girl whose experiences with institutions such as school, work, and marriage contribute to her mental illness. As the poet himself moves through the streets of New York, he sees his mother, too, moving these same streets while her life extends "[t]oward education marriage nervous breakdown, operation, teaching school, and learning to be mad." Section II documents her fall into madness and its effects on the Ginsberg family. The young Ginsberg tries to flee his mother's madness at the same time that he is drawn into it as one of her family caretakers. Her illness produces great anxiety in him; yet her condition and the way she is treated by doctors invoke in him seeds of understanding the social inequities of illness and treatment. Ginsberg's earliest research into his homosexuality and his first homosexual feelings, for a classmate whom he followed to Columbia University, coincide with what he describes as his mother's harrowing "mad idealism." Still, she remains as an inspiration to him. Like the Hindu goddess Kali about whom he writes in the poem "Stotras to Kali Destroyer of Illusions," Naomi is a destructive and liberating figure in "Kaddish." She is both a figure who frightens him and one who inspires visionary poetry—she is his "glorious muse that bore me from the womb, gave suck first mystic life & taught me talk and music, from whose pained head I first took Vision." Indeed, in eulogizing Naomi's madness, she begins to appear at times less mad than the culture that seeks to treat her. "Kaddish" emerges from Ginsberg's own interest in the antipsychiatric movement of the 1960s, an effort to reveal the environmental causes of mental illness and to hold the psychiatric community accountable for the consequences of treatments, such as electroshock and lobotomy, that could worsen patients' conditions. *Madness* in "Kaddish" eventually comes to be defined as actions that are bereft of human compassion—such as those performed by medical authorities whose treatments leave Naomi "tortured and beaten in the skull."

The final sections of the poem transform the language of Naomi's illness into sacred poetry in the Western and Eastern religious traditions that frame the poem. Invoking the god of Judaism within the illusory "dream" of the world taught by Buddhism, Ginsberg closes his revisionary prayer with language that combines the metaphysics of monotheism with the material pragmatism of Eastern thought. This West–East fusion is dramatized in the crows circling Naomi's grave in Long Island

and the speaker's cries to his god to hear his prayer for the dead: "Lord Lord Lord caw caw caw Lord Lord Lord caw caw caw Lord." Ginsberg's language for sacred experience is one scarred by loss and the failure of metaphysical models to redeem. He resorts to a prayer that weighs language and nonreferentiality (*Lord* and *caw*) equally. Such a strategy forecasts his interest later in his career of the asemantic one-syllable breath exhalation, "Ah," as a Buddhist-inspired principle for, in his words, the "purification of speech." For Ginsberg, who represented himself in the poetic tradition of prophecy as it manifests through poets such as Blake, the purification of speech cannot be separated from the purification of thought and action.

Bibliography
Breslin, James. "The Origins of 'Howl' and 'Kaddish.'" *Iowa Review* 8, no. 2 (Spring 1977): 82–108.
Ginsberg, Allen. "How *Kaddish* Happened." In *Poetics of the New American Poetry,* edited by Donald Allen and Warren Tallman, 344–347. New York: Grove, 1973.
Herring, Scott. "'Her Brothers Dead in Riverside or Russia': 'Kaddish' and the Holocaust." *Contemporary Literature* 42, no. 3 (Fall 2001): 535–556.
Hyde, Lewis, ed. *On the Poetry of Allen Ginsberg.* Ann Arbor: University of Michigan Press, 1984.
Trigilio, Tony. *"Strange Prophecies Anew": Rereading Apocalypse in Blake, H. D., and Ginsberg.* Madison, N.J.: Fairleigh Dickinson University Press, 2000.

Tony Trigilio

Kaddish and Other Poems
Allen Ginsberg (1961)

ALLEN GINSBERG's second book of poems, *Kaddish and Other Poems* follows so closely the pitch and tone of *HOWL AND OTHER POEMS* that it is easy to forget the differences between the two books. Both are written from the perspective of Western prophecy; both fuse religious and political concerns to redeem protagonists who are alienated by cold-war social containment. Moreover, both privilege an autobiographical poetics in which social agony and spiritual crisis can be redeemed through a poetry of visionary experience. Nevertheless, it is important to note major differences between the two books. *Kaddish and Other Poems* was composed in the wake of the enormous international success of *Howl and Other Poems*. Ginsberg himself had become something of a media figure, given the attention that he received from the 1957 "HOWL" obscenity trial and from the attention bestowed on the Beats as a result of the combined success of both *Howl and Other Poems* and JACK KEROUAC's ON THE ROAD. Thus, *Kaddish and Other Poems* should be seen within the social and cultural framework of Ginsberg's increased public visibility as a writer and a public figure. Ginsberg's international travel in the period after *Howl and Other Poems* confirms how the shift from private to public life affected the composition of *Kaddish and Other Poems*. Biographer Michael Schumacher notes that during Ginsberg's 1957 trip to Tangier, the period when *Howl and Other Poems* was seized in San Francisco, the poet started to feel that "Howl" was too private and singular for the public persona necessitated by his self-representation as a poet–prophet. As Schumacher describes it, Ginsberg was "shaken" by his direct experiences with colonialism and state-sponsored police brutality during his trip and that he "vowed" to produce poetry in response to global struggle. Especially in its title poem, this book reshapes his career as a writer from a poetry of private statement to one of public statement. Yet this movement from private to public in *Kaddish and Other Poems* is enacted through a poetry that pays close attention to the integrity of each individual's imagination—and emphasizes, moreover, what Ginsberg saw as the necessity of shaping a public voice from nevertheless inward pilgrimages. As often is the case with Ginsberg, the autobiographical is rarely removed from the prophetic.

Ginsberg's epigraph to the book can serve as a symbol for this combined private–public voice. Preceding the table of contents, he writes, "Magic Psalm, The Reply, & The End *record visions experienced after drinking Ayahuasca, an Amazon spiritual potion. The message is: Widen the area of consciousness*" [emphasis Ginsberg's]. The importance of selfhood in these poems, the final three in the book, would seem to suggest that *Kaddish and Other Poems* does not extend further than the boundaries of the poet's mind and body. Yet in the

book as a whole and in its final three poems, the impulse to "*[w]iden the area of consciousness*" is by necessity for Ginsberg a public one. Widening the boundaries of mental experience is a crucial step in all the poems of this book toward transforming the cultural conditions of the poet's historical moment. As an exercise in the expansion of these boundaries, *Kaddish and Other Poems* attempts, in the language of Ginsberg's back-cover afterword, to "reconstitute" the "broken consciousness of mid twentieth century suffering."

The title poem of the book, for Ginsberg's mother, Naomi, is as much a private elegy as it is a public epic. In his afterword, Ginsberg describes "KADDISH" as a response to seeing "my self my own mother and my very nation trapped desolate our worlds of consciousness homeless and at war except for the original trembling of bliss in breast and belly of every body." To redeem body and mind, "Kaddish" must first acknowledge how the individual integrity of both are beaten down, for Ginsberg, by contemporary U.S. capitalism. Naomi's life is outlined in the opening section of the poem, a veritable overture, as Naomi, the young Russian immigrant from a Communist family, grows into womanhood in what she perceives as a hostile country. Borrowing one of the dominant symbols of vision in "Sunflower Sutra" and "Transcription of Organ Music" (both from *Howl and Other Poems*), Naomi's life is a "flower burning in the Day"; she is a flower "which knew itself in the garden, and fought the knife—lost." This first section, written in a long-strophe form resembling "Howl," ends with a revision of the Hebrew Kaddish prayer for the dead. Section II chronicles the pain suffered by Naomi and the extended Ginsberg family as her illness worsened. It closes with appropriated material from a letter that Naomi sent right before her death, which Ginsberg, living on the opposite coast, did not receive until he already knew that she had died. Her final message, then, motherly advice to "[g]et married" and "don't take drugs," resembles a voice from beyond the grave. Immediately thereafter, a new section, "Hymmnn," continues Ginsberg's revision of the Kaddish prayer. Section III reviews Naomi's life, borrowing at times from the language and imagery of Naomi's final letter. Section IV is a litany of bodily description of the depredations Naomi suffered at the hands of doctors—a section framed by discussion of the cultural conditions in which Naomi lived "with Communist Party and a broken stocking" and "with your eyes of Czechoslovakia attacked by robots" (a nod to the political satire of playwright Karl Capek). Section V continues to merge public and private life, with Ginsberg reimagining Naomi's otherwise private burial as a public visionary experience.

This fusion of individual and communal spheres continues in "At Apollinaire's Grave," one of six poems in the book that Ginsberg composed from 1957–58 while residing at the Beat Hotel in Paris (the others were "Poem Rocket," "Europe! Europe!," "To Aunt Rose," "The Lion for Real," and "Death to Van Gogh's Ear!"). "At Apollinaire's Grave" is especially important because of Ginsberg's incorporation of the surrealist tradition in his efforts to "widen" private and public consciousness. Surrealism and Dada already were part of the literary heritage that led to *Howl and Other Poems,* but Ginsberg's life as an expatriate in 1957–58 also included meetings with noted surrealists and dadaists. The poems of this period continue the theme of "divine madness" central to "Kaddish," where mental illness is both a danger and a welcome evasion of the rational mind. "At Apollinaire's Grave" eulogizes the early 20th-century European avant-garde at the same time that it hails their legacy in contemporary experimental art. Ginsberg evokes Guillaume Apollinaire as his surrealist muse. Walking hand-in-hand at Pére Lachaise cemetery with Peter Orlovsky, Ginsberg implores Apollinaire to "come out of the grave and talk thru the door of my mind." His imagined muse is, urgently, both a personal and a historical force, for Apollinaire's "madness is only around the corner and [Jean] Genet is with us stealing books / the West is at war again and whose lucid suicide will set it all right." As if to suggest the potential for failed individual self-obsession—the potential for narcissism in all autobiographical verse—the speaker of this poem never leaves the cemetery. "At Apollinaire's Grave" ends with a disjunctive collage: A burning cigarette sends the poet's book in flames, an ant crawls on him, and he *feels* a tree growing. The poet seems trapped in the graveyard despite the potential of the voice of prophecy to redeem. "I am buried here," the poem

closes, "and sit by my grave beneath a tree." The Western world may be "at war again," but in the face of his desire to "set it all right," the poet never leaves the place of the dead and is buried alongside those whom he wishes to eulogize.

The next two poems, "The Lion for Real" and "Ignu" revisit Ginsberg's 1948 William Blake vision to reconstitute a speaking self for *Kaddish and Other Poems* that can perform in the same collage–voice as "At Apollinaire's Grave" but without the self-obsession that burdens the social urgency of poetic prophecy. Both poems serve an important function by constructing a self who speaks with believability the opening line of "Death to Van Gogh's Ear!," where the poet, echoing Whitman's preface to *Leaves of Grass,* declares, "Poet is Priest." The conflict in "Death to Van Gogh's Ear!" is more consistent with Whitman's *Democratic Vistas,* where a culture that is unable to integrate its materialist present with its idealistic origins will doom its own "best minds." Ginsberg borrows Whitman's famous warning in *Democratic Vistas* that the United States is "on the road to a destiny, a status, equivalent, in its real world, to that of the fabled damned." With poets and presumably with all artists, being seen as priests among the "fabled damned," then it follows, for Ginsberg, that an image of Van Gogh's ear should be placed on paper currency at the same time that Vachel Lindsay should be named Secretary of the Interior, Edgar Allan Poe placed in a new cabinet position as Secretary of the Imagination, and Ezra Pound named Secretary of Economics. The exhortation is satirical, as in a poem from the same year, "American Change," where Ginsberg ruminates on the images of Washington and Eisenhower on the loose change that he has taken from his pocket; "O Fathers," he exclaims in that poem, "No movie star dark beauty—O thou bignoses." The satire of "Death to Van Gogh's Ear!" reaches resolution when Ginsberg borrows from Blake. The final line recasts the familiar battle between the artist and utilitarian culture, echoing the "dark Satanic mills" that destroy the imagination in Blake's prophecies: "Money against Eternity! and eternity's strong mills grind out vast paper of Illusion!"

"Magic Psalm," "The Reply," and "The End" are the result of Ginsberg's private trip to Peru in 1960 searching for the drug *ayahuasca,* part of his effort through the early 1960s to replicate his Blake vision. Ginsberg's 1966 testimony in the U.S. Senate on the effects of hallucinogenic drugs suggests that the influence of Ginsberg's mother echoes in these final poems that were written with the aid of *ayahuasca*. Of his experiments with the drug, Ginsberg told the Senate: "In a trance state I experienced . . . a very poignant memory of my mother's self, and how much I had lost in my distance from her[. . . .] The human universe became more complete for me—my own feelings more complete." Of these three poems, "Magic Psalm" explicitly extends the effects of *ayahuasca* into the tradition of Western literary prayer. Echoing John Donne's Holy Sonnet XIV ("Batter my heart, three-person'd God"), Ginsberg writes, "Drive me crazy, God I'm ready for disintegration of my mind, disgrace me in the eye of the earth, / attack my hairy heart with terror eat my cock." Where the traditional Western psalm would separate body from soul, with the body a fallen shadow of the soul, Ginsberg's spiritual poetics, like Blake's and Whitman's, demands the unification of the two. His speaker prays so that God "at once in one huge Mouth of Universe" might "make meat reply." "Magic Psalm" vocalizes the overarching lament in *Kaddish and Other Poems* to fuse the world—mother and son, community and individual, soul and body, God and pilgrim—into a unified whole.

Bibliography
Breslin, James. "The Origins of 'Howl' and 'Kaddish.'" *Iowa Review* 8, no. 2 (Spring 1977): 82–108.
Ginsberg, Allen. "How *Kaddish* Happened." In *Poetics of the New American Poetry*, edited by Donald Allen and Warren Tallman, 344–347. New York: Grove, 1973.
Hyde, Lewis, ed. *On the Poetry of Allen Ginsberg*. Ann Arbor: Univerity of Michigan Press, 1984.
Schumacher, Michael. *Dharma Lion: A Critical Biography of Allen Ginsberg*. New York: St. Martin's, 1992.
Trigilio, Tony. *"Strange Prophecies Anew": Rereading Apocalypse in Blake, H. D., and Ginsberg*. Madison, N.J.: Fairleigh Dickinson University Press, 2000.
United States Senate. Special Subcommittee of the Committee on the Judiciary. *The Narcotic Rehabilitation Act of 1966*. 89th Cong., 2nd sess. Washington, D.C.: GPO, 1966.

Tony Trigilio

Kandel, Lenore (1932–   )

Lenore Kandel is a second generation Beat poet whose life and work articulate the connection between the Beat movement of the 1950s and the hippie counterculture of the 1960s. Bringing avant-garde impulses of Beat poetics into the radical 1960s counterculture, Kandel expressed an emerging feminism in her poems, which are cool and streetwise, existential and mystical, prophetic and incantatory, erotic and psychedelic. This distinctive blend marks Kandel's transfiguration of Beat writing and anticipation of the hippie ethos. Kandel was born in New York City in 1932 and spent her adolescence in Los Angeles. After studying at the New School for Social Research in New York in the 1950s, she returned to California in the 1960s and has resided in the San Francisco area since. Part of the North Beach Beat scene, Kandel lived in East–West House, had a relationship with the poet LEW WELCH, and was immortalized by JACK KEROUAC as Ramona Schwarz in his 1962 novel *BIG SUR*. When she moved into Haight–Ashbury in the early 1960s, Kandel brought a female Beat bohemian experience and sensibility to that scene, reincarnating the 1950s hipster as a 1960s peace-and-love hippie. In her poetry, sited in women's and sexual liberation movements of the 1960s, Kandel transforms the Beat Generation's beaten-down exhaustion to the love generation's postcoital exaltation and transfers feminine junkie malaise to the feminist sexual revolution. Kandel's distinction is her contribution to these two related countercultures, her embodiment of the conjunction and overlap of Beat Generation social critiques and 1960s movements for personal and political liberation.

Kandel's poems of her North Beach period, first published in mimeographed broadsides, are distinctively Beat Generation/New York hipster in mood and texture. Beat Generation skepticism is felt in elegies such as "FIRST THEY SLAUGHTERED THE ANGELS," "Junk/Angel" or "Blues for Sister Sally," which bear the hip street smarts and incantatory rhythms, the contempt of conformity and anti-authority contentiousness of ALLEN GINSBERG and the nihilism of Welch. Through perspectives rooted in female sexuality and women's lives, Kandel's expression of iconic Beat subjects, forms, and dictions makes visible the usually dismissed women of Beat bohemia and reinvents Beat movement aesthetics to fit her feminist slant.

Living in the Haight–Ashbury community, Kandel transformed her Beat voice to speak in the liberated radical and psychedelic tones of the new countercultural movement, shifting her aesthetics to challenge the 1950s "Age of Anxiety" with the sexual ecstasy of the 1960s "Age of Aquarius." Her 1966 collection, *The LOVE BOOK*, a graphic paean to heterosexual love that is grounded in Beat poetics and Eastern mysticism, was a groundbreaking expression of female sexual freedom and psychedelic ethics. Its hippie-inflected love diction and erotic outlook offer Beat Generation sex, drugs, and mysticism not as palliatives for cold-war paranoia but as blissful panaceas. The book made Kandel a local celebrity and became notorious when it was confiscated by San Francisco police for obscenity, repeating a decade later the seminal Beat event of the seizure and trial of Ginsberg's *HOWL* on the same grounds. As the only female speaker among such men as Ginsberg, GARY SNYDER, and TIMOTHY LEARY, Kandel read *The Love Book* poems at the 1967 Human Be-In at Golden Gate Park, defiantly resisting the ban on her erotica and free speech. The case against the book and its sellers was ultimately dropped, and in 2004 *The Love Book* was reissued. The unabashed sexually descriptive lyrics and uninhibited vernacular diction—which caused attempts to censor the book—accord with the hippie emergence, heralding sexually liberated women and psychedelic communal consciousness in the literature of the new antiwar, free love counterculture.

In 1967 Grove Press published Kandel's second and last book of poetry to date, *Word Alchemy*. Her introduction to this volume addresses *The Love Book* controversy from a clearly Beat perspective, as Kandel pronounces, "Poetry is never compromise. It is a manifestation/translation of a vision, an illumination, an experience." At the same time, she condemns the Vietnam War and its slaughters, identifying the poet's vocation with the central concerns of her age. Never far from her mind is women's liberation from oppression and stereotype. With the open, desirous eroticism of "Love–Lust Poem," the female poet–speaker seizes the freedom to demand and relish sexual gratification, voicing

Lenore Kandel and Dr. Timothy Leary, Be-In, San Francisco, 1967. Photographer Larry Keenan: "Poet Lenore Kandel and guru Timothy Leary are talking together on stage at the 'Gathering of the Tribes: The Human Be-In.'" *(courtesy of Larry Keenan)*

her desire and yearning with sex words that are frank and free: "I want you to explode that hot spurt of pleasure inside me / and I want to lie there with you / smelling the good smell of fuck that's all over us." Taking a different tack toward a similar end, the prose poem "Morning Song" makes a claim for women's emancipation through mocking images of feminine and domestic culture and, by poetic play on the word *wife*, rejects bourgeois marriage as demeaning to women: "Eyes shut as an unborn bird he lay unmoving and examined the presence of his wife. wife. WIFE. wIFe. wife." Kandel's 1960s art revises male Beat misogyny with feminist assertion, effecting the continuity of Beat Generation and hippie countercultures by making women count in both.

Kandel did not achieve mainstream or academic literary recognition, if for no other reason than her de facto disappearance from literary publication and communities. Presciently, in the introduction to *Word Alchemy*, Kandel warns of the death or disappearance of the poet by means of forces outside poetry, such as censorship or compromise: "To compromise poetry through expedience is the soft, small murder of the soul." In 1970 Kandel suffered a serious motorcycle accident with her then-husband, Hell's Angel Billy Fritsch (Sweet William), and at this time withdrew from public literary activity. Freewheeling sexual imagery and language, ethical recoil from war, and all-encompassing defense of women's autonomy and personhood distinguish the poetry of Lenore Kandel. Her transformation of hipster cool with female sexual energy made her a Beat poet of 1960s countercultural consequence. Her transgression of cultural and legal restrictions on speech and female decorum made her an icon of liberation.

Bibliography

Cook, Bruce. *The Beat Generation: The Tumultuous '50s Movement and Its Impact on Today.* New York: Scribner, 1971.

Gifford, Barry, and Lawrence Lee. *Jack's Book: An Oral Biography of Jack Kerouac.* New York: St. Martin's Press, 1978.

Johnson, Ronna C. "Lenore Kandel's *The Love Book:* Psychedelic Poetics, Cosmic Erotica, and Sexual Politics in the Mid-sixties Counterculture." In *Reconstructing the Beats*, edited by Jennie Skerl, 89–104. New York: Palgrave Macmillan, 2004.

Wolf, Leonard. *Voices from the Love Generation.* Boston: Little, Brown, 1968.

Ronna C. Johnson

Kaufman, Bob (1925–1986)

Kaufman was a multiethnic poet, an African-American poet, a Beat poet, a surrealist poet, a jazz poet, a *poète maudit*, a New Orleans poet, a San Francisco poet, a street poet, a people's poet, and a poet's poet. One of the founding architects and "living examples" of the Beat Generation as a literary, historical, and existential phenomenon, he has until recently been overshadowed in reputation by his white and formally educated contemporaries such as ALLEN GINSBERG, JACK KEROUAC, GARY SNYDER, and WILLIAM S. BURROUGHS. To some extent this reflects a business-as-usual neglect of black writers by the mainstream; to some extent it reflects Kaufman's own stated ambition to become "completely anonymous." Partly by choice, partly out of disillusionment and the ravages of street life, he turned his back on fame and respectability, implicitly declaring solidarity with the world's anonymous poor. While African-American writers and scholars have been familiar with his work, it is only in the last several years that he is gaining wider recognition.

One of 13 children, Robert Garnell Kaufman was born in New Orleans to a well-respected, high-achieving, middle-class, black-identified Catholic family. His mother, a member of the Vigne family (one of whose members was Louis Armstrong's upper-school teacher at the Colored Waifs' Home for Boys), was a schoolteacher who insisted that the children develop sophisticated literary capacities: their reading included Henry James, Marcel Proust, Herman Melville, and Gustave Flaubert. According to Kaufman's older brother George, their father was a Pullman porter and thus participated in one of the most heroic labor efforts in American history: The Brotherhood of Sleeping Car Porters, the Pullman porter union, was the first black union to organize successfully. It was, in the words of Franklin Rosemont, "more than a union," as it used the railroad system to disseminate black culture, education, and political power throughout the United States. (Other research has suggested that Kaufman's father was a waiter at elegant restaurants that catered to whites; another oral-history source claims he was a bar owner.) At age 18, in 1945, Kaufman, like several of his older brothers, joined the merchant marines and participated in the turbulent organizing activities of several overlapping maritime unions. He became an impassioned, militantly leftist labor orator for the National Maritime Union. When the American Federation of Labor (AFL) and the Congress of Industrial Organizations (CIO) merged in the 1950s, he was purged from the union, a casualty of the anticommunism that swept through the labor movement during the Eisenhower-McCarthy years.

During this period of the cold war, political dissent was crushed; cultural/aesthetic dissent seemed the only way to publicly affirm one's right to be different. The Beat literary movement was born under these circumstances. Kaufman left New York, which had been his prime organizing territory, for California where he met Kerouac, moved to San Francisco, and became a familiar figure in the North Beach literary and street scene. In a brilliant move of spiritual survival, he reinvented himself as a poet—a half-black, half-Jewish Beat poet with an Orthodox Jewish and "voodoo" upbringing (his Jewishness remains apocryphal, though there is some possibility that his great-grandfather, Abraham Kaufman, was a Jew who converted to Catholicism; there is no basis in the claim, made in several biographical sketches, that his mother was Martiniquaine). Embodying dissent in his lifestyle (not working) and writing—or not writing but living "poetically"—became his form of labor, as outlined in "The Poet." A much-beloved and brilliant extemporizer, he blended original rapid-fire aphorisms and wisecracks with the considerable store of modernist poetry that he recited from memory. This ability to "sample" other writers in an original and inventive context is evident in his poetry, which reworks and defamiliarizes that of Samuel Taylor Coleridge, Federico García Lorca, Tennessee Williams, Hart Crane, Langston Hughes, and others. In its adventurous imagery, sonorous qualities, and biting wit, moreover, Kaufman's poetry has much in common with other New World black surrealists such as TED JOANS, Aimé Cesaire, Will Alexander, and Wilson Harris, as well as with the jazz-inspired poetry and fiction of Leroi Jones/AMIRI BARAKA and Nathaniel Mackey.

Kaufman's first book, *Solitudes Crowded with Loneliness* (1965) was compiled, edited, and sent off to the publisher (New Directions) by his wife Eileen Kaufman. Many of the poems in this volume describe the North Beach scene in San Francisco's bohemian pathos, humor, posturing, and genuine utopian yearnings ("ABOMUNIST MANIFESTO," "Bagel Shop Jazz"); others chronicle the ongoing social hassles of being African American ("Jail Poems," and "I, Too, Know What I Am Not," which was selected by Clarence Major for his 1970's anthology *The New Black Poetry*); still others are modeled on jazz compositional principles ("Second April") or invoke jazz themes. Many lyrics express an intense desire to live beyond oneself or acute dissociation ("For My Son Parker, Asleep in the Next Room," "Would You Wear My Eyes?"). *Golden Sardine* (City Lights, 1967) continues many of these themes and continues to experiment, as did "Abomunist Manifesto" and "Second April," with new versions of the long poem ("Caryl Chessman Interviews the PTA from his Swank Gas Chamber"). After a three-year sojourn in New York City (1960–63), during which time he experienced the hardships of addiction and poverty, Kaufman returned to San Francisco, abruptly withdrawing from public life. Where he had been animated and gregarious, spouting his witty raps from cafes and street corners, he became elusive and shadowy, desiring only "anonymity" and "uninvolvement," which he maintained for the remainder of the 1960s and early 1970s. Some accounts characterize this period as a "ten-year Buddhist vow of silence" lasting from John F. Kennedy's assassination to the end of the Vietnam War. Others point to the locating of his son Parker, who had been lost for several years, in the Khyber Pass, as the moment when Kaufman "began to speak again." A second period of productive engagement with the literary and social world in the mid-1970s through the 1980s produced "The Ancient Rain," a bicentennial dark-night-of-the-soul, and several other beautiful poems, some of which derive their power from the increasingly decentered, fragmented vision of apocalyptic liberation and/or destruction that the poet's psychic, physical and political/aesthetic life embody; they are both historical allegories and personal accounts of nightmarish experiences and intuitions. This era culminated in the publication of *The Ancient Rain: Poems 1956–1978* (New Directions, 1981), edited by Raymond Foye, who had to demonstrate his commitment to the project to convince Kaufman to break his own commitment to silence and anonymity but who ultimately won the poet's approval. In January 1986 Kaufman died of emphysema and cirrhosis. The Bob Kaufman Collective published the posthumous *Closing Time Till Dawn* (1986), a poetic dialogue between Kaufman and San Francisco poet Janice Blue. In 1996 Coffee House Press republished *Golden Sardine* and a selection from the other books under the title *Cranial Guitar: Selected Poems by Bob Kaufman*.

Bibliography

Damon, Maria. "Unmeaning Jargon/Uncanonized Beatitude: Bob Kaufman, Poet." *The Dark End of the Street: Margins in American Vanguard Poetry*. Minneapolis: Minnesota University Press, 1993: 32–76.

Edwards, Brent Hayes, et al., eds. *Callaloo* 25, no. 1. Special Issue on Jazz Poetics: Special Section on Bob Kaufman.

Kaufman, Bob. *The Ancient Rain: Poems 1956–1978*. New York: New Directions, 1981.

———. *Cranial Guitar*. Edited by Gerald Nicosia. Introduction by David Henderson. Minneapolis: Coffee House Press, 1996.

———. *Solitudes Crowded with Loneliness*. New York: New Directions, 1965.

Maria Damon

Kerouac, Jack (1922–1969)

Architect and cofounder of the Beat Generation, Jack Kerouac was the innovator of Beat literature's distinctive poetics. His legacy of associational composition techniques and hybrid forms—African-American styles of culture, language, and music amalgamated with European literary ones—reflects his ambition both to join canonical literary tradition and also to reinvent it. This dual impulse epitomizes his pivotal position on the 20th-century modern/postmodern divide. Though his seminal status in post–World War II U.S. culture and literature has been underestimated by many critics, Kerouac's oeuvre—comprised of 14 published novels forming "The Duluoz Legend" (a multivolume extended narrative of the life of a U.S. American postwar writer), books of poetry, various essays, two writing manifestos, and posthumously published texts—had wide influence on Beat movement contemporaries such as ALLEN GINSBERG, WILLIAM S. BURROUGHS, RUTH WEISS, BRENDA FRAZER, and JOHN CLELLON HOLMES, and on succeeding artists, such as BOB DYLAN, KEN KESEY, ED SANDERS, HUNTER S. THOMPSON, and Jerry Garcia of the Grateful Dead, as well as giving rise to literary modes such as New Journalism and forms

of historiographic metafiction. Kerouac has been dismissed as simply an autobiographical writer, and numerous, often erroneous, biographies and memoirs in thrall to his Beat-Generation reputation have fetishized his personal history. However, his works themselves argue against reading his life as a literal source for or influence on his writing because the originality of his writing's aesthetics of mind, or consciousness, complicates simplistic ideas about reading his literature as a mirror of life. Rather, Kerouac's books narrate the workings of his mind as he composed, not merely his conjured memories of the past. Therefore, Kerouac's most

Jack Kerouac smokes a cigarette on an apartment's fire escape in the Lower East Side with R. R. Brakeman's Rule Book in his pocket, while visiting Burroughs and Ginsberg at 206 East 7th Street, New York City, 1953. *(Photo by Allen Ginsberg, courtesy of Corbis Images)*

salient Beat-Generation story is told not by the exaggerated emphasis placed by fans and overzealous biographers on his life's facts but by recounting his development of his literary inventions, which helped transform American writing to meet the emerging postmodern era. The books, far more than the man or what is speculated about the man, are the lasting legacy and influence of the writer Jack Kerouac.

Jean-Louis Kerouac was born on March 12, 1922, in Lowell, Massachusetts, the grandson of French-Canadian immigrants who settled in Nashua, New Hampshire, where his parents met and married. An intense connection to America that often marks children of immigrants and the influence of Catholic myth and dogma reflect his formative experience of Lowell's French-Canadian, Irish, and Greek immigrant communities between the two world wars. His first language was *joual*, the French of Quebec, and he did not routinely speak or write English until he entered junior high school. The death of his older brother Gerard in 1926 at age nine from rheumatic fever and the family's struggles during the Depression attuned Kerouac to suffering and hardship. Dependent on his mother, Gabrielle (Mémère), he lived with her through his three marriages and more than 30 moves. He died in 1969 of alcoholism and the effects of a barroom fight in St. Petersburg, Florida, where he and Gabrielle, still together, lived with his third wife, Stella, the sister of his close boyhood friend, Sebastian Sampas. At his funeral, his Beat-Generation friends mingled with the Greek- and Franco-American families of his Lowell life, embodying the two worlds that he commemorated in his 1950 debut novel, *The TOWN AND THE CITY.*

Kerouac was a writing prodigy. His earliest compositions, handwritten and illustrated one-page home newspapers and magazines, are from 1933–34. At age 11 he wrote his first novel, "Jack Kerouac Explores the Merrimack." He left Lowell in 1939, at 17, to attend Horace Mann School in New York City before matriculating to Columbia University on a football scholarship in 1940. The next year he left Columbia found a job in Hartford, Connecticut and wrote "Atop an Underwood," a lost story collection whose title has been reused. After Pearl Harbor in December 1941, Kerouac

enrolled in a navy V-2 program; while awaiting qualification he was a sportswriter for the Lowell *Sun* and then signed on as a scullion on the S.S. *Dorchester.* He attended Columbia in fall 1942 but quit football. At Christmas in Lowell, he handprinted the novel that had been begun on the *Dorchester,* "The Sea Is My Brother" (never published). In 1943 at naval boot camp in Newport, Rhode Island, Kerouac rebelled against military authority, walking away during a drill session. He received an honorable discharge on psychiatric grounds in June and later caught another ship, the S.S. *George Weems,* bound for Liverpool. During the October crossing Kerouac read John Galsworthy's *Forsyte Saga,* a multivolume prose epic that inspired "The Duluoz Legend."

In winter 1943–44 Kerouac lived with Edie Parker and her roommate Joan Vollmer Adams at 421 West 188th Street, and they attracted a volatile bohemian crowd that included Lucien Carr, David Kammerer, Burroughs, and Ginsberg. Kerouac's arrest as a material witness in Carr's notorious murder of Kammerer in the early morning of August 14, 1943, galvanized his marriage to Parker, whose family bailed him out (he was ultimately exonerated). Kammerer's murder fit with the bizarre "Self-Ultimacy" ritual of purgation and suffering that Kerouac developed in 1944 that included writing notes in his own blood and burning manuscript pages as they were written; resonated with Ginsberg's arrest for involvement with stolen property and sentence to Columbia Presbyterian Psychiatric Institute for "rehabilitation"; and matched Bill Cannastra's decapitation in a 1950 subway-train accident and Burroughs's reckless shooting of his wife Joan Vollmer Adams Burroughs during a game of William Tell in Mexico City in September 1951. As a neophyte writer Kerouac was engrossed in this violent cycle, although of the deaths, only Kammerer's turned up in his published work, veiled as a suicide.

His marriage to Edie Parker disintegrating, Kerouac fraternized in New York with HERBERT HUNCKE and Ginsberg. He collaborated with Burroughs on the unpublished novel "And the Hippos Were Boiled in Their Tanks," each writing successive chapters in Dashiell Hammett detective style about a murder based on the Carr/Kammerer episode. As his father Leo lay dying in December 1945, Kerouac made notes for *The Town and the City*. Late in 1946 with the novel underway, he first met NEAL CASSADY, who, like Carr and Huncke, would exert considerable effect on his writing. In 1947 Kerouac hitchhiked to California, stopping in Denver. This trip, and another the next year with Cassady, provided the inspiration for ON THE ROAD. In 1948 Kerouac finished *The Town and the City* at some 1,100 handprinted pages "a perfect Niagara of a novel," and began to attend classes in literature and writing at the New School for Social Research on the G.I. Bill.

In fall 1948 Kerouac wrote an account of his 1947 travels with a narrator called Ray Smith, a first attempt at *On the Road*. In a conversation with Holmes, Kerouac coined the term *Beat Generation* from a phrase used by Huncke—"Man, I'm beat." Traveling cross-country with Cassady in early 1949, as always he kept a detailed journal; these notes of observations, incidents, and American landscapes grounded several works that he wrote in the 1950s. In March 1949 Kerouac began a second version of *On the Road* with a narrator called Red Moultrie. That month, Robert Giroux, then an editor at Harcourt Brace, accepted *The Town and the City*, which debuted in 1950 to mixed reviews. In 1949 Kerouac met Cassady in Denver for what he called their last great trip to Mexico City. On his return Kerouac started another road tale using a first person narrator, a southern black boy named Pictorial Review Jackson, which later became *Pic*. On November 17, 1950, Kerouac married Cannastra's ex-girlfriend, Joan Haverty, after a month's courtship. The couple parted in May 1951.

Kerouac's failed marriage to Haverty was fruitful nevertheless. Their daughter Janet Michele was born on February 16, 1952, and while living with Haverty, Kerouac wrote what became the published version of *On the Road* to answer her questions about his adventures with Cassady. Typing on a continuous paper roll that was made from taped-together teletype sheets, Kerouac ingeniously invented the physical correlative to his aesthetic of spontaneous composition. This April 1951 version narrated by "Sal Paradise" was preceded by one using the third-person "Ray Smith" narrator again and by Kerouac's receipt, in February 1951, of the

legendary (and now lost) "Joan Anderson letter," in which Cassady detailed his early sexual experiences in a directly confessional style—this inspired Kerouac to write *On the Road* as an "autobiography of self-image" following Herman Melville. But the novel surpasses the sum of its influences to anticipate its postmodern moment: Figuring the hero "Dean Moriarty" both "mad Ahab at the wheel" and "Groucho Marx," the novel collapses distinctions between high and mass culture; celebrating the "mad ones" who chafe against postwar conventions, it questions "white ambitions" to the American dream.

Major breakthroughs followed from Kerouac's devotion to his art. Attaining the scroll version of *On the Road* after three attempts (and a draft of *Pic*), he persisted to further postmodern forms with VISIONS OF CODY. He began this fifth version of the Cassady road tale in May–June 1951, pursuing "deep form," a way to blend linear (*On the Road*) and metaphysical (*DOCTOR SAX*) material. In October 1951 painter Ed White helped Kerouac conceive of "sketching." This fleet notational style, the foundation of spontaneous prose and vehicle for "deep form," began as a technique to capture real-life events as they happened, but the style was extended to writing about remembered and imagined ones. In December Kerouac stayed with Neal and his second wife Carolyn in San Francisco, embarking on a ménage à trois and continuing the "Neal book," completing it in April 1952. Kerouac conceived *Visions of Cody* as a "vertical" successor to the "horizontal" *On the Road*. It featured interior confessions, treated pop culture forms and icons (the Three Stooges) with high culture seriousness, and mixed nonfiction ("Frisco: The Tape") and improvisational ("Imitation of the Tape") genres to achieve an unprecedented postmodern prose narrative. In Mexico City in May, while Burroughs was being investigated for killing Joan, Kerouac wrote, in longhand in a month of afternoon writing sessions, another experimental work, *Doctor Sax*. Articulating a philosophy for sketching the remembered and invented past, narrator "Jack Duluoz" counsels "don't stop to think of words when you do stop, just stop to think of the picture better—and let your mind off yourself in this work." A metaphysical coming-of-age novel of 1930s Lowell, *Doctor Sax* amplifies "vertical" poetics.

By now Kerouac was habituated to a peripatetic existence adapted to the demands of an isolated writing life and his emotional reliance on his mother. Moving in September 1952 back to California and the Cassadys, he began to write "October in the Railroad Earth," "experimental speedwriting" about the American landscape and working man. That fall Holmes published GO, the first novel of the Beat Generation that Kerouac would later apotheosize. But for now, Kerouac was unsung and at loose ends, and in New York in early 1953, he wrote "Springtime Mary"—MAGGIE CASSIDY. Its adolescent love affair mingles with war ("No idea in 1939 that the world would turn mad") and charts the narrator's Horatio Alger ambition to be "a big hero of New York . . . incarnation of the American Super Dream Winner," traditional success Kerouac would ironically seek through literary experimentalism. His frustration at disappointed publishing opportunities was unrelieved by travels to Quebec and San Francisco, but returning to New York, he produced another breakthrough novel and a major manifesto of his composition techniques.

In three successive nights in October 1953, Kerouac wrote The SUBTERRANEANS, whose aesthetic to "just . . . start at the beginning and let the truth seep out" yields a narration of "confessional madness" that encompasses both "the conscious top and the unconscious bottom of the mind." The Subterraneans also represents postwar cultural hybridity in the mixed-race hipster community and the biracial "Mardou Fox," whose "new bop generation way of speaking"—"part Beach, part I. Magnin model, part Berkeley, part Negro highclass"—exemplifies the pastiche postmodern literary style that Kerouac helped pioneer. Burroughs and Ginsberg found the novel so exceptional that they asked Kerouac to explain his techniques. His nine-point list, "Essentials of Spontaneous Prose," describes a method that honors the private mind that speaks freely in the moment of composition by sketching or "blowing" like a jazz musician an "undisturbed flow . . . of personal secret idea–words"; that permits "free deviation (association) of mind"; and, most famously, that insists on "no revision." These demanding ideals, mastered in the compositions of 1951–53, would be the gold standard for all Kerouac's work.

In 1953 Kerouac started to study Buddhism and to meditate. In December he began SOME OF THE DHARMA as reading notes; the 100-page section that he sent to Ginsberg in 1955 evolved into a comprehensive literary work that he finished in March 1956. Visiting the Cassadys in 1954 he wrote some "sketch poems" that later were titled "San Francisco Blues." Back in New York he wrote the science-fiction meditation on global decline, "CITYCitycity." His finished novels were continually rejected by publishers, his thrombophlebitis (a chronic condition dating back to the early 1940s) flared up, and in January 1955 Joan Haverty brought him to court for child support. The Viking Press editor Malcolm Cowley, interested in On the Road, provided small funds that Kerouac used to escape to Mexico, where he wrote the first part of TRISTESSA in pencil by candlelight. Kerouac cryptically lauded its "ingrown-toenail packed mystical style," but the narrator "Jack Duluoz" is overcome by "All of us trembling in our mortality boots, born to die, BORN TO DIE," the existential preoccupation of most works Kerouac composed after embracing the practical but unflinching Buddhist thought.

Kerouac also wrote MEXICO CITY BLUES in summer 1955, "all by hand" in pencil, counterbalancing spontaneity by limiting the choruses to the page size of his pocket notebook. He moved to Berkeley, California, where Ginsberg had just completed "HOWL," obviously indebted to Kerouac's spontaneous method. Orchestrating audience fervor but not presenting his work at the pivotal Six Gallery reading on October 7, 1955, Kerouac began his important literary friendship with GARY SNYDER and alienated KENNETH REXROTH, the poet impresario who proclaimed the landmark event—at which Ginsberg premiered "Howl"—to be the birth of the San Francisco Poetry Renaissance. At his sister's in North Carolina, Kerouac wrote VISIONS OF GERARD by hand in January 1956 in 12 nights; the novel's "windblown" Shakespearean style and "soul and mind" memory temper the pitiless "born to die" ethos that the tale commemorates. With Snyder in Marin County in spring, Kerouac began The Scripture of the Golden Eternity, carefully revising because "it was a scripture. I had no right to be spontaneous." He also worked on OLD ANGEL

MIDNIGHT, styling its "sounds of the universe" "a spontaneous *Finnegans Wake*." Recommended to the post by Snyder, Kerouac spent 63 days alone in summer 1956 as a fire lookout in the Cascade Mountains in Washington, watching over Desolation Peak.

Kerouac returned to "the world" in September 1956, traveling to San Francisco and Mexico City, completing there the second part of *Tristessa* and writing Book One of DESOLATION ANGELS. The narrator's Zen recognition that "I know there's no need to tell a story and yet I know there's not even need for silence" is countered by his aesthetic of the "tic," which codifies the way narrative results from mind prompts when "a thousand memories come like tics all day . . . almost muscular spasms of clarity and recall." In New York in December Kerouac contracted with Viking Press to publish *On the Road* and met the young writer Joyce Glassman (later JOYCE JOHNSON), who became an important confidant after it came out. Visiting Burroughs in Tangier, he typed parts of the book that he named NAKED LUNCH, returning for the September 5, 1957, publication of the groundbreaking *On the Road* that marked a pivotal point in Kerouac's life and writing. Gilbert Millstein's star-making review in the *New York Times* naming *On the Road* its generation's *The Sun Also Rises*—comparing Kerouac to Ernest Hemingway—made Kerouac a high-profile culture icon, and he was never able to reclaim the privacy of mind and anonymity that his writing required. One of the first American writers to gain television exposure, he appeared on John Wingate's *Nightbeat* in September 1957, while in early 1958 he was interviewed by Mike Wallace on CBS. Henceforth, his biography as a writer is complicated by the impact on his art of his outsized public status.

Initially, Kerouac's enormous celebrity permitted wide-ranging artistic expression. In November 1957 he typed *The DHARMA BUMS* for Viking Press in 10 sessions on a long paper roll. His "Visions of Gary" Snyder novel is renowned for its "vision of a great rucksack revolution"—often interpreted as foreseeing the 1960s counterculture. A postmodern hybrid of postwar existential nihilism and Buddhist relinquishment is transmitted in the narrator "Ray Smith's" re-

frain, "I didn't know anything anymore, I didn't care, and it didn't matter, and suddenly I felt really free." The 1958 publication of *The Dharma Bums* coincided with spoken word projects. Kerouac recorded *Poetry for the Beat Generation* to Steve Allen's improvised piano accompaniment; *Blues and Haikus* with Zoot Sims and Al Cohn; and *Readings on the Beat Generation*, a solo performance. He improvised a voiceover narration for the acclaimed short film based on his writings, *Pull My Daisy*, which was shot in painter and director Alfred Leslie's New York loft in January–February 1959. The Spring 1959 issue of *Evergreen Review* carried "Belief & Technique for Modern Prose," Kerouac's other writing manifesto. When Kerouac appeared on *The Steve Allen Show* in November, he read pages of *Visions of Cody* hidden in his copy of *On the Road*, signaling his preference for its experimental aesthetics. During this period of overwhelming popular attention, Kerouac's strong artistic showing was mitigated by increased drinking and defensive loutish public conduct.

Kerouac's postfame novels emphasize the high price of "making it" in America. In early 1960 LAWRENCE FERLINGHETTI's City Lights Books published BOOK OF DREAMS, middream notes that observe the interior mind with stylishly Freudian detail. Kerouac escaped fame's oppressive scrutiny in Ferlinghetti's cabin near Big Sur, California, in July 1960, but this visit proved to be a living nightmare. Written in 10 nights almost a year later, in October 1961 in Orlando, Florida, on a roll of paper, BIG SUR depicts a breakdown under extreme alcohol sickness and debilitating celebrity. The author's claim that the book "tells a plain tale in a smooth buttery literate run" contradicts the narrator's inordinate suffering. In the preface Kerouac confidently reveals his literary master plan to make all his books "chapters in the whole work which I call *The Duluoz Legend* . . . one enormous comedy seen through the eyes of poor Ti Jean (me), otherwise known as Jack Duluoz." Signed "Jack Kerouac," this statement blurs biography of self-image and autobiography, enclosing Duluoz and Kerouac in a shared consciousness that is at once imagined and real, like the delirium hallucinations of the novel's climax.

The postmodernism of Kerouac's late writing, wherein distinctions between the writer's life and his books' legend are obscured, was galvanized by what he called the horror of literary notoriety. The existential aspect of *Big Sur*'s alcoholic suffering appears in 50,000 words that Kerouac wrote in Mexico City in July 1961 and that form Book Two: Passing Through of *Desolation Angels*. This account of fame's crisis state—Kerouac's first extended writing since publication of *On the Road* and *The Dharma Bums*—iterates a "new way of writing about life, no fiction, no craft, no revising afterthoughts" while writhing under the lost privacy of fame's exposure, a condition which undermines invention. The narrator of *Desolation Angels* styled himself a "20th Century Scrivener of Soul Stories," but in *Big Sur* the narrator laments that he is "the bloody 'King of the Beatniks,'" opposing self-images of writer and reputation that increasingly close in on each other.

In March 1962 Kerouac submitted to a court-ordered blood test that confirmed his paternity of his daughter Jan. The next year and a half was filled with drinking, distressing press reports, and negative reviews. Driving Ken Kesey and the Merry Pranksters in the psychedelic bus "Further" in 1964, Cassady engineered a meeting with Kerouac, who, underscoring the disjuncture between the man and the legend, was repulsed by the group whose counterculture his books inspired. Kerouac moved his mother from Northport, New York, to St. Petersburg, Florida, where they weathered his sister Caroline's unexpected death in fall 1964. By late that year, most of Kerouac's books were out of print and unobtainable. In July 1965 he traveled to France to study his genealogy and spent 10 days writing *SATORI IN PARIS*, which was serialized in *Evergreen Review* in 1966 and then published as a book.

In May 1966, providing the first scholarly attention to his writing, Ann Charters visited Kerouac at his home in Hyannis, Massachusetts, and catalogued his archive for a bibliography published in 1967. In September his mother was partially paralyzed by a stroke, and on November 19, 1966, Kerouac married Stella Sampas. In Lowell, in 10 sessions from March to May 1967, Kerouac wrote the last novel published during his lifetime, VAN-ITY OF DULUOZ, which he had been contemplating since 1963 and now addressed to Stella. A scathing account of the costs of fame, the novel connects prewar American innocence and postwar American Dream ideology in a single circular figure: "[Y]ou kill yourself to get to the grave before you even die, and the name of the grave is 'success,'" a destabilizing unreality in which the narrator feels that he is "not Jack Duluoz at all . . . but just a spy in somebody's body pretending." In that postmodern way that Kerouac brilliantly anticipated, Duluoz morphed with his creator in the dizzying fame that renders all aspiration "the general vanity of Duluoz." In summer 1968 Kerouac moved again to St. Petersburg, returning briefly to New York in fall for a ruinous television appearance on William F. Buckley's *Firing Line*. By November Kerouac was in an intense alcoholic downward spiral; revising *Pic* for publication in early 1969, he had no new books planned, demand for his work was at its lowest point, and he had run out of money. In late summer he published "After Me, the Deluge," a widely syndicated essay on his condition as writer. It turned out to be his last word, for Kerouac died on October 20, 1969, in a St. Petersburg hospital.

The critical neglect of Kerouac's literary innovations is partly a fluke of timing; his masterwork *Visions of Cody* was not published in its entirety until 1972 when the familiarity of American postmodernity as well as his trivializing "beatnik" reputation obscured the book's importance. Kerouac continues to be read, but his cultish fans, unremitting commercial exposure, and careless posthumous publications thwart his acceptance into canons of American writing. Nevertheless, recent fresh reception may redeem this lapse and provide the recognition that his work merits. This recovery will be greatly facilitated by the long overdue placement in the New York Public Library's Henry W. and Albert A. Berg Collection of Kerouac's large archive, that he meticulously kept for future studies of his legacy and that is reported to include about 1,800 pieces of correspondence; more than 1,050 manuscripts and typescripts; 130 notebooks for almost all his works, published and unpublished; 52 journals from 1934 to 1960 that include materials used in some novels; and 55 diaries that Kerouac wrote between 1956 and his death. With access to this trove of material, critics and scholars will be able to construct a clearer and fairer picture of Kerouac as person and as writer and to assess his rightful, pivotal place in postwar American literary history.

Bibliography

Dardess, George. "The Delicate Dynamics of Friendship: A Reconsideration of Kerouac's *On the Road*." *American Literature* 46 (May 1974): 200–206.

Grace, Nancy M. "A White Man in Love: A Study of Race, Gender, Class, and Ethnicity in Jack Kerouac's *Maggie Cassidy*, *The Subterraneans*, and *Tristessa*." *College Literature* Special Issue 27, no. 1 (Winter 2000): 39–62.

Hunt, Tim. *Kerouac's Crooked Road: Development of a Fiction*. Hamden, Conn.: Archon Books, 1981.

Johnson, Ronna C. "'You're putting me on': Jack Kerouac and the Postmodern Emergence." *College Literature* Special Issue 27, no. 1 (Winter 2000): 22–38.

Jones, James T. *A Map of Mexico City Blues: Jack Kerouac as Poet*. Carbondale: Southern Illinois University Press, 1992.

Kerouac, Jack. *Windblown World: The Journals of Jack Kerouac 1947–1954*. Edited by Douglas Brinkley. New York: Viking, 2004.

Maher, Paul. *Kerouac: The Definitive Biography*. New York: Taylor Trade, 2004.

Martinez, Manuel Luis. *Countering the Counterculture: Rereading Postwar American Dissent from Jack Kerouac to Tomas Rivera*. Madison: University of Wisconsin Press, 2003.

McNally, Dennis. *Desolate Angel: Jack Kerouac, the Beats, and America*. New York: Random House, 1979.

Tallman, Warren. "Kerouac's Sound." *The Tamarack Review* 11 (Spring 1959): 58–74.

Ronna C. Johnson

Kesey, Ken Elton (1935–2001)

Ken Kesey is best considered as a bridge between the Beats and their inheritors, the hippies, as he is associated more with the West Coast countercultural phenomenon during the 1960s than he is with the luminaries of the Beat movement. Kesey

Ken Kesey, Oakland, 1966. Photographer Larry Keenan: "Fugitive Ken Kesey was giving a talk to some students at the California College of Arts and Crafts when I shot this picture. I sent Neal Cassady some prints. The FBI intercepted Cassady's mail, found this photograph and put it on a wanted poster. It was the only current profile they had of Kesey." *(courtesy of Larry Keenan)*

is best known for his novel ONE FLEW OVER THE CUCKOO'S NEST and for being a member of the psychedelic experimentation group The Merry Pranksters, who met and befriended ALLEN GINSBERG, JACK KEROUAC, HUNTER S. THOMPSON, and TIMOTHY LEARY. The Grateful Dead were the house band for some of the Pranksters' infamous acid tests. "Furthur," the bus driven by the group, eventually found its final resting place on Kesey's Oregon farm.

Kesey was born on September 17, 1935, in La Junta, California, to Fred and Geneva Kesey. He was raised in a Baptist household in Colorado and

Oregon and studied ventriloquism, illusions, and hypnotism as a child. His father took him on hunting trips to the Pacific Northwest, where Kesey would develop a sense of respect for nature. His athleticism extended into organized sports, and he was active in sports throughout high school and college. Kesey would eventually earn a wrestling scholarship to the University of Oregon. While at Oregon, Kesey married Faye Haxby, whom he had known since high school. He majored in communications and speech, graduating with a Bachelor of Arts in 1957. During these studies, Kesey would be influenced by the technical style of television and film, such as multiple points of view and flashbacks, which would find a way into his fiction.

After graduation, Kesey moved to California and enrolled in Stanford's creative-writing program. While in California, Kesey was introduced to the Stanford Lane group, who styled their community after the North Beach Beats. At Stanford, Kesey studied with Malcolm Cowley, one of the editors at Viking who was most responsible for the publication of Kerouac's ON THE ROAD. During this time Kesey served as an aide at the Veterans Administration Hospital in Menlo Park. While there, he would participate in drug experiments where he was paid to take various hallucinogens and report on their effects. These experiences provided him with material for his first novel, *One Flew over the Cuckoo's Nest*, published in 1962. The novel details the antagonism between Randle Patrick McMurphy, a work-shirking prison inmate who has himself committed to an insane asylum, and Nurse Ratched, who controls the ward. This first novel establishes the major theme that would run throughout most of Kesey's fiction—the individual versus a repressive social structure.

Shortly after *Cuckoo's Nest*, Kesey attached himself to the group of psychedelic explorers, including NEAL CASSADY, known as The Merry Pranksters. In 1963 the group set out in their multicolored bus Furthur (a combination of *farther* and *future*) from California with the ultimate goal of attending the New York World's Fair and the publication party for Kesey's next novel, SOMETIMES A GREAT NOTION. This large novel chronicles the actions of the Stampers, a family of loggers breaking a strike in their lumber community. This second novel would seal Kesey's fame as young writer in the American countercultural movement, but it would also be his last for quite some time. Tom Wolfe chronicled the exploits of The Merry Pranksters and their famous bus trip and acid experimentations in *The Electric Kool-Aid Acid Test* (1968). Paul Newman starred in the film *Sometimes a Great Notion* released in 1971.

In 1966 Kesey fled to Mexico after staging a suicide to escape marijuana possession charges in San Mateo, California. This is chronicled in the short story "Over the Border," published in his next book in 1973, *Kesey's Garage Sale.* Kesey eventually returned to California to serve a short sentence. He expressed a desire to quit writing and turn to more experimental forms of expression at the time of his arrest, and this seemed actually to be the case for a while. After his prison and workhouse term, Kesey moved to the relatively secluded town of Pleasant Hill, Oregon, near Eugene. Although Kesey would not publish much throughout the 1960s and 1970s, he was still an active writer. He would collect the shorter works written during these decades in the collection *Demon Box* in 1986. Many of these stories center on Kesey's experience in the countercultural movement and show a more mature opinion of the somewhat radical lifestyle that he advocated in his heyday. This is perhaps because of the iconic status that Kesey had achieved by the time he moved to Pleasant Hill. Many hundreds of hippies and would-be beatniks flocked to his residence, which was surely a strain on the author's patience.

In 1974 Kesey began to publish a periodical in Oregon titled *Spit in the Ocean.* The sixth and seventh issues of the magazine are of particular importance. Number six is a tribute to Neal Cassady, the model for Kerouac's character Dean Moriarty in *On the Road.* (This is Kesey's closest biographical link to the Beat Generation.) The seventh issue is "All About Ken Kesey" himself; it was published as a book by Penguin in 2003. Each issue of *Spit in the Ocean* was guest-edited by a friend of Kesey's, such as Timothy Leary, who would choose the theme of the issue. *Seven Prayers for Grandma Whittier,* a long fictional interior monologue written by Kesey, is serialized in the seven issues of *Spit in the Ocean,* one episode per issue.

Though the stage version of *One Flew over the Cuckoo's Nest* starring Kirk Douglass had been critically panned in 1963, the critically acclaimed film version of *One Flew over the Cuckoo's Nest* starring Jack Nicholson in 1975 was a tremendous success, despite Kesey's disapproval.

Kesey was working on a novel called *Sailor Song* when his son Jed died in 1984. This inaugurated a period of writer's block that Kesey could not begin to overcome until he began to work on *Caverns,* an archaeological murder mystery written by Kesey and a group of graduate students at the University of Oregon. One year before this experimental novel was released in 1989, Kesey published a children's book, *Little Tricker the Squirrel Meets Big Double the Bear,* about a clever squirrel who thwarts a local bully. Another children's book, *The Sea Lion,* was published in 1991. Kesey eventually completely overcame his writer's block concerning "adult" audiences and published *Sailor Song* in 1992. The novel is set in the future where environmental damage that is caused by humans has reached its apex. The final work published during Kesey's life is another experiment in genre for the author: 1994's *Last Go Round* can best be described as a pulp western. One posthumous publication, *Kesey's Jail Journal* was published in 2003. This collection is a series of short prose, illustrations, and poetry, much like *Kesey's Garage Sale.* Ken Kesey died on November 10, 2001, in Eugene, Oregon, following complications from liver surgery.

Bibliography

Leeds, Barry. *Ken Kesey.* New York: Unger, 1981.
Porter, Gilbert M. *The Art of Grit: Ken Kesey's Fiction.* Columbia: University of Missouri Press, 1982.

Donovan Braud

Krishna Poems Herschel Silverman (1970)

HERSCHEL SILVERMAN's first collection remains an undiscovered minor classic of Beat poetry. Although the "big" Beats have sometimes been criticized as media creations or publicity junkies, there is little recognition that there was a community of poets who followed in their wake and who essentially remain marginal figures. Unlike the second generation of New York School poets, who carved out distinct identities away from their elders, second-generation Beat poets were vastly overshadowed by ALLEN GINSBERG, GREGORY CORSO, LAWRENCE FERLINGHETTI, GARY SNYDER, and MICHAEL McCLURE. Poets such as RAY BREMSER and JACK MICHELINE were generally found to be too "crude" and/or "anti-intellectual" to be considered by either the mainstream or the alternative poetries dominated in the 1960s by the disciples and friends of CHARLES OLSON.

Krishna Poems were written in the mid- to late 1960s and were published in 1970. They are fanciful excursions that were written and published during a period where the Vietnam War generated mountains of angry words from poets all across America. Silverman, perhaps the only published American poet to have served during World War II and the Korean War, responds to the absurdity of war with his own, albeit nonlethal, buckshots of whimsy.

> it's Krishna
> who visits me
> with warm midnight lips
> on my forehead,
> who without words
> speaks my thoughts
> and desires,
> and
> suggests
> i construct a poem
> in love
> for my children—

is how the volume begins. Silverman's Krishna is more a figure of the exotic than a religious symbol. In the late 1960s and early 1970s Krishna is guest-starring in the American religious firmament. In 1965 Ginsberg paid for the boat passage of 69-year-old A. C. Bhaktivedanta Swami Prabhupada to the United States from India. By 1966 he established the International Society for Krishna Consciousness. In a few years the "Krishna People" became ubiquitous in both the hippie neighborhoods and in the less-restrictive airports of that era. Ginsberg readings of that era often featured long rounds of Krishna chanting, with Ginsberg pumping away on his harmonium. Even the ex-Beatle George Harrison was seeing Krishna everywhere—his recording of the Radha Krishna Temple choir was a top-10 hit in London. Also still to be heard on oldie stations everywhere is Harrison's "My Sweet Lord" with its chorus chanting "Hare Krishna" behind the "quiet Beatle's" spiritual lyrics.

Silverman, who is a committed Jew who has always talked about his deep roots in his area's Jewish community, turns his Krishna into a mixture of imp, trickster, and muse:

> Krishna
> visible
> in heart of Coltrane.
> Krishna kids
> bounce
> rubber
> balls
> on
> dead-end streets.
> Krishna girls
> wear micro-skirts
> and live
> on New York's East Side
> Krishna's in the wind
> of passing
> motorbikes

An unnoticed element in Silverman's prosody is that his line actually owes less to the poetry of Ginsberg and Corso than to his longtime friend Theodore Enslin. A poet associated with the "Deep Image" group of Jerome Rothenberg and often published in Clayton Eshelman's *Caterpillar* magazine, Enslin was famous at the time for his massive poems—some of which stretched 1,200 pages. A complex, abstract writer, he was about as not-Beat as you could be at the time. However, Enslin possess one of the great musical ears in American poetry—partially owing to his youthful career

as a classical composer who studied under the great Nadia Boulanger. *Krishna Poems* borrows from Enslin's style of the period, where the poetic line is broken into musical phrases. However, Silverman's musical model is the jazz of the period—Mingus, Coltrane, Art Blakey—as opposed to Enslin's allegiance to classical.

Krishna Poems are certainly a product of its period; in fact the chapbook's "binding" simply being a plastic slide that is associated with report covers suggests a certain temporality even beyond the chisel-stapled mimeo books of the era. However, the humor and good naturedness of these poems shine through and make them far more available to the contemporary reader than the kind of excoriating anti-Vietnam poem more typical of the period. The intrepid may find a copy in a rare-book room; however, the sample presented in Silverman's selected poems may inspire some beatnik-in-training to see it back into print.

Joel Lewis

Kyger, Joanne (1934–)

The four-decade career of West Coast poet Joanne Kyger grew out of the San Francisco poetry renaissance and overlaps with several major Beat Generation writers. Kyger was active in the literary circles of the renaissance through her association with Jack Spicer and Robert Duncan and in the lives of major Beat writers including JACK KEROUAC, ALLEN GINSBERG, DIANE DI PRIMA, and from 1960 to 1964 husband GARY SNYDER. Kyger was born November 19, 1934, in Vallejo, California, to Jacob and Anne Kyger. Jacob Kyger's career as a navy officer led to frequent moves for the family, and by her father's retirement in 1949 Joanne had lived in China, Washington, Pennsylvania, Florida, and Illinois before settling in Santa Barbara, California. Kyger attended the University of California at Santa Barbara from 1952 to 1956, where classes with Hugh Kenner and Paul Wienphal encouraged her serious attention to poetry. She left the university and in 1957 moved to the San Francisco Bay

Area, spurred by her interest in poetry and her self-admitted drive for adventure.

In San Francisco's North Beach, Kyger began to work days at Brentano's Bookstore and to spend nights discussing and reading work with friends at poetry bars. In 1957 she met JOHN WIENERS at the poetry bar, The Place, and through him met Duncan and Spicer. At Duncan and Spicer's Sunday poetry group, Kyger encountered future husband Snyder in 1958. The Sunday poetry group drew the literary bohemians of North Beach and students from the then recently defunct Black Mountain College in North Carolina who had followed Duncan to California. Kyger was one of few women in this crowd, and although her work was encouraged, she described the meetings as rigorous: "They (Duncan and Spicer) would read what they had written, and everybody else would read what they had written. And you would be severely criticized. A lot of people would be so heavily criticized that they wouldn't come back." (Duncan, a founder of the San Francisco Renaissance, also encouraged the Beat-associated poets Helen Adam and Madeline Gleason.)

Kyger began to study Buddhism and moved to the East-West House, a co-op begun by Snyder and other Zen students, where Kerouac, LE-NORE KANDEL, LEW WELCH, and PHILIP WHALEN were occasional residents. In 1960 she moved with Snyder to Japan, where they were married on February 23, first at the American consul and then at the Daitoku ji monastery in Kyoto. *The Japan and India Journals 1960–64* chronicles her life with Snyder in Japan, as well as their travels in India from December 1961 to April 1962 with Ginsberg and Peter Orlovsky. She also worked on the poems that became her first book, *The TAP-ESTRY AND THE WEB,* published by Donald Allen after her divorce from Snyder and return to the Bay area in 1964.

In 1966 Kyger married the painter Jack Boyce, and made a lengthy tour of Europe. In 1968 the pair purchased land in the community of Bolinas, north of San Francisco Bay, where Kyger has continued to live (she and Boyce separated in 1970). Since the 1970s Bolinas has been known as a liberal and arts-oriented community,

Joanne Kyger, Cody's Books, Berkeley, 2004. *(courtesy of Larry Keenan)*

attracting artists, writers, and editors such as Donald Allen, Whalen, and ROBERT CREELEY. Kyger began to teach at the Jack Kerouac School of Disembodied Poetics, at the Buddhist Naropa Institute in Boulder, Colorado, with ANNE WALD-MAN and Ginsberg in 1975. While teaching at Naropa in 1978, Kyger met Donald Guravich, a Canadian writer and artist who joined her in Bolinas. *Going On, Selected Poems 1958–80* was one of the winners of the United States National Poetry Series competition in 1983. Kyger remains active in Bolinas community and environmental issues and has continued her practice of Buddhism, and to write, publish, give readings, and teach.

Bibliography
Charters, Ann. "Beat Poetry and the San Francisco Renaissance." In *The Colombia History of American*

Poetry, edited by Jay Parini, 581–604. New York: Columbia University Press, 1993.

Friedman, Amy L. "Joanne Kyger, Beat Generation Poet: 'a porcupine moving at the speed of light.'" In *Reconstructing The Beats,* edited by Jennie Skerl, 73–88. New York: Palgrave, 2004.

Knight, Brenda. "Joanne Kyger: Dharma Sister." In *Women of the Beat Generation,* 197–204. Berkeley, California: Conari Press, 1996.

Amy L. Friedman

L

Lamantia, Philip (1927–2005)

A misfit and a rebel for most of his life, and certainly from the time he became a teenager, Philip Lamantia achieved fame as a poet a full decade before his Beat contemporaries. "To rebel! That is the immediate objective of poets!," he wrote in 1943 at the age of 16. For the rest of his life he continued to rebel in as many different ways as he could imagine. From the mid-1940s until the late-1990s, he wrote hundreds of poems—many destroyed by his own hand. He published nearly a dozen books, but his complex and enigmatic poetry never reached a wide audience, and he remained the least known of the major poets of the Beat Generation. Born in San Francisco on October 23, 1927, to a working-class Catholic family, Lamantia broke from the church, discovered the world of the macabre and the grotesque in the work of Edgar Allan Poe, and as a precocious adolescent wrote inspired love poetry. After viewing an exhibit of the paintings of Juan Miró and Salvador Dali, he cast himself as a member of the avant-garde and left San Francisco, which struck him as a cultural wasteland. During World War II, he settled in New York where the exiled French surrealist poet André Breton took him under his wing and promoted him as a literary genius.

His first book, *Erotic Poems* (1946), exhibits the visionary surrealist element that Breton found compelling. But the lukewarm, largely patronizing introduction by KENNETH REXROTH, then the leading advocate for California artists and writers, hardly helped Lamantia or his work. As the title suggests, these poems explore sex and love, often in the manner of Arthur Rimbaud, the French poet who wrote *The Drunken Boat.* The cautious poetry world of the mid-1940s refused to embrace the young, iconoclastic Lamantia, and he became notorious for such lines as, "I am a criminal when your body is bare upon the universe."

In California again, he finally graduated from high school, then studied at the University of California at Berkeley, and moved in anarchist circles. In the mid-1950s, he gravitated toward the poetry scene that was just then emerging in San Francisco's North Beach—energized by LAWRENCE FERLINGHETTI's fledgling City Lights Bookstore and publishing company and by the arrival from the East Coast of two young poets, JACK KEROUAC and ALLEN GINSBERG. Lamantia appeared onstage at the legendary poetry reading that took place at the Six Gallery in San Francisco on October 7, 1955, when Rexroth served as M.C. and Ginsberg first performed the first part of his signature Beat poem "HOWL." Oddly enough, Lamantia did not read his own work, though he was the only poet on the program with a published book of poems to his name. (John Suiter has revealed that after experiencing what he thought was a near-death experience after a scorpion bite in Mexico in early 1955, Lamantia called to the Madonna of Guadalupe for help. Questioning his renunciation of Catholicism when Lamantia read at the Six Gallery, he did not feel comfortable reading his earlier poetry and read the work of John Hoffman, a friend who was rumored to have died from a peyote overdose.) From that moment on, until his death at the age of 78 on March 7, 2005, Lamantia played an integral and influential role in the San Francisco literary scene—occasionally teaching poetry and reading his own poems in public—but he rarely assumed a commanding presence at the center of the literary scene. In 1970 he married Nancy Peters, an editor at City Lights, which published several of his works, including *Selected Poems 1943–1966* (1967), *Becoming Visible* (1981), *Meadowlark West* (1986), and *Bed of Sphinxes: New and Selected Poems, 1943–1993* (1997). Lamantia published five other volumes: *Ekstasis* (1959), *Narcotica* (1959)—an unapologetic defense of narcotics—*Destroyed Work* (1962), *Touch of the Marvelous* (1966), and *The Blood of the Air* (1970). The titles hint at the author's preoccupations with visibility and invisibility, extreme states of consciousness, the mysterious and the occult.

Like many of his Beat contemporaries, Lamantia experimented with illegal drugs—including heroin and peyote—embraced jazz—especially the music of Charlie Parker and Thelonious Monk—and traveled to Mexico and Morocco, eulogizing the downtrodden of the Earth and lambasting global capitalism. Like Ginsberg, he explored the apocalyptic and the catastrophic. Like GARY SNYDER, he captured California's rare natural beauty—its mountains, rivers, and forests. What makes Lamantia's poetry unique is his willingness to blend the opaque and the transparent and to experiment unremittingly with language, form, and voice. Eschewing the linear, his poetry achieves its power and beauty through digression and accretion, weaving odd bits and strange pieces into asymmetrical wholes. Reading a Lamantia poem often feels like hearing a series of dissonant voices, not one single, harmonious voice.

The author described his own ideas about poetry in a seminal 1976 essay entitled "Notes Toward a Rigorous Interpretation of Surrealist Occultation," but his clearest, most precise views on poetry can be found in his own poems. In *Meadowlark West*, for example, he notes that "poetry is wedded to silence" and that "poetry knows in the unknowing." Students who approach Lamantia's poetry for the first time will find it difficult. Those who have enjoyed his work—including Ginsberg and Ferlinghetti—have insisted that the effort needed to com-

prehend his work is worthwhile. Almost all of his poetry, even the most erotic, is infused with a sense of the spiritual, and it is not surprising that near the end of his life he returned, in some measure, to the Catholic faith and the Catholic Church into which he was born.

Bibliography

Frattali, Steven. *Hypodermic Light: The Poetry of Philip Lamantia and the Question of Surrealism.* New York: Peter Lang, 2005.

Raskin, Jonah. *American Scream: Allen Ginsberg's "Howl" and the Making of the Beat Generation.* Berkeley: University of California Press, 2004.

Suiter, John. *Poets on the Peaks: Gary Snyder, Philip Whalen & Jack Kerouac in the North Cascades.* Washington, D.C.: Counterpoint, 2002.

Jonah Raskin

Last of the Moccasins Charles Plymell (1971)

First published in 1971 by City Lights Books, *Last of the Moccasins* is an impressionistic novel which chronicles CHARLES PLYMELL's experiences in and out of San Francisco in the early 1960s when the "Wichita Vortex" collided with the Beat Generation. Though sharing some thematic and stylistic concerns with other works in the Beat pantheon, Plymell's novel is a unique expression that is shaped by the picaresque sensibilities of the car, bop, and Benzedrine cultures of the Midwest. The critic Hugh Fox wrote, "The only 'beat' novels that approach the stylistic stature of *Last of the Moccasins* are, in fact, NAKED LUNCH and (to a much lesser degree) Kerouac's DOCTOR SAX." However, it could be argued that Plymell's energy and outlook are more in tune with manic rhythms of the works (both aural and written) of seminal Beat NEAL CASSADY.

Plymell began work on *Last of the Moccasins* while attending the writing seminars at Johns Hopkins University where he had been awarded a fellowship. When the novel was published in 1971, it was praised by WILLIAM S. BURROUGHS who wrote, "From the first paragraph the reader is drawn into the writer's space. Plymell has as much in depth to say about death as Hemingway did and a lot more to say about it in terms of the present generation. . . . He is saying a lot about life, which has become the chewed over leftovers of death. . . ." The death of Plymell's prodigal sister Betty early in the book foreshadows the premature demise of not only the psychedelic scene in San Francisco but also the entire American experiment in the 1960s. As Plymell restlessly shuttles between Kansas and California, the novel "keens with an alternating sense of apocalyptic portent and hopeful renaissance." Similarly, Plymell's focus shifts seamlessly from the intimate to the panoramic, an iteration in structure and tone of nature's double helix, which the author perceives as a central metaphor for the cycle(s) of life.

Last of the Moccasins also addresses issues that would be further developed in Plymell's subsequent poetry and essays: the despoilment of the environment, America's karmic debt to the Native Americans, and the dehumanization of the worker. In one moving passage describing a wheat harvest in Kansas, Plymell paints an elegiac portrait of middle America fading beneath a dying sun. Plymell's sharp insights into the Vortex resonate today: "When the Indians lived there, the sun was God. Now there is an unseen God. This God is everyone's extreme image of himself as righteousness personified."

Last of the Moccasins was reprinted in 1996 by Mother Road Publications. A reproduction of a phantasmagoric painting by Plymell's friend Robert Williams adorns the cover of this edition. This mesmerizing cover intimates the wild ride that awaits the reader.

Bibliography

Atherton, Wayne. "Interview with Charles Plymell." *The Café Review* (Summer 2001): 17–23.

Laki Vazakas

Leary, Timothy Francis (1920–1996)

A former Harvard professor and counterculture figure for nearly 40 years, Timothy Leary is best known as the leading advocate for use of psychedelic drugs. Leary was born in Springfield, Massa-

chusetts, in 1920, and after attending West Point and attaining a master's degree from Washington State University, he received a Ph.D. in psychology from the University of California at Berkeley. After the suicide of his first wife, he accepted a teaching position at Harvard and in 1960 first took hallucinogenic psilocybin mushroom while on a trip to Mexico. He then shifted his work to focus on the effects on humans, of psilocybin, a synthetic of the psychedelic mushrooms obtained through Sandoz Laboratories, beginning the Harvard Psilocybin Project that included volunteer test subjects ALLEN GINSBERG, JACK KEROUAC, NEAL CASSADY, WILLIAM S. BURROUGHS, and CHARLES OLSON. Though Kerouac (quipping, "Walking on water wasn't built in a day") and Burroughs (warning, "That bastard wants to control the minds of the next generation") were not persuaded that the drug could bring about a revolution of the mind, Ginsberg, Cassady, and Olson were strong advocates.

Introduced to LSD soon after, Leary became a vocal advocate of the drug, coining the phrase, "tune in, turn on, drop out." He was dismissed from his position at Harvard in 1963 and founded the Castalia Institute in Millbrook, New York, to continue controlled experiments with LSD. Leary's approach was diametrically opposite that of KEN KESEY, another high-profile LSD advocate and counterculture icon. Where Kesey, who visited Leary with Cassady and the Merry Pranksters during their famous bus trip across America, distributed LSD in chaotic warehouse "acid test" parties, Leary's Millbrook experiments were in controlled environments, ostensibly for the purposes of spiritual, even sacramental enlightenment. Leary documented his opinions on the quasi-religious uses of LSD in several books, including *The Psychedelic Experience* (with colleagues Ralph Metzner and Richard Alpert, 1964) and *Psychedelic Prayers from the Tau Te Ching* (1966). While he did take LSD as both a therapeutic and recreational drug, Leary's official opinion on the substance was one of caution, saying, "Acid is not for every brain—only the healthy, happy, wholesome, handsome, hopeful, humorous, high-velocity should seek these experiences. . . . Unless you are self-confident, self-directed, self-selected, please abstain." Occasional

Dr. Timothy Leary, Human Be-In, San Francisco, 1967. Photographer Larry Keenan: "This is my reverent portrait of Dr. Tim at the Be-In in the Polo Fields in Golden Gate Park." *(courtesy of Larry Keenan)*

residents at Millbrook included Ginsberg, Burroughs, and ABBIE HOFFMAN.

In 1968 Leary published perhaps his most important work, HIGH PRIEST, which chronicles experiences on 16 LSD trips taken before the drug was made illegal and tells of goings on in Milbrook during the middle 1960s. Trip "guides" noted in the book include Ginsberg, Burroughs, Olson, and Aldous Huxley among others and each chapter includes an I Ching reading as well as various marginalia to expand further on the experience described therein.

Leary had been invited as an emcee at the January 1967 Human Be-In. The Moody Blues wrote the song "Legend of a Mind" about Leary in 1968, and JOHN LENNON wrote the song "Come Together" for Leary's 1969 gubernatorial campaign against Ronald Reagan in California. Leary joined Lennon and Yoko Ono at their 1969 Bed-In.

Leary spent much of the late 1960s and 1970s either running from the law or incarcerated. Though he did successfully challenge the constitutionality of the Marijuana Tax Act (which the U.S. Supreme Court declared unconstitutional in 1969), he eventually served several years in prison for various drug charges, having fled to Algeria, Switzerland, and Afghanistan before being caught after he had escaped prison with the help of the Weather Underground. For a short period of time he was placed in the cell next to Charles Manson

at Folsom Prison. In 1970 he published *Jail Notes* as record of his thoughts through this period.

Late in life, Leary became very interested in cyber culture and virtual reality, seeing many similarities in these types to his own concepts of "reality as opinion." His writings on this include *Chaos & Cyber Culture* (1994), which conveys his philosophy of humanism with an emphasis on questioning authority, independent thinking, and individual creativity in the framework of computers and other technologies. This work and others helped make him a counterculture icon in the emerging cyber–punk subculture as well as keep his philosophies in the contemporary consciousness. He then worked with a group of friends and colleagues to document his own death from prostate cancer in 1996, published as *Designs for Dying* (1997). The following year, part of his cremated remains were launched into outer space.

Bibliography

Forte, Robert, ed. *Timothy Leary: Outside Looking In.* Rochester, Vt.: Park Street Press, 1999.

Greenfield, Robert. *Timothy Leary: An Experimental Life.* New York: Harcourt, 2006.

Leary, Timothy. *Flashbacks: An Autobiography.* Los Angeles: J. P. Tarcher, Inc., 1983.

Chuck Carlise

Lennon, John Winston (later Ono)
(1940–1980)

Eccentric, rock and roll legend, artist, poet, and social activist, John Lennon, together with Paul McCartney, George Harrison, and Ringo Starr, forged the most successful and beloved pop music group of the 20th century, The Beatles. Born on October 9, 1940, in Liverpool, England—inconveniently so during a bombing raid by the Luftwaffe—he was given the British prime minister's name in a fit of patriotism and then summarily was shoved under the bed as a precaution after a bomb exploded outside the Oxford Street maternity ward in Liverpool, England. His father, Freddie Lennon, a ship's waiter, skipped off to sea, leaving a young wife Julia penniless. Julia's sister Mimi took the responsibility of raising John, giving him a proper home in the posh suburb called Woolton. (Those fables of Lennon coming from a tough working-class Liverpool background are just that, fables.) A rather stern surrogate mother, Mimi kept a close eye on her nephew's whereabouts and activities, and she even parceled out sweets meagerly to keep from spoiling the boy. Lennon rebelled at an early age, first at Dovedale Primary School and later at Quarry Bank High School, where he was frequently placed on detention and suffered regular canings by the headmasters. But even while intractable as a student, Lennon developed a love of literature, whiling away hours in Mimi's home reading Lewis Carroll's *Alice's Adventures in Wonderland* and *Alice Through the Looking Glass.* He took to lampooning his teachers in a handwritten publication that he dubbed "The Daily Howl," which was frequently confiscated and passed around by bemused faculty members—they were slightly proud of their student's burgeoning talent, though his talent presented itself in the most defiant of ways. These early drawings and stories were the seeds for his later parodies that eventually grew into his first published book, *IN HIS OWN WRITE.*

That would wait, however, until long after the fateful day of July 6, 1957, when Ivan Vaughan led his unsuspecting friend Paul McCartney to the Woolton fete to hear a local skiffle group, The Quarry Men. Onstage, in a red checkered shirt, Lennon played guitar and sang "Be-Bop-A-Lula" while a transfixed McCartney looked on. When later that day they were introduced, the first incarnation of The Beatles was born. McCartney remembers, in his original introduction to *In His Own Write,* "At Woolton Village fete I met him. I was a schoolboy and as he leaned an arm on my shoulder I realised he was drunk. We were twelve then [sic] but in spite of his sideboards we went on to become teenage pals."

In the year that followed, Lennon entered the Liverpool College of Art and came under the influence of the pop-cultural icons of his time: Elvis Presley, Carl Perkins, Marlon Brando, and James Dean. Increasingly angry and made more so by the needless death of his mother Julia, with whom he had been sharing a newfound and treasured relationship, he moved into a Victorian flat with fellow art students Stu Sutcliffe and Bill Harry. Harry would lecture his two roommates about such Beat writers as JACK KEROUAC, LAWRENCE FERLINGHETTI, and GREGORY CORSO and was determined that they all should write something significant to put Liverpool on the literary map. Lennon's contributions were his word-play nonsense and sketches. According to biographer Ray Coleman, "John's work was to presage the rise of Liverpool beat poets and can now be seen as an indicator of the assertiveness of Liverpool people in various arts, away from the American influence of the time."

Edgy, iconoclastic, Lennon with his razor-sharp wit lashed out at those who disapproved of his teddy-boy appearance, winning over disciples and droves of smitten girls as well, such as Cynthia Powell, who later became his first wife. His drive and personal magnetism certainly helped propel The Beatles to ever-greater musical accomplishments, though it would be a mistake to discount the innate talent of each group member, which was considerable. Add to that the extravagantly fortuitous associations with people the likes of impresario Brian Epstein, record producer George Martin, and music publisher Dick James, and fame and fortune for the pop group, especially for Lennon (long considered the "leader"), was secured—at an unprecedented level.

The year Lennon became a multimillionaire rock and roll idol and Al Aronowitz introduced Lennon to BOB DYLAN and marijuana, 1964 also witnessed his assent into the upper crust of Great Britain's literary world. *In His Own Write* sold 100,000 hardcover copies in its first printing, garnered rave reviews on both sides of the Atlantic, and won the Foyles Literary Prize. Followed the next year by a second volume, *A Spaniard in the Works,* and in 1966 by his solo acting debut in Richard Lester's surrealistic *How I Won the War,* Lennon established himself as a bona-fide artist and came to be regarded internationally as something of a neorenaissance man.

When the bottom fell out (as bottoms so often do), it did so with the BBC Television release of *Magical Mystery Tour,* the day after Christmas 1967. Though chiefly McCartney's inspiration, the film, especially when shown in black and white, was an unwatchable, dismal entanglement of undeveloped sketch ideas and inside jokes. Ironically, in an art-imitates-life-imitating-art sort of way, the idea of going for a "magical trip" on a bus was influenced by KEN KESEY's Merry Pranksters, true Beats themselves who, as popular rumor has it, dropped acid one night in the parking lot outside The Beatles' final performance in San Francisco in 1966. In the late 1960s Kesey would be given a record contract by Apple, The Beatles' new production company, for their spoken-word series.

Lennon's association with the avant-garde predated even his life association with Yoko Ono; in fact it led directly to his first meeting with Yoko. Late nights out with the fast Chelsea crowd in 1966 brought him in contact with John Dunbar, brother of ED DORN's wife Jennifer, ex-husband of Marianne Faithfull and owner of the Indica Art Gallery in Mason's Yard. Lennon began to frequent Dunbar's gallery, as did poet ALLEN GINSBERG, who lived around the corner. Dunbar managed to get an acid-besotted Lennon (he had been tripping for days) to come to Ono's show, "Unfinished Paintings and Objects." And so the second great partnership in the life of Lennon had begun, humbly enough.

After the inevitable break up of The Beatles, John and Yoko took their bed-peace campaign overseas, first landing in Toronto and then moving to Montreal where they met with Ginsberg and TIMOTHY LEARY at bedside in their hotel suite. Ginsberg and Lennon, cultural leaders of the respective Beat and hippie movements, risked the wrath of the current Nixon administration by holding public demonstrations against the war in Vietnam, even though they were a country away. (This would lead to an attempt on behalf of J. Edgar Hoover and Nixon alike to deport Lennon because of the perceived danger of his political ideology and his influence on youth.) But it was in fall 1971, during a meeting with ABBIE HOFFMAN and Jerry Rubin, when Ginsberg and Lennon, the two artists of the pack, formally parted with the radical politicos when it was suggested that they go to San Diego to disrupt the Republican National Convention. They did not want to expose young people to the kind of violence that had erupted at the 1968 Democratic National Convention in Chicago.

Lennon's so-called "lost weekend" began in late 1973 when he was ordered out of the apartment that he shared with his wife, Yoko Ono. The circumstances surrounding the break-up of the celebrity couple are beclouded, though it is agreed by many who knew Lennon that he was in trouble emotionally and not ready to continue a serious husband–wife relationship. He moved to Los Angeles along with Ono-assistant May Pang and for the next 11 months humiliated himself in public drunken scenes with Harry Nillson and others, at times alienating even close friends. Lennon had rocketed to stardom, fallen from public grace, and now appeared a lost and broken man, though only 33 years old.

Encouraged by the success of his album *Walls and Bridges* and the number-one song collaboration with Elton John, "Whatever Gets You Through the Night," Lennon made good on a bet by appearing live at Madison Square Garden to perform with Elton. Unbeknownst to him, Yoko was backstage, waiting. Thus the Lennons' reconciliation was ensured, and John began his new life as a house husband and a full-time father to their son Sean, who was born on John's birthday in 1975.

After coming out of retirement with the new album *Double Fantasy*, John Lennon was shot to death on December 8, 1980, in front of the Dakota Building in Manhattan, by a disturbed man.

Bibliography
The Beatles Anthology, edited by Brian Roylance et al. San Francisco: Chronicle Books, 2000.
Brown, Peter, and Steven Gaines. *The Love You Make: An Insider's Story of The Beatles.* New York: Signet, 1983.
Coleman, Ray. *Lennon.* New York: McGraw Hill, 1986.
Norman, Philip. *Shout!: The Beatles in Their Generation.* New York: MJF, 1981.

Greg Herriges

Loba Diane di Prima (1998)

It took DIANE DI PRIMA 28 years to determine that her master work, *Loba,* is about "the feralness of the core of women, of the feminine in everything, in everyone." The collection of 205 oracular and mysterious poems, titled for the Spanish word meaning "she-wolf," uses Navajo wolf mythology to represent female and feminine consciousness over thousands of year. Through the trope of loba in the form of the Virgin Mary, Lillith, Kali-Ma, Shiva, a bag lady, a young woman dancing at a bar, and many others both secular and spiritual, di Prima reveals the process by which all humans—innately artists—create themselves. Book I was published in 1978 by Wingbow Press, and Books I and II were published in 1998 by Penguin.

Di Prima began the poem in the early 1970s, using a process that she describes the intuitive "receiving" of "broadcasts" that she then records. As she worked on the collection making visual collages of images of women, wild animals, and strange scenery, individual poems emerged through the juxtaposition of forms. These images and words eventually coalesced into a portrait of female and feminine power symbolized by the wolf.

In method and content, *Loba* exemplifies many of the passions in di Prima's life, especially the poetry of John Keats, the alchemical and hermetic arts, Zen and Tibetan Buddhism, the blues and jazz, autobiographies and memoirs, motherhood, the female body, and world mythologies. The style relies upon short imagistic lines balanced with longer prose lines, vernacular language mixed with the esoteric, playful use of the page as canvas, shorthand such as *&* and *yr*, and quick dancelike rhythms modulated with slow dreamlike rhythms. Book I deals with the physical and sexual life of a woman and Book II with the soul. The collection epitomizes a postmodern form called a rhizome—a nonlinear text with multiple sites of entry and exit.

Loba testifies to an essentialist philosophy that characterizes second-wave feminism: recognition and celebration of an essential "femaleness" at the core of all women. One argument that *Loba* makes vociferously is that female power has remained steadfast throughout history and that every woman possesses the ability to tap this common essence:

> were it not for the ring of fur
> around her ankles
> just over her bobby socks
> there's no one
> wd ever guess her name. . . .

While this argument has great value, contemporary psychological and sociological identity research has shown that race, class, ethnicity, relationships, and individual biochemistry complicate the formation of self. Di Prima's essentialist perspective is mitigated somewhat by the integration of poems that represent critical reviews of *Loba*, poets' and painters' renderings of loba, and male-centered visions such as the "Tahuti Poems" that portray the lover of Isis in Egyptian mythology. These decenter the concept of the essential female nature, lending credence to di Prima's statement that *Loba* is about the wildness in all humans.

Di Prima continues to work on Book III of *Loba*, which focuses on the journey of the spirit.

Bibliography

di Prima, Diane. "The Tapestry of Possibility" (Interview). *Whole Earth.* (Fall 1999) http://www.findarticles.com/p/articles/mi_m0GER/is_1999_Fall/ai_56457596.

Foley, Jack. "Diane di Prima." *Poetry Previews.* Available online. URL: http://www.poetrypreviews.com/poets/poet-diprima.html. Accessed May 5, 2005.

Libby, Anthony. "Diane di Prima: 'Nothing Is Lost; It Shines In Our Eyes.'" In *Girls Who Wore Black: Women Writing the Beat Generation,* edited by Ronna C. Johnson and Nancy M. Grace, 45–68. New Jersey: Rutgers University Press, 2002.

Nancy M. Grace

Lonesome Traveler   Jack Kerouac   (1960)

Lonesome Traveler began as a novel called "Beat Traveler," but JACK KEROUAC abandoned it after 40,000 words and, instead, put together this collection of mostly previously written travel pieces. Still, *Lonesome Traveler* holds up as a good collection of Kerouac's most accessible and popular short works. Several of the essays that are collected in *Lonesome Traveler* were written for the popular, mainstream magazine *Holiday*. He wrote them for money both for himself and his friends. "New York Scene" (originally titled "The Roaming Beatniks") was written with ALLEN GINSBERG, GREGORY CORSO, and Peter Orlovsky, and it financed Ginsberg and Orlovksy's trip to India. Corso lost his share at the racetrack. Other pieces are far more challenging, such as the stream-of-consciousness "The Railroad Earth" (originally published in the *Evergreen*

Review), which was performed by Kerouac at his rare public readings and works best when read aloud. It is printed here with new chapters. For serious Kerouac enthusiasts, the book has an additional value in that essays such as "Slobs of the Kitchen Sea" (one of the new pieces that he wrote for the book) fill in gaps in Kerouac's "The Legend of Duluoz," his fictional story of his life. Kerouac wrote to Ginsberg describing the contents of the book and said that *Lonesome Traveler* was "not a bad book." Kerouac is right not to say that it is one of his best books. All of the pieces are successful and entertaining, but most are conventionally written (by Kerouac's standards). Yet, Daniel Talbot, in the *New York Times Book Review,* called it "vintage Kerouac" and said that it would make any nine-to-five office worker long for a freewheeling life such as Kerouac's. The book did not enjoy good sales, however, and was remaindered by 1961. McGraw-Hill melted the plates for the book in 1962, preventing any paperback reprint. David Amram set a section of the book to music in 1968, and Kerouac wrote to him that he found it "beautiful."

"Piers of the Homeless Night" covers December 1951. Kerouac misses his boat, the S.S. *Roamer;* takes a bus cross-country from New York to San Pedro, California, to meet Henri Cru at the other end of the *Roamer*'s voyage; spends a few mad days partying in Los Angeles with Cru; and, once again, is unable to ship out on the *Roamer* with Cru, this time because of a difficulty with the union. Cru was an old friend of Kerouac's from his Horace Mann days; he is a main character in the Oakland/San Francisco section of ON THE ROAD. Here, even more so than in *On the Road,* Cru's storytelling ability comes through strongly and reveals why Kerouac believed that Cru was "the funniest man I have ever known." Cru had a magnetic pull on Kerouac similar to that exercised by NEAL CASSADY. Kerouac would follow Cru anywhere, he says.

In early 1952 Kerouac had been living with the Cassadys in San Francisco, writing DOCTOR SAX and VISIONS OF CODY. He finished typing *Visions of Cody* in April 1952, and decided to visit WILLIAM S. BURROUGHS in Mexico and write a book about him, called "Down." The Cassadys took a trip of their own, to Tennessee, and dropped Kerouac off

on the border of Mexico at Nogales. Taking a bus to Mexico City, he became friends with a young Mexican hipster named Enrique, who guided him to Culiacán, near Mazatlán, where they smoked hashish with a medicine man in an Indian grass hut. Their host, after being convinced that Kerouac was not a cop, expressed the opinion that all of the Americas belonged to the Indians and that they would in due time return to them. Kerouac agreed. From Spengler he saw these people as the "fellaheen," hence the title of this section "Mexico Fellaheen," Indian peoples of the Earth who survive all catastrophes and continue living untouched by decadent civilizations. Kerouac continued on to Mexico City with Enrique, but he abandoned him there, fearful of involving Burroughs in any complications that might jeopardize Burroughs's parole status: Burroughs had accidentally shot his wife Joan the previous year. Kerouac's portrait of his first bullfight in this section reveals a darker side of Mexico. He sees the bull's doomed situation in the ring as analogous to the human condition. Kerouac's distaste for bullfights is one of the ways in which he distinguishes himself as a writer and as a person from one of his earliest influences, Ernest Hemingway.

"October in the Railroad Earth" was written in San Francisco in 1952, just after Kerouac completed *Visions of Cody.* The first half of it was published in the "San Francisco Scene" issue of the *Evergreen Review.* Kerouac had already withdrawn an excerpt from *The* SUBTERRANEANS from this issue because Ginsberg had punctuated his prose; Kerouac feared the same would happen to "The Railroad Earth"; therefore, he instructed his agent, Sterling Lord, to defend the piece against any significant changes. He also published excerpts from the same piece titled "October in the Railroad Earth" in the "Beat" issue of the *Black Mountain Review.* It was published alongside his "Essentials of Spontaneous Prose" and was intended to be an example of a piece written using the technique described in that essay. Kerouac liked to perform from "The Railroad Earth" and read from it as part of his Vanguard performance in December 1957; in 1958 he recorded a section of it with Steve Allen accompanying him on piano for the album *Poetry of the Beat Generation.* McGraw-Hill included both

parts I and II of "The Railroad Earth" in the hardback edition of *Lonesome Traveler.* Kerouac gave
in and let them change his dash style of punctuation (restored in the Grove edition), but he would
not allow any other changes. In 1960 he wrote to
Ginsberg that the railroad men forgot what a lousy
brakeman he was and wanted to rehire him after
reading "The Railroad Earth." The prose style of
"The Railroad Earth" came to represent for him
a style of writing that he knew was extreme for
most readers and required too much attention, as
opposed to his style in *The DHARMA BUMS,* which
was, perhaps, too accessible. In his *Paris Review* interview, Kerouac described the style of "The Railroad Earth" as "highly experimental speedwriting."
Gerald Nicosia champions the piece in his biography of Kerouac, *Memory Babe,* saying that "the dili-
gent reader [of Kerouac's long sentences] is almost
rewarded with an unexpected increment of meaning that no series of simple sentences could have
provided."

The story is set in September of 1952 when
Kerouac had returned to the West to live with
Neal and CAROLYN CASSADY in San Jose, California. They promised him a room in which to write,
a railroad job, and the resumption of their previous
relationship in which both Neal and Kerouac were
"husbands" to Carolyn. The relationship did not
work out this time, and Kerouac moved out to live
in a San Francisco skid-row hotel that he favored
called the Cameo. There he wrote "The Railroad
Earth" after work on the rails. The railroad job
revived old dreams that he had of settling down
with a good hometown girl, such as Mary Carney
of whom he wrote in *MAGGIE CASSIDY.* In most biographies of Kerouac, "The Railroad Earth" is the
primary source for information about this period of
Kerouac's life on skid row and on the railroad. He
was making as much as $600 a month, but to save
money to go to Mexico, he restricted himself to living on $17 a week. Although he loves the skid-row
life, he tries not to romanticize it overly. In fact, he
distinguishes his own fierce mental activity from
that of the bums around him. Living in the Cameo
also helped Kerouac to imagine San Francisco's
past and the days of the Gold Rush and (charac-
teristically) to become nostalgic for the past. His
railroad run took him from Third and Townsend,

where the Coast Division line began, to the halfway point at San Jose (where Neal and Carolyn
Cassady lived for Neal's convenience as a railroad
man himself), to the end of the line in Watson-
ville (where Neal had an apartment he was at one
point sharing with LuAnne Henderson). The 50-
mile ride to San Jose was eventless and allowed
Kerouac to read and to write. He also studied the
countryside, and in stream-of-consciousness style
he allowed himself to write lengthy asides on topics
such as the plight of the braceros (legal Mexican
workers), who pick vegetables in the fields border-
ing the tracks.

"Slobs of the Kitchen Sea" covers June 1953
when Kerouac, no longer living with the Cassadys,
was living at the Cameo and working out of San
Luis Obispo (250 miles from San Francisco). Kerouac had to admit that he was not particularly
good at railroad work, and one night in San Francisco after drinking heavily with Al Sublette, he
signed on as a porter on the S.S. *William Carruth,*
bound for Alabama, New York, and Korea. Kerouac served, in a rather surly manner, as a steward
in the officer's mess. When he was caught with a
prostitute in Mobile, Alabama, while he was supposed to be on duty, Kerouac had to agree to leave
the ship at the next port, New Orleans. From New
Orleans, Kerouac headed back to New York and
the events that are covered in his novel *The Subterraneans.* About this adventure at sea, he wrote
to Carolyn Cassady that he began to feel that the
ship was a "steel trap" and that he began "lush-
ing tremendously" and had to stop drinking for a
month to recover. Kerouac does not write in detail
about this voyage anywhere else, and thus "Slobs
of the Kitchen Seas" fills a gap in "The Legend of
Duluoz." It is an entertaining if somewhat evasive
sketch, in that Kerouac is not nearly as honest
about his true mental situation in the story as he is
in his letter to Carolyn Cassady.

By 1959 Kerouac's character had been so thoroughly destroyed in print by his many critics that
he could only publish in lascivious magazines such
as *Swank* or in travel magazines like *Holiday,* edited
by his friends Ted Patrick and John Knowles. Originally titled "The Roaming Beatniks," "New York
Scenes" was a group of spontaneous compositions
written by Kerouac, Ginsberg, Corso and Orlovsky

and published in the October 1959 issue of *Holiday*. Ginsberg, Corso, and Orlovsky all received a much-needed $500 check for their contribution to this essay and to a second, titled "The Vanishing Hobo." "New York Scenes" is particularly valuable for its detailed descriptions of familiar Beat hangouts often referred to in the works of Kerouac, Ginsberg, and Corso—Bickford's Cafeteria, The Cedar Bar, and The Five Spot. There are also anecdotes about Corso, Ginsberg, Orlovsky, Lester Young, Bill Heine, and LeRoi Jones/AMIRI BARAKA.

"Alone on a Mountaintop" covers June to August 1956 when Kerouac spent 63 days as a fire lookout in the Mount Baker National Forest. A much longer description of this disheartening experiment in solitary living appears in *DESOLATION ANGELS.* It is interesting to examine this account alongside the ones in *The Dharma Bums* and *Desolation Angels* to see how Kerouac's perspective changed.

"Big Trip to Europe" is a different version of Kerouac's spring 1957 trip to Europe than covered in *Desolation Angels.* The major difference between the two accounts is that Kerouac provides a much longer description of his stay in Paris in "Big Trip to Europe." The woman he leaves on the docks in New York in February 1957 is JOYCE JOHNSON.

"The Vanishing American Hobo" is the second *Holiday* magazine collaboration with Ginsberg, Corso, and Orlovsky. Unlike "New York Scenes," however, this essay appears to be written mostly by Kerouac, who knew much more about this side of American life than the other three did. Kerouac bemoans the loss of W. C. Fields and Charlie Chaplin-type bums in America, the "motherland of bumdom." Television and newspapers and radios have demonized the drifter as a child molester or thief, he says, and underemployed police officers in the U.S. police state mercilessly hassle them. In a larger sense, he sees the move to outlaw bums as part of a corporate plot to force everyone into conformism. Such conformity will eradicate the hobo saints whom Kerouac met. Jesus was hobo, Kerouac says, as was Li-Po and Buddha. As in most of the pieces from this collection, the general feel one receives after finishing it is a melancholy nostalgia. Oddly, of all of Kerouac's thousands of pages of prose and poetry, the magazine-made "Hobo" is

the only work by Kerouac included in the influential *Heath Anthology of American Literature.*

Rob Johnson

Love Book, The   Lenore Kandel (1966)

In 1966 *The Love Book*, a small collection of cosmic erotic lyrics, was published by Beat poet LENORE KANDEL. Like *HOWL AND OTHER POEMS* a decade earlier, *The Love Book* was confiscated in San Francisco on charges of obscenity, iterating for the new countercultural generation of hippies and activists the free speech issues that Beat movement writing had confronted. *The Love Book*'s origins in female sexuality and sexual emancipation, its publicized seizure and obscenity trial, and its female author's controversial use of profane sex words in poetry are the hallmarks of this pivotal text's transmutation of Beat Generation ethics into the rebel freedoms of the 1960s counterculture.

The Love Book was published privately by a small Haight–Ashbury press, Jeff Berner's Stolen Paper Review, in November 1966, just months before the January 1967 Human Be-In and the epoch-making Summer of Love. The volume was handprinted and sold for a dollar; it had nearly translucent dry-paper pages, and its cover featured a wood-blocked image, an Eastern-inspired likeness of Krishna embracing a naked woman from behind. The tripped-out, love-saturated design of the book exemplifies the psychedelic hippie counterculture to which it spoke. A testament to its mid-1960s era, *The Love Book* merges hippie romanticism and women's orgasmic pleasure with four-letter sex words, spinning these in a mystical, psychedelic love chant. The legal controversy focused on the book's subject matter—heterosexual intercourse—and diction, which made free use of the verb *fuck* as well as slang for genitalia such as *cock* and *cunt,* which Kandel regarded as beautiful, not obscene, words.

Four poems constitute *The Love Book:* "God/ Love Poem" and three phases of "To Fuck With Love." The poems' distinctive 1960s ambience is in their sexual candor and ardor, their focus on orgasm, their allusions to Hindu cosmology, and their psychedelic register, which offered LSD-inflected hallucinatory descriptions. The influence of consciousness-altering drugs is apparent in the poems' mind-bending perspectives, visions seen through a crystal haze in multiple linguistic reflections: "fuck—the fuck of love-fuck—the yes entire— / love out of ours—the cock in the cunt fuck— / the fuck of pore into pore—the smell of fuck / taste it—love dripping from skin to skin— . . . I/you / reflected in the golden mirror we are avatars of / Krishna and Radha . . . carnal incarnate." The psychedelia of prismatically overlapping frames of repeated words and images in trippy kaleidoscopic wholes functions visually, aurally, and imaginatively to alter consciousness as might a hallucinogenic drug. The sex talk of *The Love Book* wallows in the body, and it is spoken for women's orgasmic benefit by a free-love female mystic, who embodies the way pleasure is freed in the vibrant Jungian 1960s from the confinement of the dour Freudian 1950s.

The Love Book flaunts radical freedoms to depict heterosexual intercourse through explicit sex language in poetry, adumbrating aspects of second-wave feminism by exalting the sexual revolution from the position of the female lover in the cosmic act of love. The uninhibited sex language achieves a liberation that models the sexual freedom *The Love Book* advocates taking. Kandel adapted the countercultural ethic of free love to serve poetry's liberation, just as *The Love Book*'s literary liberation served women's sexual freedom.

Bibliography

Cook, Bruce. *The Beat Generation: The Tumultuous '50s Movement and Its Impact on Today.* New York: Scribner, 1971.

Gifford, Barry, and Lawrence Lee. *Jack's Book: An Oral Biography of Jack Kerouac.* New York: St. Martin's Press, 1978.

Johnson, Ronna C. "Lenore Kandel's *The Love Book:* Psychedelic Poetics, Cosmic Erotica, and Sexual Politics in the Mid-sixties Counterculture." *Reconstructing the Beats,* edited by Jennie Skerl, 89–104. New York: Palgrave Macmillan, 2004.

Wolf, Leonard. *Voices From the Love Generation.* Boston: Little, Brown, 1968.

Ronna C. Johnson

M

"Mad Dogs of Trieste" Janine Pommy Vega (2000)

JANINE POMMY VEGA's signature poem was written in Willow, New York, in August 1998 for ANDY CLAUSEN, but its intended audience can be seen as all the fellow travelers of the Beat movement and their compatriots. It can be found in *Mad Dogs of Trieste: New & Selected Poems* published by Black Sparrow Press in 2000. It is a lament for the passing of a generation of poets and political activists, the "mad dogs of Trieste," whose "words crept / under the curtains of power, made little changes, / tilted precarious balance, and brought relief." These poets and political activists "have faded like stories." It is significant that the poem was written not long after the death of the politically active poet ALLEN GINSBERG, who was one of Vega's mentors.

It might be assumed that the "Trieste" Vega is referring to is the Caffé Trieste in San Francisco mentioned in ED SANDERS's poem "HYMN TO THE REBEL CAFE," that was frequented by Ginsberg, GREGORY CORSO, BOB KAUFMAN, JACK KEROUAC, LAWRENCE FERLINGHETTI, and HAROLD NORSE. Vega herself suggests that the symbolic name is actually in reference to the city in northeastern Italy, Trieste. This city has long been a commercial and cultural hub. It was a free port from 1719 to 1891. This border town was a creative refuge for James Joyce and Rainer Maria Rilke among others. From 1947 to 1954 it was the capital of the Free Territory of Trieste. Thus the "Trieste" of this poem can be seen as a symbolic place that is free from the corruption and philistinism of centrally located and dominating governments.

The poem suggests that the "war" between the establishment and the counterculture has taken a turn for the worse. Senseless violence ("kids lobbing cherry bombs into garbage cans"), isolation ("the last hookers heading toward home"), and police brutality ("Cops square off against teenagers in the village square / take the most pliant as lovers, and reroute the rest / into chutes of incarceration") are now commonplace. The Paris of Vega's youth, where many Beat poets lived and wrote during the late 1950s and 1960s, is conjured in the poem. Vega reminisces about Les Halles, the colorful wholesale marketplace known as the "stomach of Paris" that was the setting of Émile Zola's *Le Ventre de Paris* (1873) and was demolished in 1971 to be turned into a soulless modern shopping center; La Chat Qui Peche ("The Fishing Cat"), the famous Paris jazz club where Miles Davis played and TED JOANS performed; and Le Chien Que Fume ("The Smoking Dog"), the celebrated Parisian bistro named after a poem by the French surrealist André Breton. But what is truly missing is "The mad dogs of Trieste / we counted on to bring down the dead / and rotting status quo, give a shove here / and there, marauder the fattened and calcified order."

The ambiguous ending of the poem ("your friends my friends nobody left / but the mad dogs of Trieste as we / cover the streets") suggests that while the older "mad dogs of Trieste" have passed away, their memory can inspire the surviving poets and generations of new poets to take their place.

Kurt Hemmer

Maggie Cassidy Jack Kerouac (1959)

This novel might not get the respect it deserves because its subject matter is so different from JACK KEROUAC's more famous novels and its style comparatively conventional. Still, its frank handling of delicate emotional experiences is highly original. Chronologically, *Maggie Cassidy* is the third volume of Kerouac's "Duluoz Legend," following *VISIONS OF GERARD* and *DOCTOR SAX*. *Visions of Gerard* covers Kerouac's early childhood, and *Doctor Sax* covers his late childhood and early adolescence. *Maggie Cassidy* is the record of Kerouac's first serious love affair, beginning in the summer when he was 16. All three of these books were originally sketched out in several long, confessional letters that Kerouac wrote to NEAL CASSADY in December 1950 and January 1951. The book is not just about Maggie but is also about Kerouac's family during the years following his father's loss of his printing business. Emil (Leo Kerouac) is proud and resourceful and careful to tell his son about the world without embittering him.

The inspiration for the real-life Maggie was Mary Carney, a young woman who lived in a house with rosebushes along the river in South Lowell. In Kerouac's actual life, Mémêre, his mother Gabrielle Kerouac, always had a say about both his girlfriends and (later) his wives, and Mary Carney was only the first in a long line of women who would not pass Mémêre's inspection. Kerouac's relationship with Mary was mostly over by the time he went off to Columbia in 1940, but Kerouac would still walk by her house on trips back to Lowell. To him, she represented the possibility of a life he missed leading—one of home and family, a stable, steady job on the railroad.

Instead of Mary and the railroad job, Kerouac went on the road with Cassady. It is no accident that Maggie and Neal share similar last names; they are the two sides of the coin of Kerouac's life. For if Kerouac saw Mary as someone who could have provided him with a much-needed stability, he saw Neal—at least at the time he was writing *Maggie Cassidy*—as the opposite. In October 1952 Kerouac wrote to JOHN CLELLON HOLMES, "and how I loved Mary Carney's dark sad face, & wanted to marry her at 16 and be a brakeman on the Boston & Maine railroad . . . to have a real

asshole like Cassady come along & con me like a yokel into listening to his crap & believing in his kind of franticness & silly sexfiend ideas." Kerouac's choice of *Cassidy* for Maggie's name is also suggestive of his homosexual desire for Cassady: in essence, he makes "Maggie" Neal's sister, a strategy that Kerouac admitted to Ellis Amburn was typical of his way of expressing sexual desire for men such as Sammy Sampas (Jack's third wife was Sammy's sister) and GARY SNYDER.

Although written at the same time as the experimental novels *The SUBTERRANEANS* and *Doctor Sax*, *Maggie Cassidy* is often called Kerouac's most accessible novel because of its traditional, linear style—almost a return to the style of *The TOWN AND THE CITY*. The book even begins in the third person, a rarity in Kerouac. Kerouac appears to have written the book consciously to resemble a movie scenario or to resemble more of a conventional novel, perhaps because his persona, Jack Duluoz, perceived the world in such terms. Kerouac even went so far as to rewrite the "spontaneously" written sections of the novel to fit them in with the other more conventionally written sections.

Written in the third person, the first four chapters capture the last moments before Duluoz and his friends mature into men with jobs and wives and a war to fight. The fifth chapter is elegiac and sets the tone for the rest of book. He meets Maggie, and she plays many roles in the book: sister, mother, witch, and Madonna. Later, Kerouac outlines his confused relationship with religion. He says he has "exchanged the angel of life for the other," presumably the dark angel with whom he often associates Cassady. He also writes frankly here of his love for a little boy when he was nine and says that we do not notice the "little dramas" of love that children play out. Such observations, analyses, and descriptions make the novel much more than the simple "adolescent love story" advertised on its cover.

Kerouac is also an excellent sports writer, and here he re-creates an indoor track meet in which Duluoz competes against an African-American runner. Although Duluoz is intimidated by the black runner, when they meet at the starting line, he sees that they are in fact similar: "The Canuck Fellaheen Indian and the Fellaheen Negro face to face." Later,

Jack realizes that "love" is ruining his sports life with the boys and regrets having ever met Maggie.

Reading this novel, you have to wonder why Malcolm Cowley and other editors turned down a story with such universal appeal, one that Kerouac says captures "the enormous sad dream of high school deaths you die at sixteen." Behind the "typical" awkward scenes between high school lovers, Kerouac creates a tension between harmless teenage small talk and Duluoz's hidden mind. This tension is felt throughout the book and makes for anything but a typical romance novel. His love for Maggie is presented as imprisonment and torture, and the imagery of love carefully includes only nature's harsh elements—rock, ice, fire. We see Maggie draw Duluoz away from his family and from his love of sports in sirenlike fashion.

The book was published in 1959 as an Avon paperback with the tag line, "The Bard of the Beat Generation reveals a startling new dimension to his personality in this brilliant and profoundly moving novel of adolescence and first love." It received no serious reviews, and to this day it is one of the least commented-upon novels by Kerouac. However, critics would do well to examine the relationship between Kerouac and Neal and Carolyn Cassady in terms of how it may have influenced the novel: Their threesome broke up just before Kerouac sat down in his mother's kitchen in New York and wrote *Maggie Cassidy.*

Bibliography
Amburn, Ellis. *Subterranean Kerouac: The Hidden Life of Jack Kerouac.* New York: St. Martin's Press, 1998.
Grace, Nancy McCampbell. "A White Man in Love: A Study of Race, Gender, Class, and Ethnicity in Jack Kerouac's *Maggie Cassidy, The Subterraneans,* and *Tristessa.*" In *The Beat Generation: Critical Essays,* edited by Kostas Myrsiades. 93–120. New York: Peter Lang, 2002.
Kerouac, Jack. *Selected Letters, 1940–1956,* edited by Ann Charters. New York: Viking, 1995.

Rob Johnson

"Marriage" Gregory Corso (1959)
The theme of marriage is in poetry an ancient and honored one, which through the centuries has been treated in a consistently celebratory fashion. But in his poem "Marriage," GREGORY CORSO brings a somewhat skeptical spirit to the theme and adds to the tradition of the marriage poem a note of zany humor.

Written by Corso in 1958, published in the *Evergreen Review* Summer 1959 edition, and included in his collection *The HAPPY BIRTHDAY OF DEATH* (1960), "Marriage" has been widely anthologized and is probably the poet's best-known work. The poem takes the form of a monologue in which the poet–speaker addresses to himself a series of questions and by imagining dramatic situations relevant to those questions seeks to answer them. The questions that he poses and ponders in the course of the poem are fundamental to his future happiness and his fate in the world: "Should I get married? Should I be good?"

Clearly, the questions imply feelings of uncertainty on the part of the speaker, who is both attracted by the possibility of marriage and fearful of it. The second question clarifies the first, identifying what is ultimately at issue—a clash of values between individual freedom and social norms, for to will oneself to be good necessitates conforming to a standard of right, and it is this standard that the speaker is unsure he accepts or is capable of meeting or maintaining.

Much of the fun of the poem derives from the voice of the chaplinesque first-person narrator, whose eccentricity and sincerity and self-deflating candor arouse a sympathetic response in the reader. The narrator or speaker is all too keenly aware of his shortcomings, his inadequacies, his irremediably impractical nature, and the irrepressibility of his extravagant, insurgent imagination. While he fantasizes longingly about the kinds of fulfillment that are to be found in marriage and parenthood, he wonders anxiously whether he is equal to the challenges that courtship, marriage, and fatherhood will present.

The first stanza illustrates the nature of the conflict within the speaker as he imagines the challenges and frustrations of courtship. The speaker is concerned that he may "astound" the girl next door if he begins to woo her, and given his eccentric sartorial tastes and his quirky notions of what constitutes an entertaining evening and a romantic setting, his concerns would seem well founded.

This initial conflict suggests the crux of the matter: The speaker's behavior and interests clearly diverge from all conventions and accepted usages, and so he must either suppress his desires and values or by indulging them and risking alienating others, including the object of his affections. The issue is that of integrity versus conformity.

In the stanzas that follow, the speaker imagines what the consequences for him might be if for the sake of marriage he consents to conform, to dress, and to conduct himself in an acceptable manner. Each stage of the courtship and the marriage is envisioned by him as an ordeal: the examination and evaluation by the parents of his betrothed, the wedding ceremony, the honeymoon. He imagines committing social blunders and enduring discomfort, unease and embarrassment.

Moreover, he recognizes that there is in him an unrestrainable streak of rebellion against the mundane, the bland, and the banal. His poetic imagination, he foresees, would inevitably erupt, taking the form of surreal phrases spoken or cried, and he would soon be driven to acts of defiance and subversion. Even were the marriage to be Hollywood-idyllic and were fatherhood to follow, the narrator knows that he could not suppress his idiosyncrasies, his outbursts of poetic babble, his compulsive forays into dada-sabotage of the quotidian. And what, he wonders, if the marriage were far from idyllic and he found his poetic spirit being suffocated by poverty and squalor? Accordingly, he rejects all thoughts of marriage.

No sooner has he done so, however, than he reconsiders the notion, envisioning a *Vogue* magazine kind of marriage: sophisticated, affluent, fashionable, comfortable. Yet even so thoroughly satisfactory a situation, he concludes, would ultimately be for him no more than a "pleasant prison." In such an atmosphere, his imaginative spirit would be stifled, would wither. But the alternative to all of these unsatisfactory scenarios, the narrator realizes, is at least equally unsatisfactory—a life of isolation and loneliness.

The poem concludes with reflections on love, the ideal woman, and the ideal marriage, all of which are for the speaker epitomized in the figure of "SHE"—the sorceress Ayesha from H. Rider Haggard's novel. In the novel, Ayesha's love for Kallikrates is so passionate and intense that in a jealous rage it drives her to kill him and then to wait 2,000 years for him to be reincarnated and return to her. (In the interim, she maintains her youthful beauty by bathing in the Flame of Immortality, a mysterious life-giving fire.) This is the kind of fierce, unconstrained love, untainted by convention, that would—in the poet–speaker's view—make for the perfect mate and the perfect marriage.

Corso's "Marriage" suggests that social conventions often serve to tame and attenuate our purest impulses and as well to subdue and starve in us all that is most vital and most vivid. Yet, though playfully and pointedly critical of the social institution of marriage and its associated customs, Corso's poem ultimately affirms marriage as a human, heart-to-heart pact and upholds the animating principle underlying true marriage—the precious, perilous, primal mystery of love.

Bibliography

Corso, Gregory. *An Accidental Autobiography: The Selected Letters of Gregory Corso.* Edited by Bill Morgan. New York: New Directions, 2003.

Olson, Kirby. *Gregory Corso: Doubting Thomist.* Carbondale: Southern Illinois University Press, 2002.

Miles, Barry. *The Beat Hotel: Ginsberg, Burroughs, and Corso in Paris, 1957–1963.* New York: Grove Press, 2000.

Skau, Michael. *"A Clown in a Grave": Complexities and Tensions in the Works of Gregory Corso.* Carbondale: Southern Illinois University Press, 1999.

Stephenson, Gregory. *Exiled Angel: A Study of the Work of Gregory Corso.* London: Hearing Eye, 1989.

Gregory Stephenson

Matz, Martin (1934–2001)

A self-proclaimed "perpetual wanderer" who did not taste the admiration of a wider audience until late in his life, Martin Matz was a streetwise poet who savored close friendships with GREGORY CORSO, BOB KAUFMAN, and HERBERT HUNCKE. Like his comrades, Matz was an autodidact, whose love of intoxicating substances led to a long bit in Mexico's notorious Lecumberri Prison in the 1970s, and like his friend Huncke, Matz was a gifted raconteur and storyteller with a keen appreciation of the surreal and absurd.

Martin Matz was born on July 16, 1934, in Brooklyn. His father died in 1944, and Marty spent his adolescence with his mother and her second husband in Nebraska. After a year at the University of Nebraska, Matz entered the army, serving as an alpine instructor in Colorado during the Korean War. While in the service, he was seriously injured in a car accident and spent nearly nine months recuperating in an army hospital. Following his discharge, Matz arrived in San Francisco, where he studied Buddhism and met JACK KEROUAC, NEAL CASSADY, and ALLEN GINSBERG. Just as he was becoming part of the incipient North Beach poetry scene in the late 1950s, Matz hit the road, traveling in Mexico and South America for the next 15 years. Alluding to his time in Mexico, Matz later recalled, "I got tired of it after the first year, but it took me 14 years to get out of the hammock."

After collecting pre-Columbian art for the film director John Huston, Matz began to collect for himself, occasionally returning to the States to sell some artifacts. He moved on to drug smuggling for which he was incarcerated in the abominable Lecumberri, which he described as "the closest thing to Hell to be found on earth." Matz detailed the horrors he endured and his attempted escape from the prison in "The Escape Was Impossible," a story (from his partially completed autobiographical novel) published in the Panther Books edition *In the Seasons of My Eye: Selected Writings 1953–2001* (2005).

In 1978 Matz returned to the United States as part of a prisoner exchange with Mexico, and he again settled in San Francisco where he renewed old friendships with the city's poets. Matz's *Time Waits: Selected Poems 1956–1986* was published in 1987. In the late 1980s, he married filmmaker Barbara Alexander, and they spent the better part of eight years in northern Thailand, living on Barbara's inheritance. In a small hill tribe village north of Chiang Mai, Matz wrote a suite of opium poems that became PIPE DREAMS (1989), a privately published gem with an introduction by Huncke, who wrote that Matz "draws support for the solidity of his statements from the earth, the soil—all of nature; trees, rocks and gems—upheaval and restless winds—strange, dream-producing flowers. His is an awareness of the endless mystery we are all so much a part of."

In 1990 and early 1991 Marty and Barbara Matz spent eight months in the Chelsea Hotel, where they hosted a convivial salon which included Huncke, painter Vali Myers, poet Ira Cohen, and literateur Roger Richards. The Matzes separated in the late 1990s, and he again hit the road, living for a time in Oaxaca, Mexico. He found a warm receptiveness for his poetry in Italy, where he joined a "Beat Bus" tour of poets, including Ira Cohen, LAWRENCE FERLINGHETTI, and ANNE WALDMAN. In 2000 Matz found himself back full circle in his native Brooklyn. He recorded a CD of his poetry, *A Sky of Fractured Feathers*, with musicians Chris Rael and Deep Singh. Marty spent his final months on the New York's Lower East Side, where he graciously received a new generation of admirers. He died on October 28, 2001, in the hospice unit of Cabrini Hospital.

Bibliography

Matz, Marty. *In the Seasons of My Eye: Selected Writings 1953–2001.* Edited by Romy Ashby. New York: Panther Books, 2005.

Laki Vazakas

Maximus Poems, The   Charles Olson (1983)

These poems, composed between 1950 and 1970, rank as one of the profoundly brilliant epics of 20th-century American poetry, alongside William Carlos Williams's *Paterson* and Ezra Pound's *Cantos*. The focus of CHARLES OLSON's epic is the history of a New England fishing town—Gloucester, Massachusetts, where Olson's family would spend their summers when the poet was a child and where he lived during the final decades of his life.

Olson completed his important manifesto on poetics, "Projective Verse," in 1950. In it he proposes a poetry that creates itself projectively through high energy grids of writing that draw the eye of the mind through its complexities. The first volume of *The Maximus Poems* was published in 1960. Other volumes followed in 1963, 1968, and posthumously in 1975. All of *The Maximus Poems* has been published as a single volume of more than 600 pages by the University of California Press. It remains in print.

Olson had been trained as a scholar, with important research on Herman Melville behind him when he began his epic. This sense of scholarship suffuses *The Maximus Poems*, which are highly referential, but no more difficult than the verse of other top rank bards of his century, such as T. S. Eliot, Robert Duncan, Hart Crane, Rainer Maria Rilke, or Wallace Stevens.

In its essence, *The Maximus Poems* narrates through the voice of Maximus the beginnings of a fishery off Cape Ann that became the Plymouth Bay Colony and then Massachusetts. Olson investigated the actual raw historical records to trace how the village of fishermen was co-opted by British investors, and thus America itself came under corporate control in its earliest decades. In his sometimes angry denunciation of the loss of local economy, Olson carried into epic writing the principles of social democracy that he learned while occupying a fairly high position in the Franklin Roosevelt New Deal administration of the early 1940s.

The idea for the name Maximus came from Maximus from Tyre, a second-century A.D. philosopher, Platonist and moralist, whom Olson discovered when researching Sappho in the late 1940s. Ancient Tyre had similarities to Gloucester in that it was a main port of the Phoenicians, just as Gloucester was a leading location of the burgeoning fishing industry in the New England colonies. Tyre was forced to be connected to the mainland by a bridge, just as Gloucester became connected by a bridge and modern roadway. Another source for the name Maximus was Olson's size—he was six feet eight inches tall, added to which was an intellectual intensity that made him seem even taller than that and which gave the voice of Maximus in his epic even greater force.

Olson was deeply religious and felt a religious sacredness in the buildings and land forms of Gloucester and its churches. To the end of the poet's life, his hunger for a United States with a just economy and brightness for all burned in his poems. ROBERT CREELEY believes that ED DORN's

essay "What I See in *The Maximus Poems*" is still the gate through which one enters *The Maximus Poems.*

Bibliography
Butterick, George F. *A Guide to* The Maximus Poems *of Charles Olson.* Berkeley: University of California Press, 1980.

Edward Sanders

McClure, Michael (1932–)

Since his literary debut at the Six Gallery reading, Michael McClure has been one of the most enduring and influential writers of the Beat movement. As one of five poets who began his career on that night in 1955, he shares a long and rich history with ALLEN GINSBERG, PHILIP WHALEN, LAWRENCE FERLINGHETTI, GARY SNYDER, PHILIP LAMANTIA, and many other writers of San Francisco's Beat period. As one of the youngest members of the Beat circle, McClure played an important role as a bridge between writers and artists of the Beat movement and the region's youth counterculture of the 1960s and has been a close friend and collaborator with figures such as JIM MORRISON, RICHARD BRAUTIGAN, BOB DYLAN, and Janis Joplin.

The author of more than 20 volumes of poetry, more than 20 plays, two novels, and three collections of essays, McClure's most powerful and persistent message is that humans must strive to regain their biological identity as mammals. Writing in what his friend Snyder calls a "biological / wild / unconscious / fairytale / new / scientific / imagination form," McClure pushes his readers to reconsider their place in the world, to question and revolt against humanmade political structures, and to reexamine their relationship to the rest of nature. "LET US THROW OUT THE WORD MAN!," he urges, and seek in place of this limited role the "mammalian possibility" of "a larger place" in the world.

McClure was born October 20, 1932, in Marysville, Kansas, to parents Thomas and Marian Dixie Johnston McClure. He began his university education in 1951 at the University of Wichita and later transferred to the University of Arizona before moving to San Francisco, where he enrolled in a writing workshop with poet Robert Duncan at San Francisco State University. Through his friendship with Duncan and later with poet KENNETH REXROTH, he began to find his place in the city's literary community in the early 1950s.

In fall 1955 McClure took part in the now famous Six Gallery Reading—the foundation of what would soon be called the San Francisco Poetry Renaissance. Here, in his first public reading, McClure, along with Lamantia, Snyder, Whalen, and Ginsberg, helped to launch the Beat movement, and his presence at the event helped to instill in the fledgling movement his lifelong fascination with the natural world.

In the months following the Six Gallery reading, McClure began in earnest to publish his work. In 1956 his first small collection of poems, *Passage*, was published by Jonathan Williams's Jargon Books series. Other collections soon followed, including McClure's first major collection, *Hymns to Saint Geryon* (1958), *The New Book / A Book of Torture* (1961), his powerfully erotic long poem *DARK BROWN* (1961), the wildly experimental "beast language" poems contained in *GHOST TANTRAS* (1964), and his vitriolic condemnation of the Vietnam War, *POISONED WHEAT* (1965). During these early years, McClure also took an active role in seeing that the words and ideas of other writers of the Beat movement and the Black Mountain School made it into print; he coedited two influential literary journals of the period: *Arc II / Moby I* and *Journal for the Protection of All Beings*.

Although early in his apprenticeship as a poet McClure experimented with formal verse, his published work from the 1950s to the present has often been written in a bold projective-verse style that features abundant use of capital letters and of lines centered on the page, a form that quickly became a recognizable trademark of his poetry. By moving away from the blocky stanza, anchored to the left margin, and moving his lines to the center of the page, McClure's poems became representations of symmetrical forms found in the natural world. Visually, they came to resemble strands of DNA, whirlpools, blossoms, and—according to the poet—"the lengthwise symmetry found in higher animals."

Michael McClure with autoharp, San Francisco, 1965. Photographer Larry Keenan: "I photographed McClure for his poster to announce a reading he was giving. The classic photograph turned out so well that McClure did not want to use it. It took a week to convince him to go with it. Bob Dylan gave him the autoharp." *(courtesy of Larry Keenan)*

While McClure is perhaps best known for his talents as a poet, his work as a playwright has earned him a reputation as one of America's most innovative dramatists. Heavily influenced by the writings of French playwright Antonin Artaud, McClure's plays often reject traditional dramatic staging and dialog and rely instead on what Artaud termed "a language of signs" that is designed to cut through the audience's social conditioning, thus replacing the standard more linear and rational theater experience with imagery akin to that of a powerful dream. His first major play *The Blossom; Or, Billy the Kid* was staged in 1964, to be followed a year later by his erotically charged masterpiece *The BEARD*, a play that resulted in no fewer than 19

Michael McClure and Ray Manzarek in performance, San Francisco, 2000. Photographer Larry Keenan: "Poet Michael McClure and former Doors keyboard player Ray Manzarek teamed up as a duo performing all over the U.S." *(courtesy of Larry Keenan)*

censorship trials as a result of its graphic sexuality. The whimsical *Gargoyle Cartoons* followed in 1969, a set of 11 short plays that included the comic but powerful antiwar play *Spider Rabbit*. McClure's most successful theatrical endeavor came in 1978 with his play JOSEPHINE: THE MOUSE SINGER, an adaptation of a short story by Kafka.

McClure's impact as a writer extends far beyond the Beat era. During the later 1960s, he served as an important mentor to the emergent youth counterculture of San Francisco, as well as a friend and adviser to rock music luminaries such as Dylan, Joplin, and Morrison. From the 1970s onward, his concerns have often turned toward global environmental issues, and his poetry has served as a key source for those who struggle for environmental justice. In recent years, he has often collaborated with musicians such as The Doors' keyboardist Ray Manzarek and composer Terry Riley, blending his poetry with music to reach new audiences, a half-century after he first read his poems at the Six Gallery.

Bibliography

Bartlett, Lee. "Meat Science to Wolf Net: Michael McClure's Poetics of Revolt." *The Sun Is But a Morning Star: Studies in West Coast Poetry and Poetics.* Albuquerque: University of New Mexico Press, 1989: 107–123.

Phillips, Rod. *Michael McClure.* Western Writers Series Vol. 159. Boise, Idaho: Boise State University, 2003.

Rebel Roar: The Sound of Michael McClure. Film written by Kurt Hemmer, produced by Tom Knoff. Palatine, Ill.: Harper College, 2004.

Stephenson, Gregory. "From the Substrate: Notes on Michael McClure." *The Daybreak Boys: Essays on the Literature of the Beat Generation.* Carbondale: Southern Illinois University Press, 1990: 105–130.

Rod Phillips

Meltzer, David (1937–)

When Donald Allen edited his landmark anthology *The NEW AMERICAN POETRY, 1945–1960*, little did he realize the critical trouble that he was creating when he divided his poets among "schools" and regional allegiances. Most notably was the placing of Denise Levertov and Larry Eigner among the poets of Black Mountain College—an institution that they had never visited and that had tenuous prosodic connection.

Equally confusing was the placement of David Meltzer in Allen's catch-all Section Five—despite his strong connections to the San Francisco Bay Area and to the circle of writers around Jack Spicer. What does stand out was that Meltzer, along with Ron Loewinsohn, was the only poet under 25 in an anthology whose oldest poet was born in 1903.

Meltzer is sometimes viewed as one of the last Beat poets standing, which is, hardly an accurate categorization. However, he was part of Los Angeles's early Beat scene that was made up of a mix of artists and actors that included Dennis Hopper and Wallace Berman. His move up the coast put him in contact with the lively San Francisco scene, which by the late 1960s transformed from beatnik to hippie. Meltzer caught the *Zeitgeist* when he formed a rock band that was popular enough to open up for The Doors and to record two albums for a national label.

Meltzer's journey begins in Rochester, New York, in 1937. Four year later the family moves to Brooklyn and in 1952 moves again to Los Angeles. Meltzer termed himself a "compulsive dropout since thirteen" and though he saw himself as a writer, assumed that it was "a private enterprise, nearly impossible to learn or teach within the school format." This attitude abruptly changed in 1954 when he met the artist Ed Kleinholz, who was renting a space off Santa Monica Boulevard from Meltzer's girlfriend. Soon, Meltzer came into contact with a group of artists that included George Herms, Robert Alexander, and, most importantly, Wallace Berman. A remarkable figure, whose influence caused him to appear as part of the cover art of The Beatles' *Sgt. Pepper's Lonely Hearts Club Band* and in a small part in Hopper's film *Easy Rider*, Berman was deeply interested in mysticism in general and kabbalah in particular, elements that continue on in Meltzer's work.

Meltzer married in 1958 and moved to San Francisco in 1959. He became involved in the jazz and poetry-reading movement and made contact with all the major figures of that community—including Robert Duncan, LEW WELCH, and KENNETH REXROTH.

His first book, *Ragas*, was issued by Discovery Books in 1959. Meltzer is the author of many additional volumes of poetry including *The Clown* (Semina 1960), *The Process* (Oyez 1965), *Yesod* (Trigram 1969), *Arrows: Selected Poetry, 1957–1992* (Black Sparrow Press 1994), and *No Eyes: Lester Young* (Black Sparrow 2000). He has also published fiction including *The Agency Trilogy* (Brandon House 1968; reprinted by Richard Kasak 1994), *Orf* (Brandon House 1969; reprinted by Masquerade Books 1995), and *Under* (Rhinoceros Books 1997) and book-length essays including *Two-Way Mirror: A Poetry Notebook* (Oyez 1977). He has edited numerous anthologies and collections of interviews including *The Secret Garden: An Anthology in the Kabala* (Continuum Press 1976; reprinted, Station Hill Press 1998), *Birth: Anthology of Ancients Texts, Songs, Prayers, and Stories* (North Point Press 1981), *Death: Anthology of Texts, Songs, Charms, Prayers, and Tales* (North Point Press 1984), *Reading Jazz* (Mercury House 1996), *Writing Jazz* (Mercury House 1999), and *San Francisco Beat: Talking With the Poets* (City Lights 2001). His musical recordings include *Serpent Power* (Vanguard Records 1968; reissued on CD in 1996) and *Poet Song* (Vanguard Records 1969). He teaches in the humanities and graduate poetics programs at the New College

of California. He lives in the Bay area. His most recent venture has been the jazz magazine *Shuffle Boil*, which he coedits with Steve Dickson.

Meltzer himself is quite uneasy about the notion of a Beat "movement" and its current revival. In an interview in the *NY Press* he noted, "I think the local press and then the national media created it more than it created itself, at least self-consciously. [ALLEN] GINSBERG, of course, was a notorious promoter—wonderfully so, for his friends—but I think the taking up of the whole 'Beat' and 'beatnik' stereotypes that came out of that period, that was all media-created, and unfortunately it's that image that seemingly many people still believe in and are nostalgic for. But they're nostalgic for something that never really existed in the sense in which the media represented it. Movements, as we understand them historically, are always labeled as such after the fact—they're easier to nail down that way, when they're over and when these guys aren't in your face anymore. Then you can place them and you can basically study them—take them off the streets and into the more formal institutions."

Although Meltzer's own work shares much with what it is considered Beat writing, his stance is a bit more introspective. In his "Tell them I'm struggling to sing with angels," a popular anthology piece, the tone is far removed from Ginsberg's "bop kabala" or JACK KEROUAC's catholicized version of Buddhism:

> Tell them I'm struggling to sing with angels
> who hint at it in black words printed on old
>   paper gold-edged by time
> Tell them I wrestle the mirror every morning
> Tell them I sit here invisible in space
> nose running, coffee cold & bitter
> Tell them I tell them everything
> & everything is never enough. . . .

It is perhaps Meltzer's rather distinctive writing project that has created a critical void in the reception of his work. The kabbalah-laden texts of books such as *Yesod* lacked the greater context that is now available with current Hollywood-driven interest in kabbalah. Likewise, his continual thematic reference to jazz limits such works as *No Eyes: Lester Young* to an even narrow slice of readership. Perhaps this accounts for his exclusion from some of the more recent anthologies of postmodern and alternative poetries.

Like one of his intellectual heroes, kabbalah scholar Gershon Schoelem, Meltzer's work—the poetry, the prose, the music, the anthologies—act as an authentic counterhistory of life as lived out in his own imagination and in the imagination of the artists of the Bay area.

Joel Lewis

Memoirs of a Beatnik Diane di Prima (1969)

DIANE DI PRIMA has often called *Memoirs of a Beatnik* a "pot-boiler." As fictionalized autobiography, *Memoirs of a Beatnik* is a mixture of life writing and erotic fiction through which di Prima explores life as bohemian poet and sexual adventurer in the cold-war 1950s. It was published in 1969 by Olympia Press—The Traveler's Companion, Inc., reissued in 1988 by Last Gap Press, and reprinted in 1998 by Penguin Books.

Although di Prima began her vocation as a poet long before meeting JACK KEROUAC, ALLEN GINSBERG, and GREGORY CORSO, *Memoirs of a Beatnik* illustrates how her literary proclivities and her bohemian lifestyle situated her within the Beat Generation, shaping her poetic voice to become an important representation of Beat politics and aesthetics as well as an essential female perspective in this heavily male-dominated movement.

Many readers have initially turned to *Memoirs of a Beatnik*, which has sold more than any of di Prima's books, to gather primary historical material about the core male Beat figures and the Greenwich Village milieu. In this respect, *Memoirs of a Beatnik*, organized according to the movement of the seasons from 1953 through 1956, provides a valuable historical function. A reader can hear the authentic voices of Kerouac and Ginsberg discussing poetry and can find fascinating descriptions of the Village bar scene, lofts, and pads—Beat Bohemia in all its elegance and poverty. More importantly, however, *Memoirs of a Beatnik* speaks strongly for the rights of women to practice their art with the same freedom as men. Di Prima's dis-

cussion of the "Rule of Cool" that transformed women into silent bystanders explains why so many of the women artists of the movement have long remained invisible. One also learns a great deal about di Prima herself: her study habits, her reading lists, her love of poetry, her correspondence and visit with Ezra Pound who was then at St. Elizabeth's Hospital in Washington, D.C., and the composition of her first collection of poems, *This Kind of Bird Flies Backwards*. The book also records her memories of the significance of first reading Ginsberg's "HOWL," an experience through which she came to find her Beat kinsfolk.

While *Memoirs of a Beatnik* stands as an essential historical document of Beat culture, as a book written for hire, its original function as part of the Olympia Press offerings was to provide sexual entertainment. As such, the text is often classified as erotica. It relies on fiction to explore sexual practices and mores, and as di Prima states in the afterword to the 1988 edition, most of the sex scenes are fabrications that were written to placate her Olympia publisher, Maurice Grodias, who kept returning her drafts with the editorial comment that "more sex" was needed. Di Prima complied, and the book follows the form of standard male-focused erotic fiction by using flashbacks and dreamscapes to introduce serial sex scenes. Plot and character are subordinate to long scenes of explicit sex, which feature the sexual vernacular, such as *cocks, cum, prick,* and *fuck*. A wide range of sexual acts is featured as well, including heterosexual and lesbian sex, rape, incest, and a stereotypic Beat orgy with Kerouac, Ginsberg, and Peter Orlovsky, Ginsberg's lover. Ironically, this last scene is for many readers the least convincing sex scene in the book.

The self that di Prima created, then, exists as a sex object and a male fantasy. For instance, the lesbian scenes act to trigger male sexual arousal, and the rape and incest scenes use the abuse of the female body for male sexual gratification, particularly as di Prima's fictive persona at one point persuades herself that she enjoys the violation.

As a feminist, however, di Prima used the book to critique the angel/whore image of women that characterizes much Beat literature authored by men. Many of the sex stories, while ratifying male power, also suggest that women can assert their sexual identity in ways that defy male power. Di Prima uses literary devices to reject the cultural mandate that a woman is defined in her relationship to a man. For instance, she refers to most of the males in the book by their first names only, thus stripping them of patriarchal heritage and their fuller identities as individuals. As narrator, she leaves whatever man she is with whenever she wants. She also concludes the memoir with what might be the most radical Beat scene ever written: a reversal of the masculine pattern of men on the road and women at home. Happily realizing that she is pregnant, the unmarried di Prima watches her lover leave for the day; then she serenely packs her books and prepares herself to head out with her unborn child into the unknown future.

It is also important to understand that *Memoirs of a Beatnik* subverts not only stereotypic portraits of women and Beat writers but also subverts expectations of nonfiction prose. Most explicitly, di Prima does this by using and acknowledging the use of fiction in a genre that is grounded on an implicit reader–author contract of fidelity to historical truth. She also freely breaks the narrative voice to disrupt the chronological point of view, such as her diatribe against contraception (an antipill passage that in later editions she amends with a warning not to eschew contraception in a world plagued with AIDS) and an interactive passage in which the narrator directs readers to use a blank space that is provided to list their favorite kisses. The most dramatic device is the use of two subchapters that break the erotic and historical template, making explicit the relationship between fantasy and audience. The first describes a mid-November evening during which the narrator and her friends have a hot and wild Beat sex orgy; the subsequent subchapter exposes this as myth, revealing the reality to be a freezing apartment that is void of sex and is populated with cold noses, indifference, and boredom.

By embracing and rejecting its erotic as well as historic content, *Memoirs of a Beatnik* stands as an important example of the experimental drive that characterizes both Beat literature and the women's movement of the 1960s and 1970s, suggesting that both erotic fiction and memoir, while having a place in both myth and reality, are not the primary substance by which either *Beat* or *woman* is defined.

Bibliography
di Prima, Diane. "Pieces of a Song: Diane di Prima" Interview by Tony Moffeit. *Breaking the Rule of Cool: Interviewing and Reading Women Beat Writers,* edited by Nancy Grace and Ronna C. Johnson, 83–106. Jackson: University of Mississippi Press, 2004.
Friedman, Amy L. "'I say my new name': Women Writers of the Beat Generation." In *The Beat Generation Writers,* edited by A. Robert Lee, 200–216. London: Pluto, 1996.
Grace, Nancy M. "Snapshots, Sandpaintings, and Celluloid: Life Writing of Women of the Beat Generation." In *Girls Who Wore Black: Women Writing the Beat Generation,* edited by Ronna C. Johnson and Nancy M. Grace, 141–147. New Brunswick, N.J.: Rutgers University Press, 2002.
Kirschenbaum, Blossom S. "Diane di Prima: Extending La Famiglia." *MELUS* 14, nos. 3–4 (Fall–Winter 1987): 53–67.
Libby, Anthony. "Diane di Prima: 'Nothing Is Lost; It Shines In Our Eyes.'" In *Girls Who Wore Black: Women Writing the Beat Generation,* edited by Ronna C. Johnson and Nancy M. Grace, 45–68. New Brunswick, N.J.: Rutgers University Press, 2002.
McNeil, Helen. "The Archaeology of Gender in the Beat Movement." In *The Beat Generation Writers,* edited by A. Robert Lee, 178–199. London: Pluto, 1996.

Nancy M. Grace

Mexico City Blues Jack Kerouac (1959)

JACK KEROUAC's book-length poem *Mexico City Blues,* now more than 45 years old, remains in print, a result of the continued phenomenal interest in its author's life and work. It has been joined in recent years by a growing number of books of Kerouac's poetry—most recently an anthology of his haiku—and previously unpublished fiction and nonfiction so that it is now possible to view his first published poetry in a much broader perspective. It is obvious now, for instance, that Kerouac was a much more serious poet than was first thought. Books of poems weave through the industrious middle of his career like golden threads. It is also much easier now to document the course of his study of Buddhism and to understand how *Mexico City Blues* emanated from that study. An ever-increasing number of biographies trace and retrace the course of his career. Two volumes of his letters help flesh out the personal background of his fictional and poetic compositions. Clearly, we are in a better position now to evaluate his work.

Yet, without access to autograph drafts of *Mexico City Blues*, revised typescripts, and proofread galleys, it is impossible for scholars to describe accurately Kerouac's composition process, to identify literary influences on the poem, and finally to say with any degree of certainty what the author's intentions were in the most obscure or ambiguous passages. Consequently, 45 years down the road from the initial publication of the poem, we have a clearer picture of how it fits into the entire body of Kerouac's work, but we are still in the dark about the actual process by which the poem was created. Ironically, this situation is likely to persist until interest in Kerouac's writing dies down, until all the money that is to be made from his unpublished manuscripts has been made, and until the kind of materials that scholars need to do their work is freely and easily available (and can be quoted without payment of exorbitant fees and royalties).

Having said all this in a prefatory way, we are now in a position to evaluate the poem provisionally.

First, a word about its position in American literary history. Much debate has been given to the question of when the modernist era ended and when the postmodern era began. Many of Kerouac's contemporaries, such as the novelist William Gaddis (the model for Harold Sand in *The SUBTERRANEANS*), can be viewed as transitional figures, some of their works satisfying late modernist criteria and others moving into postmodernist territory. *Mexico City Blues* is clearly such a transitional work. It bears the obvious influence of Ezra Pound's *Cantos* and William Carlos Williams's *Patterson,* but like its Beat companions, ALLEN GINSBERG's "HOWL" and "KADDISH," it shows signs of self-parody, the mixing of high, middle, and low culture, and the incorporation of autobiography, all qualities associated with postmodernism. In *The DHARMA BUMS,* written just two years after *Mexico City Blues,* Ray Smith, the Kerouac character, in an argument with the GARY

SNYDER character, Japhy Ryder, calls Pound "a pretentious nut," perhaps in an attempt to distance himself from his modernist forbearer. Directly, the Ginsberg character quotes one of the best known lines from Kerouac's poem, "the wheel of the quivering meat conception" that begins the 211th Chorus. It is worth remembering, too, that *The Dharma Bums* is dedicated to Han Shan, the Chinese poet whom Snyder was translating when he and Kerouac met. In the novel, Kerouac provides a brief synopsis of the literary milieu in which the poem was written. The influence of high modernism was beginning to give way to postmodern innovation—but only beginning to give way. It would take another 20 years or more for postmodernism to come into its own, and *Mexico City Blues* helped pave the way from one era to the next.

As far as the form of the poem is concerned, it follows one of two major trends in Western long poems: the epic and the sequence. In the United States, Walt Whitman galvanized 19th-century attempts to write an American epic by founding "Song of Myself" on the theme of individuality, a cherished national value. As different as *The Waste Land* is from Whitman, T. S. Eliot followed in the same vein, basing his condensed epic on the theme of the wreck of Western culture. H.D.'s *Trilogy* and Hart Crane's *The Bridge,* likewise, are organized around a central theme or image. Kerouac chose the alternate route, the form of the sequence. For him, the concept of a blues, a musical form in jazz susceptible of endless improvisations on a basic chord progression, provided the flexibility that his wandering lifestyle required for composition. By adopting a sequence structure—musical rather than literary, like Pound's *Cantos*—Kerouac was able to exercise his lyric gifts while still composing at length. Thus, a moment like the one described in the 78th Chorus can flame into being in the context of the book-length improvisation without losing its individual intensity. Looked at in this way, *Mexico City Blues* can be seen as an accumulation of such lyric moments, an accumulation that could not be strung out indefinitely but that had to conform to the demands of its analogy to musical performance. Unlike the musical form of Louis Zukovsky's "A", which results in a tightly constructed poem in the epic tradition, the jazz form favored by

Kerouac allowed him to add units as they occurred to him in much the same way that Edgar Lee Masters—though with an entirely different model (the Greek Anthology) and a much stricter theme (the life-in-death of the residents of one small town)—was able to expand his *Spoon River Anthology*.

The Beats, as is well known, were among the few U.S. writers who were influenced by the European school of surrealism. Improvisation is the main aspect of the surrealism that was employed by Kerouac in *Mexico City Blues*, but he also subjected himself to arbitrariness by confining each chorus to the length of a single notebook page. The result is similar to another contemporary, long, sequence poem, John Berryman's *Dream Songs*. Berryman's poems, of course, are all 15 lines long, showing the advantages and drawbacks of uniform length when contrasted to the variable length of Kerouac's choruses, but Berryman's sonnetlike poems avail themselves of the same lyric possibilities while spinning out the story of Henry. Altered states also played a part in the composition of Kerouac's poem, and many of the choruses, such as the 81st and 82nd, employ a stoned-out free association to achieve their effects, not the least of which is humor.

The poem itself has four, perhaps five, themes: Kerouac's life; the culture, geography, and language of Mexico; the analogy between poetry and jazz; the doctrines and terminology of Buddhism; and possibly the spontaneous method of composing the poem itself.

Kerouac's main failing as a novelist—which he ingeniously converted into a tremendous asset—was his inability to invent characters, plots, or scenes, the very kind of invention at which most fiction writers excel. As long as he was young and resilient, capable of traveling and experiencing new adventures, this failing was overshadowed by the exciting prose of his thinly disguised autobiographical novels. But when middle age began to come on him in the early 1960s, the drawbacks of his method of converting his own escapades into fiction became more and more apparent. Kerouac announced his awareness of the problem first in BIG SUR, which begins with an aging narrator who is meditating on the misperception of his readers that he is still young and vigorous. This awareness culminates in the pathetic narrative of *SATORI IN*

PARIS. Near the end of his life, however, Kerouac seemed to discover, first in *VANITY OF DULUOZ* and then in *Pic*, that he could refashion his life again from a greater distance in retrospect. If he had not succumbed to alcoholism, most likely he would have proceeded to fill in the gaps in the Duluoz Legend on the model of the new postmodern beginning that was signaled by *Vanity of Duluoz*.

Like his fiction, Kerouac's poetry also relies heavily on a direct rendering of his personal experience, and because of the intersection of its condensed poetic form and his spontaneous method of composition, *Mexico City Blues* contains one of the most revealing versions of his life.

Mexico City Blues treats these recollections in a more systematic way: It gathers into a group of choruses (the 87th to the 104th) the kernel of Kerouac's youth; then it touches on various important events in his adult life; finally it merges with the present to capture the "future memories," so to speak, memories as they are being made. The importance of the poem hinges to some degree on this observation. Since *Mexico City Blues* presents the Duluoz Legend—Kerouac's fictional autobiography—in a nutshell, the poem must have special significance among Kerouac's works from the point of view of both writer and readers. In this long poem, Kerouac found a way to encapsulate his past, represent it in a symbolic religious dimension, and thus use ego—the product of family, memory, and individual desire—as a means to transcend itself. His family members become figures of legend, and he himself becomes a Tathagata, one who has "passed through," as he calls himself in the 216th-B Chorus, the "Venerable Kerouac."

More than a fourth of the choruses of *Mexico City Blues* contain references to events in Kerouac's life, and this sheer bulk, if nothing else, makes autobiography one of the most important themes in the poem. Beyond that, however, the autobiography in the poem is very carefully developed, having three distinct time frames and a religious significance all its own. The time frames function almost spatially to create perspective: close-up, medium range, and far distance. The religious motif also connects autobiography to the most important theme of the poem, Kerouac's exploration of the concept of anatta, the possibility of annihilating the self. As the singer of the poem delves deep into his past, recalls significant moments in his adult life, and tries to capture experience as it is happening in the present, he learns that the cost of selflessness is the recognition that even memory is an arbitrary conception. For Kerouac, who was called Memory Baby by his boyhood companions, this must have been a shocking realization.

The function of Mexican words, settings, and myths in *Mexico City Blues*, though much simpler than the function of the autobiographical theme, is far less obvious. At first, it seems to serve merely as a binding agent, a rather convenient, superficial element that serves to connect various aspects of the poem—some of them highly abstract—to a concrete sense of place. This is particularly true with respect to the Buddhist theme. While Mexico—especially the Native American side of it—does serve to ground the poem, as it grounded *On the Road*, DOCTOR SAX, TRISTESSA, and DESOLATION ANGELS, it plays other roles as well. Chief among these are the sound effects that the Spanish language provides, the opportunity that life in an ancient society gives the singer to illustrate his views on reincarnation, and the images that foreign landscape and folkways contribute to the surrealism of the poem.

Only in retrospect, in the last section of *Desolation Angels*, did Kerouac himself come to understand fully that the great faith that he placed in Mexico derived from his own personal vision. In the process of an ill-fated move to California to be near his newfound Buddhist friends, including the poet PHILIP WHALEN, Duluoz stops at the Mexican border with his mother, and together they walk over into Juarez. After lighting a votive candle for her dead husband in the church of Maria de Guadalupe and observing the penitents in devotion there, Duluoz's mother exclaims, "These are people who have heart!" They are, in short, the "Mexico Fellaheen" Kerouac celebrated in *Lonesome Traveler*, kinfolk under the skin to the poor French Canadians from which the Kerouacs were descended and fellow Catholics to boot. While Catholicism may have gained the upper hand in Kerouac's ideology during the later years of his life, it is clear that his memory of Mexico here is the memory of a time during which, thanks in large part to Bud-

dhist doctrine, he had managed to suspend for a while the many conflicts of his consciousness. The narrator concludes this episode of *Desolation Angels* on a note of satisfaction with his mother's intuition about the place: "Now she understood Mexico and why I had to come there so often." Kerouac's feeling for Mexico, to which he erected many guideposts in his novels, was a feeling for the people, their religion, their way of life, their earth. In 1955, he made a monument to the feeling, and as the art that manipulates and finally masters the divisions of his consciousness demonstrates, *Mexico City Blues* deserves a permanent place among our other literary monuments to that ancient land.

By a fateful coincidence, the great bop saxophonist Charlie Parker died on Kerouac's 33rd birthday, March 12, 1955. Bird himself was only a year and a half older than Kerouac, and his death must have set the seal on Kerouac's already acute sense of mortality. Though mention of the recently deceased musician is severely limited to the 239th, 240th, and 241st choruses, *Mexico City Blues* is clearly an elegy for Parker, and the inspiration of his saxophone work suffuses the poem. Kerouac has come to a realization of the art that binds them as well as the art that separates them. He makes it clear in the epigraph to *Mexico City Blues* that he wishes both to identify himself as a jazz musician and to distinguish himself as a poet. He accomplishes this feat by discovering a new voice for himself, a voice with its origins in the stylings of bop instrumentals, a voice that takes on profound religious significance in the course of the poem.

That is—and this holds true for much of Kerouac's writing, including *Mexico City Blues*—that the style of the blues, presumably both the composition and the performance, puts both singer and audience in touch with the most elemental workings of the mind. This contact with the unconscious accounts, I suspect, for the sense that Barry Gifford and Lawrence Lee, among others, report with respect to *Mexico City Blues*: "Some of the choruses read like scat singing played back at low speed, words 'blown' for their musical values or their punning link to the subject matter that Kerouac had in mind." The form of the blues, which LeRoi Jones [AMIRI BARAKA] once called primarily a verse form, provided Kerouac with an analog to his intuition about poetics. He recalled to us that words are fundamentally sounds, and he committed himself to exploring their deepest significance by returning signs to song.

Buddhism seems to have served as the dynamo that powered Kerouac's poetic impulse. The first book he wrote after beginning his study of the sutras, *San Francisco Blues,* was composed in the Cameo Hotel during spring 1954 while Kerouac was working as a brakeman on the Southern Pacific. While it has neither the coherence nor the magnitude of *Mexico City Blues,* it does indicate the direction in which Kerouac's writing was impelled by his newfound religion. A certain stillness in these blues poems contrasts markedly with the motion of his novels. The observation of detail, which is great in both the fiction and the poetry, seems to be externalized, objectified, detached. The philosophical content, which is much more apparent in the poems than in the novels, flows directly from Kerouac's focus on the details of daily life on skid row. He gives a strong sense that the characters, their actions, and the world in which they occur are all illusory. In short, Buddhism provided Kerouac with a new mode of imagination, one that complemented and supplemented his fiction.

In Mahayana Buddhism, Kerouac also found a fatalism that corresponded to his own Celtic nostalgia, with the important difference that the inevitable extinction of the ego, instead of an event to be feared, became the object and goal of his study and meditation—and of his writing. Oswald Spengler (who was no fan of Buddhism) embodied a similar fatalism, so Kerouac, in having read *The Decline of the West,* had previous experience of a profound resonance to this theme in a powerful text. Like *The Decline,* the Buddhist scriptures confirm the universality of two terms of the Kerouac family motto: work and suffer. Unlike Spengler's organic determinism, however, Buddhism makes a place for the third term: love. In fact, the impact of Buddha's Four Noble Truths— the omnipresence of suffering—is counterbalanced in Kerouac's writing only by the need for compassion. If suffering is life's given, the compassion for all sufferers must form the basis for an active response to human relations. In this sense, Kerouac's Buddhism might indeed be said to have provided him with an ethics.

There is really no way to know exactly how Kerouac felt when he wrote *Mexico City Blues* during the months of August and September 1955, and in some ways Kerouac's spiritual quest is just one more literary issue, available to readers only through other texts, such as biographies. The really pressing question is how his Buddhism functions in the poem to create a formal unity, one that can be perceived and experienced as unity by a compassionate reader. Kerouac's need was not unique, however. In his devotion to Buddhism, as in so many things, he seems to have captured the spirit of his age. *Mexico City Blues* is a profound cry uttered on behalf of American culture for meanings that our way of life—and therefore our individual ways of life—lacks. That is what helps give the poem its power and living value. The Buddhism of *Mexico City Blues,* like the Buddhism of *Tristessa* and VISIONS OF GERARD, is a Buddhism in perfect equipoise with Catholicism. By contrast, the Buddhism of *The Dharma Bums,* written only two years after the poem, often seems preachy, even sappy. The Buddhism of *Mexico City Blues,* on the other hand, appears in its finest spiritual and literary bloom. In fact, it enlivens Kerouac's Catholicism, which was frequently so stale and dogmatic and is vibrant in the literary sense only in *Visions of Gerard,* another remarkable product of Kerouac's Buddhist period. Regardless of Kerouac's failure to build on, solidify, practice, and renew his study during the last decade of his life, for a few years in the 1950s Buddhism became an agent of equilibrium in his life and clearly provided the direct impetus for him to become a poet. The openness of Kerouac's spiritual quest and his passion in the crisis of it are only the most immediate values of his religious poetry. The balance between the two religions—effectively a new religion, at once both private and public—helps make *Mexico City Blues* an extraordinary work of literature. In it, as in so much of Kerouac's fiction, the personal is transmuted into the representative, though the language of his poetry never loses its distinctive accent. Buddhism provided a counterbalance against Catholicism that allowed Kerouac to move forward into totally new fields of perception.

Obviously, then, *Mexico City Blues* holds an important place among Kerouac's works, both as a highly condensed poetic exploration of his own life and also as the consummate literary expression of his Buddhist beliefs. In a broader sense, it also exemplifies the influence of both surrealism and jazz on his spontaneous method of composition and makes a contribution to the long series of literary homages to the country of Mexico. But is the poem important in a literary sense?

Ironically, it seems likely that Kerouac's reputation as a novelist and his notoriety as a cultural icon may continue to work against his stature as a poet. Very few novelists writing in English have established a dual reputation as poets. Herman Melville and Thomas Hardy come to mind, but few others. Perhaps Kerouac was reaching back to his cultural roots to imitate the great Victor Hugo. But poetry in America is a much more elite field than fiction, largely because of the size and nature of its audience. Also, despite the fanaticism of some Kerouac fans, it will be difficult to convince that audience to invite Kerouac into the ranks of the major 20th-century poets, to allow him to share the limelight with the writers who composed the important long poems of that era. Kerouac himself was often at odds with contemporary poets, such as James Merrill (the model for Merrill Randall of *Desolation Angels*). Nevertheless, when viewed in the context of literary history, *Mexico City Blues* can be seen to play a crucial part in the transition from modernism to postmodernism (a transition that paved the way for poems such as Merrill's epic, *The Changing Light at Sandover*). Kerouac's poem, then, takes its place alongside *The Dream Songs, Howl, Kaddish,* and CHARLES OLSON's *THE MAXIMUS POEMS* as a mediator between Eliot's *Four Quartets,* the later *Cantos* of Pound, and especially William Carlos Williams's *Paterson* and the long poems that were to come in the 1960s and the following decades.

Mexico City Blues may be, as Beat poet MICHAEL McCLURE once claimed, "a religious poem startling in its majesty and comedy and gentleness and vision," but we can now see that its importance is even greater than that. *Mexico City Blues* has only now begun to take its place among the major poetic works of late modernism, and perhaps, after the long overdue foundational work has finally been done on Kerouac's texts, we may be able to say that it not only stands among the major works of the 20th century but also among the major long poems in English of any era.

Bibliography

Jones, James T. A *Map of* Mexico City Blues: *Jack Kerouac as Poet.* Carbondale: Southern Illinois University Press, 1992.

James T. Jones

Micheline, Jack (1929–1998)

Known as a street poet, a Beat poet, an outlaw, an outsider, a self-taught writer and artist, and a powerful performance poet, Jack Micheline was loved at home and abroad. Though unaccepted by the major publishers of his time, he published more than 20 books of poetry and stories, edited others, and has been included in hundreds of important anthologies and magazines, journals, and small press publications.

Said to be extremely underweight at birth, Micheline was born Harold Silver on November 6, 1929, in the East Bronx, New York, to Herman and Helen Silver, a postal worker and a housewife respectively. He had an older brother, Edward. The family followed the old Jewish tradition of changing his name in an attempt to fool the Angel of Death—and he became Harvey Martin Silver. Sometime later he chose Jack Micheline as the name by which he would write and paint—Jack, he said, for one of his earliest favorite writers Jack London, and Micheline from his mother's maiden name. The name change was legalized in the early 1960s.

Micheline served in the U.S. Army Medical Corps in 1947–48. He worked on a kibbutz in Israel in 1949, and back in America he began to roam the country in the 1950s, doing a variety of blue-collar jobs such as pushing a cart in the garment district, washing dishes, union organizing, panhandling, and selling his penny poems in the street. He taught art at his brother's day-care center on Long Island and later worked for him as a cook at his amusement park in Puerto Rico. During these years and throughout his life, Micheline read many of the great writers and philosophers but did not seek a formal education.

In 1957 Micheline won the "Revolt In Literature Award" at a poetry reading contest at the Half Note Cafe in the Village in New York. The judges were Charles Mingus, Jean Shepard and Nat Hentoff. A lover of jazz and classical music, Micheline sang his poems in his head as he wrote them. In 1958 he published a poem in the premier issue of *Yugen*, which was put out by LeRoi Jones (AMIRI BARAKA) and his wife HETTIE JONES. Also appearing in the first issue of *Yugen* were PHILIP WHALEN, DIANE DI PRIMA, and ALLEN GINSBERG. Micheline's first book of poetry, *RIVER OF RED WINE*, was published in 1958 with the introduction written by JACK KEROUAC. It was reviewed by Dorothy Parker in *Esquire* magazine.

Micheline was an active writer till the end of his life, much of his work scribbled on bits and pieces of paper, napkins, and notebooks. He published individual broadsides and chapbooks, and in 1962 his second book of poems *I Kiss Angels* came out and he edited *Six American Poets* in 1964. Meanwhile he was being included in many of the anthologies of Beat poetry and magazines.

Franz Kline financed his stay in Mexico in 1961–62, and it was there that he began to paint his unique childlike portraits, showing an astounding use of colors. He continued painting and drawing throughout his life, often doing a spontaneous piece of art alongside his signature in his books of poetry and short stories. Many of his paintings were dotted with words, bits of philosophy and poetry—some of his most interesting work was done on the walls of an entire room in the Abandoned Planet Bookstore in San Francisco.

Micheline's first collection of stories, *In the Bronx and Other Stories*, was published 1965, followed by the production of his play *East Bleeker* at the Café La Mama in New York. In 1968 publisher John Bryan was arrested on obscenity charges in connection with Micheline's story "Skinny Dynamite." The case was dismissed after letters were written by Ginsberg and other well-known writers and representation by civil-rights attorney Stanley Fleishman.

Micheline had copious correspondences with many people throughout the world. Included were hundreds of writers, some famous such as CHARLES BUKOWSKI and HAROLD NORSE, and many unknown. He also wrote and received boxes of letters from a variety of women who answered ads that he placed in personals.

Purple Submarine, a story in book form, was published in 1976, as was his collected poems *North of Manhattan, Collected Poems, Ballads and Songs: 1954–1975*. In 1979 the publication of "Skinny Dynamite" by A. D. Winan's Second Coming Press was accomplished. Throughout these years Micheline, who like Kerouac, did not drive, continued to travel the United States by bus and train, dropping in unexpectedly on friends and family. He also traveled to Europe where he received wide acceptance, was invited to festivals and readings, and was published in several countries.

Micheline received the "Most Valuable Performance" award at the Naropa Institute's "25 Years On The Road" conference in Boulder, Colorado, commemorating the 25th anniversary of Kerouac's *ON THE ROAD*. In addition to videos including Micheline or about him, Micheline appeared with saxophonist Bob Feldman on NBC's *Late Night With Conan O'Brien* in 1994. Micheline continued writing, painting, exhibiting, and publishing during the 1990s, despite being ill from diabetes. Beloved by so many yet always known as cantankerous, Micheline continued ranting, nearly always about the "establishment" publishers and gallery owners, reflecting his bitterness at not being more accepted in his own time. He predicted that he would come into his own after his death. His buddy Bukowski agreed: "He's right: they'll find him after he's dead, he's fought hard. . . ."

His last book, a major collection of his work, which was compiled and edited by Matt Gonzalez, was *67 Poems for Downtrodden Saints*, published in 1997. A revised second edition was published in 1999, and it includes additional poems, photos, art, and ephemera from the Beat era. Also in 1999 two important works were published: *The Outlaw Bible of American Poetry*, edited by Alan Kaufman and contributing editor S. A. Griffin and dedicated to "Jack Micheline, the greatest Outlaw poet of all time," and *Ragged Lion: A Tribute to Jack Micheline*, edited by John Bennett, which contains poems and commentary by many poets and friends.

Jack Micheline was found dead of a heart attack on a subway train in San Francisco at the end of the line on February 27, 1998, at the age of 68. He was one of the youngest of the Beats. Hundreds of people of all ages and every conceivable kind turned out to celebrate his life at memorials in San Francisco, New York, Boston, and Los Angeles. A little street in North Beach was renamed for him and is now Jack Micheline Place.

A "rare bird," what you saw was what you got—he was simply who he was, no more, no less. He railed at "the dead . . . the goddamned dead who rule this world" and paused to note the passing of a pigeon. He is survived by his son Vince Silvaer and his grandchildren Nicole and Dustin Silvaer.

Bibliography

Bennett, John, ed. *Ragged Lion: A Tribute To Jack Micheline.* Brooklyn/Ellensburg: The Smith Publishers and Vagabond Press, 1999.

Kaufman, Alan, ed. *The Outlaw Bible of American Poetry.* New York: Thunder's Mouth Press, 1999.

Micheline, Jack. *North of Manhattan, Collected Poems, Ballads and Songs: 1954–1975.* San Francisco: Man Root Press, 1976.

———. *67 Poems for Downtrodden Saints.* San Francisco: FMSBW, 1999.

———. *River of Red Wine and Other Poems.* 1958. Sudbury, Me.: Water Row Press, 1986.

pat cherkin alexander

"Milton by Firelight"   Gary Snyder (1958)

First published in the inaugural issue of the small literary magazine *The Fifties*, most readers did not see this remarkable poem until the publication of GARY SNYDER's first book-length collection, *RIPRAP*.

The title sets up a relationship between Puritan poet John Milton and "firelight," with the "by" of the title clearly indicating that the condition of reading the poet's work will inform the discussion of it in the poem. Snyder further emphasizes the context of the experience with the location and date of composition, "Piute Creek, August 1955." In the afterword to the 1990 and 2004 editions of *RIPRAP AND COLD MOUNTAIN POEMS,* Snyder describes the locale and states that it proved the source for a new class of poems that he began to

write that year. Doing trail restoration work for the Parks Service, Snyder spent the summer in the northern section of Yosemite National Park. Studious as always, Snyder would have taken books along to read, apparently including Milton's *Paradise Lost.* The poem opens with a quotation from that epic work: "O hell, what do mine eyes / with grief behold?" In Milton's poem "hell" is to be understood literally, and "grief" is to be felt with a deep religious conviction. But here, we can also imagine the speaker saying these lines out loud with a tone of exasperation, not at his surroundings but at what he sees before him now—this epic poem, illuminated only by a campfire. Throughout the rest of the first of four stanzas, Snyder describes the skill and vision of the "old / Singlejack miner" with whom he works and then poses a fundamental philosophical and religious question that critiques not only Milton but the entire Judeo–Christian postlapsarian tradition: "What use, Milton, a silly story / Of our lost general parents, / eaters of fruit?"

Gary Snyder, Black Oaks Books, Berkeley, 2004. *(courtesy of Larry Keenan)*

As if in answer, the next stanza describes "The Indian" arriving in camp with a mule team, hungry for, among other things, "green apples." This co-worker comes out of a different religious tradition than the one that Milton represents. He forms part of the daily life and work that continues in this place at this time. The third stanza invokes in its opening line, "In ten thousand years the Sierra," a geological sense of history that exceeds that of Christian human time and depicts a future in which nature goes about its own evolutionary and geological development, independent of human concerns. Accepting that the planet will outlast people frees the speaker: "No paradise, no fall, / Only the weathering land."

In the final stanza, natural activity, the burning down of the fire, leaves too little light for further reading. This action saves the speaker from being overly concerned with Milton's dark brooding and from being overly concerned with events out in civilization in the present time, since he is "miles from a road." The mundane activities of the "bell-mare" that he can hear following "an old trail" places his own activities in the framework of ceremonial time. He and his coworkers build up trails that nature breaks down that were built up by others before them, to be restored again by others after them, "All of a summer's day."

Snyder stakes out a fundamental opposition to modern civilization and the Puritan foundations of American culture. At the same time, he implies that one can sidestep civilization and reconnect with larger and historically longer natural and cultural forces. Although he elides his presence in the poem through no use of the first-person pronoun and only that one fleeting "our" in the first stanza, the poem also demonstrates a strong assertion of individuality and the possibility of charting one's own path in life.

Patrick Murphy

Minor Characters: A Memoir of a Young Woman of the 1950s in the Beat Orbit of Jack Kerouac Joyce Johnson (1983)

When writer JOYCE JOHNSON accepted a serendipitous invitation to a London café in the early 1980s, little did she suspect that the evening would lead to the resurrection of women writers of the Beat Generation. Johnson remembers that she found herself at The Pizza Express listening to "these old guys, very nattily dressed, who played this wonderful music, and I began reflecting on the fact that here were these septuagenarians, still on the road, [while] others in their generation are dead—people like Charlie Parker. . . ." The experience convinced Johnson to write a memoir of her early years in Beat Greenwich Village. *Minor Characters* was published by Houghton Mifflin in 1983, winning the National Book Critics Circle Award the same year. It was reissued by Simon and Shuster in 1990 and in 1999 by Viking Penguin.

Minor Characters is a traditional memoir in that it chronicles the story of someone who had an intimate relationship with a cultural hero or someone famous, a subgenre termed a "marginal memoir" by James Atlas. Many readers have been attracted to the book's original subtitle: "A Memoir of a Young Woman of the 1950s in the Beat Orbit of Jack Kerouac." (The subtitle was later changed to "A Young Woman's Coming-of-Age in the Beat Orbit of Jack Kerouac" and later to "A Beat Memoir.") Johnson, then Joyce Glassman, met JACK KEROUAC in 1957 after ALLEN GINSBERG encouraged Kerouac to call her. Their first date took place at the Howard Johnson's on West Eighth Street. Kerouac had no money on that auspicious occasion, so Johnson paid for his meal: hotdogs, home fries, and baked beans. She also recounts that when she opened the heavy glass door of the restaurant, Kerouac was the only person there "in color," a black-haired young man in a flannel lumberjack shirt with "amazingly blues eyes."

More importantly, however—and unlike many "marginal" memoirs—*Minor Characters* is much more about its author than it is about the Beat icon with whom she had a two-year romance. A reader will find glimpses of the private Kerouac and the tumultuous days following the publication of ON THE ROAD, but what one learns about the heroism of young women in midcentury America far outshines the other. Johnson credits the women's movement with helping her recognize the importance of her own story, so to grant justice to both her life and Kerouac's, she constructed *Minor Characters* as two distinct narratives that converge and then diverge at the end. The stories that emerge create a lyrical and painterly vision that blurs the boundary between fact and fiction to foreground the truth of how a self(s) is created.

The self that tells Johnson's story is never didactic, apologetic, or self-impressed, but she does make certain that she speaks as a gendered being. The memoir opens from a moment in the present, the narrator looking at a 1945 photograph of Kerouac, Ginsberg, and WILLIAM S. BURROUGHS and thinking about all those who are missing from the portrait—especially the women, such as Joan Vollmer Adams Burroughs (Burroughs's second wife), and Edie Parker (Kerouac's first wife). Through a tone of detached intimacy, she then begins her own story as a young girl who at the age of 13 rode the bus to Greenwich Village, unbeknownst to her middle-class Jewish parents, to spend afternoons with her friends. The narrative takes her to Barnard College, where she became close friends with the poet Elise Cowen, who introduced her to Ginsberg and Peter Orlovsky. After Barnard, which she left one credit short of the degree requirements, we see her struggle to forge a career as a novelist and her valiant efforts to live independently. We also witness the efforts of Cowen to do the same as well as Johnson's other female friends and acquaintances, such as the writer HETTIE JONES (the first wife of LeRoi Jones/AMIRI BARAKA) and the painter and sculptor Mary Frank (the wife of photographer Robert Frank), respectively.

In the process, Johnson illustrates how dangerous and yet necessary it was for young single women after World War II to live alone (they ran the risk of being mistaken for prostitutes), of acting as full sexual beings (they ran the risk of unwanted pregnancy and life-threatening abortions), and of daring to actualize their own artistic talents (they ran the risk of being told to get their M.R.S. degree and of working in stultifying isolation). The ironic, point-counterpoint copula technique that Johnson employs subtly effects these political arguments. For example, by juxtaposing a description of Ginsberg traveling in 1954 in the Yucatán with her own memories of a creative writing instructor at Barnard telling the all-female class that they should instead "be hopping freight trains," Johnson poignantly wields indirection to clarify the difficul-

ties the aspiring females artists of her generation endured. In like manner, she connects a trip she took to have an abortion with Kerouac's journey to Desolation Peak; while he spent the summer in meditative isolation as a firewatcher, an experience recorded in *The DHARMA BUMS* and *DESOLATION ANGELS*, she endured the shame and ridicule of an illegal and dangerous medical procedure, a strikingly different isolation.

Johnson's memories of Cowen are perhaps the most dramatic in the memoir, which provided the first published examples of Cowen's raw power as a metaphysical poet. Cowen's unrequited love for Ginsberg, her elision by her Beat male friends who nicknamed her "ellipse," her bouts of depression—which were not effectively treated and which became increasingly severe—her desperate experiments with sexuality, and her eventual suicide in 1962 are treated by Johnson with tender dignity. Johnson's narrative of Cowen ultimately embraces the myth of the tragic artist while transforming it to accommodate the female experience, suggesting that within the masculine Beat community the female tragedy often went unrecognized.

Minor Characters is not, however, a sad and tragic tale; rather it is remarkable testimony to the power of the artist to remember and imagine—and thereby to create knowledge that was heretofore nonexistent or inaccessible. Through memories and imaginative reconstructions, Johnson resurrects Cowen as a worthy human being; she also presents a sympathetic portrait of Kerouac's mother, Gabrielle, generally characterized in Beat histories as paranoid and nasty; and she makes visible the intangible bonds of female friendship that have guided the women artists of the Beat area into the 21st century. Fittingly, it is not the break-up of her relationship with Kerouac in late 1958 that concludes *Minor Characters*; it is instead an image of muted young women in cold-war United States— Hettie Jones, Elise Cowen, and Joyce Glassman, in particular—whose silence has finally been broken.

Bibliography

Atlas, James. "Marginal Memoirs." *The Atlantic Monthly.* 251 (1983): 100–101.

Grace, Nancy M., and Ronna C. Johnson, eds. *Breaking the Rule of Cool: Interviewing and Reading Beat*

Women Writers. Jackson: University Press of Mississippi, 2003.

Johnson, Joyce. *Minor Characters: A Memoir of a Young Woman in the 1950s in the Beat Orbit of Jack Kerouac.* Boston: Houghton Mifflin, 1983. Reprint, New York: Washington Square Press, 1990. Expanded ed. New York: Penguin Books, 1999.

Johnson, Ronna C., and Nancy M. Grace, eds. *Girls Who Wore Black: Women Writing the Beat Generation.* New Brunswick, N.J.: Rutgers University Press, 2002.

Nancy M. Grace

Morrison, Jim (1943–1971)

One of the most glamorous and intellectually challenging rock stars of his generation, Jim Morrison was also an accomplished poet. According to Stephen Davis, "He was arguably *the* major poet to emerge from the turmoil of the legendary American sixties."

James Douglas Morrison was born in Melbourne, Florida, on December 8, 1943. His family moved around, following his father's assignments as a professional navy man. As a young boy traveling with his family between Albuquerque, New Mexico, and Santa Fe, Morrison saw the aftermath of a horrific automobile accident that left Native Americans dying on the road. Morrison believed the soul of one merged with his own. When Morrison saw James Dean in *Rebel Without a Cause* (1955), a fascination with film began that would last the rest of his life. While in high school in San Francisco in the late 1950s, Morrison spent time in LAWRENCE FERLINGHETTI's City Lights Books, where he met Ferlinghetti and was exposed to the works of MICHAEL McCLURE, ALLEN GINSBERG, and JACK KEROUAC. Ray Manzarek would write, "I suppose if Jack Kerouac had never written ON THE ROAD, the Doors would never have existed." The young Morrison liked to copy the mannerisms of Dean Moriarty (Kerouac's character based on NEAL CASSADY). Morrison was later influenced by Robert Frank's underground film *Pull My Daisy*, which was narrated by Kerouac and starred Ginsberg and GREGORY CORSO. After spending time at Florida State University, where he continued to read such Beat writers as WILLIAM S. BURROUGHS, Morrison attended

the University of California at Los Angeles, where he met Manzarek, to study film. One of Morrison's classmates was Francis Ford Coppola. Morrison also took a writing class at UCLA with Jack Hirschman. Morrison would not see his parents again after December 1964. He began to indulge in LSD, the drug promoted by TIMOTHY LEARY for consciousness expanding. In the summer of 1965 Morrison and Manzarek formed The Doors, later to include Robby Krieger and John Densmore. The band's name derived from Aldous Huxley's *The Doors of Perception*, which was derived from William Blake's "The Marriage of Heaven and Hell": "If the doors of perception were cleansed every thing would appear to man as it is: infinite."

Morrison met Ginsberg in late 1965, and The Doors became the house band at the London Fog, where Morrison met the love of his life, Pamela Courson, on the Sunset Strip. By May 1966 The Doors had become the house band at the famous Whisky-A-Go-Go. During this time Morrison met Andy Warhol, who was in Los Angeles with the Velvet Underground, and Nico, the band's chanteuse, fell in love with Morrison. That summer the band was signed to Elektra Records.

In January 1967 The Doors attended the Human Be-In at Golden Gate Park and saw Ginsberg, McClure, Leary, and LENORE KANDEL usher in the Hippie Generation. The Door's first album would reach the top of the charts during the Summer of Love. During the next few years The Doors would be the biggest band in the United States, and Morrison would have legendary encounters with Jimi Hendrix, Janis Joplin, and Mick Jagger. The image of bare-chested Jim Morrison, hair by Jay Sebring (who was later murdered by the followers of Charles Manson), would become one of the indelible icons of the 1960s. Morrison became very close with Michael McClure, who encouraged Morrison to publish his poetry, and the two of them worked on a screenplay after abandoning a project to make McClure's play *The BEARD* into a film starring Morrison.

Alcoholism plagued Morrison during his years of fame, and after being arrested for supposedly exposing himself onstage in Miami in 1969 (an act he did not do despite the legend), Morrison found less interest in being a pop star and eventually moved to Paris to become a poet. Books of poetry by Morrison include *The Lords* (1969), *The NEW CREATURES* (1970), *An American Prayer* (1970), *Wilderness—The Lost Writings of Jim Morrison* (1988), and *The American Night—The Writings of Jim Morrison Volume 2* (1990).

Morrison died probably of a heroin overdose on July 3, 1971, in an apartment he shared with Pamela Courson in Paris. His grave in Père Lachaise Cemetery is one of the most often visited sites in the City of Light. The Greek epitaph on his grave, *kata ton daimona eaytoy,* can be translated as "To the divine spirit within himself," "The devil within himself," "The genius in his mind," and "He caused his own demons." Michael McClure writes of Morrison the poet,

"As to his potential for growth—well, he started out so good that I don't know how much better he could've gotten. He started off like a heavyweight. . . . I liked Jim's complexity, his brilliance. I think he was one of the finest, clearest spirits of our times."

Bibliography

Davis, Stephen. *Jim Morrison: Life, Death, Legend.* New York: Gotham Books, 2004.

Manzarek, Ray. *Light My Fire: My Life with The Doors.* New York: G. P. Putnam's Sons, 1998.

McClure, Michael. "Michael McClure Recalls an Old Friend." *Rolling Stone,* 8 August 1971, 40.

Kurt Hemmer

N

Naked Lunch William S. Burroughs (1959)

Naked Lunch is WILLIAM S. BURROUGHS's masterpiece and one of the most influential novels of the 20th century. It is also the most infamous novel to come out of the Beat Generation. In his dedication to HOWL AND OTHER POEMS, published three years before Burroughs's novel, ALLEN GINSBERG called *Naked Lunch* "an endless novel which will drive everybody mad." JACK KEROUAC, whom Burroughs credited with coming up with the title, had nightmares after typing part of the original manuscript. The publication of *Naked Lunch* inspired Norman Mailer to declare, "Burroughs is the only American novelist living today who may conceivably be possessed by genius."

The novel first materialized as letters from Burroughs to Ginsberg, prompting Burroughs to write to his friend, "Maybe the real novel is letters to you." LAWRENCE FERLINGHETTI rejected the original manuscript, called "Interzone," for publication by City Lights. ROBERT CREELEY published the first excerpt to come from the novel in the *Black Mountain Review* appearing in 1958. Another chapter was published by LeRoi Jones/AMIRI BARAKA in *Yugen*. Two issues of the student-run *Chicago Review* also carried excerpts. The second issue, autumn 1958, was attacked by a Chicago newspaper columnist, which led to the faculty of the University of Chicago preventing the publication of the winter 1958 issue, which was to have another excerpt by Burroughs. Student editors started *Big Table*, another title credited to Kerouac, to publish the censored material. Copies of the journal were seized by the U.S. Post Office in Chicago for obscenity. The controversy surrounding Burroughs's unpublished novel inspired Maurice Girodias of Olympia Press to publish it in Paris as *The Naked Lunch* in 1959. Other censorship battles prevented Barney Rosset at Grove Press from releasing a U.S. edition of *Naked Lunch* until 1962. Boston police arrested a man for selling the book in 1963. The case, initially lost, was appealed to the Massachusetts Supreme Court, which ruled that the book was not obscene in 1966. David Cronenberg's film *Naked Lunch* (1992) starring Peter Weller and Judy Davis, is a fictional, surrealistic interpretation of how the novel was written rather than a strict adaptation of the novel itself. Most pointedly, it lacks the wild humor of the novel.

Although randomness is the principal of organization in *Naked Lunch*, there is a type of narrative frame. At the beginning, William Lee (Burroughs's persona) is being pursued by narcotics detectives (the "heat"); toward the end of the book, he is arrested by the detectives Hauser and O'Brien. The major theme of the novel is the attempted escape from various forms of control. The opening scenes in the novel come from Burroughs's experiences as a junky in 1946. Readers familiar with JUNKY will recognize similar scenes at the beginning of *Naked Lunch* in the sections "And Start West," "The Vigilante," and "The Rube," but the scenes soon change into more elaborate and surrealistic "routines," disjointed and often brutal depictions of nightmarish visions and episodes of black comedy. Also of particular note is the antiromantic tone of the novel, which is in stark contrast to Kerouac's ON THE ROAD. Burroughs writes, "America is not a young land: it is old and dirty and evil before the settlers, before the Indians. The evil is there waiting."

The rapid shifting of locales is a characteristic of *Naked Lunch*. Scenes set in the United States, Mexico, South America, Europe, and Tangier seem to open up into each other. In this fashion the novel moves from New Orleans ("a dead museum") and East Texas, south to the border and beyond into Mexico. In Mexico, Lupita (based on Lola "La Chata," Burroughs's connection in Mexico City in the early 1950s) makes the remark, "Selling [heroin] is more of a habit than buying." This leads to the story of Bradley the Buyer. Pushers and narcotics agents who do not "use" become addicted nonetheless—to watching junkies use. Bradley needs more and more "contact" with junkies to satisfy his "yen," a craving for "contact." Bradley's need is so desperate that he moves from contact to direct invasion. The story is one of many variations on forms of addiction in the novel. This section ends with visions of Mexico, circa 1953. Perhaps Joan Burroughs, the wife Burroughs accidentally shot and killed in 1951, is referenced obliquely when a character called Jane is briefly introduced. The section ends with the cryptic line: "A year later in Tangier I heard she was dead." Thus Burroughs depicts Joan with even more obliqueness than in *Junky* and QUEER.

In the "Benway" section, Burroughs introduces one of his most famous characters, Dr. Benway, "a manipulator and coordinator of symbol systems, an expert on all phases of interrogation, brainwashing and control." Benway shows Lee around the reconditioning center that he has established in Freeland. With Benway as tour guide, Lee is introduced to a wide variety of modern (and future) methods of enslavement—including psychological, chemical, and sexual means. The ultimate addiction is the "control" to which the members of the emerging police state are addicted. This section highlights Benway's misadventures in medicine, but some of Benway's routines here are serious; for example, Benway's theories about why junkies have a low incidence of schizophrenia is a theory that Burroughs himself had researched. In the middle of Benway's guided tour of the Reconditioning Center, the INDs (Irreversible Neural Damage patients) are accidentally set free. These include "rampant bores," "Rock and Roll hoodlums," and an "intellectual avant-gardist" who thinks that scientific reports are "the only writing worth considering now." The scenes of "over-liberated" INDs, the gentle narrator tells us, "I fain would spare you." But nothing is spared: "A beastly young hooligan has gouged out the eye of his confrere and fuck him in the brain." These revolting passages appear to be a reflection of the kind of writing that Burroughs often did to "free" himself of such images and obsessions (a primary motivation for his writing at this time—his "word horde" let loose). The section ends with the INDs storming the Freeland government in protest of the current "unspeakable conditions," the moral being that in a controlled society, all who rebel must be branded "lunatics." Benway, meanwhile, and in typical fashion, has long since made his escape.

The narrative jumps to the next section, "Joselito," where Carl watches a German doctor examine a young man named Joselito, who is diagnosed with lesions in both lungs. Carl asks if he will receive "chemical therapy," and the words and the doctor's manner ("seedy and furtive as an old junky") create an intersection or digression (the major plot device in the book) with a separate storyline involving a junky. Conversations in the sanitarium take on a double meaning: a comparison is drawn between chemical cures for lung ailments versus sanitariums, and medical cures for heroin addiction versus incarceration.

"The Black Meat" section begins with The Sailor (based on Phil White) looking to score, and it is written in the hard-boiled style of *Junky*. However, the setting—a Times Square cafeteria—transforms into a surreal, other-worldly setting where the addicts are "Reptiles" and "Meat Eaters," and the pushers are creatures called Mugwumps. (*Mugwump*, actually an Algonquian word that literally means "great man," was used as a term to describe those members of the Republican Party who refused to support James G. Blaine, the presidential party nominee, in 1884. The term has come to mean someone who is independent or neutral politically.) The Mugwumps produce an addictive substance that they secrete from their penis and that addicts the Reptiles by slowing their metabolism and thus prolonging life (the secret of all addictive drugs, says Burroughs). Periodically the Dream Police create a panic among the Heavy Fluid addicts, and the Mugwumps go into hibernation until the scene is clear.

The "Hospital" section is mostly made up of the letters that Burroughs wrote to Ginsberg under the title "Selections from Lee's Letters and Journals." In late 1955 Burroughs checked into a hospital in Tangier, and began a two-month junk "cure." He intended the letters that he wrote about the experience to be part of "Interzone," an early draft of *Naked Lunch*. Burroughs wrote to Ginsberg, "The 'Selection' chapters form a sort of mosaic with the cryptic significance of juxtaposition, like objects abandoned in a hotel drawer, a form of still life." This description fits not only this section but the book as a whole. The hospital stay inspired a further chapter in Dr. Benway's career, also. Here surgery is compared to bullfighting, hilariously. In the following paragraphs, Lee's musings on "bedpans full of blood" and monstrous births covered up by the State Department turn into a "routine" in which a U.S. diplomat's denials are cut in with a technician's attempts to stop a "swish fart" from mangling his performance of "The Star-Spangled Banner." A subsection of "Hospital" called Habit Notes is based on Burroughs's off-and-on addiction for three years to a synthetic drug called Eukodol.

Lazarus, the title character of the "Lazarus Go Home" section, is a young man who has kicked junk (thus has come back to life), but Lee gets him addicted again with a snort of heroin off a nail file. The section introduces the concept of Bang-utot (literally "attempting to get up and groaning"), nightmares that are so intense that they have killed a number of Southeast Asians. The concept strengthens Burroughs's theme of the ways in which the dream world can break into the real world. In a November 1, 1955, letter to Kerouac and Ginsberg, Burroughs says, "The meaning of Interzone, its space-time location is at a point where three-dimensional fact merges into dream, and dream erupt into the real world. . . . The very exaggeration of routines is intended to create this feeling. In Interzone dreams can kill—like Bangutot—and solid objects and persons can be unreal as dreams."

"Hassan's Rumpus Room" is one of two notorious pornographic sections in the book. Burroughs agreed to publish *Naked Lunch* with Olympia Press in part because he knew Girodias would keep these sections in the book: They were unpublishable practically anywhere else. The Rumpus Room features a show in which a Mugwump first hangs and then has sex with a boy, to the delight of the crowd. In his introduction to *Naked Lunch*, Burroughs disingenuously tried to pass off these scenes as a satire on capital punishment in the style of Swift's "A Modest Proposal." Yet the graphic sex that labeled the section as pornographic should not overshadow the weird, beautiful poetry of many passages: "Satyr and naked Greek lad in aqualungs trace a ballet of pursuit in a monster vase of transparent alabaster. The Satyr catches the boy from in front and whirls him around. They move in fish jerks. The boy releases a silver stream of bubbles from his mouth. White sperm ejaculates into green water and floats lazily around the twisting bodies." The party at the Rumpus Room is broken up by an invasion of "lust-mad American women." Hassan blames A. J. for the disaster. A. J. screams, "Guard me from these she-foxes!" and defends himself with a cutlass, decapitating the American women. A fear of American women and matriarchal power (as it threatens homosexual expression) runs throughout this novel and other works by Burroughs.

The Interzone University of the "Campus of Interzone University" section is apparently based on Mexico City College where Burroughs studied the Mayan religion and language. The Professor has a "nostalgia fit," and instead of lecturing on "The Rime of the Ancient Mariner" by Samuel Taylor Coleridge tells the students Ma Lottie stories from East Texas, where Burroughs lived from 1949 to 1950. In the Professor's analysis of "The Rime of the Ancient Mariner," the Mariner is the analyst, the Wedding Guest the analysand. Paradoxically, the analyst does all of the talking: *"You can find out more about someone by talking than by listening."*

The second "pornographic" section of the novel is called "A.J.'s Annual Party." A. J. introduces the "Blue Movie" director Slashtubitch. He screens a film that stars Johnny and Mary: "Clothes and hair-do suggest existentialist bar of all the world cities." In the film, Mary "rims" Johnny and sodomizes him with a strap-on dildo. Mark watches from a doorway and then joins in, sodomizing Johnny. Johnny's orgasm releases a flood of images, many taken from Burroughs's South American trips, ending in a scene that takes place in deserted midwestern farmhouse where "rats run over the floor and boys jack off in the dark musty bedroom." The point-of-view changes to that of an old junky, who has found a vein and hallucinates the farm scene from his past. As the "old queer" stares at adolescents who walk by him in Chapultepec Park in Mexico City, the scene returns to Johnny and Mark. Repeating the earlier scene in "Hassan's Rumpus Room," Mark and Mary hang Johnny; Mary has sex with the hanged body, biting off parts of Johnny's face in her ecstasy. Mark next hangs Mary, and he turns back into Johnny as her neck snaps. Johnny then douses Mary with gasoline; they roll under a great magnifying glass and burst into flames. The burlesque repeats a variation on the hanging, with Johnny being hanged by a county sheriff who promises that onlookers will see a "young boy come three times at least . . . *completely against his will.*" The movie ends, and Mary, Johnny, and Mark take a bow, looking older than they do in the film. Several "blue movie" projects inspired by *Naked Lunch* have been considered over the years, but none (understandably) has been produced.

The "Meeting on International Conference of Technological Psychiatry" section is a "routine" with Doctor "Fingers" Schaefer, the Lobotomy Kid. Schaefer has created "The Complete All American Deanxietized Man," a monstrous black centipede. Centipede imagery, first seen by Burroughs in Chimu pottery, occurs throughout his work and signifies for Burroughs the most debased form of life—the horror at the root of what went wrong with human beings.

The city of Interzone in "The Market" section is based on Tangier, and the market is based on the *soco chico* ("little market") that is the center of life in Tangier. Burroughs felt more at home there primarily because he was free to do there as he pleased. It is also a pleasantly disorienting city, where dreams and reality fade into one another (a key to the technique of the book), and a place where there is potential for change, evolution, and

accidents. Although this picture of Tangier is fairly close to that in his nonfictional account the narrator claims that it was written under the influence of *yage*. In fact, the passage comes from a letter to Ginsberg in which Burroughs described hallucinations that he had while under the influence of the vine. The connection between *yage* visions and Tangier is that *yage* facilitates "space–time travel," and Tangier, Burroughs believed, existed in such space–time. The *yage* section segues into a very funny skit in which Indian medicine men talk about drugs, using the lexicon of the American underworld: "Let's hope Old Xiuptutol don't wig and name one of the boys." "The Prophet's Hour" subsection comes from a letter to Ginsberg and needs to be seen in the context of Burroughs's views on Kerouac's Buddhism, NEAL CASSADY discovering the mystical teachings of Edgar Cayce, and the emergence of a school of Buddhist-inspired poetry on the West Coast. The major world religions here are all portrayed as carnival sideshow attractions, as cons used on the gullible.

The "Ordinary Men and Women" section addresses the political unrest in Tangier while Burroughs lived there (Morocco was taking control of the former International Zone). Burroughs maintained that there was much less dissatisfaction than the papers published. (In letters from the time period, he tries to allay the fears of Kerouac, who is planning a trip to Tangier.) A self-contained story recounts how Brad, a jeweler with a gambling problem, uses fake jewels to cover his losses and ends up in prison, where he meets and falls in love with Jim. Brad and Jim are released at the same time, but Lucy Bradshinkle—an "old moth-eaten tigress"—tries to lure Brad back with her money. The "happy ending" shows Brad and Jim sitting down to eat dinner; the main course is Lucy's "cunt."

The "talking asshole" "routine," performed by Dr. Benway in this section, is perhaps the most famous routine in the novel for its outrageous humor. Such irreverence and invention opened up the field for later American humorists such as Robert Coover, Don Delillo, Ishmael Reed, Thomas Pynchon, Kurt Vonnegut, KATHY ACKER and HUNTER S. THOMPSON. This routine runs into a critique of American bureaucracy as cancer. The reader who looks for a connection between the talking asshole and this critique of bureaucracies may find that they are both examples of the disruption of the "evolutionary direction of infinite potential": The asshole evolves and takes over the host. Burroughs felt that government bureaucracies were malignant because they discouraged change and spontaneity, essentials for continued human evolution (the goal being to evolve beyond the body and into "space").

In "Dr. Berger's Mental Health Hour" Berger specializes in reconditioning people—psychopaths, homosexuals, writers. The psychoanalyst who offers to "cure" homosexuality is a parody of doctors who tried to cure Burroughs and Ginsberg of their homosexuality. The writer is cured by Buddhism, a reference to Burroughs's objections to Kerouac's newfound Buddhist lifestyle and philosophy. The model for the reconditioned person is the "Latah," who is defined by Burroughs in a letter to Ginsberg: "Latah is condition occurring in S.E. Asia. Otherwise normal, the Latah can not help doing what anyone tells him to do once his attention has been attracted by calling his name or touching him." The following scene shows the Party Leader creating a riot: "goes off like a football play. We have imported a thousand bone fed, blue ribbon Latahs from Indochina. All we need is one riot leader for the whole unit."

In "Islam Incorporated and the Parties of the Interzone," the narrator says that he is working for Islam, Inc., an outfit financed by A. J., who, the narrator says, "is an agent like me, but for whom or for what no one has ever been able to discover." A. J.'s cover is that of an "international playboy." This section includes scenes of Arab violence about which Burroughs had read in the Tangier newspaper. A. J. pulls all kinds of pranks on the stuffy members of the upper classes around the world—ordering ketchup in a fine restaurant; releasing grasshoppers that emit an aphrodisiac on the opening night of the New York Metropolitan Opera. A cinematic fade-out moves the scene to Venice. A. J., in admiral's uniform, sails a preposterous gondola that crashes and sinks in the canals. This section is a series of absurd skits whose humor comes from A. J.'s outrageously overblown homosexual mannerisms. Involved with A. J. in Islam, Inc. is Salvador Hassan O'Leary, who reaps profits from misery all over the world. He "hit the jack-

pot" with "slunks" (miscarried cattle fetuses) during World War II. He also profited from the sale of such items as condemned parachutes and leaking lifeboats. Clem and Jody, two more of the cast, are Russians impersonating Americans to make Americans look bad around the world. This routine—in which they kidnap a sacred black stone—is one that Burroughs developed with Kells Elvins. Islam, Inc. comes to resemble the complex trading, bartering, and bribing that Burroughs observed in the International Zone of Tangier.

A major subsection of "Islam Incorporated" details "the parties of Interzone," referred to throughout the book and defined here. Because the book was randomly arranged, the information casts new lights on the preceding two-thirds of the book (which then takes on a slightly more coherent meaning). Ginsberg calls this "the political meat of the book," although Burroughs would later call his political classifications "tentative." The Divisionists are paranoid, homosexual "moderates." The Factualists, the party to which Burroughs himself can be said to belong, see the world as it is, not as they believe it to be. Factualists are conservatives who oppose the spread of both government bureaucracy and the police state. Burroughs first used the term in letters to Ginsberg in the late 1940s to distinguish his own political philosophy from "liberal" thinkers. Factualists, as opposed to the FDR New Dealers whom Burroughs considered to be "communists," support total freedom from all control and believe that only difference, variety, and accident can save the human race in the process of the continuing evolution of the species. The "human virus," a "degraded" version of humanity, threatens to do the opposite by producing copies of degraded humans and thus cuts off the ability of the species to evolve. To the far left on this political spectrum are the Liquefactionists, who are the opposite of the Factualists in that "except for one man," they are "entirely composed of dupes." Senders, another group, are the "most dangerous, evil men in the world," who threaten to control the thoughts and actions of others (such as Benway or the Mayan priests who use the religious calendar to control their subjects completely).

In "The County Clerk" section Burroughs creates a routine about a Southern racist from his experiences on his farm in New Waverly, Texas, as well as from his arrest by a sheriff in Beeville, Texas. His time spent as a cotton farmer in the valley of South Texas is also an influence here. In this routine, Lee has to file an affidavit to keep from being evicted from his property, and the only man who can help him is the County Clerk, who tells endless, racist stories. Ginsberg argued during the *Naked Lunch* trial that a major redeeming feature of the book was its forward-looking attack on racists. Lee convinces the Clerk he is a "good old boy" by telling him an anti-Semitic joke.

Andrew Keif in the "Interzone" section is based on PAUL BOWLES, and the jokes about Bowles's chauffeur are related in Burroughs's Tangier letters. Keif is a young writer who is a resident of The Zone. The rest of this section describes the unlucky adventures of Leif and Marvie, who run Interzone Imports Unlimited. Leif the Unlucky is based on an acquaintance of Burroughs who was always down on his luck. Burroughs suggested he repatriate to Denmark, and the ship that he took home sank en route.

Burroughs's trip to see his friend Kells Elvins in Denmark inspired the section "The Examination," which takes place in Freeland, a socialist state. Dr. Benway is in charge of controlling the citizens, reconditioning them if necessary. Benway calls in a young man named Carl and examines him for signs of homosexuality, which is compared to a disease such as tuberculosis. At his second interview, Carl is apparently drugged by Benway, and the narrative intersects with that of The Fag, a junky being interrogated by two cops who offer him an Old Gold Cigarette (a detail connecting the scene to the Hauser and O'Brien episodes at the beginning and end of the novel). Carl reawakens, and it is apparent that Benway is attempting to condition him as a homosexual by locating (or planting) latent homosexual behavior. The chapter reflects the then-current methods of psychologists (such as Ginsberg's) who tried to cure homosexuals. By implication, if you can cure them, you can also "create" them along the line of infection—transmission of a disease. The section is also a more general attack on communistic governments that seek to control people physically and mentally for their own purposes.

The sections "Have You Seen Pantopon Rose," "Coke Bugs," and "The Exterminator Does a Good Job" are interconnected and seem to anticipate in style, if not in method, the cut-ups trilogy. The section ties in with the opening scenes of the novel. The Sailor connects for a boy who approaches him in a cafeteria. He wants the boy's time (literally), not his money. In Burroughs, one of the biggest "highs" that characters are after is immortality.

Burroughs defines the title of the next section, "The Algebra of Need," in his "Deposition: Testimony Concerning a Sickness," a type of foreword for some editions of *Naked Lunch*: "Junk yields a basic formula of 'evil' virus: The Algebra of Need. The face of 'evil' is always the face of total need. A dope fiend is a man in total need of dope." In respect to the "need" it creates, "Junk is the ideal product," says Burroughs. "Fats" lives by learning the "The Algebra of Need" and grows into a substance that drains all of the addicts of the world back into him. Burroughs believed that there could be drugs that were powerful enough to enslave all of humanity, with one man doling out the supply and thus controlling everyone else. This section seems to be based on such a scenario. It is followed by a prose poem about this worldwide "network of junkies."

The "Hauser and O'Brien" section is a Mickey Spillane-style story of Lee getting busted in his apartment by two cops. The two show up in several of Burroughs's books. This section continues the opening lines of the book: "I can feel the heat closing in. . . ." Lee manages to distract the cops as they avert their eyes while he fixes. He grabs a gun and kills them both. Lee is an "agent," it turns out, and a key to the book is a something Kerouac told Burroughs—that he felt like an agent from another planet who did not know his mission. With a sufficient supply of heroin, Lee makes plans to flee the city. When he tries to confirm Hauser and O'Brien's death, Lee realizes they are not simply dead, they no longer exist, as is true of him, too: "I had been occluded from space-timed. . . . Never again would I have a key, a point-of-intersection." This particular version of Lee is now stuck in a "landlocked junk past"—perhaps a dramatization of Burroughs's sincere desire to leave junk behind at this point in his life.

The book ends with the penultimate section "Atrophied Preface," an explanation of how to read the novel, which is appropriate for a book that has little or no chronology or linearity, and a small section called "Quick. . . ." Burroughs writes cryptically, "Naked Lunch is a blueprint, a How-To Book." Representing a bridge to the next three "cut-up" novels, the cut-up method appears to be used here, and ominously so: "raw peeled winds of hate and mischance / blew the shot." Burroughs thought this cut-up (one of the first he created) was in reference to a blown shot of morphine, but Brion Gysin interpreted it as a reference to Joan Burroughs's death. Much of the "Atrophied Preface" does in fact decode the novel for the reader, even if it is a bit late. Most revealing to the lost reader is the admission by the writer that all of his characters are basically the same character and are, of course, the author. This explains why one character is "subject to say the same thing in the same words to occupy, at that intersection point, the same position in space-time." As to the method used in *Naked Lunch*, Burroughs says, "There is only one thing a writer can write about: *what is in front of his senses at the moment of writing.* . . . I am a recording instrumental. . . . I do not presume to impose 'story' 'plot' 'continuity.'. . . Insofar as I succeed in *Direct* recording of certain areas of psychic process I may have limited function. . . . I am not an entertainer."

Years later, Burroughs would argue that in fact there was a great deal of craft used in the construction of *Naked Lunch.* Today, reading these pages, the expert reader cannot help but be aware of the ways in which Burroughs's methods—so incomprehensible at the time to many readers—now address our central, critical concerns about language and culture. The novel lends itself to poststructuralist readings popularized in the academies during the 1970s and 1980s, and to many critics, Burroughs can now be seen as a pioneer of postmodernism. Certainly Burroughs opened up an entirely new form of the novel as well as a vast field of previously untouchable subjects for future writers. Burroughs set out as a writer to write anything but something literary. Ultimately, *Naked Lunch* is an antinovel that thwarts nearly every expectation the reader has of what a "novel" should be. Presently,

there are more than a million copies in circulation throughout the world.

Bibliography

Burroughs, William S. *The Letters of William S. Burroughs: 1945–1959.* Edited by Oliver Harris. New York: Viking Penguin, 1993.

Goodman, Michael Barry. *Contemporary Literary Censorship: The Case History of Burroughs' Naked Lunch.* Metuchen, N.J.: Scarecrow, 1981.

Lydenberg, Robin. *Word Cultures: Radical Theory and Practice in William S. Burroughs' Fiction.* Chicago: University of Illinois Press, 1987.

Miles, Barry, and James Grauerholz. Editors' Note. *Naked Lunch: The Restored Text,* by William S. Burroughs. New York: Grove Press, 2001, 233–247.

Murphy, Timothy S. *Wising Up the Marks: The Amodern William Burroughs.* Berkeley: University of California Press, 1997.

Rob Johnson and Kurt Hemmer

New American Poetry, 1945–1960, The Donald Allen, ed. (1960)

This landmark anthology, edited by Donald M(erriam) Allen (1912–2004), introduced Beat poets and other avant-garde post–World War II poets to a wide reading audience on its publication by Grove Press in 1960. It stands as one of the most influential—perhaps *the* most influential—poetry anthology ever published in the United States.

Presenting the work of 44 young, groundbreaking versifiers, it "was one of the first countercultural collections of American verse" according to Wolfgang Saxon. The anthology offered a stunning variety of verse forms, from a disturbing, ancient-sounding ballad by Helen Adam to ROBERT CREELEY's modernized ballad of Dr. Seusslike rhythms and rhymes scattered with profanities, from JACK KEROUAC's blues-based songs to ALLEN GINSBERG's Whitmanesque long lines, from CHARLES OLSON's mythic pronouncements to GREGORY CORSO's bizarre effusions of irreverent word play.

Before its publication, most of the works included were known to only a limited audience through broadsheets, pamphlets, circulating manuscripts, poetry readings, and the like. Following its publication, several of the poets featured—John Ashberry, Creeley, Robert Duncan, LAWRENCE FER-LINGHETTI, Ginsberg, Kerouac, Denise Levertov, Olson, GARY SNYDER—have become so established in the postmodern canon that it may be difficult to imagine a time when they were largely unknown, marginal figures.

Spotlighting what has been called the poetic equivalent of abstract expressionism in painting, *The New American Poetry* was received as a manifesto, and it revolutionized the course of poetry in the second half of the 20th century as much as Jackson Pollock revolutionized art.

The anthology was the brainchild of its editor, Donald M. Allen. Born in Iowa in 1912, Allen became an editor at Grove Press in the mid-1950s, and he stayed with the press for 16 years. His long career would be devoted to bringing innovative poetry out of the shadows, and among other projects he founded the Grey Fox Press and the Four Seasons Foundation (the latter following an unsuccessful attempt to launch his own magazine of contemporary U.S. poetry, the *Four Seasons Quarterly*). But even at the start of his career with Grove, Allen worked with writing on the edge, editing books by Kerouac and others, and translating plays (including *The Bald Soprano*) by the absurdist Eugène Ionesco. One early project, in 1957, involved a special issue of Grove's *Evergreen Review,* for which Allen collected work by poets associated with the "San Francisco Renaissance." The special issue featured poems by Brother Antoninus (WIL-LIAM EVERSON), Duncan, Snyder, Jack Spicer—all of whom would later appear in *The New American Poetry*—as well as KENNETH REXROTH.

In 1958 Allen began the project that would culminate in the publication of *The New American Poetry.* He set out to present the wide range of experimental poetry that had flourished since World War II. As Allen himself put it in the "Preface" to the anthology, he chose work united by "one common characteristic: a total rejection of all those qualities typical of academic verse." Poetry from what had been the cultural and sexual margins would take center stage in Allen's new anthology, and he would push conventional, Europeanized verse beyond the margins—the latter would have no place in his volume.

During the next two years, Allen corresponded frequently with poets, editors, and literary agents. Some of the correspondence that he received appeared in the anthology in two closing sections containing "Statements on Poetics" and "Biographical Notes" that were supplied by the poets themselves. The role of this correspondence in shaping the final product leads critic Alan Golding to caution against regarding *The New American Poetry* as the work of Allen alone: "The collection is as much the product of multiple, interacting poetic communities and affiliations, of correspondence among contributors and editor, as it is the work of an individual editor himself. In this sense, *The New American Poetry* is very much a communal construction or shared enterprise."

Allen's anthology as it appeared in 1960 consists of a "Preface," the poems themselves, a section of "Statements on Poetics," "Biographical Notes," and a bibliography. In the preface, Allen identifies as the focus of his anthology an emerging third generation of postwar writers. In the first generation, he places William Carlos Williams, Ezra Pound, H. D., e. e. cummings, Marianne Moore, and Wallace Stevens. These poets formed an "older generation," but Allen notes that some of their most notable work was done after the war (including Williams's *Paterson,* Pound's *Pisan Cantos,* and H. D.'s *Helen in Egypt*). In the second generation, Allen situates poets who emerged in the 1930s and 1940s but reached artistic maturity after the war: Elizabeth Bishop, Edwin Denby, Robert Lowell, Kenneth Rexroth, and Louis Zukofsky. The third generation consists of those contained in the anthology, a younger group of little-known poets whom Allen hopes to vault to prominence. These younger poets have built on the achievements of Pound and Williams and have "gone on to evolve new conceptions of the poem. . . . They are our avant-garde, the true continuers of the modern movement in American poetry," Allen says.

Allen then divides his 44 third-generation writers into five large groups. He concedes that these groupings are overlapping and arbitrary and that they "can be justified finally only as a means to give the reader some sense of milieu and to make the anthology more a readable book and less still another collection of 'anthology pieces.'" The first group is what we now know as the Black Mountain group. Allen represents this group with Olson, Duncan, and Creeley (who all taught at Black Mountain College); EDWARD DORN, Joel Oppenheimer, and Jonathan Williams (who all studied at Black Mountain College); and Paul Blackburn, Paul Carroll, Larry Eigner, and Denise Levertov (who had no connection with the college but who published in the magazines *Origin* and *Black Mountain Review*). The second group contains poets of the San Francisco Renaissance. Here we find Helen Adam, Brother Antoninus (William Everson), Robin Blaser, Ebbe Borregaard, Bruce Boyd, James Broughton, Kirby Doyle, Richard Duerden, Ferlinghetti, Madeline Gleason, PHILIP LAMANTIA, Jack Spicer, and LEW WELCH. The Beat Generation forms the third group. Allen includes Corso, Ginsberg, Kerouac, and Peter Orlovsky. Allen notes their close connections to both the "San Francisco Scene" and the Black Mountain group and also to individual poets such as PHILIP WHALEN and Gary Snyder whom he includes elsewhere. The fourth group consists of the New York poets John Ashberry, Edward Field, Barbara Guest, Kenneth Koch, Frank O'Hara, and James Schuyler. The grab-bag fifth group, as Allen explains, "has no geographical definition; it includes younger poets who have been associated with and in some cases influenced by the leading writers of the preceding groups, but who have evolved their own original styles and new conceptions of poetry." Featured here are RAY BREMSER, LeRoi Jones (who later changed his name to AMIRI BARAKA), Ron Loewisohn, Edward Marshall, MICHAEL McCLURE, David Meltzer, Stuart Z. Perkoff, Gary Snyder, Gilbert Sorrentino, PHILIP WHALEN, and JOHN WIENERS.

After explaining these groupings, Allen expresses the hope that the statements on poetics, biographical notes, and bibliography will lead back to the poems themselves, helping readers to achieve a fuller understanding of a "field [that] is almost completely uncharted."

The five-part grouping described in the preface is subtle and unintrusive. Each of the five sections is given a roman numeral in the table of contents, but no section name accompanies the numeral. There is a page break with just the roman numeral before each section, but no section numbers or headings appear over the poems in the main part of the book. Within each section, writers are organized chronologically by year of birth; within each writer's selections the arrangement is also chronological, with dates of composition following most poems.

As the firstborn member of the first group (Black Mountain), Charles Olson appears first. Olson stands as a titan—even without reference being made to his imposing physical stature—by virtue of his first position, the arresting majesty and authority of his poems ("I, Maximus of Gloucester, to You," "Maximus, to Himself," and "A Newly Discovered 'Homeric' Hymn," "The Lordly and Isolate Satyrs"), and the fact that Allen devotes more space to Olson than to any other poet (38 pages for Olson, with Frank O'Hara second at 32 pages, and Allen Ginsberg third at 24 pages). When combined with Olson's long essay on "projective verse" and his letter to Elaine Feinstein leading off and dominating the section of "Statements on Poetics," Olson seems positioned as a new Homer, a poet/prophet whose voice looms over the entire anthology.

Major poems in section I include Olson's MAXIMUS POEMS and "The Kingfisher" and Duncan's "A Poem Beginning with a Line by Pindar." Several poems are metapoems, or poems about the art of poetry itself, thus eliding the distinction between the poems and the statements on poetics. Duncan's "An Owl is an Only Bird of Poetry," complete with line drawings, is one such example.

Major poems in section II (San Francisco Renaissance) include selections from Ferlinghetti's *PICTURES OF THE GONE WORLD* ("Sarolla's women in their picture hats" and "Dada would have liked a day like this") and *A CONEY ISLAND OF THE MIND* ("In Goya's greatest scenes we seem to see," "The wounded wilderness of Morris Graves," and "Constantly risking absurdity") and from Spicer's "Imaginary Elegies, I–IV." Notable for Beat scholars is Ferlinghetti's "HE," a portrait of Allen Ginsberg. The poem mixes apparently positive observations ("He is one of the wiggy prophets come back") with negative ("He is a talking asshole on a stick"). Ferlinghetti elevates Ginsberg to the status of mythic and eternal poet while simultaneously caricaturing him as the writer of "KADDISH" "whose every third thought is Death." Ferlinghetti sprinkles the word

Death throughout the poem with increasing frequency until it forms a rhythmic refrain and then concludes with *Death* deployed across the page more than 25 times.

Section III (the Beat Generation) opens with 12 choruses from Kerouac's MEXICO CITY BLUES. Inhabited by rhythms as spirited as those in Kerouac's prose, these song/poems are broken into short lines—some just one syllable—that visually reinforce the beat. Many of the 12 choruses grapple with Buddhist concepts as Kerouac searches for elusive Buddhist calm and detachment. For example, "219th Chorus" begins with an attempt at self-abnegation and ends still searching for stasis, balance, acceptance. In "225th Chorus," "restless mental searching" continues despite an intellectual acceptance of Buddhist ideals; in the end, the speaker says, "I've lost my way." In the closing lines of "230th Chorus," the speaker remains very much of this world; his Buddhism does not prevent him from recognizing human suffering or from savoring the soft pleasures of physical contact.

Next in section II is Ginsberg. The Ginsberg selections are as follows: "The Shrouded Stranger," "Malest Cornifici Tuo Catullo," "Sunflower Sutra," "A Supermarket in California," "Howl," Parts I and II, "Sather Gate Illumination," "Message," and "Kaddish," Parts I, III, IV, and V. Ginsberg springs from these pages as a major poetic voice who has already produced multiple major works, the clear heir to Walt Whitman. First among the Ginsberg selections is "The Shrouded Stranger," which sets the tone for his poems of then-startling sexual frankness. The speaker is a combination modern-day equivalent of Wordsworth's Old Cumberland Beggar, a Wordsworthian poet transforming the romantic and poetic tradition, and a fallen angel ("and on my back a broken wing"). Written in ballad form, this poem contains all the seediness of urban poverty and lonely people who are trolling for love, or at least sex.

"Malest Cornifici Tuo Catullo" is addressed to Kerouac. It derives its title from poem 38 by the Roman poet Catullus (circa 84 B.C.E.–54 B.C.E.). Cornificius was a friend of Catullus and a fellow poet. In Catullus's poem, Catullus craves Cornificius's pity and asks Cornificius to write a poem to cheer him up; the line that Ginsberg takes for his title translates as "Your Catullus is ill at ease, Cornificius." In Ginsberg's poem, he craves Kerouac's pity and asks Kerouac not to be disgusted with him for his many lovers. "It's hard to eat shit, without having visions, / & when they have eyes for me it's Heaven," he pleads. As he does elsewhere in the volume, editor Donald M. Allen refrains from supplying explanatory notes to even the most richly allusive, personal, or obscure poems.

"Sunflower Sutra," like the Kerouac poems, reflects the interest in Eastern religion that was shared by this circle of writers. The long, Whitmanesque lines reveal one strain of poetic influence, but another influence surfaces in the romantic poet and visionary William Blake. Ginsberg begins by describing a blighted urban hell to rival Blake's London, a world in which nature has become mechanized. He then sees a lone sunflower; it is a dead and gray sunflower, but it triggers his memory of Blake, and with the visionary power of the poet Ginsberg, transforms the sunflower into an emblem of perfect beauty. In a triumph of the imagination, and of the pathetic fallacy, he even finds unity with it: "Unholy battered old thing you were, my sunflower O my soul, / I loved you then!" In the closing lines, the unity spreads, with all of humanity celebrated: "we're all beautiful golden sunflowers / inside, we're blessed by our own seed & golden hairy naked / accomplishment-bodies. . . ."

"Sather Gate Illumination" begins with the spiritual Ginsberg as a love song to his own soul but quickly moves to sexual ecstasy. Like Whitman's, Ginsberg's poetic world encompasses all, from mundane physical details to ethereal spirit. Yet Ginsberg can also jar the reader, as with this nakedly emotional line that forms a stanza in itself: "My grief at Peter's not loving me was grief at not loving myself."

The Ginsberg section provides one of the clearest examples of Donald M. Allen's brilliance as an editor. This is no haphazard assemblage of poems. Following "Sather Gate Illumination" with "Message" works masterfully to illuminate both poems—as well as the space between them. "Sather Gate Illumination" had ended with a revelatory pronouncement, arrived at after much groping and grieving, that whoever loves himself loves him

(Ginsberg) as well since they are united by self-love. This epiphany, followed by the title "Message," sets up an expectation that another prophetic statement will be forthcoming. Instead, "Message" offers nothing profound, no transcendent Buddhist detachment or acceptance, but rather a simple, personal longing for love. The speaker, too long alone in Paris, aches for the time two months hence when he will be home and able to once again look his beloved in the eyes. For now, the poem delivers the message that the eyes cannot.

Corso appears third in section III. Corso receives a fairly generous 11 page representation, with these poems: "Birthplace Revisited," "Poets Hitchhiking on the Highway," "Zizi's Lament," "Uccello," "But I Do Not Need Kindness," "Dialogue—2 Dollmakers," "Paranoia in Crete," "A Dreamed Realization," "From Another Room," "Notes After Blacking Out," and "MARRIAGE." Corso's gifts are on full display here, the product of an unruly, scrappy street urchin with a Keatsian love of language, a brilliant ear for sound, and a mind that is capable of summoning stunning juxtapositions of words and images.

"Uccello" celebrates immortality achieved through art with reference to battlefield deaths and the Italian painter Paolo Uccello. In "Dialogue—2 Dollmakers," Corso uses imaginative chaos and absurdity as creative forces. Two dollmakers converse, one suggesting absurd improvisations in doll making (a chair for the nose, a sink for the hair) while the other objects to such nonsense—but eventually the rationalist is swayed and joins in the fun, suggesting an aesthetic in which creativity is achieved through nonsense. In "From Another Room," Corso refers to "dumb genius," and in all of these poems he seems, like the surrealists, to have drawn his images from somewhere outside, beyond, or beneath the conscious mind. From where else could he have drawn the final stanza of "A Dreamed Realization"?:

Life. It was Life jabbed a spoon in their mouths.
Crow jackal hyena vulture worm woke to necessity
—dipping into Death like a soup.

Although Allen did not include Corso's controversial pull-out poem "BOMB," he did include Corso's other most-famous work, "Marriage."

Sharing Corso's feel for stunning combinations of images is Peter Orlovsky, the final poet in section III. This is the "Peter" whom Ginsberg addresses in "Sather Gate Illumination," and he is probably the object of Ginsberg's longing "Message" as well. Allen includes one Orlovsky poem, titled simply "Second Poem." Orlovsky displays not just a gift for metaphor ("life splits faster than scissors") but also for alternate spellings that add humor and enrich possibilities of meaning. "Second Poem" concludes with Orlovsky speaking as the innocent poet of nature, emerging from the urban grime that coated Ginsberg and Corso's verses to discover that "I was born to remember a song about love—on a hill a butterfly / makes a cup that I drink from, walking over a bridge of / flowers."

The sexual frankness of the Beat writers seeps into section IV (New York poets) through such poems as Frank O'Hara's "You Are Gorgeous and I'm Coming." O'Hara dominates this section, both in terms of page count and of long poems that appear to be major poetic statements. These long poems include "In Memory of My Feelings" and "Ode to Michael Goldberg ('s Birth and Other Births)." Goldberg, a painter, is also the subject of O'Hara's humorous poem "Why I Am Not a Painter." Corso had dedicated his poem "Marriage" to this same Mike Goldberg and his wife.

Other notable works in section IV include Guest's soaring "Parachutes, My Love, Could Carry Us Higher"; Koch's long poem "Fresh Air," and his short, amusing "Mending Sump," a parody of Robert Frost's "Mending Wall"; and Ashberry's "A Boy," "The Instruction Manual," and "'How Much Longer Will I Be Able to Inhabit the Divine Sepulcher . . .'"

Section V (no geographical definition) offers generous samplings of work by Whalen (16 pages), Snyder (16 pages), and McClure (18 pages). These three poets had strong personal connections with Beat Generation writers: When Ginsberg gave his first public reading of "Howl" Part I on October 7, 1955, at the Six Gallery, Whalen, Snyder, and McClure were the other readers on the bill (along with Lamantia).

Notable works in section V include Whalen's "SOURDOUGH MOUNTAIN LOOKOUT" and the riproaring "Denunciation: Or, Unfrock'd Again"; Stuart Z. Perkoff's "Feasts of Death, Feasts of Love"; a selection from Part III of Snyder's *Myths and Texts;* Marshall's "Leave the World Alone," which, like Ginsberg's "Kaddish," gives a searing confessional account of a family drama involving madness and trauma; McClure's "Hymn to St. Geryon, I" and "For Artaud"; and Jones's "IN MEMORY OF RADIO." Jones's "For Hettie" is a chilling lyric of a superstitious husband who is mistrustful of his pregnant wife, HETTIE JONES.

As section V moves to a close, we encounter more metapoems that blur the distinction between poetry and poetics. These include Loewisohn's "The Stillness of the Poem" and the very last poem in the collection, Meltzer's "Prayerwheel / 2," and they help to bridge the five sections of poetry and the "Statements on Poetics" that form section VI. Meltzer's poem completes the bridge by concluding with its own statement on poetics and the role of the poet:

> Is anything ever gone
> to the poet who works up everything
> eventually? Somewhere, without mind,
> Love begins. The poet begins
> to examine the dissolution of Love.
> The sea continues. We continue
> talking, growing nervous, drinking,
> too much coffee.

The fact that Allen gives poetic statements their own section number rather than relegating them to an appendix indicates the importance that he accorded them. The section begins with Olson's thoughts on projective verse and then contains reflections by Duncan, Creeley, Levertov, Ferlinghetti, Spicer, Kerouac, Ginsberg, Schuyler, O'Hara, Whalen, Snyder, McClure, Jones, and Wieners. With the exception of Olson and Duncan's essays, most contributions are a couple of pages or less.

An excerpt from *Fantasy 7004* makes clear Ferlinghetti's differences from, and with, the Beat writers. He states that Beat writers tell him that he cannot be Beat and socially engaged at the same time. Ferlinghetti notes that Sartre, an inspiration for the Beats, insisted upon the artist's engagement with social issues and adds, "that Abominable Snowman of modern poetry, Allen Ginsberg, would probably say the same. Only the dead are disen-

gaged." The "wiggy nihilism of the Beat hipster," he continues, will lead to the death of the creative artist, as will disengagement or "non-commitment."

A brief statement by Kerouac from 1959 insists on the value of the irrational "because poetry is NOT a science." He sees rhythm as the essence of truthful expression, whether in poetry or in "an endless one-line poem called prose."

In "Notes for *Howl and Other Poems*," Ginsberg relates his own inspirations and processes of composition from 1955 on. Finding a poetic line that captures his breath preoccupied him from the start. He says that he began "Howl" with patterns of speech that he picked up from William Carlos Williams and that he followed "my romantic inspiration—Hebraic-Melvillian bardic breath." Each line of "Howl" should be a single breath unit, he says, adding that "my breath is long." Ginsberg mentions the vision of Blake that is recounted in "Sunflower Sutra" and recounts his experiments with long and short lines in "Supermarket in California," "Cottage in Berkeley," and "Kaddish." He argues for rhythm of "Promethian [sic] natural measure, not in mechanical count of accent." Ginsberg takes a swipe at academics and politicians who do not understand poetry and then concludes with an image of a gay creator dancing in eternity.

Most of the biographical notes were written by the poets themselves. Many of the poets confine themselves to three or four lines of basic biographical fact. Corso takes two pages, relating the horrors of his boyhood from a broken home to a boy's home to Bellevue. Prison follows, and Corso tells how he began to read serious literature and to write poetry while incarcerated. He speaks of the innocent 12-year-old Gregory whom he has lost. Following his release from prison, he takes a job in the Garment District; meets Ginsberg and is introduced to noninstitutional, literary society; embarks on a series of odd jobs; and finally begins to publish. Corso takes his story up to his time in Paris.

After one conventional sentence that list his birth date, birthplace, and parents, Ginsberg's brief self-penned biography proceeds to a series of place names, job descriptions, and career milestones. He leaves a smoky wisp of mystery behind him, saying that in 1959 he "returned to SF & made record to leave behind and fade awhile in Orient."

This final part of the book, "Short Bibliography," consists of the following: I. Books and Broadsheets, arranged alphabetically by poet, giving press and date of publication along with titles; II. Anthologies in which the works of these poets appear; III. Recordings of readings; IV. Chief Periodicals, as well as others of value; V. Addresses of Publishers.

Allen's anthology drew significant attention to these unheralded new voices. Not all the attention was positive. The book upset the literary establishment. Critic John Simon wrote, "Mr. Allen's anthology divides all gall into five parts."

Alan Golding encapsulates the long-term influence of Allen's anthology:

> In terms of its defining "anti-academic" role in the 1960s anthology wars, its impact on later collection and editors, its importance for later poets, and its central place in most readings or structurings of postwar literary history, Donald Allen's *The New American Poetry* (1960) is generally considered the single most influential poetry anthology of the post–World War II period.

Golding goes on to say that the volume remains such "an anthological touchstone for alternative poetries that editors of avant-garde anthologies continue to invoke it as a model over thirty years after its publication."

In 1998 the New York Public Library devoted a six-month exhibit to the poetry "mimeo revolution" of the 1960s and 1970s. This movement was characterized by poets who duplicated their self-published work with the aid of mimeograph machines. A library press release observes, "It was Donald Allen's watershed 1960 anthology *The New American Poetry* that stimulated the flood of poetry that led to the mimeo movement." The press release singled out City Lights as "among the most important precursors" to the mimeo movement. The exhibit prominently featured Ginsberg's self-published works.

Marjorie Perloff states that *The New American Poetry* is "still acknowledged by all later anthologists as the fountainhead of radical American poetics." Perloff identifies five new anthologies in 1993–94 alone for which *The New American Poetry*

served as precursor. Perloff also points to the then-forthcoming publication of Jerome Rothenberg and Pierre Joris's two-volume *Poems for the Millenium*. She could have also included Carolyn Forché's *Against Forgetting: Twentieth-Century Poetry of Witness* (New York: Norton, 1993).

Perloff notes that *The New American Poetry* became so influential because there was a clear, acknowledged tradition that made Allen's anthology stand in stark relief. That tradition was best exemplified by the chief rival to Allen's volume, *New Poets of England and America*, edited by Donald Hall, Robert Pack, and Louis Simpson (New York: Meridian, 1957). The current lack of canonical consensus may prevent any future collection from having the impact that Allen's did. "It is no longer possible, as it was for Donald Allen, to present readers with an anthology of *the* or even *a* definitive New American Poetry," says Perloff.

Information concerning exact sales figures and number of printings is considered proprietary and is therefore unavailable from the publisher. In addition, the number of times that Grove Press has changed hands since 1960 makes such data difficult if not impossible to obtain. A sales figure of more than 100,000 is generally accepted, but how much more than 100,000 could not be determined. Golding reports that within 10 years it had gone through 16 printings and 112,500 copies; by 1978 it reached its 22nd printing. In July 1999 the University of California Press became the publisher of *The New American Poetry, 1945–1960,* and the book remains in print.

Allen originally intended to publish a revised edition every two to three years. That did not happen. In 1982 Grove published a revised volume called *The Postmoderns: The New American Poetry Revisited*, which Allen coedited with Charles Olson-expert George F. Butterick. *The Postmoderns* introduces nine new poets, including three women, to the anthology: DIANE DI PRIMA, Anselm Hollo, Robert Kelly, James Koller, JOANNE KYGER, Jackson Mac Low, Jerome Rothenberg, EDWARD SANDERS, and ANNE WALDMAN. Fifteen poets from the original volume no longer appear: Helen Adam, Ebbe Borregaard, Bruce Boyd, Ray Bremser, James Broughton, Paul Carroll, Kirby Doyle, Richard Duerden, Edward Field, Michael Gleason, Philip Lamantia,

Edward Marshall, Peter Orlovsky, Stuart Z. Perkoff, and Gilbert Sorrentino.

Allen and Butterick explain these choices in a new preface:

> Our purpose was to consolidate the gains of the previous anthology and confirm its predictions, by taking the best of the poets represented there, who have, by every indication, achieved a certain recognition. The present volume does not seek to be all-inclusive, or exclusionary. . . . Yet it does offer a sharpened focus to represent an era. . . .

In *The Postmoderns,* Allen and Butterick removed the sectional divisions, subtle as they were. Authors appear in the table of contents ordered by year of birth. The new preface explains this choice, saying that the "earlier designations, if they were ever anything more than terms of convenience, have been rendered obsolete and unnecessary by the poets' subsequent activities and associations. Postmodernism is a more encompassing designation, while still having its own precisions." They observe that Olson first used the term *postmodernism,* meaning by it "an instant-by-instant engagement with reality."

In addition to this engagement and "instantism," Allen and Butterick note other unifying characteristics of the writers selected; these include "formal freedom or openness as opposed to academic, formalistic, strictly rhymed and metered verse"; "a spontaneous utilization of subject and technique"; "freely maneuvering among the inherited traditions, time-honored lore, and proven practices"; an unflinching willingness to confront "previously held convictions and proprieties, while seeking a restoration of some very ancient ones"; and various matters of style and subject.

Allen and Butterick altered and updated the selections of poets whose work had appeared in *The New American Poetry.* For example, seven previous Corso poems, including "Marriage," have been dropped, but two new poems have been added. The Ginsberg section drops five poems, including "Sunflower Sutra," and drops parts III, IV, and V of "Kaddish," while adding Part III of "Howl," "America," "Kral Majales," and "On Neal's Ashes."

The arrangement of the back matter has also changed in *The Postmoderns.* In one comprehensive list, for each poet Allen and Butterick list biographical information (adding to the poets' own accounts when necessary), poetry books published, bibliography, and secondary sources. For some authors, information also appears for recordings and "other" (such as non-poetry books that an author may have written). Finally, there is a general bibliography.

The "Statements on Poetics" section has been removed since such items appeared separately in *The Poetics of the New American Poetry* in 1973. *The Poetics* reached back to include statements from Whitman, Pound, D. H. Lawrence, Gertrude Stein, Williams, H. D., and Zukofsky. Beat writers are represented by Ginsberg, who has eight selections included. Corso and Kerouac's contributions have been dropped. However, statements appear from a number of figures who were allied with the Beat writers, including Dorn, Ferlinghetti, McClure, Snyder, and Whalen.

Even before the curriculum and canon wars erupted in the 1980s and 1990s, even before it was published, *The New American Poetry* came under fire for its reifying, canonizing potential from one of its chief contributors, Robert Duncan. "He rejects a venture that he sees as dominated by aspirations toward taste-making, career-building, influence, and representation of a period—all of which, at least in retrospect, *The New American Poetry* could lay claim to," explains Alan Golding.

Eventually, Duncan allowed Allen to include his work when he became convinced of Allen's seriousness of purpose. Subsequent detractors have not always been mollified, particularly with regard to "the anthology's race and gender lacunae," as mentioned by Golding.

Ironically, then, an anthology that intended to present an alternative tradition became canonical itself, made mainstream by its own success. Widely imitated even by those who in the 40-plus years since its publication have found it insufficiently radical or inclusive, it retains a stature and influence unmatched by anything else of its kind.

Bibliography

Allen, Donald M., and George F. Butterick, eds. *The Postmoderns: The New American Poetry Revisited,* with a new preface by Donald Allen and George F. Butterick. New York: Grove, 1982.

Allen, Donald M., and Warren Tallman. *The Poetics of the New American Poetry.* New York: Grove, 1973.

"Background." Donald Allen Collection Online. University of California, San Diego. Available online. URL: http://orpheus.ucsd.edu/speccoll/testing/html/mss0003a.html. Accessed September 3, 2004.

Golding, Alan. *From Outlaw to Classic: Canons in American Poetry.* Madison: University of Wisconsin Press, 1996.

———. "*The New American Poetry* Revisited, Again." *Contemporary Literature* 39, no. 2 (Summer 1998): 180–211.

Olson, Charles. *Poet to Publisher: Charles Olson's Correspondence with Donald Allen.* Edited by Ralph Maud. Vancouver, B.C.: Talon, 2003.

Perloff, Marjorie. "Whose New American Poetry? Anthologizing in the Nineties." *Diacritics* 26, nos. 3–4 (1996): 104–123.

Saxon, Wolfgang. "Donald Allen, 92, Book Editor of Bold New Voices in Poetry, Dies." The New York Times on the Web. Available online. URL: http://www.nytimes.com/2004/09/09/books/09allen.html. Accessed September 9, 2004.

"Underground Publications Document Poetry's 'Mimeo Revolution' in Exhibition at The New York Public Library." Press release (November 26, 1997). The New York Public Library. Available online. URL: http://www.nypl.org/press/secret.cfm. Accessed September 3, 2004.

Richard Middleton-Kaplan

New Creatures, The Jim Morrison (1969)

MICHAEL McCLURE writes, "In the lucid mescaline-like light of a hangover, I found his manuscript of *The New Creatures* on the coffee table of his Belgravia apartment [in London] and was excited by what I read. . . . I suggested that Jim do a private edition for friends only and then give the book to a commercial publisher if he chose." JIM MORRISON privately published a limited edition of 100 copies of *The New Creatures,* finished July 24, 1968, dedicated to Pamela Courson, printed by Western Lithographers in summer 1970. Simon & Schuster published the book combined with *The Lords* (1969), Morrison's Nietzschean poetic-philosophical musings on film, as *The Lords & The New Creatures,* in 1970. Stephen Davis writes:

> *The New Creatures* compiled more recent poetic interpretation of his adventures and persona as a rock star, charting the psychic territory of national legend and celebrity that no poet since Lord Byron had been able to investigate firsthand. Sometimes stabbingly acute, sometimes banal and derivative, these poems hung together as the inner workings of a rebel and outlaw self-exiled to a spiritual landscape of exaltation and despair.

McClure calls *The New Creatures*

> a book of imagistic poetry with hints of seventeenth century, hints of Elizabethan drama, tastes of classical mythology. It's a kind of romantic personal viewpoint in a nineteenth-century Shelleyan/Keatsian sense. . . . Very nineteenth-century, very personal. Yet the poetry itself is almost mainstream twentieth-century imagist poetry. It's good poetry, real fine poetry, as good as anybody in his generation was writing. . . . Some of them could be Roman poems, except for their very Englishness—goddess hunters, bows and arrows, people with green hair walking by the side of the sea. It's a little bit like science fiction. A little bit like some Roman poet writing in Latin had been reading nineteenth-century poetry.

The "new creatures" of Morrison's book are mutants that were spawned by the violence and the revolutionary changes occurring in the late 1960s. The opening image could be of Morrison himself:

> Snakeskin jacket
> Indian eyes
> Brilliant hair
>
> He moves in disturbed
> Nile Insect
> Air

The military industrial complex is destroying itself and the world. The new creatures of the counter-culture are being born. While the cold war spoils the planet, the spirits of ancient peoples are returning. The youth questions the destructiveness of the old. Morrison uses Hieronymous Bosch-like images of chaos. Disturbing hallucinations, like a Native-American shaman seeing the terrible future on peyote, make visible the spirit world damaged by capitalism, consumerism, colonialism, and soul-lessness. African Americans riot in the streets of America after "The assassin's bullet / Marries the King," an allusion to the assassination of Martin Luther King in April 1968. These are visions from a trance that was induced by the horrors of a civilization gone wrong.

In these poems Morrison becomes the Beat poet that he wanted to be. According to Ray Manzarek, "Jim has that same kind of aura about him that the Beats had." McClure states, "I know of no better poet of Jim's generation."

Bibliography

Davis, Stephen. *Jim Morrison: Life, Death, Legend.* New York: Gotham Books, 2004.

Manzarek, Ray. *Light My Fire: My Life with The Doors.* New York: G. P. Putnam's Sons, 1998.

McClure, Michael. Afterword. *No One Here Gets Out Alive,* by Jerry Hopkins and Danny Sugerman. New York: Warner Books, 1981.

———. "Nile Insect Eyes: Talking on Jim Morrison." Interview with Frank Lisciandro. *Lighting the Corners: On Art, Nature, and the Visionary—Essays and Interviews,* by Michael McClure. Albuquerque: University of New Mexico College of Arts and Sciences, 1993.

Kurt Hemmer

Norse, Harold (1916–   )

An important avant-garde poet, translator, and memoirist, Harold Norse first became connected to the Beat movement while living in the Beat Hotel in Paris in the early 1960s. Having already become a member of W. H. Auden's inner circle through a mutual lover, Norse had also established a relationship with William Carlos Williams by the early 1950s, one that was later documented in *The American Idiom: A Correspondence, William Carlos Williams & Harold Norse 1951–61* (1990). Following the publication of Norse's first book of poems (*The Undersea Mountain* 1953), he moved to Rome and began the extremely ambitious project of translating the poems of Guiseppi Gianchino Belli (a task which both James Joyce and D. H. Lawrence had attempted and abandoned). While there, Williams, who was also mentoring a young ALLEN GINSBERG, wrote to tell Norse of the European expedition that Ginsberg, JACK KEROUAC, GREGORY CORSO, and WILLIAM S. BURROUGHS had undertaken. Norse, whose street lifestyle, homosexuality, interest in Zen Buddhism, and spontaneous poetics of lyricism and confession mixed very well with the budding Beat aesthetic, checked into the legendary Beat Hotel in 1960 at the suggestion of Burroughs. Once there, he began a cut-up novel in the style of Burroughs and Brion Gyson, which was later compiled and published as *The BEAT HOTEL* (1983).

Norse left the Beat Hotel in 1963 and began to receive critical attention by middecade. He continued to publish poems in journals such as the *Evergreen Review,* a literary review that also published much Beat poetry as well as the likes of Samuel Beckett and Octavio Paz, and in 1966 an entire issue of the avant-garde journal *Ole* was devoted to his work.

By 1969 Norse had settled in San Francisco, becoming a key member of the San Francisco literary movement as well as the 1970s gay-liberation movement. In 1974 Beat poet LAWRENCE FERLINGHETTI's City Lights Pocket Poets series (the same series in which Ginsberg's HOWL AND OTHER POEMS first appeared) published Norse's *Hotel Nirvana: Selected Poems, 1953–1973,* which was nominated for the 1974 National Book Award. Three years later, his book *Carnivorous Saint: Gay Poems 1941–1976* was published, maintaining the then 61-year-old poet's place in 20th-century counterculture.

In 1989 his *Memoirs of a Bastard Angel* was published (James Baldwin wrote the preface), attempting to break down myths and legends about the famous and admired. In it Norse, who was always surrounded by the mythologized, documents encounters with the Beats, as well as with Auden,

Tennessee Williams, Gore Vidal, Marlon Brando, Ezra Pound, Anaïs Nin, Jackson Pollock, Dylan Thomas, Robert De Niro, PAUL BOWLES, CHARLES BUKOWSKI, and numerous others. This memoir fits Norse's style in its frankness and tone, but it also does so thematically as Norse had always strived to create a poetry not of novelty and myth but of lived experience, finding the extraordinary in the deeply genuine.

Norse received a lifetime achievement award from the National Poetry Association in 1991 and continues to live and work in San Francisco.

Bibliography

Norse, Harold. *Memoirs of a Bastard Angel: A Fifty-Year Literary and Erotic Odyssey.* New York: Thunder's Mouth Press, 1989.

Chuck Carlise

Nova Express William S. Burroughs (1964)

This third book in WILLIAM S. BURROUGHS's cut-up trilogy of science fiction was written in the 1960s.

In the first section, "Last Words," the last words are ascribed by Burroughs to Hassan i Sabbah, the eighth-century leader of a group of assassins who targeted fundamentalist religious leaders. Burroughs extends Hassan i Sabbah's opposition to religious fundamentalism to an opposition to corporations, monopolies, and syndicates that dominate the globe at the expense of individuals. A letter from Inspector J. Lee of the Nova Police explains in more detail that the "boards syndicates and governments of the world" represent an intergalactic conspiracy to enslave human beings to their vices. In parasitic form, these control agents thus use human beings and the planet Earth until they are sucked dry, at which time they abandon the planet to "nova"—total destruction. The Nova Police are out to arrest the "Nova Mob" that is controlling the planet by means of a film that was created in the Reality Studio. Compared to the previous two books in this trilogy (*The SOFT MACHINE* and *The TICKET THAT EXPLODED*), the message here is far more urgent: We have only "minutes to go" to prevent the catastrophe of nova. Nova conditions are fomented by The Intolerable Kid, who ignores the

signs that the Nova Police are moving in. Much of this action has been described in the two previous books, but a new character is introduced as the planet's savior, The Mayan God of Pain and Fear. From his seat of power on the surface of Venus, he shuts down the con game that is played by the board members.

In the section "So Pack Your Ermines," Burroughs raises environmental themes in this book that look forward to the environmental movement of the 1970s: The Board's "Green Deal" (a metaphor for the destruction of the environment by profit-minded global corporations) involves sucking the oxygen out of the Earth's atmosphere to create a carbon-dioxide atmosphere that can be breathed by the Vegetable People, who have formed an alliance with the Insect People of Minraud. When the carbon dioxide runs thin, the effects are similar to those of withdrawal from heroin, and Burroughs brings in his old drug partner, Phil White (the Sailor), and creates a variation on their days "working the hole" (the subway) in 1946 (described in *JUNKY*). KiKi, based on Burroughs's boy companion Kiki in Tangier, narrates a scene as he did in *The Ticket That Exploded*. He tells "Meester William" that his theories on writing are "loco." The many references to bread knives refer to the fact that the real-life Kiki was stabbed to death with a bread knife. Another boy narrates a scene from Burroughs's *yage* expedition to South America where the "Meester locates a Brujo and pays him to prepare ayahuasca" (a hallucinogenic potion containing DMT). The characters here shift "coordinate points," meaning that they travel from body to body, making it possible for KiKi to show up as a boy in South America. Dr. Benway makes an appearance at the end of this chapter. He is conducting experiments with a "green drug," and when the patient dies, he concludes that "orgones" are "blue" not green.

The "Chinese Laundry" section has Inspector Lee of the Nova Police interrogate a suspected Nova Mob member named Winkhorst, who describes the ways in which apomorphine can be used to short-circuit mechanisms of addiction and control. He tells Lee that the planet is going nova and offers to obtain a "lifeboat" for him if he will send back reports saying that conditions on Earth are normal. Lee's District Supervisor tells him that Winkhorst has lied to him about the Mob's interest in chemicals: They are interested in using "images" to control subjects, a method far more effective than chemical addiction and a method that cannot be counteracted with apomorphine. A death dwarf is brought on stage to describe addictive images of sex and violence. Winkhorst is further interrogated about apomorphine. Burroughs compares morphine to police, for both "stick around" after they are not needed, and he compares apomorphine to the Nova Police, who leave when their job is done. This explains the need of the police for drug addicts and drug laws: Without them, the police cease to exist, an analysis of the Police State that was first made by Burroughs in *Junky.* One of the agents of the Nova Police is posing as writer. He is a defector called Uranian Willy (based on Burroughs). Uranian Willy institutes Plan D—"Total Exposure"—and blows up the reality film, allowing everyone to see behind the scenes of the control universe.

In the "Crab Nebula" section the Crab Nebula is described as the result of a star gone supernova and that was first observed by the Chinese in A.D. 1054. Burroughs locates the Insect People of Minraud there, as well as their "Elders," superbrains that are suspended in jars filled with spinal fluid. These jars are guarded by "crab" people. From the Crab Nebula, the controllers have loosed a language "virus" on Earth, which works much the same way a biological virus does or the way an adding machine does—"like the cylinder gimmick in the adding machine." As the grandson of the man who perfected the adding machine, Burroughs is able to decode the language virus, and he suggests ways that we can deprogram ourselves from its influence. "The old mind tapes can be wiped clean," he says.

A Nova criminal gives a deposition before the Biologic courts, and the transcript of his deposition fills in more information about the intergalactic set-up. Earth, in fact, was a set-up for the Nova Criminals who were able to stay just a few light-years ahead of the Nova Police. But they are caught on Earth. Their plan had been to escape by banking hours that were built up through "short timing" the inhabitants of Earth, who cannot figure out why they have less time to do things than they used to. The inhabitants of Earth need to stay duped for the controllers to suck them dry; most importantly, they must be kept ignorant of how to move into space because once they do this, they will no longer be manageable.

Agent K9 (also based on Burroughs) is with the Biologic Police and has been assigned the task of cutting off the death dwarfs from the influence of the controllers in the Crab Nebula. He discusses how language can be robbed of its ability to control us by reteaching us to think not in words but in association patterns. This is thinking at "the speed of light." The cut-up method demonstrated in several passages throughout the book exemplifies how we can read in "association blocks" rather than "in words."

In the section entitled "Remember I Was Carbon Dioxide," Burroughs creates a "fold-in" using his own text and the text of T. S. Eliot's "The Waste Land." The fold-in technique, an extension of the cut-up technique created by Brion Gysin, is described in *The Third Mind.*

"From a Land of Grass Without Mirrors" takes evolution as the key theme in the opening chapters of this section. Lee awakens after the battle for the Control Room with no body, a new state to which he adapts easily. He sees that other lifeforms have had to evolve on an Earth with a carbon-dioxide atmosphere. Lee evidently has been aided in his evolution by apomorphine, which releases him from the control of parasites. The "cure" resembles Burroughs's treatment for morphine addiction in Lexington, Kentucky, or later in Morocco and London.

The "Gave Proof Through the Night" section begins with a version of the first "routine" Burroughs ever wrote, with Kells Elvins in 1938, entitled "Twilight's Last Gleamings." Amazingly, this first routine anticipates the plot of the cut-up trilogy in that both are about passengers who are abandoned by the crew and captain of a sinking ship. (The circumstances of the sinking of the *Titanic* and of the *Morro Castle* fascinated Burroughs.) Here, the captain of the ship murders his way onto the lifeboat, much as the Nova Criminals abandon planet Earth as it goes nova. The character Perkins is based on Kells Elvins's father Politte Elvins, who suffered from paresis and lisped.

"This Horrible Case" section was written in collaboration with "Mr. Ian Sommerville, a mathematician," Burroughs informs us in the front notes. Here, the "horrible case" of the planet Earth is brought before the courts. The key question is whether or not the alien invaders of Earth can be excused for killing the inhabitants of Earth out of a "biologic need." Was it survival or murder? The parasitic invaders lose in the biologic courts because they made no effort to adapt to the conditions of the planet where they supposedly crash landed. Instead, they simply milked its inhabitants of life, awaiting new travel arrangements. Writers are the Biologic Counselors who prosecute and defend such cases. One of the greatest Biologic Counselors was Franz Kafka. His "briefs" are "classics." To make a judgment, Burroughs folds in parts of Kafka's nightmare study of bureaucracy, *The Castle,* with the facts of the "horrible case."

"Pay Color," the final section, has the colors red, blue, and green corresponding respectively to (among other things) blood, sky, and jungle. Hassan i Sabbah demands that the boards and syndicates pay back all that they have stolen from the planet. Benway, in antibiotic handcuffs, says, "It goes against my deepest instincts to pay off the marks—But under the uh circumstances." The Subliminal Kid breaks down images and sounds with playback techniques, freeing up the narrative for a fantasy sequence that begins when agent K9 (a character introduced in *The Soft Machine*)

enters a sensory deprivation tank with a Chinese youth and emerges himself as a Mexican street boy. On the outskirts of the city he encounters wild boys who are performing acrobatic sex. Later, Burroughs folds in sections from John Yerbury Dent's treatise on apomorphine, "Anxiety and Its Treatments." Burroughs makes the metaphor of addiction in the book (and in all of his books) explicit by saying that "Mr. Martin" (the head of the Nova Mob) is "morphine." The District Supervisor asks an agent to detail his knowledge of scientology (the Logos group in the book). This is one of Burroughs's longest discussions of the controversial religion that was founded by L. Ron Hubbard. He extends Hubbard's methods to show how we can literally "laugh off" childhood and other traumas by cutting them into an absurd context and viewing/listening to them repeatedly.

Burroughs states, as he did in the "Atrophied Preface" to *NAKED LUNCH,* that all of the characters in the book are the same. He reiterates the basic Nova technique of feedback—two groups' hateful statements about each other played before them, back and forth—and says that the trick to avoiding nova is simply not to respond: *"Silence."* The author has no more "junk scripts, no more word scripts" and tells the reader to "Clom Fliday," the old Chinese heroin dealer's way of getting rid of deadbeat occidental junkies.

Rob Johnson

Off the Road: My Years with Cassady, Kerouac, and Ginsberg Carolyn Cassady (1990)

Though CAROLYN CASSADY does not consider herself a Beat, this is one of the most important memoirs that was written about the Beat era. Carolyn was commissioned by a publisher to write her memoirs in 1970, but she was unable to receive permission to publish the letters that JACK KEROUAC had sent her. Excerpts of the memoir appeared in magazines. A large excerpt called *Heart Beat: My Life with Jack and Neal* was published in 1976 by Creative Arts Books in Berkeley, California, and inspired the 1980 Orion Pictures film *Heart Beat* starring Nick Nolte, John Heard, and Sissy Spacek. The full memoir was finally published by Black Spring Press in England and later the same year by William Morrow in the United States.

Carolyn first meets NEAL CASSADY in March 1947. She has already heard of his exploits through Neal's friend Bill Tomson, who is infatuated with Carolyn. Tomson brings Neal to Carolyn's apartment unannounced, and Neal sweeps in looking for good jazz records to play. She is impressed more by his clothes than by his physical appearance. Still, she is attracted to him and is disappointed when a few hours later she discovers that he is married to a 16-year-old waitress named LuAnne. LuAnne, Neal, Al Hinkle, and Tomson all go back to Carolyn's apartment for a party. LuAnne gushes about their perfect marriage, but Neal is sullen. Neal later returns to Carolyn's apartment at 2 A.M., and fearing a scene with her landlord, she sneaks him in. They sleep chastely together in her

bed, and this begins their relationship. She values how he listens to her and likes that their relationship is intellectual rather than sexual. However, part of the plot of this memoir is Carolyn's gradual understanding of how much Neal and his friends lie to her. ALLEN GINSBERG, she learned too late, was in love with Neal, and that fall they had had an intense sexual relationship in New York. Ginsberg's jealousy of Carolyn begins here when Neal begs off on a promised trip to Texas to visit WILLIAM S. BURROUGHS because he wants to stay with Carolyn. This love triangle results in an odd scene. With Ginsberg asleep on the couch, Neal chooses to end their chaste relationship and forces sex on Carolyn. Carolyn wants to return to her "former state of bliss" so much that she represses the implications of this act. She believes that their love is "predestined," but at the same time she feels herself losing her own free will.

Neal introduces her to the mind-altering effects of Benzedrine, and they lie next to each other in a hotel bed, uninhibitedly talking about their past for hours. Neal makes love to her for the second time, and Carolyn once again feels only pain. In spite of their uninhibited conversation that night, she cannot bring herself to communicate her ideas about pleasurable sex to him. Neal seems not to notice her reaction and asks her to marry him. She replies that he is already married, and the subject does not come up again, although Neal does force LuAnne to file for an annulment. Kerouac arrives from New York about this time, and with him Carolyn feels the kind of warmth that she cannot feel with Neal. He whispers in her ear that it is too bad that Neal saw her first. Carolyn enjoys "playing house" with Neal, but he begins to disappear and does not provide explanations. Neal's erratic behavior leads to her accepting an invitation from her former boyfriend to go to California, where she can pursue a costume-design career. Neal responds by saying that he will go with Ginsberg to Burroughs's ranch in Texas.

In Los Angeles, Carolyn finds herself haunted by thoughts of Neal as she dances with Cyril in the Biltmore Hotel. Cyril leaves for a trip to Mexico, and Carolyn moves to San Francisco where her older sister lives; there she awaits word on a potential job in Hollywood. From New Waverly, Texas, Neal writes her about life on Burroughs's ranch. He tells her that he and Ginsberg have been unable to have a satisfactory physical relation and that Ginsberg was shipping out for Dakar, Senegal. Neal promises to join her in San Francisco after he drives Burroughs back to New York. They have only been separated five weeks when Neal arrives in San Francisco in October 1947. He still has not gotten the annulment, but as a consolation, he teaches her how to smoke marijuana that night, a drug that she eventually gave up because she did not like the feeling of losing control of her mind. Their first few months in San Francisco are fulfilling. However, on December 1 LuAnne arrives, looking very sophisticated. For the next few months, LuAnne teases Neal mercilessly and shows off the clothes and jewelry that another man is buying her. They resume a sexual relationship that Carolyn only finds out about years later through letters and Kerouac's novels. Neal wrote to Kerouac that he needed to figure out a way to call off his impending marriage to Carolyn. It is too late: Carolyn is pregnant. When Neal finds a doctor who will perform an abortion, Carolyn cannot believe that he did not first discuss it with her. Lack of communication between men and women is a refrain in the book. The various pressures in his life—LuAnne, Carolyn's pregnancy, Ginsberg's letters from overseas—lead Neal to try to commit suicide on his birthday, February 8, 1948. Al Hinkle and Carolyn talk him out of it.

Neal goes to Denver to secure the annulment in late February 1948. Carolyn, alone and

pregnant, fears that he will not return. But he does, with the annulment, and with a hair-raising story about crossing the Donner Pass. Neal now settles down to get married and to raise a family. Their wedding day falls on April 1. It is a comedy of errors, and they end up having to use fake silver rings that had been purchased from Woolworth's as their wedding bands. Al Hinkle helps Neal get a job on the railroad, but to get work, he has to go to Bakersfield. Carolyn is left alone, six months pregnant, the lease on her apartment up, and with only five dollars to last her two weeks. Soon, the work is steadier, and Neal regains his old energies, writing to Kerouac, "God has once again touched my seed—it blooms, I blossom"—perhaps an image that Kerouac incorporated into his description of Dean Moriarty that was based on Neal in *On the Road* from around this time, that Neal had developed into a "strange flower." Neal begins some writing (possibly early versions of *The FIRST THIRD*), and Carolyn begins to paint again.

Cathleen Joanne Cassady is born just after midnight September 7, 1949. Hospital rules forbid Neal witnessing the birth and kept Carolyn confined to the hospital for eight days—eight days that she feared Neal was spending in the company of LuAnne. Neal proves to be a doting father, however, writing enthusiastic letters to Ginsberg and Kerouac about parenthood. Two months after Cathy's birth, Neal brings Al Hinkle with his new wife, Helen Hinkle. Carolyn is surprised that Al has married a woman whom she has never met and who does not appear to be his type. Her surprise becomes anger when Neal announces that he has bought a new car and will be taking the newlyweds on a honeymoon tour. Helen is rich, and Neal and Al are using her to finance a senseless trip back East to pick up Kerouac. Carolyn is furious with Neal's irresponsibility and says that she would have broken up with Neal for good at that point were it not for two-month-old Cathy.

Carolyn finds out that Neal has stopped off in Denver and knows that this means that he has picked up LuAnne (which, in fact, he has). Neal returns in late January 1949 after being on the road for more than two months. Carolyn throws him out. The next morning Neal calls Carolyn and convinces her that he is not seeing LuAnne.

He comes home with Kerouac in tow. Kerouac is embarrassed that he is a big part of Carolyn's problem with Neal. Still, he stays with them for about a week. Neal tries to work as a door-to-door salesman but fails. Carolyn tries to tolerate their antics and ends up letting them go out at night to hear jazz in San Francisco. A phone call from LuAnne ends her tolerance. Neal and Kerouac both swear that LuAnne is a whore, and Carolyn realizes that she actually envies LuAnne's freedom. She kicks Kerouac out and tells Neal to go with him. Neal calls her a few days later, frantic and hurt: He has broken his hand hitting LuAnne; it is all over between them, he swears. When they go to the hospital, LuAnne is there, and Carolyn and LuAnne leave him there and go back to her house—one of the many scenes where Carolyn actually sides against Neal with his girlfriends. LuAnne tells her side of the trip East, and it turns out that she has conned both Jack and Neal: The only reason that she rides with them is to get a trip back to California where she is to meet her fiancé. Neal now has nowhere to stay, and Carolyn takes him back.

With his injured hand, Neal cannot work and stays home with the baby while Carolyn works at a doctor's office. During this period (March 1949) he is writing *The First Third*. Neal recovers sufficiently to get a job recapping tires. Word from the East and from Texas is that both Ginsberg and Burroughs have been arrested. They are not to hear from Ginsberg who was institutionalized for almost a year, and it is only through reading JOHN CLELLON HOLMES's novel GO that they learn the story of his arrest. Carolyn learns of her second pregnancy and is almost fired from her job by a male doctor because of her condition, but his partner, a woman general practitioner, starts her own office and takes Carolyn with her. Neal is writing long letters to Kerouac and persuades him to come to San Francisco. Carolyn finds herself having to watch over them as if they are children, but they invite her out one night to see the town with them. Her description of this night reveals the myth of the Beat lifestyle. Most of the night is spent standing around trying to score for marijuana and being entertained by pathetic strippers. Still, Carolyn is upset that her conventional upbringing prevents her from enjoying this scene the way Neal and

Kerouac can. Another friend shows up, Henri Cru, and his enthusiasm over Neal's seemingly perfect domestic life heightens Carolyn's fury. She throws them all out; the next day, a note from Neal written by Helen Hinkle tells Carolyn that this time he is gone for good. Carolyn is now a single mother with another child on the way and has neither a husband nor reliable friends.

Helen Hinkle emerges as one of the heroes of the book. When Carolyn is at her lowest and starting to use amphetamines, Helen shows up at her doorstep. Carolyn shares her amphetamines with Helen and they talk nonstop for two days, mainly about their grievances against their husbands. Helen and Carolyn decide to be roommates and for Helen to take care of Cathy while Carolyn continues to work until her pregnancy keeps her from doing so.

In January 1950 Carolyn received a phone call from Diana Hansen, a woman who identified herself as Neal's New York girlfriend and who was pregnant with his child. Diana wants Carolyn to get a divorce, but Carolyn demands that Neal ask for it himself. Jami is born to Carolyn on January 26, 1950. Later that year, Neal goes to Mexico with Kerouac in part to obtain a divorce from Carolyn to marry Diana, but he evidently never files the papers and lies about it to Diana when they bigamously marry on July 10. Two hours after this marriage, he is back on the road to seek work out West—and to reunite with Carolyn.

Neal is called away to a railroad job in San Luis Obispo, and Carolyn writes to him about their relationship. At this time a struggle is going on between Carolyn and Diana for Neal as husband and provider, although Diana is in the weaker position. Diana's son is born in November 1950. The other news from New York is that Kerouac has married Joan Haverty, the former girlfriend of the recently deceased Bill Cannastra. In December 1950 Carolyn and Neal celebrate their first Christmas together as a family. Carolyn discovers that she is pregnant again. To her relief, Neal is enthusiastic about the situation.

Neal and Carolyn celebrate their third anniversary in comparative harmony. They go into therapy together to keep their marriage functioning. Neal starts to write long Proust-like letters to

Kerouac, including the famous Joan Anderson letter (December 17, 1951). This letter influenced Kerouac's writing style. Carolyn's son is born on September 9, and they name him after Kerouac and Ginsberg: John Allen Cassady. Carolyn felt relieved that she had finally given Neal a son, but Neal would be plagued by guilt because of his inadequacy as a role model for John Allen. In January 1952, Kerouac moved in with the Cassadys. He is initially shy around Carolyn. He moves into the attic where Carolyn has made him a desk for writing, and he works as a brakeman during these months. Carolyn's ability to live with both men is tested when Neal and Kerouac sneak home a prostitute one night. Kerouac later apologizes to her by inscribing a copy of The TOWN AND THE CITY with a message that says "it will never happen again." Later they all sit around, drink, and talk into a tape recorder. This conversation might be included in the transcripts from Kerouac's VISIONS OF CODY, in which Carolyn makes a brief appearance.

Neal draws a two-week stay in San Luis Obispo. Carolyn and Kerouac are nervous about being left alone together, but Neal actually encourages their intimacy. This embarrasses both Carolyn and Kerouac, and Kerouac spends most of the two weeks staying with a friend. When Neal returns, he casually says he is disappointed that Carolyn and Kerouac did not make love. Carolyn is furious and decides to seduce Kerouac.

Kerouac is initially shy, and Carolyn calculatedly seduces him with wine and jazz. The relationship works: she finally feels included in Neal's and Kerouac's lives; even more, she feels central. She speculates that Neal likes the set-up because he feels less tied down when a rival lover is with her. Carolyn finds her self-confidence growing. But Kerouac's ex-wife Joan Haverty pressures him for child support, and he decides to go to Mexico. Carolyn and Neal move to San Jose in August 1952. Kerouac moves back in with them. Neal has taken a job on the railroad and has to leave that first night, leaving Kerouac and Carolyn alone. He tells Carolyn sentiments that never occur between him and Carolyn in his novels. Kerouac seems to love the children, too. Eventually, Neal resents that Kerouac wishes to spend more time with his wife and children than with him, and they have a

falling out. Kerouac retreats to a skid-row hotel in San Francisco but soon rejoins Carolyn and Neal. In December 1952, Kerouac is laid off from the railroad. He plans to go to Mexico and to take Carolyn with him. In spite of Neal's seeming openness to the affair, he comes up with a counterplan. He takes Kerouac to Mexico himself. In Mexico City, Kerouac writes to Carolyn to join him. Carolyn hesitates, Kerouac grows lonely, and he goes back to his family in North Carolina.

Neal seriously injures his foot while working in April 1953. They invite Kerouac to stay with them while he recovers. However, the three-way relationship no longer works. Kerouac moves in with a student named Al Sublette and returns to New York. Depressed by his injury and prolonged legal battles, Neal's personality goes blank. In 1954 Neal and Carolyn jointly and powerfully embrace Edgar Cayce's philosophy. In sum, Cayce says that self-condemnation or guilt only keeps one on the same path that led to these feelings. Cayce teaches substituting a positive attitude about life—expect the best, not the worst. Cayce also believed in reincarnation as an evolutionary path, a concept that the Cassadys embraced as well. For Neal, his self-destructive acts revealed the guilt that he felt from his actions in previous lives. For Carolyn, Cayce taught her to let go of her anger over Neal's actions. In an odd synchronicity, Kerouac arrives in January 1954 ready to share his newfound spiritual enthusiasm, Buddhism. However, Kerouac cannot make Buddhism compatible with Cayce, and the "magic circle" of 1952 breaks down.

In March 1954 the railroad settled with Neal for a sum amounting to $16,000 after lawyer fees. Ginsberg finally arrives, fresh from his adventures in Mexico. Carolyn has not seen him for seven years since the scene in her Denver apartment, and she is nervous, but he puts her at ease by being the perfect guest. She assumes that his passion for Neal is over. She is wrong and walks in on them for the second time. This time, she is sorry to see Ginsberg go. With the insurance settlement, they buy a house in Los Gatos in August 1954. In retrospect, Carolyn realizes that there is no room for Kerouac in this house, and indeed Kerouac never feels comfortable in the house. Carolyn says that their first year in the house was among her best with Neal.

Unfortunately, Neal's job gives him more and more opportunities for extended visits to San Francisco. He falls in love with Natalie Jackson after falling in love with a portrait of her by Robert LaVigne (just as Ginsberg had fallen in love with LaVigne's portrait of Peter Orlovsky before meeting him). In spite of Carolyn's attempts to be tolerant, Neal moves to San Francisco to share an apartment with Ginsberg and Orlovsky.

Kerouac returns to San Francisco, and Neal brings him to Carolyn's for a visit. A scene develops on which Kerouac's play *The Beat Generation* and the film *Pull My Daisy* are based. Neal leaves Kerouac alone with Carolyn that night, and they resume their intimacy. The next day, they all go to the racetrack, and Neal explains his sure-fire betting scheme: Always bet the third-choice horse. Carolyn is soon to find out that Neal has been raiding their savings account to finance his gambling habit. He has manipulated Natalie into posing as Carolyn and forging her signature on withdrawal slips. Neal hits bottom soon. Natalie commits suicide while eluding a police officer who is trying to help her down from a fire escape.

Soon after, Ginsberg and Kerouac become famous (or infamous) with the publications of *HOWL AND OTHER POEMS* and *ON THE ROAD* respectively. Neal, on the other hand, continues to battle his demons and tries to expiate his guilt over Natalie's death by making a fortune at the racetrack. Of course, he loses. Neal actually attends the famous "Howl" censorship trial during layovers in San Francisco. No one knows that he is the famous "secret hero" of the poem. When the reviews of *On the Road* come out, Neal and Carolyn are shocked by the viciousness of many of the critics. Neal is upset by their psychoanalysis of Dean Moriarty as a "madman." In February 1958 Neal is arrested for possession of two marijuana cigarettes and is accused of being involved in a drug-smuggling ring on the railroad. Neal's celebrity as the model for Dean Moriarty was seen by him and Carolyn as a factor in the arrest. Carolyn watches in horror as Neal is handcuffed in the living room of their house and taken off to jail. In the next few chapters, she writes an indictment of America's police and legal system. Neal is released from prison—but only briefly. The feds obtain a new warrant, and

Neal goes back to jail. He becomes desperate. To obtain a separate trial, he needs to be released on bail, but bail is set exorbitantly high. To raise bail, Carolyn would have to take out a mortgage on the house. She refuses, in spite of Neal's pleas. This decision, which results in Neal unnecessarily receiving a lengthy prison sentence, she regrets. He is sentenced for five years to life and will actually serve about two and a half years.

Carolyn supports the family by doing make-up and costumes for a Wild West show and by working for the drama club at the University of Santa Cruz. She admits to feeling an odd security while Neal is in prison because she always knows where he is. Kerouac offers to help with money, but none materializes. In prison Neal meets Gavin Arthur, a friend of GARY SNYDER. Through Arthur, both Snyder and Ginsberg give prison readings. Kerouac is invited to read but drinks too much the night before and is unable to keep the date.

Neal is released on June 3, 1960. Kerouac visits in July 1960 in the company of LEW WELCH. Neal breaks his parole on day trips to Big Sur with Kerouac, Welch, LAWRENCE FERLINGHETTI, and PHILIP WHALEN. Carolyn, Neal, and the children drive up to Big Sur one day and surprise Kerouac, his girlfriend, MICHAEL McCLURE, and his wife Joanna. Kerouac openly flirts with Carolyn. Unfortunately, this would be the last time that she would ever see him. Carolyn eventually reads Kerouac's portrait of her in *BIG SUR* and is once again upset that he never portrays his love for her honestly.

Neal's parole lasts three years. The last straw for Carolyn comes in fall 1962 when she is encouraged by Neal to take the children to a Cayce conference. Left at home, Neal brings home a woman (later identified as Anne Murphy, Neal's girlfriend from 1961 to his death) and her disturbed child, who tears up the house. Carolyn tells Neal that it is time for a divorce. Kerouac advises them against it, believing that the root of their problems is simply financial. Divorced and no longer on parole in summer 1963, Neal quite naturally embarks on a road trip, this time with a group called The Merry Pranksters whose leader is KEN KESEY. Neal becomes a famous counterculture figure with the Pranksters, and Carolyn struggles to raise teenagers who idolize Neal for his irreverent behavior. Carolyn and Helen Hinkle are invited to the final "acid test" by the Pranksters, who are now fugitives from the law, which is depicted as quite dull. Carolyn struggles to keep Neal's influence on his teenage children to a minimum, but he is irresistible. She decides that the best way to break the spell cast by his fame is to throw a birthday party for him and to invite all of the famous people whom her children and their friends want to meet. This party, held in spring 1966, draws Ginsberg, Kesey, members of the Grateful Dead, and other heroes of the counterculture. Already tending toward psychosis and under the influence of drugs, Neal degenerates mentally. Carolyn last sees him at a New Year's Eve dinner party in 1967. Neal is disoriented and barely recognizes her. Soon thereafter, he moves to San Miguel de Allende, Mexico, to escape the law. On February 4, 1968, Carolyn receives a call that Neal is dead.

Carolyn does not want Ginsberg and Kerouac to find out about Neal's death through the newspapers and tells them personally by phone. Ginsberg is subdued by the news. Kerouac is drunk. Carolyn asks that Neal's body be cremated. After four months of confusing negotiations, the ashes arrive in an urn. The eulogies for Neal in the official press are brief, but in the underground press they are fervent. Kerouac calls Carolyn and tells her that he will be joining Neal soon; he does, in fact, seven months later. The eulogies for Kerouac are lengthier but mixed. The final section of the book returns to Carolyn's feud with Diana Hansen. She tries to get Carolyn to split Neal's ashes with her. Carolyn is furious, and only after many phone calls does she relent and give her a spoonful. Diane then surprises her with the sensible suggestion that she will have Neal's ashes sprinkled on Kerouac's grave. The book ends on this note of resolution to the decades-long quarrel between the two women.

For those interested in hearing a woman's perspective regarding the Beat scene, Carolyn Cassady's book is particularly insightful. It is also a memoir that sheds some light on the events not depicted by the Beat writers. Maybe most importantly it also shows to some extent how the Beats fictionalized and romanticized their lives in their works.

Rob Johnson

Old Angel Midnight Jack Kerouac (1993)

Old Angel Midnight might be the purest instance of JACK KEROUAC's spontaneous prose to reach publication. Indefinable in terms of genre—one cannot accurately label it novel, memoir, or poem—*Old Angel Midnight* remains one of Kerouac's least known works. Unpublished in one volume until 1993, the book blends word play and the unfocused musings of a poet's mind as Kerouac attempts to record "the sounds of the entire world . . . swimming" through his window. Kerouac worked on the project on and off for several years and later wrote that "it is the only book I've ever written in which I allow myself the right to say anything I want, absolutely and positively anything." Seen in that light, *Old Angel Midnight* may stand as one of the loosest, least edited books ever published. The book offers an unadulterated look into the fluid associations in the nexus of incidental sounds and Kerouac's imagination.

Biographer Ann Charters reports that Kerouac began to write *Old Angel Midnight* on May 28, 1956, after a night of drinking with two companions, Bob Donlin and Al Sublette, to whom he had boasted that he was William Shakespeare reincarnated. To make good on his boast, he set about producing a jazzy, rambling, pun-loaded prose that was inflected by what he thought of as Shakespearean tone. Kerouac initially wrote in a cottage in Mill Valley on the slopes of Mount Tamalpais on the California coast, where he had been staying with GARY SNYDER. When Snyder sailed for Japan on May 15, Kerouac remained in the cottage for another month before departing for a fire lookout job in the Cascade Range. MICHAEL McCLURE, who spent time with Kerouac during his time at the cottage, recalls that Kerouac read to him some portions of *Old Angel Midnight* and told him that it was a long, spontaneous project that he hoped to work on for years. McClure states, "*Old Angel Midnight* is a pirate's treasure chest. I can sit for a long time running the fingers of my mind through the shining doubloons and emeralds and pull out a crusty necklace of pearls and precious stones draped with sea moss." The writing became an ongoing project that provided Kerouac with release for his creative energies and also helped him maintain his spontaneous prose style during the times when he was not writing books actively. Kerouac's working title for the project was *Lucien Midnight,* for by 1956 Kerouac had determined to write books about his friends, and the speaker's voice is influenced in part by Lucien Carr. In various other writings, Kerouac had captured Carr's intonation as part menacing snarl, part insinuation, part playful bully. The language also features toss-off Shakespearean mimicry, such as "ending up nowhere & ne'er e'en born." The prose also is flavored by Buddhist terms and concepts throughout, from "Visions of the Tathagata's Seat of Purity & Womb" to made-up phrases that vaguely echo Hindu terms, such as *paryoumemga sikarem nora sarkadium.* Clearly, however, the biggest influence in the language comes from James Joyce, whom Kerouac greatly admired. Biographer Gerald Nicosia wrote that "in its ambitious scope as well as verbal ingenuity, *Old Angel Midnight* may indeed be the closest thing to *Finnegans Wake* in American literature."

Old Angel Midnight is divided into 67 sections. Although the sections vary in length, they average roughly one section per published page. The first section begins "Friday afternoon in the universe" and announces the rationale, such as it is, for the writing. The speaker sets out to tell a "vast" tale that includes everything in the universe as witnessed through his window. Initially, the speaker focuses on the sounds that roll in as one word leads to the next in terms of sound rather than semantics: "pones tics perts parts pans pools palls pails parturiences and petty Thieveries." The first section ends with a reference to Carr, personified as "old Sound," who comes home after work to "drink his beer & tweak his children's eyes—." The second section intensifies the speaker's reliance on sound, "the sonora de madrigal," by introducing onomatopeia: *bardoush* and *flaki;* the latter may represent the sound of a chain saw stalling in the log, but one may also experience the word simply for its sound. Kerouac repeatedly sets up the reader to anticipate actual meaning, only to undercut the reader's expectation. For example, "—God why did you make the world? Answer:—Because I gwt pokla renamash ta va in ming the atss are you forever with it?" The reply may represent a riddle that implies that God will not answer the question, at least not in a way that average people understand.

The reply may also be interpreted in various ways, depending on how one "translates" the language. Is *gwt* merely a mistyping of *get* (*e* and *w* are adjacent on the keypad) that set the writer off in a new direction? Ought one rearrange various letters to find new words such as *renaming* and *ass?* James Joyce's readers have been rewarded by dissecting *Finnegans Wake* to identify various languages that work together with puns and neologisms to reveal the ordered whole of the novel. Kerouac's work is not unified in that way. Instead, he is telling his reader, among other things, to move along with the sounds of words as one might with the sounds of the evening, to experience it without trying to make sense of the story.

Sections 1 through 49 were published as "Old Angel Midnight" in *Big Table* I (Spring 1959), edited by Irving Rosenthal. Kerouac not only gave the magazine its title but was indirectly responsible for its creation. Rosenthal edited the *Chicago Review,* published under the auspices of the University of Chicago. The Winter 1958 issue would have featured Kerouac's "Old Angel Midnight," along with 10 episodes of WILLIAM S. BURROUGHS's *NAKED LUNCH,* had it not been suppressed by the university's administration. According to Rosenthal, the administrators refused to allow the publication of "four-letter words," and when negotiations broke down, Rosenthal and six of seven staff members quit. Rosenthal went on to found *Big Table* and published the suppressed works in its first issue. Kerouac hoped that the publication of "Old Angel Midnight," along with the concurrent publication of selections from what would become *VISIONS OF CODY,* would convince literary critics of his artistic merit. The recent publication of *The DHARMA BUMS* had given some critics the impression that Kerouac was merely cashing in on the success of *ON THE ROAD* and not producing serious artistic literature.

In spring 1959, LAWRENCE FERLINGHETTI was interested in publishing "Old Angel Midnight" in book form, and Kerouac told him that he had 5,000 new words to add, making the new publication distinct from the *Big Table* publication. Kerouac assessed his ongoing project for Ginsberg: "I feel silly writing Old Angel tho because it is an awful raving madness, could make me go mad, I'm ashamed of it, but must admit it reads great, I wish other writers wd [sic] join me I feel lonely in my silliness writing like this is space prose for the future and people of the present time will only laugh at me, o well let em laugh." Kerouac even rendered an ink-and-pastel drawing for the cover. Copyright complications doomed the City Lights publication, though, as Rosenthal insisted that *Big Table* owned the rights to the work. *Evergreen Review* later published "Old Angel Midnight Part Two" (sections 50 through 67) in the August/September 1964 issue.

Old Angel Midnight held high value for its creator. Kerouac sometimes regretted his experimentation with language because he believed that his experimental style took a toll on his popular acceptance as a writer. However, after an experience with Mescaline in October 1959, Kerouac found confirmation of his artistic instincts. Recounting the profundity of the experience, he wrote to ALLEN GINSBERG, "Most miraculous of all was the sensational revelation that I've been on the right track with spontaneous never-touch-up poetry of immediate report, and Old Angel Midnight most especially, opening out a new world connection in literature with the endless spaces of Shakti Maya illusion."

Bibliography

Kerouac, Jack. *Selected Letters, 1957–1969.* Edited by Ann Charters. New York: Viking, 1999.

McClure, Michael. "Jack's *Old Angel Midnight.*" *Old Angel Midnight,* by Jack Kerouac. San Francisco: Grey Fox Press, 1993, xiii–xxi.

Nicosia, Gerald. *Memory Babe: A Critical Biography of Jack Kerouac.* New York: Grove Press, 1983.

Matt Theado

Olson, Charles (1910–1970)

If KENNETH REXROTH can be seen as a father figure of the Beat Generation on the West Coast, then Charles Olson can be seen as a father figure of the Beat Generation on the East Coast. He was mentor to ROBERT CREELEY, ED DORN (who wrote "What I See in *The MAXIMUS POEMS,*" one of the most important critical evaluations of Olson's masterpiece), JOHN WIENERS, and ED SANDERS (who tried to romantically involve Olson with the great blues singer Janis Joplin). His groundbreaking essay

"Projective Verse" appeared in 1950. It opened up the field of poetry and continues to stimulate poetic imaginations to this day. Olson writes:

> It is the advantage of the typewriter that, due to its rigidity and its space precisions, it can, for a poet, indicate exactly the breath, the pauses, the suspensions even of syllables, the juxtapositions even of parts of phrases, which he intends. For the first time the poet has the stave and the bar a musician has had. For the first time he can, without the convention of rime and meter, record the listening he has done to his own speech and by that one act indicate how he would want any reader, silently or otherwise, to voice his work.

The imagination of the poet, argues Olson, should be conveyed through the poet's breath. This essay helped modern American poetry, like that of the Beats and their contemporaries, become something more for the ears than something for the eyes.

On December 27, 1910, Olson was born in Worcester, Massachusetts, also the home of ABBIE HOFFMAN and not far from JACK KEROUAC's Lowell. After being highly involved in the Democratic Party, Olson was inspired to pursue a literary career by his visits to St. Elizabeth's Hospital to see Ezra Pound, for whom he acted as an informal literary secretary. (DIANE DI PRIMA would also visit Pound in the hospital where the treasonable old poet was kept by the government after World War II.) *Call Me Ishmael,* Olson's seminal study of Herman Melville's *Moby-Dick* appeared in 1947, which Pound helped him publish. Olson eventually broke ties with Pound over Pound's anti-Semitism. As the rector of Black Mountain College in North Carolina, Olson would become the central figure of the poets known as the Black Mountain School, which included, according to Donald Allen's *The NEW AMERICAN POETRY, 1945–1960,* Creeley, Dorn, Robert Duncan, Joel Oppenheimer, Jonathan Williams, Paul Blackburn, Paul Carroll, Larry Eigner, and Denise Levertov. These were poets published in the important magazines *Origin* and *Black Mountain Review.* Olson also saw the Beats as fellow travelers in his poetic movement (though he would be spurred into head-butting GREGORY CORSO after a poetry reading and was jealous of the Beats' media attention) and even predicted the success of WIL-LIAM S. BURROUGHS's prose. Ginsberg, an admirer of Olson's poetry (though Corso was not), convinced Olson to partake in TIMOTHY LEARY's psilocybin experiments, and Olson became an advocate of the drug. Dorn claims that Olson "never met a substance he didn't like." Leary called Olson "the father of modern poetry." Olson also was a guide for Arthur Koestler's psilocybin trip with Leary, though he startled the author of *Darkness at Noon* with a toy gun. Olson later tripped with Sanders on psilocybin that he received from Leary.

Near the end of his life, Olson taught at the University of Connecticut at Storrs, where the esteemed Beat scholar Ann Charters later taught, but he had to resign due to illness. Kerouac, another admirer of Olson, made a pilgrimage to visit Olson near the end of their lives. From 1950 until Olson's death on January 10, 1970, from liver cancer, Olson worked on his masterpiece, *The Maximus Poems*, a monumental epic poem that examined Gloucester, Massachusetts, a place of high significance for Olson both as a child and as a dying giant of letters. Sanders, one of Olson's poetic heirs, put a section of the poem to music to be performed by his folk-rock band The Fugs. Duncan, Creeley, and Dorn visited the dying poet near the end. Ginsberg, Wieners, and Sanders attended his funeral.

Bibliography

Clark, Tom. *Charles Olson: The Allegory of a Poet's Life.* New York: W. W. Norton, 1991.

Olson, Charles. "Projective Verse." *The New American Poetry, 1945–1960,* edited by Donald Allen. 1960. Reprint, Berkeley: University of California Press, 1999, 386–397.

Kurt Hemmer

One Flew over the Cuckoo's Nest
Ken Kesey (1962)

This novel is KEN KESEY's first and most commercially successful novel. The immediate success of this work pushed the young author into the countercultural spotlight where he would serve as a bridge between the earlier Beats and the hippies of

the 1960s. The novel was inspired by Kesey's stint as a hospital aide for the Veteran's Administration in Menlo Park, California. While working there, Kesey was introduced to hallucinogens as a volunteer test subject.

In this novel, Kesey establishes one of the major themes that he will develop in his later fiction, the conflict between a strong-willed individual and a community that demands conformity to a universal standard. The characters Randle Patrick McMurphy and Nurse Mildred Ratched represent these two opposing forces in *Cuckoo's Nest,* as does Hank Stamper and the community of union loggers in SOMETIMES A GREAT NOTION. Although some commentators have described McMurphy as irresponsible to a fault, he is perhaps best seen as a trickster figure, something completely antithetical to the values of conformist 1950s America, the setting of the novel. Kesey's narrator is Chief Bromden, a schizophrenic half Native-American inmate at a Portland, Oregon, mental hospital. He is suspicious of Nurse Ratched, the "Big Nurse," who is in charge of the Chief's ward. This somewhat unreliable narrator allows Kesey to create a claustrophobic and paranoid depiction of the hospital's staff, who represent the conformity-driven society outside the institution with which all of the inmates must fall in line if they are to "fit in." They are, according to the Chief, the "Combine" of America.

Into this situation comes Randle Patrick McMurphy, a prisoner at a local labor camp who has had himself committed to shirk his duties. McMurphy is the classic American hero, larger than life and full of contempt for Big Nurse and the control she represents. He is also a Beat hero, similar to Dean Morarity in JACK KEROUAC's ON THE ROAD, whose almost excessive exuberance has a positive influence on those around him, even as it destroys him. As the novel progresses, McMurphy and Ratched engage in a series of head-to-head conflicts that eventually make the inmates devoted disciples of McMurphy and threaten to erode the control that Ratched has over them.

While the inmates such as Chief Bromden start out as observers of McMurphy's seemingly bizarre behavior, they are soon willing participants in his antics. After a series of adventures including a fishing trip, McMurphy is subjected to electroshock treatments. This torture session makes him into even more of a Christ figure, suffering for his followers. (McMurphy himself asks if he is to receive a crown of thorns for the session.) Despite the electric shocks to his skull, McMurphy returns to his nonconformist activities. To top the fishing trip, McMurphy organizes a party, complete with alcohol and prostitutes that are smuggled into the ward. The sexual component to this scene is important for the characters in the novel, who seem to be emasculated. Dale Harding is afraid of his own sexuality despite being married to a beautiful woman, and Billy Bibbit is as much under his mother's control as he is under Nurse Ratched's. After their exposure to this wilder side of masculinity, Dale hatches a plan for escape, and Billy becomes more assertive.

This is not to last, though, as Big Nurse steps in. Reasserting her control over the inmates, she belittles Billy into a state resembling his earlier childlike self. This regression pushes Billy to suicide. This precipitates a final confrontation between Ratched and McMurphy, during which he physically attacks her. In this fight McMurphy rips open Big Nurse's uniform, revealing her previously hidden breasts, symbolically revealing her as a "real" woman rather than a controlling figure. McMurphy is overpowered in the fight by an attendant. His punishment for this violent outburst is severe: a lobotomy. When McMurphy is returned to the ward in a vegetative state, he can no longer serve as an inspiration for the inmates. Following his Christ-figure path, McMurphy must be martyred. Chief Bromden uses his massive physical strength to smother McMurphy with a pillow. The Chief then symbolically breaks out of his self-imposed silence by breaking out of the asylum and running across the hospital's lawn toward the highway in the distance.

One Flew over the Cuckoo's Nest was extremely popular from the time of its publication and was one of the most assigned contemporary American novels in college-level courses during the 1970s. The continued success of the novel is perhaps due to the dichotomy between Ratched and McMurphy, which can be reinterpreted to incorporate successive social concerns. The novel is set in the 1950s when reaction against middle-class sub-

urbanite conformity was a major concern for many of the Beat writers. During the 1960s and early 1970s Ratched could stand for the "establishment" against which the hippies were reacting. In the 1980s and into the 21st century, Ratched can stand for the increasing presence of controlling technology in everyday life. Against all of these symbols for a repressive social structure stands McMurphy, the symbol of old-fashioned American individuality at the core of the Beat and hippie ethos.

One Flew over the Cuckoo's Nest was adapted for film in 1975 and directed by Milos Forman. The film, starring Jack Nicholson as McMurphy was a popular and critical success and earned six Academy Awards. The film is told with McMurphy as the central character, so Kesey's use of Bromden as a schizophrenic, filtering narrator is all but lost. The book was also adapted as a play on Broadway with Kirk Douglas as McMurphy in 1963. It was later revived by the Steppenwolf Theatre Company in Chicago in 2001.

Bibliography
Leeds, Barry, *Ken Kesey*, New York: Unger, 1981.
Porter, Gilbert M. *The Art of Grit: Ken Kesey's Fiction.* Columbia: University of Missouri Press, 1982.

Donovan Braud

On the Road Jack Kerouac (1957)

JACK KEROUAC's *On the Road* has been called the Bible of the Beat Generation and is arguably the most important literary text to come out of that movement. In his review of the book in 1957 for the *New York Times*, Gilbert Millstein wrote, "Just as more than any other novel of the Twenties, *The Sun Also Rises* came to be regarded as the testament of the 'Lost Generation,' so it seems certain that *On the Road* will come to be known as that of the 'Beat Generation.'" Kerouac wrote the original manuscript of the novel in three weeks as one continuous paragraph on taped-together 12-foot strips of onionskin paper. The novel would not be published until six years later.

The novel begins by introducing the main relationship between Sal Paradise (based on Kerouac) and Dean Moriarty (based on NEAL CASSADY). Sal has just divorced his wife, just as Kerouac had divorced his first wife, Edie Parker, and feels "that everything was dead." (In fact, *On the Road* was written in part to Kerouac's second wife, Joan Haverty, as a way of explaining his life to her.) Dean becomes the rejuvenating spark of life that Sal needs. Dean, who meets Sal through Chad King (based on Hal Chase), is portrayed as an irresistible but harmless con man who wants Sal to teach him how to write. He watches Sal write and enthuses about writing that is not "all hung-up on like literary inhibitions and grammatical fears" (sentiments straight from letters Cassady sent to Kerouac). Dean is a breath of fresh air from the West who says "Yes" as opposed to the East's "No." He has a cowboy's charm and freshness and even looks like a young Gene Autry. He also reminds Sal of a "long lost brother," an aspect of Cassady's relationship with Kerouac that is emphasized in letters from this time. Kerouac saw a mystical significance in the fact that Cassady was born about the same time that Kerouac's brother Gerard, immortalized in VISIONS OF GERARD, died. Sal's primary interest in Dean is explained in one of the novel's most memorable lines that describes Dean and Carlo Marx (based on ALLEN GINSBERG): "But then they danced down the streets like dingledodies, and I shambled after as I've been doing all my life after people who interest me, because the only people for me are the mad ones, the ones who are mad to live, mad to talk, mad to be saved, desirous of everything at the same time, the ones who never yawn or say a commonplace thing, but burn, burn, burn like fabulous yellow roman candles exploding like spiders across the stars and in the middle you see the blue centerlight pop and everybody goes 'Awww!'" Dean and Carlo take to each other to the exclusion of Sal. Yet the sexual nature of the relationship between Cassady and Ginsberg is only hinted at in the novel.

Sal is invited by a prep-school friend, Remi Boncoeur (based on Henri Cru), to join him in San Francisco, where they can then ship out together. On the way, he plans to stop off in Denver to see Chad, Carlo, and Dean. His plan is to hitch all the way from New York to California by following Route 6. His first day ends in disappointment as he is stranded 40 miles north of New York City in the countryside near Bear Mountain.

After Bear Mountain, he takes a bus (instead of hitching) to Chicago, where he briefly samples the bop nightclubs before beginning his travels proper. The following chapters are travelogues recreated from notebooks that Kerouac kept during his 1947 journey west. He hitches from Chicago west into Iowa, where he sees the Mississippi River for the first time. A series of rides in trucks take him across the Iowa prairies. In Des Moines, he spends the night in a YMCA and wakes up disoriented, unable to remember who he is or where he is. He feels like a "ghost," and marks this point as being "the dividing line between the East of my youth and the West of my future." He rides across the Midwest entertained by a truck driver who tells him about the Depression; Kerouac recorded such unembellished tales in his notebooks from the time. In Shelton, Nebraska, he is temporarily stranded.

The book is a youthful one and is full of superlatives. Such sentiments turned off some early readers (as Dan Wakefield says of himself in *New York in the Fifties*) who did not understand that this language accurately captures Sal's enthusiasm. For example, Kerouac describes "the greatest ride of his life" with two young blond farmers who are delivering farm machinery to California and who pick up every hitchhiker along the way, allowing them to sit out the long journey on a flatbed trailer. With Denver as his destination, he leaves the farmlands of the Platte behind and descends into the rangelands. In Wyoming he congratulates himself on how far he has come since Bear Mountain. However, in Cheyenne, Wyoming, he witnesses "Wild West Week" and is depressed at how the West had betrayed its traditions for entertainment.

Sal says good-bye to the Minnesotans and stays in Cheyenne, wandering through the street party. He meets a beautiful blond and wants to pick prairie flowers for her, but all she wants to do is leave Wyoming and head to New York. He tells her that there is nothing there. He spends all his money on this fruitless romance and laments that he has tarnished the spiritual nature of his pilgrimage. He hitches out of Cheyenne the next morning and sees the Rocky Mountains for the first time. He is let off in Denver on Larimer Street.

Because he does not know Dean that well at the time, he first looks up Chad in Denver. Chad is an anthropology student and works at a local museum. When he asks about Dean, he finds that Dean and Carlo are in exile in the Denver community. Dean was the son of a Denver wino, and Chad and his crowd come from Denver society, including Roland Major.

Roland Major (based on Bob Burford), is a Hemingwayesque writer who represents the "arty" types that alienate Dean, even if Roland himself makes fun of them in his stories. Sal finally contacts Dean through Carlo, who tells him all about Dean's schedule, which includes having relationships with two or three women at the same time. Camille (based on CAROLYN CASSADY), then a Denver art student, and Marylou (based on Lu-Anne Henderson), are the important women in Dean's life. Dean answers Sal's knock on his apartment door naked, and Sal sees an undressed Camille on the couch and also a nude study that she has drawn of Dean. Sal refers to Carlo's "Denver Doldrum" poems, which is the title of a series of poems that Ginsberg wrote in the late 1940s in Denver and that dramatize (albeit indirectly) his frustrated desire for the promiscuous Cassady.

Kerouac re-creates Cassady and Ginsberg's nightlong conversations in which they attempted to be completely honest and straight with each other. Both men shared a capacity for this kind of extended analysis and debate, but Sal falls asleep listening to them. Carlo dismisses Sal as a "Wolfean" (a term derived from the name of author Thomas Wolfe)—a reference to the division between Wolfeans (heterosexual, all-American types) and non-Wolfeans (homosexual, cosmopolitan types) that was made one night in the fall of 1945 by Kerouac, Ginsberg, Hal Chase, and WILLIAM S. BURROUGHS.

Sal mingles with the "arty" types who put on an opera every season in Central City, two miles up in the mountains in rich silver-mining country. The opera that year is *Fidelio,* and Sal relates to the "gloom" of the central character, who rises up onstage carrying a boulder on his back. He wishes that Carlo and Dean were there, but he

knows that they would feel out of place, even if they could understand his feelings of gloom. Sal says, "They were like the man with the dungeon stone and the gloom, rising from underground, the sordid hipsters of America, a new beat generation that I was slowly joining." Sal celebrates wildly that night in an abandoned mining shack, and there he looks east and imagines their raucous laughter being silenced. Throughout the book, the East is associated with repression and a silencing of Sal's enthusiasm. By the time he wrote *On the Road,* Kerouac was embittered by the East with its New York publishing industry and by the poor sales of his first book, *The TOWN AND THE CITY,* which he believed his editors had destroyed with extensive cuts and forced revision.

Sal realizes that during his entire Denver stay he has not talked to Dean enough—a refrain of the book, which has the structure of an obstructed romance. Talk is more important than sex here. Sal sleeps with a woman named Rita and despairs that, postcoitus, they cannot talk honestly.

Sal takes the bus from Denver to San Francisco and is dropped off at Market and Fourth. In nearby Mill City, he stays with Remi, whom is living with a sour woman named Lee Ann. Sal wants to write a screenplay that he will sell to Hollywood, but he can only write a gloomy story. The screenplay a failure, he has to go to work with Remi as a security guard. In an ill-fitting uniform, he looks like Charlie Chaplin playing a cop. He works at a dockside barracks, and his job is to make sure that drunken sailors who are shipping out to Okinawa do not tear down the quarters. Sal critiques America's police-state mentality, similar to Burroughs's views in *JUNKY.* His stay with Remi and Lee Ann falls apart when the money runs out; then Sal embarrasses Remi at a dinner with Remi's stepfather. At the end of his stay, as he did in Denver, he climbs a mountain and looks east, this time seeing something "holy" there and finding California by comparison "emptyheaded."

He hitches south to Los Angeles and is stranded in Bakersfield, where, at the bus station, he instantly falls in love with the "cutest little Mexican girl," Terry. She is on the run from an abusive husband back in Fresno, and Terry and Sal take to each other in their mutual loneliness. However, both suspect each other: He thinks that she may be a prostitute, and she thinks that he might be a clever pimp. They confess their suspicions in a hotel room and afterward make love. This part of the novel was excerpted in *The Paris Review* (Winter 1955) and titled "The Mexican Girl" and can be found in *The Best American Short Stories 1956*. It was one of Kerouac's few publications in the period between *The Town and the City* and *On the Road*.

Terry and Sal decide to hitchhike to New York together, and they first head south to Los Angeles where Terry can get some money and clothes. In Los Angeles's crowded main street Sal is reminded of Elmer Hassel (based on HERBERT HUNCKE). Various plans fall through, and they hitch back to Sabinal, where Terry has left her son, and they meet up with her brother Ricky. For a week or so, Sal lives the shiftless life of a migrant farm worker in California's San Joaquin Valley. They think that he is a Mexican, and he says "in a way I am," a reference to Kerouac's belief that his "Canuck" ethnicity links him to other immigrant Americans. Sal is a poor fieldhand, though, and cannot pick enough cotton to support Terry and her son (who is a better cotton picker than Sal). When winter comes and they have no stove in their tent, Sal's old life of writing in New York begins to call him back. They make vague plans to reunite in New York. The separation from Terry is quick and, on Sal's part, callous: "Well, lackadaddy, I was on the road again."

Sal returns from the West Coast to the home of his aunt (based on Kerouac's mother), who lives in Paterson, New Jersey. He takes a bus all the way to Pittsburgh but has to hitchhike the last part of the journey. Wandering in the dark on a back country road that follows a river, he meets a crazy old man whom he calls the Ghost of the Susquehanna. His strange stories teach Sal that "there is a wilderness in the East," not just out West. By this point he is near starving; unfortunately, he hitches a ride with a man who believes in the revitalizing power of voluntary starvation. Before he knows it, he is dropped off in the middle of Times Square, and his road-wasted eyes see it clearly as a place where materialism has gone mad, an important theme in this and subsequent works by Kerouac. At his aunt's house he learns that Dean had re-

cently been there. Once again, they just miss each other.

Sal does not see Dean again for a year. He finishes his novel (based on *The Town and the City*) and is staying with his brother (based on Kerouac's sister) in Virginia when Dean shows up, driving a brand new 1948 Hudson. Marylou and Ed and Galatea Dunkel (based on Al and Helen Hinkle) go along for the ride. They plan to visit the East Coast and bring Sal back west with them. This begins life on the road for Sal and Dean. The original plan is crazy: Dean will help move some furniture back to Paterson, where they will pick up Sal's aunt and bring her back to Virginia. On the trip, Dean describes the heroic drive from the West Coast, and Sal realizes that Dean has changed in a year "into a weird flower." On the drive to New Jersey, Sal tells Dean that what he really wants is to settle down. Dean, on the other hand, has abandoned his wife and children to "go on the road." (Carolyn Cassady's *OFF THE ROAD* tells the far less romantic "homefront" side of this story.)

They sleep at his aunt's house in Paterson; the next morning Sal receives a phone call from Old Bull Lee (based on Burroughs) in Algiers, Louisiana, where Galatea is stranded, waiting for Ed to come get her. Sal says that they will come for her soon. Instead, they call Carlo, who has had visionary experiences (based on Ginsberg's visions of William Blake) that are recorded in his poetry known as the "Harlem Doldrums." Carlo is openly skeptical of their road trips, which appear to have no purpose. They leave Carlo in Times Square and drive back to Virginia in 10 hours. On the road, Dean and Sal have the long talk that they both wanted to have since meeting. Dean has become a mystic in the last year and declares God's existence.

They make it back to New York in time for New Year's Eve, 1948. Along the road, Sal and Dean discuss the "Shrouded Traveler," an allegorical death figure that was invented by Sal and Carlo. Dean wants nothing to do with such concepts because he is interested only in life—unlike his two brooding writer friends. The parties go on for days, with Dean saying "Yes" ecstatically in response to everything. At a George Shearing concert at Birdland, he yells "Go!" and is possessed by Shearing's piano playing. Such descriptive passages lead some critics to say that *On the Road* is one of the best jazz novels.

Off the road the gang grows "sloppy," as Sal says. His aunt warns him away from Dean and his friends, and Carlo questions their behavior as well. They hang out in a bar (probably the San Remo) that is notorious as a rendezvous for criminals, sex deviants, and adulterers. In such bars Alfred Kinsey interviewed some of the Beats about their sexual behavior. Dean even suggests a three-way with Sal and Marylou. However, Sal finds himself overcome by his shyness and cannot perform.

Old Bull calls again about Galatea, and they head out West with a stop off in New Orleans to reunite Ed with Galatea. Now on the move, the gang loses its sloppiness. In Virginia they are ticketed by a cop and have to spend most of their money on the fine. For the rest of the trip they pick up hitchhikers for money and steal gas and food at every opportunity. Dean tells Sal stories from when he was being raised by his wino father, material found both in Cassady's *The FIRST THIRD* and in Kerouac's *VISIONS OF CODY*. They arrive in New Orleans and take the ferry to Algiers, where Old Bull lives. Kerouac's account of Bull's life with his wife Jane (based on Joan Burroughs) and their two children is the most detailed account that we have of the life of Burroughs in Louisiana and covers material that Burroughs left out of *Junky*. Bull is their teacher, Sal says, and all of them sit at his feet listening to his philosophical discussions. Old Bull in 1948 is already ranting against the police state, government bureaucracies, and unions. In Burroughs's letters to Kerouac in the late 1940s, it is apparent that he knew such rants would find a sympathetic audience with Kerouac. In fact, Old Bull's opinions can be seen to inform *On the Road*, particularly Kerouac's repeated indictments of America's emerging police state. Sal's description of Bull's relationship with Jane is as good a description of Burroughs and his wife that exists: Sal says Jane "loved that man madly," and that they stayed up all night talking.

Readers of Burroughs will be interested to see here a much more lively and interesting Burroughs than the self-portrait he created in *Junky*—emotionless and factual. Old Bull rants against the planned obsolescence of American manufactured goods and explains the revivifying powers of Wilhelm Reich's orgone accumulator. A scene at the racetrack describes Old Bull missing the jackpot on a slot machine by a hair and saying, "Damn! They got these things adjusted. . . . I had the jackpot and the mechanism clicked it back. Well, what you gonna do." When Sal's GI check comes through, they are able to leave Algiers but not before Dean tries to con Old Bull out of some money, but Old Bull, who knows Dean well from their Texas days, is not fooled. Old Bull says to Sal about Dean, "He seems to me to be headed for his ideal fate, which is compulsive psychosis dashed with a jigger of psychopathic irresponsibility and violence. . . . If you go to California with this madman you'll never make it." A close reader of *On the Road* will notice that, surprisingly, only Sal and Dean romanticize their road lives.

They head West through Louisiana and into Texas. When they reach Beaumont and Houston, Dean tells stories of his Texas days with Old Bull, Carlo, and Hassel. Marylou tells Sal that when they get to San Francisco, she will be his girl. At one point, they are all naked in the car, with Marylou applying cold cream to the men, causing rubbernecking truck drivers almost to lose control of their rigs. (LuAnne Henderson, in *Jack's Book*, says they took their clothes off because they were hot and that they had no cold cream, although she would have loved to have had some.)

They pick up hitchhikers through El Paso and on to Tucson. There is a spectacular description of Dean saving precious gas by driving with the engine dead for 30 miles as they descend from the Tehachapi Pass into the San Joaquin Valley of California. They make it to San Francisco, and Dean, anxious to get back to Camille, strands Sal and Marylou, leaving them off in downtown without money and without a place to stay. "Dean will leave you out in the cold any time it's in his interest," says Marylou, who knows him well.

Sal says of the inconsiderate Dean that he "lost faith in him that year." He spends the "beatest time" of his life on the streets of San Francisco with Marylou. She eventually leaves him for a man who will pay her for sex. Sal is nearly starving when he has a vision that reveals to him the numberless lives which he has lived and that allows him to confront the idea of death, an issue with which he was struggling before he met Dean.

Dean rescues Sal from starvation and moves him in with him and Camille, "a well-bred polite woman"—as opposed to Marylou. Dean and Sal hit San Francisco's jazz clubs, which Sal describes as featuring the wildest musicians in America. Eventually, Camille asks him to leave. Sal makes 10 sandwiches for himself and buys a bus ticket to New York. He does not expect to see Dean again. Their lives seem to have moved off in different directions.

In spring 1949 Sal heads back to Denver but can find none of the old gang. In a controversial passage, Sal states, "At lilac evening I walked with every muscle aching among the lights of 27th and Welton in the Denver colored section, wishing I were a Negro, feeling that the best the white world had offered was not enough ecstasy for me, not enough life, joy, kicks, darkness, music, not enough night. . . . I wished I were a Denver Mexican, or even a poor overworked Jap, anything but what I was so drearily, a 'white man' disillusioned." This passage inspired James Baldwin to write in *Nobody Knows My Name: More Notes of a Native Son* (1961), "Now, this is absolute nonsense, of course, objectively considered, and offensive nonsense at that: I would hate to be in Kerouac's shoes if he should ever be mad enough to read this aloud from the stage of Harlem's Apollo Theater." In one of the most scathing attacks against Kerouac and the Beats, Norman Podhoretz in the Spring 1958 *Partisan Review* singled out this passage and wrote, "It will be news to the Negroes to learn that they are so happy and ecstatic; I doubt if a more idyllic picture of Negro life has been painted since certain Southern ideologues tried to convince the world that things were just as fine as could be for slaves on the old plantation." The African-American Beat poet LeRoi Jones/AMIRI BARAKA came to Kerouac's defense in a letter found in the Summer 1958 edition of the *Partsan Review* where he says *On the Road* "breaks new ground, and plants new seeds." Eldridge Cleaver, in *Soul on Ice,* called the passage that Baldwin found offensive "remarkable," and cited it as an example of one of the stages whites needed to go through in the fight against racism.

Later, Sal shares a ride to San Francisco with two pimps and arrives at Dean and Camille's house. Dean is sincerely impressed that finally Sal has come to him, not vice versa. The nights are spent talking and drinking, but Camille soon throws them out. Sal tells Dean that he has a little money and will finance their trip back to New York; there, he will pick up his advance on his recently accepted novel, and they will go to Italy. This is a pivotal moment in their friendship, for Dean realizes that Sal has spent some time thinking about his welfare—a rare experience for this child of a Denver wino.

Before they leave San Francisco, they decide to hit the town for a few nights. They go to Galatea's apartment to see about a place to sleep. Ed has left her again, and she is in no mood for the two happy-go-lucky men. She and several other women circle Dean and lay into him about how irresponsible he is to leave Camille and their young daughter and run off on another adventure. Dean can only simper and mug comically in response. Sal defends him by trying to get them to admit how fascinated they are by Dean. Kerouac said that Helen Hinkle was the only woman whom he knew who could tell off Cassady and get away with it.

After Galatea has laid into Dean, they all go to hear some jazz. Kerouac published this section as "Jazz of the Beat Generation" under the name Jean-Louis in the 1955 *New World Writing.* It features Kerouac's best extended attempt in the novel to render into prose the sounds of jazz. In an odd coincidence, they encounter a young man who looks just like Carlo, playing tenor saxophone. After the round of nightclubs, Dean and Sal head back to the East Coast.

They share a ride East with a "thin fag" who drives an "effeminate" car. The owner drives, and Sal and Dean sit in back talking nonstop. Dean tells Sal that the alto man the previous night had "IT" and Sal wants to know what "it" is. "It" is when "time stops" for everyone, says Dean; one of Dean's refrains in the book is that they "know" time and others do not—others spend their lives worrying about the future, but Sal and Dean "know what IT is and we know TIME and we know that everything is really FINE." Dean feels that he has IT at that moment and "blows" a story of his Denver days. When they stop for the night, the "thin fag" tries to get Dean into bed, but Dean cons him for some money with vague promises of sex favors when they reach Denver. (In *Visions of Cody*, Kerouac describes another version of this story: Cody agrees to the deal, and Duluoz spends a long night in the bathroom listening to Cody sodomize this man.) With the "thin fag" in his confidence, Dean takes the wheel and terrifies the passengers with a demonstration of how "not to drive."

Dean and Sal have their first falling out, and there is no good explanation for it in the book. Dean kids Sal about being older than he is and having kidney problems, and Sal responds, "I'm no old fag like that fag"—perhaps in reference to his disgust with Dean's bisexuality. In telling off Dean, he realizes that he is actually wounding himself by projecting his repressed animosity. Sal apologizes for this odd episode, and they go to stay with a woman named Frankie whom Sal had met previously in Denver. Dean gets in touch with a cousin who meets him at a bar but will not drink with him; he tells Dean that the family wants nothing more to do with him. Sal sticks up for him and reassures Dean that he trusts him if no one else does. Denver brings back bad memories for Dean, and he gets drunk and goes on a car-stealing rampage.

They leave the crime spree and drunkenness of Denver behind and are fortunate enough to find a 1947 Cadillac that they are hired to drive to Chicago. The Cadillac is a dream machine for Dean, and he drives it at a steady 110 miles per hour. They are making such good time that they stop off at a ranch where Dean worked while on probation from reform school, but his old friend there no longer trusts him and believes that the Cadillac is stolen.

They tear across the state of Nebraska while Dean tells stories of his days in Hollywood in the early 1940s and of his meeting Marylou in a Denver drugstore when she was only 15. There are also descriptions of Dean's incredible feats as a driver. He is so daring on the road that Sal crawls into the backseat. When the trip to Chicago is done, they have gone 1,180 miles in 17 hours—"a kind of crazy record." In Chicago, they of course head to the jazz clubs. They follow a group of young musicians into a bar, and their music allows Sal to give a

brief history of jazz and bop. They return the Cadillac to its wealthy Chicago owner; it is so battered that the man's mechanic does not recognize it.

They take a bus in Detroit, and Sal reveals to the reader in a description of a bored beautiful girl that the meaning of life is to be passionate about what you are doing, even if it is only making popcorn on a porch. It is important for readers to note that Sal does not believe that the only way to live passionately is through the recklessness of Dean. Another ride gets them to his aunt's new house in Long Island, but she will not let Dean stay. Sal hooks up Dean with a girl named Inez (based on Diane Hansen) who always wanted to meet a "cowboy," and Dean's romantic complications keep Sal and Dean from ever making it to Italy.

It is springtime, and Sal needs to go on a pilgrimage. Dean is living with Inez, who is pregnant, and he has a job parking cars. Sal leaves Dean in New York and goes West without him. Everyone is older and has responsibilities, children, jobs, a family—everyone except Sal. In parting, Dean expresses their mutual wish that they would grow old together with their families, living on the same street.

Sal takes a bus west, and in Terre Haute he befriends a young ex-con just released from prison. He promises to set him up on a straight path when they get to Denver: the kid reminds him of a young Dean. In Denver, he hooks up with Tim Gray, Babe Rawlins, and a young man named Stan Shephard, who has heard of the legendary tales of Sal and Dean. Stan knows that Sal is going to Mexico and gets Sal's permission to go along. Word from the East arrives that Dean is coming. Sal says, "Suddenly I had a vision of Dean, a burning shuddering frightful Angel, palpitating toward me across the road, approaching like a cloud, with enormous speed, pursuing me like the Shrouded Traveler on the plain, bearing down on me."

Dean arrives driving a 1937 Ford in which he will drive them to Mexico City. For him, the trip will be partly for business. He intends to get a Mexican divorce from Camille to marry Inez. With the old Denver gang reunited, Dean reflects on how they are all older now but little changed. However, that night, he gets drunk in an old gold rush saloon above which he and his father once lived, and high and raving he appears to Sal as if he is "the ghost of his father." The axis of their journey has finally changed. Now they go South, rather than West and East.

They drive down through Texas, each of them telling their story on the long trip, made longer by the 1937 Ford's top speed of 40 miles an hour. In San Antonio, Sal looks at the Mexican-Americans on the streets and thinks of the fate of Terry. San Antonio only inspires Dean to keep going to Mexico, and they head to Laredo. This border town is "sinister," "the bottom and dregs of America where all the heavy villains sink." They feel differently almost immediately after the enter Mexico. Dean observes that the cops are kindhearted.

This famous section of the book inspired thousands of young Americans to make a pilgrimage to Mexico in the 1950s and 1960s, and to this day Kerouac's infectious account of Mexico's charms and allurements is a guide and inspiration for youthful adventurers who are heading south of the border. Burroughs criticized Kerouac for romanticizing Mexico, which Burroughs called a "place of death," but Kerouac's description of Mexico is very similar to and perhaps, in part, is inspired by Burroughs's early letters to Kerouac from Mexico City: The cops are benign, the whorehouses are exciting, drugs are readily available, and expenses are ridiculously cheap. Dean intends to be the first American who comes to Mexico not to conquer or exploit it but to "understand" it. Dean sees himself in the Mexican Indians. While Dean sleeps, Sal takes the wheel and applies Oswald Spengler's idea of the "fellaheen," primitive cultures from *The Decline of the West* to what he sees in Mexico: These Indians are "the essential strain of the primitive" who will survive the coming apocalypse. They arrive in a town where an obliging and charming young man named Victor provides them with marijuana and prostitutes. At last, their desires are satisfied completely, and they believe that they are in a dream. Stan has to be dragged away from the whorehouse.

They press on to Mexico City and spend the night in a jungle town where they sleep outside, their bodies covered with insects. They study the Indians whom they see by the roadside on the Pan American Highway and stop and trade with them for rock crystals. To the children, says Sal, Dean appears as

if he is a prophet of some kind. Sal ponders the fact that these people have no idea that a bomb has been invented that could "reduce them to jumbles." They cross over the mountains and descend to Mexico City. Sal says little of this city, as if they were already too exhausted to experience it fully. He becomes ill with dysentery, and Dean, having obtained his Mexican divorce from Camille, abandons him to the care of Stan. Only after his fever breaks does Sal consider what a rat Dean is, but he forgives him, knowing that he needs to get back to his two families.

The final section of the book is a brief coda. Sal is back in New York and is in love with a girl named Laura (based on Joan Haverty). He is going to a Duke Ellington concert with Laura, Remi, and Remi's girl in a chauffeured Cadillac. Sal has to leave Dean on the cold sidewalks of New York because Remi, still wary of Sal's friends, will not give Dean a ride. This is a far cry from going to bop nightclubs with Dean in a beaten-up car. Many detractors and fans of the novel fail to see that *On the Road* has a sober ending, with Sal getting off the road and Dean appearing defeated, "eyes on the street ahead, and bent to it again."

The novel thus ends with this, one of the greatest lost lines in American literature: "So in America when the sun goes down and I sit on the old broken-down river pier watching the long, long skies over New Jersey and sense all that raw land that rolls in one unbelievable huge bulge over to the West Coast, and all that road going, all the people dreaming in the immensity of it, and in Iowa I know by now the children must be crying in the land where they let the children cry, and tonight the stars'll be out, and don't you know that God is Pooh Bear? the evening star must be drooping and shedding her sparkler dims on the prairie, which is just before the coming of complete night that blesses the earth, darkens all rivers, cups the peaks and folds the final shore in, and nobody, nobody knows what's going to happen to anybody besides the forlorn rags of growing old, I think of Dean Moriarty, I even think of Old Dean Moriarty the father we never found, I think of Dean Moriarty."

A movie based on Kerouac's novel, directed by Walter Salles with screenplay by Jose Rivera, is in production, with an anticipated 2007 release date. In 2000 Caedmon Audio released an excellent 11-hour unabridged reading of *On the Road* by Matt Dillon on 10 CDs. Jim Irsay, owner of the Indianapolis Colts, bought the original scroll manuscript of *On the Road* for $2.43 million, a record for a literary manuscript at auction. He put the scroll on a 13-stop, four-year national tour. A book version of the *On the Road* scroll is scheduled for publication in 2007 to celebrate the 50th anniersary of the novel's original publication. It is believed that the various editions of *On the Road* worldwide sell more than 100,000 copies annually.

Bibliography

Charters, Ann. Introduction. *On the Road,* by Jack Kerouac. New York: Penguin Books, 1991.

Hunt, Tim. *Kerouac's Crooked Road: The Development of a Fiction.* Hamden, Conn.: Archon Books, 1981.

Kerouac, Jack. *Selected Letters 1940–1956.* Edited by Ann Charters. New York: Viking, 1995.

———. *Windblown World: The Journals of Jack Kerouac 1947–1954.* Edited by Douglas Brinkley. New York: Viking, 2004.

Millstein, Gilbert. "Books of The Times." *New York Times,* 5 September 1957: 27.

Swartz, Omar. *The View from* On the Road: *The Rhetorical Vision of Jack Kerouac.* Carbondale: Southern Illinois University Press, 1999.

Rob Johnson and Kurt Hemmer

Pictures of the Gone World
Lawrence Ferlinghetti (1955)

The first book of poems by LAWRENCE FERLING-HETTI is *Pictures of the Gone World,* a plain and slender 5" × 6 ¼" volume of 27 imagistic poems in open forms. The poems express Ferlinghetti's views of love, art, time, death, great cities, nature, animals, memories, and literature.

The book is the first volume produced in the Pocket Poets Series of City Lights Books, the publication company that was established by Ferlinghetti and was dedicated to inexpensive editions of artists whose experimental methods or political dissidence makes publication through other outlets unlikely.

In June 1952 Ferlinghetti and his friend Peter Martin, the publisher of *City Lights,* a literary magazine, each invested $500 to open City Lights Bookstore in San Francisco. The store began as a means to provide funds for the continuation of the magazine but with an emphasis on inexpensive, avant-garde books and an evening schedule that made the bookstore a cultural center, City Lights Bookstore endured and eventually became a landmark in San Francisco.

In 1955 Martin sold his interest in the store to Ferlinghetti, making him sole director; on August 10, 1955, Ferlinghetti published *Pictures of the Gone World.* The poems have endured: the original text was reprinted numerous times; a selection of the poems were reprinted in A CONEY ISLAND OF THE MIND (1958); an enlarged edition of *Pictures of the Gone World* was published in 1995; and numerous selections were included in *These Are My Rivers: New and Selected Poems* (1994).

The title of the collection is apparently based on two key ideas. First, the poems are meant to be pictures. In that sense, the poems are like paintings or photographs—in the tradition of the imagists, the poems are meant to convey a strong visual impression. Second, the title refers to the "Gone World," invoking the hip idiom and its sense of "gone," which can connote a positive sort of craziness but can also suggest a desperate emptiness.

Among the most familiar poems in *Pictures of the Gone World* are "Away above a Harborful," "The World Is a Beautiful Place," and "Reading Yeats." Because these poems are included in A *Coney Island of the Mind,* discussion of these poems is found in the entry for A *Coney Island of the Mind.*

Another poem of special interest in *Pictures of the Gone World* is "8," also known as "Sorolla's Women in Their Picture Hats." The poem reveals Ferlinghetti's frequently used technique of referring to famous works of visual art to create a springboard for his own imaginative flight. Ferlinghetti opens his poem with a reference to the women with large hats in *Promenade on the Beach* (1907), a painting by Joaquin Sorolla. Ferlinghetti says that Spanish Impressionists admired Sorolla's works, particularly "the way the light played on them," but Ferlinghetti doubts the realism of Sorolla's painting, noting "illusions / of love." Ferlinghetti's own memory of his own experience seems more realistic to him as he describes the lovemaking of "the last picnickers," who exquisitely delay the culmination of their engagement. In recognition of the fulfillment that the picnickers finally experience, "night's trees" stand up.

"London," which is titled "18" in *Pictures of the Gone World,* pursues the fantastic rather than the realistic. Ferlinghetti admits that the setting for the poem could be "anyplace," but it is in fact London. Street artists on a Sunday afternoon seek a model, but when one woman volunteers and begins to disrobe, she finds the uncovered parts of her body absent. "I mean to say," Ferlinghetti writes, that "she took off her shoes / and found no feet." She is "ASTOUNDED" to witness her corporal incompleteness. When she puts her clothes back on, she is "completely / all right." An artist calls out to her to repeat the amazing performance, but she is "afraid," gives up being a model, and "forever after" sleeps "in her clothes." On one hand, the poem is comic, fantastic, and surreal; on the other hand, if one considers the symbolism of someone who is corporally absent beneath her clothes and who is so frightened by the experience that she remains dressed when she sleeps, one sees that Ferlinghetti's poem is about a woman who cannot be naked. Since "nakedness" to a Beat writer involves frankness, candor, and openness on both physical and spiritual levels, this failed model must be fundamentally and sadly unable to reveal herself.

The issue of reality versus fantasy continues in *Pictures of the Gone World* in "23," which is also known as "Dada Would Have Loved a Day Like This." Dada refers to an antiart movement in Europe and New York in about 1916. Dadaists saw no meaning in a European culture that perpetuated hatred and war, and therefore the Dadaists sought to dismantle the forces of control so that art could go forward freely. In Ferlinghetti's poem, the day features "realistic / unrealities," but each of these apparent contradictions is "about to become / too real for its locality." The "light-bulb sun" shines "so differently / for different people," but "still shines the same / on everyone / and everything." Ferlinghetti refers to "a bird on a bench," an airplane "in a gilded cloud," a "dishpan hand," and "a phone about to ring," but he proceeds to his principal example, the "cancerous dancer," whose "too real funeral" amidst a "sweet street carnival" leaves "her last lover lost / in the unlonely crowd" and leaves the "dancer's darling baby / about to say Dada." A "passing priest" may "pray / Dada" and utter "transcendental apologies," but Ferlinghetti insists that the day belongs to Dada because of "not so accidental / analogies." This poem, with its reference to death, the bereaved, and the unaffected surroundings, is dark in its outlook, but true to life.

Pictures of the Gone World remains a key publication in the history of the Beat Generation. The poems seem easy to read and accessible to all readers; yet their references to art and cultural history demand careful attention, and the subtle effects of rhyme and wordplay deserve appreciation.

William Lawlor

Pipe Dreams Martin Matz (1989)

An exquisite collection of 11 opium poems, privately published in an edition of 100, with 10 signed and lettered copies, *Pipe Dreams* is Martin Matz's hallucinatory suite of his odyssey in Thailand in the late 1980s. With cover art by Don Martin and an introduction by HERBERT HUNCKE, *Pipe Dreams* marks a collaboration between Matz and two friends who, like Marty, possessed outlaw sensibilities. The book also features two tipped-in photographs and a glossary by Barbara Alexander Matz, Marty's wife. Don Martin, an artist whom Marty described in the book's dedication as "my soul brother," had lived and traveled with Matz in Mexico in the 1950s. Huncke, a storyteller who, like Marty, was a longtime user of opiates, was a neighbor and close friend of Matz's in the Chelsea Hotel in the 1980s.

In his introduction, Huncke writes, "Mr. Matz can successfully blend the strange and fascinating dream level reality with the mundane daily experience most perfectly, weaving perfect magic." The magic commenced in 1988 when Marty and Barbara were invited to the Tenth World Congress of Poets in Bangkok, Thailand. On their third day in Bangkok, Matz was hit by a truck and broke his collarbone. He and Barbara then headed to northern Thailand and settled in Ban Muang Noi, a remote hill tribe village north of Chiang Mai.

Finding inspiration in the undulating poppy fields that ringed his bamboo hut, Matz wrote most of *Pipe Dreams* during the course of several languid months during the monsoon season. In addition to savoring the ritual and effects of opium smoking, Marty and Barbara enjoyed elephant treks in the jungle and visits to the local Lahu village.

The title *Pipe Dreams,* perhaps, has a dual meaning: It refers to the visions evoked by smoking opium out of a long stemmed pipe, but it may also refer to dreams unfulfilled. The first five poems in *Pipe Dreams* reflect Matz's exuberant embrace of the poppy's alchemical effects, while the last six poems are darker in tone, addressing themes of suffering, addiction, and mortality. In "The Writing of Pipe Dreams," Barbara A. Matz writes, "The whole of the *Pipe Dreams* poems are [sic] an autobiography of Marty's experiences during our first stay in Thailand. *Pipe Dreams* #9 and #10 were written in a hospital in Chiang Mai where Marty and I were trying to clean up our wonderfully immense drug habits."

Though a rare and elusive artifact, *Pipe Dreams* is a prime example of the Beat sensibility being fused with elements of surrealism and lyricism. Martin Matz, the self-proclaimed "insatiable traveler," found a Shangri-la in northern Thailand, only to discover that one must pay a high price for an extended stay in Paradise.

Bibliography
Matz, Marty. *In the Seasons of My Eye: Selected Writings 1953–2001.* Edited by Romy Ashby. New York: Panther Books, 2005.

Laki Vazakas

Place of Dead Roads, The   William S. Burroughs (1983)

Perhaps the masterpiece of WILLIAM S. BURROUGHS's "the Red Night trilogy," which includes CITIES OF THE RED NIGHT (1981) and *The WESTERN LANDS* (1987), *The Place of Dead Roads* is Burroughs's first and only Western. Burroughs moved into a house in Lawrence, Kansas, to finish writing the book. He would live in Lawrence until his death on August 2, 1997. Lawrence was the stronghold of the Jayhawkers, Union guerrillas

during the Civil War who were the archenemies of Quantrill's Confederate marauders. The outlaw gang that Burroughs imagines in *The Place of Dead Roads,* called the Johnson Family, loosely resembles the legendary James–Younger gang that sprang from Quantrill's raiders. In Burroughs's novel the detractors of the Johnson Family compare the outlaw gang to the Confederate guerrillas by starting a defamation campaign with the slogan "QUANTRILL RIDES AGAIN." One of the Johnsons, Denton Brady, "rode with the James boys and he was a child prodigy under Quantrill." In this novel Burroughs creates a political model for the counterculture of the future that is based on the legends of supposedly egalitarian outlaws such as Frank and Jesse James and Cole Younger.

The Place of Dead Roads can be read as a rewriting of Burroughs's favorite childhood book *You Can't Win* (1926) by Jack Black. Burroughs writes:

> Stultified and confined by middle class St. Louis mores, I was fascinated by this glimpse of an underworld of seedy rooming-houses, pool parlors, cat houses and opium dens, of bull pens and cat burglars and hobo jungles. I learned about the Johnson Family of good bums and thieves, with a code of conduct that made more sense to me than the arbitrary, hypocritical rules that were taken for granted as being "right" by my peers.

Ted Morgan claims that Black's book "would have an enormous impact on the unfolding of [Burroughs's] life and work." "In *You Can't Win,*" writes Morgan, "there is a set of values . . . that Burroughs would make his own." Yet in the harsh world of Black's picaresque autobiography, even the outlaws who stand by an honorable code of conduct are destined to fail as victims of a hypocritical society. Burroughs's childhood dream of actually finding a successful and righteous community of outlaws, similar to the one depicted in Black's book, haunted Burroughs's imagination throughout his literary career. Barry Miles argues, "In *The Place of Dead Roads,* Jack Black's Johnson Family stand a good chance of winning. . . . Here [Burroughs] is doing his best to make it happen by writing it into existence." Timothy S. Murphy describes *The Place of Dead Roads* as concerned "with the possibilities for a subversive social order along the 'lawless' American frontier." Though often a loner and depicted as apolitical, Burroughs in *The Place of Dead Roads* makes his most rigorous attempt to imagine a successful outlaw community.

Burroughs places his alter-ego, Kim Carsons, at the center of the Johnson Family in *The Place of Dead Roads.* Carsons is a gay shootist whose struggle is against all forces that control the individual. Carsons also writes Westerns under the name William Seward Hall.

In the middle of the novel, Burroughs states the political agenda of the Johnsons, who have been forced out of their position of tolerance by alien forces seeking to destroy humanity:

> We will take every opportunity to weaken the power of the church. We will lobby in Congress for heavy taxes on all churches. We will provide more interesting avenues for the young. We will destroy the church with ridicule. We will secularize the church out of existence. . . . Far from seeing an atheistic world as the communists do, we will force Christianity to compete for the human spirit.
>
> We will fight any extension of federal authority and support States' Rights. We will resist any attempt to penalize or legislate against so-called victimless crimes . . . gambling, sexual behavior, drinking, drugs.
>
> We will give all our attention to experiments designed to produce asexual offspring, to cloning, use of artificial wombs, and transfer operations.
>
> We will endeavor to halt the Industrial Revolution before it is too late, to regulate populations at a reasonable point, to eventually replace quantitative money with qualitative money, to decentralize, to conserve resources.

With this clear sense of purpose, the Johnson Family becomes a political entity that is capable of defeating the alien presence. The agenda of the Johnsons is something in which Burroughs truly believed and hoped that it would be implemented in society. For Burroughs this agenda was a practical means of creating a better world. Burroughs even imagines sources for the Johnsons to support themselves in their subversive struggle: "The Family has set up a number of posts in America and northern Mexico. They are already very rich, mostly from real estate. They own newspapers, a chemical company, a gun factory, and a factory for making photographic equipment, which will become one of the first film studios."

Rather than having static roles within the Johnson Family, the members periodically exchange positions of greater and lesser power in the community: "The Johnson Family is a cooperative structure. There isn't any boss man. People know what they are supposed to do and they do it. We're all actors and we change roles." Kim Carsons goes underground to help the Johnson cause and has himself cloned. When Kim reflects on the society that he is helping establish, he thinks that "his dream of a take-over by the Johnson Family, by those who actually do the work, the reactive thinkers and artists and technicians, was not just science fiction. It could happen."

Yet Burroughs ends his novel with the assassination of his hero. In *The Western Lands,* the sequel to *The Place of Dead Roads,* we find out that Joe the Dead has killed Kim Carsons. Perhaps Burroughs's fatalistic and pessimistic attitude prevented him from allowing Kim Carsons to live. Despite the sense that the Johnson Family, with the death of Kim, will not be capable of organizing itself well enough to be successful, Burroughs does suggest another avenue for them out of defeat. The events of the novel are portrayed as being scenes in a film that is controlled by a mysterious director. At the beginning of the novel there is the suggestion that the film can be broken, liberating the characters involved, and altering their fates.

Bibliography

Burroughs, William S. Foreword. *You Can't Win,* by Jack Black. 1926. Reprint, New York: Amok Press, 1988, v–viii.

Miles, Barry. *William Burroughs, El Hombre Invisible: A Portrait.* New York: Hyperion, 1992.

Morgan, Ted. *Literary Outlaw: The Life and Times of William S. Burroughs.* New York: Henry Holt, 1988.

Murphy, Timothy S. *Wising Up the Marks: The Amodern William Burroughs*. Berkeley: University of California Press, 1997.

Kurt Hemmer

Plymell, Charles (1935–)

Poet, essayist, publisher, printer, artist, laborer, teacher—Charles Plymell has worn almost as many hats as his friend Hat Man Jack, the legendary Wichita hat maker, has fashioned. According to ALLEN GINSBERG, Plymell and his friends invented the "Wichita Vortex," a free flowing sensibility and loose artistic agglomeration that emerged from the local car, music, and Benzedrine cultures in the 1950s. Although associated with the Beat Generation writers, Plymell has always forged his own literary path as a writer and as a major catalyst in the small-press renaissance of the 1960s and 1970s.

Plymell was born in Holcomb, Kansas, in 1935 and spent his formative years in Wichita and California. After dropping out of a military academy in San Antonio at the age of 15, Plymell spent the better part of the next decade crisscrossing the country in various automobiles, including a "lowered and leaded in" 1951 Chevy. He worked in mines, on pipelines, and on dams and has written incisively about his experiences as a manual laborer. After years of roaming the western states, Plymell enrolled in Wichita State University in 1955. While at Wichita State, he worked as a printer, and in 1959 he began to edit and publish literary magazines, including *Poets' Corner* and *Mikrokosmos*.

In the early 1960s Plymell gravitated to San Francisco, where he befriended NEAL CASSADY, Ginsberg, and other writers, as the Beats collided with the "Vortex." From 1963 to 1965 Plymell published three issues of the literary journal *Now*. He also had a successful show of his collage work at the infamous Batman Gallery on Fillmore Street in San Francisco at this time. In 1966 he married Pamela Beach, with whom he would have two children, Elizabeth and William. That same year saw the publication by Dave Haselwood of Auerhahn Press, another seminal figure in the small-press revolution of Plymell's first book of poetry, *Apocalypse Rose*, with an introduction by Ginsberg.

In 1967 Plymell edited and published *The Last Times*, an experimental literary journal, designed and printed the first issue of *Zap Comix* (which featured the work of Robert Crumb), and guest-edited and published *Grist Magazine*. In 1970 he earned a Masters degree in Arts and Science from Johns Hopkins University. At Hopkins, he began to write his novel LAST OF THE MOCCASINS (1971), which was published by City Lights Books. An impressionistic chronicle of his restless years in and out of the incipient psychedelic scene in San Francisco, Plymell's novel was praised by WILLIAM S. BURROUGHS and Ginsberg.

In 1974 the Plymells launched Cherry Valley Editions and *Cold Spring Journal* with their friend Joshua Norton. Throughout the 1970s and into the 1980s, Cherry Valley Editions published important works by HERBERT HUNCKE, JANINE POMMY VEGA, Charles Henri Ford, and many others. During this time Plymell taught in the Poets-in-the-Schools programs and in prisons. In 1975 his poetry collection *The Trashing of America* was published.

In the 1980s and 1990s, Plymell wrote poems and philosophical essays while distancing himself from the Beats. In 1985 a second collection of his poetry was published as *Forever Wider: Poems New and Selected, 1954 to 1984*. At this time, Plymell's work took on a new urgency as he addressed such pressing issues as environmental devastation and the war on drugs.

In 2000, Water Row Books published *Hand on the Doorknob: A Charles Plymell Reader*, a collection of essays, poetry, and fiction. Plymell and his wife Pamela live in Cherry Valley with their dog Bebop. Plymell's latest book is a compilation of memoirs, poetry, and photos titled *Some Mothers' Sons*.

Bibliography
Plymell, Charles. "Interview with Charles Plymell." Interview by Wayne Atherton. *The Café Review* (Summer 2001): 17–23.

Laki Vazakas

Poems of Madness Ray Bremser (1965)

This is a collection of long poems that RAY BREM-SER wrote in prison and that not only plumb the depths of emotional experience, hence having a blues base, but also entertain with exquisite swinging musicality and both high and low humor.

The work can be difficult or free flowing, depending on the reader's receptiveness. It is a bit akin to listening to a dialect—once the mind hears the words and adjusts to the syntax, it flows like water from the Himalayas. The collection is teeming with anthropological, historical (ancient and recent), geological, biblical, and sociological insight. It is a spew of mellifluous vocabulary of prophetic connotation.

Poems of Madness are time traveling in the meditative or dream state, similar to Virginia Woolf's *Orlando* and Jack London's *The Jacket* and *Before Adam*. All psychological, religious, and philosophical questions that have plagued and amused humanity are being bandied about and answered by the mind of a self-educated young man in a cell, who is living ancient glories, disasters, illuminations, and pains.

Like Walt Whitman, there are classic admitted contradictions and such oxymorons as "brutalest forgiveness" with its "unauthenticated weight." You will find description from the primitive "blip blip dreams" to the silken "snow ensmutted wings."

Not far into *Poems of Madness* Bremser declares himself an outlaw. He showcases the desultory, dolorous conditions of his New Jersey upbringing, the sordid bleakness of the underbelly and the underworld, and the unabashed cruelty of the authorities: "Since then I have hated what / passes as law."

Then, as in most of Bremser's work, comes the affirmation, the passion for sex and love: "I would run my cool tongue / in your mouth, eat your tears, taste your difficult / washmachine beauty!"

He fantasizes, "Great edible crotch full of hermitage lore / and excusable gloom."

He explains how he became incarcerated: "And I took in my hand / in my coat and conjoined / a pistol, in case— / to decide things / best / for myself."

His poem "Blues for Bonnie," like all the poems in the collection, is full of drugs, sex, and the argot of jazz. The "phenomenoes" section of this piece is similar to the Russian Futurian Velimir Khlebnikov's "Incantation by Laughter."

If a musical key could be ascribed to this blues, it would be flatted or sharped, fit for saxophone.

He ends the piece with a long paean to love, love for Bonnie Bremser (BRENDA FRAZER).

The book includes a short-rant one-page piece about masturbating, "Hanging Like a Baboon From a Tree."

In the poem on the opposing page, "Eternity Grinding Allens Great Beyond," we are made conscious that even though Bremser's mind is on the outside, he must confront realities, like the yard, the indeterminacy of time, lack of privacy, the horrifying machine shop, and the darkening cell.

Andy Clausen

Poems to Fernando Janine Pommy Vega (1968)

This first book by JANINE POMMY VEGA contains poems that were written between 1963 and 1967. The book documents Vega's marriage to Peruvian painter, Fernando Vega, who died suddenly of a heroin overdose in November 1965 on the island of Ibiza off the coast of Spain; her grief and solitude in Paris after his death; and the aftermath on her return to the United States. The writing is devotional, spiritually intense, and charged with a blend of mortal and immortal love—that is, companionate, romantic marriage that is mediated through a strong religious intuition that there is a higher love to which all phenomena owe the ebb and flow of their temporal existence. This recourse to the rapturous language and the experience of a higher purpose acts as salvific and a means of channeling the sense of abandonment and the natural dissociation that accompanies sudden (traumatic) loss and the grief that follows. In many ways it is unique in that it combines a celebration of domestic love and marriage—usually a Beat anathema—with a wild spiritual yearning, a theme that we associate with Beat writing but not necessarily with Beat writing by women. Vega's writing is both identifiably Beat and tinged with broader female concerns that were typical of the era.

The first section of the book is the eponymous "Poems to Fernando," made up of 16 poems, most of them only one page long—and since the book is one of the City Lights Pocket Book series, a breakthrough design in minimalism that is intended for easy portability, these are very short pages indeed. This section is in turn divided into two parts: The first corresponds roughly to the period in which the couple lived together in Jerusalem and Paris, then apart as Fernando Vega travels to Ibiza while the author stays in Paris; the second, following her husband's death, traces the author's disbelief, shock, and compensatory conviction that her husband's spirit is still alive, dispersed into nature and the cosmos beyond nature. This series is characterized by a delicacy and a sensitivity of spirit and language that resonates with the compact, fragmented, intimate, oblique styles and sensibilities of other modernist women writers such as Emily Dickinson, H. D., Lorrine Niedecker, and even Edna St. Vincent Millay in its focus on the emotional phenomenology of romantic love. This genealogy is not usually associated directly with Beat literature (for example, in standard secondary literature on the Beat phenomenon, Whitman is far more often cited than Dickinson as an immediate forebear) but with movements and tendencies adjacent to it, most of which also overlapped in influence and/or personal association: namely avante-garde high modernism and its most well-known U.S. precursors, the Black Mountain School and objectivism. (However it does resonate with the work of JOANNE KYGER, another spiritually motivated Beat writer.) This first section is the emotional and aesthetic heart of the book.

The second section, appropriately titled "Other Poems," turns away from the powerful experiences and emotions associated with erotic love and its sudden end. Instead, it chronicles in looser, longer, and less coherent poems the San Francisco scene of drugs, poetry readings, friends, mentors and liaisons, and the conjunction of higher yearning and loneliness. The latter nexus (of spiritual need and loneliness) is clearly, though not overtly,

unfulfilled by the frenetic activity of the "scene." The shift in tone and focus from the first half of the book to the second enacts a transition from a Dickinsonian orientation to an attempt at Whitmanism, and it is clear where Vega's fire lies. It is in the interior, the whispered, in the domestic aspect of Bohemianism rather than in public declamation. The volume demonstrates that Vega's scale is more nuanced and intimate than that of her male counterparts and is less grandiose. Nonetheless, she shares with ALLEN GINSBERG, JACK KEROUAC, and others of her cohort a desire to turn the hell of loss or abjection to spiritual grist and seeing the "will" of the "Lord"—or a cosmic pattern—in both the minutiae of closely observed natural detail (inherited from the William Carlos Williams branch of American poetry's genealogy) and the personal tragedy of complete abandonment. Both the everyday and the catastrophic become vibrantly charged with spiritual possibilities, providing opportunities for the "marriage of Heaven and Hell" (a poem by William Blake whose title spells out a fundamental Beat ethos).

"Poems to Fernando," the poem cycle that comprises the first half of the book, is written *for*—not *about*—the painter. The poems are immediate and fresh, many taking the form of personal address that is complete with second-person pronouns, and this effect makes the emotion almost unbearably intimate for the reader, who knows what is coming. Their elegiac power comes partially from the innocence with which the poet, not knowing of the impending death of her husband in the first several poems, nonetheless revels in his already almost otherworldly significance to her—a significance that makes it possible for her to survive his loss, as she has already endowed him and their relationship with supernatural powers that transcend time and space. Before his death, she writes:

> in-here is gone forth to meet in-there, &
> we ARE bound below a sound or gesture;
> beneath distance, before time, at the foot of
>   the
> silent forest, meet me here, I love you.

and after:

For my love with you is deep as the space
   between stars
& that my song is sung before does not lessen
   its validity;
I speak to *you,* always as I would speak before
   or write letters
to the space between clouds, that patch of
   sky—
or the sky deserting me, to that place invisible
   beyond me

As we follow the poet through her early months
of widowhood, we see how her visionary tendencies stand her in good stead, enabling an ongoing reciprocity with her husband whereby they
can continue to hear and see each other through
their common apprehension of the cosmos both
natural and supernatural, physical and metaphysical. Her observations about unpeopled
landscapes, while often minimalist and hasty (a
glimpse from a moving train window, and so on),
indicate that she reads them as profoundly satu-
rated with personality and purpose, conveying a
particular message to her. That there is no resolution of this grief in the duration of the book
(the second half does not so much document a
recovery as redirect the author's energy) is entirely appropriate to the unfinishedness and fragmentation that are part of the volume's reality,
beauty, and strength.

Bibliography

Damon, Maria. "Revelations of Companionate Love, or,
   the Hurts of Women: Janine Pommy Vega's *Poems
   to Fernando.*" *Girls Who Wore Black: Women Writing
   the Beat Generation,* edited by Ronna C. Johnson
   and Nancy M. Grace. New Brunswick, N.J.: Rutgers
   University Press, 2002. 205–226.
Vega, Janine Pommy. *Tracking the Serpent: Journeys to
   Four Continents.* San Francisco: City Lights Books,
   1997.

Maria Damon

Poisoned Wheat Michael McClure (1965)

MICHAEL MCCLURE's lengthy poem *Poisoned
Wheat* is both an attack on America's growing
involvement in the Vietnam War and a harsh
indictment of the world political structures that
lead humanity toward disaster by ignoring biological realities.

   In early 1964 McClure began to learn of the
alarming potential for the use of biological weapons such as defoliants and crop poisons in the
Vietnam conflict to destroy North Vietnamese
agricultural resources for an entire growing season, thus bringing about the destruction of communist forces through widespread famine. Such
frightening information moved McClure to respond. He wrote what he calls "a lengthy blast"
on the subject in his journals in 1964, a speech
that he later shaped into a long poem titled *Poisoned Wheat.*

   McClure's intention in writing the poem
seems to have gone far beyond mere artistic expression. From the outset, he envisioned the
poem as a means of changing minds on the subject of the Vietnam War. To this end, he and
Oyez Press publisher Robert Hawley designed a
chapbook that contained McClure's single long
poem which would be distributed directly to readers whom he felt might have some influence on
U.S. policy in Southeast Asia. Together, the two
men mailed 600 copies of the poem. The document that was received by those 600 influential
Americans was striking, both in its appearance
and its content. The chapbook's cover bore the
hand-canceled portrait of Billy the Kid—a figure
that McClure equated with the American penchant for the glorification of murder and a cultural archetype who loomed large in his plays *The
Blossom* and *The BEARD.* By canceling the young
outlaw's portrait with two broad brushstrokes,
McClure symbolized the end of this fascination
with violent death, including its incarnation in
Vietnam.

   Poisoned Wheat is a poetic manifesto that
would foreshadow much of McClure's writing for
the next four decades, as it attempts to look for
solutions to the world's catastrophic problems outside the normal channels of politics and ideology.
From its very beginning, the poem blends the crisis in Southeast Asia with the "forgotten / memory that we are creatures." Although the poem is
rooted in the war in Southeast Asia, the Vietnam

conflict quickly becomes just one symptom of a much larger malaise that results when humans cling to what the poet calls the "Structural mechanisms of Society" which lead to blind conformity and political allegiance. The poet writes: "Acceptance of guilt for the acts of / entrepreneurs, capitalists and imperialists / smothers, tricks, and stupefies / the free creature." Refusing to cling to what he sees as outmoded and destructive political dogma that ignores biological realities, McClure's response is to divorce himself from the war and from the misguided and cruel society that wages it: "I AM NOT RESPONSIBLE / FOR THOSE WHO HAVE CREATED / AND / OR CAPTURED the CONTROL DEVICES / OF THE SOCIETY THAT SURROUNDS ME!" Arguing that "COMMUNISM WILL NOT WORK!" and that "CAPITALISM IS FAILURE!" McClure dismisses the ideology of both sides of the cold war and claims instead his role as an individual, divorced from the governments that wage a war he hates: "I AM INNOCENT AND FREE! / I AM A MAMMAL!"

By stating that "I have escaped politics" and that the "meanings of Marxism and Laissez faire are extinct," the poet rejects the political and social systems that have been artificially imposed upon the biological realities of life. The social and intellectual forces of the mind—in this case, the abstract notions of politics and government—have repressed the biological aspects of human life, often resulting in disastrous consequences. McClure points to the stark biological realities facing the Earth—realities that have gone unaddressed by both capitalism and communism: overpopulation, mass starvation, genocide, exploitation of resources, and an increasingly repressive and warlike society.

In place of a culture that is governed by political dogma, McClure offers what Allen Van Newkirk has called a bioculture in which biology, not political power, is the basis for action. With the poet's emphatic line near the end of *Poisoned Wheat* that declares that "POLITICS IS DEAD AND BIOLOGY IS HERE!" McClure demands nothing short of a total reorganization of society along these biocultural lines.

Bibliography

Phillips, Rod. *"Forest Beatniks" and "Urban Thoreaus": Jack Kerouac, Gary Snyder, Lew Welch, and Michael McClure.* New York: Peter Lang, 2000.

Van Newkirk, Allen. "The Protein Grail." *Margins* 18 (March 1975): 21–23.

Rod Phillips

Preface to a Twenty Volume Suicide Note Amiri Baraka (1961)

Dedicating the work to his Jewish wife and co-editor of the seminal journal *Yugen*, HETTIE JONES, AMIRI BARAKA (LeRoi Jones) published his first poetry collection, *Preface to a Twenty Volume Suicide Note* at Totem Press, the publishing house that he founded in 1958. Many of the poems—composed between roughly 1957, when Baraka returned from the air force, and 1960—had appeared in little magazines on the East and West Coasts prior to the release of the collection. Of these chronologically ordered poems, one is "IN MEMORY OF RADIO," perhaps his most notable poem.

Despite Baraka's growing reputation as a distinctive voice in "new" poetry and his fixed place in the Greenwich Village bohemian scene, augmented by his work at *Yugen* and Totem Press, *Preface* received mixed reviews. Denise Levertov praised *Preface* for its use of jazz rhythms and the influence of earlier poets on Baraka. However, she warned that its political nature undercut some of its lyrical qualities. Baraka's friend and literary associate Gilbert Sorrentino noted that the style was too full of "tricks."

It is precisely this style that demonstrates Baraka's literary heritage and "authentic voice." Baraka credits Williams Carlos Williams with teaching him "how to write in my own language—how to write the way I *speak* rather than the way I think a poem should be written." *Preface* as a whole demonstrates a Williamsesque reliance on typographical manipulations and unconventional poetic syntax and punctuation. Showing the influence of Beat precursor CHARLES OLSON and the Black Mountain School of poets, Baraka embraced free verse, with its irregular line length and absence of rhyme, in *Preface*. Though Baraka defended the Beat aesthetic in the *Partisan Review* as "less than a movement than a reaction against . . . fifteen years of sterile unreadable magazine poetry" and though he actively praised JACK KEROUAC's "Essay on Spontaneous Prose" in a 1959 letter to *Evergreen Review,* the works in *Preface* show more self-consciousness than the poetry that Kerouac envisioned. However, works such as "The Bridge" have a breathlike, jazz rhythm in the manner of what Kerouac called "blowing."

Thematically, *Preface* illustrates the poet's disaffection with American culture and his growing alienation from society. These are common currents in Beat literature, as William C. Fisher has pointed out. However, *Preface* is positioned uneasily within the Beat canon. The Beats as a group rejected the "organization man" conformist mentality of the Eisenhower–McCarthy establishment that invested truth in ideas such as the American Dream, traditional gender roles, and the conjuration of heroes from mass media. As the title of the collection suggests, the internalization of cultural myths have driven people to the brink; it is the poet's burden to exorcise these cultural demons. *Preface* purports to shatter those cultural myths but, as Fisher writes, "To bring so much heavy apparatus to bear—prefaces and volumes—on a mere note is to mock the ostensible value of the poems themselves." The duality of the poems contained in the work suggest that Baraka is not only disaffected and alienated from society as a whole but also as a lone black voice among a chorus of white Beats, he is a double outsider.

Foreshadowing his eventual break with the Beats to spearhead the black arts movement, when the title poem appeared in *The Naked Ear,* Baraka received a note from Langston Hughes that simply read, "Hail LeRoi from Harlem. I understand you're colored." The poem "Preface To A Twenty Volume Suicide Note" suggests an apocalyptic end for the poet, "the ground opens up and envelopes me," but does so with an irony at his own expense. Because he has become accustomed to his fate, the poet stands apart from the chaos, a critical observer of the "broad edged silly music." However, because he has not the faith of his daughter (to whom the

poem is dedicated), he is rendered a tragic clown, alone and unable to assign meaning to his life or hope for something better. Pleadingly, he writes, "Nobody sings anymore."

In the poem addressed "To a Publisher . . . cut out" Baraka begins by attacking publishers for their commercialism. He rails against their insistence on categorizing poetry and poets, but he then shifts to a critique of his own crowd of intelligentsia for their too-clever conversation, ending with a commentary on the possibly futile act of writing poetry. The poet in this world is both one of the "land creatures in a wet unfriendly world" who is victimized by the forces around him and a victim of his own mediocrity. He has but "talked a good match."

In "One Night Stand" which is addressed to ALLEN GINSBERG and in "Way Out West" which is addressed to GARY SNYDER, the motif of artifice runs through the poems, distancing Baraka from the other poets' respective projects. In "One Night Stand," Baraka conjures the images of indigenous poverty in stark contrast to white, Beat effeminate luxury. Baraka pits the "olives and the green buds" of the traveling poets against the "Twisted albion-horns" of the "black bond servants dazed and out of their wool heads." Interestingly, to heal the schism of his own racial disconnection, the poet chooses to identify with his white friend but does so with a lack of sincerity: "We have come a long way, & are uncertain of which of the masks / is cool." As Marlon B. Ross has written, Baraka "as a lower-class black man among upscale, slumming white beatniks" could only identify with Beats, though he expresses a tension that marks that identity as decadent and ineffectual. Images of white decadence subsumed in homoerotism lead to physical and spiritual decay in "Way Out West": "No use for beauty / collapsed, with moldy breath / done in. Insidious weight / of cankered dreams. Tiresias' / weathered cock." The poet connects these images with his own mortality, juxtaposing the passing of the seasons with the passing of his youth.

Turning his critical gaze toward the black middle classes in "Hymn for Lanie Poo," Baraka satirizes the black man who "apes" the white man by detailing the banality of his stifling, domesticated life. Unique for its distinctly racially conscious voice, "Hymn for Lanie Poo" sets up a tension between the poet and the white consciousness of American culture. In the space of this tension, the narrative takes the black bohemian as well as the black bourgeoisie to task for complicity with white hegemony. Parodying the black bohemian and effectively turning the criticism back on himself, the poet puts the weak protestations of the bohemian national consciousness into minstrel slang: "It's not that I got anything / against cotton, nosiree, by God / It just that . . . / Man lookatthatblonde / whewee! / I think they are not treating us like / Mr. Lincun said they should / or Mr. Gandhi."

In the final poem of the collection, "Notes For A Speech," the poet fully articulates his own estrangement from black culture, "African blues / does not know me." Returning to the unresolved tension of his position as a black poet in a white subculture in a white America, he sees himself as an "ugly man" to whom "Africa / is a foreign place." Unresolved,

Baraka ends the poem on a note of generic angst: "You are / as any other sad man here / american."

Bibliography

Benston, Kimberly W., ed. *Imamu Amiri Baraka (LeRoi Jones): A Collection of Critical Essays.* Englewood Cliffs, N.J.: Prentice-Hall, 1978.

Fischer, William C. "The Pre-Revolutionary Writings of Imamu Amiri Baraka." *Massachusetts Review* 14 (Spring, 1973): 259–305.

Hudson, Theodore. *From LeRoi Jones to Amiri Baraka: The Literary Works.* Durham, N.C.: Duke University Press, 1973.

Mackey, Nathaniel. "The Changing Same: Black Music in the Poetry of Amiri Baraka." *boundary 2* 6, no. 2 (Winter, 1978): 355–386.

Ross, Marlon B. "Camping the Dirty Dozens: The Queer Resources of Black Nationalist Invective." *Callaloo* 23, no. 1 (2000): 290–312.

Stephanie S. Morgan

Q

Queer William S. Burroughs (1985)

Queer is a transitional novel between the hard-boiled prose of JUNKY and the "routines" of NAKED LUNCH.

Queer can be used as an alternative to *Junky*, the text used for the junk paradigm as a blueprint for WILLIAM S. BURROUGHS's oeuvre to be read with a queer paradigm. Jamie Russell's *Queer Burroughs* (2001) and Greg Mullins's *Colonial Affairs: Bowles, Burroughs, and Chester Write Tangier* (2002) are recent scholarly texts that emphasize Burroughs's homosexuality over his drug use to analyze his writings. During the cold-war 1950s it was potentially more subversive to be a homosexual than a junky. To grasp the importance of Burroughs as a novelist, *Queer* must be examined.

Queer was first published almost 35 years after it was written (some speculate that the manuscript was either lost or suppressed by Burroughs). In his introduction to the book, something Burroughs had to write to meet the demands of the publisher for a text of adequate length and a piece of writing that happened to eclipse the novel itself on its publication, Burroughs draws heavily from his letters to ALLEN GINSBERG and JACK KEROUAC, which were written during the period when Burroughs lived in Mexico City, from late 1949 to 1954, and before he moved to Tangier, Morocco. He wrote *Junky, Queer,* and *The* YAGE LETTERS and started what would become INTERZONE. Burroughs shot his wife Joan in 1951, but with the aid of a clever lawyer working the corrupt Mexican legal system of the time, he served only 13 days in jail for her accidental murder. *Junky* covers Burroughs's years of addiction and *Queer* his years off junk in Mexico and on a South American expedition to try to find the mysterious hallucinogenic vine *yage*. Joan is barely mentioned in *Junky* and is conspicuously absent from *Queer.*

At the time when he wrote the books, Burroughs thought of *Junky* and *Queer* as part of the same book: one written on the junk and the other off it. Yet *Queer* is an odd sequel to *Junky*, written as Burroughs struggled for a form to recount his experiences. In the introduction to *Queer*, Burroughs says that while he was an addict, he "just shot up and waited for the next shot." On junk, he needs no human contact. Off junk, however, he is desperate for contact, in particular sexual contact, for when an addict kicks, the sex drive comes back in "full force." At first, Burroughs says, William Lee (Burroughs's persona in the novel) believes that the contact he seeks is merely sexual and that to lure in the sex object named Eugene Allerton (based on Lewis Marker) he devises skits, or comic routines to entertain him. As these performances intensify, however, Lee realizes that he is looking for much more than mere sexual contact: He is searching for contact with an *audience.* Later even that need is removed as he realizes that he can perform for himself, and it is at that point, says Burroughs, that "Lee is being inexorably pressed into the world of fiction." Still, Lee does not yet realize—as Burroughs did not at the time—that he is "committed to writing."

A powerful subtext of this novel is the absence of any discussion of Joan Burroughs's death. When

Carl Solomon tried to get Burroughs to include in *Junky* the "William Tell" scene in which he tried to shoot a glass off Joan's head at a Mexico City party, Burroughs begged off on the basis of how such a scene would betray his artistic intentions. Here, in his shocking and infamous introduction and after having read *Queer* again after three decades, Burroughs writes, "I am forced to the appalling conclusion that I would never have become a writer but for Joan's death, and to the realization of the extent to which this event has motivated and formulated my writing. I live with the constant threat of possession, from Control. So the death of Joan brought me in contact with the invader, the Ugly Spirit, and maneuvered me into a lifelong struggle, in which I have had no choice except to write my way out." Not all of Burroughs scholars buy this commentary as honest or accurate. It is possible to see this claim about "the Ugly Spirit" as a cover for Burroughs to take full responsibility for his foolish, drunken act.

The book begins in medias res with Lee off junk and oversexed, pursuing a boy named Carl. When Carl leaves Mexico City to rejoin his family in Uruguay, Lee makes a more desperate attempt to attract the attention of Winston Moor. Moor is based on the real-life Hal Chase, who earned Burroughs's ire not simply for rejecting Burroughs's sexual advances when Chase visited him in Mexico City but also for Chase's style of rejecting him. Burroughs pays him back here with an equally mean-spirited portrait of physical ugliness and a hypochondriac personality. Moor, he says, "had aged without experience of life, like a piece of meat rotting on a pantry shelf."

The reader follows Lee and the other G.I. Bill students and junkies from their daytime bar, Lola's, to their nighttime haunt, The Ship Ahoy. Lee meets the young ex-soldier, Eugene Allerton, who becomes his obsession. He first sees Allerton with an American girl, Mary, and believing him beyond his reach, he takes refuge in boys at the Chimu, a queer bar. (A similar scene is described in *Junky*, which shows how at one time the two books were connected). The next night Lee starts a conversation with Allerton at the Ship Ahoy. Allerton is drunk and friendly. Oversexed from junk withdrawal, Lee "licked his lips" over Allerton, wolf-

like, and stretches forth "ectoplasmic fingers" to touch him. The limitations on his ability to fulfill his desires are compared to the "bars of a cage," and the book, like all of Burroughs's works, investigates the limits of personal freedom. Lee adopts the strategy of attracting Allerton with his conversational routines.

Lee's routines for Allerton grow more elaborate. Burroughs's first sustained routine, the "Texas Oil-Man routine," is drawn from his experiences as a cotton farmer in Edinburg, Texas, and from his farming days in East Texas. The routine shows Burroughs's continued fascination with the jargon and argot of different professions (as in the underworld language of junkies and queers), but it is also a means of seducing Allerton by entertaining him (much as Burroughs used similar routines in letters to Allen Ginsberg in the late 1940s). To further seduce and "feel out" Allerton, Lee takes him to Jean Cocteau's film *Orpheus*, "cruising" him for responses that might indicate if he is interested in Lee sexually. Lee at last finds an entrée to the subject of his queerness and begins melodramatically, "A curse. Been in our family for generations. The Lees have always been perverts. I shall never forget the unspeakable horror that froze the lymph in my glands . . . when the baneful word seared my reeling brain: **I was a homosexual.** I thought of the painted, simpering female impersonators I had seen in a Baltimore night club. Could it be possible that I was one of those subhuman things?" He turns his confession into a routine that is part truth and part invention. Allerton is apparently open to homosexual experience, and he and Lee have sex in Lee's apartment. The next morning, Lee puts their relationship on a business basis by offering to get Allerton's camera out of hock.

Later Lee lectures Allerton about a South American vine called *yage* that medicine men ingest to achieve telepathic abilities and thought control. Allerton is bored, unaware that Lee wishes to control *his* thoughts. Lee eventually proposes to Allerton that he accompany him on his South American quest for *yage*. He will pay all expenses if Allerton is "nice to Papa, say twice a week." Allerton says that he will consider the offer. In a desperate attempt to capture Allerton's attention, Lee shoots the head off a mouse that is held by its tail by a busboy—perhaps another subconscious reference to Joan's accidental death.

Lee and Allerton travel to Panama City and then fly from Panama to Quito and to Manta. Lee is fighting withdrawal symptoms, and the cities seem to be the most squalid that he has ever observed. (Imagery and events from this trip recur in many of Burroughs's books, including *Naked Lunch*, and the Red Night trilogy.) Lee tells Allerton why he is interested in *yage*—"Think of it: thought control. Take anyone apart and rebuild to your taste"—but he hides his real thoughts from Allerton: "You'd be so much *nicer* after a few alterations." Lee is just one step from becoming like the monstrous Central Intelligence Agency (CIA) agents and Russians who are in South America searching for mind-controlling drugs: "Automatic obedience, synthetic schizophrenia, mass-produced to order. That is the Russian dream, and America is not far behind. The bureaucrats of both countries want the same thing: Control." The search for *yage* becomes an investigation into modern methods of control, which is ironically being practiced by Lee himself in his relationship with Allerton. Lee's invoking of the imperialism of the United States and his identity as the Ugly American demonstrates that *Queer*, far from being a slight, personal work, can be read as a political text that serves as a key for his later political commentary in *Naked Lunch*.

Lee and Allerton fly from Manta to Guayaquil. In Ecuador, he first sees the ancient Chimu pottery with its erotic imagery of men who are engaged in sodomy and of men who are changing into huge centipedes. Throughout his work, from this point on, the centipede imagery of Chimu pottery will come to represent the end of all limits, or, in later works, the horrifying original act that imprisoned human beings in their flesh form. Lee goes to Quito to obtain information about *yage* and finds that it grows on the Amazon side of the Andes. From Babahoya, they take the bus for 14 hours over the top of the Andes Mountains. On the bus, Lee meets an old prospector named Morgan who says that he can obtain any quantity of the vine for Lee. The locals are suspicious of foreigners, however, and do not come through. Lee and Allerton seek out Doctor Cotter, an American living in the jungle near Puyo. They stay with Cotter for a few days, but the botanist is evasive about Lee's questions, suspecting him of some con game to steal his discoveries. They leave without having obtained any of the vine.

There is a gap in the book here. The "Epilogue: Mexico City Return" section was grafted on to the original *Queer* manuscript of 1952 by James Grauerholz; the material here actually came from the *Yage Letters* manuscript and was an unused ending to that text, added on to *Queer* because the manuscript was too short for the publishers. Allerton apparently returns to Mexico City before Lee does. In any case, their relationship has disintegrated, and Allerton has apparently satisfied his curiosity about South America. Lee is stuck in Panama for some time. He has a recurrent dream of being back in Mexico City and asking Allerton's friends if they knew where he was. He conducts this investigation when he actually does return to the city, but he can find no one at Lola's or the other haunts who has information on Allerton. The book ends with a dream/routine, with Lee playing the part of the Skip Tracer, sent by the Friendly Finance Company to collect on Allerton's "debt" to Lee—"Haven't you forgotten something, Gene? You're supposed to come see us every third Tuesday." (The Skip Tracer will show up in many of Burroughs's books, from *Naked Lunch* to the Red Night trilogy).

Joan's death is suppressed in the novel, an absence that may account for the many dreams that are recounted at the end. The last line of the novel eerily suggests the Ugly Spirit that killed her: "The door opened and wind blew through the room. The door closed and the curtains settled back, one curtain trailing over a sofa as though someone had taken it and tossed it there."

Since *Queer* was published in 1985, the book cannot be seen as having influenced queer writing from the 1960s through the early 1980s, but it can be seen as part of the great interest in gay literature in the age of AIDS, and it was published during the rise of queer theory during this time period. *Queer* laid the groundwork for the writing of *Naked Lunch* precisely in terms of Burroughs using a particular audience (unreciprocated objects of desire) as the recipients of his material. Routines from *Queer* can be found first in letters to Marker, just as routines from *Naked Lunch* were initially written in letters to Ginsberg.

Bibliography

Harris, Oliver. "Can You See a Virus? The Queer Cold War of William Burroughs." *Journal of American Studies* 33, no. 2 (1999): 243–266.

Johnson, Rob. "William S. Burroughs: South Texas Farmer, *Junky,* and *Queer.*" *Southwestern American Literature* (Spring 2001): 7–35.

Russell, Jamie. *Queer Burroughs.* New York: Palgrave, 2001.

Rob Johnson and Oliver Harris

R

"Rant" Diane Di Prima (1985)

This marvelous example of late Beat poetry was written in 1985 and included in the 1990 collection *Pieces of a Song*. By title, form, and spirit DIANE DI PRIMA's "Rant" evokes ALLEN GINSBERG's "HOWL." Di Prima has contended this conclusion, insisting rather that CHARLES OLSON is the contemporary inspiration for the piece. The poem also brings to mind the influence of Ezra Pound, whom di Prima made a pilgrimage to visit at St. Elizabeth's Hospital in Washington, D.C., in 1955. In January 1967, di Prima wrote a related poem, "Rant from a Cool Place," which was included in the 1971 volume *Revolutionary Letters* and which offers a vernacular prequel of "cold prosaic fact" that is specified in its moment ("genocide in Southeast Asia now in progress Laos Vietnam / Thailand Cambodia O soft-spoken Sukarno") in contrast to the more generally existential and spiritual discontents of the successor "Rant." The two poems intimate the invention of a genre, the preslam rant, which in di Prima's hand is a fervent, hectoring poem of protest and demand.

The 1985 "Rant" is a jeremiad that is a defense of art, spirituality, and intellectual pursuit, a defense of interiority, as "*intellectus* means 'light of the mind.'" The title of the poem in the context of its claims and calls for correction suggest the unbottled rage of the subaltern, here the poet-speaker/activist. The verses are specifically encompassing ("every man / every woman carries a firmament inside," "A woman's life / a man's life is an allegory"), and the poem stipulates a wholeness of sentience—"there is nothing to integrate, you are a presence / you are an appendage of the work"—through which mind labors to produce art, to express imagination. Formulating an exemplary Beat movement and postmodern aesthetic, the poem dismisses boundaries that divide poetry making from daily life-processes: "there is no part of yourself you can separate out / saying, this is memory, this is sensation / this is work I care about, this is how / I make a living." Rejecting tendencies to separate everyday from existential or artistic pursuits, articulating a poetics in which distinctions among self, labor, and aesthetics are erased, the speaker contends that manual labor, everyday forms of creative expression, have poetics and contain techniques for engendering consciousness:

> There is no way you can *not* have a poetics
> no matter what you do: plumber, baker, teacher
>
> you do it in the consciousness of making
> or not making yr world

The poem rejects gender, class, and vocational limits about what merits the label "art" and who may be called an artist to include the caste of persons who have been by their work excluded. Everyday activities transferred from the historical/cultural record to the discourses of literary production are themselves poetic discoveries. All are implicated in the soul combat this poem defines and joins, for "There is no way out of the spiritual battle / the war is the war against the imagination / you can't

271

sign up as a conscientious objector." Defending the "holy" and "precise" imagination, this "Rant" defends and honors the "inner sun," the "central" fire of consciousness.

Bibliography

Johnson, Ronna C., and Maria Damon. "Recapturing the Skipped Beats." *Chronicle of Higher Education* 46, no. 6 (October 1, 1999): B4, B6.

Kirschenbaum, Blossom S. "Diane di Prima: Extending La Famiglia." *MELUS* 14, nos. 3–4 (Fall–Winter 1987).

Libby, Anthony. "Diane di Prima: 'Nothing Is Lost; It Shines In Our Eyes.'" In *Girls Who Wore Black: Women Writing the Beat Generation,* edited by Ronna C. Johnson and Nancy M. Grace, 45–68. New Brunswick, N.J.: Rutgers University Press, 2002.

McNeil, Helen. "The Archaeology of Gender in the Beat Movement." In *The Beat Generation Writers,* edited by A. Robert Lee, 178–199. East Haven, Conn.: Pluto Press, 1996.

Moffeit, Tony. "Pieces of a Song: Diane di Prima." In *Breaking the Rule of Cool: Interviewing and Reading Women Beat Writers,* edited by Nancy M. Grace and Ronna C. Johnson, 83–106. Jackson: University Press of Mississippi, 2004.

Ronna C. Johnson

Red Wagon Ted Berrigan (1976)

This collection of poems captures TED BERRIGAN in the mode that has made him something of a cult figure among young poets 20-plus years after his death—the uncanny ability to juggle the highs and lows of culture while being simultaneously populist and avant-garde.

The book was published at the end of a fairly stable period in the poet's life. He had married the poet Alice Notley a few years earlier and was once again raising a family (his sons Anselm and Edmund, who grew up to become poets themselves). He was at the end of a four-year poet-in-residence position at Northeastern Illinois University in Chicago, the longest teaching post of his career. A large community of poets gathered about Berrigan, including Bob Rosenthal (later to become Ginsberg's personal assistant), Rochelle Kraut, Art Lange, Rose Lesniak, and Barbara Barg. Many of these poets followed Berrigan to Manhattan when his Chicago job ended.

The title of the volume refers to the famed wagon of the William Carlos Williams poem "The Red Wheelbarrow." This image is usually taken by the doctor–poet's disciples as a return to a focus on the daily drama of everyday life, as opposed to the rarified ether of Williams's bête noire T. S. Eliot. This volume seems to bring in a more the Williamesque strain of Berrigan's poetry into play. One of the best known poems in the volume is "Things to Do in Providence." The "things to do" motif was derived from the entry "things to do in the capitol" in *The Pillow Book of Sei Shonagon* (English translation by Ivan Morris), a prose commonplace book that was popular around New York School poets and often was used in writing exercises in the workshops that were given at the Poetry Project at Saint Mark's Church. The setting of the poem is his native Providence, Rhode Island. Berrigan has returned home because his grandmother is dying. The poet reads the newspaper ("No one you knew / got married / had children / got divorced / died), eats ("swallow / pepsi / meatballs"), takes drugs ("give yourself the needle"), and watches television.

The almost journallike rendering of the extreme quotidian is offset by Berrigan's use of a composition-by-field technique that is reminiscent of both CHARLES OLSON and William's "The Desert Music." Berrigan watches a Western on TV, answers a phone call ("'Hello! I'm drunk! & / I have no clothes on!' / '"My goodness,' I say. / 'See you tomorrow.'"), and reads all night.

Berrigan's use of dailiness is a radical extension of PHILIP WHALEN's poetry. The language is speech-like, and the lack of artifice that is common to the mainstream poem of the period is stark. However, Berrigan is also like a good poker player: He refuses to telegraph "the winning hand" that he is holding. In reference to his grandmother's impending death he notes:

> The heart stops briefly when someone dies,
> a quick pain as you hear the news, & someone
>   passes
> from your outside life to inside. Slowly the heart
>   adjusts

to its new weight, & slowly everything continues
sanely.

As his widow Alice Notley noted: "I have heard
these lines recited at funerals; people use them, the
lines say 'that thing' right. Why or how? Because
the words 'briefly' and 'sanely' are farther apart
than the two 'slowlys,' and the word 'heart' is accurate and free of sentiment? Or because, as you
might say, he knows what he's talking about? Well,
both."

Other poems in *Red Wagon* extend the poet's
interest in cut-ups, borrowings, and collage. "From
a List of Delusions the Insane What They Are
Afraid Of" is a digest of a longer poem by David
Antin (and Antin's source was from a psychiatric
text). Berrigan would quip, "I just used David's
most interesting lines!" when he read this poem in
public. A similar technique is used in "The Complete Prelude: Title Not Yet Fixed Upon," which
samples Wordsworth. A number of poems are recognizable as products of writing exercises found in
the "teaching writing" books of Kenneth Koch.

The spirit of JACK KEROUAC is present in
the poem "Goodbye Address." Using an ALLEN
GINSBERG-like stanza, the poem is a ritual for leaving a temporary home—a situation with which
Berrigan was familiar as he traveled around the
country doing various writing residencies:

> Goodbye House, 24 Hungtington, one block past
> Hertel
> on the downtown side of Main, second house on
> the left.
> Your good spirit kept me cool this summer, your
> ample space.
> Goodbye house.

When he read this poem in public, Berrigan usually
prefaced it by saying that the genesis of the poem
was reading that Kerouac, during the height of his
interest in Buddhism, had a farewell ritual that he
enacted every time he left a space in which he had
resided.

Red Wagon was an influential and popular
volume among young poets of its era. Against the
backdrop of the high-minded moralism that was
typical of the immediate post-Vietnam mainstream

poetry, the pleasure that Berrigan's poetry takes in
the incidentals of the day world are almost revelatory. Similarly, Berrigan's radical poetry techniques
are unaccompanied by the sort of manifestos and
exegesis that would be commonplace with the
then-nascent language poetry movement (many
former students of Berrigan's). Paul Carroll was
more than on-target when he declares on the back
of *Red Wagon*, "Ted Berrigan is one of Whitman's
most legitimate sons."

Joel Lewis

Revolt of the Cockroach People, The
Oscar Zeta Acosta (1973)

This second volume of fact–fiction memoir continues all the high-wire verve of its predecessor *The
AUTOBIOGRAPHY OF A BROWN BUFFALO* (1972).
The Chicano–Beat antic pose again holds, "Oscar"
or "Zeta" as at once first- and third-person participant in the Chicano upheavals of the 1960s.
OSCAR ZETA ACOSTA's account, thus, overlappingly
can be historic, confessional, self-monitoring, foul-
mouthed and, as it were, Beat-fantastical: "I stand
and observe them all. I who have been running
around with my head hanging for so long. I who
have been lost in my own excesses, drowned in my
own confusion. A faded beatnik, a flower vato, an
aspiring writer, a thirty-three-year old kid full of
buffalo chips is supposed to defend these bastards."
As the voice of *The Revolt of the Cockroach People*,
he so positions himself in relation to the Chicano
militants who are involved in the local school
strikes of 1968. The lawyer–radical blends with
the "faded beatnik," the "aspiring writer" with the
"flower vato." Chicano or Beat, Chicano and Beat,
this authorial self-pairing could not again be more
striking.

On the one hand and as autobiography-
cum-novel, the text yields an "actual" Acosta of
Los Angeles courtrooms and barricades. This is
Acosta as counsel in the "St. Basil's Cathedral
21" and "Los Angeles 13" Chicano militant trials, the would-be exposer of the jail death of the
youth Robert Fernandez and the police shooting of
"Roland Zanzibar" (based on the award-winning
Chicano radio and print journalist Reuben Salazar

of station KMEX), the political cospirit of legendary leadership such as César Chávez and Denver's "Corky" Gonzalez, and the independent La Raza Unida candidate for sheriff of Los Angeles County.

On the other hand, this is the Acosta who relishes his own writer's distance from the events at hand, a figure of mask, persona, and almost self-invention who sees his silhouette in the Aztec warrior–founder–god Huitzilopochtli, speaks of himself as "Vato Número Uno" and "singer of songs," and uses the court to give a parallel history of *chicanismo* with due allusion to Quetzacoatl, Moctezuma, Córtes, and La Malinche through to 1848 and the Anglo appropriation of the Southwest and its latter-day aftermath. He thus recalls his part in the bombing by Chicano activists of a Safeway store and a Bank of America branch, and yet he stands back to monitor it, the participant–observer both as *carnal* (brother/dude) and yet edging into madness at the petty conspirators and fifth columnists within Chicano activism.

Throughout, and in an address to the court that as much serves as an appeal to history as to the law, he again emphasizes his Chicano–Beat outsider status: "A hippie is like a cockroach. So are the beatniks. So are the Chicanos. We are all around, Judge. And Judges do not pick us to serve on Grand Juries." The text, appropriately, becomes near-hallucinatory. The Chicano poor who protest Cardinal McIntyre's high-tier cathedral in Los Angeles transpose into a "gang of cockroaches." Placards read "YANKEES OUT OF AZTLAN," "MENUDO EVERY DAY," and "VIVA EL ZETA!" As the "religious war" erupts, "Oscar" envisions himself as both his own familiar and his own stranger: "'Come on,' our lawyer exhorts. I, strange fate, am this lawyer."

The trials, his own contempt-of-court imprisonments, and the political campaign for sheriff are assuredly real enough, but there is, throughout, more than a suggestion of Beat phantasmagoria, be it his ingestions of Quaalude–400s, would-be subpoena of the entire Californian judicial bench on grounds of racism, love trysts, or image of the arrest, self-hanging and autopsy of Robert Fernandez as if it were the abused larger body of *chicanismo*. It could not be more appropriate that questing, as he says, for "my Chicano soul," he associates with "my beatnik days."

Bibliography
Lee, A. Robert. "Chicanismo's Beat Outrider?: The Texts and Contexts of Oscar Zeta Acosta." *The Beat Generation: Critical Essays,* edited by Kostas Myrsiades, 259–280. New York: Peter Lang, 2002.

A. Robert Lee

Revolution for the Hell of It Abbie Hoffman (1967)

Only ABBIE HOFFMAN would open a Beat/jazz/hip/revolutionary/yippie masterpiece like *Revolution for the Hell of It* with a letter supposedly from his mother. It is dated November 1, 1967, and in it Mrs. Hoffman, real or imagined, frets over *Time* magazine's coverage of Abbie's latest plans to levitate the Pentagon. As his "mother" chides him for his irresponsible hippie ways (he is even thinking about moving to California!), we get the full blast of *Time*'s bewilderment at Abbie's application for a permit to raise the Pentagon 30 feet off the ground by surrounding it and chanting, no doubt while under the influence of illegal drugs.

Abbie Hoffman's *Revolution for the Hell of It* thus blasts its way into literary history as a stream-of-consciousness riff on a society that is ravaged by war and a revolutionary movement that is led by stoned youngsters with absolutely no idea what they were doing.

After those words from Mrs. Hoffman, Abbie quotes the legendary revolutionary Ernesto "Che" Guevara as telling us that "In Revolution, one wins or dies." Then he presents us with a televison commercial touting Dash as a "revolution" in cleansing powder.

The intense media/political schizophrenia of the 1960s is thus epitomized and skewered as its leading street psychotherapist tears off on an introductory rant.

As a literary pioneer, Hoffman is alternatively coherent and babbling, brilliant and baffled. "There is no way to run a revolution," he says, and then he repeats "do your thing" six times. He writes: "There are no rules, only images. Only a System has boundaries. Eichmann lived by rules."

It is tempting to call the stream-of-consciousness rant that opens *Revolution for the Hell of It* a

Beat brand of anarchism, but Hoffman would have rejected that; he wrote repeatedly that "isms are wasms."

Instead the book relies on mantralike ALLEN GINSBERGian chants that stem from a deep faith in the one thing Hoffman trusts: the inner human spirit.

"TRUST YOUR INSTINCTS. TRUST. TRUST. TRUST . . ." is repeated many times.

After he finishes his opening rant, Hoffman fills *Revolution for the Hell of It* with scraps of press releases, sectarian arguments, logistical instructions for getting to Chicago for the infamous 1968 Democratic Convention, acid-based definitions of *Yippie,* and a crazed account of how he kicked in Sergeant Fink's trophy case to get himself arrested in solidarity with "spades" who were being harassed on the Lower East Side.

Revolution for the Hell of It becomes a zen koan as Abbie answers a reporter's question "Is that a club?" by answering that it is "a part of a tree. It symbolizes my love for nature."

Today *Revolution for the Hell of It* can seem dated, so deeply is it rooted in its time, but it bridges the ages in its hectic, eclectic style and never shies from the universal, transcendent issues of war, love, and existence. As a condensation/concentration of the mindset of an astonishing era, *Revolution for the Hell of It* will be around for a long, long time.

Harvey Wasserman

Rexroth, Kenneth (1905–1982)

Popularly known as "the godfather of the Beats," Kenneth Rexroth criticized them as wisely as he inspired and promoted them. Born a generation before ALLEN GINSBERG, GARY SNYDER, MICHAEL McCLURE, PHILIP LAMANTIA, and PHILIP WHALEN, all of whom he enthusiastically introduced in San Francisco as the M. C. of the famous Six Gallery poetry reading of October 7, 1955, Rexroth was already achieving international fame as a leader of the San Francisco Poetry Renaissance. He was a philosophical, mystical, intensely erotic poet of love and rebellion, a translator from Asian and European languages, a cubist painter, and an in-

fluential cultural critic. He had also published poetic dramas on classical subjects, had advocated anarchism as an alternative to both capitalism and communism, and had been active in the Industrial Workers of the World.

Though the exact influence of Rexroth's "THOU SHALT NOT KILL: A MEMORIAL FOR DYLAN THOMAS" (written 1953–54, published 1955) on Ginsberg's "HOWL" (1956) is debatable, the older poet's comprehensive outraged lament for visionary poets who were destroyed by the culture of death intensified underground rebellion against the cold-war nuclear arms race. Recorded with jazz accompaniment, it remains the most powerful reminder of his many innovative performances with music. Remaining closest to Snyder, with whom he profoundly shared the values of Buddhism and environmentalism, Rexroth cheered Beat poets for their boldly individualistic creativity, but he ridiculed the commercialized stereotypes of beatniks and, later, hippies.

Born on December 22, 1905, in South Bend, Indiana, Rexroth grew up in Chicago. After his parents, cosmopolitan bohemians who encouraged his genius, died when he was a child, he precociously developed as a poet, a painter, and a revolutionary orator during the Chicago literary renaissance and lived in poverty. Expelled from public high school, he visited some classes at the University of Chicago, began to learn and translate Chinese and Japanese, but never matriculated or received a degree. In *An Autobiographical Novel* (1966) he tells of his adventurous development in Chicago and elsewhere until 1927 when he hitchhiked with his bride Andre Dutcher, an anarchist painter, to San Francisco where he lived until, disgusted by the prevailing drug culture, he moved to Santa Barbara in 1968. There he resided, except for frequent poetry tours to Europe and Asia, until his death 14 years later at the peak of his international fame. Meanwhile, he had been married three more times and had two daughters.

Readers have converged on Rexroth's work from several directions. Those primarily interested in the art of poetry discover in his a remarkable range of forms and techniques: haiku, tanka, ballads, love lyrics, elegies, free verse, hilarious satires, bawdy limericks, song lyrics, travel poems, epistolary poems, cubist poems, philosophical epics, Buddhist meditations, even a bestiary, on and on. Besides *The Complete Poems* (2003), his tetralogy of tragic verse plays was published as *Beyond the Mountains* (1951).

Moreover, many readers who are interested in poetry from non-English cultures have delighted in Rexroth's manifold and popular translations from Japanese, Chinese, French, Spanish, Latin, and Greek. Though his translations have not yet been collected in a single volume, many of his books from individual languages are still in print.

Even readers who do not ordinarily read poetry have become fans of Rexroth's brilliant cultural criticism, which originally were published in many periodicals and then were collected in a dozen books such as *Bird in the Bush* (1959) and *Assays* (1961), which accurately predicted 1960's countercultural movements from underground rumblings. *Classics Revisited* (1968) and *Communalism: Its Origins to the Twentieth Century* (1974) profoundly link certain traditional values with contemporary countercultural values: love, beauty, prophetic vision, justice, aesthetic creativity, and cooperative utopianism, among others. His long article on literature in the 1974 *Encyclopedia Britannica* and his books of literary criticism established him as an erudite literary scholar and influential critic outside the academy, challenging its cant, canons, fads, and dogmas. A selection of Rexroth's most widely read essays is *World Outside the Window* (1987).

Rexroth's exploration and expression of Japanese culture deepened during his poetry tours of Asian nations between 1967 and 1982, accompanied by the poet Carol Tinker after their marriage in 1974. His major creations from this experience of Asia were a long Zen poem called *The Heart's Garden, the Garden's Heart* and a sequence of erotic, tantric poems that he published as his translations from a Japanese woman, though he had actually created them as well as the persona in *The Love Songs of Marichiko* (1978).

Readers of much of Rexroth's work have been intrigued by his synthesis of diverse values from Asian and Western traditions, such as Buddhism and Christianity, expressing them in a variety of poetic forms and avant-garde innovations. He was a poet of love and justice, philosophical rationality and mystical realization, individuality that voluntarily cooperates with others for the common good, and nonviolent rebellion against oppression. The achievements and limitations of Beat writers can be more deeply understood in the context of his worldview.

Books and papers by and about Rexroth are in libraries at UCLA, SUNY–Buffalo, the University of Chicago (The Morgan Gibson Collection in the Regenstein Library), and Kanda University of International Studies (where 13,000 volumes of his personal library are in a special collection, with some information online).

Bibliography

Gibson, Morgan. *Revolutionary Rexroth: Poet of East-West Wisdom.* Hamden, Conn.: The Shoe String Press, 1985. The Expanded Internet Edition (2000) with Rexroth's Letters to Gibson (1957–79) is at Karl Young's *Light & Dust* site. Available online. URL: http://www.thing.net/~grist/ld/rexroth/gibson.htm.

Gutierrez, Donald. *"The Holiness of the Real": the Short Verse of Kenneth Rexroth.* Madison and Teaneck, N.J.: Associated University Presses, 1996.

Hamalian, Linda. A *Life of Kenneth Rexroth.* New York: W. W. Norton, 1991.

Knabb, Ken. *The Relevance of Rexroth* and *Rexroth Archives.* The best source on and about Rexroth's work is available online at the Bureau of Public Secret. URL: http://www.bopsecrets.org/rexroth. Of special interest is the survey of worldwide celebrations of the 2005 centenary of Rexroth's birth, organized by John Solt and others.

Morgan Gibson

Riprap Gary Snyder (1959)

While GARY SNYDER was in Japan, Cid Corman visited from Italy and, with financial support from LAWRENCE FERLINGHETTI, arranged for the first edition of this book, Snyder's first published volume of poetry, to be printed in Kyoto under the imprint Origin Press. In 1965 Donald Allen published it in his series for the Four Seasons Foundation and added Snyder's translations of Han Shan, which had originally appeared in *Evergreen Review* in 1958. In 1969 a new edition was published with a photo of Snyder replacing the plain cover of the earlier editions; it remained in print until 1990. In that year a new edition appeared from Jack Shoemaker's North Point Press with a photo of a riprap trail on the cover, and Snyder added an afterword about the genesis and aesthetics of the poems. In 2004 Shoemaker reissued this version under the Shoemaker and Hoard imprint.

Riprap and TURTLE ISLAND are the two best-known volumes of Snyder's poetry. *Riprap* establishes one major strand of Snyder's poetics. In contrast to the (Ezra) Poundian, highly allusive and esoteric poetics that define *Myths & Texts* and a significant portion of *Mountains and Rivers Without End*, his two book-length sequences, the poetics of *Riprap* generate relatively short lyric poems that average a half to one page in length. The majority of the poems also contain equally short lines of a half-dozen or so words, many of them monosyllabic. Identification of the speaker is generally omitted through frequent reliance on participles and infinitives, or it only appears late in the poem. While high in alliteration, there is little rhyme, and rhythm is established by means of syllable count, punctuation, and line breaks that are designed to mimic the described activity, such as walking, meditating, or running. Themes develop through accretion across the poems as a group, with some containing literal images that only take on added resonance when considered in the context of other poems in the collection.

The poems of *Riprap,* although they can be read discretely as separate lyrics, can also be read as a loose sequence, unfolding in both time and space, encompassing Snyder's time in the Sierra Nevada in the mid-1950s, his first years in Japan, and his return trip to the United States as a worker on the oil tanker, *Sappa Creek.* The sequence character of the collection is reinforced by Snyder's placing the title poem, "Riprap," at the end of the volume, functioning as a metapoetic statement that is directly addressed to the reader.

The opening two-stanza poem, "Mid-August at Sourdough Mountain Lookout," describes a moment in one of his work experiences as fire lookout for the Forest Service. The poem may be read entirely literally with the opening stanza describing the vision that the speaker has from his lookout tower on a specific day, with this specificity directing readers toward a literal rather than symbolic reading. In contrast, the second stanza opens with a reflective statement, "I cannot remember things I once read." He can, however, remember friends, but they are beyond his vision in cities far removed from the wilderness in which he is immersed. The poem closes: "Looking down for miles / through high still air." That is, he is working at the moment of the poem. It is the forgetting depicted that urges readers to add a layer of interpretation to the literal description, but the pace of the poem and the lack of evidently emotive words render it difficult to discern a specific tone. He has taken the time to take stock of what he is forgetting and what he is remembering, but only the "but" suggests that he may very well miss them, and clearly he is not brooding on his separation from other people. More than anything else, this poem provides a setting with the most significant word, probably the "still" of the last line, a reading that is encouraged by the highly emotional and agitated tone of the poem that follows it, "The Late Snow & Lumber Strike of the Summer of Fifty-Four."

By the time snow has fallen in the forested mountains, the speaker's job as a lookout has ended for the season, and he must find other work to live through the winter. But the strike precludes finding a job anywhere in the Pacific Northwest. As a result, although he can climb Mount Baker and have the same solitude that he experienced as a lookout, he cannot gain a meditative state because he is "Thinking of work / . . . / I must turn and go back." The emphasis on the disquiet that the work silencing strike causes encourages an interpretation that the city and its economy define the character of human life, even high on a mountain, from which there is no escape. Yet the speaker would like to escape such determinism, not because he does not wish to work, since the previous poem and lines in this one imply that work provides the basis for being able "to think," whereas a lack of work disrupts it. Rather, the speaker pits the cities and their synthetic economies against the natural economies of the mountains.

Here in these first two poems Snyder defines a signal difference between the West Coast and the East Coast Beat movements. The latter, as evident from its major figures, was urban focused and idealized the freedom of traveling by car on the open road. The former was nature focused and idealized the freedom of mountain climbing and getting away from the city into the wilderness. JACK KEROUAC captures the essence of this distinction in his two most famous books, *ON THE ROAD* and *The DHARMA BUMS*. At the same time, Kerouac, ALLEN GINSBERG, and others were quite open to undergoing the wilderness experience because underneath this initial urban/wilderness dichotomy lay the fundamental appeal of the rejection of 1950s consumerism that was reflected in their lifestyles and work decisions, whether living in the woods or living in the city, and the common interest in Eastern alternatives to Western philosophy and culture.

Riprap also contains four poems set in Japan. The last of these, "A Stone Garden," bears little resemblance to any of the others. The language is formal, the pace is measured and slow, it has four numbered movements, and it closes with a couplet. Snyder attempts to take in the land and the people as a cultural whole. The strong tone of nostalgia and longing for personal relationships and familial love, in contrast to the solitude and independence of spirit in the American poems, is explained by the place and date lines at the end: "Red Sea / December, 1957." Snyder has left Japan, not knowing when or if he will return. Until the title poem at the end, "A Stone Garden" is followed by the other poems written aboard the tanker on which he worked as it made its way from Japan to the Middle East before heading to the United States. Like so much other Beat literature, *Riprap* records a journey, both physical and spiritual.

Patrick Murphy

River of Red Wine and Other Poems
Jack Micheline (1958)

Covering a wide variety of subjects and styles, JACK MICHELINE's first published book of poetry must be seen against the background of its time. The rebellion for which the author became well-known is more of a statement than a shout. We see more of his power of observation, his youthful excitement, and his feelings about nature. Behind this though, we remember that these were the times of *Sputnik*

and science and the space race—of *Happy Days*, of the flight to suburbia, of alcohol, and before drugs. During these times we see Micheline dealing with inner space—almost his own race to keep the humane alive in this world.

River of Red Wine was blessed with an introduction by JACK KEROUAC. The book's proposed publisher at Troubadour Press told Micheline that he had to rearrange the graphics of the lines to look more interesting and had to get a "famous person" to write an introduction. Quite by coincidence Micheline and Kerouac were both living in the same apartment building for a brief time, and one Jack approached the other Jack, who in his exuberant wine-imbibed state, said "Wow" and then "Yes." Kerouac clearly liked Micheline's work and writes, "Micheline is a fine new poet, and that's something to crow about. Doctor William Carlos Williams I think would like him, if he heard him read out loud. He has that swinging free style I like... . See? There is some poetry I don't like, and that's the poetry that's premeditated and crafted and revised. . . . I like the free rhyme, and these sweet lines revive the poetry of open hope in America, by Micheline, tho Whitman and Ginsberg know all that jive, and me too, and there are so many other great poets swinging nowadays. . . ."

River of Red Wine contains only 27 poems. The title poem uses a sort of stream-of-consciousness form that is so often evident in Micheline's writing. From one subject to another, his mind races; it all makes perfect sense to him—the connections are obvious. It was all about go, go, go—move to the beat—be alive—BE. He describes the world around him breathlessly, perhaps in imitation or implication of speech when drunk: "covered in glories / of scream filled nights / you've played games / with bed bugs / musicians blew trumpets / down back alleys." His words are more sound than thought—global than linear—jazz poetry—improvisation in language: "five bucks a pint / for a river of red wine / we are bleeding in the / deserts of your world."

The first poem in the collection, "Let's Sing A Song," embodies, perhaps, the essence of his message—simple and profound—let's sing a song—be happy, don't worry—and for singing a song he was carted away, the plight that he wants us to understand: Singing is crazy, smiling not okay. Be serious.

In "Tenant Farmer" we see one of Micheline's frequent interesting juxtapositions—first a sweet pastoral scene—then suddenly the suffocating ending: "Green grass / in the summertime / noises of frogs / in a creek / a plow striking / the earth / sun's rays / against his back. / Sixteen years / in a two room shack." "Lost Child" also deals in juxtaposition—the beauty of nature while hearing the sounds of bottles crashing against walls in the street.

"Lower Depths" showers the reader with sounds and sights and smells and feelings from "Fists / slamming / against / a / man's / face" to "rivers flow / in never / ending stream." "Wasteland," written in a different form, is a hypnotic exploration of reality and depression. In "Give Bird Love," invoking Charlie Parker, one of the jazz musicians who had a profound impact on the Beats, Micheline shows us the beauty that there is in spite of harsh reality. Micheline often read his poetry with jazz musicians such as Charlie Mingus or Bob Feldman. He was primarily a performance poet.

In "On the Curbstones" we begin to see the rhythm that naturally guides the poet: "To wail a beat / on a tin can / deaf to the sounds / of the deceivers / enclosed in steel / shelters of the mind / . . . Who saw the unbelievable sunset / which sang a song of songs? / No-one heard / but the winos / and the poets. / . . . to be born again / to the beauty no one saw / but the lovers and the insane." We hear his budding anger and sadness against the world that he sees and his frustration that most of the world does not see. One hears the beat in this poem, the cadence with which Micheline and other poets of his time became identified—it is the sound, the dance, the walk—look at the words on the page.

"Shoe Shine Joe" is one of the poet's early word portraits where he brings to life the whole of a person with an economy of words. These portraits are little poems about people whom he encountered in all walks of life. "Wanderer" is another hint of poems to come, where he speaks for the ordinary man and those who hurt. Some of his strongest lines are in this poem: "Did you ever see people / waiting to die in the heat of / coffee house and automats in late evenings? / . . . In the early dawn of Gary, Indiana / the steel mill shoots firey slag / orange and black into the sky. / In the white

houses / families die choked and strangled / thirsting for trinkets of joy / to fill their hollow spaces."

A Breughel painting in words, "Carnival in Pardeesville" is a wonderful little vignette of childhood. Another sweet poem–painting in this collection is "To My Grandfather." Micheline has written often of his grandfather, describing him as somewhat of a pied piper, a roaming storyteller in Romania—a learned Jewish Gypsy. He was apparently an important influence on Micheline and his writing.

"Imagination Saturday Night" is a poem that embodies the poet's thinking and his rhythm and style and the hip and the bop of the day: "oh baby / send me / send me / oh baby send me too / send me / send me / send me/ to another / world that's true." Sam Cooke's song "You Send Me" topped the rhythm-and-blues and top 40 charts of 1957.

River of Red Wine (there is such a place in Spain) is an excellent first collection for a young poet. It received notice from Dorothy Parker in *Esquire* magazine and raves from CHARLES BUKOWSKI with whom Micheline had a long-term correspondence and friendship. Another friend and supporter, Father Alberto Huerta, S.J., says, "Jack Micheline's poetic diction, unencumbered by the trappings of spiritual violation and rupture, salvages lost innocence and simplicity." John Bennett in *Ragged Lion* speaks of "the enormity of who Jack Micheline had been. . . ." Micheline speaks best for himself in a statement called Censorship In America that was written in 1985: "When I began to write in the early fifties my work was full of anger and raw energy. I roamed America like a mad dog. . . . By some lucky accident my first book of poems was published 'River of Red Wine' with an introduction by Jack Kerouac. I was launched on a Rocket ship called hope into a literary jungle loaded with shit, far worse than the garment center where I pushed a hand truck years before, nonetheless I began to discover myself the process of being my own man had begun. It was a time when Henry Miller, ALLEN GINSBERG, Jack Kerouac, [WILLIAM S.] BURROUGHS were influencing young writers. A time of great energy in New York and San Francisco. Out of the slime pits of America new voices were emerging in all the arts. Poetry, Painting, Jazz, Dance, Theatre. . . . A time of revolt and breaking down of old values. McCarthy was gone and John Kennedy was making his rise to the Presidency of the United States. A time of hope . . . [but] the dollar bill emerged as king rat. Nothing emerged from the mass protest but the enrichment of those controlling it."

Bibliography

Bennett, John, ed. *Ragged Lion: A Tribute To Jack Micheline.* Brooklyn/and Ellensburg, N.Y.: The Smith Publishers and Vagabond Press, 1999.

Micheline, Jack. *67 Poems For Downtrodden Saints.* 1997. 2d ed. San Francisco: FMSBW, 1999.

patricia cherkin alexander

"River-Root: A Syzygy" William Everson (Brother Antoninus) (1976)

WILLIAM EVERSON's long narrative poem, "River-Root: A Syzygy," is said to have been written in response to ALLEN GINSBERG's "HOWL," which appeared in the 1957 second number of *Evergreen Review*—and to which Everson reportedly responded in horror. The report emphasizes his revulsion from Ginsberg's autoeroticism, thus occasioning this 173 strophe, 32-page counterpoint that celebrates heterosexual love. Perhaps this is true but, as thus bluntly stated, it is certainly as to the essence of the piece insufficient and short-sighted.

The poem seems more appropriately described as a paean to the erotic fullness of the world itself, the masculine and feminine sexual drives reflecting the very dynamism of God's creation and of God Himself/Herself—as personified in the extremely explicit lovemaking of a Catholic couple, who are the parents of four children and who become the poem's centerpiece only after establishing a geologic—in fact, a cosmic—reach that recognizes the interacting opposites that allow for a dynamic existence that is sacrament itself.

The "River" is the Missouri–Mississippi, and the "Root" is a kind of inverted tree of creation, the multirivered, multistreamed origin and feed of the Father of Waters. This torrential creative force is also the cosmic source of galaxies, stars, and planets. And, of course, by homonym it is the "Route," or way, by which all creation is fashioned and directed. In this metaphor of creation all things are sexual:

> For the River is male. He is raking down ridges,
> And sucks up mud from alluvial flats, far muck-
> bottomed valleys.
> He drags cold silt a long way, a passion to bring,
> Keeps reaching back for what he has left and
> channeling on.
> All head: but nonetheless his roots are restless.
> They have need of suckling, the passion to fulfill.
> In the glut of hunger
> He chews down the kneecaps of mountains.
>
> And bringing down to bring on has but one
> resolve: to deliver.
> It is this that makes up his elemental need,
> Constitutes his primal ground, the under-aching
> sex of the River.

The poem is archetypal. It is the cry of all life that is intent on multiplying—buck and doe, buffalo and cow, squirrel, coyote, rabbit, drake, pike, turtle, and bullfrog—culminating in a mixed-race couple who represent consciousness with brain capacity and immortal soul, is able to give glory to the maker of it all. The couple is resolving their recent quarrel of wills in sacramental coitus, repeating, varying, fast and slow paced, aggressive and gentle, in a whole night of lovemaking, intermittently dreaming of separate childhoods and ongoing burgeoning in children. It is sex at its most explicit.

One thinks of two pornography trials in San Francisco, the first for Ginsberg's "Howl" in 1956, the second for LENORE KANDEL's *LOVE BOOK* in 1967; the first cleared, the second judged guilty of obscenity, though later a mistrial was declared. The second was precisely the same ecstatic and specific word spilling as in "River-Root" with its "phallos–thrust" and "labial door," "scrotum" and "vulva," but "River-Root" outdistanced the second by 24 pages with 151 verse paragraphs of explicit sex compared to the *Love Book*'s six pages and 12 verse paragraphs. All three poems, candid to an extreme but upright, would constitute a significant test of whether discernment and justice were possible from a jury of peers. The essence is not in the details but in their moral purpose.

Everson's poem at any rate is intended not as a rejection of the Beat world nor as a condemnation of Ginsberg. It is a desperate expedient to widen and deepen the context of sex and love in that world and to give a counterpoint to "Howl," where sex is a symbol of the alienation caused by society. Everson would offer assonance to the prevailing dissonance:

Beyond him [that is, the lover] the River,
And beyond the river the continental mass,
And beyond the humped hemisphere,
    somnolent, awash like a whale on its primal
    sea,
And beyond the hemisphere the globed earth,
    female, . . .
Each one is seized,
As the God so seizes in the act of existence, in
    the swept fire,
The excellence of the creative act, . . .

Everson echoes Ginsberg's "Howl" but challenges his fellow poet:

For the phallos is holy
And holy is the womb: the holy phallos
In the sacred womb. And they melt.
And flowing they merge, the incarnational join
Oned with the Christ.

This sexual love, though lost in the world of established superficiality, gray flannel suits, conformity, mediocrity, deaf and dumb response, materialism, repression, exclusion, and so on that the Beats reject, exists beatifically in God—presence, wholeness of spirit, worship, mystery, and incarnated God.

The great mystery for Everson is the Incarnation, God entering and becoming part of the world, a world in which Ginsberg perhaps wants to believe but that is obscured by the time's all-flattening veil of post-World War II willful forgetfulness and even forgery of mystery.

The word *Syzygy* closing the title has a dictionary meaning: "the conjunction or opposition of two heavenly bodies," "any two related things, either alike or opposite," from the Greek "yoked," "union," "pair." The poem was published in 1976 (though written in 1957) as a celebration of the bicentennial of the United States, but its original context, though meaningful also to the national persona, was the Jungian joining of male and female, animus and anima, a wholeness that Everson found missing both in the postwar country and in the Beat response to that disjunction.

"River-Root: A Syzygy" was a breakthrough for Everson/Antoninus. After a two-year dryness or writer's block in the monastery, the poetry flowed once more in that year 1957 with all its breakthrough events. Although the poem was not immediately published (one wonders what his priory officials and the order's censors would have thought of it!), it prepared him for the later 1967 *Rose of Solitude* and the 1973 *Tendril in the Mesh* integrations, which freed Everson more clearly and cleanly to choose to leave a monastic life that was not congenial to his nature. The nine-year publication delay, however, also blocked any response from his confreres, the Beats. How they would have judged it must remain only a guess. Everson's own words on "River-Root" and its relationship to his other poems should be read in the essay "The Priapic Image," which is most readily available in two collections of his forewords and interviews.

Bibliography

Everson, William. "The Priapic Image." In *Earth Poetry: Selected Essays & Interviews of William Everson*, edited by Lee Bartlett, 205–218. Berkeley: Oyez, 1980.

Robert Brophy

S

Sanders, Ed (1939–)

ED DORN writes, "Whereas movie stars *think of* themselves as movie stars, Ed Sanders *is* a movie star." If Sanders had to pick his own gravestone, he would want it to read, "Ed Sanders, American Bard" because a bard, he explains, is a poet who takes public stances. Though poetry and public stances are two things that characterize Sanders's life, they are two of dozens. American Bard, though apt, is a grave understatement.

Much younger than most of the first Beats, Sanders discovered ALLEN GINSBERG's "HOWL" as a 17 year old in Kansas City, Missouri. He was, as he tells it, overnight reborn, quoting from the poem (which his teachers proclaimed "filth") in his classes, questioning authority at every turn, even being suspended for a time. After high school graduation he headed to New York to become a poet himself, kicking off a head-spinning list of achievements from poet activist to musical inventor to rock star.

After earning his degree in Classics from New York University in 1964, Sanders founded the Peace Eye Book Store on Manhattan's Lower East Side, where he ran a free press that was dedicated to helping renegade magazines and insurgent leaflets blanket the streets with their messages. One such magazine was Sanders's own *Fuck You!: A Magazine of the Arts,* a venture that proclaimed itself "a total assault on the culture" and as such garnered much notice from the police at a time when perceived obscenity, like that of comedian Lenny Bruce, was literally being put on trial. Then,

along with Tuli Kupferburg, Sanders formed the controversial "folk-rock poetry satire group" The Fugs. As he writes in the liner notes to *The Fugs Second Album,* "We vowed to live from our art, to have fun and party continuously, and somehow to translate our creativity to tape." The band was a shock to the system with loads of satirical songs such as "Kill For Peace," had a penchant for using envelope-pushing "dirty" words and sexual innuendo, and had an honest desire to draw attention to "the oodles of freedom guaranteed by the United States Constitution that was not being used." True to their 1985 album title, *Refuse to be Burnt Out,* The Fugs still perform occasionally and released *The Fugs Final CD* in 2003.

As Cuthbert Mayerson, a character from Sanders's "The Poetry Reading" in TALES OF BEATNIK GLORY, believed, "if you piss off the cultural frontal lobes of *Time Mag,* you must be doing something right." It seems one of Sanders's goals has always been in service to just such an idea. As Brooke Horvath writes in "Introducing Ed Sanders," "Ed was the stuff of counterlegend, up there with [KEN] KESEY and [BOB] DYLAN, Ginsberg and Emmett Grogan." More than even a writer/poet, rocker, bookstore owner, and controversial magazine editor, he has been a tireless social and political activist. With his doctrine of "fierce pacifism," he has walked the South for racial equality and marched on the Pentagon literally attempting to exorcise it. In 1961 he was jailed for attempting to board the *Ethan Allen,* a submarine carrying enough Polaris missiles to kill, he estimated, "about thirty million

Beat trio/Ginsberg Memorial, Los Angeles, 1997. Photographer Larry Keenan: "Steven Taylor (guitar player for Ginsberg and for The Fugs), poet Anne Waldman and Ed Sanders (also of The Fugs) are performing in this photograph in front of an art-in-action painting at the Ginsberg Memorial. The Memorial event went on until the wee hours in the morning and still about a third of the speakers had not spoken or performed. They got cancelled." *(courtesy of Larry Keenan)*

people." In jail he penned his first book of poetry, "Poem From Jail," on wads of toilet paper, which he transferred to sections of cigarette packs.

Of his many writings, what has possibly gained Sanders the most fame (and infamy) is his investigative book *The FAMILY: THE STORY OF CHARLES MANSON'S DUNE BUGGY ATTACK BATTALION*. Interested not only in the warped psychosis that bloomed in Manson's circle but also in the circumstances and the society that allowed such a blooming, Sanders went undercover to shed light on the Manson Family's exploits. As Thomas Myers writes in "Rerunning the Creepy Crawl: Ed Sanders and Charles Manson," "Sanders discovered in his grisly data one possible destination of his own journey as activist and anarchist, where his idea of 'total

assault' might also be interpreted in the writing of DEATH TO PIGS, RISE, and HEALTER SKELTER [*sic*] on walls with the blood of random victims." Not deterred by the horror of the Manson Family but enlightened by his own self-discoveries, Sanders continued with his own bardic brand of cultural assault.

Sanders speaks both Greek and Latin, translating songs like The Byrd's "Turn Turn Turn," into "Tropei Tropei Tropei" for his 1990 album, *Songs in Ancient Greek*. Other solo albums include *Sanders Truckstop* (1970), *Beer Cans on the Moon* (1972), and *American Bard* (1995). He is the author of four musical dramas and three volumes of *Tales of Beatnik Glory*, a series of short stories that chronicle underground city life of the 1950s and

1960s. In addition to many prestigious fellowships and honors, his 1987 poetry collection THIRSTING FOR PEACE IN A RAGING CENTURY won him an American Book Award. For his long list of published poems, he has even invented instruments to facilitate their proper reading, among them the Pulse Lyre, the Microlyre, and the Talking Tie, an instrument literally worn as a tie.

Sanders continues his writing and activism in his hometown of Woodstock, New York, where, along with his wife Miriam, he writes and edits for the local *Woodstock Journal* and hosts a local cable-access talk show where he discusses such topics as water pollution and a place to dispose of such waste as old tires and paint and where he conducts interviews with rockers and poets. Keeping to his belief in the transformative power of the bard, Sanders lectures on investigative poetry, insisting that "poetry should again assume responsibility for the description of history." As such, he is currently working on a nine-volume *America, A History in Verse*. The first three volumes, 1900–39, 1940–61, and 1962–70, have already been published by Black Sparrow Press.

Bibliography

Horvath, Brook. "Edward Sanders on His Fiction: An Interview." *Review of Contemporary Fiction.* 19, no. 1 (1999): 23–30.

———— "Introducing Ed Sanders." *Review of Contemporary Fiction.* 19, no. 1 (1999): 7–12.

Myers, Thomas. "Rerunnng the Creepy Crawl: Ed Sanders and Charles Manson." *Review of Contemporary Fiction.* 19, no. 1 (1999): 81–90.

Sanders, Edward. *Tales of Beatnik Glory.* New York: Stonehill, 1975.

———— "The Fugs Second Album." Liner Notes. *The Fugs Second Album.* Fugs Records, 1993.

————. *Thirsting for Peace in a Raging Century: Selected Poems 1961–1985.* Minneapolis: Coffee House Press, 1987.

Jennifer Cooper

Satori in Paris Jack Kerouac (1966)

Though arguably the weakest novel in the "Duluoz Legend," *Satori in Paris* does offer some important insights regarding the state of JACK KEROUAC's mind at the end of his career. In 1965 Kerouac took a trip to Paris to research his family history. In particular, he hoped to find the military records of the first Kerouac who came to Canada as a soldier. *Satori in Paris* dramatizes this 10-day misadventure in which he fails to find the origins of his family but does drink very good old cognac. He wrote *Satori in Paris*, he told JOHN CLELLON HOLMES, in seven days in longhand with a pencil. To get into the mood of the trip, he drank old cognac as he wrote, and he later told the *Paris Review* that *Satori in Paris* was thus the only novel he ever wrote while drunk. The novel was first published in three installments in the *Evergreen Review* and later as a complete novel in hardback by Grove Press.

In the first chapter Kerouac defines a *satori* as a Japanese term meaning "sudden illumination" or literally a "kick in the eye," thus relating a satori to what the Beats referred to in the 1940s as "eyeball kicks." What exactly has been illuminated for him is unclear even to him, although it relates to the simple kindness of a cab driver driving on Sundays to support his family. Kerouac uses the cabby's real name as well as his own real name in this book (as he does in LONESOME TRAVELER), for this is a book about names. He states the plot of the book simply: "I had come to France and Brittany just to look up this old name of mine which is just about three thousand years old and was never changed in all that time." The book will be a "non-fiction" one he says, dismissing "fiction" as being "made-up stories and romances about what would happen IF" which "are for children and adult cretins." As one of his last works and one that centers on his ethnic origins, it thus stands in contrast to his first novel, The TOWN AND THE CITY, in which almost all traces of his French-Canadian, Catholic heritage have been eliminated. Even in ON THE ROAD, Sal Paradise is Italian.

At La Bibliotheque Nationale, Kerouac's research is stymied by uncooperative librarians and by the fact that the Nazis destroyed the list of the officers in Montcalm's army of 1756 in Quebec; one of those soldiers was Kerouac's first North American forbearer. He finds Paris to be "a tough town." A gendarme intentionally misdirects him, and he ends up facing a government building where the guards eye him suspiciously as he lights a cigarette. The scene is a recurring one in Kerouac's work in which society (America and now Paris) is increasingly becoming a police state that does not permit the wanderings of the likes of Kerouac.

In spite of the wrong turns the trip takes, Kerouac has actually planned it very carefully. He intends to stay at an Inn in Finistère on the Atlantic coast and write "Sea: Part II," a sequel to his sound–poem of the Pacific Ocean that was published at the end of BIG SUR. He has even included a plastic bag in which to write in case the weather is bad.

Satori in Paris is a book about language, and Kerouac shows himself throughout the book to be a brilliant and witty linguist. In a cross-table dinner conversation with a Paris art dealer, Kerouac lectures on the evolution of the French language. Kerouac's French is "Canuck" French, and it sounds the way French did 300 years earlier in Paris. Paris French in 1965, he has to admit, has been corrupted by other European influences that did not corrupt Canadian French. Still, the old French men and women at the restaurant listen to him with pleasure, slightly embarrassed by his old-fashioned tongue, but laughing with him and enjoying him. He has a satori at this point about language: "That people actually understand what their tongues are babbling. And that eyes do shine to understand, and that responses are made which indicate a soul in all this matter and mess of tongues and teeth." He also showcases his talent for linguistic play by translating a conversation between himself and a French mystery writer into a formal sounding English that renders their dialogue comic and stilted.

Kerouac wonders, "Why do people change their names?" The question is of interest to Kerouac and his readers, for Kerouac is known for his cleverly disguised names in his fiction, all done to protect him from libel suits. His name, he says, means "House" (*Ker*) "In the Field" (*Ouac*). Later, in Brittany, he searches for the old Breton name *Daoulas*, saying that "Duluoz" was a variation on that name he invented as a pseudonym for his "non-fiction" writings. As the book comes to a close, he starts to imagine that strangers are calling out his name, referring to him derisively as Kerouac the King, for Kerouac maintains that he has a royal lineage. The book thus ends with repeated echoes of the name that Kerouac came to find. In the final chapter, he once again circles the subject of why people are ashamed of their names, and he answers his question by having the most simple of human exchanges take place between strangers: "He [his taxi driver] tells me his name, of Auvergne, I mine, of Brittany." Breaking his longstanding policy of creating an alias for his characters, he refers to his cab driver by his actual name. It is worth noting that Kerouac often said that in his old age he intended to rewrite all of his books and put in the real names; however, he died in middle age before he could act on this intention.

Rob Johnson

"Sermon, The" Ted Joans (1961)

Written in Greenwich Village, "The Sermon" might be considered a kind of early Afro-Beat credo. Though the composition date in *Teducation: Selected Poems 1949–1999* says 1955, references in the poem make that date impossible. The poem can be found in *All of Ted Joans and No More* (1961). TED JOANS affects the voice of the flirtatious, beckoning Beat-scene hipster, the counselor of middle-class young white American womanhood as to the pathway to becoming a "swinger," an "in-chick." Chauvinist as some of the argot can now look, not to mention dated (*dig, square, split,* and the like), "The Sermon" looks to the freeing up of body and senses from 1950s Main Street conformism and nice-girl sexual gridlock. It is a call for self-liberation very much of its Village time and place, and it carries Joans's typical verve, the speaking-voice rhythm, the companionable tease, and the seams of bop and jazz reference. It is also underwritten by his insider sense of himself as co-spirit with ALLEN GINSBERG, JACK KEROUAC, Norman Mailer, and GREGORY CORSO—all of whom are named—in the making of Beat as counterculture, another kind of America.

"So you want to be hip little girls? / You want to learn to swing?" run the opening lines. There follows a Joans instruction manual in verse form of "how to" become suitably "cool" and thereby gain existential entry into Beat-hipster ranks. Ginsberg is immediately invoked ("And you want to be able to dig and take in everything / Yes dig everything as the poet Ginsberg said?") and linked to the call for abandonment of "antique anglo-saxon / puritanical philosophy." The time is due, avers the poem, to head for "swinging surroundings" and "creative activity," for "Action!!" and "Jazzaction!" and to do so by learning to "Dig this sermon." Sex should be plentiful but not without condom or diaphragm. Drink should be had but only to the point of a "high." "If you want to be popular with real hipsters" there should be a curb on too much talk or argument. But the essential core lies in the references to jazz and the works of the Beat writers, which are intimately connected. Each ingredient to come into play, whether jazz, bop, Jelly Roll Morton, rhythm and blues, Ginsberg's *HOWL*, Kerouac's *ON THE ROAD*, or Mailer's "The White Negro" serves to create the identifying Beat insignia.

The remainder of the poem adds supporting weight and detail: no fake bras, lipstick to be worn for kissing, Hollywood to be subverted by applause in the wrong places, vegetarianism a must, reading to include Corso's "MARRIAGE," the Bible, Koran, and Torah, and life to be lived as affirmative energy ("you must learn to say YES YES YES more often"). In a closing lines the speaker asks his women reader–listeners ("You sweet angelic chicklets, chicks, and you too / lovely past forty old hens") to "dig my sermon. . . . pick up on what / I've just / wailed. . . ." Joans's "The Sermon" will likely not satisfy postfeminist readers, but it arises out of a willingness to examine gender roles and sexual life as part of the larger Beat renegotiation of America's cultural mores.

A. Robert Lee

Silverman, Herschel (1927–)

Can Herschel Silverman make an authentic claim to being the "last of the beatniks?" Possibly so, though he has a better claim to being last of the Beat-era poets to achieve widespread recognition. Until Longshot Books published his selected poems in his 75th year he was the classic "local poet," his locale being the city of Bayonne, New Jersey—an oddly isolated working-class town that is located on Upper New York Bay—where he encouraged younger poets, publishes himself and others using a balky home photocopy machine plus a velo-binder, and is respected enough locally to have read at a mayoral inauguration.

Born in California, Silverman was orphaned by age five and was sent East to be raised by an aunt in Jersey City (a city adjacent to Bayonne). After serving as a navy seabee during World War II and marrying young to his wife Laura, he opened a candy store called Hersch's Beehive (the store was opposite the city high school whose sport teams were called the Bees). Despite the seven-day-a-week grind that such a profession entails, Silverman developed an interest in poetry, taking classes at the 92nd Street "Y" and attending readings of such poets as e. e. cummings, Dylan Thomas, and Robert Frost.

In 1957 Silverman read an article about ALLEN GINSBERG and his Beat compatriots as well as reading his work in the *Evergreen Review*'s West Coast issue (access to myriad magazines being a bonus of running a candy store). Fired up by their adventures across Europe and America, he was tempted to join them on the road. However, the reality of a wife and two kids stopped this. (Silverman is one of few male Beats to be have been married at length and to not have alienated his children.) Silverman instead corresponded with Ginsberg and GREGORY CORSO, often sending them much-needed funds.

Silverman soon became active in the Lower East Side poetry scene, reading at such famed spaces as the Metro, Le Deux Maggots, and Doctor Generosity's and publishing in magazines such as *Nomad* and *El Corno Emplunado*. He became friendly with many poets who were involved in the downtown scene such as Paul Blackburn and Susan Sherman. He developed a lifelong friendship with Theodore Enslin and their 30-plus years of correspondence is part of the SUNY–Buffalo Library's Enslin holdings.

However, the demands of his job and family could not be ignored, and Silverman's activities were more and more confined to the west side of New York Harbor. He was actively involved in the North Jersey poetry community, mentoring two generations of poets and managing to give poetry readings around the car-centric Garden State despite not possessing a drivers license.

Silverman's "discovery" came after he turned 60. A hefty rent increase forced him to give up the Beehive, and he spent the next couple of years nursing his wife through a long struggle with cancer that ended with her death in 1988. A bit unanchored, he then took a workshop with Bernadette Mayer at the Poetry Project and soon was discovered by a new generation of younger poets. It was the beginning of the era of both the poetry slam and the revival of all things Beat, and Silverman's Beat-influenced poetry was suddenly au courant. He began to read all over Manhattan, usually with poets more than half his age.

Silverman's work shifted at this late, more active stage into works that more increasingly served as a score for performance. A frequent collaborator in the 1990s was the great jazz clarinetist Perry Robinson, recently, Silverman has performed with Gunter Hampel's Galaxy Dream Band.

It has only been in the last few years that Silverman's work has found a reliable tenancy on the printed page. His appearance in the very popular neo-Beat *Outlaw Bible of American Poetry* (2000) raised his visibility on the national poetry scene, and his book of selected poems finally offered a comprehensive body of his mostly fugitive work. All the while, Silverman has remained deeply attached to the Beats, especially the legacy of Ginsberg, who in "Television Was a Baby Crawling Towards That Deathchamber" declared, "candy store emperor Hersh Silverman in Bayonne, dreaming of telling the *Truth*, but his Karma is selling jellybeans & being / kind." Perhaps, an even greater testimony to Silverman's kindness came at his surprise 75th birthday party that brought together poets, neighbors, and grown-up versions of the students to whom he once sold Yoo-Hoos and comic books. Not only did the tenants of his Bayonne townhouse show up, but they also offered testimonial as to what a great landlord he was.

Joel Lewis

Snyder, Gary (1930–)

Gary Snyder became connected with the Beat movement as a result of his participation in the famous October 1955 Six Gallery reading in San Francisco where ALLEN GINSBERG first performed the first section of HOWL. Part of the West Coast wing of the movement, which also is referred to as the San Francisco Renaissance, Snyder viewed his wing as "cool," while he viewed the New York wing as "hot." This distinction can be seen clearly in the selections for that famous poetry gathering. While Ginsberg focused on anguish, despair, and the destructive oppressive forces of the American cultural and political system, Snyder read "A Berry Feast." This poem, first published in *The Evergreen Review* in 1957, later became the opening poem of "The Far West" section of *The Back Country*. In contrast to Ginsberg's poem, "A Berry Feast" alludes to positive Native American myths and the trickster figure of coyote. Human connection with nature is emphasized through mating with bears and coyote, and ancient wisdom and contemporary knowledge are married in a new hunter–gatherer consciousness. The poem ends: "Dead city in dry summer, / Where berries grow." Clearly Snyder and Ginsberg's selections at this reading display the differences in sensibility and poetics that Michael Davidson sees as distinguishing the East Coast and West Coast movements. Yet, Snyder will forever be associated with the East Coast Beats as a result of his immortalization by JACK KEROUAC as Japhy Ryder in *The DHARMA BUMS* (1958) as well as his long friendships with Ginsberg and Kerouac.

Born toward the beginning of the Great Depression on May 8, 1930, Snyder experienced financial poverty and material deprivation as a child. His father was away looking for work when he was born and they soon moved to a small farm in Washington state where they eked out a living through a combination of subsistence activities, jobs, and small enterprises, such as cutting shake shingles. In 1942, as jobs became more plentiful, the Snyders moved to Portland. His parents separated a few years later, and his mother worked for the newspaper where Gary also found employment. On the farm Gary had developed two very intimate relationships: one with nature, particularly with the woods, and one with books, which his mother persistently borrowed from the public library. In Portland he became the youngest member of a mountain-climbing club and extended his engagement with nature into true wilderness. In high school he began to write poems and articles for the club magazine. He also became interested in anthropology, particularly in relation to the native peoples of the northwest. In 1947 he entered Reed College in Portland on a scholarship and pursued a double major in literature and anthropology. There he was influenced by various progressive professors and developed a wide circle of friends, many of them aspiring writers and some of them quite interested in Eastern philosophy and religions. Like all Reed students, he wrote an undergraduate thesis, "He Who Hunted Birds in His Father's Village," which was published in book form in 1979. His love of myth and many of his own poetic themes are revealed in it. When he graduated in 1951 he was truly a working-class intellectual, squarely opposed to U.S. imperialism and highly critical of mainstream U.S. culture. After a brief stint in graduate school at Indiana University, he headed back to the city of his birth, San Francisco, intent on becoming a poet.

With the Bay area as his home base, Snyder ventured into the wilderness of a variety of work experiences, including becoming a forest-service fire lookout on Crater Mountain in the summer of 1952. In the winter months he studied Chinese and Japanese at Berkeley and became involved with the Berkeley Buddhist Church. In 1954 he worked as a choke setter for a logging operation on the Warm Springs Indian Reservation, an experience that was detailed in his essays which are collected in *The Practice of The Wild.* He had been blacklisted from working for the forest service because the coast guard had labeled him a subversive as a result of his membership in a left-wing seamen's union, which he had had to join to ship out in summer 1948. Also, his affiliations with various radical teachers and other students at Reed College led to the same charge by the Federal Bureau of Investigation (FBI). Of course, the FBI was correct in defining Snyder, as they would numerous other intellectuals who were associated with the Beats, as subversive: Snyder had already taken a stand against the Korean War and throughout his life would oppose large, centralized nation states. Somehow, though, Snyder was able to slip through the bureaucracy and obtain a position with the park service, clearing trails in Yosemite in 1955. During this summer

Snyder began to write relatively short poems that were quite different in style from the segments of the mythopoeic sequence *Myths and Texts* that he had begun to write in 1952 and would not finish until 1956. These new poems, as David Robertson relates, became the core for his published collection, RIPRAP, which appeared in 1959.

The year 1955 proved to be a crucial one for Snyder. He began to write the poems that persuaded him of his own talent and his ability to sustain his vocation as a poet. He became more committed to Buddhism and determined to travel to Japan to study it more seriously. Also, he participated in the October 7 Six Gallery poetry reading, establishing himself as one of the rising stars of the San Francisco Renaissance and also linking himself and that group with the East Coast Beats. In 1956, he left San Francisco to study Buddhism in Kyoto and lived in Japan on and off into the late 1960s. Two poems in *Riprap* record his preparations for that journey: "Nooksack Valley," written in Feburary 1956, and "Migration of Birds," written in April. The latter makes a comparison between himself and Kerouac, with whom he was sharing a cabin in Mill Valley. Snyder had already begun to publish mature poems by 1954 and continued to do so while in Japan, with the result that he was already building up a reputation with readers of such journals as the *Evergreen Review,* which published his Han Shan/Cold Mountain translations in 1958. Then LAWRENCE FERLINGHETTI started to distribute *Riprap* from City Lights Books in 1959. The following year, *Myths & Texts* was published, letting readers see both of Snyder's major poetic styles in book-length collections.

Also in 1960 while back in the States Snyder became involved with fellow poet JOANNE KYGER and invited her to Japan, where he was returning for further Buddhist study. On her arrival she learned that the First Zen Institute of America, which financially supported Snyder, expected the couple to marry if they were to live together. Kyger has written of their life together in Japan, as well as their historic trip to India in *The Japan and India Journals 1960–1964.* On their six-month sojourn to India, which Snyder treats in *Passage Through India* (1983), Snyder and Kyger hooked up with Ginsberg and Peter Orlovsky for part of the trip. Kyger left

Snyder and Japan in early 1964, and Snyder did not return to San Francisco until the fall of that year. For the year that he stayed in the United States, Snyder participated in pacifist protests against the Vietnam War and briefly taught creative writing at the University of California in Berkeley.

Snyder spent another year in Japan and returned to San Francisco in early 1967 in time to help provide leadership along with Ginsberg for the Human Be-In at Golden Gate Park. By this time he had gained significant notoriety as a counterculture figure and as a proponent of an American Buddhism that was quite congenial to the developing Hippie movement. Back in Japan, Snyder hooked up with a commune movement that was headed by Nanao Sakaki and a small group of people who were engaged in subsistence living on an island south of Kyushu. There he married Masa Uehara, and in 1968 she gave birth to their first son, Kai. The first sections of *Regarding Wave* record the commune period, their marriage, and the period leading up to Kai's birth. Shortly after that Snyder ended his years of living in Japan when the three of them returned to the United States, lived in San Francisco for a while, and then settled near Nevada City, California, where Snyder built a house on land that he, Ginsberg, and Jerry Brown had purchased. In 1969 Masa and Gary's second son, Gen, was born. During the years 1968–70 Snyder published, now with New Directions, *The Back Country* (poems), *Earth House Hold* (prose), and an expanded edition of *Regarding Wave* (poems). His books were also being published in England. At this time translations of his poems began to appear in a variety of European and Asian languages.

With his permanent return to the States, Snyder received every increasing attention, including various awards and numerous speaking and reading invitations. As Dan McLeod notes, "The example of Snyder's life and values offered a constructive, albeit underground, alternative to mainstream American culture." In particular, McLeod accurately concludes that Snyder's "main impact on the Beat Generation, and on American literature since, has been as a spokesperson for the natural world and the values associated with primitive cultures" (487–488). As people might say today, Snyder was someone who "walked the talk" of the beliefs and actions that he presented in his poetry. Also, Snyder offered people a way forward, an alternative to, and not just a reaction against, mainstream American culture. His return to the States also coincided with an increasing global attention to environmental issues, ones that were linked to a critique of the Vietnam War and U.S. imperialism but also extended beyond that particular issue. His recognition as a spokesperson for new ways to think about how to live in the world can be seen in his invitation to give the Earth Day address in 1970 at Colorado State College and in his 1971 invitation to speak at the Center for the Study of Democratic Institutions in Santa Barbara. His environmental internationalism was also demonstrated by his 1972 participation in the United Nations Conference on Human Environment that was held in Stockholm, and his angry poem on the behavior of most of the delegations to that conference, "Mother Earth" (later retitled "Mother Earth: Her Whales"), was published in the *New York Times* on July 13, 1972, and reprinted in *TURTLE ISLAND*.

That volume of poetry and prose won Snyder the Pulitzer Prize for Poetry in 1975. Like *The Back Country* and *Regarding Wave*, this large collection is organized into sections, including a gathering of short prose pieces, the most culturally important of which is "Four Changes." This essay had been written in summer 1969 and was distributed as a broadside by the tens of thousands around the country. After 1975 Snyder put more time into environmental politics, particularly bioregionalism, and less time into poetry, if his rate of publication is any indication. In fact, nine years passed between the publication of *Turtle Island* and *Axe Handles*, which although popular was less well received than his previous books of poetry. By 1983 Snyder's tone had changed considerably. Unlike many writers associated with the Beat movement, Snyder neither burned out nor turned bitter and cynical; rather he became a homesteader, a father, and a responsible local citizen. Many of the poems in *Axe Handles* reflect those multiple responsibilities and also offer a long-term, long-range vision for social change rather than the kind of revolution-around-the-corner attitude that energized the Hippie movement and much of the New Left of the 1960s. In 1983 Snyder became a professor at the University of California, Davis, spending less time on the road and paying greater attention to writing prose than he had in the past. *Left Out in the Rain: New Poems 1947–1985* was published in 1986. It contained some 150 poems either previously unpublished or uncollected in other books. His main publications in the decade after taking up his teaching position consisted of the two prose volumes, *The Practice of the Wild* (1990) and *A Place in Space* (1995), which collected early and new essays. He also published in 1992 the equivalent of a selected poems titled *No Nature: New and Selected Poems* so that it and *Left Out* together contained the majority of his poems that had been written up to that time. In these years also, Snyder and Masa Uehara divorced, and Snyder married Carole Koda, who brought two daughters into the marriage.

In the early 1990s many readers and not a few critics wondered if Snyder had peaked as a poet, even as his status as an international spokesperson for environmental issues continued to rise. Then in 1996 he stunned and pleased people with the publication of *Mountains and Rivers Without End,* a book-length poetic sequence 40 years in the making. Anthony Hunt has written a companion to this volume, *Genesis, Structure, and Meaning in Gary Snyder's* Mountains and Rivers Without End, which provides a comprehensive study guide to Snyder's masterpiece. Then in 1999 he published *The Gary Snyder Reader,* which contains a variety of poems, essays, and translations covering the years 1992 through 1998. Having retired in the early years of the new millennium from his teaching position, Snyder has not retired either from his writing or from his international reading and lecturing, as demonstrated by the 2004 publication of a book of new poems that are written in a variety of styles (some new for Snyder), titled *Danger On Peaks.* The septuagenarian Snyder continues to remain active as a writer and a speaker, one of the last of the Beats still standing.

Bibliography

Davidson, Michael. *The San Francisco Renaissance: Poetics and Community at Mid-Century.* 1989. New York: Cambridge University Press, 1991.
Halper, Jon, ed. *Gary Snyder: Dimensions of a Life.* San Francisco: Sierra Club Books, 1991.
Hunt, Anthony. *Genesis, Structure, and Meaning in Gary Snyder's* Mountains and Rivers Without End. Reno: University of Nevada Press, 2004.
Kyger, Joanne. *The Japan and India Journals 1960–1964.* Bolinas, California: Tombouctas Books, 1981.
McNeil, Katherine. *Gary Snyder: A Bibliography.* New York: The Phoenix Bookshop, 1983.
Murphy, Patrick D. *A Place for Wayfaring: The Poetry and Prose of Gary Snyder.* Corvallis: University of Oregon Press, 2000.
Robertson, David. "Gary Snyder Riprapping in Yosemite, 1955." *American Poetry* 2, no. 1 (1984): 52–59.

Patrick Murphy

Soft Machine, The Wiliam S. Burroughs (1961)

The Soft Machine is the first volume of what is popularly called WILLIAM S. BURROUGHS's cut-ups trilogy—*The Soft Machine, The TICKET THAT EXPLODED,* and *NOVA EXPRESS.* Although these books are formed from material that was part of the NAKED LUNCH "word hoard" (and thus have many overlapping scenes and characters from *Naked Lunch*), the cut-up technique introduced in the trilogy distinguishes it from the earlier novel. Cut-ups were "discovered" by Brion Gysin in 1959 when he pieced together the sections of a newspaper that he had been using as a cutting surface for artwork. Burroughs had become convinced that language was a virus that controlled consciousness, and the cut-ups showed him a way to "cut word lines" and restore truth to writing. The cut-up thus provided Burroughs with an experimental literary technique that matched his ambitions to write a "new myth for the space age." Readers of these difficult books must keep in mind that Burroughs saw himself in a line of experimental writers who were particularly engaged by language itself, such as James Joyce, Gertrude Stein, and John Dos Passos.

Burroughs described *The Soft Machine* as mainly being a surreal retelling of his 1953 South American expedition in search of *yage.* In fact, much of the book is set in Mexico, Panama, Colombia, and Peru. Readers wishing background on this trip should read *The YAGE LETTERS* and the

"1953" section of Oliver Harris's *The Letters of William S. Burroughs, 1945–1959*.

The book was first published in 1961 by Olympia Press. Grove Press published a revised version in 1966 in America. Another edition was published in England as well. The British version is, according to Barry Miles, the most accessible. For that edition (as well as the American edition) Burroughs added more "straight narrative" in an attempt to make the book more comprehensible. The original book was also color coded, while later editions were not. Burroughs defined the title of the book in an afterword to the British edition: "The soft machine is the human body under constant siege from a vast hungry host of parasites with many names but one nature being hungry and one intention to eat."

The "Dead on Arrival" chapter samples scenes of Burroughs's addiction from Mexico City, Tangier, and New York City. The characters include "the sailor" (based on Phil White, who hanged himself in the Tombs), Bill Gains (based on Bill Garver, who dies in Mexico City in this chapter), and Kiki (based on Bill's young lover in Tangier who was killed by a jealous bandleader when he found Kiki in bed with one of his female players). "Esperanza," based on the same woman whom Jack Kerouac calls Tristessa in the novel *TRISTESSA* and who was a drug connection for the American Beats living in Mexico City, makes a brief appearance. The chapter ends with Bill and Johnny en route to the Federal Narcotics Farm in Lexington, Kentucky, where Burroughs took the "cure" in 1948.

In the "Who Am I To Be Critical" chapter, Bill and Johnny (who turn out to be the same person) never make it to Lexington; instead they go south into Mexico where they join up with revolutionary soldiers and continue further south for a series of adventures. Bill meets an Indian boy named Xolotl (also a character in *THE WILD BOYS*) who shows him how to transmigrate into his body through sex magic. Now in Xolotl's body (his body has been hanged), he travels into the land of the Maya where he meets up with a "foreigner" who is a "technical sergeant." Technical Tilly teaches Xolotl how to overcome the powerful conditioning of the Mayan priests, but the two are caught and sentenced to "centipede

death." Xolotl frees them with intense mental concentration—"something I inherit from Uranus where my grandfather invented the adding machine." He continues his adventures with Technical Tilly, now called Iam, whose "moaning about the equipment the way he always does" reveals him as based on Burroughs's young mathematician friend in England, Ian Sommerville.

In the cut-ups trilogy, Burroughs's narrative identity is frequently that of an "agent" or an "inspector" (Inspector Lee). Here, he busts queers who have a James Dean addiction. "Public Agent" introduces cut-up sections of text that are thematically linked to the following "Trak Trak Trak" chapter. Cut-ups are used by Burroughs in these two chapters to cut "control" lines and to exorcise sexual obsessions (by replaying them in various cut-up forms). "Trak Trak Trak" has a variety of meanings, but in general it refers to a giant police state/bureaucracy/global corporation that enforces worldwide conformity. Cutting up language—as is the dominant style of this chapter—cuts these lines of control. Johnny from *Naked Lunch*'s blue movies makes a reappearance here, an example of how much of the cut-up novels came from the *Naked Lunch* "word horde." There are even cut-ups from the *INTERZONE* period ("Wetback asleep with a hardon was taken care of that way"). The author himself makes an appearance and reveals his seemingly haphazard methods. The jungle setting of this chapter (and others) is South America, and the time setting is 1951 when Burroughs went in search of *yage*.

Burroughs has compared his cut-up style to what the eye sees (and the brain interprets) as one takes a walk around the block: images associate, break, synthesize, multiply. The "Early Answer" chapter is an excellent example of such a style. While taking a walk on North End Road (in London, where Burroughs lived during much of the composition of this book), "Jimmy" flashes on World's End in South America, and London and South American settings cut in and out of the narrative. Fading photos also inspire the chain of memories, here involving Kiki in Tangier.

The "Case of the Celluloid Kali" chapter marks the first appearance of one of Burroughs's most famous characters, Clem Snide, the Private Ass-Hole.

The chapter parodies the hardboiled style of Raymond Chandler. Clem takes a case from Mr. Martin (sometimes Mr. Bradly), the Uranian heavy-metal addict, and contacts the Venus Mob through a Venusian sex addict, Johnny Yen. The Venusians are set to blow up the planet ("nova"). In *The Ticket That Exploded,* the Venusians are foiled in their plot to cause a "nova" on Earth and to escape through transmigration of souls. Johnny Yen's "3000 years in showbiz" routine is in this chapter and is a send-up of borscht-belt humor. Clem infiltrates the palace of the Venusian Queen, the Contessa di Vile, who projects pornographic films of boys being hanged for a sex-addicted audience. Snide speeds up the projector—which causes fits in the crowd—and subdues the Venusians in time for the Nova police to move in for the bust.

The overall theme of the cut-up trilogy is that of "control," and in "The Mayan Caper" chapter Burroughs explicates one of the world's most efficient control systems—the Mayan calendar. According to Burroughs, who studied Mayan language and culture at Mexico City College in 1950–51, the Mayan priests invented a calendar that kept the people occupied with agricultural labor and cultural festivals virtually every day of the year. Only the priests knew the order of the calendar, and thus their control over the people was total. In "The Mayan Caper," Burroughs creates a time traveler who returns to the time of the Mayans, destroys the calendar, and overthrows the priests. Time travel is explained through the use of Burroughs and Brion Gysin's "fold-in" technique of creating texts (discussed at length in their book *The Third Mind*). In fact, fold-ins are used extensively in *The Soft Machine*. The actual time travel is accomplished first by transferring the scientist into the body of an Indian boy, a medical process that was accomplished by Dr. Bradly/Martin; and second, the Indian boy goes back in time a thousand years by drinking a potion prepared by a *curandero*, a ceremony similar to Burroughs's description of drinking *ayahuasca* in *The Yage Letters*. This chapter is an important one in Burroughs's project of creating a new "myth for the space age," as it cleverly narrates time and space travel.

The chapters "I Sekuin," "Pretend an Interest," and "Last Hints" are based on Burroughs's experiences on his South American trip in 1953 in search of *yage*. Parts of this section are written as a mock travelogue that is authored by the invented explorer Greenbaum. Carl, from *Naked Lunch*, is a character, and he is still being experimented on by Dr. Benway. Here he undergoes a sex-change operation. The grotesque chimu pottery that so fascinated Burroughs—with its sense of a world taken to horrible extremes—comes alive in the final scenes of "Pretend an Interest," in which Carl undergoes "Centipede Death." The description of the teetering catwalk city in "Last Hints" comes from Burroughs's *yage* visions.

Much of the chapter "Where the Awning Flaps" is inspired by Burroughs's experiences in Panama. Burroughs did not like Panama at all. "The Panamanians are about the crummiest people in the Hemisphere," he wrote to Allen Ginsberg.

Burroughs wrote "blue movie" sections into many of his books of this period, part of his campaign to replace the "word" with images. In the "1920 Movies" chapter, Johnny and Jose (Joselito) have sex in a Mexican prison. Erotic scenes in Burroughs frequently cause a loss of control, and in the following scene, without transition, Burroughs switches to a narrative about Salt Chunk Mary, who fences stolen goods. She (along with the Johnsons) is a character from Jack Black's *You Can't Win,* a book about "good bums and thieves" that impressed Burroughs in his youth. The last section of the chapter is broken down into color-coded "units." The original book was printed in different colors, and the "units" here are a leftover from that scheme. They also are part of Burroughs's project of replacing language through cut-ups, images, and colors. Silence, the aim of Burroughs's work during these years, is colored "blue." Blue is the color of his *yage* visions as well—so prominent in this book.

The chapters "Where You Belong," "Uranian Willy," and "Gongs of Violence" sketch out Burroughs's "myth for the space age," a science-fiction plot that underlies the cut-up novels as well as *The Wild Boys* and later works. In "Where You Belong," Burroughs is hired to write for the Trak News Agency, the motto of which is "We don't report the news—we write it." He falls in with "the Subliminal Kid" (based on Ian Sommerville) who teaches him how to plant subliminal, subversive messages in the Trak copy. Through words and images they destroy Trak's hold on public consciousness: "Word falling—Photo falling—Break through in the Grey Room." (Trak is based on the Time–Life word-image bank often referred to by Burroughs). "Uranium Willy" continues this plot. "Willy the Rat" (based on Burroughs) "wises up the marks" about how they are being controlled. When the reality film buckles, what is revealed is an interplanetary battle underway in which humans are mere pawns. "Gongs of Violence" appears to describe the reenvisioning of society after the Board Books ("symbol books of the all-powerful Board that had controlled thought feeling and movement of a planet") are destroyed. There is chaos but also evolution. The sexes split, no longer needing each other. With the reality film destroyed, the real universe is revealed to be a dreamlike city of precarious catwalks, bridges, and ladders. This city closely corresponds to the city Burroughs envisioned under the influence of *yage*. The end of this chapter shows humanity evolving to escape from the poisoned Earth.

In the "Dead Fingers Talk" chapter, the "reader" is directly addressed by the "Captain" (presumably of spaceship earth) introduced at the end of the previous chapter. We see the "deserted transmitter" that had been used to broadcast the language of control. The rest of the chapter—as if demonstrating the freedom of language no longer subject to control—is a seamless collage of routines set in East Texas (where Burroughs raised marijuana within sight of the farm of his neighbor, Mr. Gilley), London, and even in Herman Melville's *Billy Budd* (which receives what is probably its first "queer" reading).

The final chapter, "Cross the Wounded Galaxies," dramatizes Burroughs's theory of what went wrong with the human species. Two aspects of his theory are important here: First, Burroughs believes that our cave dwelling ancestors were infected by a language "virus" that controlled them (here, the "white worm"); second, he believed that our present age of violence stems from the fact that only one strain of primitive humanoid survived the ice age. As he told Robert Palmer in 1972, "Have you read *African Genesis* [by Robert Butler]? Well, there was the aggressive Southern ape, who survived because he was a killer, and has really in a sense forced his way of life on the whole species."

Burroughs would expand on this plot in CITIES OF THE RED NIGHT (1981), the first book in a second trilogy, the Red Night trilogy. Such interconnections among his past and future books reveal what amounts to a cosmology. Difficult works, such as *The Soft Machine,* thus become more comprehensible to readers willing to explore Burroughs's entire oeuvre.

Rob Johnson

Some of the Dharma Jack Kerouac (1997)

Some of the Dharma began as a series of notes that JACK KEROUAC made of his studies in Buddhism beginning in December 1953 and concluding in May 1956. Initially, Buddhism offered solace to Kerouac when he was going through a difficult time. Recovering emotionally from the 1953 love affair that was recounted in The SUBTERRANEANS, Kerouac sought respite in the library, reading some works of Henry David Thoreau; Thoreau's references to Hindu philosophy lead Kerouac to *The Life of Buddha* by Ashvaghosa. Kerouac identified instantly with the Buddhist philosophies, especially the notion that life consists of suffering or sorrow, and he continued to read Buddhist texts after he traveled to San Jose to stay with NEAL and CAROLYN CASSADY. Kerouac intently studied the Buddhist texts, even compiling a bibliography of works that he considered essential, but he may have been hindered in his progress toward enlightenment by his go-it-alone approach. He never had a teacher, and as he had since the school days of his youth, he assembled his own education by reading and responding to books. Kerouac steadfastly continued his dedication to the understanding of Buddhism for years to come, in San Francisco, New York, and Mexico City, but his favorite location for meditation and journal writing was rural Rocky Mount, North Carolina, where he often stayed at the home of his sister and brother-in-law. In the woods near his brother-in-law's house, Kerouac was free to roam and to meditate and to come home in the evenings to the sanctity of his family.

In February 1954 Kerouac typed up 100 pages of his Buddhist study notes so that he could collate them and send them with ALLEN GINSBERG. Ever eager to share the discovery of new ideas, Kerouac initially assumed the role of teacher and considered Ginsberg his student; he addresses Ginsberg directly several times in the notes. Soon, though, Kerouac came to understand inherent dangers in professing to be a teacher of enlightenment, and he dropped the role except to the degree that he positioned himself as a conduit for the voice of the great Buddhist teachers of the past. His notes continued to grow and to open out into new areas as Kerouac continued to learn about Buddhism and to expand his personal responses to his spiritual study. While the published *Some of the Dharma* may not be as popular a book for readers as, say, ON THE ROAD or the The DHARMA BUMS, its writing—that is, the ongoing act of its creation—was vitally important to Kerouac's thematic development as a writer. The seeds of Buddhist influence that begin in *Some of the Dharma* fully bloom in such later works as MEXICO CITY BLUES, TRISTESSA, VISIONS OF GERARD, *The Scripture of the Golden Eternity*, and DESOLATION ANGELS. Even in his earlier, pre-Buddhist books a strong spiritual drive had been evident; after spring 1954, Buddhism became the driving force of Kerouac's output, so much so that in January 1955, Kerouac asked his literary agent to return to him his various pre-1954 manuscripts that he had been trying to publish. He wished instead to substitute his story of the life of the Buddha: "I won't need money the way I'm going to live. And from now on all my writing is going to have a basis of Buddhist Teaching free of all worldly & literary motives. . . . I couldn't publish [*On the Road*] except as 'Pre-enlightenment' work." His heart may have been in the right place, but "right livelihood" could not overwhelm entirely his desire to be a successfully published author, and several months later Kerouac again was engaged in the business of trying to get his work published.

Kerouac did not live to see the publication of *Some of the Dharma*. He had hoped to usher in a new age of American Buddhism with *Some of the Dharma* and "Wake Up," the Buddha story, and he foresaw a groundswell of new and enlightened attitudes from the general citizenry right up to the U.S. president. *The Dharma Bums*, however, came as close to shifting the current American cultural landscape as one had any reason to expect, and it demonstrates the power of Kerouac's narrative art to convey the ideas about which he had been ruminating in his nonfiction study. Some contemporary critics belittled Kerouac's apparent dabbling in Buddhism in *The Dharma Bums*, but the 1997 publication of *Some of the Dharma* finally allows readers to trace the influence of Buddhism in Kerouac's life and his work.

Some of the Dharma consists of 10 "books" of varying length, based on the spiral ring notebooks in which Kerouac originally composed the notes. Readers who are interested primarily in learning about Buddhism might be terribly frustrated if they rely on *Some of the Dharma* as their starting point. On the other hand, maybe some readers would be powerfully rewarded in a way that they might miss if they had taken a more conventional approach, and this seems to be Kerouac's aim. The published book is not a guide to Buddhism; it is instead a guide to how Kerouac approached the subject and how his understanding of Buddhism contended with his Christianity and also with his lust for women and alcohol. There is much repetition of themes throughout the book, and in fact one might say that there is only one theme—reality is an illusion—that echoes repeatedly in seemingly endless variations. That Kerouac is painfully aware of suffering is fully evidenced throughout the book, and Buddhistic beliefs help Kerouac to see that pain, too, is an illusion.

In Book One, Kerouac lists what he believes to be an essential bibliography for the study of Buddhism and also lists important Hindu terms along with their meanings in English. Beyond that, one cannot discern what thoughts are Kerouac's and what ideas are his gleanings from his bibliography. Occasionally quotations are cited, but more typically they are not. Kerouac uses language that at times sounds as if it were lifted from the King James Bible (*thy* and *thou* and so on) when he is purportedly stating Buddhist precepts. At other times, he brings Buddhism and Christianity into close proximity: "Tathagata in Us All / The Lord Hath Mercy." Shakespearean language play and a blend of Buddhism and Catholicism are present in future works as well. In addition to Christianity, other featured themes are also particularly Kerouacian. Numerous times, he refers to his Beat-

Generation friends by name, and in Book Two, he astutely perceives his own situation: "I don't want to be a drunken hero of the generation of suffering. I want to be a quiet saint living in a shack meditation of universal mind." These references to both the Beat Generation and to his position in society (versus his yearning to retire from society) place *Some of the Dharma* firmly in the Kerouac canon. Throughout the book, Kerouac wrestles with his attachments to friendships, his addiction to alcohol, and his eagerness for critical and monetary success as a writer. He cannot reckon how to adhere to Buddhist precepts and satisfy his desires, and many of his notes record his ongoing battles to balance them. Finally he determines to eat but one meal per day, to quit drinking, and to drop all friendships. When he finds that he cannot maintain this regimen, he decides that he might live a double life, which he calls The City and the Path. In the City, he will indulge in sex, wine, friends, and the business of writing the Duluoz Legend to earn money. The Path represents solitude and a do-nothing philosophy. To some degree, Kerouac was able to carry on this lifestyle.

Buddhism influenced more than Kerouac's lifestyle; it also helped him develop a scheme for his writing. When he fully conceived his Duluoz Legend, he foresaw his work divided into six categories: Visions, Dreams, Dharmas, Blues, Prayers, and Ecstasies. This list provides serviceable divisions for his life's work. Readers will find numerous insights to the ways that *Some of the Dharma* influenced Kerouac's life and his work.

Matt Theado

Sometimes a Great Notion　Ken Kesey
(1964)

This second novel by KEN KESEY, which is often considered to be his masterpiece, exhibits a concern with local color that is reminiscent of many of America's best regionalist writers such as William Faulkner and John Steinbeck. Kesey went to the Oregon logging country for several weeks in 1961 and rode with loggers in their trucks and frequented their bars. The novel was begun in Stanford and completed in La Honda, California.

The publication party for this novel was one of the ultimate destinations for the group known as The Merry Pranksters, a collection of psychedelic experimenters based in La Honda and led by Kesey and NEAL CASSADY. The Pranksters started in California in their colorful bus "Furthur" and traveled across the United States to New York. This moment, which is captured in Tom Wolfe's *The Electric Kool-Aid Acid Test* (1968), is seen by some as the transition between the Beats and the hippies, their countercultural inheritors.

Sometimes a Great Notion follows the saga of the Stampers, a family of strike-breaking loggers on the Wakonda Auga River in southwest Oregon. This is done at the behest of Hank Stamper, the novel's protagonist. Kesey manipulates the novel's narration through Hank and various characters who are connected to him, showing their emotional and psychological relationship to him through flashbacks. The novel opens with Jonathan Draeger, national representative for the logging union on strike. Floyd Evenwrite, the local representative, informs Draeger that the Stampers have broken the strike. This opening sequence is illustrative of Kesey's technique, as Draeger and Evenwrite become secondary to Vivian, Hank's wife, as the focal narrative character; she then gives way to a third person who retells of the clan's migration West. The novel's plot is told as a recapitulation of the past and through a series of point-of-view shifts which are often abrupt. In some cases, there are several of these shifts in one paragraph.

The plot first centers around Hank's decision to do "wildcat" logging to fill an order to a sawmill. When the novel opens, none of the timber has been delivered, and only some of the contract's quota has been cut. Due to the strike in the Wakonda community, there is a shortage of help for Hank and his family. They must therefore send for Leland "Lee" Stamper, Hank's half-brother, who is currently a graduate student at Yale University. Lee attempts suicide before receiving his invitation West. This establishes a contrast between Lee as the bookish easterner who has no sense of self-worth, and Hank as a self-reliant western-frontier type who is secure in his own individuality. In an interview with Gordon Lish in 1963, Kesey stated that there were some autobiographical elements in

Colors, San Francisco, 1997. Photographer Larry Keenan: "Ken Kesey talking to a Hell's Angel at the Fillmore for The Grandfurthur Tour party. He is celebrating the bringing of the Magic Bus back to Cleveland to be inducted into the Rock-and-Roll Hall of Fame and Museum." *(courtesy of Larry Keenan)*

each of these two characters. The entire Stamper clan eventually goes to work on the lumber contract: Hank, Lee, their father Henry, and their cousin Joe Ben, who helps run the family business. This close family work environment is soon disturbed by ghosts from the past. When Hank was a teenager, he had an affair with his stepmother Myra, Lee's mother. Myra would commit suicide, and Lee blames Hank for contributing to her death. This background story soon leads to the conflict between Lee and Hank over Vivian. She has become a substitute for Myra, as Lee seduces her in revenge for Hank's earlier indiscretion. During the novel's action, Joe Ben serves as more of a brother for Hank than Lee, a change of roles that

will have dramatic consequences for Hank's emotional and psychic health.

The climax of the novel takes place during one of several logging accidents on the river, some of which are caused by the union workers. During the pivotal accident, Joe Ben is trapped underwater. Hank tries to bring him air but is unsuccessful in his surrogate breathing and Joe Ben drowns. In the same accident, Hank's father Henry loses his arm and is left on his hospital deathbed. Hank is left to take the logging run down the river with one helper at the novel's close. The climax of the love triangle culminates in Lee's successful seduction of Vivian, who then realizes that she loves both brothers. Now aware of the full scope of the conflict between Hank and Lee, Vivian decides to leave the Wakonda community and begin her life anew. Vivian is portrayed as alienated from the community throughout the novel, a state that is made worse by the loss of her unborn child. The relationship between Vivian and Hank is complex, and many critics see her as one of Kesey's most realistically portrayed women characters.

Kesey's technique of changing points-of-view in quick succession makes a first reading of the novel a bit difficult. However, many of Kesey's recurrent themes come through in *Sometimes a Great Notion*. Hank Stamper is the archetypal rugged individualist. As a wildcat logger, he is paid based on the amount of lumber that he delivers to a sawmill; the union loggers surrounding him are paid an hourly wage. This fundamental difference is illustrative of Kesey's concern with the value of the individual in the face of a group that demands conformity, much like McMurphy's defiance in *ONE FLEW OVER THE CUCKOO'S NEST*. Draeger, the national union man, is representative of the larger system at work beyond the local Wakonda community. This is a hallmark of many of America's great regionalists. They are able to expand the concerns of a small community outward to the larger society as a whole.

Sometimes a Great Notion was made into an underrated film released in 1971 by Universal Studios starring Paul Newman and Henry Fonda. The film was rebroadcast on television under the title *Never Give an Inch*.

Bibliography

Leeds, Barry, *Ken Kesey*, New York: Unger, 1981.
Lish, Gordon. "What the Hell You Looking in Here For, Daisy Mae?: An Interview with Ken Kesey." *Genesis West* 2 (Fall 1963): 17–29.
Porter, Gilbert M., *The Art of Grit: Ken Kesey's Fiction*, Columbia: University of Missouri Press, 1982.

Donovan Braud

"Sourdough Mountain Lookout" Philip Whalen (1958)

One of PHILIP WHALEN's most anthologized poems, "Sourdough Mountain Lookout" is representative of themes and techniques central to Whalen's work as a whole: a love of the natural world; an interest in Buddhist and Western philosophy; the use of the long poem as a format; and the inclusion of a variety of kinds and levels of language in his poetry. The poem's dedication to KENNETH REXROTH not only credits the encouragement that Rexroth gave Whalen early in his career but also indicates both Whalen's affiliation with the San Francisco renaissance and the inspirational role that Rexroth played in the Beat turn to Asian poetry. The poem was first published as an excerpt in the *Chicago Review* Zen issue of 1958, thereby associating Whalen with Beat Zen and writers such as GARY SNYDER, JACK KEROUAC, and Alan Watts. It is also included as the last poem in Whalen's first published book of poetry, *Like I Say*, 1960, and represented Whalen in Donald Allen's seminal anthology of *The NEW AMERICAN POETRY, 1945–1960* of that year.

"Sourdough Mountain Lookout" is based on Whalen's experience working as a fire lookout during the summers of 1953–55 in the Mount Baker National Forest in Washington. In an interview with John Suiter, Whalen noted that the poem came from "bits and pieces" of writing that he did up on the mountain, adding that ALLEN GINSBERG's "HOWL" was a model and inspiration as he put the poem together from journal entries the following year in Berkeley. The poem is similar to other poems of this period in that it is written in an open form. Often a rough blank verse in rhythm predominates with somewhat irregular stanzas, usually ranging from three to six lines each with occasional instances of rhyming couplet and even a nursery-rhymelike ditty about the miracle of the egg. Whalen varies the tone and the language of the poem, too, mixing casual conversational colloquialisms and slang with homespun sayings of his grandmother, philosophic musings, ironic self-reflections, and quotes from books that he is reading, making for a rich mixture of voices. The poem is thus an example of how Whalen's poetry graphs the mind's movement, although it does not contain the daring linear experiments of such later poems as "Self Portrait, From Another Direction."

The speaker of the poem is a fire lookout (recalling Whalen's experience) who also acts as a contemporary version of the Chinese or Japanese hermit poet or Buddhist priest who spends time in the mountains contemplating and communing with nature. The poem begins in a conversational and humorous tone as the speaker climbs the mountain to the lookout at the beginning of summer: "I always say I won't go back to the mountains / I am too old and fat there are bugs mean mules / And pancakes every morning of the world." It ends as he closes up for winter and comes back down the mountain. In between, the speaker recounts his solitary life on the mountaintop in company of a bear, a mouse, a deer, and stars, juxtaposed with philosophical musings on the nature of the universe in flux. Critic Geoffrey Thurley notes of this poem that "reflections upon the relations between the mind and the outer world constitute Whalen's major theme." Throughout the poem, the speaker contrasts opposites: the hot sun of midday with the starry night and the speaker's memories and meditations with his view of mountains and lakes.

As he meditates further from his rock lookout, reflection becomes more focused on Buddhist tenets. He compares the surrounding mountains to the circle of beads of a Buddhist rosary, which the speaker imagined as the Buddha meditating in the center's void. Toward the end of the poem, Whalen refers to the Prajnaparamita Sutra, a key text of Zen Buddhism whose message is that the seeming opposites of form and emptiness are one. His hip translation of the closing lines of the sutra describe his departure from the lookout, while suggesting the loss of ego experienced in meditation: "Gone / Gone / REALLY gone / Into the cool / O MAMA!" Whalen's Beat use of slang here is a more effective way to express alternative consciousness than ordinary language. The last two lines of the poem also play with meaning, characteristic of the way Whalen ends many of his poems: "Like they say, 'Four times up, / Three times down.' I'm still on the mountain." The speaker may suggest that though he is leaving, he takes the mountain state of mind with him or that he has never really left the mountaintop. Such a paradoxical ending can challenge, but for Whalen, such challenges, including his use of quotes from other writers, are ways to educate and encourage readers to further research and deeper thought. The idea of education also relates to "Since You Ask Me," Whalen's statement of po-

etics and his claim to the title of Doctor or teacher: "I do not put down the academy but have assumed its function in my own person. . . ." Thus, "Sourdough Mountain Lookout" is not only deservedly one of Whalen's most well-known poems but also an important early expression of his poetics, Buddhist interests, and role as poet and teacher.

Bibliography
Holsapple, Bruce. "A Dirty Bird in a Square Time: Whalen's Poetry." In *Continuous Flame*, edited by Michael Rothenberg and Suzi Winson, 129–149. New York: Fish Drum, Inc., 2004.
Suiter, John. *Poets on the Peaks*. Washington, D.C.: Counterpoint, 2002.
Thurley, Geoffrey. "The Development of the New Language: Michael McClure, Philip Whalen, and Gregory Corso." In *The Beats: Essays in Criticism*, edited by Lee Bartlett, 165–180. Jefferson, N.C.: McFarland, 1981.

Jane Falk

Subterraneans, The Jack Kerouac (1958)
This novel is about interracial love, JACK KEROUAC's obsessive relationship with his mother, and his confrontation with his homosexual tendencies. Kerouac wrote it in three days while fueled by Benzedrine, and it is perhaps the best example of his spontaneous prose style. JOYCE JOHNSON found the book astonishing in that she had no idea how conscious Kerouac was that his wild behavior and all-night drinking caused him to lose the women in his life. *The Subterraneans* is emotionally raw and heartbreaking and is Kerouac's most sexually explicit novel. Charles Frazier, author of *Cold Mountain* (1997), writes, "In *The Subterraneans* the theory and the practice mesh perfectly, and Kerouac—before the train wreck of fame and self-destruction—created a remarkable writing style capable of capturing the manic energy flooding the country just after World War II, when, contrary to the stereotype of the period, many different elements of the nation emerged from the Depression and the war years wild for life."

Soon after the events that were fictionalized in the novel occurred, Kerouac sat down and wrote

The Subterraneans in three October nights in 1953 at his mother's kitchen table. This amazing feat of spontaneous writing impressed even Kerouac, who reported that he lost several pounds in the process and ended up white as a sheet. ALLEN GINSBERG and WILLIAM S. BURROUGHS, astonished at how the book was created, asked Kerouac to write an essay on his methods. Kerouac's famous "The Essentials of Spontaneous Prose" was the result.

The Subterraneans details Leo Percepied's (based on Kerouac) love affair with Mardou Fox (based on Alene Lee) in Summer 1953. Lee was the half American Indian and half African American girlfriend of Allen Ginsberg; when Kerouac first met her, she was typing copies of Burroughs's JUNKY and QUEER, which Ginsberg was trying to sell for Burroughs. Ginsberg (the inspiration for Adam Moorad in the novel) dubbed Alene and her ultracool friends at the San Remo bar "the subterraneans" (from which BOB DYLAN derived the title of his song "Subterranean Homesick Blues," the video of which includes Ginsberg). Primarily, though, the book is a deep Oedipal confession by Kerouac. Gerald Nicosia, Kerouac biographer, writes in the introduction to the 1981 edition, "*Leo* was the first name of Kerouac's father, and *Percepied* is French for 'pierced foot,' an equivalent of the Greek *oedipus*. Leo Percepied has the classic Oedipal complex as described by Freud: he has replaced his father in his mother's affections, and has in turn accepted her as his wife." Nicosia informs his readers that Kerouac had recently read Wilhelm Reich's *The Function of the Orgasm* before starting his relationship with Alene Lee. James T. Jones argues, "*The Subterraneans* presents an argument against Freudian psychoananlysis based on Kerouac's recent reading of Wilhelm Reich's *Function of the Orgasm.*"

Commentators and biographers have pointed out the extensive fictionalizing of this supposedly uncensored, unrevised confession by Kerouac. Some of these alterations were made to avoid a libel suit. Alene Lee, for example, was horrified by the personal details that Kerouac revealed about her. New York City thus becomes, rather implausibly at points, San Francisco. Other "truths" in the book are obscured, such as Kerouac's one-night stand with Gore Vidal, discussed in Vidal's memoir *Palimpsest.* A film

version of the novel, released in 1960 by MGM and starring George Peppard, made Kerouac cringe as Mardou is changed into a white woman.

The book's style is its most famous feature, Kerouac's bop prosody at its best. Kerouac had to battle with Donald Allen at Grove Press to print the book as he wrote it, with his dash punctuation intact. The novel was first published in both paperback and hardback editions and received few serious reviews until decades later. Today it is considered one of Kerouac's masterpieces.

The book centers around a group of artists and intellectuals. Leo is more of an observer of this group than a member and has hidden motives for hanging out with them: He is consciously seeking out a great love affair and is immediately struck by the "fellaheen" princess of this group, who is called Mardou. From the beginning, it is evident that this romance will fail; in fact, the book's interest is exactly that. Leo realizes that he is "hot" and that her crowd, younger than he, is "cool." He also fears that he is too brash and roughly masculine to fit in with this effeminate crowd. Leo, fresh from his lover's betrayal as he writes these opening pages, questions whether or not he wanted her simply because he felt the need as a great writer to have a great love or if it is simply that he is courting rejection by choosing an impossible partner.

Moorad tells Leo of his aborted affair with Mardou. She is, he tells Leo, in therapy and subject to hallucinations. The three of them—Leo, Mardou, and Moorad—go out for jazz and beers, and Leo sketches a portrait of this moment. Charlie Parker sees Mardou and Leo dancing, and Leo thinks the jazz great can see how it will all end. Moorad leaves the two alone (as planned), and Leo and Mardou return to her apartment. They dance and inevitably make love. In their postcoitus conversation, Mardou wants to know why men find their essence in women but rush away from it to build things and start wars. Leo makes a graceless exit the next morning, feigning a hangover and the need to work on his books. She finds him in Moorad's apartment a few days later and sits in his lap and tells him the story of her life.

Her story sends Leo off on a reverie about Mardou's Cherokee father. Leo, too, is part Native American. He transcribes her story as well as he can remember it, confessing that he has probably forgotten much, an admission that matches Alene Lee's claim after reading the book that Kerouac mostly put his own words into her mouth in the novel. Percepied blames Mardou's neurosis on the other subterraneans. She loses her identity living with these men and one night ends up wandering naked on the San Francisco streets. Mardou recounts the days in her life when she verges on psychosis from too much Benzedrine, marijuana, and general exposure. She has an epiphany about the endless depth of reality and the interconnectedness of things, but this beautiful vision eventually becomes sinister. She is put in a hospital, where, once and for all, she realizes that she must not risk her freedom by going too far out.

Mardou stays overnight with Leo at Adam's and the next day misses her appointment with her analyst at the county hospital. Moorad tries to tell Leo how serious this oversight is, but Leo misses the significance of such events as they unfold. That night, after a round of parties in literary San Francisco, Leo makes another crucial error. Drunk and in the company of some witty gay men, he sends Mardou home in a taxi at 3 A.M. while he continues partying. On the surface, the fault of the narrator lies in his alcoholism and late-night habits—both hardly conducive to a long-term relationship. However, there is the suggestion that Leo prefers the company of homosexuals to the company of women. Leo's failure here leads directly to Mardou beginning an affair the next night with Yuri Gligoric (based on GREGORY CORSO). For the rest of his life Corso felt the need to defend himself about this relationship, which he claims happened before he was truly friends with Kerouac. Other pressures separate Leo and Mardou as well, particularly Leo's need to go back to the domestic stability of his mother's apartment, where he can dry out and write. Mardou resents that he has such a stable place to which to return.

The second half of the book begins with a long self-examination by the narrator regarding his feelings about Mardou as a "Negro" and how that might have been affecting their relationship. He notes that it will be impossible for him to visit his family in the South with a half Cherokee, half African-American girlfriend. He also confesses

his childish fears of Mardou's black body, and she allows him to closely study her anatomy in full daylight. Leo exorcises all kinds of fears and hang-ups in his portrait of their relationship. He feels a competition between Mardou and his mother. The subterraneans also question his sexual orientation, calling him a fag, and Leo even compares himself to the "little fag whose broken to bits" at the hand of the African-American masseur in Tennessee Williams's short story "Desire and the Black Masseur."

Leo recounts the night that he spent with Arial Lavalina (based on Gore Vidal). (The details of his one-night stand with Kerouac were later revealed by Vidal in his memoir *Palimpsest*.) The evening begins with Leo meeting up with Frank Carmody (based on Burroughs), who is just back from Africa. Leo takes the opportunity to introduce Carmody to Lavalina, who is across the bar from them. Leo once again puts Mardou in a cab and stays out partying. Carmody leaves the two to their own fun, and Leo and Arial go back to his hotel. Leo wakes up the next morning guilt-ridden but unspecific about the details of the night. He later writes Lavalina a letter apologizing for being drunk and acting the way he did.

Mardou does not stay mad at Leo because of this incident, but a few days later she writes a rather abstract letter to him, which he analyzes for the next several pages. In the letter he reads between the lines that she hates to see him making himself sick with drink, and Leo recalls a disastrous drunken party with Yuri and Mardou at the house of Sam Vedder (based on Lucien Carr), ending up with Sam falling-down drunk next to his wife, who is holding their newborn. The letter also reveals to Leo what he sees as Mardou's fear of losing her sanity.

The next section of the book centers on a dream that Leo has following a long night of drinking with Mardou, Moorad, Carmody, and Yuri. Leo makes a fool of himself by insisting that a beautiful young man in a red shirt accompany them on their rounds—further fueling speculation regarding his sexuality. They become completely inebriated, and back at Mardou's apartment, she rolls around with a balloon, pantomiming lovemaking and trying to arouse jealousy in Leo. That morning, they both have the same dream that features all of their friends; most significantly, Leo sees Mardou making love to Yuri in the dream. Later, it becomes clear that Leo has, in a way, created a love affair between the two—dreamed it into existence. In fact, he tells Yuri and the rest of the subterraneans about the dream. Mardou, too, seems to understand that Yuri will provide her a way out of the affair with Leo. Later, he tells Yuri that he is in love with Mardou, a fact that makes the young poet even more heartless in his betrayal. Leo believes that he betrays him because the younger poet wants the status of older poets Leo, Carmody, and Moorad, and he can show his mastery of them by taking Mardou.

Leo admires Mardou for her deep understanding of jazz and literature. He dreams of the two of them disappearing as Indians down into Mexico. But he later stands her up on a date, disappears for no reason, and tortures her unnecessarily by telling her that Moorad broke it off with her because she is a "Negro." When she goes off on a date with a young black man, he takes it out on Mardou's neighbor. Later, in an infamous passage Leo describes performing cunnilingus on Mardou. One drunken evening, Yuri steals a pushcart and pushes Mardou and Leo all the way to Moorad's apartment. Moorad is upset that stolen property has been parked in front of his apartment, but Leo is less upset about this situation than he is at discovering Yuri and Mardou playing intimately like children in the next room. Leo feels the age difference keenly. His instinct to be jealous conflicts with his desire to break-up with Mardou to return to his mother and the writing of his books.

As the book moves between good and bad times, Leo describes the "most awful [night] of all." Yuri accompanies him and Mardou, and Leo discusses Yuri's emerging vision as a poet. Throughout the evening, various men approach Leo and ask him if Mardou is his girl, and each time he draws up short of claiming her. They drive out of the city with a young novelist and visit an estate. Leo, knowing how out-of-place Mardou is becoming in his drunken wanderings, sees his relationship with her falling apart. He knows that he is in trouble when even the dawn birds sound bleak. He chastises himself for past infidelities and for dragging along Mardou, who is unstable at best, on an exhausting alcohol-fueled nightmare in which she figures as an outsider.

The book takes on a tragic tone. Leo sees the relationship breaking up, but it is already too late to stop. Race really does come between them. Mardou will not let Leo hold her hand in public for fear that people will think that she is a prostitute. His attitude toward her blackness changes from loving her as an "essential" woman to now seeing her as the "hustler" whom she dreads resembling. (Readers should note that Kerouac portrays Leo's changing attitude with self-awareness.) They go to a birthday party for Balliol MacJones (based on JOHN CLELLON HOLMES), and in the subsequent scene in a downtown bar Leo bounces off the crowd delivering half insults and embarrassing people at random, such as Julien Alexander, whom he hits on in mock-homosexual interest. The night of the party for MacJones ends with Leo insisting on continuing on to one more bar and leaving Mardou stranded in a cab with no fare for home. Having made a dreadful mistake, Leo remembers her kind words in a letter, wishing he were not a drunk.

Leo has lost all ability to balance the tensions in his life and thus loses Mardou. She seems to have honestly hoped that someday they would be together. Knowing that he is on the brink of despair, Leo, with Sam, heads to Adam's apartment where he and Sam become intoxicated. He awakens the next morning truly ill and heads out of the city where, at the end of one of Kerouac's greatest long sentences, he "went in the San Francisco railyard and cried." Staring at the moon, he sees his mother's face, and it is apparent to him that only a mother, quite literally, could love him in this state.

Leo and Mardou reunite only to discuss their break-up. She tells him that she has had sex with Yuri, a fact that almost completely undercuts Leo. Mardou explains to him how she knows that women are only trophies to men and that she now has less value in Yuri's eyes for having slept with him. Originally the novel ended with Leo breaking a chair over the knife-wielding Yuri's head. Corso himself convinced Kerouac to render this in a fantasy that merely flashes in the narrator's mind. Mardou has the last calm word: "I want to be independent like I say." Then the narrator goes home to his mother—as did Kerouac—and writes this book.

Jon Panish criticizes Kerouac's portrayal of Mardou in *The Subterraneans*: "Not recognizing their own complicity in perpetuating racist ideology, Kerouac and others continued the tradition of primitivizing and romanticizing the experiences of racial minorities (particularly African Americans) and raiding their culture and contemporary experience for the purpose of enhancing their own position as white outsiders." Nancy McCampbell Grace reminds us that "It's critical that we not lose sight of Kerouac's [ethnic] hybrid status." In recent years more attention has been spent looking at Kerouac's portrayal of race than in his use of language. Yet during its time Henry Miller praised Kerouac's artistry: "Jack Kerouac has done something to our immaculate prose from which it may never recover. A passionate lover of language, he knows how to use it. Born virtuoso that he is, he takes pleasure in defying the laws and conventions of literary expression which cripple genuine, untrammeled communication between reader and writer."

Bibliography

Grace, Nancy McCampbell. "A White Man in Love: A Study of Race, Gender, Class, and Ethnicity in Jack Kerouac's *Maggie Cassidy, The Subterraneans,* and *Tristessa.*" In *The Beat Generation: Critical Essays,* edited by Kostas Myrsiades, 93–120. New York: Peter Lang, 2002.

Jones, James T. *Jack Kerouac's Duluoz Legend: The Mythic Form of an Autobiographical Fiction.* Carbondale: Southern Illinois University Press, 1999.

Miller, Henry. Preface. *The Subterraneans,* by Jack Kerouac. New York: Avon, 1959. i–iii.

Nicosia, Gerald. Introduction. *The Subterraneans,* by Jack Kerouac. New York: Grove Press, 1981, i–iv.

Panish, Jon. "Kerouac's *The Subterraneans:* A Study of 'Romantic Primitivism.'" *MELUS* 19, no. 3 (Fall 1994): 107–123.

Rob Johnson and Kurt Hemmer

T

Tales of Beatnik Glory Edward Sanders
(1975)

Described as a "cluster novel," *Tales of Beatnik Glory* illustrates the lives of those who roamed the Beat streets of 1960s New York. Taking a hindsight vision of the Beat Generation as it melded slowly into hippiedom, EDWARD SANDERS investigates a time when poetry and folk singing were radical acts and everyone, from university professors to distraught mothers-in-law, came face to face with the "deviants" of the "rucksack revolution." As he writes in "The Filmmaker," "With a generation readily present who viewed their lives as on a set, there was no need to hunt afar for actors and actresses. What a cast of characters was roaming the village streets of 1962!"

Sanders writes in "The Poetry Reading," the novel's opening story, that "it was impossible for the pulse-grabbers at the throat of culture to deny the beats." They became a palpable force during the 1950s and 1960s in cities like New York where rebellion against all forms of social control was the norm of the day. From protests against injustices such as racism and war to illicit drug use and free love, Sanders maps the "scene" in its often bizarre and hilarious transformations where the main propulsion, he writes, "came from a desperate search for some indication that the universe was more than a berserk sewer."

A master of satire, Sanders pokes fun equally at authority figures and at his Beat characters. In "The Mother-in-Law" the denizens of the "beat scene" miss "no poetry reading, no art show, no concert in an obscure loft, no lecture, no event of sufficiently rebellious nature," and when looking for an apartment, a prime consideration was "how long the door would hold up in a dope raid." Thus, from the authorities who would not allow poetry in a café without a cabaret license to the "weekend beatniks" who would "pay a pretty penny for genuine flip-out garb," to the "microfilmed transcriptions" of the Central Intelligence Agency (CIA) Poetry Operations Division, Sanders surrounds the era in an aura of the ridiculous. In "The Cube of Potato Soaring through Vastness," Sanders even chronicles a university conference on "The Death of the Beat Generation," a typical academic farce of co-option at which Sanders's book flatly sticks its tongue out.

Yet, in the midst of the fun, Sanders does not shy away from the sensitive subjects of the time. For every Beat accomplishment, for every social more that was wounded, there was a victim of oppression and excess, an amphetamine-wasted body, bragging "I lose trillions of cells everyday, man, grooo-VY," or shrieking as does Uncle Thrills, one of the novel's many strung out junkies, "I've puked my life away here, I tell you. . . ."

In "A Book of Verse," the novel comes full circle. Sanders autobiographically describes his first run-in with ALLEN GINSBERG's "HOWL," describing the shock it delivered to his placid, midwestern worldview. The novel ends with Sanders leaving for New York to become a poet, pointing the reader right back to page one.

Jennifer Cooper

Tapestry and the Web, The Joanne Kyger
(1965)

In her first poetry collection, JOANNE KYGER revisits and revises Homeric epic myth, adding layers of personal, reflective imagery and references. The backdrop to the composition of her poems gives a snapshot of the West Coast Beat scene. Arriving at age 22 in San Francisco in 1957, Kyger was quickly swept up into the North Beach arts milieu, meeting poets and attending readings at the numerous lively venues that were popularized by members of the San Francisco Poetry Renaissance. Writers visited from Greenwich Village, and there was an influx of students who had previously studied at the experimental Black Mountain College in North Carolina.

Kyger began to attend the poetry circle that grouped around Jack Spicer and Robert Duncan, and it was there, on February 23, 1958, that she first read material that would become part of *The Tapestry and the Web*, the work that Kyger has identified as her breakthrough in establishing her own poetic "voice." Duncan later described the scene: Kyger, in her habitual stance of kneeling and holding the text before her, intensely focused on her words, reads to the mostly male assemblage "The Maze," a poem about a woman who was driven mad by expectations of passive fidelity. The response, said Duncan, was an immediate "furore" as Kyger's passionate and iconoclastic vision registered with the usually highly critical group.

Drawing on Homer's tale, Kyger creates a dynamic Penelope who was more fueled by eros than the nobly stoic spouse of Homer's epic; the latter guards her wifely virtue and nightly unweaves her daily tapestry work. Kyger reevaluates the passivity of Penelope's patience for Odysseus, asking in the poem "Pan as the Son of Penelope," "Just HOW / solitary was her wait?" Kyger portrays Penelope as wily and in control, and he essays new versions of Penelope's long wait for the return of her husband, imagining more and more daring accounts: Penelope as a cheating wife; Penelope giving birth to a son fathered by all the suitors; Penelope slowly going mad. Through the central metaphor of dreaming and weaving, Kyger explores burgeoning female creativity. The poems of *The Tapestry and The Web* grow from the centering mythic narratives, which, in Kyger's chatty,

colloquial, Beat-influenced idiom, are grounded in personal concerns and a sense of immediacy.

Critic and chronicler of the San Francisco Poetry Renaissance Michael Davidson has argued that in some ways Kyger is herself analogous to Penelope, citing her position as a singular female in a largely male artistic enclave, surrounded by suitors/male writers whom she "enchants" with her poetry. Certainly there is something both playful and subversive in Kyger's challenge to Homeric and patriarchal authority. Influences in Kyger's work include both the late modernism of Duncan and the nature-oriented, Zen-inflected work of GARY SNYDER (Kyger's husband from 1960 to 1964 whom she met in 1958).

Ultimately it is the personal narrative in Kyger's work, an impulsive and exhilarating voice, that bridges her navigation of these various influences. Kyger's achievement in *The Tapestry and The Web* is the creation of a book-length, cohesive work that is autobiographical, laconic, colloquial, grounded in classical mythology, and yet personal.

Bibliography
Davidson, Michael. "Appropriations: Women and the San Francisco Renaissance." In *The San Francisco Poetry Renaissance: Poetics and Community at Midcentury.* New York: Cambridge University Press, 1989, 172–199.

Duncan, Robert. *As Testimony: The Poem & The Scene.* San Francisco: White Rabbit, 1964.

Friedman, Amy L. "Joanne Kyger, Beat Generation Poet: 'a porcupine traveling at the speed of light.'" In *Reconstructing The Beats,* edited by Jennie Skerl, 73–88. New York: Palgrave, 2004.

Amy L. Friedman

Tarantula Bob Dylan (1971)

Drafted in late 1964 and early 1965, bootlegged from early promo copies in 1966, commercially released by Macmillan in 1971, BOB DYLAN's *Tarantula* is a confounding text that, like much of the best work of Dylan, defies expectations and facile explication. Debate in regard to what genre it inhabits has roiled from the time of its clandestine release. It has been variously deemed a novel (Shelton

1986/1997), poems (St Martin's 1994 reissue), and "a book of words" (Heylin 1991). Joan Baez at one time suggested an alternative title for the collection: "Fuck You." Dylan himself seems to have taken up the composition of *Tarantula* as an open-ended commercial and artistic opportunity. His contract for the book appears to have been signed prior to settling on a fully conceived notion of how its content might be manifested—in May 1964 he described the book as "pictures and words" that focus on Hollywood.

Dylan's writing, and especially his writing in the mid-1960s, was clearly influenced by the Beats, never more transparently so than in *Tarantula*. Ann Charters excerpted a part of it in her *The Portable Beat Reader* (1992). Dylan's first serious discussion

in regard to publishing his work was with LAWRENCE FERLINGHETTI and City Lights in 1963. Liner notes that support his album releases, beginning with *The Times They Are a-Changin'* in 1963, exhibited Dylan's propensity for free-form verse and the exercise of JACK KEROUAC's spontaneous prose method.

Dylan's composing process in *Tarantula* was clearly indebted to WILLIAM S. BURROUGHS's cut-up techniques. Speaking in early 1965 about *Tarantula* (then tentatively titled "Bob Dylan Off the Record"), Dylan asks interviewer Paul Jay Robbins of the *LA Free Press* whether he "dig[s] something like cutups" and describes his writing as "[s]omething that had no rhyme, all cut up, no nothing except something happening which is

McClure, Dylan, and Ginsberg, North Beach, San Francisco, 1965. Photographer Larry Keenan: "This session was arranged the night before at a party after Bob Dylan's concert at the Berkeley Community Theater. Allen Ginsberg introduced me to Dylan and we arranged to do a photo session (for the *Blonde on Blonde* album) the same day as the Beat's last gathering at City Lights Books. At City Lights we hid out in the basement with Dylan and when the people started to break the door down we climbed out a window and ran down the alley and took this photograph." *(courtesy of Larry Keenan)*

words." Dylan's propensity for exaggerated American plain-speak and his carnivalesque description of "atomic fag bars being looted and Bishops disguised as chocolate prisoners" is deeply redolent of NAKED LUNCH–era Burroughs. Dylan's exposure in 1960 to Kerouac's MEXICO CITY BLUES appears also to have had a bearing on both its free-form verse and the Spanish language and bordertown episodes of Tarantula's fractured narrative.

Perhaps the clearest line between the Beats and the Dylan of this period might be drawn between Tarantula and GREGORY CORSO's The HAPPY BIRTHDAY OF DEATH (1960), opening as it does: "Lady of the legless world I have refused to go beyond self-disappearance." Tarantula, which road-tests hundreds of personas and masks, behind any of which might lurk (or not) "Bob Dylan," is as much a book about self-abrogation as revelation. It is one of Dylan's earliest exercises in "self-disappearance." Corso makes a cameo appearance late in Tarantula: "I could tell at a glance that he had no need for Sonny Rollins but I asked him anyway 'whatever happened to gregory corso?'" Much of the language, syntax, and headlong velocity of Tarantula seems to be channeling Corso's "BOMB," with its "tomahawk Cochise flintlock Kidd dagger Rathbone," its suggestion that "To die by cobra is not to die by bad pork," and its clear nod to Rimbaud and French symbolist poetry.

Bibliography

Corso, Gregory. *Mindfield: New & Selected Poems.* New York: Thunder's Mouth, 1989.

Hajdu, David. *Positively 4th Street: The Lives and Times of Joan Baez, Bob Dylan, Mimi Baez Fariña, and Richard Fariña.* New York: North Point, 2001.

Heylin, Clinton. *Bob Dylan: Behind the Shades.* New York: Summit, 1991.

Shelton, Robert. *No Direction Home: The Life and Music of Bob Dylan.* New York: Da Capo, 1997.

Tracy Santa

Thirsting for Peace in a Raging Century: Selected Poems 1961–1985 Ed Sanders
(1987)

For ED SANDERS, the phrase "thirsting for peace in a raging century" was definitive of any act that questioned the myriad inconsistencies and injustices of its age; thus it becomes the unifying theme to the six sections that make up the volume. *Thirsting for Peace in a Raging Century* poetically challenges areas of social control, from missile carrying submarines to sexual repression to an investigation of control and rebellion in ancient cultures. In 1988 this volume won the American Book Award.

The first section, "Poem From Jail," was written during the poet's 1961 incarceration after attempting to board a missile-bearing submarine off the coast of Connecticut. Written on toilet paper and transcribed to sections of cigarette packages, it had to remain hidden because paper, pencils, and, of course, poetry were strictly forbidden in prison. Many of the themes carried through in this volume are established in this first poem.

As a "sort of secular version of the rather more mystic crawl at the end of 'Poem From Jail,'" "The V.F.W. Crawling Contest" continues the idea that was later articulated in "The Thirty-Fourth Year" that the poet "can't face life like a fist fight / must crawl down lonely arroyos." One of his most popular poems, it depicts an epic crawl past vast spaces of American mud, through dumps and fast food restaurants, along litter-strewn highways in the fumes of "rusty monsters roaring past." At the poem's end, though near dead, limbs reduced to stubs, the poet has declared victory over the pervasive American cultural machine, saying "I crawled / I groveled / I conquered."

By 1973, just as Sanders was working on the first volume of TALES OF BEATNIK GLORY while writing many of these poems, he had also just begun his poems for *Egyptian Hieroglyphics.* Thus, many of the poems also illustrate Sanders's interest in ancient cultures, specifically the artist rebels of dictatorial Egypt. He explains in the notes that he "was looking for Lost Generations, for sistra-shaking Dadaists in tent towns on the edge of half-finished pyramids, for cubists in basalt, for free-speech movements on papyrus." As David Herd suggests in "'After All What Else is There to Say': Ed Sanders and the Beat Aesthetic," Sanders was looking "for a genealogy of dissent, for a historical angle of vision that shows the Beat project to be not a momentary aberration but a further eruption of a vibrant radical tradition." He then continues this "genealogy" through to New York's Lower East Side and on to "A.D. 20,000."

As a final theme that was articulated in *Thirsting for Peace in a Raging Century,* in such poems as "Homage to Love-Zap," "Yiddish-Speaking Socialists of the Lower East Side," and "The Time of Perf-Po," Sanders encourages the power of the poem as a historicizing device, where all history should be caught in "sweet nets / of barb babble" to create a "poem zone" used to "love-zap" injustice and "make a New World / inside the New World."

Bibliography

Herd, David. "'After All What Else Is There to Say': Ed Sanders and the Beat Aesthetic." *Review of Contemporary Fiction* 19, no. 1 (1999): 123–137.

Jennifer Cooper

Thompson, Hunter S(tockton) (1937–2005)
Although not usually considered a full-fledged member of the Beat Generation, Hunter S. Thompson maintained an association with several principle Beat figures. Thompson's body of work would seem at first to be at odds ideologically with that of the Beats in that he did not embrace the spirituality and communal living that were usually associated with Beat writers, but he shares several vital characteristics with them. Above all, Thompson and the Beats write with an uncompromising, truth-seeking intensity that does not shy from unauthorized accounts of American culture and unconventional views of the individual's place in American society. Ultimately, Thompson differs ideologically from some of the main currents of thought in Beat writing and, in fact, became one of their most outstanding critics. Nevertheless, Thompson and such Beats as ALLEN GINSBERG, NEAL CASSADY, and KEN KESEY always maintained a respectful admiration of each other due to the earnestness and integrity of their respective attempts to investigate, critique, and influence their surrounding culture.

Thompson was probably born on July 18, 1937, in Louisville, Kentucky. Most sources agree upon 1937 as his birth year, although several sources claim it was 1939. True to character, Thomp-

son himself never provided clarification on this matter. From the start he was someone who took unconventional routes and someone who had a conflicted relationship with traditional values and authority. In high school, Thompson was a gifted athlete but was also prone to run-ins with the local authorities. Several arrests and a 30-day jail sentence for robbery in 1956 prevented Thompson from graduating, although he later received his diploma through the air force, which he joined a week after leaving high school. It was in the air force that Thompson began his work in journalism. While assigned to Eglin Air Force Base in Florida, he became a staff writer and sports editor for the base newspaper. Following an honorable discharge due to general insubordination and his moonlighting activities on a local civilian paper, Thompson briefly held a reporting job in Pennsylvania before winding up in New York City where he first worked as a low-level copy writer for *Time* magazine and where he also took a few formal classes in journalism at Columbia University. But the *Time* job did not last long either, and due to his continual unruly, defiant behavior, Thompson would continue to migrate from job to job throughout the late 1950s and early 1960s (he was fired from one paper for driving a writer's car into the river, another for destroying the office candy machine). During this period, Thompson also fell under the influence of the Beats and embarked on a cross-country journey of discovery inspired by JACK KEROUAC's ON THE ROAD.

Despite his notoriously difficult nature, Thompson began to amass a prolific body of journalistic work and a reputation as a highly competent, if highly eccentric, reporter. Among other publications, he wrote for the *New York Herald Tribune,* the *Chicago Tribune,* and the *National Observer,* for which he became the South American correspondent from 1961 to 1963. Returning to the United States, Thompson settled in the Bay area on the West Coast where he became acquainted with Beat writers Kesey and Ginsberg. He began to write for the *Nation* after once again being fired, this time from the *Observer,* for inflammatory remarks. All the while, Thompson was carving a niche as a reporter of the burgeoning counterculture movement and was asked to write a piece for the *Nation* on the motorcycle gang known as the Hell's Angels. This assignment led him to immerse himself in the culture of the Hell's Angels for almost a year and ultimately resulted in the publication of his first book, HELL'S ANGELS: A STRANGE AND TERRIBLE SAGA (1967). While the book provided an intimate glimpse inside the gang's activities, it also examined the media's role in the creation of the gang's notorious reputation and featured Thompson's unique, novelistic, and subjective style of reportage that he eventually coined "gonzo journalism." In gonzo journalism, the reporter's involvement in the story becomes as crucial to the story as the subject being reported. During the research for his book, Thompson introduced the Angels to the San Francisco Beat world of Kesey, Ginsberg, and Cassady. The association between the Angels and the Beats was short-lived, but Thompson makes his observations on their ideological differences that were central to his conclusions in *Hell's Angels,* and the book furthermore cemented Thompson as one of the foremost cultural critics of the 1960s.

Thompson's newfound journalistic celebrity resulted in a *Pageant* magazine assignment to interview Republican presidential nominee Richard Nixon in 1968 and to follow him on the campaign trail. He wound up at the Democratic National Convention that year in Chicago and both witnessed and was victimized by the police brutality during the rioting. It was a pivotal moment for Thompson. As he later remarked, "I went to the Democratic Convention as a journalist and returned as a raving beast." Thompson became increasingly wary of politics but also much more critical of its reach: "We have to get into politics—if only in self-defense." This stance actually led Thompson to run for the office of sheriff in his new home, Aspen, Colorado, in 1970. He did not win, but he was one of the strongest voices in Aspen's famous ongoing "Freak Power" campaign that hoped to ban all commercial exploitation of the region, preserve its natural splendor, and establish a haven of antiauthoritarian civil rights for its residents. Earlier that year, in June 1970, Thompson published "The Kentucky Derby Is Decadent and Depraved" for *Scanlan's Monthly.* British illustrator Ralph Steadman worked with Thompson on

the piece. The result of Thompson's quick editing of his notes resulted in an accidental breakthrough in journalistic writing that furthered Thompson's gonzo style.

Thompson worked for several publications before finding a home at *Rolling Stone,* where he worked from 1970 until 1984. His first piece in the magazine was an account of the political struggle in Aspen. His second article covered the murder of a Hispanic *Los Angeles Times* reporter, Reuben Salazar, and the consequent volatile response throughout the Hispanic community. During his research he befriended the activist attorney OSCAR ZETA ACOSTA, and after accepting an offer from *Sports Illustrated* to cover the Mint 400 motorcycle race in Las Vegas, Thompson invited Acosta along with him. The resulting article, based on their experiences in Las Vegas, was rejected outright by *Sports Illustrated,* but was printed in *Rolling Stone* in 1971. The article was soon published in book form with Steadman's illustrations: FEAR AND LOATHING IN LAS VEGAS: A SAVAGE JOURNEY TO THE HEART OF THE AMERICAN DREAM.

Fear and Loathing in Las Vegas catapulted Thompson to the heights of literary fame, and, aside from being one of the best-loved books of its time, it remains one of the most trenchant examinations of late 20th-century American culture. In December 1971 the editors at *Rolling Stone* decided to finance Thompson as their correspondent for the Nixon–McGovern campaign trail of 1972. The resulting book, *Fear and Loathing: On the Campaign Trail '72* (1973) is considered one of the most controversial, subjective, and hilarious pieces of political journalism to be ever written. Thompson used his gonzo journalism in an effort to get 18-year-olds, who had recently been given the right to vote, to defy Nixon's reelection. McGovern became friendly with Thompson despite the futility of Thompson's efforts, and McGovern's campaign chief, Frank Mankiewicz, called Thompson's take on the campaign "the most accurate and least factual account of the campaign."

In addition to articles for *Rolling Stone* and other magazines, Thompson went on to publish eight more books (mostly anthologies of previously published articles) that catalogued political corruption and the disillusionment of the times, but none ever again achieved the astounding cultural resonance of the two *Fear and Loathing* books. His writing remained insightful and uncompromising—and gonzo as ever—but failed to find the same kind of mass audience as his masterpiece. In a 1979 preface Thompson wrote that he had "already lived and finished the life [he] had planned to live" and that he may as well end it all. He may not have been serious at the time, but 25 years later he certainly was. On February 20, 2005, Thompson took his own life with a handgun blast to the head. Uncompromising in his writing, he was equally uncompromising in how he lived and how he ended, his life. Like the greatest of the Beat authors, Thompson had the rare ability to give succinct voice to the unarticulated thoughts and concerns of his own generation and of those to follow him. He was able to crystallize in writing the spirit of an age, to show us a vision of ourselves that, while perhaps unappealing, is nonetheless honest. Finally, he showed us how to tolerate, or even defiantly rejoice in, our degenerate civilization, and he exposed lives of willing complicity.

Bibliography

Carroll, E. Jean. *Hunter: The Strange and Savage Life of Hunter S. Thompson.* New York: Dutton, 1993.

McKeen, William. *Hunter S. Thompson.* Boston: Twayne, 1991.

Perry, Paul. *Fear and Loathing: The Strange and Terrible Saga of Hunter S. Thompson.* New York: Thunder's Mouth, 1992.

Thompson, Hunter S. *The Proud Highway: Saga of a Desperate Southern Gentleman, 1955–1967 (The Fear and Loathing Letter, Volume One).* Edited by Douglas Brinkley. New York: Ballantine Books, 1998.

Whitmer, Peter O. *When the Going Gets Weird: The Twisted Life and Times of Hunter S. Thompson.* New York: Hyperion, 1993.

Luther Riedel

"Thou Shalt Not Kill: A Memorial for Dylan Thomas" Kenneth Rexroth (1955)

"Thou Shalt Not Kill," written in 1953–54, is a long, elegiac poem mourning the death of the charismatic Welsh poet Dylan Thomas (1917–53), who drank himself to death during his last orgiastic poetry tour of the United States. It is also much more: a prophetic poem of enraged protest denouncing the destruction of many poets in the worldwide culture of power, violence, and death and tragically affirming the creative, artistic imagination. By combining diverse poetic techniques, forms, and traditions KENNETH REXROTH—who was not himself a Beat but strongly influenced the Beat movement—produced this unique poem, which he performed with the accompaniment of a live jazz band. Indeed, Rexroth was a pioneer, with Kenneth Patchen (1911–72) and others, of performing poetry with musical accompaniment (some commercially recorded). This ferocious poem helped to mobilize the San Francisco Poetry Renaissance in which Beat poetry was born in the 1950s, a decade of cold war, the Korean War, the black struggle against racism, and the terrifying threat of nuclear annihilation.

The poem begins, "They are murdering all the young men" all over the world: Youth are being destroyed as ruthlessly as, for example, early Christian martyrs who prophetically denounced the lies and oppression of their society:

> They are stoning Stephen . . .
> He did great wonders among the people,
> They could not stand against his wisdom.

And:

> You are broiling Lawrence on his gridiron,
> When you demanded he divulge
> The hidden treasures of the spirit,
> He showed you the poor.

And:

> You are shooting Sebastian with arrows.
> He kept the faithful steadfast under persecution.

Who is guilty of murdering men of prophetic vision? Rexroth accuses the reader or listener of participating in the "social lie" of coercion and destruction:

> You!
> The hyena with polished face and bow tie . . .

The vulture dripping with carrion,
Carefully and carelessly robed in imported
    tweeds . . .
The jackal in double breasted gabardine . . .

In corporations, in the United Nations,:

The Superego in a thousand uniforms;
You, the finger man of behemoth,
The murderer of the young men.

Behemoth, the monstrous demon of the Bible
and John Milton's *Paradise Lost,* is an influential
precursor of Moloch in Allen Ginsberg's "HOWL,"
which seems influenced by Rexroth's poem in
terms of subject, themes, prophetic rhetoric, and
righteous passion. Rexroth even writes in Part III of
this poem: "Three generations of infants / Stuffed
down the maw of Moloch."

In Part II Rexroth laments the untimely deaths
of more than many American poets, each suc-
cinctly memorialized. Each stanza, whose theme
and form are derived from those in "Lament for
the Makeris" by the medieval Scottish poet William Dunbar, ends with a Latin line meaning "The
fear of death disturbs me."

In Part III Rexroth's vision expands in a series
of terrifying anecdotes of the destruction of individual poets of many nations in two World Wars:

Here is a mountain of death.
A hill of heads like the Khan piled up,
The first-born of a century
Slaughtered by Herod.

In the final part, which focuses on the death
of Dylan Thomas—"The little spellbinder of Cader
Idris"—Rexroth denounces the murderers in the
culture of death, one by one:

There he lies dead,
By the iceberg of the United Nations.
There he lies sandbagged,
At the foot of the Statue of Liberty.
The Gulf Stream smells of blood.

The poem has been unfairly denounced as
crudely rhetorical, motivated by self-righteous in-

sanity. In this intense, far-reaching, and complex
poem, did Rexroth explode from his own success
in the deadly culture that he attacked? Aesthetic
and ethical controversies concerning this important poem, which explored in such critical studies
as those listed below, have crucial implications for
Beat poetry in general.

Bibliography
Gibson, Morgan. *Kenneth Rexroth.* New York. Twayne
    Publishers, 1972.
———. *Revolutionary Rexroth: Poet of East-West Wis-
    dom.* Hamden Conn.: The Shoe String Press, 1985.
    The Expanded Internet Edition (2000) containing
    Rexroth's Letters to Gibson (1957–79) is available
    on Karl Young's *Light & Dust* site at http://www.
    thing.net/~grist/ld/rexroth/gibson.htm.
Hamalian, Linda. A *Life of Kenneth Rexroth.* New York:
    W. W. Norton, 1991.
Knabb, Ken. *The Relevance of Rexroth* and *Rexroth Ar-
    chives.* The best work on the political meaning of
    Rexroth's work. Much work by and about Rexroth
    is available online from the Bureau of Public Secrets
    at http://www.bopsecrets.org/rexroth.
Rexroth, Kenneth. *The Complete Poems of Kenneth
    Rexroth.* Edited by Sam Hamill and Bradford Mor-
    row. Port Townsend, Wash.: Copper Canyon Press,
    2003.

Morgan Gibson

Ticket That Exploded, The William S. Burroughs (1961)

This is the second installment in WILLIAM S. BUR-
ROUGHS's cut-ups trilogy. Burroughs described the
plot of the book as follows: "*The Ticket That Exploded* involves the Nova conspiracy to blow up
the earth and then leave it through reincarnation
by projected image onto another planet. The plot
failed, so the title has both meanings." Stylistically,
the book takes the cut-up method that Burroughs
developed with Brion Gysin in *The* SOFT MACHINE
and extends it by creating collages of image and
sound, a technique that Burroughs developed in
collaboration with Ian Sommerville and British
filmmaker Anthony Balch. The first version of the
book was published by Olympia Press in Paris in

1961. A revised version, meant to be more accessible, incorporated more of the Sommerville/Balch material and was published by Grove Press in 1966.

The opening chapter recalls Burroughs's South American trip and is based in part on his days in Panama with Bill Garver. By the time Garver returned to Mexico City, Burroughs had decided that his old friend was self-serving and even "vicious." Burroughs introduces the idea of the "reality film" being directed by behind-the-scenes characters. The director is B.J., and a screenwriter pitches him an idea that is based closely on the novel's reality: A virus has enslaved humanity, and renegades are trying to break through the control lines. The screenwriter periodically will break into the novel to heighten the "pitch."

Hassan i Sabbah was the head of a group of assassins who operated out of a mountain castle in Northern Persia in the 11th and 12th century. Legend has it that when his assassins successfully completed a mission, they were treated to rest and relaxation in the sumptuous and sensuous "Garden of Delights." Burroughs uses the Garden of Delights as a metaphor for the many sensual traps and addictions that entice the unwary traveler on life's path. Inspector Lee is involved in a plot to find a similar group of assassins in 1962, and he must pass through the garden to experience its temptations and thus inoculate himself against the "virus." The district supervisor gives him his "orders"—a series of antiorders that require him to avoid joining any group and also to look for his orders in a "series of oblique references." These take the form of "cut-up" knowledge that is similar to the cut-up style of the book, as the book itself points out: "This is a novel presented in a series of oblique references." Lee is ordered to investigate the suicide of the roommate of a man named Genial. He discovers that Genial subliminally influenced his roommate's death with a series of clever tape-recorded messages. Burroughs's knowledge of such tape effects is attributed to Ian Sommerville in the opening of the book. The subliminal message is discovered to be just the surface of a larger plot—"a carefully worked out blueprint for invasion of the planet." This is in fact the larger plot of the novel (and of the trilogy as a whole). The deconditioning methods of the "Logos" group (based on Scientologists) are described but are ultimately rejected as a means of breaking through the "control" of the invaders.

A separate storyline shows Brad and Iam (based on Ian Sommerville) on Venus (the home planet for the invasion) trapped in a semen dairy—which has human males for cows. Iam arms them with a camera gun, and they blast their way out. The plot returns to Inspector Lee's appointed meeting with Genial, who cannot speak with Lee until Lee pays the screenwriter a fee for his dialogue. He finds Genial detained by police over a passport issue, a scenario very close to Burroughs's detainment for similar reasons in Puerto Assis. The chapter ends as do many in the book—with a cut-up re-creation of the preceding events.

Many of the characters in the book are actually the same character. Here Bradly and Lykin are exploring the green boys' planet, and this scenario turns out to be a dream of Ali (later identified as the God of Street Boys and Hustlers). A second dream awakens Ali. The characters are constantly moved forward and backward in time and space. Ali, for example, "flashes" back on the passport episode involving "Genial." In Panama, Ali is fitted with a pair of gills by a shopkeeper, who points to the sky: In Burroughs's cosmology, human beings must evolve as they once did from fish into lunged mammals by evolving yet again into a creature that is capable of space–time travel.

A good part of the "do you love me" chapter cuts up the trite lyrics of popular love songs. In 1964, Burroughs told Eric Mottram, "I feel that what we call love is largely a fraud—a mixture of sentimentality and sex that has been systematically degraded and vulgarized by the virus power." Burroughs thus believed that love was a virus and that the "original engineering flaw" in human beings was the duality of nature created by the "word" (which established self-consciousness) and the dual sexes: "The human organism is literally consisting of two halves from the beginning word and all human sex is this unsanitary arrangement whereby two entities attempt to occupy the same three-dimensional coordinate points." This duality is the source of the planet's conflicts and wars, and this flaw has left us open to invasion by intergalactic parasites. "Operation Rewrite" is meant to fix this flaw in human nature, but there are too many viruses that are "addicted" to the human condition, and they mightily resist being thrown out of their hosts. These "Gods" are "vampires."

The nova police are called in because the "addicts" keep breaking into the Rewrite office. The basic "nova" techniques are described, the primary one being to create insoluble problems on a planet by stocking it with incompatible inhabitants. The members of the Nova Mob are listed for the first time. The leader of the Mob is Mr. Bradly/Mr. Martin, also known as "the Ugly Spirit." (It is important to note that Burroughs later identified the "ugly spirit" as the entity that invaded him and caused him to shoot his wife, making the Nova Mob a metaphor, at least in part, for Burroughs's own addictions and making "nova" the mistakes and tragedies that stem from these addictions.) In this myth for the new space age, our planet can be taken over because of a "blockade" on thought that was engineered by the Venusians, but partisans from Saturn cut through the word and image lines (again, a reference to Burroughs's cut-up technique in the novel). While the blockade was in effect, alien parasites invaded human beings through "coordinate points" that were defined by the individual's addictions. Heroin addicts, for example, were invaded by "heavy metal junkies" from Uranus. The planet is freed by shutting down the coordinate points, and the "ugly spirit" is dragged kicking and screaming from Hollywood, *Time* magazine, and Madison Avenue.

This book is self-referential, meaning that it is often about the writing of the book itself, and in one chapter Burroughs demonstrates his own cut-up technique, cutting up classic literary texts with his own texts.

The "substitute flesh" chapter cuts up images. Both the image and the soundtrack have to be cut up to free human beings from the control of the reality film. The main subject of the chapter is the Garden of Delights. The garden has a sex area for which Bradly is prepared by being photographed, measured, and then by having his image intercut with that of thousands of sex partners. The sex area of the garden is intended to negate the allurements of sex, for sexual frustration and sentimentality only feed the viruses living inside us. The chapter

ends with a description of how sensory deprivation tanks can be used to free us of these parasites as well. The tank reveals to us the parasite inside as many participants in tank experiments report feeling a "second" body.

Lykin is a coordinate point that is used by parasites throughout the galaxy. Bradly's adventures in the jungle ("in a strange bed") continue. He encounters a naked young man with a bow and a quiver, who observes Bradly's disheveled appearance and surmises that the "blockade" has been broken. The young man expects more of Bradly's type to arrive. His attitude is not one of "contempt," but the tone is that of British colonialism.

In the fake journal "all members are worst a century," an explorer and his "boy" Johnny encounter a virus that causes sexual delirium. Burroughs wrote several versions of this story that were based on an account that he heard in South America of a grasshopper with a sting that acted as a powerful aphrodisiac: If "you can't get a woman right away you will die."

Dr. Dent's apomorphine cure for heroin addiction, which Burroughs underwent in London in 1955, is analyzed in an afterward to the British edition of *The Soft Machine* which is entitled "A Treatment that Cancels Addiction." Apomorphine was thus part of Burroughs's arsenal of methods that are used to vanquish "control" of any sort. Here, apomorphine breaks the control lines of the Venusians, the Mercurians, and the Uranians: "Good bye parasite invasion with weakness of dual structure, as the shot of apomorphine exploded the mold of their claws in vomit." The fight in the Control Room is replayed from the point of view of Burroughs's Tangier companion Kiki, the street boy who is aided by Ali (from the liberating planet of Saturn). Kiki is advised that "retreat" is the better part of valor in some battles with evil forces of Minraud and that space–time travel allows retreat. Such "time travel on association lines" leads Burroughs back into his St. Louis boyhood days when Bill and John build a crystal radio. Bill asks John, "Is it true if we were ten light years away we could see ourselves here ten years from now?" The scene demonstrates this possibility by cutting in moments from 10 years in the future, which are then played out in a linear scene. Only afterward does the reader realize that he/she has been given a glimpse into the future in the previous pages.

The chapter "vaudeville voices" is in part of pure "association lines," as Burroughs calls his literary representation of consciousness. The screenwriter continues his pitch to B.J. and dreams up a plot where writers *"write history as it happens in present time."* Burroughs believed that writers (as he said of JACK KEROUAC) could actually write history into being through the influence of their works.

Bradly's adventures in "the black fruit" are continued in "terminal street." He is walking the streets of Minraud after the Reality Studio has burned, and he is introduced to The Elder (later called The Old Man) who was behind the hoax on Earth. He tells Bradly that his race will have to make "alterations" to itself now that the blockade has been broken. Minraud's inhabitants live without emotion and include centipedes and scorpions. These creatures personify deep horror in Burroughs's work.

In *Moby-Dick,* Herman Melville catalogs all of the horrors that are associated with "whiteness" in a famous chapter entitled "The Whiteness of the Whale." The chapter "last round over" is Burroughs's extension of that idea. Here, whiteness is heroin, yetis, monopolies, anglo-saxons, and Time/Life/Fortune, Inc. "Drain off the prop ocean and leave the White Whale stranded," he demands. Now that the control game has been exposed, he wants restitution from all of the "Mr Martins who are buying something for nothing."

The rant turns to ridicule of the failed intergalactic con men: "You had every weapon in three galaxies you couldn't roll a paralyzed flop." The marks have wised up, and the "collaborators" with the insect trust will be punished. Still, the "marks" brought it on themselves by being weak and easily addicted: "If you have to have it well you've had it." The two parasites that worked to control us were "word" and "sex," and Burroughs asks just what exactly "word" and "sex" are. Other writers, from Jacques Derrida (the famous deconstructionist) to Norman Mailer (in *The Prisoner of Sex*) would take up these questions. The con worked for a while because it was pleasurable, rather like the 19th-century America to which Burroughs always looks back nostalgically. Back then, the Reality Film was never exposed because everyone had a "part" written into it; however, when the roles gave out, the film existed primarily to silence those who began to question the Reality Film (writers and artists).

With the con exposed, the controllers rush to leave the planet like passengers abandoning a sinking ship. One of Burroughs's favorite metaphors is that of the ship's captain abandoning his ship disguised as a woman. The "marks" now see environmental destruction at the hand of monopolies and "boards" (the "Green Deal"), drug deaths, sexual obsessions, and subliminal messages all as part of the con: "technical brains melted the law—control machine is disconnected by nova police."

The Fluoroscopic Kid (one of the defectors from the Nova Mob, along with the Subliminal Kid) lectures about the invisible "Other Half" that is parasitically attached to us: "The body is two halves stuck together like a mold—That is, it consists of two organisms—See 'the Other Half' invisible—(to eyes that haven't learned to watch)." He shows the "marks" the Board Books (control system similar to the Mayan calendar) and challenges them to rewrite them. The Subliminal Kid disempowers the books by "cutting" them up, thereby exposing their naked mechanisms of control. Control can also be exposed (and broken) by simple exercises that are made with the aid of tape recorders. Ian Sommerville demonstrated to Burroughs the ways in which tape loops and feedback allowed participants to gain control over their responses to conflicts and arguments: "Get it out of your head and into the machines." The recorder experiments make a basic Burroughs point: Recordings can be just as "real" as reality.

The defectors from the Nova Mob "silence" Mr. Bradly/Mr. Martin. Silence is the end result of the eradication of the "word" virus. Inspector Lee has been working throughout the book in "Rewrite" to cut in on the messages of the "collaborators"—a metaphor for Burroughs's role as writer of the novel.

"Now some words about the image track," begins the chapter "let them see us." Just as sound has been manipulated in the Reality Film, so too has image been used to control us. Burroughs discusses slow-motion projection techniques, which he believes create an image more real than flesh and could be used to hoodwink human sensory systems. Burroughs had worked extensively in film experiments by this time, particularly with the filmmaker Anthony Balch.

The characters in the book (if one can refer to characters in a Burroughs book) make their exit in Shakespearean fashion in "silence to say good bye": "our actors bid you a long last goodbye." The final chapter, "the invisible generation," is a cut-up explanation to wise up the marks.

Rob Johnson

Town and the City, The Jack Kerouac (1950)

Inspired by John Galsworthy's *The Forsyte Saga* and the lyrical prose of Thomas Wolfe, author of *Look Homeward, Angel* (1929), JACK KEROUAC wrote what would be his first published novel from 1946 to 1949 to tell everything he knew about life up to that point. Perhaps that is why the manuscript ran to more than 1,000 pages. The edition published by Harcourt, Brace cut more than half of it. Though not part of "The Duluoz Legend" proper, the fictionalized autobiography of Kerouac's life, *The Town and the City*, can be read as Ur-text that reveals many of the themes to which Kerouac would return in his later novels when he broke from Wolfe's influence and found his own voice.

The novel introduces the Martin family, who live in Galloway, Massachusetts, and who are closely modeled on Kerouac's own family in Lowell, Massachusetts. Presumably to expand the book's scope and also to hide the autobiographical basis of the book, Kerouac made the Martins a large family—Mickey, Charley, Elizabeth, Peter, Julian, Francis, Joe, Ruth, and Rose. Each of these characters receives careful development in the novel. Kerouac emphasizes that although they are a close family, each is an individual, and each has a secret life separate from the rest of the family.

Francis is portrayed as a sickly youth whose twin brother Julian dies. Peter's reaction to Julian's death can be seen as parallel to Kerouac's feelings of his brother's death as depicted in VISIONS OF GERARD. Francis, says Kerouac, was modeled slightly on WILLIAM S. BURROUGHS and is portrayed as bookish and cold natured. But there are other sources for Francis's personality: Kerouac has the 16-year-old Francis play out his own broken love affair with beautiful, dark-haired Mary, who is based on Mary Carney about and whom he later wrote in MAGGIE CASSIDY.

Peter is the character who most closely resembles Kerouac, and the novel recounts Peter's rise as a high school football star, ending in his scoring the only touchdown in the Thanksgiving Day game. Peter realizes that his own victories are the loss of someone else's (he resembles a Boddhisattva, Buddhist holy man, already). After the victory, he wishes that he were anonymous again and feels as if he has betrayed his friends by making them praise him.

The oldest brother Joe can be seen as an early version of the NEAL CASSADY characters in ON THE ROAD and VISIONS OF CODY: He has the same cowboy image and passion for cross-country driving. In this respect he personifies the spirit of uprootedness and dislocation that many Beat writers say was the major note of their times.

In real life, Kerouac had only two siblings, and by expanding the Martin children to nine members, Kerouac has in many ways created the additional characters from his own experiences at different stages in his life. Thus, the Martin children are a kind of exploded version of Kerouac. For example, the oldest brother Joe quits a good trucking job on a whim and ends up working as a grease monkey in the lube pits, as did Kerouac after he walked away from his football career at Columbia. The youngest boy, Mickey, precociously prints his own newspaper and handicaps horse races, as Kerouac did as a youth.

Francis, on the other hand, comes more and more to resemble Burroughs. He meets Wilfred Engels, whose European sophistication masks his homosexuality. He shows Francis that there are others like him in Boston and New York. That same summer, Peter spends his time before he enters Pine Hall (Kerouac's version of the prep school Horace Mann) imagining all of his future glories. These scenes are recreated in *The* VANITY OF DULUOZ and emphasize his self-delusion. At Pine Hall, Peter initially fears that he will not be able to live up to his promise, but he later understands that all the freshmen felt the same fear that he did. This leads him to the conclusion that the world "was so much more beautiful and amazing because it was so really, strangely, sad."

In the summer after his first year at Pine Hall, Peter meets the most important friend of his youth, Alex Panos (based on Sebastian "Sammy" Sampas), who teaches him how to be interested in literature and how to be kind to others. Panos's old mother treats Peter like a son, almost as if she realizes that someday her family will play the role for Peter that the Sampas's did for Kerouac. Stella Sampas, Sammy's sister, would be Kerouac's third wife. The Sampas family are presently Kerouac's literary executors.

Peter attends Penn for his sophomore year and plays football; however, he breaks his leg in the game against Columbia. The injury allows him time for deep thought and study, which parallels Kerouac's own injury and his embrace of the life of the artist. By Christmas Peter realizes that he can learn more by studying the city and its people than he can learn at the university. Back home, Peter and Francis have arguments about philosophy, and their differences are remarkably similar to arguments that Kerouac and Burroughs carried through their correspondence of the 1940s.

George Martin loses his printing business, and the family's closeness is tested. This novel suggests that Kerouac had something that many of the other Beat writers did not—a real home that he loved and a close family. Readers can see why Kerouac's girlfriend JOYCE JOHNSON called this book Kerouac's "sweetest" one.

Wartime America becomes the setting, and Kerouac shows the effect of the war on his generation of Americans and, more specifically, its effect on the Martin family and the town of Galloway. An overlooked feature of the book is Liz's story. Through her, Kerouac shows the story of the women of this generation, too. Liz falls in love with a jazz pianist, Buddy. A notable scene shows her entering a roadhouse by herself for the first time in her life. Liz and Buddy develop a serious relationship, and when she becomes pregnant, they elope. Peter helps her in her getaway. George Martin is devastated by Liz's elopement and blames himself for having lost his business and uprooted the family.

Peter, the football hero, must now shoulder the family's hopes for success in the world. However, he rejects the university and its professors for "the world itself." When his father finds out that he has quit football and school, he despairs for Peter, who does not know the pain that he will cause himself by changing his future. Peter can see no future because of the looming war. When the Japanese bomb Pearl Harbor, George Martin is furious that his sons will be sacrificed. Joe is the first of the Martins to enlist. Kerouac uses Joe's experiences to illustrate the "great wartime wanderings of Americans" and the sense of displacement that affected his generation to the point of actual derangement: "No one could see it, yet everyone was . . . grown fantastic and homeless in war, and strangely haunted."

Liz and Buddy move to Grosse Point Park in Detroit, and their married life is a version of Kerouac and his first wife Edie Parker's life in Detroit. Liz's miscarriage parallels Kerouac and Edie's inability to have children, which is described in *The Vanity of Duluoz*. Seeing the younger boys of Galloway going off to fight, Peter joins the merchant marines out of shame. His voyage to Greenland is based on Kerouac's *Dorchester* voyage in 1941. When he returns, he learns that his girlfriend Judie (based on Edie Parker) is living in an apartment in New York.

Francis joins the navy, and his experiences are based on Kerouac's failure to pass the mechanical aptitude test for training as a naval officer. Forced to go through boot camp with the enlisted men, Francis finds that he is incapable of submitting to military discipline. As was true of Kerouac, he is sent to the asylum and eventually is discharged from the navy.

The Martins move to Brooklyn, where George has found a printing job. George Martin is lost in the huge city, and the remainder of his life is spent trying to comprehend how he has arrived there. He is also concerned about Peter's friends, who are based on Burroughs, ALLEN GINSBERG, HERBERT HUNCKE, Lucien Carr, Dave Kammerer, Joan Burroughs, and Phil White. Peter arrives back in New York after a trip to Guam and is eager to start a "new season." Kerouac describes in detail the Times Square scene of 1943–44. The central orchestrator of his group of friends is the poet Leon

Levinsky (based on Ginsberg), who reminds Peter of Alexander Panos. Kenneth Wood and Waldo Meister (based on Lucien Carr and Dave Kammerer respectively) are the main topic of conversation. Wood enjoys making fun of Meister, who has lost an arm in a car accident in which Wood himself was the driver. In spite of this, Meister finds himself irresistibly drawn to his torturer Wood. Although Burroughs liked the detail of Meister's lost arm, the preposterous set-up here is a clear cover-up of the true story of the homosexual Kammerer's obsession with the beautiful Carr.

The portrait of his group of criminals and bohemians mirrors W. H. Auden's view that this generation was living in the "age of anxiety." Mary Dennison (portrayed as Will Dennison's sister but based on Joan Vollmer Burroughs) popularizes the theory that their neurotic feelings and actions stem from "the atomic disease, everyone's radioactive." Judie dislikes this crowd: "All they can do is talk about books." The description of Peter and Judie's relationship is Kerouac's lengthiest portrait of the wife of his youth, Edie Parker. Judie's apartment is often burst into by the crowd. She particularly dislikes the effeminate poet Levinsky and Waldo Meister. Peter has a dream in this apartment one night that Kerouac later told Neal Cassady represented his fear of becoming a homosexual. Heterosexuality and masculinity are represented in the dream by Joe, Charley, and George Martin. Kerouac told Cassady that he secretly modeled Joe on Cassady.

Peter divides his time between Judie's Manhattan apartment and his parent's apartment in Brooklyn. En route to Brooklyn, he stops off at Dennison's apartment and watches him shoot morphine. The scene includes snapshot portraits of Herbert Huncke (portrayed as Junkey) that Huncke resented. At home, Peter's father lectures him about the moral relativism that is practiced by his generation. The subtext of this lecture is that he does not like his son running around with homosexuals, and George even appears to have read Gore Vidal's sensational gay novel *The Pillar and the City* (1948). Much of the last part of the book is about George's frustrated attempts to tell his son what he knows about life to save him from suffering unnecessarily. When Waldo Meister commits suicide (Kerouac displaces Carr's stabbing of Kammerer) and Peter is brought in for police questioning, his father's warning appears justified. Then there is news of a second death—Alex Panos has been killed in the war.

The final part of the book begins with the arrival in New York of the troopships carrying the returning soldiers who had survived World War II. Peter is living with his mother and father, who is ill, and his sister Liz is living elsewhere in the city. Liz's character is of particular interest here, for it is through her that Peter learns the new language of the hipster. She shows him her most cherished picture of him, from 1941, in which, she says, he looks as if life has slapped him in the face. Liz's philosophy here is an early expression of Beat, a term is even used near the end of the novel. Her character is at least partly based on Kerouac's friend Vicki Russell, who appaers in *On the Road*, JOHN CLELLON HOLMES's *GO*, and is sketched in Herbert Huncke's books. She represents the women of the Beat Generation.

The final section also follows Francis, who resembles Burroughs in his interest in "Orgone Theory" and Jean Genet. Still, Francis leaves the Greenwich Village crowd and moves to the East Side, where he is more comfortable in the world of intellectuals. He has an affair with a married woman who is heavily into Benzedrine use. Their dialogue is farcical and is acidly exposed by Kerouac.

Peter watches his father die slowly and painfully. At last, he begins to absorb the life lessons that his father has tried to teach him. These lessons echo throughout Kerouac's later works. George Martin is buried in New Hampshire, and the funeral sets up a meeting between the two brothers who are so at odds philosophically—Peter and Francis. Joe is also present. Peter finds himself playing the role of George Martin, getting the brothers to talk in the open about themselves and their lives. Something of the debate between Burroughs and Kerouac is replayed here, with Peter quoting from the Bible and showing a deep understanding of Christ's sermons of compassion and Francis studying him coldly as if he were an interesting psychiatric case. The confrontation relaxes all three brothers, though, and they are once again able to fall into a natural family relationship with each other.

The novel ends with Peter hitchhiking across the country, a scene that anticipates *On the Road*. In fact, Kerouac writes that Peter was "on the road again." Thus, the final pages of this novel set up Kerouac's next novel, published seven years later. Though *The Town and the City* received some critical praise, it did not sell well. When *On the Road* was published, *The Town and the City* had been virtually forgotten.

Bibliography

Charters, Ann. *Kerouac: A Biography*. San Francisco: Straight Arrow Books, 1973.

Rob Johnson

Tracking the Serpent: Journeys to Four Continents Janine Pommy Vega (1997)

JANINE POMMY VEGA's work has received scant critical attention, despite the fact that she has published roughly a dozen books since her first work, POEMS TO FERNANDO, appeared in 1968. What makes this omission even more surprising is that Vega was not a latter-day Beat follower but was intimately connected with the Beat circle in New York City during the late 1950s. In 1958, after graduating as the valedictorian of her class, Vega moved to New York, where she met GREGORY CORSO, ALLEN GINSBERG, HERBERT HUNCKE, Elise Cowen, and Cowen's lover Peter Orlovsky. Vega would later meet the Peruvian painter Fernando Vega, traveling with him until his sudden death from a heroin overdose in November 1965. While Vega's attempt to develop her own brand of spirituality in the face of social and cultural constraints mirrors the work of fellow Beats, the ways in which she develops such Beat themes as individuality, spontaneity, sexuality, and particularly mobility deserve more critical investigation.

As its subtitle suggests, *Tracking the Serpent* is a book about travel. Vega journeys to British castles, the cathedral at Chartres, the Irish countryside, the Amazon jungle, and the mountains of Peru and Nepal to discover what she terms the "Goddess." The goal, according to Vega, is to "let my personal history be overtaken by a present that was conscious of itself and infinitely alive. That consciousness I call the Mother or serpent power or Goddess." Vega's novel chronicles this search and, in the process, reveals not only what this interaction with the Goddess looks like but, perhaps more importantly, how it is achieved. The key for Vega is to remain open to the possibilities of the moment in both body and soul. Ultimately, Vega experiences this spiritual connection, though not always where and when she plans for it to happen. The Goddess reveals herself when you least expect it during those moments that you cede control over the world and offer yourself up for change and revelation.

By invoking the term *Mother* or *Goddess*, Vega also raises the important question of gender that is beginning to receive the attention it deserves in Beat scholarship. In *Tracking the Serpent*, Vega is repeatedly disappointed to discover that many of the sites in which she hopes to find the Goddess are actually governed by a patriarchal mindset that closes off the possibility for communion with the divine. Male space is often enclosed, hierarchical, and exclusionary, as many poems in her collection *Mad Dogs of Trieste* likewise demonstrate. The space of the Goddess, by contrast, is characterized by an openness and egalitarianism that is the hallmark of Vega's work. The lesson for Vega is to always remain open, whether trekking up the side of a mountain, making love, or simply meeting someone for the first time.

Tracking the Serpent is an important Beat work. Although it was written after the Beat heyday of the 1950s and 1960s by a woman who has yet to receive the sort of accolades accorded to male writers like Ginsberg, JACK KEROUAC, and WILLIAM S. BURROUGHS, Vega's book seriously engages the desire for personal transformation through interaction with the divine that animates much Beat writing. Vega gives us a means of understanding not only how such a connection is forged, but the pitfalls of relying on a purely masculine model of transcendence, and in the process sheds light on what it means to be "Beat."

Erik Mortenson

Tristessa Jack Kerouac (1960)

MICHAEL McCLURE feels that this novel is one of JACK KEROUAC's most beautiful pieces of writing.

Though it has been criticized for its romanticization of a Mexican woman, it is also one of the most passionate portrayals of a woman that Kerouac ever wrote. Kerouac wrote this romance about his relationship with a beautiful morphine addict in two installments as the story unfolded in Mexico City in 1955 and 1956. Kerouac was living on the rooftop in the Orizaba Street apartment where he had first visited WILLIAM S. BURROUGHS in 1950. Burroughs's and Kerouac's friend, the old-time junky Bill Garver who is called Old Bull Gaines in this novel, was living in the building, and his morphine connection was a young Indian woman named Esperanza. Interestingly, Kerouac changes her name in the novel from one that means "hope" to one that means "sadness," which reflects how Kerouac saw the world. Esperanza had been an addict since she was 16, and she had married Dave Tercerero, Burroughs's heroin connection. When Tercerero died, Esperanza started a relationship with Garver. Theirs was a relationship of mutual dependency. Garver needed her to move through the Mexican underworld in search of morphine, and she needed his money. Kerouac fell in love with her and felt that he was trying to save her from the destructive life that she was living.

The book is written in a spontaneous prose style, similar to that of the first part of DESOLATION ANGELS (which he was also writing in 1956) and *The* SUBTERRANEANS, a novel whose interracial romantic relationship parallels the one in *Tristessa*. The novel is a sustained moving sketchbook of Mexico City's slums, junkies, prostitutes, and drunks. Intermixed with this description is Kerouac's own philosophical take on his surroundings. Kerouac's Buddhism allowed him to see the world as an illusion and a dream; thus he could move in a society that to most people would be repulsive and even terrifying—moaning, sick junkies stumbling into the dawn in search of another fix, smiling bandits with their hands in their wallets. One of the readers for Viking said of this book that it should not only be turned down for publication at Viking, but also it should be kept from being published at all. Kerouac enthusiasts, of course, are glad it was not. This is pure Kerouac.

Once again, Kerouac's persona is Jack Duluoz. At the center of this novel is Duluoz's love

for Tristessa. But this is no simple love story. Duluoz is still a practicing Buddhist who is denying himself sex (a practice that is derided by Burroughs in letters to Kerouac), and his lust for Tristessa is sublimated into affectionate interplay with animals. Tristessa runs a fingernail down his arm, and it nearly makes him jump out of his chair. At one point, she tries to explain to him, with a pantomime of lunging hips, that friends show their affection in bed. Even then, Duluoz imagines that her tone is girlish, not seriously sexual, and he believes that the blame will all be on him if he seduces her.

Duluoz returns after a year and finds Tristessa ill and self-destructive. He has given up his vow of chastity and feels that had he been sexually involved with her the year before, he might have been able to save her. Now, it appears to be too late. In one horrifying scene, after a night of drinking and morphine shooting, Tristessa falls unconscious and splits her head open. Duluoz thinks that she is dead, but she recovers, and he takes her back to Orizaba Street for help. There Kerouac slowly comes to realize that it makes much more sense for Tristessa to marry Old Bull Gaines than it does to marry him. To marry an addict, you have to be one, he says, and he cannot. In an effort to understand where Old Bull Gaines and Tristessa are coming from, he shoots morphine with them.

The book is a fascinating twist on the obstructed romance motif of much of Western literature. At first, Duluoz's Buddhism prevents him from being with Tristessa. Later, it is Tristessa's addiction that thwarts the romance. One darkly funny scene has Duluoz trying to pass, with Tristessa, through a kitchen that is full of women to get to his rooftop bed with her, but the women will not let her in. She has been known to throw violent fits, breaking glasses and kitchenware. Tristessa's own sincerity is also questioned by Duluoz when he suspects that she might be the leader of a gang of thieves who have robbed him, even taking his pad of poems. The book and their relationship ends with Duluoz showing his immaturity in a way that is similar to the relationship between Sal Paradise and the Mexican girl Terry in ON THE ROAD. Kerouac's own appraisal of the novel was that it was not as bleak as BIG SUR. Tristessa's tragedy appears far less so in light of the inevitability of her relationship with another addict, Old Bull Gaines. At times Duluoz loses his Buddhist calm and feels dismayed at a God who would treat his children this way.

Literary critics can use this book to support the view of Kerouac as a writer who romanticized what he called the fellaheen, the indigenous peoples of the world. Yet, Kerouac honestly felt connected to the fellaheen. It is important to note that Kerouac was able to mix fairly well with these people and does so without trying to convert them to his own Buddhist philosophy. The book was published as a 35-cent paperback by Avon in July 1960. The cover proclaimed it as a "new and hauntingly different novel about a morphine-racked prostitute," and the salacious cover art suggested a very different story than the one that Kerouac had written.

Bibliography

Grace, Nancy McCampbell. "A White Man in Love: A Study of Race, Gender, Class, and Ethnicity in Jack Kerouac's *Maggie Cassidy, The Subterraneans,* and *Tristessa.*" In *The Beat Generation: Critical Essays,* edited by Kostas Myrsiades, 93–120. New York: Peter Lang, 2002.

Rob Johnson

Troia: Mexican Memoirs Brenda Frazer (Bonnie Bremser) (1969)

Lauded as "a female ON THE ROAD," *Troia: Mexican Memoirs* is one of the most extraordinary works of Beat literature that was produced by a woman. Nancy Grace writes, "*Troia* stands apart as a memoir that in form and content may be the most troubling and provocative of the Beat female life stories." The title comes from French slang meaning "whore," derived from a negative association with Helen of Troy, but it also means "adventuress." The memoir was republished in London as *For the Love of Ray* (1971), a more appropriate title that reflects the motivation for Frazer's struggles. Sadly, it has been out of print since the first edition, but it continues to be considered an underground masterpiece by Beat enthusiasts and scholars.

BRENDA FRAZER started writing the book as a series of letters from March to November 1963 to her husband, Beat poet RAY BREMSER, while he was serving a prison sentence in New Jersey. Her editor, Michael Perkins, arranged the material into a four-part narrative. A section of the book was published in 1967 by the literary magazine *Down Here,* which was put out by the Tompkins Square Press. Ann Charters's *Beat Reader* (1992) excerpts the opening pages of the memoir; Frazer credits Charters with reinvigorating interest in her work. Brenda Knight's *Women of the Beat Generation* (1996) includes the same section that Charters used, along with part of the book's introduction. Another selection from *Troia* appears in the fifth edition of *The Heath Anthology of American Literature* (2006). Work on a prequel and a sequel to *Troia* was begun several years ago. The trilogy is tentatively entitled "Troia: Beat Chronicles." Part of the first book of the trilogy, "Breaking out of D.C.," was published in Richard Peabody's *A Different Beat: Writings by Women of the Beat Generation* (1997).

Beat scholars have often asked, "Why were there no female Kerouacs?" The general answer is that women of the time were silenced through incarceration and the social restraints of postwar U.S. society. But Frazer's memoir defied the times. It is a candid examination of her life as a prostitute, an occupation that she feels forced to take in an effort to support her husband and their daughter, Rachel. Frazer asserts, "I thought that I was doing a revolutionary thing. . . . I felt righteous about being a prostitute. I felt like what I was doing was more honest than free love. . . . I thought prostitutes needed a spokesperson." The memoir rejects middle-class moral codes and disfigures the codes of pornography to become a text of resistance against the conformity of what has come to be known as the "containment culture" of the American 1950s and early 1960s.

Influenced by the prose of JACK KEROUAC and the poetry of her husband, Frazer created a work that allowed her to become part of the Beats' "boy gang" that she admired. Frazer says, "If I sound like Kerouac, it's because I tried to. I read him while I was writing." But she was also one of the handful of female Beat artists who gave a much-needed woman's perspective of her times. Her masochism and subservience to Ray mirrors the sacrifices that women were expected to make in the dominant culture. What truly separates Frazer is her affinity for a lifestyle of risk rather than a lifestyle of security. *Troia* is ultimately a more radical text than *On the Road.* It shares with Kerouac's novel the desire for solidarity with the indigenous people of Mexico. Unlike Kerouac's *On the Road,* where the protagonist reenters society, *Troia* ends with Frazer embracing life on the bohemian streets.

Bibliography

Grace, Nancy M. "Artista: Brenda (Bonnie) Frazer." In *Breaking the Rule of Cool: Interviewing And Reading Women Beat Writers,* edited by Nancy M. Grace and Ronna C. Johnson, 109–130. Jackson: University Press of Mississippi, 2004.

———. "Snapshots, Sand Paintings, and Celluloid: Formal Considerations in the Life Writing of Women Writers from the Beat Generation." In *Girls Who Wore Black: Women Writing the Beat Generation,* edited by Ronna C. Johnson and Nancy M. Grace, 141–177. New Brunswick, N.J.: Rutgers University Press, 2002.

Hemmer, Kurt. "The Prostitute Speaks: Brenda Frazer's *Troia: Mexican Memoirs.*" *Paradoxa* 18 (2003): 99–117.

Kurt Hemmer

Trout Fishing in America Richard Brautigan (1967)

The best-known work of RICHARD BRAUTIGAN, *Trout Fishing in America* is often considered the novel that best captures the zeitgeist of the social, cultural, and political change that was centered in San Francisco, California, during the late 1960s which was known as the counterculture or the Summer of Love. *Trout Fishing in America* features an anonymous narrator who relates witty observations and stories through an episodic narrative structure that is full of unconventional but vivid images that are powered by whimsy and metaphor. The result, says John Cooley, is a "highly stylized kaleidoscope of little fictions" that seem to suggest a transformative healing for the American pastoral ideal which had been lost to commercialism, environmental degradation, and social decay. Cooley notes that the idea of trout fishing in America represents the book itself being written

by Brautigan, a character in the novel, a place, an outdoor sport, a religion, and a state of mind. Despite lacking sustained narrative, plot or characterization and despite its short length, *Trout Fishing in America* yielded to many critics and readers alike a sense of immediate satisfaction, an in-the-moment thrill that required no context or frame of reference other than the power of imagination. Newton Smith called *Trout Fishing in America* "one of the first popular representations of the postmodern novel" and said that it altered the shape of American literature. Other critics compared *Trout Fishing in America* to Henry David Thoreau's *Walden* and welcomed Brautigan to the tradition of Ernest Hemingway, Wallace Stevens, and Mark Twain.

Brautigan wrote *Trout Fishing in America* in 1961 during a summer camping trip in Idaho's Stanley Basin with his wife Virginia and daughter Ianthe. Jack Spicer worked with Brautigan to edit the *Trout Fishing in America* manuscript line-by-line and arranged for Brautigan to give public readings of the novel at a San Francisco church. Several excerpts were published in *Evergreen Review* and *The New Writing in the USA,* edited by Donald Allen and ROBERT CREELEY. All these opportunities provided important early exposure for Brautigan and his writing. After rejection by several other publishers, Donald M. Allen, the West Coast representative of New York–based Grove Press, published *Trout Fishing in America* in 1967 under the imprint of his own San Francisco nonprofit press, Four Seasons Foundation. The novel was an immediate best-seller, and Brautigan was rocketed from cult status to international fame as a new writer with a fresh, visionary voice.

In subsequent novels Brautigan vowed not to write sequels to *Trout Fishing in America* and, instead, experimented with different literary genres. General dismissal by literary critics reversed Brautigan's initial literary success, and his popularity waned throughout the 1970s and early 1980s. However, *Trout Fishing in America,* continually translated into other languages, remains popular for its unique prose style.

Bibliography

Barber, John. *The Brautigan Bibliography plus+* Available online. URL: http://www.brautigan.net/brautigan/. Accessed January 3, 2005.

Cooley, John. "The Garden in the Machine: Three Postmodern Pastorals." *Michigan Academician* 13, no. 4 (Spring 1981): 405–420.

Smith, Newton. *Encyclopedia of American Literature*, edited by Steven R. Serafin, 122–123. New York: Continuum, 1999.

John F. Barber

Turtle Island Gary Snyder (1974)

Awarded the Pulitzer Prize for Poetry in 1975, this volume of poetry brought expanded national attention to GARY SNYDER. While in his previous two collections of poetry, *The Back Country* (1968) and *Regarding Wave* (1970), he tended to delineate himself as an international traveler and transient counterculture practitioner, he defined himself unmistakably as an inhabitant of North America, a person who was settling in for a long process of cultural transformation through the promotion of reinhabitation. For the first time since *Myths & Texts* (1960), Snyder published a collection that consists of poems that were written entirely in the United States from the point of his permanent return from Japan with his wife Masa and their son Kai through 1974. This sense of reinhabitation is reinforced by some of the prose pieces that make up the final section of the volume.

The title of the book alludes to Native American depictions of the North American continent as a giant turtle, and its symbolic function as a counter to the concepts of the United States, Canada, and Mexico are made explicit in Snyder's "Introductory Note": "the old/new name for the continent, based on many creation myths of the people who have been living here for millennia. . . . The 'U.S.A.' and its states and counties are arbitrary and inaccurate impositions on what is really here." He also clarifies the purpose of that title and his orientation in the book toward reinhabitation as a political and environmental strategy: "A name: that we may see ourselves more accurately on this continent of watersheds and life-communities—plant zones, physiographic provinces, culture areas; following natural boundaries. . . . Hark again to those roots, to see our ancient solidarity, and then to the work of being together on Turtle Island."

Turtle Island contains nearly 60 poems and is divided into three sections: "Manzanita," "Magpie's Song," and "For the Children." The prose section is titled "Plain Talk." Snyder mixes together a variety of poetic styles in these pages, including the two very distinct kinds of poems that are displayed first in *Riprap* and *Myths & Texts* but also other types of poems, such as songs (for example, "Without" and "Magpie's Song"), prayers (for example, "Prayer for the Great Family"), and histories (for example, "What Happened Here Before") as well as diatribes ("Front Lines" and "LMFBR" and narratives (for example, "Two Immortals" and "The Call of the Wild"). Readers will also find here the majority of the Snyder poems that are most often quoted and reprinted in anthologies, such as "I Went Into the Maverick Bar," "Front Lines," "For the Children," and "Tomorrow's Song."

The "Manzanita" section was originally published as a separate chapbook and has a clearly Western focus. The first two poems look back to the history of the Anasazi in the American Southwest and then link Native American history with the circumpolar bear cult, emphasizing the global linkages of primitive cultures, which nevertheless remained highly place specific. He also has a pair of poems that contrast the use of road kills as an act of conservation and ecological responsibility in opposition to the wasteful and cruel treatment of animals by modern agribusiness and sport hunting. The fifth poem of this section, "I Went into The Maverick Bar," is a bit unusual for Snyder in the way that it emphasizes the "I" of the poem from the outset. In this poem, Snyder both describes his differences as a long-haired, earring-wearing freak from the heartland cowboys in the bar, but he also emphasizes his kinship with them and their shared heritage. They are not the enemy, on the one hand, but his invocation of Lenin's revolutionary politics in the closing quote of the poem, "What is to be done," on the other hand emphasizes his sense of the need to transform the contemporary culture that he believes they blindly uphold. Snyder also reiterates the importance of harmonious family life in "The Bath" and extends that sense of family to encompass other creatures in "Prayer for the Great Family." In the middle of the "Manzanita" section, Snyder reprints "Spell Against

Demons" from *The Fudo Trilogy,* a chapbook that was originally published in a limited edition in 1973. Both humorous and serious in intent, it is a Buddhist-based poem that is meant to exorcize the demons that are plaguing this continent, reminding readers that Snyder intends to integrate his practice of Buddhism with the native spiritual beliefs that he has upheld in the earlier poems. But let there be no doubt: Snyder has not eschewed direct action, as evident in the poem "Front Lines," which opposes destructive urban development and concludes: "And here we must draw / Our line." But Snyder is careful not to suggest that militancy guarantees victory, as evidenced by the concern reflected in "The Call of the Wild." In this poem he worries about the destruction that is already being accomplished by contemporary consumer culture's "war against earth." The last three poems of this section, "Source," "Manzanita," and "Charms," taken together, suggest that salvation, victory, and true knowledge will come from close attention to the nonhuman world that people must reinhabit in order to transform the United States into Turtle Island.

This attitude is further developed through many of the poems of the next section, "Magpie's Song." Here the magpie has a function similar to that of the coyote as a trickster who speaks to and interacts with the human world. As with the first section, this one contains an eclectic mixture of different types of poems. The second and third poems of this section are "The Real Work" and "Pine Tree Tops." The first poems emphasizes the idea that all life is engaged in survival and is just getting by, whether they are seagulls or humans, riding the waves and looking for food. The second poem ends with the ambiguous line, "what do we know." If read in complementary fashion, the two likely meanings of these words combine. The first functions as a summary of the descriptions in the poem of the speaker who is out at night, paying close attention to the life in the woods and learning the details of Turtle Island. The second can be understood as a question through which the speaker admits that regardless of how much we learn we will remain students of the wild, always ignorant of the mysteries that surround us. This admission of ignorance, then, becomes one of the

things that "we" must know if people are to reinhabit the land. "Night Herons" continues this type of theme. The speaker is visiting San Francisco and while he and his friends go for a walk at night, he notices all of the animals living amid the machinery of modern society. As the poet celebrates the coincidence of his return to the city alongside the return of the night herons, he feels an optimistic sense of self-renewal as a result of the possibility for ecological renewal.

The poems mentioned in the previous paragraph all reflect a meditative mood on the part of the poet. With "The Uses of Light" he shifts into a more playful, rhyming poetry. Heavily indebted to Buddhism—particularly Vairocana, the sun Buddha—the poem also reflects the recognition that the sun remains the primary source of energy and, therefore, food and links virtually all life on the surface of the planet in one interconnected web. But the poem does not stop there. In the final stanza, it invokes a Chinese saying about climbing up one level of a tower to expand dramatically one's perspective on the surrounding world. This stanza, then, comments not only on the rest of the poem and its point about recognizing the interdependence of human life on other life-forms but it also reiterates the point in "Pine Tree Tops" and other poems in this section regarding the new to break out of the perceptual habits promoted by contemporary culture and to look at life in fresh ways, such as being thinking of the sun in terms of the reactions of the "stones," "trees," "moths" and "deer" of the poem. Part of this new perception is reflected in "It Pleases," where the poet dismisses the apparent power of Washington, D.C., because it does not hold jurisdiction over the material world that "does what it pleases."

"Mother Earth: Her Whales," the most far reaching of the political poems in *Turtle Island,* however, does not take such a sanguine view of the power of wild nature in the face of governments and bureaucracies. As Hwa Yol and Petee Jung note, "It began with a terse foreword in which he said that everyone came to Stockholm not to give but rather to take, not to save the planet but to argue how to divide it up. . . . The poem meant to defend all the creatures of the earth." It does so by pitting the lives in nature against the destruction of various civilizations, both historic and contemporary, east and west as well as north and south. It is important to note that Snyder closes with attention to the survival of animals, while nation states are represented by a dead knight whose eyes vultures are homing in to eat.

The third section of *Turtle Island,* "For The Children," contains just nine poems. Here Snyder wishes to pass on something to the next generation and so focuses not on condemnation, concern, or doubt but on reassurance and practical wisdom. The opening poem, "O Waters," functions as a prayer that invokes rituals of purification and concludes by declaring that all planetary life shares a mutual fellowship. "Tomorrow's Song" then turns to the future. It begins by declaring that the United States has lost its alleged "mandate" as a governing body because it refused to include the nonhuman in its deliberations and laws. The future, therefore, must rectify this omission and also move beyond a fossil-fuel-based excessive-consumption culture. The new future in which the children "will grow strong on less" will require hard work that is based on a wilderness-centered philosophy of life. The next poem, "What Happened Here Before," provides some historical background for how human beings came to live the way they do in the part of California that Snyder, his family, and his community are seeking to reinhabit. The "white man" is specifically criticized for his exploitation of nature and the destruction of native cultures. The poem ends with a challenge: *WE SHALL SEE / WHO KNOWS / HOW TO BE.*"

"Toward Climax," which logically follows from the preceding poem, responds to this challenge through a set of contrasts between a historically destructive way of looking at the world and an alternative life-affirming—all life, not just that of humans—worldview. The penultimate and title poem for the section, "For the Children," presents a lyrical utopian view of the future and contains an often repeated closing refrain: "stay together / learn the flowers / go light." Some critics have scoffed at the simplicity of this slogan, but it contains just the kind of statement that is appropriate for its audience. The next generation must unite and remain united through all kinds of political, economic, and cultural adversity and setbacks; they must

learn where they live and what else lives there and through that learn to respect that life; and they must abandon the consumerism that is literally choking Americans to death. "As For Poets" ends this section and the poetry sections of *Turtle Island* in much the way that "Riprap" ended Snyder's first volume. It makes a metapoetic statement about the role of poems and their diversity through the images of a variety of poets, who are not people so much as they are whorls of energy in the larger flow of matter that is seeking consciousness.

"Plain Talk," the prose section that closes *Turtle Island,* contains five short pieces, with the longest one, "Four Changes," also being the most important. Snyder provides a brief introduction to this essay, which was originally written and distributed in 1969 by means of some 50,000 broadsides and pamphlets that were distributed freely across the United States. Here Snyder reprints the original edition with bracketed comments that were added in 1974. Through sections titled "Population," "Pollution," "Consumption," and "Transportation," he first describes the crisis in each category as he sees it unfolding, and then he posits a guide to action for each. Many of the statements in this essay elaborate on or clarify themes that are explored in the *Turtle Island* poems.

"'Energy Is Eternal Delight,'" although alluding to William Blake, does not focus on romanticism or poetry, but instead it addresses a general issue that is already raised throughout the volume—the looming energy crisis and the danger of a turn to nuclear power—as well as a specific action—the resistance of Native Americans to uranium mining in the U.S. Southwest. "The Wilderness" focuses on the issue of figuring out how to represent the interests of the nonhuman in governmental deliberations and turns to the examples of so-called primitive cultures for examples of proper practice. This essay in many ways prefigures the slim prose collection *The Old Ways,* which appeared in 1977, and is reprinted as a section of *A Place in Space.* "What's Meant By 'Here'" makes an excellent companion to the poem, "What Happeed Here Before" and serves as a demonstration of bioregional history. "On 'As For Poets'" provides a gloss of the poem that ended the "For the Children" section of the volume and functions, as well, as a commentary on the volume as a whole. Snyder concludes, "The power within—the more you give, the more you have to give—will still be our source when coal and oil are long gone, and atoms are left to spin in peace." As Katsunori Yamazato so eloquently sums it up, "'how to be' is the central question that Snyder asks and tries to answer throughout *Turtle Island*," and clearly this closing sentence defines a certain mode of being. *Turtle Island* is unquestionably the most programmatic of all of Snyder's collections of poetry; nevertheless, it displays a wide variety of poetic styles and devices, as aesthetic as it is thematic. Also, it is as humorous and visionary as it is serious and focused on the moment.

Bibliography

Jung, Hwa Yol, and Petee Jung. "Gary Snyder's Ecopiety." *Environmental History Review* 14.3 (1990): 75–87.

Murphy, Patrick D. *A Place for Wayfaring: The Poetry and Prose of Gary Snyder.* Corvallis: University of Oregon Press, 2000.

Snyder, Gary. *The Back Country.* New York: New Directions, 1968.

———. *The Fudo Trilogy.* Berkeley, Calif.: Shaman Drum, 1973.

———. *Myths & Texts.* 1960. New York: New Directions, 1978.

———. *The Old Ways.* San Francisco: City Lights Books, 1977.

———. *A Place in Space: Ethics, Aesthetics, and Watersheds.* Washington, D.C.: Counterpoint, 1995.

———. *Regarding Wave.* New York: New Directions, 1970.

———. *Turtle Island.* New York: New Directions, 1974.

Yamazato, Katsunori. "How to Be in This Crisis: Gary Snyder's Cross-Cultural Vision in *Turtle Island*." In *Critical Essays on Gary Snyder,* edited by Patrick D. Murphy, 230–247. Boston: G. K. Hall, 1990.

Patrick Murphy

V

Vanity of Duluoz: An Adventurous Education, 1935–1946 Jack Kerouac (1968)

This novel is JACK KEROUAC's final entry in what he called "The Duluoz Legend," his fictional autobiography. The book is an account of much of the material Kerouac had previously covered in his first novel, *The TOWN AND THE CITY*. Yet this revised account takes on a different tone. *Vanity of Duluoz* is considered one of Kerouac's most accessible novels because of his self-described attempt to write plainly and to use normal punctuation (he somewhat bitterly chooses to eliminate his characteristic dash-style of punctuation). The book also covers aspects of the Kerouac's life that are calculated to interest his readers, in particular the Columbia years and the scene around Joan Vollmer's apartment at the time of the famous murder of Dave Kammerer by Lucien Carr. Kerouac's letters to his agent at the time of the writing of this book show that he was under severe financial pressure for it to be a success, and perhaps this is why he finally ignored the plea of Carr, who had for years asked him not to discuss Kammerer's death. Still, the book succeeds on its own terms, establishing a ruthless truthfulness and fullness of disclosure that is the trademark of Kerouac's best work.

Kerouac addresses the book to his third wife, Stella Sampas, for one of reasons that he wrote *ON THE ROAD*—to explain to his wife, Joan Haverty in the case of *On the Road,* how he had come to be who he was. It is also worth noting that Kerouac wrote to Stella throughout the years that are covered in the book, although it would be many years before he would marry and move back to Lowell with her. The word *vanity* seems to be hanging before Kerouac as he writes the book. He points out to Stella that all his success as a writer has really brought him more trouble than happiness.

Jack Duluoz is Kerouac's persona again, and his decision to attend Columbia costs his father his job with Calloway printers in Lowell, which had offered him a promotion if Duluoz played football for the Jesuits at Boston College. Accordingly, in the years to come, Duluoz feels pressure to justify his decision. He spends a year at Horace Mann prep school to make up his high school deficiencies. There his fellow football players, who are mostly from working-class backgrounds, are suspicious of his friendship with the nonathletic, rich Jewish students who comprise the majority of the student body. Duluoz's city friends introduce him to literature, avant-garde film, and jazz. He skips classes to study New York City. The original title of the book was "The Adventurous Education of Jack Duluoz," and Duluoz recommends letting "a kid learn his own way, see what happens." Kerouac's nickname was "Memory Babe," and he demonstrates a facility for recalling events and details of his teenage years, particularly his experiences in New York.

War will disrupt what appears to be a clear path to success as a football player and a scholar at Columbia: Duluoz does play the 1940 season at Columbia. However, a spectacular run-back makes him overconfident in a game against St. Benedict, and he has his leg broken on the next play, foolishly fielding an unreturnable punt. The broken leg gives him the leisure to study, and he immerses himself in the works of the writer who will most influence him in his early years—Thomas Wolfe. Late one night, crossing the Brooklyn Bridge in a blizzard, he actually sees Wolfe stride past him, deep in meditation, not noticing Duluoz.

Duluoz returns to Columbia for this sophomore year, and his sense of fatalism is reinforced by Lu Libble's (based on coach Lou Little) obvious intentions to keep Duluoz benched, playing lesser players in his place. Duluoz walks away from the team with a resolution to "go after being a writer, tell the truth," and to "go into the Thomas Wolfe darkness" of America. He returns to Hartford and his disappointed father, takes a job at a gas station, and rents a typewriter. His father's job ends in New Haven, and the family returns to Lowell, where Duluoz has the appearance of a returning prodigal son. He takes a job as a sportswriter for the *Lowell Sun* and spends his afternoons there writing a Joyce-influenced novel. In the evenings, he embarks on a program of self-education, working through H. G. Wells's *Outline of History* and the 11th edition of the *Encyclopedia Britannica.* He fights with his father. His mother tells him not to listen to his father and that his father is only afraid that Duluoz might succeed in life by following his own path. Duluoz claims for the first time that he will support his mother no matter what comes. He quits the sports-writing job and goes South, where he works a construction job on the military's new Pentagon outside Washington, D.C., in Virginia. War broke out in December, and Duluoz inevitably enlists—in the marines—but he ends up signing on with the merchant marines as a scullion, bound for the North Pole. Kerouac's most important friend of his youth, Sebastian "Sammy" Sampas, brother of Stella, is portrayed here as Sabbas "Sabby" Savakis. Sabby tries to sign on with him, but Duluoz tells him he wants to be on his own. Duluoz laments that if Sabby had been able to sail with him, it might have changed his fate and saved his life. Sabby is later killed on the beach at Anzio. Much of the book quotes from Kerouac's sea diary on board the ship, which he interrupts with wry, parenthetical comments about the style of his prose. Kerouac, at the time he wrote the novel, disliked communism, but in spite of the fact that he deplored anti-Vietnam war protesters, this book has

a strong antiwar message. He is in the ship's mess, cooking 2,000 strips of bacon for the crew, when he hears a depth-charge attack against a German submarine. Instead of feeling fear, he thinks of the German boy on the submarine who is doing the same thing he is—cooking breakfast.

He arrives back home to find a telegram from Lu Libble, telling him it is time to come back and play football for Columbia. Duluoz does, on the condition that he gets to play and that Libble help his father get a job. Neither happens, and Duluoz implies that Libble keeps him benched in the Army game because the mob has a fix on the outcome. While listening to Beethoven's Fifth Symphony on the radio in his dorm room, he decides to quit football. Duluoz returns to Lowell, gets sick with the German measles, and spends his time hand-printing a novel entitled "The Sea is My Brother." After recovering, he reports to the navy for duty, flunks his Naval Air Force Test, and is sent to boot camp.

Duluoz's problem with the navy was that he could not submit to the arbitrary discipline of his superiors. In the middle of the daily drills, he throws his gun down and walks off the field. They find him in the library. Although it was determined after psychiatric testing that he had the highest IQ of any soldier in the history of the Newport Navy Base, he is shipped off to the "nuthouse." Duluoz explains to no avail that he was perfectly willing to serve his country in the merchant marine. In the psychiatric ward, he meets "Big Slim" from Louisiana, a man whose ambition from childhood was to become a hobo. Naturally, Duluoz hits it off with him. Duluoz is visited by his father, who tells him that he did the right thing in throwing down his rifle. Sabby also visits him, eyes big with tears, not understanding Duluoz's actions. This is the last time that he sees Sabby. The navy discovers that Duluoz and Slim have hidden away knives to attempt an escape and sends them both, straight jacketed, to Bethesda Naval Hospital. There they are thrown in with seriously mentally ill patients. Duluoz tells the doctors that he constitutionally is incapable of submitting to discipline. They discharge him honorably but make him sign an affidavit that he will make no claims on the military thereafter.

Kerouac now regrets that he felt compelled to balk the navy and even admits that he might have learned something useful in the service—something more useful, he says, than writing. He begins his "adventurous education" anew, going to live with his parents who now reside in Ozone Park in New York City. Big Slim visits and with Duluoz's father they spend a day at the horse races and a night drinking. This is the last time he sees Big Slim. Duluoz makes good on his promise to the navy psychiatrists and signs on a merchant-marine ship. While making this voyage, he reads John Galsworthy's *The Forsyte Saga* and comes up with the idea to write his own saga of interconnected books. The chief mate has it in for Duluoz, and assigns him to life-threatening duties that enraged the other crew members. Duluoz compares his situation to Billy Budd. After the ship docks in Liverpool he sees enough of the extreme poverty of the city and buys a train ticket to London on a two-day pass.

Duluoz manages to visit London during a lull in the German air war. He visits museums and hears the symphony at the Royal Albert Hall. The day before sailing, he imagines fully the idea of "The Duluoz Legend"—"a lifetime of writing about what I'd seen with my own eyes." Back in Brooklyn, he continues a romance with Johnnie (based on Edie Parker). Johnnie lived with a Barnard journalism student named June (based on Joan Burroughs) whose Columbia-adjacent apartment was the center of a group of bohemians. Here begins a long account of the events that are based on Lucien Carr's relationship with Dave Kammerer. Here Carr is Claude de Maubris, and Kammerer is Franz Mueller. Kerouac had never previously published his version of the famous killing that signaled the beginning of the Beat Generation. Here he gives a detailed account of the older man Mueller stalking the beautiful, blond Claude and of Claude's bemused response to Mueller that finally turned to desperation and murderous rage. For libel reasons, Kerouac has WILLIAM S. BURROUGHS, Kammerer, Carr, and Kells Elvins all come from New Orleans, instead of St. Louis. Kerouac writes that this "clique was the most evil and intelligent buncha bastards and shits in America but had to admire in my admiring youth." Kerouac also writes a detailed portrait of Burroughs and of the beginning of their long friendship. It is as close as Kerouac ever came to writing his long-promised novel based on Burroughs.

This book gives the most detailed account of the Carr/Kammerer murder that was written by any of the Beats, and it is the basis of most of the accounts that are found in other books. It is a very literary retelling (Duluoz says of Claude and Mueller that their past was "exactly like Rimbaud and Verlaine"), almost as if the real-life story were scripted to be included one day as the first installment in the legend of the Beats. Mueller follows Claude from school to school and from city to city. At one point, Claude is so depressed by Mueller's pursuit and his own confused sexuality that he attempts suicide by sticking his head in a gas oven—only to be saved at the last instant by Mueller. The pursuit continues in New York, where Claude attends Columbia and Mueller befriends Claude's friends. Duluoz and Claude plot to shake Mueller for good by shipping out to France on a merchant-marine ship. The trip to France falls through when the first mate of the ship runs off most of the crew, including Duluoz and Claude. Claude awakens Duluoz at six the next morning, saying that he has "disposed of the old man last night." The motive was self-defense. According to Claude, Mueller said that he would kill him if he could not have him. Claude stabbed him 12 times with his Boy Scout knife. Claude weighted the body and submerged it in the river. At some point earlier that morning, he found Will Hubbard, based on Burroughs, who advised Claude to get a good lawyer and turn himself in, which he planned to do. But first, Claude and Duluoz dispose of the evidence and go on a two-day drunk in Manhattan for one last time before, as Claude believes, he goes to the electric chair. After Claude turns himself in, Duluoz is arrested as an accessory to murder. The case immediately makes the newspapers. Duluoz is put in a cell with Mafia men who are being held as material witnesses, and one by one these hardened criminals try to take him into their confidence to find out if Claude is a homosexual. If his friends, including Duluoz, do not testify that Claude is heterosexual, he is almost certain to be convicted of murder, rather than manslaughter, for which he would receive only a two-year sentence. Duluoz is bailed out by Johnnie's mother (Duluoz's father had angrily refused bail money), and in return he marries Johnnie. Duluoz's arresting detective was the best man, bought them several rounds of drinks, and escorted Duluoz back to jail. Duluoz's summary comment on the murder is that Mueller got what he deserved for threatening Claude.

To pay back Johnnie's mother the bail money, Duluoz moves with his wife to Detroit where his father-in-law finds him an easy, well-paying job in a ball-bearing factory. He works for two months until the money is repaid and then goes to New York to ship out. Aboard the S.S. *Robert Treat Pain,* the bosun makes Duluoz's life miserable by referring to him as a pretty boy, and Duluoz—still sensitive to the issues of sexuality raised in the Claude/Mueller affair—suspects the man's hatred of him as some kind of homosexual infatuation. He jumps ship in Norfolk, Virginia, and heads back to the Columbia campus, where he dedicates himself to becoming a serious writer. After Benzedrine use lands him in the hospital, he rejects his Beat friends. This is the beginning of Duluoz's ambition to explore America and signals his break from New York. The final chapters of the book focus on the death of Duluoz's father, Duluoz's vow to support his mother, and the writing of a novel. His biggest "vanity" is revealed as his ambition to be a great writer.

An excellent account of Kerouac's writing of *Vanity of Duluoz* appears in Ellis Amburn's *Subterranean Kerouac.* Amburn was Kerouac's editor for *DESOLATION ANGELS* and *Vanity of Duluoz,* which is dedicated to Kerouac's wife Stella and to Amburn. Amburn says that it was his idea that Kerouac address the book to his wife and that this helped him find a form and a voice for the novel. Kerouac completed the novel in 10 marathon sessions at the typewriter. Amburn was disappointed by the book's sexist and racist statements. The book was poorly reviewed, with the notable exception of JOHN CLELLON HOLMES's review, but it has since become a classic example of Kerouac's misanthropy and bitterness at the end of his life. Kerouac's portrait of Ginsberg as Irwin Garden seems particularly harsh. Yet, the book is still a tour de force of memory.

Bibliography

Amburn, Ellis. *Subterranean Kerouac: The Hidden Life of Jack Kerouac.* New York: St. Martin's Press, 1998.

Rob Johnson

Vega, Janine Pommy (1942–   )

Janine Pommy Vega continues to be a major figure in contemporary American poetry, as is evident in her remarkable recent collection, *The Green Piano* (Black Sparrow 2005). While JACK KEROUAC's road took him all across America, Vega's road has taken her all across the world.

Janine Pommy was born in Jersey City, New Jersey, on February 5, 1942, to a working-class family. She was inspired to join the Beat movement after reading Kerouac's ON THE ROAD in 1958. "All the characters seemed to move with an intensity that was missing in my life," she recalls. She met GREGORY CORSO in the Cedar Bar when an article on the Beat Generation prompted her to check out the scene in Greenwich Village, and she would eventually meet Kerouac himself. She has been associated with the Beats ever since. She was romantically involved with Peter Orlovsky (ALLEN GINSBERG's partner) and became friends with RAY BREMSER and his wife Bonnie (BRENDA FRAZER), and HERBERT HUNCKE became her mentor. Of all the Beats, Vega admired Huncke the most for resisting the male chauvinism of the times. Though

Janine Pommy Vega, San Francisco, 1996. Photographer Larry Keenan: "The *Women of the Beat Generation* book-signing party. Poet Janine Pommy Vega is shown in this photograph reading some of her powerful work, at the Tosco in North Beach." *(courtesy of Larry Keenan)*

she graduated valedictorian of her high school class, Vega decided to live a life of a poet. For a time she lived with Ginsberg's assistant Elise Cowen. She had an amphetamine-fueled relationship with Bill Heine, who would later be arrested with Huncke, and briefly lived in the same apartment as novelist Alexander Trocchi and his wife.

In 1962 she met Fernando Vega, a talented Peruvian Jewish painter who took her to Israel. Fernando, the inspiration for Vega's first book of poetry, POEMS TO FERNANDO (1968), died of a heroin overdose on the island of Ibiza off the coast of Spain in November 1965. She traveled (spending time with LENORE KANDEL in Hawaii) and lived in New York City, San Francisco (with Huncke and, later, a member of the Hell's Angels), and Woodstock, New York. In the 1970s she read poetry with BOB KAUFMAN, JACK MICHELINE, DAVID MELTZER, and ED SANDERS, among others. She travelled with BOB DYLAN's Rolling Thunder Revue in 1975.

In 1982 she barely escaped death after a horrendous car crash. After recovering, she continued to travel, write, and work with prison programs to bring poetic inspiration to inmates. Her superb travelog, *TRACKING THE SERPENT: JOURNEYS TO FOUR CONTINENTS*, was published by City Lights, the publisher of her first book of poetry, in 1997. Her signature poem, "MAD DOGS OF TRIESTE," which was published in a volume under that name by Black Sparrow Press, appeared in 2000. One of the most, if not *the* most, peripatetic members of the Beat movement that she helped establish, Vega continues to be socially, politically, and artistically active today.

Bibliography

As We Cover the Streets: Janine Pommy Vega. Film written by Kurt Hemmer, produced by Tom Knoff. Palatine, Ill.: Harper College, 2003.
Vega, Janine Pommy. *Tracking the Serpent: Journeys to Four Continents*. San Francisco: City Lights, 1997.

Kurt Hemmer

Visions of Cody Jack Kerouac (1972)

JACK KEROUAC's *Visions of Cody*, his tribute novel to NEAL CASSADY, is, arguably, Kerouac's greatest book, although at the time it was written, Kerouac's best reader ALLEN GINSBERG told Cassady that it was a "holy mess." No one who had not "blown" Kerouac, said Ginsberg, could ever make sense of *Visions of Cody* because of the book's deeply personal material. What Ginsberg did not understand at the time, but came to understand later, was that Kerouac was writing his books with the clear sense that they were all one long book, "The Duluoz Legend," as he called it. Therefore, any personal references in *Visions of Cody* would in due course be explained through reference to other installments in "The Duluoz Legend." Regardless, the reader who comes to *Visions of Cody* after having read ON THE ROAD, *The DHARMA BUMS*, or some of Kerouac's other works of conventional prose will find the book as difficult to read in parts as James Joyce's *Ulysses*. Yet *Visions of Cody* is the version of Kerouac's book about his life on the road with Cassady that Kerouac himself thought was the best.

The novel is unique as a literary achievement if properly seen in the context of Kerouac's life and how his life led to his development as an artist. Kerouac started to write the book in October 1951 in Queens, New York, incorporating some of his Denver descriptions from summer 1950, and finished it in the Cassady's attic in May 1952. He wrote most of the book after having written *On the Road*, which, although it is a book with a freewheeling style, is hardly as experimental as *Visions of Cody*. Even so, Kerouac found no publisher willing to touch *On the Road*, including his friend Robert Giroux, who rejected *On the Road* out of hand. Most writers would have taken that as a message to restrain their style. Kerouac saw such rejection as liberating. If *On the Road*, a book that he knew was great, would never be published, then he may as well write for himself and write in as pure a form as he could imagine. This new form was spontaneous prose.

Spontaneous prose can be seen as the literary equivalent of the improvisational jazz solos of Lester Young and Charlie Parker or the "drip" paintings of Jackson Pollock. Kerouac would throw out all of the rules about form and create a literature that substituted images for plot—a breakthrough that would have a profound influence not only on Ginsberg (whose poems, he admits, were influenced deeply by *Visions of Cody*) but also on WIL-

LIAM S. BURROUGHS (who by the mid-1950s had come to the same conclusion about images versus plot as had Kerouac). A comparison of "A Supermarket in California," "HOWL," and the later "road" poems in *The FALL OF AMERICA* to the prose of *Visions of Cody*, and the dash-style punctuation of Burroughs's prose in *Naked Lunch* and the cut-up trilogy to *Visions of Cody* make it clear how influential Kerouac's book was on the writing of his two friends. Both read it in 1952. Ginsberg worked as an agent for the book (unsuccessfully), and Kerouac typed the manuscript while living with Burroughs in Mexico City in 1952.

The book is divided into three parts. The first part contains Kerouac's "sketches" of New York City in November 1951 with references to Cody Pomeray's (based on Cassady) childhood mixed in. Part Two recounts Cody's childhood and early pool-hall days; it also describes Kerouac's trip West to visit Cody and Evelyn (based on CAROLYN CASSADY) in December 1951. Part Three is a transcript of several days of tape-recorded conversations between Cody, Jack Duluoz (based on Kerouac), and Evelyn at Cody and Evelyn's house in San Francisco. It also includes Kerouac's imitation of the tape in spontaneous prose, along with spontaneous-prose sketches, including a description of Cody. Part of the book was published by New Directions in 1959. The entire book was published posthumously in 1972 when it was issued with an afterword by Ginsberg entitled "The Visions of The Great Rememberer," one of the best readings of Kerouac's prose by any critic.

Kerouac was friends with a Columbia architecture student named Ed White (the model for Ed Gray in *Visions of Cody*), who was an old Denver friend of Cassady's. In October 1951 White showed Kerouac some of his sketches on a notepad and, as White says, "suggested that he could do the same with notes." White says Kerouac could write extremely quickly, and he saw him carrying around pocket notebooks after their conversation. In a letter to Cassady, Kerouac calls these sketches "everything I sense as it stands in front of me and activates all around, in portable breast shirtpocket notebooks slapping."

The "sketches" of New York recorded in Part One of *Visions of Cody* were made by Kerouac in

November 1951. The sketches include the men's room in the Third Avenue El railway station, reflections in the window of a bakery in Jamaica, Queens, and St. Patrick's Cathedral. Throughout, comparisons are made to the perceptions of the hero of this book, Cody. For example, the sketch of Hector's Cafeteria was an important setting in Cody's first visit to New York in 1946. The overall connection between the "sketching" style and the storyline of the book is that unlike *On the Road*, this book will be the "complete Cody," with few details left out.

Kerouac says that in "the Autumn of 1951 I began thinking of Cody," and we know that Kerouac had been receiving letters from Neal and Carolyn Cassady asking him—even pleading with him—to come visit them, offering Kerouac their attic as a writing space. As Carolyn describes in *OFF THE ROAD*, she and Neal had come to the conclusion that Kerouac was an essential part of their life and was a necessary element in their marriage. Kerouac's attempts to travel West to see the Cassadys were slowed by his impulsive (and short-lived) marriage to Joan Haverty and by returning bouts of thrombophlebitis, which led to his hospitalization in September and early October 1951.

Part One ends with what in many ways is a love letter from Duluoz to Cody. Duluoz believes that only Cody understands him and that he is "haunted" by Cody. They have wasted too much time, and he almost lost everything by going to Mexico with Julien Love (based on Lucien Carr), a reference to Ginsberg and Carr's trip to Mexico in August 1951, just a few weeks before Joan Burroughs was accidentally shot by William Burroughs in a game of "William Tell." He adds a postscript to Evelyn assuring her that he is "Cody's friend, not his devil," for in the past Duluoz's arrival has signaled domestic chaos.

In summer 1949, financed by his $1,000 advance on *The TOWN AND THE CITY*, Kerouac moved himself and his mother to Westwood in the foothills of Denver. His mother did not like Denver and left almost immediately, but Kerouac stayed and took the opportunity to visit the old haunts of Cassady and his pool-hall gang. In fall 1950, while staying with his mother and his sister in Richmond Hill, Kerouac wrote these experiences. Before sitting down at the kitchen table to write, he would sneak into the bathroom and smoke several joints which rolled were from marijuana that he had smuggled back from Mexico on the trip with Cassady that is described at the end of *On the Road*. The marijuana-inspired style of these passages—which constitute much of Part II of *Visions of Cody*—were a breakthrough, Kerouac felt. Ginsberg and Cassady disagreed, saying that the marijuana was obscuring Kerouac's judgment. Certainly, the marijuana allowed Kerouac to focus on details to a level that he had never done before. He wrote 20,000 words alone about the day when Cassady first met his friend Jim Holmes in Peterson's Pool Hall in Denver. In *Visions of Cody,* Kerouac refers to this section as "where in North Carolina tea dreams I also saw Cody and tried to write a 'story' about it."

Cody's history as its retold in *Visions of Cody* has at least two sources. Readers of Cassady's incomplete memoir *The FIRST THIRD* will find considerable overlap between Kerouac's account and Cassady's. Kerouac probably saw the beginnings of *The First Third* when he stayed with Neal and Carolyn in 1950 and 1951. Cassady's letters to Kerouac also contain a good deal of the information— and also approximate the spontaneous style—in the first part of Book II of Cody. In fact, it was Cassady who apparently taught Kerouac to smoke marijuana and take Benzedrine to write nonstop, free-flowing prose.

The principal characters in Kerouac's history of Cody are Tom Watson (based on Jim Holmes), Slim Buckle (based on Al Hinkle), and Earl Johnson (based on Bill Tomson). Holmes remained in Denver his entire life, playing pool and betting on the horses. Hinkle is the basis for the character Ed Dunkel in *On the Road,* and his wife Helen (the model for the character Helen Buckle) is the basis of a character Galatea Dunkel in *On The Road* and is an important friend to Carolyn Cassady as is described in *Off the Road*. Tomson, who was dating Carolyn, introduced her to Neal.

A quarter of the way into the book, Kerouac begins a new section that is unrelated to Cody's past. Here, Duluoz develops his own story about himself and how he came to be heading West again to be with Cody. He recounts writing the opening section of book two and of his days at the hospital recuperating from thrombophlebitis. Increasingly the book becomes Duluoz's rather than Cody's story. Duluoz feels himself to be at the height of his powers as a writer because not only is he the "maddest *liver* in the world" but he is also the "best watcher and that's no sneezing thing." He tells us that the book will resemble Proust's great work, but he will not have the luxury of writing it in bed; instead he will write it on the fly. It will be "the most complete record in the world," a description that reveals Kerouac's immense ambitions as a writer in 1951. Kerouac is writing with such confidence of the immortality of his work in progress that he even refers cryptically to passages of his unpublished novel *On the Road*—as if any reader could know the source. Still, he seems to know that one day all of his works will be in print and that readers will be able to put the entire thing together.

To visit Cody, Duluoz plans to ship out of New Jersey on the *President Adams*. Deni Bleu (based on Henri Cru) already has a place on board, and they will travel together. However, Duluoz is unable to get a position on the ship and watches it leave without him. Deni tells him to travel overland and to meet the ship when it arrives in Port at San Pedro, south of Los Angeles. Duluoz borrows $70 for the trip, procures a supply of Benzedrine and Dexedrine, and hits the road. He arrives in San Francisco, and he, Slim Buckle, and Cody hit the saloons on Mission Street. Facing the ocean at San Pedro at the end of Part II, Duluoz listens to Deni lecture him about how Duluoz does not love anyone but himself. In Part I, however, Duluoz has written to Cody that he does love him, and it is to Cody that Duluoz returns.

Kerouac and Cassady had long discussed using a tape recorder as opposed to a typewriter or pencil and paper to capture in the raw spontaneity of their marathon discussions and monologues. Cassady bought an Ekotape recorder, and when Kerouac visited in December 1951, they let it run as they sat around in the kitchen of Neal and Carolyn's apartment smoking marijuana, drinking wine, playing records and musical instruments, and getting high on Benzedrine. Part III of *Visions of Cody* is a transcript of five such nights in early 1952.

Most critics find this section more interesting as an idea than as a written text. Ginsberg admits that the tape is "hung up and boring" at times, but he says that the "art lies in the consciousness of doing the thing, in the attention to the happening in the sacramentalization of everyday reality, the God-worship in the present conversation, no matter what." The tape, he says, is thus a very direct application of Kerouac's theories of spontaneous prosody: "It's art because at that point in progress of Jack's art he began transcribing *first* thoughts of true mind in American speech." Kerouac himself was self-conscious about the ultimate failure of the tape experiment, but maybe that was the point. "You're not going to get hardly any of this recorded, you know," says Cody to Duluoz, and Duluoz replies, "Well, that's the sadness of it all."

Inarguably, though "Frisco: The Tape" is, in terms of its content, an extremely valuable document. For the transcript, Kerouac presciently selected topics of discussion that fill in some of the gaps in the early history of the Beats. Many biographers of the Beats seem to have overlooked the material here, for many of the stories that are buried in the 150 pages of often drunken and stoned conversation have not found their way into the narratives of the lives of Burroughs, Kerouac, and Ginsberg, in particular.

Duluoz has never heard from Cody about his experiences on Hubbard's (based on Burroughs) ranch in East Texas in 1948. He has only heard Irwin Garden's (based on Ginsberg) side of the story. Cody is evasive about what Ginsberg identifies in the notes at the end of *Visions of Cody* as their "Green Automobile Vow"—a vow of love, for Ginsberg but not for Cassady, evidently, that they made in the middle of a road in Oklahoma as they hitchhiked to East Texas. Cody tells the story of the bed that Huck (based on HERBERT HUNCKE) and Irwin make for Cody and Irwin to sleep in, a famous Beat legend also recounted in Huncke's memoir *The EVENING SUN TURNED CRIMSON.*

Another part of the transcription documents the culture of marijuana smoking that would become widespread in America 15 years later. The Beats were a direct link between the drug culture and the drug language of the jazz artists of the 1930s and the 1940s and the hippie counterculture

of the 1960s. Already, in this transcript, the reader can see that a very specific ritual has emerged.

Cody talks the majority of the time in these tapes, but Duluoz tells the story of his first meeting of Julien and Hubbard and June (based on Joan Burroughs). He also discusses the relationship between Julien and Stroheim (Dave Kammerer). Carr's murder of Kammerer is a key part of Beat history. There are also details about Duluoz's early days around Huck and Phil Blackman (based on Phil White) and, in particular, the real-life Vicki Russell that are not available in any other Beat book. For example, Duluoz is quite candid about the fact that they all knew that Blackman was a murderer. In this unexpurgated account of the Times Square/Columbia scene of the early and mid-1940s, it is clear that Duluoz, Garden, and Hubbard kept company with fairly hardened criminals. Other highlights of these pages include Duluoz's memories of New Year's Eve 1947 in the company of Vicki and Julien and also of Cody's thoughts on the deaths of Finistra (based on Bill Cannastra) and June.

Cody takes the tape back and at Duluoz's urging tells about how he met his Denver "gang" in the early 1940s. They talk about their mutual friend Ed Gray, and Cody tells about meeting Tom Watson. He tells Duluoz of the breaks that he was given by Justin Mannerly (based on Justin Brierly), who helped him get a job out of reform school recapping tires. On the tire job, he met Val Hayes (based on Hal Chase), with whom he began to have deep conversations about poetry and philosophy. Ginsberg believed that Chase convinced Cassady that poetry was more important than philosophy. This fact convinced Cassady to go to New York and meet Chase's poet friends, including Ginsberg and Kerouac.

Evelyn has been in and out of the conversation, but she joins them after coming home from her nighttime job as a photographer in the nightclubs that are located in the old Barbary Coast district of San Francisco. Carolyn Cassady writes about this job and those days in *Off the Road.* Both accounts reflect Carolyn's view that these were some of the happiest times that Kerouac, Neal, and she spent together.

Duluoz becomes drunk and drops out of the conversation, giving Cody the floor with Evelyn.

These pages capture Cody's natural storytelling style as well as any in Beat literature. Cody tells Evelyn about his days in Los Angeles before he met her, the only such account available in Beat literature. Such stories are made safe for Evelyn. Cody has to be careful not to discuss parts of his life when he knew Evelyn but which did not include her. For example, earlier she asks about when he, Slim, and Duluoz were all together in New Orleans, but the subject is quickly dropped because the story includes another woman.

Cody and Duluoz discuss June's death and Hubbard's fascination with guns. They then speculate about how Irwin and Hubbard might die. Significantly, they do not speculate about their own deaths, although later in the book Cody says that he will die on a railroad track (Neal actually did).

Another section of the transcription fills in a key part of the history of Hubbard and June. Burroughs moved to South Texas in late 1946 but returned almost immediately to New York when he heard that Joan had been institutionalized. Cody tells the story of Hubbard's return. This part of Burroughs's history (as it intersects with Cassady's) is not available in any other Beat book. Though Cassady seems to have confused this time with a later return to New York by Burroughs when he and Cassady drove Burroughs's jeep from East Texas to New York and attempted to sell the marijuana that Burroughs had raised on his New Waverly farm.

In the "Imitation of the Tape" section of the book, Duluoz breaks in at one point and makes one of his most memorable statements about why he is a writer: "I'm writing this book because we're all going to die—In the loneliness of my life . . . my heart broke open in the general despair and opened up inwards to the Lord, I made a supplication in this dream." The book has been written out of the loneliness following his extended farewell to Cody. "Adios, King," he ends the novel.

Still, although he loves Cody, he resents how Cody has come to be the very eyes through which he sees the world. Cody also has become increasingly unperceptive about life in general. As Ginsberg says in his notes to the book, part of their problem was that with Cody married and with two children, he and Duluoz simply did not have any-

thing to do together. "The Imitation of the Tape" is meant to be a tribute to Cody that is more complete than *On the Road,* but it is also meant to purge Cassady from the pages of Kerouac's future books.

Kerouac tries on all kinds of styles in this section and adopts dozens of voices. He adopts Cody's voice and even his thoughts. There are whole sections written in the style of Shakespeare, for at the time Kerouac, Neal, and Carolyn liked to perform Shakespeare's plays in the living room at night. The stream of consciousness that runs throughout led Kerouac to question if "in the morning, if there is a way of abstracting the interesting paragraphs of material in all this running consciousness stream that can be used as the progressing lightning chapters of a great essay about the wonders of the world as it continually flashes up in retrospect." He even reverts to the style of *The Town and the City* for a while and imitates his own voice in *On the Road.*

A major influence on the style of *Visions of Cody* is jazz. Kerouac always wanted to write a jazz novel, and parts of *Visions of Cody* are as close to jazz as he ever came. Says Duluoz parenthetically, "this is all like bop, we're getting to it indirectly and too late but completely from every angle except the angle we all don't know." As is true of the solos of the great jazz musicians whom Kerouac and Cassady admired, Kerouac never repeats himself even when writing the same story. He often repeats stories from *On the Road,* but they are told differently, leading the thorough reader of Kerouac to the conclusion that he truly could have spontaneously written these books in any number of ways, all of them successful "solos."

Part of *Visions of Cody* corresponds to *On the Road* when Sal Paradise (based on Kerouac) stays in Denver in spring/summer 1949. The Denver gang is all elsewhere, so, left on his own, he visits Cody's old haunts and walks through Denver's African-American neighborhoods, wishing he were a "Negro." Kerouac has been accused of romanticizing African-Americans in this passage in *On the Road;* however, in *Visions of Cody,* he interviews "one poor Negro soldier" about "Denver niggertown," and when the soldier does not know about it or will not tell him, Duluoz shows self-awareness by realizing that the soldier could not possibly be "involved in a white man's preoccupation about what colored life must be." The *Visions of Cody* version is also notable for its inclusion of a section on Robert Giroux (the "mysterious Boisvert") in Denver. Giroux, Kerouac's editor on *The Town and the City*, was attracted to Kerouac and followed him to Denver, but Kerouac was ultimately depressed by Giroux's "successful young executive" mentality.

Visions of Cody also describes Duluoz, Cody, and Joanna Dawson's (based on LuAnne Henderson) on the road trip through the deserts of West Texas in 1949. Kerouac describes Marylou (based on Henderson) in *On the Road* applying cold cream to Sal and Dean's naked bodies as they drove. He is much more explicit in *Cody*: Joanna "applied cold cream to our organs." Henderson's far less erotic account (she says they had no cold cream although she would have loved to have some lotion in the dry heat) can be found in her interview with Barry Gifford and Lawrence Lee in *Jack's Book: An Oral Biography of Jack Kerouac* (1978). The ménage à trois suggested by Cassady is covered in *On the Road*.

Another passage that corresponds to a section of *On the Road* involves Cassady and a homosexual. In *On the Road* Dean tricks the homosexual into giving him money for sexual favors, which he promises but on which he reneges. In *Visions of Cody*, Duluoz cowers in a motel bathroom as Cody performs "slambanging big sodomies that made me sick"—and the homosexual never gives Cody his money. In his notes to *Visions of Cody*, Ginsberg asserts that Kerouac would have been a lot happier if he had simply joined the sex party.

Visions of Cody, just as *On the Road*, describes a version of Kerouac and Cassady's destruction of a Cadillac by driving it from Denver to Chicago in 17 hours. In *On the Road*, Kerouac leaves out a side trip that the two made to Detroit, where Kerouac tried to revive his relationship with his first wife, Edie Parker. She sends him away curtly. In *Visions of Cody*, Kerouac also describes Cassady's first meeting with Diana Hansen in New York: "She was a raving fucking beauty the first moment we saw her walk in."

The section "Joan Rawshanks in the Fog" is one of Kerouac's most popular and most frequently anthologized pieces. While living with Neal and Carolyn in San Francisco in winter 1952, he took a walk one night, and just a few blocks from the Cassady's apartment he encountered a Hollywood crew shooting a Joan Crawford film called *Sudden Fear*. He rushed back to the Cassadys to tell them, but they were not impressed, and Kerouac went back alone with his notebook. Kerouac's description of the Hollywood shoot needs to be seen in the context of his theory of spontaneous art. The "vastly planned action" of the scene that Crawford repeatedly rehearses is the opposite of how Kerouac believes that the best art is created. "Blow, baby, blow!" he says he yelled at Crawford, urging her to cut loose with an unrehearsed moment of true living in the same way that a jazz artist "blows" a solo or that a writer such as Kerouac "blows" long, spontaneously written works such as "Joan Rawshanks in the Fog." He says "the movies have nothing now but great technique to show," a comment that could apply equally well to technically proficient fiction and poetry of the type that are valued by most of the critics of his age. By contrast, the kind of film that he loves reflects the "wild form" that he told JOHN CLELLON HOLMES he was seeking in fiction. The Three Stooges captured that wild form early in their career, he says, but in their "baroque period" they were repeating themselves, a falling-off in inspiration that was reflected in the more violent style of the later Stooge films. Similarly, Crawford's faking of emotion contrasts greatly with the self-consciousness of Cody, who dislikes telling stories that he has told before because he remembers the way he told it and thus has lost his fresh perspective. Through passages such as "Joan Rawshanks in the Fog," Kerouac reveals that his ideas about spontaneous writing are not just about technique but embody an entire philosophy of life.

In both *Visions of Cody* and *On the Road*, Kerouac describes the characters that are based on Cassady as having simply talked themselves out. In *Visions of Cody*, not only has Cody talked himself out but also Kerouac apparently has finally written himself out about Cassady. His next book, DOCTOR SAX (which begins to surface in several references at the end of *Visions of Cody*), will be his most personal book, one about the imaginary, mythic landscape of his childhood.

Bibliography
Gifford, Barry and Lawrence Lee. *Jack's Book: An Oral Biography of Jack Kerouac.* New York: St. Martin's Press, 1978.
Hunt, Tim. *Kerouac's Crooked Road: The Development of a Fiction.* Hamden, Conn.: Archon Books, 1981.

Rob Johnson

Visions of Gerard Jack Kerouac (1963)

This is chronologically the first novel in JACK KEROUAC's fictionalized autobiography, "The Duluoz Legend." It takes place between 1922 and 1926, the first four years of Kerouac's life, and recounts his memories of his brother Gerard. In 1926 Kerouac's brother Gerard died at the age of nine after two years of suffering from rheumatic fever. Charles E. Jarvis writes, "Though Kerouac, in his 'on the road' existence, met many meaningful people, the most significant relationship of his life was with his brother, Gerard." Other scholars debate whether or not Kerouac's *relationship* with Gerard was the most significant, but few doubt that his romanticization of this relationship was not central to his understanding of himself. Kerouac wrote *Visions of Gerard* in early 1956 while staying at his sister's home in Rocky Mount, North Carolina. He had just returned from the West Coast where he had met fellow Buddhists GARY SNYDER and PHILIP WHALEN and witnessed the birth of the San Francisco Poetry Renaissance. He had also seen death: Natalie Jackson's suicide abruptly ended a season of camaraderie among the Beats. After hitchhiking back to North Carolina, Kerouac arrived just as his mother received the news that her stepmother had died. She left to attend the funeral, and Kerouac's sister's family also left for vacation in Florida. These two deaths may well have sent Kerouac back to the memories of his brother's death as he sat alone in the Rocky Mountain cabin and wrote for 15 days, using Benzedrine and smoking marijuana. Ellis Amburn writes, "Tightly focused on the final year of Gerard's life, 1925, and drawn from nothing but dim, dewy memories of Jack's fourth year, Mémère's [his mother's] stories, and a few old letters of Leo's [his father's], *Visions of Gerard* would probably never have been written had Mémère not

gone to New York to attend a funeral. . . . With its jewel-like clarity and sure, unimpeded narrative line, *Visions of Gerard* is as pure and distilled as Hemingway's *The Old Man and the Sea*. . . . [Kerouac] achieved in *Gerard* a kind of requiem mass in novel form, and often called it his favorite work."

The style of the book is "windblown and Shakespearian," says Kerouac in a letter to CAROLYN CASSADY: "Enough to make Shakespeare raise an eyebrow." In fact, he had been reading *Henry V* just before writing the book, but there are also echoes of *Hamlet, Macbeth,* and *King Lear* and probably numerous other Shakespeare borrowings in the book. Still, Shakespeare's influence is not as profound as the influence that Buddhist thought was exerting on Kerouac at this time. His experiences in San Francisco had sharpened his already keen understanding of Buddhist thought; he had completed writing the fascinating spiritual autobiography SOME OF THE DHARMA and at Gary Snyder's suggestion had written his own sutra, *The Scripture of the Golden Eternity.* Now as he faced his brother's death, he projected Buddhist thought onto the "saint" Gerard. In fact Gerard comes to stand in a line of holy men who learn from suffering that suffering is caused by craving for life and that we can end suffering by realizing that life is an illusion and that eternal happiness is already before us. The book thus demonstrates through the life and death of Gerard the first three of the Four Noble Truths of Buddha: All life is sorrowful, the cause of suffering is ignorant craving, and the suppression of suffering can be achieved. Recalling this family tragedy puts Kerouac's Buddhist belief that "all is illusion" to the test. Among others, Malcolm Cowley felt that the Buddhism in the book jarred with the Catholic, French-Canadian background of the novel, and at one point, Kerouac even agreed to change all of the Buddhist references to Catholic ones (he evidently saw them as basically interchangeable).

The publication of Kerouac's letters in 1995 revealed a fascinating record of Kerouac's first attempts at writing about his brother. In a December 28, 1950, letter to NEAL CASSADY, which Kerouac calls a "full confession of my life," Kerouac tells him that he cannot understand his life story unless he knows that his brother Gerard had, literally, been a saint—"and that explains all." He recounts the hagiographic stories of Gerard and the birds and of Gerard and the mouse. He also explores the resentment that he felt for his brother, who, as an invalid, received much more attention than young Kerouac did. A key scene in this letter and in *Visions of Gerard* takes place when Gerard slaps his young brother for knocking over a giant ferris wheel that he had constructed with his erector set. Later, undergoing amateur psychoanalysis with WILLIAM S. BURROUGHS, Kerouac revealed that he continued to hold a grudge against his brother for this offense and also felt guilt because of the happiness that he felt when his brother died. The letter also reveals that Kerouac's pre-Buddhist thoughts about his brother and post-Buddhist writing of the novel about him are essentially in line.

Gerard shows uncommon tenderness for animals and for less-fortunate children, bringing one boy home for supper because he knew that he was hungry. Gerard's frail health allowed him to instinctively know that, above all, one must "Practice Kindness"—the central precept of Buddhism but also key in Christian thought, as well. Through Gerard, Kerouac sees that the world is an illusion and a dream that is already over. Kerouac writes that Gerard finds a mouse in a trap, brings it home, and bandages its wounded leg. Unfortunately, the Kerouacs' cat has less sympathy for the wounded mouse and eats it. Gerard, in great seriousness, lectures the cat, saying, "We'll never go to heaven if we go on eating each other and destroying each other." The incident must be understood in light of the first directive of Buddhism, "Cause the least harm." Kerouac's mother told the story of Gerard and the cat many times, recalling the speech that the boy made to the cat in fond detail. Kerouac creates a similar scene of compassion for a mouse in *The DHARMA BUMS* and *DESOLATION ANGELS*. Gerard's saintliness is also revealed in the fact that birds come to the windowsill of his sick room. Still, he despairs that they will not sit in his hands because they know that little boys kill birds sometimes. Gerard cannot comprehend a God who made human beings who are mean. Kerouac's fictionalization of his brother's inner life turns Gerard into a young Buddha. Asks the narrator, "[W]ho will be the human being who will ever be able to deliver the world from its idea of itself that it actually exists in this crystal ball of the mind? One meek little Gerard. . . ." Yet the book is not straightforward hagiography. Even Gerard sins. At confession, Gerard admits to pushing a boy who knocked down a card house that he had built, to looking at another boy's penis as they stood at the urinal, and to lying about having studied a Bible lesson even though he already knew the lesson from previous study. Kerouac also does not dwell exclusively on Gerard's sufferings and says that he has his "holidays." When Gerard falls asleep at school, he dreams that he sees the Virgin Mary who tells him that they have been looking for him and then transports him to heaven. Before he can see heaven in any detail, a nun awakens him. He describes his dream to the nun and to his classmates, and they are deeply impressed. His message to them is similar to Kerouac's belief, at times, that we are always in heaven already but do not know it. Gerard often sounds like Kerouac in this novel. Gerard thinks to himself, "And me, big nut, I can't explain what they're dying to know." Eventually, Kerouac thinks that his mother must undoubtedly love the saintlike Gerard more than she loves him.

Though Gerard is the principal character in the book, his father, Emil, takes second place of importance. Emil has business and health problems and must also endure watching his firstborn slowly die. Kerouac must acknowledge that the realities of making a living and of backbreaking work are quite real. Emil is portrayed as capable of being a "tragic philosopher," and this quality of mind links him to Gerard. Emil escapes from the death watch in his home on the pretext that he has extra work to do with his assistant Manuel. The two men hit the road in Manuel's sidecar motorcycle and end up playing cards with some old vaudevillians in downtown Lowell. Legend has it in the Kerouac family that Leo Kerouac met W. C. Fields a time or two and that they played poker together. Fields is a key father figure for the Beats. Here, under the name Old Bull Balloon, he is, as JOHN CLELLON HOLMES called him, his generation's Dutch Uncle, but Old Bull is also something of a Buddha figure as well. After he and Emil get drunk, Bull reflects Kerouac's Buddhist philosophy by saying, "It's a dream, lads, it's a dream." The book runs the hardest reality—Gerard's impending death—up against Buddhism's "all is illusion" and tests the spiritual comfort that is (or is not) provided by such a view. The drunken, darkly comic philosophizing of Emil and Bull reflects Shakespeare's influence on Kerouac at this time.

The scene shifts from the pool hall to the death room of Gerard, who is entering his last days. Kerouac declares the subject of his book: "death is the only decent subject, since it marks the end of illusion and delusion." Gerard instinctively knows the illusion of reality and practices "nothing." He advises Ti Jean to be kind and says that when he struck him the other morning, he did not know what he was doing. The four-year-old Ti Jean, Kerouac, cannot understand the grief that was going on around him and even makes fun of his uncle's hysterical crying. Gerard dies, and the nuns take down his secret last words, whispered to them. Ti Jean continues to act perversely in the face of death and runs excitedly down the street to tell his father that "Gerard est mort!" What he wants to tell his father is that he believes that Gerard will return, stronger than ever. Before the funeral, while the body is in view, he has a vision that all of the grief which he witnesses exists only in the mind. At the house, where relative and friends gather, he tries to communicate this as well as a four year old can, but he is sent upstairs because he is acting too "gleeful." Gerard's death, Kerouac says, marks the beginning of his ambition to be a writer. All that he has written, he says, he has done in his memory and in an attempt to explain Gerard's saintliness. The formal funeral attracts lines of curious schoolchildren and a host of nuns and priests who believe that Gerard was a saint. Kerouac undercuts the solemnity with his version of Shakespeare's comic gravediggers, a painter and a plasterer, who speculate callously on the identity of the corpse. Individual readers will have to decide how much solace Kerouac's Buddhism actually provided him in the remembering of this story, for he does not end the book on any note of glory.

Kerouac thought that this book may well have been his best, and he expressed this in letters to Snyder and Carolyn Cassady. The critics disagreed. When the book was finally published seven years after it was written, they lambasted Kerouac for writing what they thought was a lachrymose book that tugged at the heartstrings of the reader—in other words, a cheaply emotional, sentimental book. Kerouac was reportedly more distressed with these negative reviews than with any other reviews that he received in his career.

Bibliography

Amburn, Ellis. *Subterranean Kerouac: The Hidden Life of Jack Kerouac.* New York: St. Martin's Press, 1998.

Jarvis, Charles E. *Visions of Kerouac: A Biography.* Lowell, Mass.: Ithaca Press, 1974.

Rob Johnson

W

Waldman, Anne (1945–)

Anne Waldman is a third-generation Beat poet whose affiliations with the New York School and the 1960s radical causes exemplify the hybrid postmodern political and artistic legacies of Beat-movement culture and aesthetics. Encompassing diverse literary schools and eras in her work, Waldman cites ALLEN GINSBERG, GREGORY CORSO, and WILLIAM S. BURROUGHS as early influences, draws from Sappho, Gertrude Stein, and the Mazatec shamaness Maria Sabina, and produces list-chant poems, Poundian epics, and slam poetry. Waldman's aesthetic advocates both personal expression and political activism, and she has frequently collaborated with writers, musicians, and dancers in works that were created to be performed. She is the author of more than a dozen works, including *Giant Night* (1968); *Baby Breakdown* (1970); *FAST SPEAKING WOMAN* (1975); *Journals & Dreams* (1976); *Talking Naropa Poetics*, volumes I and II (1978); *Helping the Dreamer: New and Selected Poems, 1966–1988* (1989); *Out of This World: An Anthology of the St. Mark's Poetry Project, 1966–1991* (1991); *Kill or Cure* (1994); *The Beat Book: Poems & Fiction from the Beat Generation* (1996); *IOVIS, volumes I and II* (1993, 1997); *Vow to Poetry: Essays, Interviews & Manifestos* (2001); *The Angel Hair Anthology* (with Lewis Warsh, 2002); and *In the Room of Never Grieve: New and Selected Poems, 1985–2003* (2003).

Waldman was born in 1945 in Millville, New Jersey, grew up in Greenwich Village, and graduated from Bennington College in 1966, where she was influenced by Howard Nemerov, Bernard Malamud, and Stanley Edgar Hyman. She wrote her senior thesis on Theodore Roethke and edited the literary magazine *Silo*. She met the poet Lewis Warsh, with whom she founded the literary journal and press *Angel Hair*, at Robert Duncan's reading at the 1965 Berkeley Poetry Conference. The conference was a powerful germinating experience for Waldman, who credits CHARLES OLSON's wrenching extemporaneous performance with galvanizing her to dynamic public readings of her work, for which she is renowned. Waldman became involved in grassroots poetry efforts throughout the late 1960s and early 1970s, fraternizing with Ted Berrigan, ED SANDERS, and Ron Padget in the Lower East Side community of younger New York poets. Waldman met Frank O'Hara before he died in 1966, and he famously welcomed her to poetry. She also met Ginsberg in Berkeley that year and became his protégée through a "mutual connection to dharma and politics," as she says. She has been acclaimed for her offices as director of the Poetry Project at St. Mark's Church in the Bowery from 1968 to 1977 and, since 1975, as founder and director (until his death in 1997 with Allen Ginsberg) of the Jack Kerouac School of Disembodied Poetics at Naropa Institute (now Naropa University) in Boulder, Colorado. A high-profile countercultural presence, Waldman was poet-in-residence on Bob Dylan's legendary Rolling Thunder Review tour of 1975–76. She participated in the antiwar movement of the 1960s and, through her poetry and activism, has been an outspoken opponent of nuclear energy, helping to close Colorado's Rocky Flats power plant. As spoken-word poetry has become more prominent in the last decades, Waldman has been part of this movement, too, which is an obvious extension of her performance-based work, and she has won twice the Taos (New Mexico) Poetry Circus slam.

Waldman brings to the Beat Generation's antiestablishment impulses the challenges and the resistances of second-wave feminism. She embodies Buddhist spirituality and Beat's spontaneous confessional poetics, cut-up methods of composition, and penchant for oration and public performance. But she contributes a woman-centered sensibility to the Beat and New York school movements, consciously taking the works of women poets as models—among Beat movement writers she acknowledges DIANE DI PRIMA, JOANNE KYGER, and LENORE KANDEL—and enacting a belief that, in spite of signs to the contrary, manifestations of feminine energy can be felt in contemporary culture. Her seminal Beat-indebted work, the long list poem "Fast Speaking Woman," was published in 1975 by City Lights Books in *Fast Speaking Woman: Chants and Essays* (number 33 of the Pocket Poet Series) and came out in a revised edition in 1996. It takes as its central subject the elucidation and expression of female energy and identity.

Waldman's masterwork, *Iovis*, published in two volumes with a third in progress, turns from Beat poetics to the use of multiple voices and typographies that are more typically associated with late high modernist and full-blown postmodern texts. Although the look and substance of the epic seem to deviate from Beat-movement writing, the poet fills the numerous texts of *Iovis* with political and poetic concerns that are continuous with those of her earlier works. *Iovis* in some instances seems destined to be sung/performed, as in Waldman's homage to John Cage; it demands action, as in the numerous unanswered letters that were sent to the poet and which she uses; it self-reflexively and self-consciously erects and performs the consciousness that it calls "poet." In contrast, charting an alternative poetics direction, Waldman produced *Marriage: A Sentence* (2000), which she "conceived of as a 'serial' poem under one rubric" and whose touchstones are Stein, Corso, and Denise Levertov,

Anne Waldman reading her work at the Allen Ginsberg Memorial in Los Angeles, 1997. *(courtesy of Larry Keenan)*

with shamanic references drawn from Mircea Eliade. This work is erudite, provocative, and formally innovative and is based on the traditional form of the *haibun* in which a proselike poem is coupled with a condensed lyric poem of the same theme, an experimental rendering that departs from the improvisational conventions of the epic *Iovis*.

Waldman is a national and international literary influence; she teaches in Boulder, Europe, and Asia and gives readings widely. In 2002 her archive was housed at the University of Michigan in Ann Arbor and honored with a convocation. Recently she resumed residence in New York City, site of her first poetry community and salon.

Bibliography
Buschendorf, Christa. "Gods and Heroes Revised: Mythological Concepts of Masculinity in Contemporary

Women's Poetry" *Amerikastudien/American Studies* 43. 4 (1998).

Johnson, Ronna C., and Nancy M. Grace. "Fast Speaking Woman: Anne Waldman." In *Breaking the Rule of Cool: Interviewing and Reading Women Beat Writers*, edited by Nancy M. Grace and Ronna C. Johnson, 255–281. Jackson: University Press of Mississippi, 2004.

McNeil, Helen. "The Archaeology of Gender in the Beat Movement." *The Beat Generation Writers.* Edited by A. Robert Lee, 178–99. East Haven, Conn.: Pluto Press, 1996.

Puchek, Peter. "From Revolution to Creation: Beat Desire and Body Poetics in Anne Waldman's Poetry." In *Girls Who Wore Black: Women Writing the Beat Generation*, edited by Ronna C. Johnson and Nancy M. Grace, 227–250. New Brunswick, N.J.: Rutgers University Press, 2002.

Talisman: Anne Waldman Issue. 13 (Fall 1994/Winter 1995).

Ronna C. Johnson

weiss, ruth (1928–   )

The outcast and the alien are concepts that are long associated with the Beat Generation, but perhaps no one exemplifies these tropes as dramatically as Berlin-born poet ruth weiss. She was an only child of Jewish parents: her father, Oscar Weiss, was a night editor for the Wolfburo news agency and of Hungarian decent; her mother Fani Zlata Weiss was a homemaker whose family was Yugoslavian. By the time weiss was 10, the family had moved to Vienna where she attended a Jewish elementary school. The family's efforts to escape the repression of Adolf Hitler's regime failed at that point, however, when weiss and other Jewish children were brutally expelled from their school. Her father was imprisoned for two weeks. After his release and fearing for their lives, the Weiss family fled Austria in December 1938, taking a train to Holland where they boarded the ship *Westerland* which ferried them to safety in the United States in 1939. Many of weiss's poems return to memories of these traumatic childhood experiences. As a survivor of the Holocaust, she later registered her antipathy for Nazi totalitarianism by rejecting the conventions of her native language, electing in the 1960s to spell her name in all lower case. This was not her only form of rebellion, however, as she soon mapped out a life devoted to art, self-definition, and cosmic liberation.

During the war, New York City, Iowa City, and Chicago became sites of refuge for the Weisses, her father supporting the family as a bookkeeper and her mother as a seamstress in various sweatshops. After they moved to Chicago, Oscar and Fani enrolled ruth in a private Catholic high school in Chicago, from which she graduated in 1942. To this day, weiss credits Sister Eulogia, one of the teachers at the school, for encouraging her to write. By 1946 her parents had returned to Europe to work as Americans with the occupation forces. weiss attended school in Switzerland, but she has said that she spent much of this time hitchhiking across Europe, where she had no difficulty finding safe rides from American soldiers: "I wore my saddle shoes and jeans, and they knew I was American." In 1948 she returned to Chicago with her parents.

By that time, weiss had set out to find an environment in which she could evolve as a writer. Whether riding the "L" in Chicago, where she lived in the Art Circle, or sitting in a jazz club, weiss made time to write poetry, a vocation that she had practiced since penning her first poem at age five. She supported herself by working as a dice girl, a waitress, and a nude model. She tried living in New York City and New Orleans as well, but it was not until 1952, when she hitched from Chicago to San Francisco, that she began to establish more permanent roots. After learning that weiss was a poet, her ride decided that bohemian North Beach was where she belonged, dropping her off at the heart of Broadway and Columbus.

weiss quickly settled into the area's avant-garde poetry and arts scene, introducing jazz–poetry readings at The Cellar in 1956, a blending of the two art forms that she had pursued since her Art Circle days in Chicago. Never aligning herself with any single art coterie, weiss says that she was more like a hummingbird, skipping and hopping from one group to another. She attended a few of KENNETH REXROTH's evening salons; met Scottish poet Helen Adam; was a close friend of painter Wallace Berman and poet Madeline Gleason; associated with LAWRENCE FERLINGHETTI, JACK MICHELINE, and PHILIP LAMANTIA; worked for musicians Jack Minger, Wil Carlson, and Sonny Wayne (now Sonny Nelson) at The Cellar; and married Mel Weitsman, a Zen priest. She also knew JACK KEROUAC, with whom she has said she wrote haiku in the 1950s.

Despite the connection to Kerouac in those early years, weiss never associated herself specifically with the Beat Generation or with pseudo-artists known as beatniks—"that was a very bad word," she later recalled. "Really, an insult." But in true Beat fashion, she made her own way as an artist, unencumbered by conventional boundaries. She would read on the streets and in bars, doing whatever she could to write poetry and plays, make films, and paint.

weiss published her first collection of poems, *Steps,* in 1958 and her second collection, *Gallery of Women,* in 1959. The latter, a small but elegant assemblage of short poems, showcases weiss's gratitude to female friends and feminist pioneers. In 1961 weiss became screenplay writer and director for a film version of her long poem "The Brink." The black-and-white film, featuring a "he" and "she" who wonder whimsically around San Francicso, draws upon spontaneity, improvisation, and found objects—an unintentional yet effective West Coast partner for the Robert Frank/Albert Leslie Beat film *Pull My Daisy* which was set in New York City.

weiss has remained a prolific writer and performer, not only in California but also in Europe. She has produced seven plays and numerous poem–prints, performed in at least a half-dozen films by Steven Arnold, been published in more than 150 magazines and anthologies, and written 10 books. Since 1998 she has returned to Vienna several times to perform. The North Beach Chamber of Commerce also presented her with its Community Enrichment Award in 1999 for her "lifetime of dedication and commitment to the muses of poetry and jazz."

Selections from her collected works were published as *A NEW VIEW OF MATTER,* a Czech-English edition by Mata Press in 1999. Her most recent work, *full circle,* is a German-English edition that includes a touching memoir of weiss's early years in Austria and the United States; it

was brought out in 2002 by the Austrian publisher Edition Exil. The most comprehensive collection of her work is housed in the Bancroft Library, the University of California, Berkeley.

Bibliography

Grace, Nancy M. "Single Out: ruth weiss." In *Breaking the Rule of Cool: Interviewing and Reading Women Beat Writers,* edited by Nancy M. Grace and Ronna C. Johnson, 55–80. Jackson: University Press of Mississippi, 2004.

Knight, Brenda. "ruth weiss: The Survivor." In *Women of the Beat Generation: The Writers, Artists and Muses at the Heart of a Revolution.* Berkeley: Conari Press, 1996, 241–256.

weiss, ruth. *The Brink.* 1961 16mm film. 1986 videocassette. San Francisco, Calif.

Nancy M. Grace

Welch, Lew (1926–1971)

A writer who successfully bridged the Beat era of the 1950s and the San Francisco youth counterculture of the late 1960s, Lew Welch left behind a body of work that is among the most precise and beautifully crafted of any poet of his generation.

Born in 1926 in Phoenix, Arizona, to an intelligent, often overbearing mother and a free-spirited, often absent father, Welch's childhood was marked by a sense of alienation and detachment. He moved frequently, spending much of his youth in several small towns along the California coastline where he was raised by his mother following his parents' divorce. After a brief term in the army air corps at the end of World War II, he took advantage of the G.I. Bill and enrolled in college, first at Stockton Junior College in California and in 1948 as an English major at Reed College in Portland, Oregon.

At Reed, he met and roomed with fellow students GARY SNYDER and PHILIP WHALEN. The three shared common interests in poetry and Eastern spirituality and formed a lasting friendship that played a significant role in the development of the West Coast Beat movement. While at Reed, Welch published his first poems in the school literary magazine, *Janus,* and along with Snyder and

The last gathering of Beat poets and artists, City Lights Books, North Beach, San Francisco, 1965. Photographer Larry Keenan: "Lawrence Ferlinghetti wanted to document the 1965 Beat scene in San Francisco in the spirit of the early 20th century classic photographs of the Bohemian artists and writers in Paris. The Beats, front row, left to right: Robert LaVigne, Shig Murao, Larry Fagin, Leland Meyezove (lying down), Lew Welch, Peter Orlovsky. Second row: David Meltzer, Michael McClure, Allen Ginsberg, Daniel Langton, Steve (friend of Ginsberg), Richard Brautigan, Gary Goodrow, Nemi Frost. Back row: Stella Levy, Lawrence Ferlinghetti. Because this is a vertical image about half of the Beats attending are not shown." *(courtesy of Larry Keenan)*

Whalen, he hosted a campus visit by poet William Carlos Williams. The elder poet encouraged Welch to publish his B.A. thesis on the work of Gertrude Stein and to continue to follow his ambitions as a poet.

The years after Welch's graduation from college provided the grist for much of the discontent with urban America that would figure so prominently in the poet's mature work. In the mid-1950s, as the West Coast was in the midst of a literary renaissance, he moved to Chicago, married, and worked as an advertising writer. (Welch is credited with writing the famous slogan "Raid Kills Bugs Dead.") He found the job, the marriage, and the city (which he called a "pitiless, unparalleled monstrocity [sic]") unbearable, a situation that he later captured in one of his finest works, "CHICAGO POEM" (1958).

By 1957 Welch returned to San Francisco where he worked at numerous part time jobs—cab driver, longshoreman, commercial fisherman—to support his career as a writer. He began a serious but short-lived course of Buddhist study with Snyder, and many of his poems from the late 1950s, including his powerful Pacific coast meditation "Wobbly Rock" (1960), draw heavily from Buddhist imagery. He published several small collections of poems in the 1960s, writing with clarity, precision, and an ear for American speech that sometimes escaped his colleagues in the Beat movement. The finest of these small collections, *Hermit Poems* (1965) chronicles his solitary withdrawal into the California foothills in the early 1960s. During the heyday of the San Francisco counterculture in the late 1960s, Welch was affiliated with members of the Digger commune, an experience that is reflected in many of his later poems and essays.

Despite growing success and recognition as a poet in the late 1960s, Welch was plagued by a battle with alcohol, and on May 23, 1971, he left behind a cryptic suicide note and wandered into the California foothills, carrying a gun. His body has never been found. His volume of collected poems, *Ring of Bone*, was published in 1973.

Bibliography

Meltzer, David. "Interview with Lew Welch." *San Francisco Beat: Talking with the Poets.* San Francisco: City Lights Books, 2001, 294–324.

Phillips, Rod. *"Forest Beatniks" and "Urban Thoreaus": Jack Kerouac, Gary Snyder, Lew Welch, and Michael McClure.* New York: Peter Lang, 2000.

Saroyan, Aram. *Genesis Angels: The Saga of Lew Welch and the Beat Generation.* New York: Morrow, 1979.

Rod Phillips

Western Lands, The William S. Burroughs
(1987)

The Western Lands is the final volume of WILLIAM S. BURROUGHS's cut-up trilogy that also includes *CITIES OF THE RED NIGHT* (1981) and *The PLACE OF DEAD ROADS* (1984). In his acknowledgments, he credits Norman Mailer's *Ancient Evenings* (1983) for "inspiration." Burroughs must have been excited to discover in Mailer's book a cosmology that was so close to his own personal mythology, for through Mailer's description of Egyptian myth and ritual, Burroughs was able to recast his previous work in a new and vital form. There must not only have been recognition here but also validation, and Burroughs takes some pains to show the ways in which his own ideas from the past 40 years of writing find their counterparts in the knowledge of the ancients.

In Egyptian mythology the Western Lands is where the soul lives on after death. The old writer who was introduced at the beginning of the novel "sets out to write his way out of death"—a strategy that Burroughs adopted quite consciously after the tragedy of his wife Joan's death in 1951. In his research on death, he learns (in Mailer's *Ancient Evenings*) that the Egyptians believed that there were seven souls and that each soul is personified. These personifications, it turns out, closely resemble the sci-fi cosmology that Burroughs had created on his own. For example, the first soul (Ren) is very much like Burroughs's "Director," the second soul (Sekem) the Director's sometimes recalcitrant "Technician," and so on. The body corresponds to Burroughs's favorite disaster metaphor—the sinking ship—and souls are deserting the ship as they leave the body. In this they resemble the "Italian steward who put on women's clothes and so filched a seat in a lifeboat" in Burroughs's various retellings of the sinking of the *Titanic* and the *Morro Castle* (such as "Twilight's Last Gleaming"). The "Venusian invasion" of Burroughs's mythology is "a takeover of the souls." The ultimate killer of souls, says Burroughs, will be the radiation from atomic blasts, for souls (following the findings of Wilhelm Reich) are seen "as electromagnetic." That is the real destructive power of the bomb, and it has been created as a "Soul killer" to keep a glut of souls out of the Western Lands.

The explanation of the seven souls provides a map of the book. In the opening storyline, Burroughs searches for an identity for his main character, starting out with Carl Peterson and then switching to Kim Carsons. The setting is Berlin in the postwar period, where Kim becomes involved with an underground group known as Margaras Unlimited, "a secret service without a country," that specializes in disrupting the plans of the victor nations and wealthy ex-Nazis. Their agenda is space exploration, inner and outer, and "expanding awareness." Anything that goes against such development "we will extirpate." Margaras Unlimited, then, closely resembles the Articulated of *Cities of the Read Night* and the Johnson Family of *The Place of Dead Roads*.

Burroughs introduces a new character, Joe the Dead, who, it turns out, was the gunman who shot Kim Carsons and Mike Chase at the end of *The Place of Dead Roads*. Joe is a Technician, the second soul. He killed Mike Chase and Kim Carsons because both were responsible, directly and indirectly, for the death of photographer Tom Dark, one of Joe's fellow guild members. He personally disliked Kim because he is an "arty type, no principle" and also because of Kim's fascination with "antiquated weaponry." Mike Chase was going to be president, which would have been a disaster. Joe the Dead is a member of a select group that is known as Natural Outlaws and is dedicated to breaking the laws of science. Joe specializes in breaking the laws of evolutionary biology: first, that only closely related species may produce hybrids and, second, that mutations are irreversible. He is also an eco-warrior who is fighting the destruction of the rainforest. In all respects, then, he is an updated, 20th-century version of Kim and the Johnsons.

Nerferti, an Egyptian scribe, is introduced as a character who is supposed to bring "drastic change," to the world. His writings, however, "are shot down by enemy critics backed by computerized thought control." The world of the book is a magical one, and Neferti practices black magic to kill Julian Chandler (based on Anatole Broyard, who savaged *The Place of Dead Roads*), a book reviewer for the *New York Times* who has "chosen for his professional rancor the so-called Beat Movement." Chandler earns his death by penning a caustic review of William Hall's *The Place of Dead Roads* (Neferti is apparently Hall). See and Prick, two goons who work for Big Picture (a plan to evacuate the select few before nova conditions set in), are also killed by magic. The cause of their death is traced back to 1959 (the year of *NAKED LUNCH*'s publication) and to William Seward Hall, "the writer, of course." The antiwriter in the book is Joe the Dead, who criticizes Kim for "irresponsible faggotry" by his "re-writes of history"—a critique of the two previous novels that holds up better than Chandler's insubstantial charges against Hall. After killing Kim, Joe goes into deep freeze for 50 years and wakes up rich from his investments. Joe, the biological outlaw, now practices magic against the medical community. He studies Reich's theories on cancer and the "retarded medical profession" that persecutes him. Hall reads the doctor's books and sees his "Doctor Benway shine forth as a model of responsibility and competence by comparison." Joe causes medical riots in 1999 by leaking information on cancer cures that were withheld by the medical establishment.

Kim returns to the novel and is "seen" in Mexico. He is apparently not dead. A little green man (later identified as the Aztec deity Ah Pook) leads him to a riverbank where they get into canoes. He will be Kim's guide in the streets of Centipede City where Kim is sent by Dimitri, the District Supervisor, on another "impossible" mission—to find out why the Western Lands were created and why they had become "bogged down" in mummies. The actual voyage to the Centipede City takes place in a dream that Kim has of Neferti. Neferti manages to break the code of the "centipede cult," and the "ancient writing" in the Mayan codex "crumbles to dust."

Neferti's knowledge of these secrets is explained. He is a scribe who fulfills Burroughs's dream as a writer—to be able to write directly in images. He is caught in an ongoing war between two religious factions, one of which worships many gods in a magical universe, the other of which is forcing the concept of One God. The One-God Universe is a "prerecorded universe" of "friction and conflict, pain, fear, sickness, famine, war, old age and Death." The Magical Universe is one of many gods who are often in conflict, so there is no paradox of an all-knowing God "who permits suffering, death." The beginning of the pilgrimage to the Western Lands is a spiritual awakening that results from the knowledge that we live in the dead, soulless universe of the One God. Neferti steals the Western Land papyrus; comically, our modern knowledge of the scrolls comes initially from *National Enquirer* stories: "Ancient Egyptian Papyrus Demonstrates That Life After Death Is Within The Reach of Everyman." The pharaohs are uproarious because of the ensuing "glut" of souls in the Western Lands.

The book takes on the form of a spiritual allegory, a pilgrim's progress/Canterbury tale on the road to the afterlife. The Great Awakening provides the blueprint for the dangerous journey—"by definition the most dangerous road in the world." Travelers first are outfitted in Waghdas, the ancient city of knowledge but also a stand-in for Burroughs's hometown of St. Louis. The road is beset by con men of every conceivable stripe and often wanders off in labyrinthine detours. Neferti is guided by a beautiful Breather (whose breath can bring both death and delight) across the Duad—"a river of excrement, one of the deadliest obstacles on the road to the Western Lands." This river represents the fatal dualism of Western thought and also the duality of the sexes, which prevents entry into the Western Lands. Neferti tells the young scribes that he can offer them freedom from "all this mummy shit." The error of the pharaohs is that they based immortality on the physical body (mummies) and built their heaven on that principle. Nerferti argues that we can create a Western Land that is made of dreams, just as artists live by thought and creativity.

Several examples of how Burroughs's previous work "fits" into the Egyptian scheme are given. For example, "Margaras," the name of the underworld organization for which Joe the Dead works, is the Sanskrit name for "the Hunter, the Investigator, the Skip Tracer"—the latter a character in *Naked Lunch* and in the cut-ups trilogy of the 1960s. There are also examples of cut-ups taken from the early 1960s (particularly in *Minutes to Go*) that now make sense 30 years later, thus proving the prophetic power of the cut-up process. Nepherti continues his journey to the Western Lands and learns that he must meet with Hassan i Sabbah, who tells him, "Life is very dangerous and few survive it. I am but a humble messenger. Ancient Egypt is the only period in history when the gates to immortality were open, the Gates of Anubis. But the gates were occupied and monopolized by unfortunate elements . . . rather low vampires."

A chapter on Hassan I Sabbah details the training of his assassins for space travel. This requires evolution on the part of human beings. Political structures, though, preclude evolution by the enforcement of a uniform (nonmagical) environment: "The punctuational theory of evolution is that mutations appear quite quickly when the equilibrium is punctuated. Fish transferred from one environment to a totally new and different context showed a number of biological alterations in a few generations." So if we change the environment, says Burroughs, we mutate. To keep humans from mutating quickly involves the enforcement of uniformity. But Burroughs comes to a key realization about the character of Hassan i Sabbah as he has been portrayed not only in this trilogy but in previous works: He realizes that he has been worshipping Hassan i Sabbah, has "invoked HIS aid, like some Catholic feeling his Saint medal." Accordingly, he can now treat HIS just like any other character or "routine" in his work, and Hassan i Sabbah becomes for the first time a true "character." He imagines a scenario where Nepherti and Hassan i Sabbah make it to the Western Lands and bring back knowledge that will destroy the Venusian Controllers. They soon have "everyone on their ass"—all the governments, churches, and powers that be. Orthodox religious leaders and some "reborn son of a bitch" accuse them of using magic because they recognize their creativity. From Alamout, HIS's hideout, he sends assassins (including AJ, from *Naked Lunch*) to kill religious leaders. The Old Man becomes the writer now who realizes "I am HIS and HIS is me." Dr. Benway has lunch with the Old Man and offers him a deal—a great place to live and potions that will restore his youth. But the Old Man presumably rejects this Faustian bargain, for the final chapter of the novel begins, "What is life when the purpose is gone?"

This book is one of Burroughs's last, and it has the feel of a winding down in this last chapter. In the Land of the Dead, Joe sees Ian Sommerville, with whom he cannot communicate, and Brion Gysin is a no-show at dinner. He recounts his days in Paris, in 1959: "We were getting messages, making contacts. Everything had meaning. . . . It reads like a sci-fi from here. Not very good sci-fi, but real enough at the time. There were casualties . . . quite a number." He realizes now that all of his paranoid fantasies about receiving "assignments"—the secret agent stuff that is in many of his novels—was wrong: "There isn't any important assignment. It's every man for himself." One scene takes place in Florida with his mother and his son Billy. He is getting older but can still say, unlike Prufrock, "At least I dare to eat a peach." Joe is now Burroughs himself, moving about the house making tea. The old writer feels his inspiration leaving him, like one soul after another escaping. The book takes on an air of finality, a last-book feel: "His self is crumbling away to shreds and tatters, bits of old songs, stray quotations, fleeting spurts of purpose and direction sputtering out to nothing and nowhere, like the body at death deserted by one soul after the other." The leaving of the seven souls is now a metaphor for the disintegrating consciousness of old age: "The old writer couldn't write anymore because he had reached the end of words, the end of what can be done with words." The Parade Bar is closed, he says, referring to his favorite haunt in Tangier in the 1950s. He actually ends the book with the words, "THE END," something he has never done before because his other books were not the end: There was still more that could be done with words. Not at the end of this book, though.

Rob Johnson

Whalen, Philip (1923–2002)

Best known as a member of the Beat Generation, Philip Whalen has also been associated with such other movements as the San Francisco Renaissance and language poetry. Born in Portland, Oregon, in 1923, Whalen grew up in The Dalles, a small town on the Columbia River. He came from a working-class background and joined the army air force soon after graduating from high school. After World War II, he attended Reed College on the G.I. Bill where he met GARY SNYDER and LEW

Philip Whalen, in his apartment in San Francisco, 1965. *(courtesy of Larry Keenan)*

WELCH and was first acknowledged as a poet by William Carlos Williams, who had come to Reed on a lecture tour. He was also introduced to Zen Buddhism at this time. Whalen graduated in 1951, his senior thesis being a book of poems.

Whalen spent the 1950s and 1960s traveling up and down the West Coast, spending considerable time in San Francisco where he participated in the Six Gallery poetry reading in 1955, meeting ALLEN GINSBERG, JACK KEROUAC, and MICHAEL McCLURE. An important year for Whalen was 1960. His first two books of poetry, *Like I Say* and *Memoirs of an Interglacial Age*, were published, and he was included in Donald Allen's *The NEW AMERICAN POETRY, 1945–1960*. At about this time, Whalen wrote "Since You Ask Me," his memorable statement of poetics that was originally meant as a press release for a reading tour which he made back East

with Michael McClure. It epitomizes his method of writing by claiming that "poetry is a picture or graph of a mind moving, which is a world body being here and now which is history . . . and you."

In 1966, at the suggestion of Snyder, Whalen first traveled to Japan where he started to practice Zen Buddhism more regularly. He also wrote prolifically in the 1960s, including three semiautobiographical novels that explore relationships between men and women and question the artist's relation to society: *You Didn't Even Try* (1967), *Imaginary Speeches for a Brazen Head* (1972), and *The Diamond Noodle* (1980). *On Bear's Head*, Whalen's first collected poems came out in 1969. Significant poems from this period include "The War Poem for DIANE DI PRIMA," a protest poem of the Vietnam War, and the longer work, *Scenes of Life at the Capital*, about his life in Kyoto amid palaces, temples, and cafés. Returning to the United States in the early 1970s, Whalen first stayed in Bolinas, north of San Francisco, where friends and fellow poets such as Donald Allen and JOANNE KYGER lived. Soon Whalen wanted to return to the city, and Richard Baker–Roshi invited him to move to the San Francisco Zen Center. He became a monk in 1973, was given dharma transmission in 1987, and became abbot of the Hartford Street Zen Center in 1991, retiring from that position in 1996. Whalen remained as a resident teacher there until his death in 2002. Even though he published less as his Buddhist responsibilities as practitioner and teacher increased, several major volumes of poetry appeared in the 1980s and 1990s: *Heavy Breathing* (1983), a collected volume of poems that was published in the 1970s; *Canoeing Up Cabarga Creek* (1996), a selection of Buddhist poems; *Some of These Days* (1999), poems from the 1970s and 1980s; and *Overtime* (1999), a final volume of selected poetry. *Off the Wall*, a collection of interviews with Whalen and an important source of information about his life and work, was published in 1978.

Whalen's poetry is known for its wit, humor, and casual, conversational style. His poems also exhibit an experimental and open form. Placement of the poem on the page is important, including the dynamic use of line breaks to graph the movement of the mind in time and space. Similar to other Beat writers, Whalen faithfully kept journals and notebooks, and many of his poems are created from journal entries, typed, rearranged, and sometimes edited and considered by some critics to exhibit a collage technique. He is also known for his elegant calligraphy and the drawings that often accompany poems when published as reproduced from his notebooks. *Highgrade* is a volume devoted to what he called his doodles and such short calligraphed poems.

Whalen's poetry may be a challenging read due to the way he combines levels of language, including slang and colloquialisms, quotations from authors whom he is reading, overheard conversations, memories, and ambient sounds, sometimes without indicating sources. His poetry is also intellectually demanding in its exploration of philosophical questions, often from a Buddhist point of view, and the wide range of ideas from the arts, sciences, and Western and Eastern culture that he includes in his poems. Some critics have claimed that his contemplative and personal poetry is lacking in drama, as he explores how the mind perceives the outer world and then records and transmits that perception through the poem. However, Whalen also addresses political issues, especially how the poet can survive in America and how poetry itself can bring change to a society of consumerism and conformity. For example, his poem "Chanson d'Outre Tombe" addresses the outsider status of the Beat poet directly, evidence that although Whalen has both denied and affirmed his Beat affiliations, his affinity with other Beat writers is certain. Important influences on Whalen include WILLIAM S. BURROUGHS, e.e. cummings, Ginsberg, Dr. Samuel Johnson, Kerouac, Kyger, CHARLES OLSON, Kenneth Patchen, Ezra Pound, Snyder, Gertrude Stein, Wallace Stevens, Welch, and William Carlos Williams, along with Chinese poet Su Tung-p'o and Zen master Dogen. Such widely ranging influences demonstrate Whalen's unique position as a poet who merges the traditions of West and East.

Bibliography

Davidson, Michael. *The San Francisco Renaissance.* Cambridge: Cambridge University Press, 1989.
Suiter, John. *Poets on the Peaks.* Washington, D.C.: Counterpoint, 2002.

Thurley, Geoffrey. "The Development of the New Language: Michael McClure, Philip Whalen, and Gregory Corso." In *The Beats: Essays in Criticism,* edited by Lee Bartlett, 165–180. Jefferson, N.C.: McFarland, 1981.

Jane Falk

"Wichita Vortex Sutra" Allen Ginsberg (1968)

Written during a 1966 poetry reading tour of Kansas that was financed with a Guggenheim grant, "Wichita Vortex Sutra" is arguably ALLEN GINSBERG's most well-known antiwar poem, written in response to the Vietnam War. The pacifist impulse of the poem is framed by Ginsberg's slow realization during this reading tour that he now was regarded, for better or worse, as a spokesperson for an emerging youth culture. The poem rewrites the U.S. government's effort to win public support for the escalation of the war in Vietnam so that the success of the war effort might be revealed as a function of the Pentagon's public-relations skill rather than any inherent moral value in the war itself. The poem borrows from Ginsberg's increasing study of Buddhism. It is written as a Western version of a sutra, or Buddhist scripture. At the same time, it borrows from Ginsberg's major Western influence, the poetry of William Blake, rendering Blake's figure of the "vortex" as a symbol for the transformative potential of the antiwar effort.

Ginsberg's compositional strategies in "Wichita Vortex Sutra" are as important as the content of the poem itself. Language is the central subject of the poem and is just as important as the war: For Ginsberg, propaganda colonizes language and meaning into wartime rhetoric that appropriates bodies for combat. Thus, the scattered spacing and line breaks of "Wichita Vortex Sutra" dramatize in broken forms and fragmented language both the physical casualties and the rhetorical causes of war. The poem was composed while he was traveling in a Volkswagen Camper that Ginsberg bought with his Guggenheim funds. Ginsberg spoke his spontaneous impressions into a tape recorder that also picked up passing sounds and radio news snippets. He included these seemingly extraneous voices in the poem and used the on–off clicking of the tape recorder to determine the poem's line structure, with the on–off tape-recorder clicks reproduced as line breaks that climb down the page. Innovations in contemporary poetry such as organic form and open-field poetics are recast in the form of what Ginsberg called auto poesy, where his immediate thoughts came out as spontaneous utterance in the transient, ever-moving space of the automobile.

Ginsberg biographer Michael Schumacher has called this poem "a 1960s poetry version of *ON THE ROAD*." True to JACK KEROUAC's vision in that novel, "Wichita Vortex Sutra" is Ginsberg's effort to reveal a visionary version of America as he travels across it. However, the poet finds that he must *create*, rather than *discover*, the America of his prophecy. Faced with the empty language of war rhetoric on the Volkswagen's radio, he creates a language for vision from his study of Buddhism. He invokes the Prajnaparamita Sutra to counter the language of the Pentagon. This is Buddhism's sutra on "emptiness"—that is, on the constructed and impermanent nature, rather than the eternal nature, of all lived experience. This is no mystical vision for Ginsberg; it is as down-to-earth as language itself, and, as such, it is introduced by the speaker of the poem casually "over coffee." The speaker's words function, then, as a form of common language that might "overwhelm" the State Department's call to war. Ginsberg begins with the premise, simply, that "[t]he war is language." Language is "abused" for commercial purposes, and is "used / like magic for power on the planet." The revisionary impulse of the poem is twofold: first, to expose the abuse of language and, second, to counter the State Department's "magic" language with linguistic sorcery of his own.

Ginsberg deploys the Buddhist mantra, a repetitive chant that is used in meditation, to counter the language of war. In a 1968 interview with Michael Aldrich, Ginsberg explained that the mantric poetics of "Wichita Vortex Sutra" emerged from the poem's historical moment, an effort to "make a series of syllables that would be identical with a historical event." This historical event was Ginsberg's imagined end of the Vietnam War, expressed by the speaker of the poem as if in the casting of a magic spell: "I lift my voice aloud , /

make Mantra of American language now, / I here declare the end of the War!" As Ginsberg said to Aldrich, this English-language mantra represents as much a belief in the power of language as an effort to test the boundaries of language. Describing the effect of President Lyndon Johnson's language, specifically his ability to escalate the war and change millions of lives with mere vocalizations, Ginsberg said, "They pronounce these words, and then they sign a piece of paper, of other words, and a hundred thousand soldiers go across the ocean. So I pronounce *my* word, and so the point is, how strong is my word?"

As often is the case in Ginsberg's prophetic poetry, Ginsberg's Buddhist influences are interconnected with his Blakean ones. "On to Wichita to prophesy! O frightful Bard!," he writes, echoing the role of the prophetic "Bard" in Blake's long poem *Milton*. Like Blake's Bard, Ginsberg's careens "into the heart of the Vortex." Young American students are trapped in the poem's Vortex; they suspect that their government lies to them as new draft notices—written in President Johnson's mantra language—arrive every day. These "boys with sexual bellies aroused" are "chilled in the heart by the mailman." As if produced by the figure of Moloch in "HOWL," Selective Service notices come "writ by machine." But always in "Wichita Vortex Sutra," the country is cursed not so much by the machine but instead by the *language* of the machine. "I search for the language / that is also yours," Ginsberg's Bard laments, adding, "almost all our language has been taxed by war."

Bibliography

Davidson, Michael. "Technologies of Presence: Orality and the Tapevoice of Contemporary Poetics." In *Sound States: Innovative Poetics and Acoustical Technologies*. Chapel Hill: University of North Carolina Press, 1997, 97–125.

Ginsberg, Allen. Interview with Michael Aldrich et al. "Improvised Poetics." *Composed on the Tongue: Literary Conversations, 1967–1977*. San Francisco: Grey Fox, 1980, 18–62.

Jarraway, David R. "'Standing by His Word': The Politics of Allen Ginsberg's Vietnam 'Vortex.'" *Journal of American Culture* 16 (Fall 1993): 81–88.

Schumacher, Michael. *Dharma Lion: A Critical Biography of Allen Ginsberg.* New York: St. Martin's, 1992.

Trigilio, Tony. "'Will You Please Stop Playing With the Mantra?': The Embodied Poetics of Ginsberg's Later Career." In *Reconstructing the Beats,* edited by Jennie Skerl, 119–140. New York: Palgrave Macmillan, 2004.

Tony Trigilio

Wieners, John (1934–2002)

John Wieners was born in Milton, Massachusetts, in 1934. After taking a B.A. at Boston College (alongside poet Steve Jonas), he attended Black Mountain College on a scholarship in spring 1955 and summer 1956 following a chance encounter with its rector CHARLES OLSON in Boston in 1954. Though Wieners was immediately drawn to Olson's forceful and energizing poetics and persona, he was quick to accommodate a broader range of then-available poetic idioms, finding equally significant orientations for his writing in the poetries of Robert Duncan (also a teacher at Black Mountain) and Frank O'Hara, who would later describe him (in "A Young Poet") as "a poet exhausted by / the insight which comes as a kiss / and follows as a curse."

After the demise of Black Mountain College in 1956 Wieners returned to Boston and published three issues of a magazine, *Measure.* In 1958 he relocated with his lover Dana Duerke to San Francisco where he wrote his great debut, *The HOTEL WENTLEY POEMS.* This volume quickly found favor among his peers and elders across the country for its determined candor, its treatment of gay and narcotic themes, and its controlled, high lyric address, traits that would consistently characterize his work. Also from this period is *707 Scott Street* (1958–59, but it was not published until 1996 by Sun and Moon Press, Los Angeles), a journal of writings—poems, aphorisms, diaristic fragments—that includes this useful statement on his project: "All I am interested in is charting the progress of my own soul. And my poetics consists of marking down how each action unrolls. Without my will. It moves. So that each man has his own poetic."

In 1960 he returned to the East Coast and during the next five years would spend time in both New York and Boston. In New York he shared an apartment with HERBERT HUNCKE and stage managed and acted in the production of three of his plays at the Judson Poets Theater. In this period Wieners read closely such kindred writers as Friedrich Hölderlin and John Clare and was composing the poems of *Ace of Pentacles* (1964), which hint at the later, more-wry developments in his writing, in such O'Haran titles as "You Talk of Going But Don't Even Have a Suitcase." His narcotic ingestion remained keen in these years. O'Hara's partner Joe LeSueur has this anecdote from a week that Wieners spent at their apartment: "Saturday afternoon John went to do some sort of research at the 42nd Street public library while we went to see *The Curse of Frankenstein* at Loew's Sheridan. That evening John, high on Benzedrine, came home and told us about the horrifying, hallucinatory experience he'd had at the library. Later I said to Frank, 'Isn't it funny? We go to a horror movie and don't feel a thing, and John just goes to the library and is scared out of his wits.'"

In 1965 Wieners's relationship with Olson regained intimacy, and he made appearances alongside Olson at two landmark poetry festivals in Spoleto, Italy, and Berkeley, California, also working as his teaching assistant at SUNY Buffalo. But his stints in mental institutions throughout the 1960s were frequent and debilitating, as the eviscerated emotions of *Pressed Wafer* (1967) and *Asylum Poems* (1969) suggest. With the support of his many friends he continued to write prolifically into the 1970s: The Jonathan Cape publication *Nerves* (1970) cemented an audience for his work in the United Kingdom, and a *Selected Poems* from Grossman in 1972 offered a valuable reckoning of his achievement to date. In the preface (itself a primary Wieners text), he restated the project of the *Hotel Wentley* years: "To stay with one's self requires position and perhaps provision, realizing quality out of strangeness."

This first *Selected Poems* was followed with the stunning *Behind the State Capitol or Cincinnati Pike* (1975), by which time Wieners had settled permanently on Boston's Beacon Hill; though continuing to experience erratic mental health, he was now active in local politics and the gay liberation movement. A local collective called The Good Gay Poets undertook publication of this collection, controversial for its pronouncedly disjunct logic, as in the poem "Understood Disbelief in Paganism, Lies and Heresy": "Brevity; yes or no arsinine Coliseum / arrogance, attrib. Constant shout / Emperor Hippocratic misaligned." Writings of such disassociated flourish, though not necessarily the book's dominant tenor, gave previous admirers such as Robert Duncan some skepticism as to its merit, while many younger writers in the United States and abroad found it exhilarating. Certainly *Behind the State Capitol* marked exciting new terrain for Wieners, but frustratingly, from this point on, very little new work would see print. Raymond Foye's editorial work on the 1986 *Selected Poems* and the 1988 *Cultural Affairs in Boston* made for crucial gatherings of previous collections and individual unpublished poems, and two wild, glamour-soaked narratives from Hanuman Books, A Superficial Estimation (1986) and *Conjugal Contraries and Quart* (1987), also served to whet readers' appetites. In his last years Wieners found support from a younger generation of writers and editors, including William Corbett, Raymond Foye, Peter Gizzi, Michael Gizzi, Fanny Howe, Kevin Killian, and Charley Shively, who ensured that his work continued to circulate. The festschrift *The Blind See Only This World* (2000) testifies to the scope of his impact.

In a statement for Who's Who (circa. 1976), Wieners wrote: "I like my poetry to have an emotional validity or veracity. If I can get something out that's emotionally true for myself and a few others that's good enough, and I would subject the form to that statement or utterance. Charles Olson, ROBERT CREELEY, Robert Duncan, ED DORN, JOANNE KYGER, PHILIP WHALEN, GARY SNYDER, [JACK] KEROUAC, [ALLEN] GINSBERG, [GREGORY] CORSO, Jack Spicer and Steve Jonas. These were the most interesting people I knew. It was not deliberate that we were influences on each other. We just did a lot of things together."

Wieners died of a stroke in Boston on March 1, 2002, on his way home from a friend's book party.

Bibliography
Corbett, William, Michael Gizzi, and Joseph Torra, eds. *The Blind See Only This World: Poems for John Wieners.* New York, Boston: Granary Books, Pressed Wafer, 2000.

Thomas Evans

Wild Boys, The William S. Burroughs (1971)
The first book that WILLIAM S. BURROUGHS published after having exhausted his original "word horde" (material composed in Morocco in the mid- to late-1950s) was *The Wild Boys*, which was the basis for NAKED LUNCH and the cut-ups trilogy— *The* SOFT MACHINE, *The* TICKET THAT EXPLODED, and NOVA EXPRESS. Unlike those novels, there are few characters in *The Wild Boys* that overlap with Burroughs's preceding works. The novel also incorporates Burroughs's "cut-up" method much more selectively (and rarely) than he does in the cut-ups trilogy. Therefore, many critics see the book as a "return to narrative" on Burroughs's part. Burroughs himself says that the book owes a debt to 19th-century narrative fiction, boy's adventure magazines, and the nostalgic novels of English writer Denton Welch. Welch inspired Burroughs's main character in the book, Audrey Carsons, who functions as Burroughs's alter ego in this book. In *The Cities of the Red Night*, Audrey matures into Kim Carsons. *The Wild Boys* is thus an important new beginning for Burroughs in the late 1960s.

Although the book's title would indicate that it concerns itself with "the wild boys," the book deals with them less than its "sequel," *Port of Saints*, does, and there are also "wild boy" sections of Burroughs's collection of short pieces from this time period, *Exterminator!* The wild boys are part of a fantasy world that is set around 1988 (20 years after the book was written) in which three-quarters of the world's population has been wiped out by radiation or by a plague, leaving the world open to a takeover by packs of roaming boys. These boys have been incubated in test tubes and thus have always lived apart from women, making them a new line in the evolution of the species. "It's all simply a personal projection," Burroughs told Robert Palmer in 1972. "A prediction? I hope so. Would I consider events similar to *The Wild Boys* scenario desirable? Yes, desirable to me."

The Wild Boys has 18 "chapters," five of which are titled "In the Penny Arcade." These sections are often startlingly visual, akin to a still life. The first has a quite famous description of a "flesh garden," some of Burroughs's best fantasy writing. The other chapters are loosely connected if at all, and some, such as the opening section on the assassin Tío Mate, should probably have been included in *Exterminator!* as Burroughs himself later suggested. Still, the book does have a strange, accruing momentum, akin to the sense that the viewer makes out of a collage. Particularly at the end, the "wild boy" scenario takes over and develops. The book is subtitled *A Book of the Dead* because, as Burroughs says, all of the characters are dead. Audrey Carsons dies at the beginning of the book in a car accident, an accident that is repeated several times in the text in different settings.

In *The Wild Boys*, Burroughs started to use material from his St. Louis (Pershing Avenue) childhood in his books, giving them a nostalgic tone. Audrey Carsons is a portrait of a deeply insecure 16-year-old Burroughs who is described by "a St. Louis aristocrat" (Politte Elvins, based on Kells Elvins's father) as looking like "a sheep-killing dog." Like Burroughs, Audrey never feels at ease around the rich men and their sons at the private school that he attends. As the narrator tells us, "He was painfully aware of being unwholesome." Audrey and a boy named John Hamlin take a Dusenberg out for a joy ride, and they are both killed in a flaming car wreck. Behind the scenes of what turns out to be one of Burroughs's "reality films," Old Sarge has gripped the wheel and caused the fatal accident.

Burroughs creates an alternative version of the "detour" wreck. John and Audrey tour a carnival, circa the 1890s. Like much of the book, it is intended to have an 1890s sepia tone to it. The wild boys roam the carnival, carrying long knives and wearing rainbow-colored jockstraps. Audrey enters a peep show. There is a good deal of dream material that is evident in the hallucinatory visions that Audrey views inside. This section makes clear the inspiration of the book in pulp magazines and boy's adventure stories: "I was waiting there pale

character in someone else's writing breathing old pulp magazines." A spectacular effect is achieved in a scene where Audrey tours a "flesh garden," which is described to him in broken English by a native naturalist: "The scene is a sketch from an explorer's notebook."

A. J. (based on Alan Ansen) reprises his role from *Naked Lunch* as the "foremost practitioner of luxury" who "thinks nothing of spending a million dollars to put a single dish on his table." The story is set in a future dystopia where the very rich have it better than ever, but the poor scrap like animals. There is a pastichelike quality, imitating turn-of-the-century British colonial narratives as the wild boys provide a "spot of bother" for the smart set.

Several chapters obsessively evoke and reinvoke sex scenes between the wild boys or the native boys in other settings. The scenes here with the wild boys appear to take place just after the "control towers" were destroyed in *The Ticket That Exploded,* for the boys frolic in the ruins of the control room.

Burroughs writes one chapter, "The Dead Child," (in part) from the point of view of his son, Billy Burroughs III. The Mexico City setting, where Burroughs shot his wife Joan in 1951 when Billy was four years old, is chilling: "I don't like to go home. My father is taking morphine and always tying up his arm and talking to this old junky who has a government scrip and mother drinks tequila all day." This story intersects with the story of an Indian boy and his friend Xolotl, who escape from the control of the Mayan priests and live in a homoerotic, boy's jungle-adventure fantasy world. When they die, they become tree spirits that urge boys to run from the "nets" cast by women—a variation of the book's wild-boy theme of men without women.

Beginning with the chapter "Just Call Me Joe" and continuing to the end of the book, the focus is more or less exclusively on the adventures of the wild boys. They begin their campaign against the status quo in Marrakech in 1969. Packs of "gasoline gangs" break into suburban living rooms and light on fire the couples who are sitting on their couches. A picture that was taken of one of these marauding youths lighting a cigarette off the match that he used to torch a gasoline-soaked suburbanite is taken up by an advertising campaign. The model is dubbed BOY, and he spawns countless merchandise and imitators. Vivien Westwood and Malcolm McLaren's seminal punk-rock boutique called BOY is said to have been inspired by this passage in *The Wild Boys.*

Colonel Arachnid Ben Driss is sent to kill the gasoline gangs, and most of the boys are eliminated but not all. From around the world, including America, young men leave home to join the wild boys. During the U.S. Bicentennial, a Colonel Greenfield rallies the troops and takes an expeditionary force to Marrakech to quash the latest wild-boy uprising. Hundreds of the wild boys surrender to the colonel, but it turns out to be an ambush, and Greenfield's army is destroyed. Only 1500 of Greenfield's 20,000 soldiers make it back alive to Casablanca.

The second generation of wild boys is actually bred by "fugitive technicians" who raise the boys in test tubes. They are the first boys never to grow up around women; their behavior is novel, and their culture is unique: "A whole generation arose that had never seen a woman's face nor heard a woman's voice." In "The Wild Boys," a Colonel Bradly describes their habits in anthropological terms, including a mystical ceremony in which the boys exhibit the power to procreate.

By 1988 the world has been taken over by fascists under the pretext of a war against drugs. The wild boys serve as the liberators of the Americas, operating out of bases in Mexico and Central and South America. Burroughs expands this storyline in *Cities of the Red Night* and *The Place of Dead Roads.* The boys' platform of liberation is based on eliminating "all dogmatic verbal systems. The family unit and its cancerous expansion into tribes, countries, nations we will eradicate at its vegetable route." This program is similar to that of the Articulated in *Cities of the Red Night* as well as that of the Johnson Family in *The Place of Dead Roads.*

Audrey Carsons reappears at the end of the book. Colonel Bradly sends him on a mission to contact the roller-skating wild boys in the suburbs of Casablanca. His contact is a shoeshine boy called The Dib. They hook up with Jimmy the Shrew, a bicycle boy who arms them with "film grenades." They toss one when a cop stops them,

and the novel goes to black. The book ends with Audrey just on the verge of discovering the wild-boy gang. *Port of Saints* picks up from this point and centers on the history of the wild boys—much more so than the book that takes its title from the name of the test–tube-incubated boy gang.

Rob Johnson

Without Doubt Andy Clausen (1991)

This lively book of poetry was published just a few years after the fall of the Berlin Wall and amid the rapid changes that were taking place within the former Soviet Union. As a poet who had been deeply influenced by the U.S. democratic tradition of Walt Whitman and ALLEN GINSBERG as well as the Russian futurist poetry of Vladimir Mayakovsky, Clausen's poems from this era were perfectly situated to offer a new and healthy internationalist vision to greet the end of the cold war. In opposition to the cynical "we won" attitude exhibited by most mainstream U.S. commentators at the time, *Without Doubt* expressed sound criticisms of the militaristic and exploitation-filled betrayals of both East and West during the previous decades and offered an imaginative literary recipe for more-enlightened social possibilities. The book is also filled with moving poems about personal dreams, desires, and loss.

The original poetic voice of *Without Doubt* leaves quite a lasting impression. In Clausen's poems, empirical perceptions mix inventively with jazzed-up surreal and modernist imagery. Tragedy is juxtaposed with well-placed humor. Lyrical modes mingle easily with narrative, epic, and oratorical ones. Carrying on the most exciting, politically progressive, and intellectually probing aspects of the Beat tradition, strings of high-speed adjectives mix with considered speculations about the unfair nature of our socioeconomic landscape.

The book includes an introduction by Ginsberg that is replete with well-deserved superlatives: "The frank friendly extravagance of his metaphor & word-connection gives Andy Clausen's poetry a reading interest rare in poetry of any generation." Ginsberg adds: "Would he were, I'd take my chance on a President Clausen!"

Without Doubt is one of the most consistently vital poetry books of its era. Just about every piece in the volume is a compelling, surprise-filled jewel. A six-page narrative poem, "The Bear," which is influenced by visionary poems like Mayakovsky's "An Extraordinary Adventure which Befell Vladimir Mayakovsky in a Summer Cottage" and Ginsberg's "The Lion for Real," is told from the point of view of a female speaker who throughout the poem is being chased by a half-fantasized, half-real bear. The chase gives the poet time to ponder questions about politics and the imagination. But when the bear inevitably catches up to the narrator, she summons "all my power" and hits the bear in the mouth, whereupon the bear turns into a man who tells the narrator with a certain amount of sincerity: "All I wanted to do was kiss you." But the narrator sees through the curtained contradictions, and a somewhat surreal tale includes the real antichauvinist message: "'You didn't want to kiss me / You wanted to own me / to dominate." When the bear-man disappears, the "blood & teeth remained," and "Word raced through the community / 'Mayakovsky is Dead.'" Utilizing a Mayakovskian style, Clausen carries on the Russian poet's radical tradition and extends its political vision by metaphorically—in a surprising twist of an ending—killing Mayakovsky himself.

"The Challenge" presents a moment of deep despair ("up & down the abandoned boiling / coastal waters of my desecrated torso") by lamenting how far the poet is from more optimistic historical moments, including the earliest days of the Russian revolution when it seemed, before Stalinism took hold, that a more progressive era might well be dawning in that country:

I will live & die never knowing
The Baroque Golden Age,
The Age of Enlightenment,
Aquarius, Ha!
Let alone the night of the
Pink Lantern
The Stall of Pegasus
& Stray Dog Cafe
There's no 1917 for me.

And yet, most of the poems, in spite of the often-gloomy times, provide at least a potential glimpse of hope, either in the substance of the text or in the way that the poems' surrealist elements convey, in the beautifully descriptive phrase of philosopher Ernst Bloch, "anticipatory illuminations"—hints or sketches of social possibilities that do not yet exist in the actual world. In "Patriotism," the second poem in the book (predating the fall of the Soviet Union), Clausen redefines love of one's country and peoples by predicting that "Russia & America / will pass in the night," implying that the end of repressive policies on both sides of the cold war would open space for more democratic and egalitarian political arrangements. In "The Iron Curtain of Love," Clausen expressionistically transforms symbols of cold-war militarism into pacifist imagery: "there's a warhead strapped to the back / of the dove / It's the iron curtain of love." In the latter poem, he also paraphrases a Russian proverb to assert that, even in dire moments, "every wall has a door." Or, as the main character in "Old Man" puts it: "All in All, it's a rough life. One not only has to surrender, one has to keep fighting after that."

Many of the poems in *Without Doubt* focus on various aspects of late 20th-century American life. Clausen writes with lyrical power about homelessness in "Sacred Relics": "red nosed busted blue derelicts / supported by lampposts & buildings / in the typewriter rain." These homeless are surviving, "gambling pain on the miracle / that's never happened yet." At the poem's end, Clausen ominously tells world leaders that a time will come when they will need these homeless folks' experience.

Clausen's poems explore the spectrum of human emotion. Love is ever-present ("Come Love, bite my brain with resplendent teeth") and, in true Mayakovskian tradition, so is heartrending lost-love ("It's an ancient and miserable wail / for the might have beens / this song of desire for one"). While "This table is supporting me / better than a lot of you ever did" (from "This Table"), Clausen ultimately retains faith in the potential of human action, empathy, and creativity, for he knows that "Our Mission is the Future" and that "this paranoia, this body hatred / this genocidal pleasure / this doctrine of might / cannot endure our wailing" (from "Wail Bar Night").

After the fall of the Soviet Union, many U.S. activists sensibly advocated for a "peace dividend," urging our government to take advantage of this historic opportunity by finally scaling back America's exorbitant military budget and prioritizing long-neglected social needs such as affordable housing, health care, education, and the environment. It was not to be. Instead, subsequent administrations continued to support the bloated military budgets and procorporate economic policies that had largely held sway throughout the cold-war era. After the atrocity of September 11, 2001, George W. Bush was able, by cynically manipulating legitimate American fears, to accelerate those regressive social priorities under the guise of a loosely defined "war on terror," a war that has included an unwarranted and disastrous military conflict in Iraq that continues to rage as I write this piece. We are living in an age in which there is still far too much poverty and violence, far too many unaccountable political and economic institutions, and far too many fundamentalist groupings within too many of the world's religions. The final poem in Clausen's *Without Doubt*, with its cautiously upbeat title "We Could," speaks poignantly to our current times:

> We wouldst rid the epic of slavery
> for women and all others
> We'd smash the caste system
> We'd put aristocrats to work!
> sacrificing this puny life
> for the Infinite Future
> We'd give Shiva something else to do. . . .
>
> We are sentenced
> there is no back to return to
> We lick the Jewel in the Lotus
> till it is human

then
We eat God alive!

Here is an imaginative tonic to the planet's dominant, rigid ideas about economic systems, the role of women, and the place of spirituality and creativity in daily life. Fundamentalism is challenged here not by metaphorically killing off the notion of an omnipotent, external god—or not by that alone—but by then taking the concept of a living, enlightened spirit and placing it inside us—not simply inside the "I" of the poet, but inside the "we" of us all. Clausen's book points the way toward poetry's emancipatory potential if only our overly dogmatic ideas and policies could be left behind on the antique cold-war trail.

Without Doubt was published by Zeitgeist Press, an independent press that was run by the fine poet Bruce Isaacson, who used to host a popular reading series with Clausen in San Francisco's Cafe Babar. As is the case with too many of the important books by writers in the Beat tradition who ought to be more well known than they are, *Without Doubt* is currently out of print. Hopefully, that will be remedied soon, and this book will more thoroughly find its way to the "Futurians" to whom the book's opening poem is aptly addressed.

Bibliography

Ginsberg, Allen. "Introduction to *Without Doubt*, by Andy Clausen." In *Deliberate Prose: Selected Essays 1952–1995*, edited by Bill Morgan, 431–433. New York: HarperCollins, 2000.

Katz, Eliot. "The Bear for Real." *Poetry Flash* 225 (December 1991): 1, 8–9.

Eliot Katz

Yage Letters, The William S. Burroughs and Allen Ginsberg (1963)

This epistolary "novel" provides early examples of WILLIAM S. BURROUGHS's writing that will later find themselves in NAKED LUNCH, and it is also a fascinating document about Burroughs's search for the ultimate drug and how it inspired ALLEN GINSBERG to follow him on this hallucinogenic journey. Though not a grand literary achievement, *The Yage Letters* nonetheless provide key insights to Burroughs's and Ginsberg's work. Letters from the book appeared in the periodicals *Big Table, Kulchur, City Lights Journal,* and *Black Mountain Review.* The "routine" "Roosevelt After Inauguration" from *The Yage Letters* was first published by LeRoi Jones/AMIRI BARAKA in *Floating Bear,* which was seized and had an obscenity case brought against it. *The Yage Letters* were also an inspiration for JANINE POMMY VEGA's *yage* experience beautifully described in TRACKING The SERPENT: JOURNEYS TO FOUR CONTINENTS. *The Yage Letters* is a key work for establishing the "pharmo-picaresque" literary genre and for popularizing the drug *yage,* which was on the margins of the ethnobotanical field at a time when such scientific research was only just emerging.

At the end of his first novel, JUNKY, Burroughs using the persona William Lee tells the reader that he is heading for South America in search of the "final fix"—a drug called *yage,* which supposedly gives one telepathic powers. *Ayahuasca,* also known as *yage* or *Banisteriopsis caapi,* is a jungle vine that is used in a psychoactive potion in South America that produces intense hallucinatory visions, has long been central to shamanic traditions throughout the region, and is still used by indigenous peoples as well as in newer vegetal churches and by Western tourists (such as the musician Sting). In the follow-up to *Junky,* Burroughs's QUEER, Lee actually makes this trip in search of *yage,* along with his paid companion, Eugene Allerton (based on Lewis Marker). However, Lee is unsuccessful in locating a supply of *yage.* The book ends with Allerton deserting Lee in the jungle and with Lee, after an unspecified period of time, returning to Mexico City to find him. This gap in time after Allerton deserts him and Lee returns to Mexico is filled in by *The Yage Letters,* which describes Burroughs's discovery of a supply of *yage* and his subsequent experiments with the drug under the tutelage of a *brujo,* or witch doctor. These experiences would supply Burroughs with some of his most powerful and original imagery in his books for many years to come.

Burroughs traveled first to Panama and then into South America in early 1953. He combined actual letters with work from notebooks that he kept of his travels in this work. The epistolary form of the work was not decided until after he returned from Latin America. Some of Ginsberg's letters are not addressed to Burroughs. The epilogue contains a Burroughs cut-up text that reworks parts of the previous text into a collage. This is a hybrid text with two authors and multiple writing forms that were written during a 10-year period—composite, collaborative, and indeterminate. *The Yage Letters* is also generally overlooked by Burroughs scholars.

In the opening scenes in Panama, Burroughs describes Bill Gains (based on Bill Garver, the junky and Times Square hustler who taught Burroughs how keep up a habit by stealing overcoats in New York in the mid-1940s). The Panama scene of boys swimming in the polluted waters of a bay that fronted the U.S. Embassy recurs in several of Burroughs's novels. As he proceeds to Colombia and Peru, he picks up other stories and images that recur in his works: A detail from these letters that surfaces frequently in his works is the street scene in Guayaquil, Colombia, where kids sell cigarettes with the cry of "A ver Luckies," meaning, "Look here, Luckies." Burroughs writes, "Nightmare fear of stasis. Horror of being finally *stuck* in this place. This fear has followed me all over South America. A horrible sick feeling of final desolation." In Putumayo, he hears of a grasshopper with a sting that induces a sex frenzy, the basis of routines in *Naked Lunch* and elsewhere. Macoa, the capitol of Putumayo, comes to stand in for all of the "end-of-the-road" towns in Burroughs's fiction (see, for example, *The PLACE OF DEAD ROADS*). He is accompanied to Macoa by a Dr. Schindler, identified by Oliver Harris as Dr. Richard Evans Schultes, the "father of ethnobotany," a pioneer botanist who conducted research on peyote at Harvard in the 1930s.

It is outside of Macao that Burroughs locates a supply of *yage* and is introduced to a *brujo* who can administer the drug. The effect of the drug is profound. Burroughs has been told that he will see a great city, and he does, the "Composite City where all human potentials are spread out in a vast silent market." These descriptions make their way directly into sections of *Naked Lunch* and other works. His experience of *yage* as "space-time travel" is crucial, for Burroughs's books become literary experiments along those lines, constantly shifting locations and time periods. He would attribute his *yage* visions as well to his development of a means of communicating beyond "words" and in juxtaposed visions, a hallmark of Burroughs's collage-style and cut-up technique of writing.

Ginsberg followed Burroughs on the *ayahuasca* trail seven years later. Ginsberg's experience with the drug was somewhat different than Burroughs's. Ginsberg felt himself facing his own death, and although death would allow him to answer the questions about the universe that obsessed him, he says

that he chose not to know these answers out of compassion for those whom he would leave behind (especially his companion Peter Orlovsky). Ginsberg's experience on the drug has recently been clinically confirmed. DMT, the active chemical compound in *yage*, has been studied for its ability to induce a so-called "near-death" experience. The experience made Ginsberg realize that he did not have the same nerve as Burroughs.

The *ayahuasca* experience for Ginsberg was important because horrific "trips" taught him that his attempts to gain a "new vision" was really a death wish and that the way to understand reality was not by leaving the body but by more consciously inhabiting it ("incarnate body feeling"). This realization was reinforced on his Indian trips and culminated in the poem "The Change: Kyoto-Tokyo Express," which marks the end of his attempts to re-create his 1948 Blake visions. Burroughs, on the other hand, had already moved beyond the kind of consciousness that Allen was seeking in 1960. He was deeply into the cut-up experiments that were inspired by Brion Gysin. Language, he says, is a virus, and the virus, he believes, is used by outside controllers to keep human beings enslaved through ignorance. Stop trying to see "the Universe," he tells Ginsberg; we are the Universe's "mark," and "whoever paid off a mark?" For Burroughs, then, the *ayahuasca* visions provide him with the imagery of space–time travel that is revealed to those who have "cut-up" the words and images that were supplied by the controller's "reality film." Burroughs's final entry in the book "I Am Dying, Meester?" overlaps the second and third revised editions but not the first edition of *The SOFT MACHINE*, and it illustrates how Burroughs made fictional use of his South American experiences in the wildly experimental "Cut-Up Trilogy" of the 1960s.

Bibliography

Burroughs, William S. *The Letters of William S. Burroughs, 1945–1959.* Edited by Oliver Harris. New York: Viking, 1993.

Burroughs, William S., and Allen Ginsberg. *The Yage Letters Redux.* Edited by Oliver Harris. San Francisco: City Lights, 2006.

Rudgley, Richard. *The Encyclopaedia of Psychoactive Substances.* New York: St. Martin's Press, 1999.

Rob Johnson and Oliver Harris

AFTERWORD

In her Foreword to this volume, Ann Charters, the dean of Beat scholars, notes that we have now been exploring the Beats for more than 50 years, and she suggests as well that this exploration has been growing significantly in recent decades. Prediction is a risky business, but this growing momentum means, I believe, that we will be exploring the Beats—reading, teaching, analyzing, arguing—for at least another 50 years. I think that it is no accident that the early Beat writers were fascinated with the writers of the so-called American Renaissance. We now recognize the achievement of Whitman, Melville, Hawthorne, Dickinson, Emerson, Thoreau, and Poe, but in the 1850s their explorations of the American scene (its possibilities and its hypocrisies), American consciousness, and the American language were regarded as threats to the cultural and social norms of the day (as was the case with Emerson and Whitman), or they were largely ignored (as were Melville and Thoreau), or they were (as in Dickinson's case) all but invisible. It took nearly 100 years for the cultural centrality and the achievement of these writers to be fully recognized. The early Beats came of age as the writers of the American Renaissance were being canonized and learned from their example both the cost of writing against the grain of what was officially condoned and the power that could be found in such imaginative self-reliance. The growing recognition of the importance of the Beat Generation and its growing influence suggests that we will eventually recognize the 1950s as another American cultural renaissance with the Beats near its center rather than at its periphery.

In the later 1950s and the early 1960s, discussions of the Beat Generation and Beat writers, whether positive or negative, tended to emphasize the extent to which the Beats stood in opposition to the cultural mainstream. In their own lives (and in the lives of the characters in their texts), they violated social norms. In their art they jettisoned the emphasis on control, precision, and ironic distance that had been explored by the high moderns in the decades before the Second World War (and which the academy of the early 1950s tried to demand) to explore the possibilities of improvisation. Instead of craft and control, they emphasized sincerity and immediacy. For the Beats, the modernism of the 1920s (especially as viewed retrospectively through the lens of the horrific destructiveness of the Second World War and the threat of nuclear holocaust) was not the redemption of the "tradition" as T. S. Eliot imagined that term in "Tradition and the Individual Talent," but it was instead a last ditch and futile attempt to evade the terms of modern society in which all cultural production and the circulation of all cultural products were increasingly intertwined with the mass media. The earliest critics of the Beats, those who embraced their work and those who denounced it, recognized that the Beats were rejecting the norms of literature.

Fifty years later, we can see, I believe, that they were also rejecting literature itself (understood as the crafting of elite aesthetic objects) to reinvent it as writing (a process that cast the reader not as a viewer as in modernism but as listener who could be a "you" in response to the writer's "I" rather than an "it"). The Beats understood that the first half of the 20th century marked the end of literature as a separate category and privileged domain, and they understood that the condition of mass mediation and popular culture had become a given that had to be engaged in some manner (whether ironically and caustically, as Burroughs did, or with ambivalent generosity, as Ginsberg did, or even with a certain enthusiasm for its possibilities, as Kerouac did) if writing was to be authentic and to reclaim some of the aesthetic power and centrality that literature had once had.

Much of our discussion of the Beats—at least that which gets beyond our fascination with the biographies of these iconic figures—still focuses on their various roles in the cultural and social changes that they helped incubate from below the seemingly placid surface of the conformity of cold-war America. The Beats were not the "man in the gray flannel suit," and even if the frontier had been closed for 50 years (as Frederick Jackson Turner declared), they showed that there were still roads that led out from the suburbs as well as inward to the wilds of Times Square and North Beach. These are significant matters. They help us see the cultural centrality of the Beats, not just their marginality. They help us see that the so-called "containment culture" of the 1950s was less a period of cultural consensus and stability than a period of cultural negotiation that paved the way for what become, in the later 1960s, a cultural fragmentation. But these approaches are not sufficient. What the Beats did, their representations of what they did, and how these have been received and "read" as cultural texts have tended to eclipse "how" they meant; that is, our focus on the activities of being Beat have tended to divert our attention from why the experience of reading them was so disruptive in the first place and why this disruptiveness has been—as the range of figures and texts covered in this encyclopedia demonstrates—so broadly influential. What's missing, still, is a sustained examination of how the Beats actually wrote and how their experimental practices have been a part of their cultural impact and cultural significance. This I think will become the agenda of the next 50 years of Beat research and criticism.

Tim Hunt

SELECTED BIBLIOGRAPHY OF MAJOR WORKS BY BEAT WRITERS

ACKER, KATHY

Blood and Guts in High School. New York: Grove Press, 1984.

Don Quixote. New York: Grove Press, 1986.

Empire of the Senseless. New York: Grove Press, 1988.

Literal Madness: Three Novels. New York: Grove Press, 1988.

In Memoriam to Identity. New York: Grove Weidenfeld, 1990.

Hannibal Lecter, My Father. New York: Semiotext(e), 1991.

Portrait of an Eye: Three Novels. New York: Pantheon Books, 1992.

My Mother: Demonology. New York: Pantheon Books, 1993.

Pussy, King of the Pirates. New York: Grove/Atlantic, 1996.

Rip-Off Red, Girl Detective and The Burning Bombing of America: The Destruction of the U.S. New York: Grove Press, 2002.

Essential Acker: The Selected Writings of Kathy Acker. New York: Grove Press, 2002.

ACOSTA, OSCAR ZETA

The Autobiography of a Brown Buffalo. San Francisco: Straight Arrow, 1972.

The Revolt of the Cockroach People. San Francisco: Straight Arrow, 1973.

Oscar "Zeta" Acosta: The Uncollected Works. Houston: Arte Publico Press, 1996.

BARAKA, AMIRI (LEROI JONES)

Cuba Libre. New York: Fair Play for Cuba Committee, 1961.

Preface to a Twenty Volume Suicide Note. New York: Totem Press/Corinth Books, 1961.

Blues People: Negro Music in White America. New York: Morrow, 1963.

Dutchman and The Slave: Two Plays. New York: Morrow, 1964.

The Dead Lecturer: Poems. New York: Grove, 1964.

The System of Dante's Hell. New York: Grove, 1965.

Home: Social Essays. New York: Morrow, 1966.

Black Art. Newark, N.J.: Jihad, 1967.

Slave Ship: A One Act Play. Newark, N.J.: Jihad, 1967.

The Baptism and The Toilet. New York: Grove, 1967.

Tales. New York: Grove, 1967.

Black Music. New York: Morrow, 1967.

Black Magic: Sabotage; Target Study; Black Art; Collected Poetry, 1961–1967. New York: Bobbs-Merrill, 1969.

Four Black Revolutionary Plays: All Praises to the Black Man. New York: Bobbs-Merrill, 1969.

It's Nation Time. Chicago: Third World Press, 1970.

Raise Race Rays Raze: Essays since 1965. New York: Random House, 1971.

What Was the Relationship of the Lone Ranger to the Means of Production? New York: Anti-Imperialist Cultural Union, 1978.

Selected Plays and Prose of Amiri Baraka/LeRoi Jones. New York: Morrow, 1979.

Selected Poetry of Amiri Baraka/LeRoi Jones. New York: Morrow, 1979.

Daggers and Javelins, Essays, 1974–1979. New York: Morrow, 1984.

The Autobiography of LeRoi Jones. New York: Freundlich Books, 1984.

The Music: Reflections on Jazz and Blues. New York: Morrow, 1987.

The LeRoi Jones/Amiri Baraka Reader. New York: Thunder's Mouth Press, 1991.

BERRIGAN, TED

The Sonnets. New York: Lorenz & Ellen Gude, 1964.
Many Happy Returns. New York: Corinth Books, 1969.
The Drunken Boat. New York: Adventures in Poetry, 1974.
A Feeling for Leaving. New York: Frontward Books, 1975.
Red Wagon. Chicago: Yellow Press, 1976.
Clear the Range. New York: Adventures in Poetry/ Coach House South, 1977.
So Going around Cities: New and Selected Poems 1958– 1979. Berkeley: Blue Wind Press, 1980.
In a Blue River. New York: Little Light, 1981.
A Certain Slant of Sunlight. Oakland: O Books, 1988.
Selected Poems. New York: Viking/Penguin, 1994.

BOWLES, PAUL

The Sheltering Sky. London: John Lehmann, 1949.
The Delicate Prey and Other Stories. New York: Random House, 1950.
Let It Come Down. London: John Lehmann, 1952.
The Spider's House. New York: Random House, 1955.
A Hundred Camels in the Courtyard. San Francisco: City Lights Books, 1962.
Up Above the World. New York: Simon & Schuster, 1966.
Scenes. Los Angeles: Black Sparrow, 1968.
Without Stopping. New York: Putnam, 1972.
Things Gone and Things Still Here. Santa Barbara, Calif.: Black Sparrow, 1977.
Collected Stories 1939–1976. Santa Barbara, Calif.: Black Sparrow, 1979.
Midnight Mass. Santa Barbara, Calif.: Black Sparrow, 1981.
Next to Nothing: Collected Poems 1926–1977. Santa Barbara, Calif.: Black Sparrow, 1981.
A Distant Episode: The Selected Stories of Paul Bowles. New York: Ecco, 1988.
Tangier Journal: 1987–1989. London: Owen, 1989.
Too Far from Home: Selected Writings of Paul Bowles. New York: Ecco, 1993.
The Portable Paul and Jane Bowles. New York: Penguin, 1994.

BRAUTIGAN, RICHARD

A Confederate General from Big Sur. New York: Grove, 1965.
Trout Fishing in America. San Francisco: Four Seasons, 1967.
In Watermelon Sugar. San Francisco: Four Seasons, 1968.
The Pill versus the Springhill Mine Disaster. San Francisco: Four Seasons, 1968.
Rommel Drives On Deep into Egypt. New York: Seymour Lawrence/Delacorte, 1970.
The Abortion: An Historical Romance 1966. New York: Simon & Schuster.
Revenge of the Lawn: Stories 1962–1970. New York: Simon & Schuster, 1971.
The Hawkline Monster. New York: Simon & Schuster, 1974.
Willard and His Bowling Trophies. New York: Simon & Schuster, 1975.
Loading Mercury with a Pitchfork. New York: Simon & Schuster, 1976.
Sombrero Fallout. New York: Simon & Schuster, 1976.

BREMSER, RAY

Poems of Madness. New York: Paper Book Gallery, 1965.
Angel. New York: Tompkins Square Press, 1967.
Drive Suite. San Francisco: Nova Broadcast Press, 1968.
Black Is Black Blues. Buffalo: Intrepid Press, 1971.
Blowing Mouth/The Jazz Poems, 1958–1970. Cherry Valley, N.Y.: Cherry Valley Editions, 1978.
Born Again. Santa Barbara: Am Here Books, 1985.
The Conquerors. Cherry Valley, N.Y.: Cherry Valley Editions, 1989.

BUKOWSKI, CHARLES

2 Poems. Los Angeles: Black Sparrow Press, 1967.
The Curtains Are Waving and People Walk through the Afternoon Here and in Berlin and in New York City and in Mexico. Los Angeles: Black Sparrow Press, 1967.
At Terror Street and Agony Way. Los Angeles: Black Sparrow Press, 1968.
Notes of a Dirty Old Man. North Hollywood, Calif.: Essex House, 1969.
If We Take. Los Angeles: Black Sparrow Press, 1969.

The Days Run Away Like Wild Horses over the Hills. Los Angeles: Black Sparrow Press, 1969.

Another Academy. Los Angeles: Black Sparrow Press, 1969.

Post Office: A Novel. Los Angeles: Black Sparrow Press, 1971.

Mockingbird Wish Me Luck. Los Angeles: Black Sparrow Press, 1972.

Erections, Ejaculations, Exhibitions and Tales of Ordinary Madness. San Francisco: City Lights Books, 1972.

While the Music Played. Los Angeles: Black Sparrow Press, 1973.

South of No North. Los Angeles: Black Sparrow Press, 1973.

Burning in Water, Drowning in Flame. Los Angeles: Black Sparrow Press, 1974.

Africa, Paris, Greece. Los Angeles: Black Sparrow Press, 1974.

Factotum. Los Angeles: Black Sparrow Press, 1975.

Scarlet. Santa Barbara, Calif.: Black Sparrow Press, 1976.

Tough Company. Santa Barbara, Calif.: Black Sparrow Press, 1976.

Maybe Tomorrow. Santa Barbara, Calif.: Black Sparrow Press, 1977.

Art. Santa Barbara, Calif.: Black Sparrow Press, 1977.

Love Is a Dog from Hell: Poems 1974–1977. Santa Barbara, Calif.: Black Sparrow Press, 1977.

Women. Santa Barbara, Calif.: Black Sparrow Press, 1978.

Play the Piano Drunk Like a Percussion Instrument Until the Fingers Begin to Bleed a Bit. Santa Barbara, Calif.: Black Sparrow Press, 1979.

Shakespeare Never Did This. San Francisco: City Lights Books, 1979.

Dangling in the Tournefortia. Santa Barbara, Calif.: Black Sparrow Press, 1981.

Ham on Rye. Santa Barbara, Calif.: Black Sparrow Press, 1982.

Bring Me Your Love. Santa Barbara, Calif.: Black Sparrow Press, 1983.

Hot Water Music. Santa Barbara, Calif.: Black Sparrow Press, 1983.

There's No Business. Santa Barbara, Calif.: Black Sparrow Press, 1984.

War All the Time: Poems 1981–1984. Santa Barbara, Calif.: Black Sparrow Press, 1984.

You Get So Alone at Times That It Just Makes Sense. Santa Rosa, Calif.: Black Sparrow Press, 1986.

The Movie, "Barfly." Santa Rosa, Calif.: Black Sparrow Press, 1987.

The Roominghouse Madrigals: Early Selected Poems 1946–1966. Santa Rosa, Calif.: Black Sparrow Press, 1988.

Hollywood: A Novel. Santa Rosa, Calif.: Black Sparrow Press, 1989.

Septuagenarian Stew: Stories & Poems. Santa Rosa, Calif.: Black Sparrow Press, 1990.

In the Shadow of the Rose. Santa Rosa, Calif.: Black Sparrow Press, 1991.

The Last Night of the Earth Poems. Santa Rosa, Calif.: Black Sparrow Press, 1992.

Run with the Hunted: A Charles Bukowski Reader. New York: HarperCollins, 1993.

Pulp. Santa Rosa, Calif.: Black Sparrow Press, 1993.

Confession of a Coward. Santa Rosa, Calif.: Black Sparrow Press, 1995.

Heat Wave. Santa Rosa, Calif.: Black Sparrow Graphic Arts, 1995.

Betting on the Muse: Poems and Stories. Santa Rosa, Calif.: Black Sparrow Press, 1996.

BURROUGHS, WILLIAM S.

Junkie. New York: Ace, 1953.

Naked Lunch. Paris: Olympia, 1959.

The Soft Machine. Paris: Olympia, 1961.

The Ticket That Exploded. Paris: Olympia, 1962.

The Yage Letters. With Allen Ginsberg. San Francisco: City Lights Books, 1963.

Nova Express. New York: Grove, 1964.

The Wild Boys: A Book of the Dead. New York: Grove, 1971.

Exterminator! New York: Seaver/Viking, 1973.

Port of Saints. London: Covent Garden, 1973.

Cities of the Red Night. New York: Holt, Rinehart & Winston, 1981.

The Place of Dead Roads. New York: Holt, Rinehart & Winston, 1983.

The Burroughs File. San Francisco: City Lights Books, 1984.

Queer. New York: Viking, 1985.

The Adding Machine: Collected Essays. London: Calder, 1985.

The Western Lands. New York: Viking/Penguin, 1987.

Interzone. New York: Viking, 1989.

The Letters of William S. Burroughs: 1945–1959. New York: Viking Penguin, 1993.

My Education: A Book of Dreams. New York: Viking, 1995.

Word Virus: The William S. Burroughs Reader. New York: Grove, 1998.

Last Words: The Final Journals of William S. Burroughs. New York: Grove, 2000.

CARROLL, JIM

Living at the Movies. New York: Grossman, 1973.

The Basketball Diaries: Age Twelve to Fifteen. Bolinas, Calif.: Tombouctou Books, 1978.

The Book of Nods. New York: Penguin Books, 1986.

Forced Entries: The Downtown Diaries, 1971–73. New York: Penguin Books, 1987.

Fear of Dreaming: The Selected Poems of Jim Carroll. New York: Penguin Books, 1993.

Void of Course: Poems 1994–1997. New York: Penguin Books, 1998.

CASSADY, CAROLYN

Heart Beat: My Life With Jack & Neal. Berkeley: Creative Arts, 1976.

Off the Road: My Years with Cassady, Kerouac, and Ginsberg. New York: Morrow, 1990.

CASSADY, NEAL

The First Third & Other Writings. San Francisco: City Lights Books, 1971.

As Ever: The Collected Correspondence of Allen Ginsberg & Neal Cassady. Berkeley: Creative Arts, 1977.

Collected Letters, 1944–1967. New York: Penguin, 2004.

CLAUSEN, ANDY

Without Doubt. Berkeley: Zeitgeist Press, 1991.

Trek to the Top of the World. Berkeley: Zeitgeist Press, 1996.

Fortieth Century Man: Selected Verse, 1996–1966. New York: Autonomedia, 1997.

CORSO, GREGORY

The Vestal Lady on Brattle, and Other Poems. Cambridge, Mass.: R. Brukenfeld, 1955.

Gasoline. San Francisco: City Lights Books, 1958.

Happy Birthday of Death. New York: New Directions, 1960.

The American Express. Paris: Olympia Press, 1961.

Long Live Man. New York: New Directions, 1962.

Elegiac Feelings American. New York: New Directions, 1970.

Herald of the Autochthonic Spirit. New York: New Direction, 1981.

Mindfield: New and Selected Poems. New York: Thunder's Mouth Press, 1989.

An Accidental Autobiography: The Selected Letters of Gregory Corso. New York: New Directions, 2003.

CREELEY, ROBERT

For Love: Poems 1950–1960. New York: Scribners, 1962.

The Island. New York: Scribners, 1963.

Poems 1950–1965. London: Calder & Boyars, 1966.

The Charm: Early and Uncollected Poems. Mount Horeb, Wis.: Perishable Press, 1967.

The Finger. Los Angeles: Black Sparrow Press, 1968.

Pieces. Los Angeles: Black Sparrow Press, 1968.

St. Martin's. Los Angeles: Black Sparrow Press, 1971.

Listen. Los Angeles: Black Sparrow Press, 1972.

The Creative. Los Angeles: Black Sparrow Press, 1973.

Inside Out. Los Angeles: Black Sparrow Press, 1973.

Thirty Things. Los Angeles: Black Sparrow Press, 1974.

Away. Santa Barbara, Calif.: Black Sparrow Press, 1976.

Presences: A Text for Marisol. New York: Scribners, 1976.

Selected Poems. New York: Scribners, 1976.

Was That a Real Poem or Did You Just Make It Up Yourself. Santa Barbara, Calif.: Black Sparrow Press, 1976.

Hello: A Journal, February 29–May 3, 1976. New York: New Directions, 1978.

Later. New York: New Directions, 1979.

The Collected Poems of Robert Creeley, 1945–1975. Berkeley: University of California Press, 1982.

Mirrors. New York: New Directions, 1983.

The Collected Prose of Robert Creeley. New York: Boyars, 1984.

Memory Gardens. New York: New Directions, 1986.

The Collected Essays of Robert Creeley. Berkeley: University of California Press, 1989.

Windows. New York: New Directions, 1990.
Selected Poems. Berkeley: University of California Press, 1991.
Echoes. New York: New Directions, 1994.

DI PRIMA, DIANE
This Kind of Bird Flies Backwards. New York: Totem Press, 1958.
Dinners and Nightmares. New York: Corinth Books, 1961.
Earthsong: Poems 1957–1959. New York: Poets Press, 1968.
Memoirs of a Beatnik. New York: Olympia Press, 1969.
Revolutionary Letters. San Francisco: City Lights Books, 1971.
Loba: Part I. Santa Barbara, Calif.: Capra Press, 1973.
Selected Poems, 1956–1975. Plainfield, Vt.: North Atlantic Books, 1975.
Loba as Eve. New York: Phoenix Book Shop, 1975.
Loba: Part II. Point Reyes, Calif.: Eidolon Editions, 1977.
Loba: Parts I–VIII. Berkeley, Calif.: Wingbow Press, 1978.
Pieces of a Song: Selected Poems. San Francisco: City Lights Books, 1990.
Loba. New York: Penguin, 1998.
Recollections of My Life as a Woman. New York: Viking Penguin, 2001.

DORN, ED
What I See in the Maximum Poems. Ventura, Calif.: Migrant Press, 1960.
The Newly Fallen. New York: Totem Press, 1961.
Hands Up! New York: Totem Press, 1964.
Idaho Out. London: Fulcrum Press, 1965.
Geography. London: Fulcrum Press, 1965.
The Rites of Passage: A Brief History. Buffalo, N.Y.: Frontier Press, 1965.
The Shoshoneans: The People of the Basin-Plateau. New York: Morrow, 1966.
The North Atlantic Turbine. London: Fulcrum Press, 1967.
Gunslinger. Los Angeles: Black Sparrow Press, 1968.
Gunslinger: Book II. Los Angeles: Black Sparrow Press, 1969.
Gunslinger I & II. London: Fulcrum Press, 1970.
By the Sound. Buffalo, N.Y.: Frontier Press, 1971.

The Cycle. Buffalo, N.Y.: Frontier Press, 1971.
Some Business Recently Transacted in the White World. Buffalo, N.Y.: Frontier Press, 1971.
Gunslinger, Book III: The Winterbook. Buffalo, N.Y.: Frontier Press, 1972.
Recollections of Gran Apacheria. San Francisco: Turtle Island Foundation, 1974.
Slinger. Berkeley, Calif.: Wingbow Press, 1975.
Collected Poems: 1956–1974. Bolinas, Calif.: Four Seasons Foundation, 1975.
Hello, La Jolla. Berkeley: Wingbow Press, 1978.
Selected Poems. San Francisco: Grey Fox Press, 1978.
Abhorrences. Santa Barbara, Calif.: Black Sparrow Press, 1989.
Way West: Stories, Essays and Verse Accounts, 1963–1993. Santa Barbara, Calif.: Black Sparrow Press, 1993.

DYLAN, BOB
Tarantula. New York: Macmillan, 1971.
Lyrics, 1962–1999. New York: Knopf, 1999.
Lyrics: 1962–2001. New York: Simon & Schuster, 2004.
Chronicles: Volume One. New York: Simon & Schuster, 2004.

EVERSON, WILLIAM (BROTHER ANTONINUS)
The Crooked Lines of God: Poems 1949–1954. Detroit: University of Detroit Press, 1959.
The Hazards of Holiness: Poems 1957–1960. Garden City, N.Y.: Doubleday, 1962.
The Poet Is Dead: A Memorial for Robinson Jeffers. San Francisco: Auerhahn Press, 1964.
Single Source: The Early Poems of William Everson, 1934–1940. Berkeley: Oyez, 1966.
The Rose of Solitude. Garden City, N.Y.: Doubleday, 1967.
In the Fictive Wish. Berkeley: Oyez, 1967.
Robinson Jeffers: Fragments of an Older Fury. Berkeley, Calif.: Oyez, 1968.
The Last Crusade. Berkeley: Oyez, 1969.
The City Does Not Die. Berkeley: Oyez, 1969.
Who Is She Who Looketh Forth as the Morning. Santa Barbara, Calif.: Black Sparrow Press, 1972.
Man-Fate: The Swan Song of Brother Antoninus. New York: New Directions, 1974.
River-Root: A Syzygy for the Bicentennial of These States. Berkeley: Oyez, 1976.

Archetype West: The Pacific Coast as a Literary Region. Berkeley: Oyez, 1976.

The Veritable Years, 1949–1966. Santa Barbara, Calif.: Black Sparrow Press, 1978.

The Masks of Drought: Poems, 1972–1979. Santa Barbara, Calif.: Black Sparrow Press, 1980.

Earth Poetry: Selected Essays and Interviews. Berkeley: Oyez, 1980.

Birth of a Poet: The Santa Cruz Meditations. Santa Rosa, Calif.: Black Sparrow Press, 1982.

On Writing the Waterbirds and Other Presentations: Collected Forewords and Afterwords. Metuchen, N.J.: Scarecrow Press, 1983.

The Excesses of God: Robinson Jeffers as a Religious Figure. Stanford, Calif.: Stanford University Press, 1988.

The Engendering Flood: Book One of Dust Shall Be the Serpent's Food (Cantos I–IV). Santa Rosa, Calif.: Black Sparrow Press, 1990.

Naked Heart: Talking on Poetry, Mysticism, and the Erotic. Albuquerque: University of New Mexico, College of Arts and Sciences, 1992.

The Blood of the Poet: Selected Poems. Seattle: Broken Moon Press, 1993.

Take Hold upon the Future: Letters on Writers and Writing, 1938–1946. Metuchen, N.J.: Scarecrow Press, 1994.

Prodigious Thrust. Santa Barbara, Calif.: Black Sparrow Press, 1996.

FARIÑA, RICHARD

Been Down So Long It Looks Like Up to Me. New York: Random House, 1966.

Long Time Coming and a Long Time Gone. New York: Random House, 1969.

FERLINGHETTI, LAWRENCE

Pictures of the Gone World. San Francisco: City Lights Books, 1955.

A Coney Island of the Mind. New York: New Directions, 1958.

Her. New York: New Directions, 1960.

The Secret Meaning of Things. New York: New Directions, 1969.

Tyrannus Nix? New York: New Directions, 1969.

Back Roads to Far Places. New York: New Directions, 1971.

Open Eye, Open Heart. New York: New Directions, 1973.

Who Are We Now? San Francisco: City Lights Books, 1976.

Landscapes of Living and Dying. New York: New Directions, 1979.

A Trip to Italy and France. New York: New Directions, 1980.

Endless Life: Selected Poems. New York: New Directions, 1984.

Over All the Obscene Boundaries: European Poems and Transitions. New York: New Directions, 1985.

Love in the Days of Rage. New York: Dutton, 1988.

These Are My Rivers: New and Selected Poems, 1955–1993. New York: New Directions, 1993.

A Far Rockaway of the Heart. New York: New Directions, 1997.

San Francisco Poems. San Francisco: City Lights Books, 2001.

How to Paint Sunlight: Lyric Poems and Others, 1997–2000. New York: New Directions, 2001.

FRAZER, BRENDA

Troia: Mexican Memoirs. New York: Croton Press, 1969.

For Love of Ray. London: London Magazine Editions, 1971.

GINSBERG, ALLEN

Howl and Other Poems. San Francisco: City Lights Pocket Books, 1956.

Kaddish and Other Poems: 1958–1960. San Francisco: City Lights Books, 1961.

Empty Mirror: Early Poems. New York: Totem Press/ Corinth Books, 1961.

Reality Sandwiches: 1953–60. San Francisco: City Lights Books, 1963.

The Yage Letters. With William S. Burroughs. San Francisco: City Lights Books, 1963.

Planet News: 1961–1967. San Francisco: City Lights Books, 1968.

Indian Journals: March 1962–May 1963. San Francisco: David Haselwood/City Lights Books, 1970.

The Fall of America: Poems of These States 1965–1971. San Francisco: City Lights Books, 1972.

Allen Verbatim: Lectures on Poetry, Politics, Consciousness. New York: McGraw-Hill, 1974.

Journals: Early Fifties Early Sixties. New York: Grove, 1977.

Mind Breaths: Poems 1972–1977. San Francisco: City Lights Books, 1978.

Plutonian Ode: Poems 1977–1980. San Francisco: City Lights Books, 1982.

Collected Poems 1947–1980. New York: Harper & Row, 1984.

Howl: Original Draft Facsimile, Transcript & Variant Versions, Fully Annotated by Author. New York: Harper & Row, 1986.

White Shroud: Poems 1980–1985. New York: Harper & Row, 1986.

Cosmopolitan Greetings: Poems 1986–1992. New York: HarperCollins, 1994.

Journals Mid-Fifties, 1954–1958. New York: HarperCollins, 1995.

Selected Poems: 1947–1995. New York: HarperCollins, 1996.

Death & Fame: Last Poems, 1993–1997. HarperFlamingo, 1999.

HOFFMAN, ABBIE

Revolution for the Hell of It. New York: Dial, 1968.

Steal This Book. New York: Pirate Editions, 1971.

Soon to Be a Major Motion Picture. New York: Putnam, 1980.

Square Dancing in the Ice Age: Underground Writings. New York: Putnam, 1982.

HOLMES, JOHN CLELLON

Go. New York: Scribners, 1952.

The Horn. New York: Random House, 1958.

Get Home Free. New York: Dutton, 1964.

Nothing More to Declare. New York: Dutton, 1967.

Displaced Person: The Travel Essays. Fayetteville: University of Arkansas Press, 1987.

Passionate Opinions: The Cultural Essays. Fayetteville: University of Arkansas Press, 1988.

Representative Men: The Biographical Essays. Fayetteville: University of Arkansas Press, 1988.

Night Music: Selected Poems. Fayetteville: University of Arkansas Press, 1989.

HUNCKE, HERBERT

Huncke's Journal. New York: Poets Press, 1965.

The Evening Sun Turned Crimson. Cherry Valley, N.Y.: Cherry Valley Editions, 1980.

Guilty of Everything: The Autobiography of Herbert Huncke. New York: Paragon House, 1990.

The Herbert Huncke Reader. New York: Morrow, 1997.

JOANS, TED

Jazz Poems. New York: Rhino Review, 1959.

All of Ted Joans and No More. New York: Excelsior, 1961.

The Hipsters. New York: Corinth, 1961.

Black Pow-Wow: Jazz Poems. New York: Hill & Wang, 1969.

Afrodisia: New Poems. New York: Hill & Wang, 1970.

A Black Manifesto in Jazz Poetry and Prose. London: Calder & Boyars, 1971.

Teducation: Selected Poems. Minneapolis, Minn.: Coffee House Press, 1999.

JOHNSON, JOYCE

Come and Join the Dance. (Under name Joyce Glassman.) New York: Atheneum, 1962.

Bad Connections. New York: Putnam, 1978.

Minor Characters: A Young Woman's Coming-of-Age in the Beat Orbit of Jack Kerouac. Boston: Houghton, 1983.

In the Night Café. New York: Dutton, 1989.

What Lisa Knew: The Truths and Lies of the Steinberg Case. New York: Putnam, 1990.

Door Wide Open: A Beat Love Affair in Letters, 1957–58. With Jack Kerouac. New York: Viking, 2000.

Missing Men: A Memoir. New York: Viking, 2004.

JONES, HETTIE

How I Became Hettie Jones. New York: Dutton, 1990.

Drive. New York: Hanging Loose Press, 1997.

KANDEL, LENORE

The Love Book. San Francisco: Stolen Paper Editions, 1966.

Word Alchemy. New York: Grove, 1967.

KAUFMAN, BOB

Abomunist Manifesto. San Francisco: City Lights Books, 1959.

Does the Secret Mind Whisper? San Francisco: City Lights Books, 1959.

Second April. San Francisco: City Lights Books, 1959.

Solitudes Crowded with Loneliness. New York: New Directions, 1965.

Golden Sardine. San Francisco: City Lights Books, 1967.

The Ancient Rain: Poems 1956–1978. New York: New Directions, 1981.

KEROUAC, JACK

On the Road. New York: Viking, 1957.
The Dharma Bums. New York: Viking, 1958.
The Subterraneans. New York: Grove, 1958.
Doctor Sax: Faust Part Three. New York: Grove, 1959.
Maggie Cassidy: A Love Story. New York: Avon, 1959.
Mexico City Blues. Grove, 1959.
Tristessa. New York: Avon, 1960.
The Scripture of the Golden Eternity. Chevy Chase, Md.:
     Corinth Books, 1960.
Lonesome Traveler. New York: McGraw, 1960.
Book of Dreams. San Francisco: City Lights Books,
     1961.
Big Sur. New York: Farrar, Straus, 1962.
Desolation Angels. New York: Coward, 1965.
Satori in Paris. New York: Grove, 1966.
Vanity of Duluoz: An Adventurous Education, 1935–46.
     New York: Coward, 1968.
Pic. New York: Grove, 1971.
Scattered Poems. San Francisco: City Lights Books,
     1971.
Visions of Cody. New York: McGraw, 1972.
Heaven and Other Poems. San Francisco: Grey Fox
     Press, 1977.
Pomes All Sizes. San Francisco: City Lights, 1992.
Old Angel Midnight. San Francisco: Grey Fox, 1993.
Good Blonde & Others. San Francisco: Grey Fox,
     1993.
Book of Blues. New York: Penguin, 1995.
Jack Kerouac: Selected Letters, 1940–1956. New York:
     Viking, 1995.
The Portable Jack Kerouac. New York: Viking Press,
     1995.
Some of the Dharma. New York: Viking, 1997.
Selected Letters, 1957–1969. New York: Viking, 1999.
Atop an Underwood: Early Stories and Other Writings.
     New York: Viking, 1999.
Door Wide Open: A Beat Love Affair in Letters. With
     Joyce Johnson. New York: Viking, 2000.
Book of Haikus. New York: Penguin, 2003.
Windblown World: The Journals of Jack Kerouac, 1947–
     1954. New York: Viking, 2004.

KESEY, KEN

One Flew over the Cuckoo's Nest. New York: Viking,
     1962.
Sometimes a Great Notion. New York: Viking, 1964.
Kesey's Garage Sale. New York: Viking, 1973.
Demon Box. New York: Viking, 1986.

Sailor Song. New York: Viking, 1992.
Last Go Round. New York: Viking, 1994.
Kesey's Jail Journal. New York: Viking, 2003.

KYGER, JOANNE

The Tapestry and the Web. San Francisco: Four Seasons
     Foundation, 1965.
Joanne. Bolinas, Calif.: Angel Hair Books, 1970.
Places to Go. Los Angeles: Black Sparrow Press, 1970.
Desecheo Notebook. Berkeley: Arif Press, 1971.
Trip Out & Fall Back. Berkeley: Arif Press, 1974.
All This Every Day. Bolinas, Calif.: Big Sky, 1975.
The Wonderful Focus of You. Calais, Vt.: Z Press,
     1980.
Up My Coast. Point Reyes, Calif.: Floating Island
     Books, 1981.
The Japan and India Journals 1960–64. Bolinas, Calif.:
     Tombouctou Books, 1981.
Mexico Blondé. Bolinas, Calif.: Evergreen Press, 1981.
Going On: Selected Poems, 1958–1980. New York:
     Dutton, 1983.
Just Space: Poems, 1979–1989. Santa Rosa: Black
     Sparrow Press, 1991.

LAMANTIA, PHILIP

Erotic Poems. Berkeley: Bern Porter Books, 1946.
Ekstasis. San Francisco: Auerhahn Press, 1959.
Destroyed Works. San Francisco: Auerhahn Press,
     1962.
Touch of the Marvelous. Berkeley: Oyez, 1966.
Selected Poems 1943–1966. San Francisco: City Lights
     Books, 1967.
The Blood of the Air. San Francisco: Four Seasons
     Foundation, 1970.
Becoming Visible. San Francisco: City Lights Books,
     1981.
Meadowlark West. San Francisco: City Lights Books,
     1986.
Bed of Sphinxes. San Francisco: City Lights Books,
     1997.

LEARY, TIMOTHY

The Politics of Ecstasy. New York: Putnam's, 1968.
High Priest. New York: World, 1968.
Jail Notes. New York: Douglas, 1970.
Confessions of a Hope Fiend. New York: Bantam,
     1973.

Changing My Mind, Among Others: Lifetime Writings. Englewood Cliffs, N.J.: Prentice Hall, 1982.

Flashbacks: An Autobiography. Boston: Tarcher, 1983.

LENNON, JOHN

In His Own Write. New York: Simon & Schuster, 1964.

A Spaniard in the Works. New York: Simon & Schuster, 1965.

MATZ, MARTY

In the Seasons of My Eye: Selected Writings 1953–2001. New York: Panther Books, 2005.

MCCLURE, MICHAEL

Passage. Big Sur, Calif.: Jonathan Williams, 1956.

For Artaud. New York: Totem Press, 1959.

Hymns to St. Geryon and Other Poems. San Francisco: Auerhahn Press, 1959.

Dark Brown. San Francisco: Auerhahn Press, 1961.

The New Book/A Book of Torture. New York: Grove, 1961.

Meat Science Essays. San Francisco: City Lights Books, 1963.

The Beard. Berkeley: Oyez, 1965.

Poisoned Wheat. San Francisco: Oyez, 1965.

Freewheelin' Frank. With Frank Reynolds. New York: Grove, 1967.

Hail Thee Who Play: A Poem. Santa Barbara, Calif.: Black Sparrow Press, 1968.

Love Lion Book. San Francisco: Four Seasons Foundation, 1968.

Ghost Tantras. San Francisco: Four Seasons Foundation, 1969.

The Sermons of Jean Harlow and the Curses of Billy the Kid. San Francisco: Four Seasons Foundation, 1969.

Star. New York: Grove, 1970.

The Adept. New York: Delacorte, 1971.

Rare Angel. Los Angeles: Black Sparrow Press, 1974.

September Blackberries. New York: New Directions, 1974.

A Fist-Full (1956–1957). Los Angeles: Black Sparrow Press, 1974.

Jaguar Skies. New York: New Directions, 1975.

Josephine: The Mouse Singer. New York: New Directions, 1980.

Scratching the Beat Surface. San Francisco: North Point, 1982.

Fragments of Perseus. New York: New Directions, 1983.

Selected Poems. New York: New Directions, 1986.

Rebel Lions. New York: New Directions, 1991.

Simple Eyes and Other Poems. New York: New Directions, 1994.

Huge Dreams: San Francisco and Beat Poems. New York: Penguin, 1999.

Rain Mirror. New York: New Directions, 1999.

Plum Stones: Cartoons of No Heaven. Oakland: O Books, 2002.

MELTZER, DAVID

We All Have Something to Say to Each Other. San Francisco: Auerhahn Press, 1962.

The Process. Berkeley: Oyez, 1965.

The Dark Continent. Berkeley: Oyez, 1967.

Journal of the Birth. Berkeley: Oyez, 1967.

The Agency. North Hollywood: Essex House, 1968.

The Agent. North Hollywood: Essex House, 1968.

Orf. North Hollywood: Essex House, 1968.

How Many Blocks in the Pile? North Hollywood: Essex House, 1968.

Abulafia Song. Santa Barbara, Calif.: Unicorn Press, 1969.

Lovely, book 1 of *Brain Plant.* North Hollywood: Essex House, 1969.

Healer, book 2 of *Brain Plant.* North Hollywood: Essex House, 1969.

Out, book 3 of *Brain Plant.* North Hollywood: Essex House, 1969.

Glue Factory, book 4 of *Brain Plant.* North Hollywood: Essex House, 1969.

The Martyr. North Hollywood: Essex House, 1969.

Luna. Los Angeles: Black Sparrow Press, 1970.

Star. North Hollywood: Brandon House, 1970.

Bark: A Polemic. Santa Barbara, Calif.: Capra Press, 1973.

French Broom. Berkeley: Oyez, 1973.

Hero / Lil. Los Angeles: Black Sparrow Press, 1973.

Tens: Selected Poems 1961–1971. New York: McGraw-Hill, 1973.

Blue Rags. Berkeley: Oyez, 1974.

Harps. Berkeley: Oyez, 1975.

Bolero: A Section from Asaph. Berkeley: Oyez, 1976.

Six. Los Angeles: Black Sparrow Press, 1976.

Two-Way Mirror: A Poetry Note-Book. Berkeley: Oyez, 1977.

The Art / The Veil. Milwaukee: Membrane Press, 1981.

The Name: Selected Poetry, 1973–1983. Santa Barbara: Black Sparrow, 1984.

Arrows: Selected Poetry, 1957–1992. Santa Rosa: Black Sparrow, 1994.

Beat Thing. Albuquerque, N. Mex.: La Alameda Press, 2004.

MICHELINE, JACK

River of Red Wine. New York: Troubadour Press, 1958.

I Kiss Angels. New York: Interim Books, 1962.

In the Bronx and Other Stories. New York: Sam Hooker Press, 1965.

Poems of Dr Innisfree. San Francisco: Beatitude Press, 1975.

Yellow Horn. San Francisco: Golden Mountain Press, 1975.

Street of Lost Fools. Mastic, N.Y.: Street Press, 1975.

Last House in America. San Francisco: Second Coming Press, 1976.

North of Manhattan: Collected Poems, Ballads and Songs 1954–1975. San Francisco: Manroot, 1976.

Purple Submarine. San Francisco: Greenlight Press, 1976.

Skinny Dynamite. San Francisco: Second Coming Press, 1980.

MORRISON, JIM

The Lords and the New Creatures. New York: Simon & Schuster, 1970.

Wilderness: The Lost Writings of Jim Morrison, Volume 1. New York: Random House, 1988.

The American Night: The Writings of Jim Morrison, Volume 2. New York: Random House, 1990.

NORSE, HAROLD

The Undersea Mountain. Denver: Swallow, 1953.

The Dancing Beasts. New York: Macmillan, 1962.

Karma Circuit: 20 Poems & A Preface. London: Nothing Doing in London, 1967.

Hotel Nirvana: Selected Poems, 1953–1973. San Francisco: City Lights Books, 1974.

I See America Daily. San Francisco: Mother's Hen, 1974.

Beat Hotel. Translated into German by Carl Weissner. Augsburg: Maro Verlag, 1975.

Carnivorous Saint: Gay Poems, 1941–1946. San Francisco: Gay Sunshine Press, 1977.

The Love Poems, 1940–1985. Trumansburg, N.Y.: Crossing Press, 1986.

Memoirs of a Bastard Angel. New York: Morrow, 1989.

OLSON, CHARLES

Call Me Ishmael. New York: Reynal & Hitchcock, 1947.

The Maximus Poems / 1–10. Stuttgart: Jonathan Williams, 1953.

The Maximus Poems / 11–22. Stuttgart: Jonathan Williams, 1956.

Projective Verse. New York: Totem Press, 1959.

The Maximus Poems. New York: Jargon/Corinth, 1960.

The Distances. New York: Grove, 1960.

Maximus, from Dogtown—I. San Francisco: Auerhahn, 1961.

A Bibliography on America for Edward Dorn. San Francisco: Four Seasons, 1964.

Human Universe and Other Essays. San Francisco: Auerhahn Society, 1965.

Selected Writings. New York: New Directions, 1966.

The Maximus Poems, IV, V, VI. New York: Grossman, 1968.

The Special View of History. Berkeley: Oyez, 1970.

Archaeologist of Morning. New York: Grossman, 1970.

Poetry and Truth: The Beloit Lectures and Poems. San Francisco: Four Seasons, 1971.

Additional Prose. Bolinas, Calif.: Four Seasons, 1974.

The Post Office. Bolinas, Calif.: Grey Fox Press, 1975.

The Maximus Poems, Volume Three. New York: Grossman, 1975.

Charles Olson and Ezra Pound: An Encounter at St. Elizabeths. New York: Grossman, 1975.

The Horses of the Sea. Santa Barbara, Calif.: Black Sparrow Press, 1976.

The Fiery Hunt and Other Plays. Bolinas, Calif.: Four Seasons, 1977.

Muthologos: The Collected Lectures and Interviews. Bolinas, Calif.: Four Seasons, 1978.

Charles Olson & Robert Creeley: The Complete Correspondence. Santa Barbara, Calif.: Black Sparrow Press, 1980.

The Maximus Poems. Berkeley: University of California Press, 1983.

The Collected Poems of Charles Olson, Excluding the Maximus Poems. Berkeley: University of California Press, 1987.

A Nation of Nothing but Poetry: Supplementary Poems. Santa Rosa: Black Sparrow, 1989.
Collected Prose. Berkeley: University of California Press, 1997.

REXROTH, KENNETH
In What Hour. New York: Macmillan, 1940.
The Phoenix and the Tortoise. Norfolk, Conn.: New Directions, 1944.
The Art of Worldly Wisdom. Prairie City, Ill.: Decker Press, 1949.
The Signature of All Things. New York: New Directions, 1950.
Beyond the Mountains. New York: New Directions, 1951.
The Dragon and the Unicorn. Norfolk, Conn.: New Directions, 1952.
In Defense of the Earth. New York: New Directions, 1956.
Bird in the Bush: Obvious Essays. New York: New Directions, 1959.
Assays. Norfolk, Conn.: New Directions, 1961.
Natural Numbers: New and Selected Poems. Norfolk, Conn.: New Directions, 1963.
The Homestead Called Damascus. New York: New Directions, 1963.
An Autobiographical Novel. Garden City, N.J.: Doubleday, 1966.
The Collected Shorter Poems. New York: New Directions, 1967.
Classics Revisited. Chicago: Quadrangle, 1968.
The Collected Longer Poems. New York: New Directions, 1968.
The Alternative Society: Essays from the Other World. New York: Herder & Herder, 1970.
With Eye and Ear. New York: Herder & Herder, 1970.
American Poetry in the Twentieth Century. New York: Herder & Herder, 1971.
Sky Sea Birds Trees Earth House Beasts Flowers. Santa Barbara, Calif.: Unicorn Press, 1971.
The Elastic Report: Essays in Literature and Ideas. New York: Seabury Press, 1973.
Communalism: From its Origins to the Twentieth Century. New York: Seabury Press, 1974.
New Poems. New York: New Directions, 1974.

SANDERS, ED
Poem from Jail. San Francisco: City Lights Books, 1963.

The Family: The Story of Charles Manson's Dune Buggy Attack Battalion. New York: Dutton, 1971.
Tales of Beatnik Glory. New York: Stonehill, 1975.
Investigative Poetry. San Francisco: City Lights Books, 1976.
Fame & Love in New York. Berkeley: Turtle Island Foundation, 1980.
Thirsting for Peace in a Raging Century: Selected Poems 1961–1985. Minneapolis: Coffee House, 1987.
Hymn to the Rebel Café. Santa Rosa, Calif.: Black Sparrow, 1993.
Chekhov. Santa Rosa, Calif.: Black Sparrow, 1995.
1968: A History in Verse. Santa Rosa, Calif.: Black Sparrow, 1997.
America: A History in Verse, Volume I, 1900–1939. Santa Rosa, Calif.: Black Sparrow, 2000.
The Poetry and Life of Allen Ginsberg: A Narrative Poem. Woodstock, N.Y.: Overlook, 2000.
America: A History in Verse, Volume II, 1940–1961. Santa Rosa: Black Sparrow, 2000.

SILVERMAN, HERSCHEL
Lift-Off: New and Selected Poems: 1961–2001. Sudbury, Mass.: Water Row Books, 2002.

SNYDER, GARY
Riprap. Kyoto, Japan: Origin, 1959.
Myths & Texts. New York: Totem/Corinth, 1960.
Six Sections from Mountains and Rivers without End. San Francisco: Four Seasons, 1965.
A Range of Poems. London: Fulcrum Press, 1966.
The Back Country. London: Fulcrum Press, 1967.
The Blue Sky. London: Fulcrum Press, 1967.
Earth House Hold: Technical Notes & Queries for Fellow Dharma Revolutionaries. New York: New Directions, 1969.
Regarding Wave. Iowa City: Windhover Press, 1969.
Manzanita. Bolinas, Calif.: Four Seasons, 1972.
Turtle Island. New York: New Directions, 1974.
The Old Ways: Six Essays. San Francisco: City Lights Books, 1977.
He Who Hunted Birds in His Father's Village: The Dimensions of a Haida Myth. Bolinas, Calif.: Grey Fox, 1979.
The Real Work: Interviews & Talks 1964–1979. New York: New Directions, 1980.
Passage through India. San Francisco: Grey Fox, 1983.

No Nature: New and Selected Poems. New York: Pantheon, 1992.

Mountains and Rivers without End. Washington, D.C.: Counterpoint, 1996.

The Gary Snyder Reader. Washington, D.C.: Counterpoint, 1999.

Look Out: A Selection of Writings. New York: New Directions, 2002.

THOMPSON, HUNTER S.

Hell's Angels: A Strange and Terrible Saga. 1967. New York: Random House, 1999.

Fear and Loathing in Las Vegas: A Savage Journey to the Heart of the American Dream. New York: Random House, 1972.

Fear and Loathing on the Campaign Trail '72. San Francisco: Straight Arrow Books, 1973.

The Great Shark Hunt: Strange Tales from a Strange Time; Gonzo Papers, Volume One. New York: Summit Books, 1979.

The Curse of Lono. New York: Bantam, 1983.

Generation of Swine: Tales of Shame and Degradation in the '80s; Gonzo Papers, Volume Two. New York: Summit Books, 1988.

Songs of the Doomed: More Notes on the Death of the American Dream; Gonzo Papers, Volume Three. New York: Summit Books, 1990.

Silk Road: Thirty-three Years in the Passing Lane. New York: Simon & Schuster, 1990.

Better Than Sex: Confessions of a Political Junkie; Gonzo Papers, Volume Four. New York: Random House, 1993.

The Proud Highway: The Saga of a Desperate Southern Gentleman, 1955–1967. New York: Villard, 1997.

The Rum Diary: The Long Lost Novel. New York: Simon & Schuster, 1998.

Screwjack and Other Stories. New York: Simon & Schuster, 2000.

Fear and Loathing in America: Brutal Odyssey of an Outlaw Journalist, 1968–1976. New York: Simon & Schuster, 2000.

The Kingdom of Fear: Loathsome Secrets of a Star-Crossed Child in the Final Days of the American Century. New York: Simon & Schuster, 2003.

Hey Rube. New York: Simon & Schuster, 2004.

VEGA, JANINE POMMY

Poems to Fernando. San Francisco: City Lights Books, 1968.

Journal of a Hermit. Cherry Valley, N.Y.: Cherry Valley Editions, 1974.

Morning Passage. New York: Telephone Books, 1976.

Tracking the Serpent: Journeys to Four Continents. San Francisco: City Lights Books, 1997.

Mad Dogs of Trieste: New & Selected Poems. Santa Rosa: Black Sparrow Press, 2000.

The Green Piano. Boston: Black Sparrow Books, 2005.

WALDMAN, ANNE

Giant Night. New York: Corinth Books, 1970.

Baby Breakdown. Indianapolis, Ind.: Bobbs-Merrill, 1970.

Spin Off. Bolinas, Calif.: Big Sky, 1972.

Life Notes. Indianapolis, Ind.: Bobbs-Merrill, 1973.

Fast Speaking Woman and Other Chants. San Francisco: City Lights Books, 1975.

Skin Meat Bones. Minneapolis, Minn.: Coffee House Press, 1985.

Helping the Dreamer: New and Selected Poems, 1966–1988. Minneapolis, Minn.: Coffee House Press, 1989.

Iovis: All Is Full of Jove. Minneapolis, Minn.: Coffee House Press, 1993.

Kill or Cure. New York: Penguin, 1994.

Iovis II. Minneapolis, Minn.: Coffee House Press, 1997.

Marriage: A Sentence. New York: Penguin, 2000.

WEISS, RUTH

GALLERY OF WOMEN. San Francisco: Adler Press, 1959.

SOUTH PACIFIC. San Francisco: Adler Press, 1959.

BLUE IN GREEN. San Francisco: Adler Press, 1960.

DESERT JOURNAL. Boston: Good Gay Poets, 1977.

SINGLE OUT. Mill Valley, Calif.: D'Aurora Press, 1978.

A NEW VIEW OF MATTER. Prague, The Czech Republic: Mata Press, 1999.

WELCH, LEW

Wobbly Rock. San Francisco: Auerhahn Press, 1960.

On Out. Berkeley: Oyez, 1965.

Hermit Poems. San Francisco: Four Seasons Foundation, 1965.

Courses. San Francisco: Dave Haselwood, 1968.

Ring of Bone. Bolinas, Calif.: Grey Fox Press, 1973.

Trip Trap: Haiku along the Road from San Francisco to New York, 1959. With Jack Kerouac and Albert Saijo. Bolinas, Calif.: Grey Fox Press, 1973.

How I Work as a Poet. Bolinas, Calif.: Grey Fox Press, 1977.

I, Leo: An Unfinished Novel. Bolinas, Calif.: Grey Fox Press, 1977.

WHALEN, PHILIP

Self-Portrait from Another Direction. San Francisco: Auerhahn Press, 1960.

Like I Say. New York: Totem Press/Corinth Books, 1960.

Memoirs of an Interglacial Age. San Francisco: Auerhahn Press, 1960.

T/O. San Francisco: Dave Haselwood, 1967.

On Bear's Head: Selected Poems. New York: Harcourt, Brace & World/Coyote, 1969.

Severance Pay: Poems 1967–1969. San Francisco: Four Seasons Foundation, 1970.

Scenes of Life at the Capital. San Francisco: Maya, 1970.

Imaginary Speeches for a Brazen Head. Los Angeles: Black Sparrow Press, 1972.

The Kindness of Strangers: Poems, 1969–1974. Bolinas, Calif.: Four Seasons Foundation, 1976.

Decompressions: Selected Poems. Bolinas, Calif.: Grey Fox Press, 1977.

Enough Said: Fluctuat Nec Mergitur: Poems 1974–1979. San Francisco: Grey Fox Press, 1980.

Heavy Breathing: Poems, 1967–1980. San Francisco: Four Seasons Foundation, 1983.

Canoeing up Cabarga Creek: Buddhist Poems, 1955–1986. Berkeley: Parallax Press, 1996.

WIENERS, JOHN

The Hotel Wentley Poems. San Francisco: Auerhahn Press, 1958.

Ace of Pentacles. New York: James F. Carr & Robert A. Wilson, 1964.

Chinoiserie. San Francisco: Dave Haselwood, 1965.

Pressed Wafer. Buffalo, N.Y.: Gallery Upstairs Press, 1967.

Unhired. Mt. Horeb, Wis.: Perishable Press, 1968.

Asylum Poems. New York: Angel Hair, 1969.

Youth. New York: Phoenix Book Shop, 1970.

Nerves. London: Cape Goliard, 1970.

Selected Poems. New York: Grossman, 1972.

Woman. Buffalo, N.Y.: Institute of Further Studies, 1972.

Hotels. New York: Angel Hair, 1974.

Behind the State Capitol, Or Cincinnati Pike. Boston: Good Gay Poets, 1975.

Selected Poems, 1958–1984. Santa Barbara, Calif.: Black Sparrow Press, 1986.

Cultural Affairs in Boston: Poetry & Prose, 1956–1985. Santa Rosa, Calif.: Black Sparrow Press, 1988.

The Journal of John Wieners Is to Be Called 707 Scott Street for Billie Holiday, 1959. Los Angeles: Sun & Moon Press, 1996.

Selected Bibliography of Secondary Sources

Compiled by Jennie Skerl

Anctil, Pierre, et al., eds. *Un Homme Grand: Jack Kerouac at the Crossroads of Many Cultures.* Ottawa: Carleton University Press, 1990.

Ansen, Alan. *William Burroughs: An Essay.* Sudbury, Mass.: Water Row, 1986.

Bartlett, Jeffrey. *One Vast Page: Essays on the Beat Writers, Their Books, and My Life, 1950–1980.* Berkeley, Calif.: J. Bartlett, 1991.

Bartlett, Lee, ed. *The Beats: Essays in Criticism.* Jefferson, N.C.: McFarland, 1981.

Beard, Richard, and Leslie Cohen Berkowitz. *Greenwich Village: Culture and Counterculture.* New York: Rutgers University Press, 1993.

Beaulieu, Victor-Lévy. *Jack Kerouac: A Chicken Essay.* Trans. Sheila Fischman. Toronto: Coach House, 1975.

Belgrad, Daniel. *The Culture of Spontaneity: Improvisation and the Arts in Postwar America.* Chicago: University of Chicago Press, 1998.

Bennett, Robert. *Deconstructing Post-WW II New York City: The Literature, Art, Jazz, and Architecture of an Emerging Global Capital.* New York: Routledge, 2003.

Berthoff, Warner. *A Literature without Qualities: American Writing since 1945.* Berkeley: University of California Press, 1979.

Bloom, Harold, ed. *Jack Kerouac's On the Road.* Bloom's Modern Critical Interpretations. Philadelphia: Chelsea House, 2004.

Breslin, James E. B. *From Modern to Contemporary: American Poetry 1945–1965.* Chicago: University of Chicago Press, 1984.

Burns, Glen. *Great Poets Howl: A Study of Allen Ginsberg's Poetry, 1943–1955.* Frankfurt am Main: Peter Lang, 1983.

Campbell, James. *This is the Beat Generation: New York–San Francisco–Paris.* Berkeley: University of California Press, 1999.

Carr, Roy. *The Hip: Hipsters, Jazz and the Beat Generation.* London: Faber, 1986.

Charters, Ann, ed. *The Beats: Literary Bohemians in Postwar America.* Dictionary of Literary Biography vol. 16: 2 vols. Detroit: Gale Research, 1983.

Charters, Samuel. *Some Poems/Some Poets: Studies in American Underground Poetry Since 1945.* Berkeley: Oyez, 1971.

Cherkovski, Neeli. *Whitman's Wild Children.* Venice, Calif.: Lapis Press, 1988.

Clay, Steven, and Rodney Phillips. *A Secret Location on the Lower East Side: Adventures in Writing, 1960–1980.* New York: The New York Public Library and Granary Books, 1998.

Cook, Bruce. The *Beat Generation: The Tumultuous '50s Movement and Its Impact on Today.* New York: Scribner, 1971.

Davidson, Michael. *The San Francisco Poetry Renaissance: Poetics and Community at Mid-Century.* New York: Cambridge University Press, 1989.

Dean, Tim. *Gary Snyder and the American Unconscious: Inhabiting the Ground.* New York: St. Martin's, 1991.

Docherty, Brian. *The Beat Generation Writers.* New York: Westview, 1995.

Donaldson, Scott, ed. On the Road: *Text and Criticism.* New York: Viking, 1979.

Duberman, Martin. *Black Mountain: An Exploration in Community.* New York: Dutton, 1972.

Duval, Jean-François. *Bukowski and the Beats: A Commentary on the Beat Generation.* Northville, Minn.: Sun Dog Press, 2002.

Ehrenreich, Barbara. *The Hearts of Men: American Dreams and the Flight from Commitment.* New York: Doubleday, 1983.

Ehrlich, J. W., ed. *Howl of the Censor.* San Carlos, Calif.: Nourse, 1961.

Ellingham, Lewis, and Kevin Killian. *Poet Be Like God: Jack Spicer and the San Francisco Renaissance.* Hanover, N.H.: University Press of New England, 1998.

Elmborg, James K. *"A Pageant of Its Time": Edward Dorn's Slinger and the Sixties.* New York: Peter Lang, 1998.

Fiedler, Leslie. *Love and Death in the American Novel.* New York: Stein & Day, 1966.

———. *Waiting for the End.* New York: Stein & Day, 1964.

Fields, Rick. *How the Swans Came to the Lake: A Narrative History of Buddhism in America.* Third ed. Boston: Shambhala, 1992.

Foster, Edward Halsey. *Understanding the Beats.* Columbia: University of South Carolina Press, 1992.

———. *Understanding the Black Mountain Poets.* Columbia: University of South Carolina Press, 1995.

French, Warren G. *Jack Kerouac.* Boston: Twayne, 1986.

———. *The San Francisco Poetry Renaissance, 1955–1960.* Boston: Twayne, 1991.

Giamo, Ben. *Kerouac, The Word and The Way: Prose Artist as Spiritual Quester.* Carbondale: Southern Illinois University Press, 2000.

Ginsberg, Allen. *To Eberhart from Ginsberg: A Letter about Howl.* Lincoln, Mass.: Penmaen, 1976.

Goodman, Michael B. *Contemporary Literary Censorship: The Case History of Burroughs' Naked Lunch.* Metuchen, N.J.: Scarecrow, 1981.

Green, Michelle. *The Dream at the End of the World: Paul Bowles and the Literary Renegades in Tangier.* New York: HarperCollins, 1991.

Harris, Oliver. *William Burroughs and the Secret of Fascination.* Carbondale: Southern Illinois University Press, 2003.

Hassan, Ihab. *Contemporary American Literature 1945–1972.* New York: Ungar, 1973.

Hrebeniak, Michael. *Action Writing: Jack Kerouac's Wild Form.* Carbondale: Southern Illinois University Press, 2006.

Hipkiss, Robert A. *Jack Kerouac: A Prophet of the New Romanticism.* Lawrence: Regents Press of Kansas, 1976.

Hoffman, Frederick J. *Marginal Manners: The Variants of Bohemia.* Evanston, Ill.: Row, Peterson, 1962.

Holton, Robert. *On the Road: Jack Kerouac's Ragged American Journey.* Boston: Twayne, 1999.

Howard, Richard. *Alone with America: Essays on the Art of Poetry in the United States since 1950.* New York: Atheneum, 1980.

Hunt, Timothy A. *Kerouac's Crooked Road: Development of a Fiction.* 1981. Berkeley: University of California Press, 1996.

Hyde, Lewis, ed. *On the Poetry of Allen Ginsberg.* Ann Arbor: University of Michigan Press, 1984.

Johnson, Rob. *The Lost Years of William S. Burroughs: Beats in South Texas.* College Station: Texas A&M University Press, 2006.

Johnson, Ronna C., and Nancy M. Grace, eds. *Girls Who Wore Black: Women Writing the Beat Generation.* New Brunswick, N.J.: Rutgers University Press, 2002.

Jones, James T. *Jack Kerouac's Duluoz Legend: The Mythic Form of an Autobiographical Fiction.* Carbondale: Southern Illinois University Press, 1999.

———. *A Map of Mexico City Blues: Jack Kerouac as Poet.* Carbondale: Southern Illinois University Press, 1992.

Knight, Brenda. *Women of the Beat Generation: The Writers, Artists and Muses at the Heart of Revolution.* Berkeley: Conari, 1996.

Lardas, John. *The Bop Apocalypse: The Religious Visions of Kerouac, Ginsberg, and Burroughs.* Urbana: University of Illinois Press, 2001.

Lauridson, Inger Thorup, and Per Dalgard. *The Beat Generation and the Russian New Wave.* Ann Arbor: Ardis, 1990.

Lawlor, William, ed. *Beat Culture: Icons, Lifestyles, and Impact.* Santa Barbara, Calif.: ABC–CLIO, 2005.

———. *The Beat Generation: A Bibliographical Teaching Guide.* Lanham, Md.: Scarecrow, 1998.

Lee, Robert A., ed. *The Beat Generation Writers.* London: Pluto Press, 1996.

Lhamon, W. T., Jr. *Deliberate Speed: The Origins of a Cultural Style in the American 1950s.* Washington, D.C.: Smithsonian Institution Press, 1990.

Lydenberg, Robin. *Word Cultures: Radical Theory and Practice in William S. Burroughs' Fiction.* Urbana: University of Illinois Press, 1987.

Martinez, Manuel Luis. *Countering the Counterculture: Rereading Postwar American Dissent from Jack Kerouac to Tomás Rivera.* Madison: The University of Wisconsin Press, 2003.

Maynard, John A. *Venice West: The Beat Generation in Southern California.* New Brunswick, N.J.: Rutgers, 1991.

Merrill, Thomas F. *Allen Ginsberg.* 1969. Boston: Twayne, 1988.

Miles, Barry. *The Beat Hotel: Ginsberg, Burroughs, and Corso in Paris, 1957–1963.* New York: Grove Press, 2000.

Miller, Douglas T., and Marion Nowack. *The Fifties: The Way We Really Were.* Garden City, N.Y.: Doubleday, 1977.

Molesworth, Charles. *Gary Snyder's Vision: Poetry and the Real Work.* Columbia: University of Missouri Press, 1983.

Morgan, Bill. *The Beat Generation in New York: A Walking Tour of Jack Kerouac's City.* San Francisco: City Lights Books, 1990.

———. *The Beat Generation in San Francisco: A Literary Tour.* San Francisco: City Lights Press, 2003.

Mottram, Eric. *Allen Ginsberg in the Sixties.* Brighton, U.K.: Unicorn Bookshop, 1972.

———. *William Burroughs: The Algebra of Need.* London: Boyars, 1977.

Mullins, Greg A. *Colonial Affairs: Bowles, Burroughs, and Chester Write Tangier.* Madison: University of Wisconsin Press, 2002.

Murphy, Patrick D., ed. *Critical Essays on Gary Snyder.* Boston: G. K. Hall, 1990.

———. *Understanding Gary Snyder.* Columbia: University of South Carolina Press, 1992.

Murphy, Timothy. *Wising Up the Marks: The Amodern William Burroughs.* Berkeley: University of California Press, 1997.

Myrsiades, Kostas, ed. *The Beat Generation: Critical Essays.* New York: Peter Lang, 2002.

Newhouse, Thomas. *The Beat Generation and the Popular Novel in the United States, 1945–1970.* Jefferson, N.C.: McFarland & Company, Inc., Publishers, 2000.

Olson, Kirby. *Gregory Corso: Doubting Thomist.* Carbondale: Southern Illinois University Press, 2002.

Panish, Jon. *The Color of Jazz: Race and Representation in Postwar American Culture.* Jackson: University Press of Mississippi, 1997.

Paul, Sherman. *In Search of the Primitive: Rereading David Antin, Jerome Rothenberg, and Gary Snyder.* Baton Rouge: Louisiana State University Press, 1986.

Phillips, Rod. *"Forest Beatniks" and "Urban Thoreaus": Gary Snyder, Jack Kerouac, Lew Welch, and Michael McClure.* New York: Peter Lang, 2000.

Phillips, Lisa, ed. *Beat Culture and the New America:1958–1965.* New York: Whitney Museum of American Art/Flammarion, 1996.

Polsky, Ned. *Beats, Hustlers and Others.* New York: Doubleday, 1967.

Portugés, Paul. *The Visionary Poetics of Allen Ginsberg.* Santa Barbara: Ross-Erikson, 1978.

Raskin, Jonah. *American Scream: Allen Ginsberg's Howl and the Making of the Beat Generation.* Berkeley: University of California Press, 2004.

Rexroth, Kenneth. *The Alternative Society: Essays from the Other World.* New York: Herder, 1970.

———. *Poetry in the Twentieth Century.* New York: Herder, 1967.

Rigney, Francis J., and L. Douglas Smith. *The Real Bohemia: A Sociological and Psychological Study of the "Beats."* New York: Basic, 1961.

Russell, Jamie. *Queer Burroughs.* New York: Palgrave, 2001.

Sargent, Jack. *Naked Lens: An Illustrated History of Beat Cinema.* London: Creation Books, 1997.

Sawyer-Lauçanno, Christopher. *The Continued Pilgrimage: American Writers in Paris 1944–1960.* San Francisco: City Lights Books, 1997.

Schneiderman, Davis, and Philip Walsh. *Retaking the Universe: William S. Burroughs in the Age of Globalization.* London: Pluto, 2004.

Schuler, Robert. *Journeys Toward the Original Mind: The Long Poems of Gary Snyder.* New York: Peter Lang, 1994.

Selerie, Gavin, ed. *Gregory Corso.* London: Binnacle, 1982.

Skau, Michael. *"A Clown in a Grave": Complexities and Tensions in the Works of Gregory Corso.* Carbondale: Southern Illinois University Press, 1999.

———. *"Constantly Risking Absurdity": The Writings of Lawrence Ferlinghetti.* Troy, N.Y.: Whitston, 1989.

Skerl, Jennie. *Reconstructing the Beats.* New York: Palgrave Macmillan, 2004.

———. *William S. Burroughs.* Boston: Twayne, 1985.

Skerl, Jennie, and Robin Lydenberg. *William S. Burroughs at the Front: Critical Reception, 1959–1989.* Carbondale: Southern Illinois University Press, 1991.

Smith, Larry. *Lawrence Ferlinghetti: Poet-at-Large.* Carbondale: Southern Illinois University Press, 1990.

Smith, Richard Cándida. *Utopia and Dissent: Art, Poetry, and Politics in California.* Berkeley: University of California Press, 1995.

Sobieszek, Robert A. *Ports of Entry: William S. Burroughs and the Arts.* Thames and Hudson: Los Angeles County Museum of Art, 1996.

Solnit, Rebecca. *Secret Exhibition: Six California Artists of the Cold War Era.* San Francisco: City Lights Books, 1990.

Stephenson, Gregory. *The Daybreak Boys: Essays on the Literature of the Beat Generation.* Carbondale: Southern Illinois University Press, 1990.

———. *Exiled Angel: A Study of the Work of Gregory Corso.* London: Hearing Eye, 1989.

Sterritt, David. *Mad to be Saved: The Beats, the '50s, and Film.* Carbondale: Southern Illinois University Press, 1998.

———. *Screening the Beats: Media Culture and the Beat Sensibility.* Carbondale: Southern Illinois University Press, 2004.

Steuding, Bob. *Gary Snyder.* Boston: Twayne, 1976.

Stiles, Bradley J. *Emerson's Contemporaries and Kerouac's Crowd: A Problem of Self-Location.* Madison, N.J.: Fairleigh Dickenson Press, 2003.

Suiter, John. *Poets on the Peaks: Gary Snyder, Philip Whalen & Jack Kerouac in the North Cascades.* Washington, D.C.: Counterpoint, 2002.

Sukenick, Ronald. *Down and In: Life in the Underground.* New York: Collier, 1987.

Swartz, Omar. *The View from On the Road: The Rhetorical Vision of Jack Kerouac.* Carbondale: Southern Illinois University Press, 1999.

Theado, Matt, ed. *The Beats: A Literary Reference.* New York: Carroll & Graf, 2003.

———. *Understanding Jack Kerouac.* Columbia: University of South Carolina Press, 2000.

Trigilio, Tony. *"Strange Prophecies Anew": Rereading Apocalypse in Blake, H. D., and Ginsberg.* Madison, N.J.: Farleigh Dickinson University Press, 2000.

Tytell, John. *Naked Angels: The Lives and Literature of the Beat Generation.* New York: McGraw-Hill, 1976.

van Minnen, Cornelius A., et al. *Beat Culture: The 1950's and Beyond.* Amsterdam: VU University Press, 1999.

Vendler, Helen. *Part of Nature, Part of Us: Modern American Poets.* Cambridge, Mass.: Harvard University Press, 1980.

Waldman, Anne, and Andrew Schelling, eds. *Disembodied Poetics: Annals of The Jack Kerouac School.* Albuquerque: University of New Mexico Press, 1994.

Watson, Steven. *The Birth of the Beat Generation: Visionaries, Rebels, and Hipsters, 1944–1960.* New York: Pantheon Books, 1995.

Weinreich, Regina. *The Spontaneous Poetics of Jack Kerouac: A Study of the Fiction.* Carbondale: Southern Illinois University Press, 1987.

White, Kenneth. *The Tribal Dharma: An Essay on the Work of Gary Snyder.* Dyfed: Unicorn, 1975.

BEAT GENERATION MOVEMENT CHRONOLOGY

As this encyclopedia attests, works by Beat writers and works espousing various Beat aesthetics continue to be produced. The following chronology focuses on the *historical* phenomenon of the Beat Generation proper. A historical beginning date and ending date for a literary period called the Beat movement is ultimately arbitrary and will certainly be contested. The purpose of the following chronology is to suggest a general time frame that can be useful for establishing an historical context for the authors and works discussed in this encyclopedia.

1944

The "New Vision," a general philosophy of the visionary, spiritual, and aesthetic values of "late civilization," forms around the intense discussions among Lucien Carr, Allen Ginsberg, and Jack Kerouac—the Beat Generation movement begins to take shape.

August 14: The first of many infamous incidents of violence that will plague the Beats occurs when Carr kills David Kammerer. Carr claims Kammerer had made unwanted and threatening advances. Kerouac and Burroughs are arrested as material witnesses. Kerouac marries Edie Parker on August 22 while still in custody, partially in an effort to raise bail money from her family. Carr is sentenced on October 6, serves two years at Elmira Reformatory, and is released in 1946.

December: Burroughs and Kerouac begin writing an unpublished collaborative novel, "And the Hippos Were Boiled in Their Tanks," about Carr and Kammerer.

1945

March 16: Columbia University suspends Ginsberg for one year for having Kerouac in his dorm room and for writing obscene words on his dorm window.

April 2: Anne Waldman is born.

1946

January: Herbert Huncke introduces Burroughs to heroin and later the Beats to the term "beat."

December: Neal Cassady meets Kerouac and Ginsberg in New York City.

1947

Gregory Corso begins his sentence at Clinton State Prison for robbery.

April 18: Kathy Acker is born.

1948

April 1: Cassady marries Carolyn Robinson.

July: Ginsberg experiences his "Blake Visions," during which he feels that the poet William Blake reads poems to him. These visions spur Ginsberg to pursue other visionary experiences through drug use for the next 15 years.

November: Kerouac tells John Clellon Holmes that their generation is a "beat generation."

December 24: William Everson has a vision that inspires him to become Brother Antoninus.

1949

April 21: Ginsberg is arrested in connection with a stolen-goods ring that includes Huncke, Vicki Russell, and Little Jack Melody.

June 29: As a condition of his arrest, Ginsberg is admitted to the Columbia Psychiatric Institute and meets Carl Solomon.

1950

February 27: Ginsberg is discharged from the Columbia Psychiatric Institute.

March: Ginsberg meets Gregory Corso at the Pony Stable in Greenwich Village.

August 1: Jim Carroll is born.

October 12: Bill Cannastra, a friend of the Beats, is killed in a subway accident.

November 17: Kerouac marries Cannastra's ex-girlfriend Joan Haverty.

December 27: Kerouac receives Cassady's "Joan Anderson Letter," which inspires Kerouac's writing style.

Kerouac publishes *The Town and the City*.

1951

April: Kerouac writes the famous scroll version of *On the Road*.

September 6: Burroughs accidently kills his common-law wife Joan Vollmer while playing "William Tell," attempting to shoot a glass off her head, in Mexico. For 13 days he is in jail.

October 25: Kerouac develops a new writing style called "spontaneous prose."

1952

November 16: "This Is the Beat Generation" by Holmes is published in the *New York Times Magazine*.

Holmes publishes *Go*.

1953

June: City Lights bookstore, owned by Lawrence Ferlinghetti and Peter Martin, opens in San Francisco.

Burroughs publishes *Junkie* under the name William Lee.

Kerouac writes "Essentials of Spontaneous Prose."

1954

January: Kerouac becomes absorbed in Buddhist study.

December: Ginsberg meets Peter Orlovsky at Robert LaVigne's apartment in San Francisco.

1955

October 7: The Six Gallery reading in San Francisco, with Kenneth Rexroth as master of ceremonies, features the poets Ginsberg (who gives his first public reading of the first part of "Howl"), Philip Lamantia, Michael McClure, Gary Snyder, and Philip Whalen. Some call this event the birth of the San Francisco Poetry Renaissance.

October 31: Natalie Jackson, Cassady's girlfriend, commits suicide.

Ferlinghetti publishes *Pictures of the Gone World*.

Kerouac publishes two excerpts from *On the Road*: "Jazz of the Beat Generation" in *New World Writing* and "The Mexican Girl" in the *Paris Review*.

1956

May 5: Snyder leaves for Japan.

June: Kerouac begins 63 days of work as a forest lookout on Desolation Peak in Washington State.

September 2: An article about the San Francisco Poetry Renaissance appears in the *New York Times Book Review*.

Ginsberg publishes *Howl and Other Poems*.

1957

January: Joyce Glassman (later Johnson) meets Kerouac.

February: An article on the San Francisco Poetry Renaissance appears in *Mademoiselle*.

February 15: Kerouac leaves to visit Burroughs in Tangier, where he is later joined by Ginsberg and Orlovsky in March. All assist Burroughs in compiling what will become *Naked Lunch*.

March 25: U.S. Customs confiscates copies of *Howl and Other Poems*.

May 21: Ferlinghetti and City Lights store manager Shigeyoshi Murao are arrested for selling *Howl and Other Poems*.

October: Ginsberg and Orlovsky move into the "Beat Hotel" at 9 rue Git-le-Coeur in Paris.

October 3: Judge Horn declares *Howl and Other Poems* not obscene.

September: *On the Road* is published, and Gilbert Millstein's review in the *New York Times* calls it a "historic occasion."

Herschel Silverman begins corresponding with Ginsberg.

Marty Matz moves to San Francisco and joins the Beat scene there.

David Meltzer moves to San Francisco and joins the Beat scene there.

1958

January: Burroughs moves into the "Beat Hotel."

April 2: Herb Caen coins the term *beatnik* in the *San Francisco Chronicle*.

April 8: Cassady is arrested for marijuana possession that will lead to two years at San Quentin.

October 13: Hettie Cohen marries LeRoi Jones.

November 16: *The Steve Allen Show* features a reading by Kerouac.

The *Chicago Review* publishes an excerpt from Burroughs's *Naked Lunch*, which leads to the censorship of the journal. Editors Paul Carroll and Irving Rosenthal start *Big Table* in order to publish the censored material, and the first issue is seized by the U.S. Postal Service in March 1959.

Corso publishes *Bomb*.

Ferlinghetti publishes *A Coney Island of the Mind*.

Holmes publishes *The Horn*.

Kerouac publishes *The Dharma Bums* and *The Subterraneans*.

Jack Micheline publishes *River of Red Wine and Other Poems*.

John Wieners publishes *The Hotel Wentley Poems*.

1959

January 2: Robert Frank and Alfred Leslie begin production of the movie *Pull My Daisy*, with Corso, Ginsberg, and Orlovsky as actors, and Kerouac as narrator.

September: "Cut-up" experiments are begun by Burroughs.

Abbie Hoffman graduates from Brandeis University.

Burroughs publishes *The Naked Lunch* in Paris.

Bob Kaufman publishes *Abomunist Manifesto*.

Kerouac publishes *Doctor Sax: Faust Part Three*, *Maggie Cassidy*, *Mexico City Blues*, and part of *Visions of Cody*.

Snyder publishes *Riprap*.

1960

April: Harold Norse moves into the "Beat Hotel."

June: MGM releases the movie *The Subterraneans*, which is loosely based on Kerouac's novel.

July 4: Cassady is released from prison.

November 26: Timothy Leary gives Ginsberg psilocybin mushrooms and plans for the psychedelic revolution begin.

Donald Allen publishes *The New American Poetry: 1945–1960*.

Corso publishes *The Happy Birthday of Death*.

Kerouac publishes *Lonesome Traveler* and *Tristessa*.

Lew Welch publishes *Wobbly Rock*.

1961

ruth weiss begins writing *DESERT JOURNAL*.

Burroughs publishes *The Soft Machine*.

di Prima publishes *Dinners and Nightmares*.

Ginsberg publishes *Kaddish and Other Poems: 1958–1960*.

Ted Joans publishes *All of Ted Joans and No More*.

LeRoi Jones publishes *Preface to a Twenty Volume Suicide Note*.

Kerouac publishes *Book of Dreams*.

McClure publishes *Dark Brown*.

1962

February 1: Elise Cowen, Ginsberg's former girlfriend, commits suicide.

Summer: Cassady meets Kesey on Perry Lane in Palo Alto.

August: Burroughs's work is praised at the International Writer's Conference in Edinburgh, Scotland.

Paul Bowles publishes *A Hundred Camels in the Courtyard*.

Burroughs publishes *Naked Lunch* in the U.S. and *The Ticket That Exploded*.

Robert Creeley publishes *For Love: Poems 1950–1960*.

Kerouac publishes *Big Sur*.

Ken Kesey publishes *One Flew over the Cuckoo's Nest*.

1963

Ginsberg receives a Guggenheim Fellowship.

Burroughs and Ginsberg publish *The Yage Letters*.

Kerouac publishes *Visions of Gerard.*
Ed Sanders publishes *Poem From Jail.*

1964

February 9: The Beatles play *The Ed Sullivan Show.*
June 14: Kesey, Cassady, and the Merry Pranksters start their journey across the country in their bus, "Further."
July 12–24: The Berkeley Poetry Conference brings together Brother Antoninus, Ted Berrigan, Creeley, Ed Dorn, Ginsberg, Joanne Kyger, Philip Lamantia, Charles Olson, Sanders, Snyder, Waldman, Welch, John Wieners, and other poets associated with the Beat movement.
August 27: Kerouac sees Cassady for the last time in New York at a Merry Pranksters party.
August 28: Al Aronowitz introduces Bob Dylan and marijuana to John Lennon and the other Beatles.
Burroughs publishes *Nova Express.*
Holmes publishes *Get Home Free.*
Jones publishes *Dutchman,* which wins an Obie Award.
Kesey publishes *Sometimes a Great Notion.*
McClure publishes *Ghost Tantras.*
John Lennon publishes *In His Own Write.*

1965

May 9: Ginsberg, as Dylan's guest, attends a party that includes Lennon after Dylan's performance at London's Albert Hall.
July: Hunter S. Thompson introduces Kesey to members of the Hell's Angels.
July 25: Dylan goes electric at the Newport Folk Festival.
Andy Clausen begins working in the American oral tradition of poetry inspired by Corso, Ginsberg, and Kerouac.
Kerouac travels to France.
Ray Bremser publishes *Poems of Madness.*
Huncke publishes *Huncke's Journal.*
Bob Kaufman publishes *Solitudes Crowded with Loneliness.*
Kerouac publishes *Desolation Angels.*
Kyger publishes *The Tapestry and the Web.*
McClure publishes *The Beard* and *Poisoned Wheat.*

1966

April 30: Richard Fariña dies in a motorcycle accident two days after publishing *Been Down So Long It Looks Like Up to Me.*
June 28: Oscar Zeta Acosta is admitted to the California bar.
July 7: *Naked Lunch* is ruled not obscene by the Massachusetts Supreme Court.
July 29: Dylan suffers a serious motorcycle accident.
November 15: Two people are arrested at The Psychedelic Shop in San Francisco for selling Lenore Kandel's recently published *The Love Book.*
November 17: A clerk at City Lights Bookstore is arrested for selling *The Love Book.* After what was at the time the longest trial in San Francisco history, *The Love Book* is banned in 1967; it is a decision that will not be overturned until 1974.
Kerouac publishes *Satori in Paris.*
Thompson publishes *Hell's Angels: A Strange and Terrible Saga.*

1967

January 14: The Human Be-In takes place in Golden Gate Park with Ginsberg, Ferlinghetti, Leary, McClure, and Kandel on stage, and Jim Morrison and The Doors among the 20,000 participants—the Beat Generation movement morphs into the Hippie movement, and an underground avant-garde movement turns into a burgeoning avant-garde popular movement.
December: Charles Bukowski meets Cassady.
Acosta meets Thompson during a cross-country trip for enlightenment.
Richard Brautigan publishes *Trout Fishing in America.*
Ray Bremser publishes *Angel.*
Holmes publishes *Nothing More to Declare.*
Kandel publishes *Word Alchemy.*
Lamantia publishes *Selected Poems: 1943–1966.*
Charles Plymell publishes *Apocalypse Rose.*
Ted Berrigan interviews Kerouac for the *Paris Review.*
Kerouac writes his last full-length book, *Vanity of Duluoz.*

CONTRIBUTORS

patricia cherkin alexander met Jack Micheline in the fountain in Washington Square in New York when she was a young writing major registering for summer classes at NYU. They were married briefly in the early 1960s and have a son, Vince Silvaer.

John F. Barber teaches science fiction within a transdisciplinary program focused on the necessary intersection of art, humanities, technology, and science at the University of Texas at Dallas. His The Brautigan Bibliography plus+, an online, interactive bio-bibliographic resource focusing on writer Richard Brautigan is noted as the most comprehensive resource of its kind.

Bebe Barefoot is currently an instructor at the University of Alabama, where she earned a Ph.D. in English literature. She is currently working on a critifictional study of Kathy Acker. Ms. Barefoot was an AAUW American Dissertation Fellow in 2002–03 and received research grants from Duke University's Sallie Bingham Center for Women's History and Culture in 2002 and 2003. Her work has appeared in HOW2: Contemporary Innovative Writing by Women, an online journal (Spring 2000), and in a special issue of Critical Matrix (1996).

Jon Blumb received a BFA in 1976 from Massachusetts College of Art and an MFA in 1981 from University of Kansas. He had worked for years photographing art when he met William S. Burroughs in 1988. Burroughs was creating and showing original paintings and drawings, shooting some of them, when Blumb photographed the art for catalogs and galleries. Shooting enthusiasts,

they visited the countryside around Lawrence, Kansas, shooting targets and photos. Appreciative of photography, Burroughs made himself accessible for Blumb's documentary photography. Blumb is still a photographer on numerous audio, video, and film projects. He documented the 1997 funeral of Burroughs. An original portfolio, "William S. Burroughs in Prints" is online at www.jonblumb.com.

Donovan S. Braud is a Ph.D. candidate at Loyola University Chicago. He has published in Teaching Basic Writing and several literature reference works.

Robert Brophy is Professor Emeritus of English at California State University Long Beach. He is author of Robinson Jeffers: Myth, Ritual, and Symbol in His Narrative Poems (Cleveland: Case Western Reserve Press, 1973) and Robinson Jeffers (Boise: Western Writer Series, 1975). He is editor of Robinson Jeffers: Dimensions of a Poet (New York: Fordham University Press, 1995) and Dear Judas and Other Poems (by Robinson Jeffers. New York: Livedright / W. W. Norton, 1977). He has been editor of The Robinson Jeffers Newsletter 1968–96 and Jeffers Studies 1997–2002. In 1995 he edited and published William Everson: Remembrances and Tributes (Long Beach).

Chuck Carlise studied literature and writing at Wittenberg University and UC-Davis and was a visiting lecturer at UC-Santa Cruz in 2004. He is currently writing poems and working as director of a national grassroots political organization based in Portland, Oregon.

Ann Charters has been teaching Beat literature and the short story as a professor of American literature at the University of Connecticut in Storrs since 1974.

Andy Clausen is a poet.

Jennifer Cooper is a writer, teacher, and Beat scholar living in Fort Worth, Texas, where she earned her M.A. in English from the University of Texas at Arlington in 2004.

Maria Damon teaches literature at the University of Minnesota. She is the author of *The Dark End of the Street: Margins in American Vanguard Poetry* (Minnesota University Press, 1993), and coauthor (with Betsy Franco) of *The Secret Life of Words* (Teaching Resource Center) and (with Miekal And) poetic hypertexts *Literature Nation, pleasureTEXTpossession, Eros/ion,* and *Semetrix.*

Thomas Evans was born in the United Kingdom and currently lives in New York. He is a poet and an editor of the monthly poetry and art magazine *Tolling Elves.*

Jane Falk is instructor in English at the University of Akron, Akron, Ohio. She has published on Beat avant-garde writing practices. Current research includes Zen and the Beats and the work of Joanne Kyger and Philip Whalen.

Amy L. Friedman teaches English at Ursinus College. She completed her doctorate at Goldsmiths College, University of London. Her publications on women writers of the Beat Generation include a chapter on Joanne Kyger in *Reconstructing the Beats,* ed. Jennie Skerl (Palgrave/Macmillan, 2004).

Morgan Gibson is a poet, an essayist, and an author of *Kenneth Rexroth* (1972) and *Revolutionary Rexroth: Poet of East-West Wisdom* (Archon, 1986), which was expanded to include correspondence between Rexroth and Gibson in the 2000 Light & Dust online edition at http://www.thing.net/~grist/ld/rexroth/gibson.htm. The latest of Gibson's essays and articles on poetry and Buddhism concern Rexroth's 15,000-volume personal library at

Kanda University of International Studies in Japan, where Gibson was a professor after teaching at the University of Wisconsin–Milwaukee and other universities in the United States and Japan. More relevant work is being gathered and catalogued in the Morgan Gibson Collection in the Regenstein Library at the University of Chicago.

Nancy Grace is a professor of English at the College of Wooster in Wooster, Ohio, where she served as the founding director of the college's program in writing. She is the author of *The Feminized Male Character in Twentieth-Century Fiction* (1995), coauthor of *Breaking the Rule of Cool: Interviewing and Reading Beat Women Writers* (2004), and coeditor of *Girls Who Wore Black: Women Writing the Beat Generation* (2002). She is secretary-treasurer of the Beat Studies Association and has published articles on Jack Kerouac, ruth weiss, and interdisciplinary approaches to teaching women studies.

Oliver Harris is a professor of American literature at Keele University and has specialized as a scholar and critic on the work of William S. Burroughs since completing a Ph.D. at Oxford in the early 1980s. In 1993 he edited *The Letters of William S. Burroughs, 1945–1959,* followed by a new edition of *Junky* in 2003. Having published the critical book *William Burroughs and the Secret of Fascination,* also in 2003, and numerous articles in the Beat field, he is also the editor of *The Yage Letters Redux* (City Lights, 2006).

Kurt Hemmer is an associate professor of English at Harper College where he teaches courses on existentialism, crime literature, literature and film, rock and roll, and Beat literature. His article "The Prostitute Speaks: Brenda Frazer's *Troia: Mexican Memoirs*" was published in *Paradoxa 18: Fifties Fictions* (2003). He wrote the award-winning documentaries *As We Cover the Streets: Janine Pommy Vega* (2003) and *Rebel Roar: The Sound of Michael McClure* (2004), which were produced by Tom Knoff.

Greg Herriges is the author of three novels, including the twice award-nominated *The Winter Dance Party Murders* (1998). His short works have appeared in the *Chicago Tribune Magazine, The Literary Review, The South Carolina Review,* and *Story Quarterly.*

Hilary Holladay is professor of English and director of the Jack and Stella Kerouac Center for American Studies at the University of Massachusetts, Lowell. She is also founding director of University of Massachusetts, Lowell's biennial Kerouac conference on Beat literature. Her books include *Ann Petry* (1996) and *Wild Blessings: The Poetry of Lucille Clifton* (2004). She is currently writing a biography of Herbert Huncke.

Tim Hunt, professor of English at Illinois State University, is the author of *Kerouac's Crooked Road: Development of a Fiction* (1996).

Rob Johnson is the author of *The Last Years of William S. Burroughs: Beats in South Texas* (Texas A&M University Press, 2006). He is currently working on a book about a sheriff who once arrested William S. Burroughs, entitled *Hell-Bent Texas Sheriff: Robert Vail Ennis and the Massacre of the Rodriguez Family.* Johnson teaches classes on South Texas literature and various courses on Beat literature at the University of Texas–Pan American.

Ronna C. Johnson is a lecturer in English and American Studies at Tufts University. She has published essays on Jack Kerouac, Joyce Johnson, Lenore Kandel, and women writers of the Beat Generation, coedited with Nancy M. Grace *Girls Who Wore Black: Women Writing the Beat Generation* (Rutgers University Press, 2002), and cowrote with Grace *Breaking the Rule of Cool: Interviewing and Reading Women Beat Writers* (University Press of Mississippi, 2004). She is currently writing *Inventing Jack Kerouac: Reception and Reputation, 1957–2002* (forthcoming from Camden House Press).

James T. Jones, professor of English at Southwest Missouri State University, is the author of four books on Jack Kerouac, as well as several chapbooks and essays on Kerouac and other Beat writers.

Eliot Katz is the author of three books of poetry, including *Unlocking the Exits* (Coffee House Press, 1999). Called "[a]nother classic New Jersey bard" by Allen Ginsberg, Katz was a cofounder of *Long Shot* literary journal and worked for many years as a housing advocate for Central Jersey homeless families. He currently lives in New York City, is serving as poetry editor of the online politics quarterly *Logos* (www.logosjournal.com), and is working on a book entitled *Radical Eyes: Political Poetics and the Work of Allen Ginsberg.*

Larry Keenan is an internationally noted San Francisco Bay area photographer. A selection of his "Beat Era" work is in the permanent collection of the Archives of American Artists in the Smithsonian Institution, Washington, D.C. His photographs are in museums and private collections throughout the world. In November 1995 Keenan's photography was exhibited in *Beat Culture and the New America: 1950–1965* at the Whitney Museum of American Art in New York. From February to June 1996 his work was featured at the National Portrait Gallery for the Smithsonian Institution's exhibit *REBELS: Artists and Poets of the 1950s.*

William Lawlor is professor of English and writing emphasis coordinator at the University of Wisconsin–Stevens Point. He is the author of *The Beat Generation: A Bibliographical Teaching Guide* (Scarecrow 1998) and the editor of *Beat Culture: Lifestyles, Icons, and Impact* (ABC–CLIO 2005).

A. Robert Lee, formerly of the University of Kent at Canterbury, UK, is professor of American literature at Nihon University, Tokyo. Recent publications include *Multicultural American Literature: Comparative Black, Native, Latino/a and Asian American Fictions* (2003), which won a 2004 American Book Award, *Designs of Blackness: Mappings in The Literature and Culture of Afro-America* (1998), *Postindian Conversations*—with Gerald Vizenor (1999), and the essay collections *Herman Melville: Critical Assessments,* 4 Vols (2001) and *Other British, Other Britain: Contemporary Multicultural Fiction* (1995). He edited *The Beat Generation Writers* (1996) and has written on Ted

Joans, International Beats, Oscar Zeta Acosta, and William S. Burroughs.

Joel Lewis is the author of *Vertical's Currency: New and Selected Poems* (1999) and *House Rent Boogie* (1992). He edited *On The Level Every Day: Selected Talks of Ted Berrigan* and *Reality Prime: Selected Poems of Walter Lowenfels* (1997).

Julie Lewis is a playwright and a professor, often using Beat texts in her literature and drama classes. She currently teaches theater at the Community College of Baltimore County. Her original plays, *Henry's Holiday, Plastic Haircut, Three Hundred Out of Hades, Quiver and Sink*, and *Jarvis Legend's Borrowed Skin* (along with others) have been published and produced in regional theaters, off-off-Broadway, and internationally.

Richard Middleton-Kaplan has a Ph.D. from UCLA and is an assistant professor in English at Harper College. His latest article, exploring the treatment of race, color, and identity in Melville's *Typee* and Toni Morrison's *The Bluest Eye*, will be published in the forthcoming volume *Melville and the Marquesas*.

Stephanie S. Morgan is a Ph.D. candidate in English at the University of North Carolina–Chapel Hill. She specializes in mid-20th-century American literature and has presented on various Beat writers at conferences throughout the country. She teaches rhetoric and composition with a focus on emerging media at UNC.

Patrick D. Murphy is professor of English at the University of Central Florida where he teaches courses in the Honors College as well as upper-division and graduate courses in American, environmental, ethnic, and international literatures and literary theory. Author and editor of numerous books, including *Farther Afield in the Study of Nature-Oriented Literature* (2000), *A Place for Wayfaring: The Poetry and Prose of Gary Snyder* (2000), and *Essentials of the Theory of Fiction 3rd Edition* (1996), he is currently editing a collection of essays on interactive hypertext fiction and writing a book on nature in the contemporary American novel.

Erik Mortenson is a postdoctoral teaching fellow in the Honors Program at Wayne State University in Detroit. He has published several articles on the Beats and is currently engaged in a book project that explores the role that the "moment" plays in Beat-Generation thought and writing. He received his M.A. in English from the University of Missouri–Columbia and his Ph.D. from Wayne State.

Rod Phillips is an associate professor of humanities, culture, and writing at Michigan State University's James Madison College. He has published broadly in the field of American literature, including articles on Herman Melville, Jack Kerouac, Lew Welch, Kathy Acker, and Tennessee Williams. His critical study of nature and ecology in the writings of the Beat movement, *"Forest Beatniks" and "Urban Thoreaus": Gary Snyder, Jack Kerouac, Lew Welch, and Michael McClure*, was published by Peter Lang in 2000. His monograph on Lew Welch will be published in 2006 as part of Boise State University's Western Writers Series.

Jonah Raskin is the author of *American Scream: Allen Ginsberg's "Howl" and the Making of the Beat Generation* (2004), and teaches media law and journalism in the communication studies department at Sonoma State University. He has a Ph.D. in English and American literature and has taught at Winston–Salem State College, at the State University of New York at Stony Brook, and at the University of Antwerp and the University of Ghent in Belgium. His other published works include *For the Hell of It: The Life and Times of Abbie Hoffman* (1998), and several poetry chapbooks, including *Jonah Raskin's Greatest Hits, More Poems Better Poems*, and *Bone Love*. He performs his poetry on stage with the bass player Claude Smith.

Luther Riedel is an assistant professor of English at the Community College of Baltimore County. He received a B.A. in politics from Whitman College and an M.A. in literature from the University of Connecticut, Storrs and is currently a doctoral candidate at Washington State University.

Edward Sanders is the author of *America: A History in Verse*, a nine-volume history of the

United States, 1450–2000, three volumes of which have been published. Other books in print include *Tales of Beatnik Glory* (all four volumes published in a single edition, 2005); *1968: A History in Verse* (1997); *The Poetry and Life of Allen Ginsberg* (2005); *The Family*, a history of the Charles Manson murder group; and *Chekhov* (1995), a biography in verse of Anton Chekhov. Sanders is the founder of the satiric folk/rock group The Fugs and has received a Guggenheim fellowship in poetry, a National Endowment for the Arts fellowship in verse, and an American Book Award for his collected poems.

Tracy Santa has taught at Loyola University, the United States Air Force Academy, and the American University in Bulgaria. He currently directs the Writing Center at Colorado College. His writing includes work on Sheri Martinelli, Anatole Broyard, Seymour Krim, and Lew Welch and most recently, "Drug/War: Anthony Loyd and the Hero(in) in Bosnia" (*War, Literature, and the Arts*, 2005).

Jennie Skerl is associate dean of the College of Arts and Sciences at West Chester University. She has published *William S. Burroughs* (Twayne 1985), *William S. Burroughs at the Front: Critical Reception, 1959–1989* (coedited with Robin Lydenberg, Southern Illinois University Press 1991), *A Tawdry Place of Salvation: The Art of Jane Bowles* (Southern Illinois University Press 1997), and *Reconstructing the Beats* (Palgrave Macmillan 2004). She edited the Winter 2000 special issue of *College Literature* on teaching Beat literature and was a major contributor to the *Dictionary of Literary Biography* volumes on the Beats (edited by Ann Charters, 1983).

Birgit Stephenson currently works with the communication team at Learning Lab Denmark in Copenhagen. She was coeditor of *PEARL*, an international literary journal, from 1975 to 1993.

Gregory Stephenson grew up in Colorado and Arizona and has lived in Denmark since 1972. He has written two books on the literature of the Beat Generation, as well as critical studies of J. G. Ballard and Robert Stone. He teaches American literature and history at the University of Copenhagen.

Matt Theado received B.A. and M.A. degrees from James Madison University and a Ph.D. from the University of South Carolina. His books include *Understanding Jack Kerouac* (2000) and *The Beats: A Literary Reference* (2003). He has written articles and given presentations on the Beat Generation and Jack Kerouac in particular. He teaches at Gardner–Webb University in North Carolina.

Tony Trigilio is the author of *"Strange Prophecies Anew": Rereading Apocalypse in Blake, H. D., and Ginsberg* (Fairleigh Dickinson University Press, 2000), and essays in *Girls Who Wore Black: Women Writing the Beat Generation* (edited by Nancy Grace and Ronna Johnson; Rutgers University Press, 2002) and *Reconstructing the Beats* (edited by Jennie Skerl; Palgrave Macmillan, 2004). His articles and reviews have appeared in *American Literature, Tulsa Studies in Women's Literature*, and *Modern Language Studies*. He has published poems in *The Spoon River Poetry Review, Hotel Amerika, The Iowa Review, Big Bridge, The Beloit Poetry Journal, Jack* magazine, and many other journals. He is an associate professor of English at Columbia College Chicago.

Laki Vazakas is a videomaker and educator. His video work includes *Huncke and Louis, Burma: Traces of the Buddha*, and *The 1998 Cherry Valley Arts Festival*.

Harvey Wasserman, a personal friend and coconspirator of Abbie Hoffman, is author of *Harvey Wasserman's History of the United States* (2004) and *A Glimpse of the Big Light: Losing Parents, Finding Spirit* (2005). He helped found the grassroots antinuclear/prosolar movement and is coauthor with Dan Juhl of *Harvesting Wind Energy as a Cash Crop* (2002).

Andrew Wilson is a professor of English at Harper College, where he teaches composition and literature classes. In 1996 he earned a Ph.D. in American literature from Kent State University. His essays have appeared in the *Mississippi Quarterly* and the *Hemingway Review.*

INDEX

Note: **Boldface** page numbers indicate main entries.

E

East Coast
    in *On the Road* 249
    in *Riprap* 277–278
"8" (Ferlinghetti) 256
"18" (Ferlinghetti) 257
"Elegies for Neal Cassady 1968"
    (Ginsberg) 91
"11" (Ferlinghetti) 53
"Elsie John" (Huncke) 86, 145
Emerson, Ralph Waldo, Holmes influ-
    enced by 131
"End, The" (Ginsberg) 169–170
"Energy Is Eternal Delight" (Snyder)
    323
Enrique 193
Enslin, Theodore 183
environmentalism
    in *Desolation Angels* 61
    in *Last of the Moccasins* 187–188
    in *Nova Express* 235
    of Snyder 289
epic, *Mexico City Blues* as 208
Erections, Ejaculations, Exhibitions and
    General Tales of Ordinary Madness
    (Bukowski) 31, **84–85**
Erotic Poems (Lamantia) 186
"Escape Was Impossible, The" (Matz)
    201
"Essentials of Spontaneous Prose, The"
    (Kerouac) 76, 177, 299
Evening Sun Turned Crimson, The
    (Huncke) **85–87**
Everson, William **87–89**
    "Howl" and 280–281
    The Residual Years 88
    "River-Root: A Syzygy" **280–281**
    The Rose of Solitude 88
evil
    in *Doctor Sax* 74–75
    Manson and 93
"Eyes Like the Sky" (Bukowski) 84–85

F

Fair Play for Cuba Committee 57
Fall of America: Poems of These States,
    1965–1971, The (Ginsberg) **90–92,**
    113
fame, in *Desolation Angels* 63
family, in "Kaddish" 166–167
Family: The Story of Charles Manson's
    Dune Buggy Attack Battalion, The
    (Sanders) **93–94,** 283
Fariña, Richard **15–16, 94–95**

Fast Speaking Woman (Waldman)
    95–97
"Fast Speaking Woman" (Waldman)
    95–96, 339
Fear and Loathing in Las Vegas: A
    Savage Journey to the Heart of the
    American Dream (Thompson) 4,
    97–98, 308
Fear and Loathing: On the Campaign
    Trail (Thompson) 308
Federal Bureau of Investigations (FBI),
    subversives labeled by 288
feminine, in *Loba* 191–192
feminism
    of Acker, in *Blood and Guts in High*
      School 20
    of di Prima, in *Loba* 192
    of Jones, in *How I Became Hettie*
      Jones 137
    of Kandel 170–172
    in *Memoirs of a Beatnik* 206–207
    of Waldman 156, 339
    of weiss 341
Ferlinghetti, Lawrence 50, 53, **98–**
    101, 99, 342
    In Americus, Book I 101
    "Autobiography" 52
    Bukowski and 85
    A Coney Island of the Mind **50–53,**
      100
    "Constantly Risking Absurdity" 52
    Corso and 55
    "Dada Would Have Loved a Day
      Like This" 257
    "Dog" 52
    "Don't Let That Horse" 51–52
    "8" 256
    "18" 257
    "11" 53
    How to Paint Sunlight 101
    "I Am Waiting" 52
    "In Goya's Greatest Scenes" 51
    Life Studies, Life Stories 101
    "London" 257
    in *The New American Poetry*
      227–228
    Old Angel Midnight and 244–245
    "1" 53
    Pictures of the Gone World 50, 51,
      53, 100, **256–257**
    on poetics 230
    "Sometime During Eternity" 51
    "Sorolla's Women in Their Picture
      Hats" 256–257

These Are My Rivers: New and
    Selected Poems 101
    "The World Is a Beautiful Place"
      53
    "12" 53
    "23" 257
    Waldman and 95
Fields, W.C. 336
"Filmmaker, The" (Sanders) 303
"Finger, The" (Burroughs) 33–34,
    153
Finnegan's Wake (Joyce) 244
"First They Slaughtered the Angels"
    (Kandel) **101–102**
First Third, The (Cassady) **102–103,**
    240
    Cassady (Carolyn) on 102
    Visions of Cody and 331
Floating Bear (newsletter) 71
flood, in *Doctor Sax* 75
fold-in technique
    in *Nova Express* 236
    in *The Soft Machine* 292
Folger, Abigail 93
"Food" (Corso) 123
food, in *Dinners and Nightmares* 73
"For K.R. Who Killed Himself in
    Charles Street Jail" (Corso) 123
For Love: Poems 1950–1960 (Creeley)
    103–104
"For the Children" (Snyder) 323
"Four Changes" (Snyder) 323
Frazer, Brenda **104–105**
    Angel and 5
    Bremser and 28, 29, 261
    Troia: Mexican Memoirs 105,
      319–320
freedom, in *Cities of the Red Night* 46
Freewheelin' Frank: Secretary of the
    Angels, as Told to Michael McClure by
    Frank Reynolds (McClure) 125
"Friends of Cuba," Baraka in 8
"Friend of the World, A" (Bowles)
    148–149
"frinky" 2
"Frisco: The Tape" 332
"Frisky" (Huncke) 147
"From a List of Delusions the Insane
    What They Are Afraid Of"
    (Berrigan) 273
"Front Lines" (Snyder) 322
Frykowski, Woyteck 93
Fugs, The 282
full circle (weiss) 341

H

Hadju, David, *Positively Fourth Street* 94

"Hair" (Corso) 123

hallucinogens. *See* drug use

"Halowe'en" (Huncke) 147

Ham on Rye (Bukowski) 30

Hansen, Diana, Cassady (Neal) and 40

　in *Off the Road* 240, 243

　in *On the Road* 253

　in *Visions of Cody* 334

Han Shan, in *The Dharma Bums* 67

Happy Birthday of Death, The (Corso) **122–124,** 199, 306

Harlem, Baraka in 80, 81

Harlow, Jean, in *The Beard* 11–12

Harper, Linda 49

Harrison, George 183

Harrison Narcotics Act 163

Harry, Bill 190

"Hart Crane" (Creeley) 104

Haverty, Joan

　in *Get Home Free* 106

　Kerouac and 176, 240

　On the Road and 248

Hawthorne, Nathaniel, *The Scarlet Letter,* in *Blood and Guts in High School* 21

Heart Beat: My Life With Jack & Neal (Cassady) 39

Heine, Bill 119, 145

Hell's Angels: A Strange and Terrible Saga (Thompson) 98, **124–126,** 308

Helter Skelter (Bugliosi) 93

Henderson, LuAnne, Cassady (Neal) and 39–40

　in *Go* 116

　in *Off the Road* 238, 239–240

　in *On the Road* 249, 251

　in *Visions of Cody* 334

"He of the Assembly" (Bowles) 148

Hermit Poems (Welch) 342

heroine. *See* drug use

Hester, Carolyn 94

"High" (Lamantia) **126–127**

High Priest (Leary) **127–128,** 189

Hinds, Willie 95

Hinkle, Al 239, 331

Hinkle, Helen 239, 240, 252

Hinman, Gary 93

hippie counterculture

　Kandel in 170, 195

　Kesey in 180, 246

history

　in *The Beat Thing* 13–14

　in "Bomb" 22

　in *The Maximus Poems* 202

　in *Memoirs of a Beatnik* 206–207

　in *Thirsting for Peace in a Raging Century* 306–307

hobos, Kerouac on 195

Hoffman, Abbie **128–129**

　Revolution for the Hell of It 128, **274–275**

　Steal This Book 128

Hollywood (Bukowski) 31

Holmes, Jim 331

Holmes, John Clellon x, **129–132**

　in *Book of Dreams* 24

　"Clearing the Field" 131

　"The Consciousness Widener" 131

　Get Home Free **106–108**

　Go 106, **114–117,** 129, 130, 131

　"The Great Rememberer" 131

　The Horn **132–136**

　Kerouac and 107–108

　Nothing More to Declare 130

　"The Philosophy of the Beat Generation" 131

　Selected Essays 130, 131

　"This Is the Beat Generation" 117, 130, 131

Holocaust, weiss in 340

Home: Social Essays, "Cuba Libre" in 57

homosexuality

　in *Book of Dreams* 24–25

　of Burroughs 267–269

　in *The City and the Town* 316

　of Ginsberg 112, 143, 167

　in *Go* 115

　in "Howl" 140

　in *Howl and Other Poems* 141–142, 143

　of Huncke 118, 144

　in *Junky* 164

　in "Kaddish" 167

　of Kerouac 198

　in *Memoirs of a Beatnik* 206

　in *Naked Lunch* 223, 224

　in *On the Road* 253, 334

　in *The Subterraneans* 300

　in *Visions of Cody* 334

　of Wieners 137

Horn, The (Holmes) **132–136**

Horowitz, Mikhail 30

Hotel Wentley Poems, The (Wieners) **136–137,** 349

House Un-American Activities Committee (HUAC), Hoffman and 128

"How Happy I Used to Be" (Corso) 123

How I Became Hettie Jones (Jones) **137–139,** 161

"Howl" (Ginsberg) **139–140,** 140–142

　Everson's response to 280–281

　Go and 114

　Kandel influenced by 101–102

　prophecy in 111

　Rexroth and 275, 310

　Sanders influenced by 282

　Six Gallery reading of 65, 100

　Trilling and 117

Howl and Other Poems (Ginsberg) 110, **140–143**

　censorship of 112, 140

　publication of 51, 100

How to Paint Sunlight (Ferlinghetti) 101

Hughes, Howard, in *Gunslinger* 120–121

Human Be-In x

humanity

　in *The Beard* 12

　in "Bomb" 22

　Bowles on 26

　in *Cities of the Red Night* 48

　in *Dark Brown* 59

　in *Desolation Angels* 61

　in *The Happy Birthday of Death* 122–123, 124

　in "High" 127

　in *Naked Lunch* 223

　in *The Western Lands* 345

humanoid 1

humor, in *The Happy Birthday of Death* 122–123

Huncke, Herbert x, **143–145**

　"Bill Burroughs" 87

　"Bill Burroughs, Part II" 87

　Burroughs and 34

　"Cat and His Girl" 146

　in *The City and the Town* 316

　"Detroit Redhead, 1943–1967" 86–87

　"Elsie John" 86, 145

　The Evening Sun Turned Crimson **85–87**